Support for the Fleet

For Vivienne

whose constant support and
encouragement were crucial to the
research and writing of this book

Support for the Fleet

Architecture and engineering of the Royal Navy's Bases 1700 – 1914

Jonathan Coad

Published by English Heritage, The Engine House, Fire Fly Avenue, Swindon SN2 2EH
www.english-heritage.org.uk
English Heritage is the Government's lead body for the historic environment.

First published 2013

ISBN 978-1-84802-055-9

Product code 51535

British Library Cataloguing in Publication data
A CIP catalogue record for this book is available from the British Library.

For more information about images from the English Heritage Archive, contact Archives Services Team, The Engine House, Fire Fly Avenue, Swindon SN2 2EH; telephone (01793) 414600.

Brought to publication by Robin Taylor, Publishing, English Heritage.

Typeset in 9.5 on 10.75 point Charter

Edited by Lesley Adkins
Indexed by Alan Rutter
Page layout by Francis & Partners
Printed in the UK by Butler, Tanner & Dennis

Front endpaper: The fleet at Spithead in 1790 with *Victory* in the foreground. The strength of the Georgian Royal Navy, vividly conveyed by Robert Dodd's painting, was utterly dependent on the navy's shore bases. (© National Maritime Museum, Greenwich, London, BHC3694)

Back endpaper: The flagship *Iron Duke* leading a procession of dreadnoughts at the Fleet Review at Spithead in July 1914. This gathering included ships of the Royal Fleet Reserve manned by some 20,000 reservists. Winston Churchill, then First Lord, described the spectacle as 'incomparably the greatest assemblage of naval power ever witnessed in the history of the world'. Behind it lay the skills and expertise of the royal dockyards. (© National Maritime Museum, Greenwich, London, N21994)

CONTENTS

Acknowledgements ... vi

Abbreviations and Measurements ... viii

Foreword by *Sir Neil Cossons* ... ix

Introduction ... xvii

1 The Royal Dockyards in Great Britain, 1700–1835 ... 1

2 The Royal Dockyards in Great Britain, 1835–1914 ... 25

3 Planning and Building the Royal Dockyards to 1795 ... 53

4 Planning and Building the Royal Dockyards, 1795–1914 ... 71

5 Engineering Works of the Sailing Navy, 1700–1835 ... 87

6 Buildings of the Sailing Navy ... 107

7 Dockyard Housing, Offices and Chapels ... 147

8 Buildings and Engineering Works of the Steam Navy, 1835–1914 ... 171

9 Growth of Empire: The Overseas Bases of the Sailing Navy, 1700–1835 ... 209

10 Heyday of Empire: The Overseas Bases, 1835–1914 ... 217

11 The Mediterranean Bases: Buildings and Engineering Works, 1700–1914 ... 233

12 The West Indies and North American Bases: Buildings and Engineering Works, 1700–1914 ... 251

13 South Atlantic and Australian Bases: Buildings and Engineering Works, 1700–1914 ... 283

14 Feeding the Fleet: The Royal Victualling Yards ... 299

15 Naval Ordnance Yards ... 315

16 Care of the Sick and Wounded: Naval Hospitals ... 343

17 Barracks and Training Establishments ... 373

Epilogue ... 391

Notes ... 395

References ... 430

Index ... 436

ACKNOWLEDGEMENTS

The research that underpins this book was spread intermittently over many years; both it and the subsequent writing would have been impossible without the help and support of many people and institutions.

At a number of the overseas bases visits and research were made feasible with the aid of grants from the British Academy, the Society of Antiquaries (William Lambarde Memorial Fund) and with support from English Heritage. I remain immensely grateful to a number of people at all the overseas bases for their help, advice and encouragement. For Bermuda I owe an especial debt of gratitude to my old friend Dr Edward Harris, Director of the National Museum of Bermuda, who has provided generous hospitality over many years, supplied much information and kindly read and commented on relevant sections of this book. In Canada, Ian Doull of Parks Canada showed me round Esquimalt and Kingston, advised on Halifax, supplied me with a great deal of Canadian material and also read and commented on a draft of Chapter 12. In Ireland Daire Brunicardi was my guide to Haulbowline and generously shared with me his own researches. Access to buildings in Malta was first arranged by the Ministry of Defence and subsequently by the Malta Drydocks Corporation. In South Africa the South African Navy hospitably welcomed me and gave me access to Simon's Town base, and Sandy Myers and Mrs A E Read with great liberality supplied me with typescript copies of their own extensive researches. For Jamaica, I am indebted to the Jamaican National Trust for access to the buildings of Port Royal and to the late Jean and Oliver Cox who shared information with me and who both did so much to help safeguard the naval hospital and other historic buildings there. In Australia my guides to the naval establishments around Sydney Harbour were Bob Clark of the Sydney Harbour Federation Trust and John Jeremy, author of the definitive history of Cockatoo Island. Subsequent to my visit, Steven Adams of the Australian National Maritime Museum helped me with a number of queries.

Visits from the mid-1960s onwards to the operational home bases of Portsmouth, Devonport and Chatham, until the latter's closure in 1984, were helped and made more rewarding by successive flag officers and many naval and civilian staff with a keen awareness of, and concern for, the historic importance of these remarkable enclaves.

Much of the information in this book comes from primary research in a number of institutions. The majority of the documents consulted are held in the National Archives. It is a pleasure to record the unfailing help and assistance over many years of the staff there. More recently, my investigations at Kew were considerably aided by Susan Lumas and her fellow researchers in the ADM/1 documents series who generously sent me transcripts of some of the fruits of their labours. At the National Maritime Museum my initial researches in the 1960s owed much to the wise guidance and profound knowledge of Alan Pearsall and the enthusiasms of George Naish. More recently Gillian Hutchinson, Pieter van der Merwe, Simon Stephens, Gareth Bellis, Martin Salmon, Richard Espley and Andrew Choong Han Lin have been unfailingly helpful. I owe especial thanks to Jeremy Michell and Bob Todd who amongst other kindnesses have identified most of the warships that appear in photographs. The staff of the British Library, the Science Museum Library and the Victoria and Albert Museum Library have been similarly knowledgeable and helpful.

At Chatham some forty years ago Royal Engineers first made me aware of the involvement in the naval bases of generations of military engineers and introduced me to the riches in their library. More recently at Portsmouth, Matthew Sheldon of the National Museum of the Royal Navy, and Jenny Wraight and her colleagues in the Naval Historical Branch have also been willing mines of information and providers of documents. Stephen Courtney of the National Museum of the Royal Navy skilfully re-photographed the Admiralty Library illustrations that appear in this book.

I owe an immense debt to the late Arnold Taylor and Andrew Saunders, successively Chief Inspectors of Ancient Monuments. They first suggested that I should investigate the historic importance of the Royal Navy's shore bases and both provided consistent support in encouraging subsequent research. In the 1960s the Cold War was at its height and security meant that little was then known about what lay behind the high walls of the royal dockyards. More recently Peter Kendall, Alan Johnston, Mike Stock, Keith Falconer, Robert Law, Peter Guillery and Michael Turner, all colleagues in English Heritage, have shared their knowledge and enthusiasms with me.

Many other individuals over the years have kindly answered my queries and volunteered suggestions and information. These include Captain Mike Barritt, former Hydrographer of the Navy, Lawrance Hurst, Brian Lavery, Roger Morriss, John Hattendorf, Roger Knight, Nicholas Rodger, Richard Linzey, Stuart Drabble, Celina Fox, Ann Coats, Honorary Secretary of the *Naval Dockyards Society,* Barry Trinder, John Powell, Librarian of the *Ironbridge Trust*, and Richard Holdsworth, Preservation and Education Director of the Chatham Historic Dockyard Trust. I am also indebted to Eric Birbeck and Ann Ryder of the Haslar Heritage Group for information and photographs of the Royal Hospital at Haslar. Janice Erskine and Helen Penman of Dunfermline Carnegie Library similarly hunted out and supplied me with rare early photographs of Rosyth Dockyard. The bibliography bears abundant witness to the debt I owe to many others working in this field. Among these, David Evans deserves especial note for his pioneering researches on the development of the steam yards and naval ordnance facilities.

I am immensely grateful to Robin Taylor, Managing Editor at English Heritage for his constant support and guidance from the inception of this book to its completion. I also owe debts of gratitude to Lesley Adkins for her constructive editing of the final text and to Paul Backhouse for masterminding the specially drawn maps. The quality of a number of the illustrations reflects Roy Adkins' digital expertise.

To all these people and organisations I remain deeply grateful. However, the responsibility for any mistakes in this book is mine alone. Last, but far from least, I owe especial thanks to my family for their constant support, tolerance and patience during many years of intermittent research and site visits.

ABBREVIATIONS AND MEASUREMENTS

Abbreviations

AdL	Admiralty Library, Naval Historical Branch, Portsmouth
BL	British Library
DoE	Department of the Environment
EH	English Heritage
GC	The Science Museum: Goodrich Collection
IWM	Imperial War Museum
MoD	Ministry of Defence
NMM	The National Maritime Museum, Greenwich
NMR	The English Heritage Archive (National Monuments Record)
NMRN	National Museum of the Royal Navy, Portsmouth
NPG	National Portrait Gallery
TNA	The National Archives, Kew

Measurements

Imperial measurements are mostly used in this book, as that was the standard system for much of this period of history.

1 inch (in) = 254 millimetres
1 foot (ft) = 0.30 metres
1 yard (yd) = 0.91 metres
1 mile = 1.609 kilometres
1 pound (lb) = 453.59 grams
1 hundredweight (cwt) = 45.36 kilograms
1 ton = 907.18 kilograms
1 gallon = 4.546 litres

FOREWORD

'It is upon the Navy under the Providence of God that the safety, honour, and welfare of this realm do chiefly depend', states the preamble to the Articles of War of the 1670s, at a time of acute tension during the Anglo-Dutch wars and in the aftermath of the disastrous raid on the Medway of June 1667. This declaration captured not only the spirit of the nation's longstanding belief in the Navy as defender of its shores, but anticipated a new understanding that there was a wider need, to protect British commerce on the high seas and, where necessary, to take war to the enemy wherever he might be. From then until the final victories at Trafalgar and Waterloo, the Royal Navy grew to become the world's largest, and to hold undisputed command of the oceans until after the entry of the United States into the Second World War following Pearl Harbour.

The unique circumstances of Britain's rise as an industrial, imperial and global power and as a trading nation put unprecedented and constantly changing demands upon the Navy. From the early 18th century until the First World War those requirements expanded progressively within a broad financial and political consensus that favoured sustained investment in ships and the complex infrastructure necessary to keep them at sea. On the one hand, a relatively small standing army, in part reflecting deep-seated domestic concerns about control of the civil population, was contrasted by an unbounded belief in and commitment to the Navy. Britain's growing self-assurance was to a great extent founded in this unquestioning confidence, that her interests, political and commercial, should and could be protected wherever the need might arise. It was also on the inferred deterrent of a global naval presence that *Pax Britannica* and thus the balance of power rested.

The climate of faith and conviction, underwritten by the Navy, encouraged mercantile endeavour and the investment of private capital, in merchant shipping and port facilities and increasingly in industrial innovation. This in turn fuelled a culture of enterprise that could progressively see the world as its open door. These synergies meant that the Royal Navy became not only the beneficiary of an increasingly wealthy nation and of the new technologies that formed part of its industrial transformation, but also the guardian of the essential security and confidence that were crucial to its longer term promotion and sustenance.

Historians have interpreted the geopolitical success of the Royal Navy in terms of superior seamanship and gunnery, courage, financial incentive, strategic and tactical knowledge and the Nelson touch, accepting too, rather as a sub-text, the presence of sound logistical support and the adoption – sometimes with reluctance – of new technologies. In this outstanding book, Jonathan Coad, without exception the leading historian of the royal dockyards, for the first time puts these assertions into broader perspective by setting out cogently and comprehensively the extraordinary nature and scale of the organisation – itself the largest industrial enterprise in the world by the middle of the 18th century – that was necessary for the Navy to emerge as the effective instrument of power that it was to become.

The design and construction of dockyards and their associated victualling and ordnance facilities were supplemented in the 18th century by naval hospitals and barracks for Royal Marines and in the 19th by specialist training establishments, naval accommodation and a worldwide chain of coaling stations. Huge engineering workshops became increasingly important as the fleet changed from sail to steam, from wood to iron and then to steel. Here could be found ground-breaking innovation, most notably at Portsmouth, where Samuel Bentham, Marc Brunel and Henry Maudslay conspired together to break the deadlock created by the insatiable demands of the Fleet for pulley blocks. By setting up what was one of the world's first mass production factories, the Navy was in the forefront of manufacturing technology at a time when Britain was becoming widely recognised as the world's first industrial nation. A century later it was in the Royal Navy's own yard, again at Portsmouth, that the revolutionary battleship HMS *Dreadnought* was built, in little over a year, at one stroke recalibrating the nature of naval warfare.

Given the scale of the Navy and its commitments over more than two centuries, all this was achieved with astonishingly modest resources and manpower. There is perhaps a moral here, for consistency of state investment and an inbuilt structure of bureaucratic continuity, often supported by sound organisation and administration, allowed naval buildings and civil engineering works to be planned and constructed on a scale and with a permanency that until the 19th century could rarely, if ever, be rivalled by commercial concerns, often subject to shorter term thinking and less predictable access to capital.

Support for the Fleet is the culmination of years of painstaking research in often neglected and unpublished archives worldwide. It charts the history of the design, construction and evolution of these naval bases over two critical centuries, between 1700 and 1914. Today, in dockyards across the world, some still in use by the Royal Navy, others by Commonwealth navies, and many now abandoned, can be found the evidence of this first global industrial network. Jonathan Coad's command of the historical sources combined with analysis of the surviving physical evidence establishes a new context within which to understand the Royal Navy's hegemony.

Sir Neil Cossons
Rushbury, Shropshire
August 2012

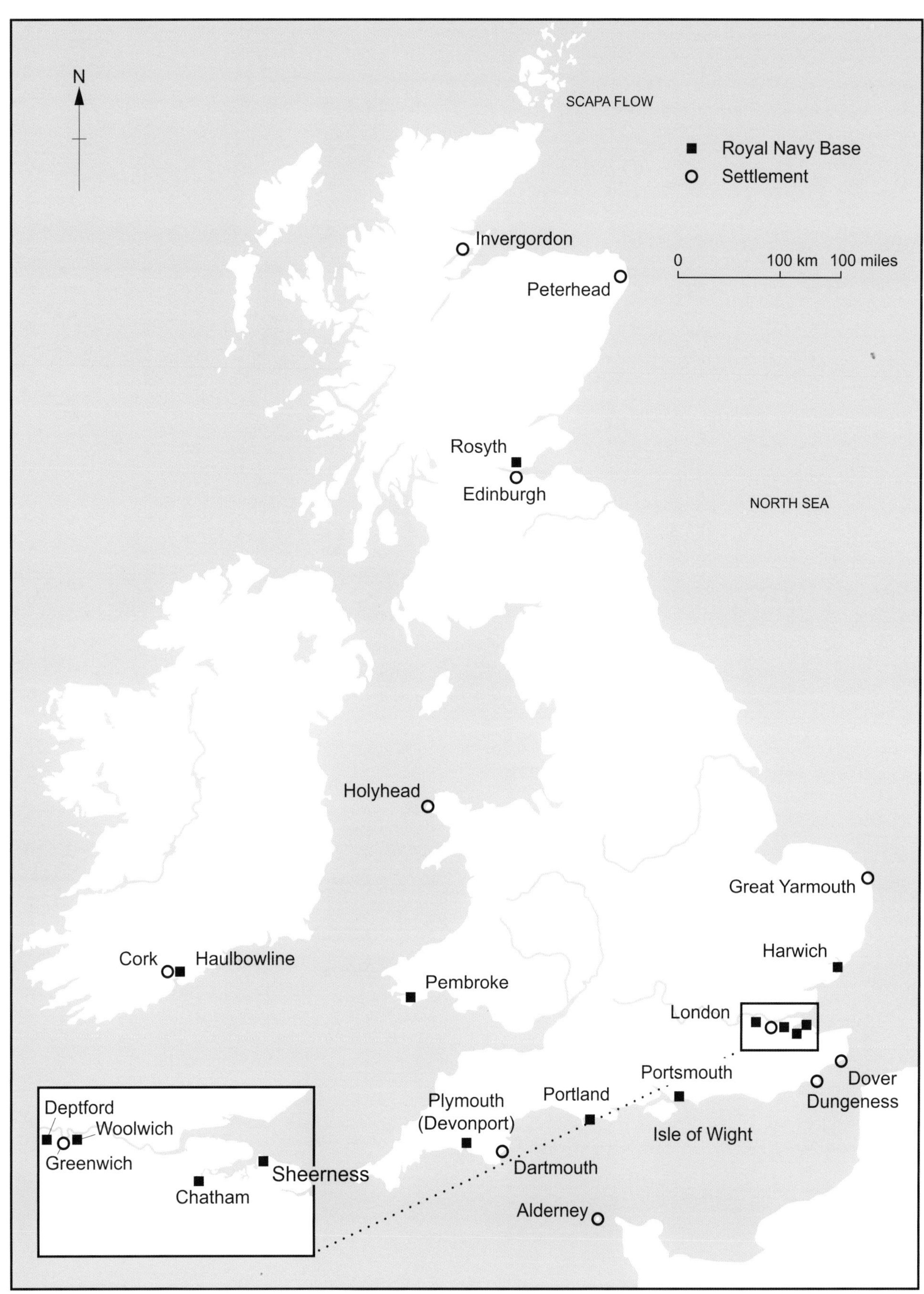

Map of Britain and Ireland with naval bases

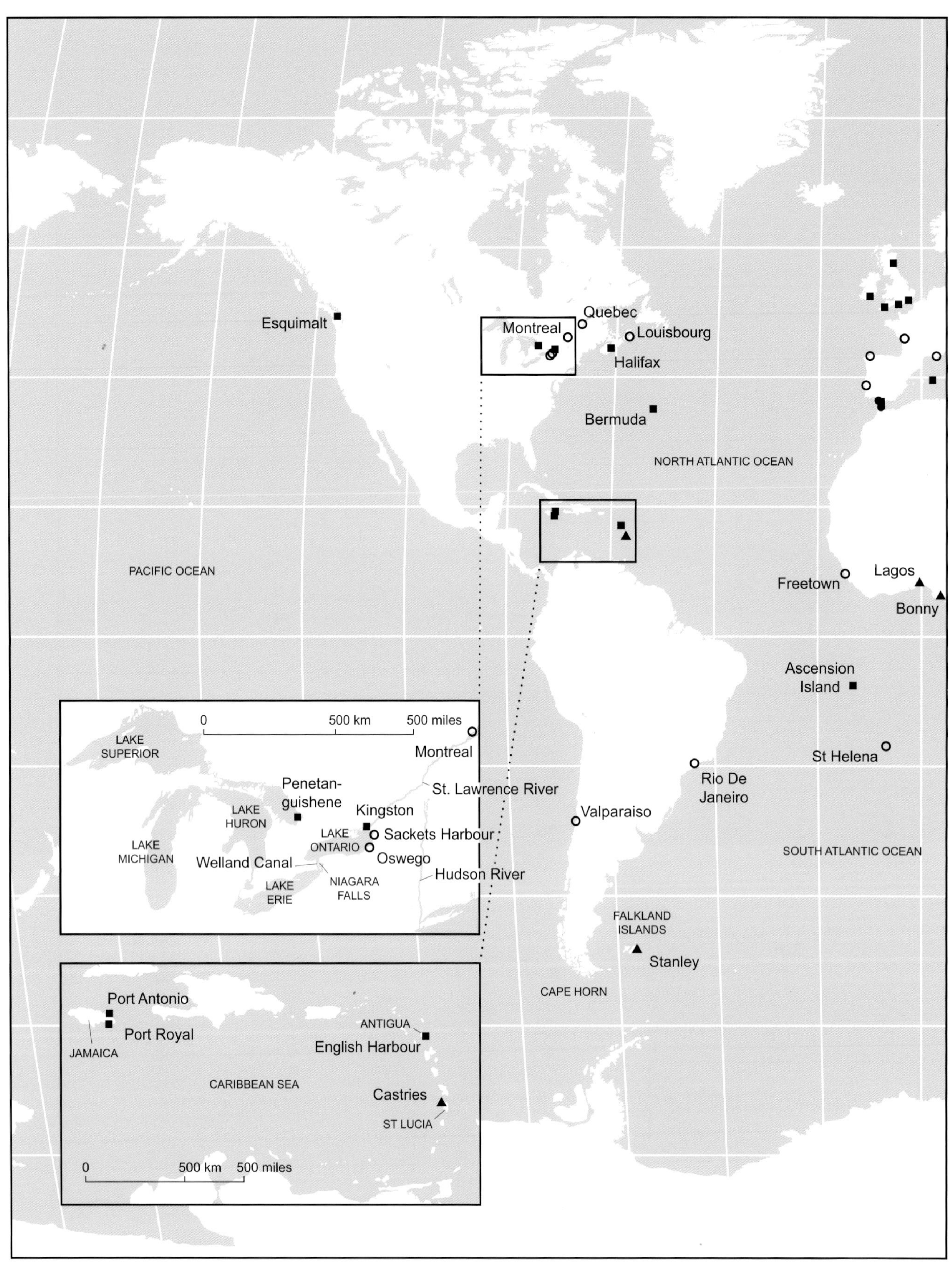

Map of the world with British naval bases

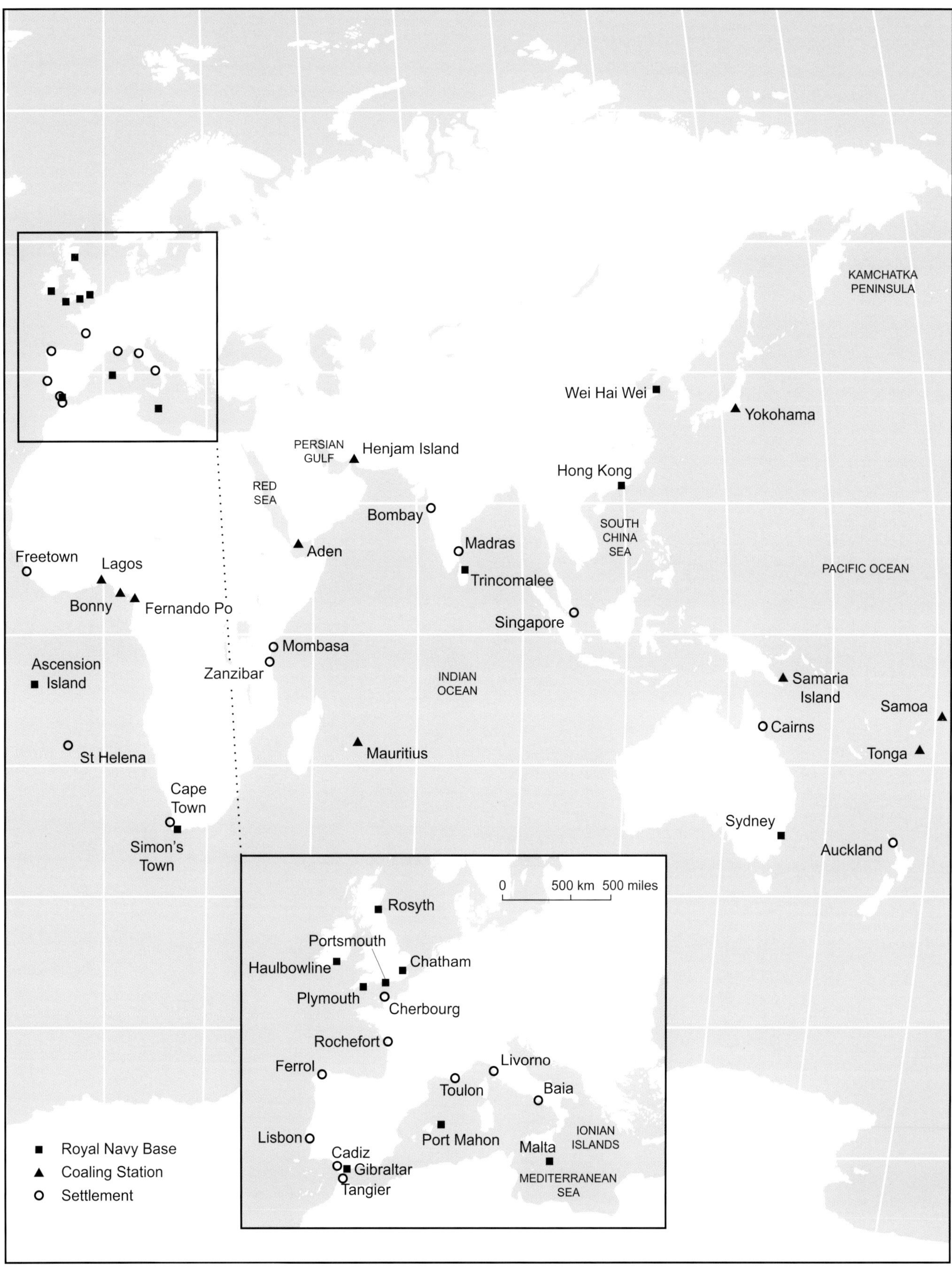

KAMCHATKA PENINSULA
Wei Hai Wei
Yokohama
PERSIAN GULF
Henjam Island
Hong Kong
RED SEA
Bombay
SOUTH CHINA SEA
Madras
Aden
Freetown
Lagos
Trincomalee
PACIFIC OCEAN
Bonny
Fernando Po
Singapore
Mombasa
Ascension Island
Zanzibar
INDIAN OCEAN
Samaria Island
Samoa
Cairns
St Helena
Mauritius
Tonga
Cape Town
Simon's Town
Sydney
Auckland
0 500 km 500 miles
Rosyth
Portsmouth
Haulbowline
Chatham
Plymouth
Cherbourg
Rochefort
Ferrol
Livorno
Toulon
Baia
Lisbon
Port Mahon
IONIAN ISLANDS
Malta
Cadiz
Gibraltar
Tangier
MEDITERRANEAN SEA
Royal Navy Base
Coaling Station
Settlement

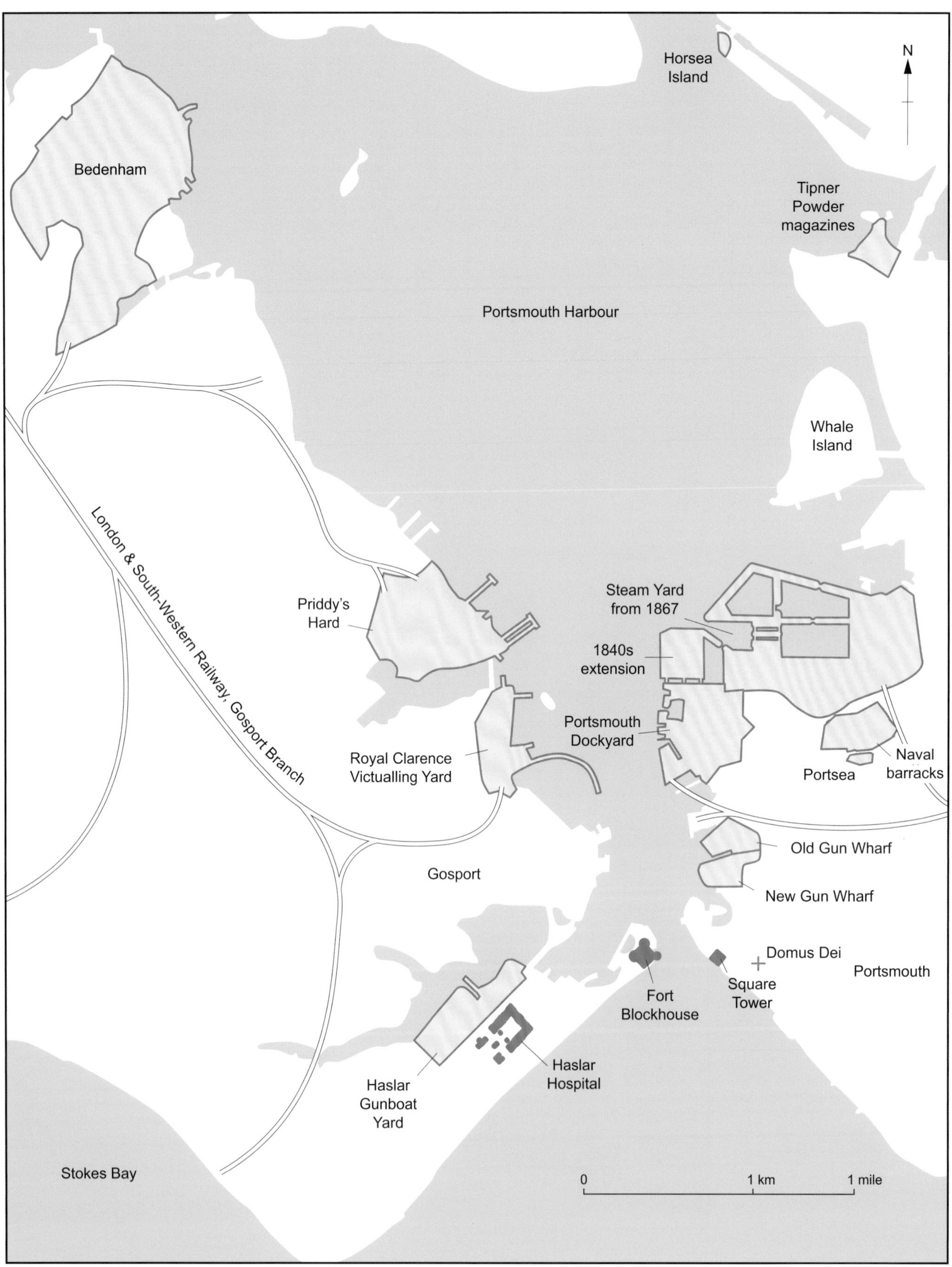

Naval installations at Portsmouth

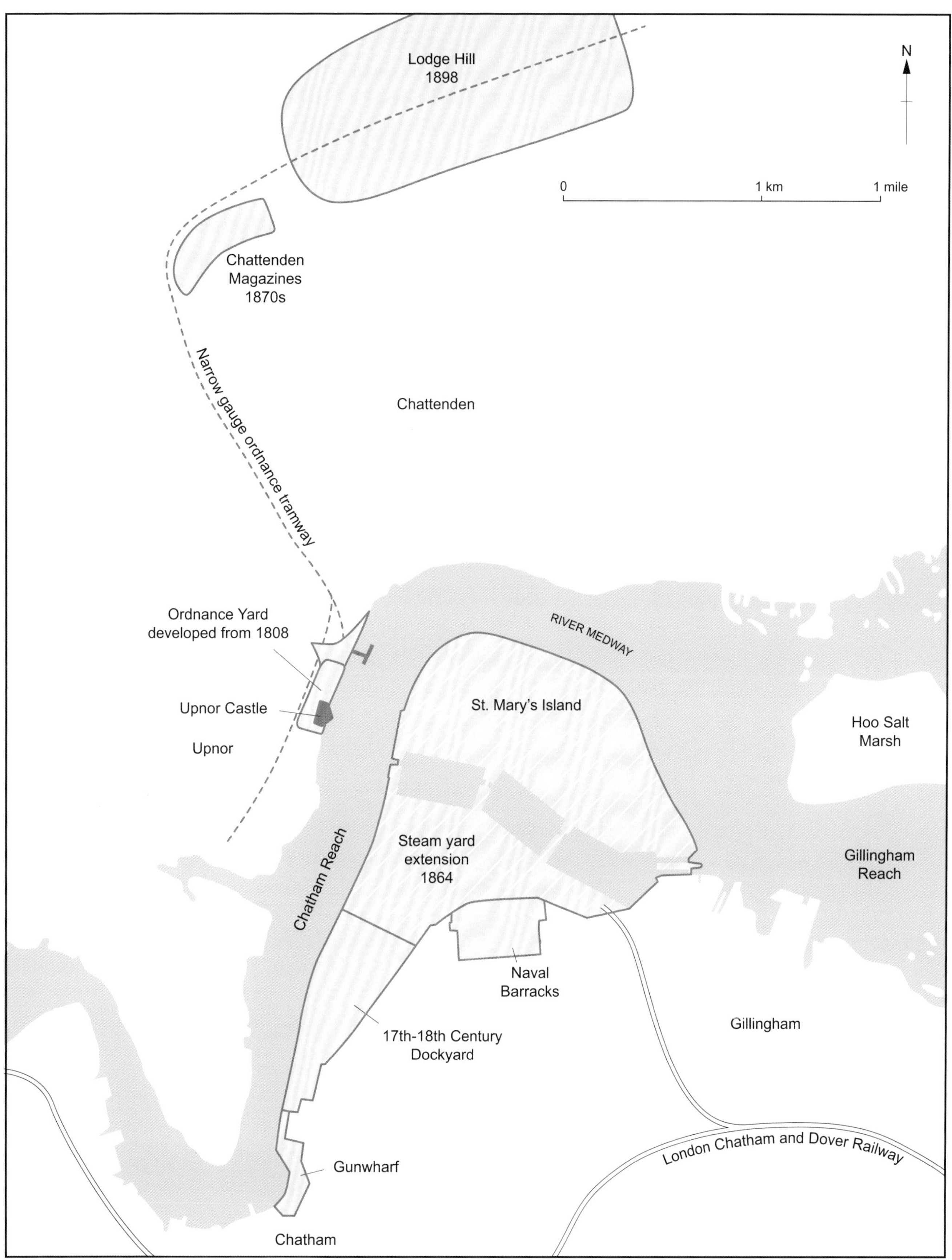

Naval installations at Chatham

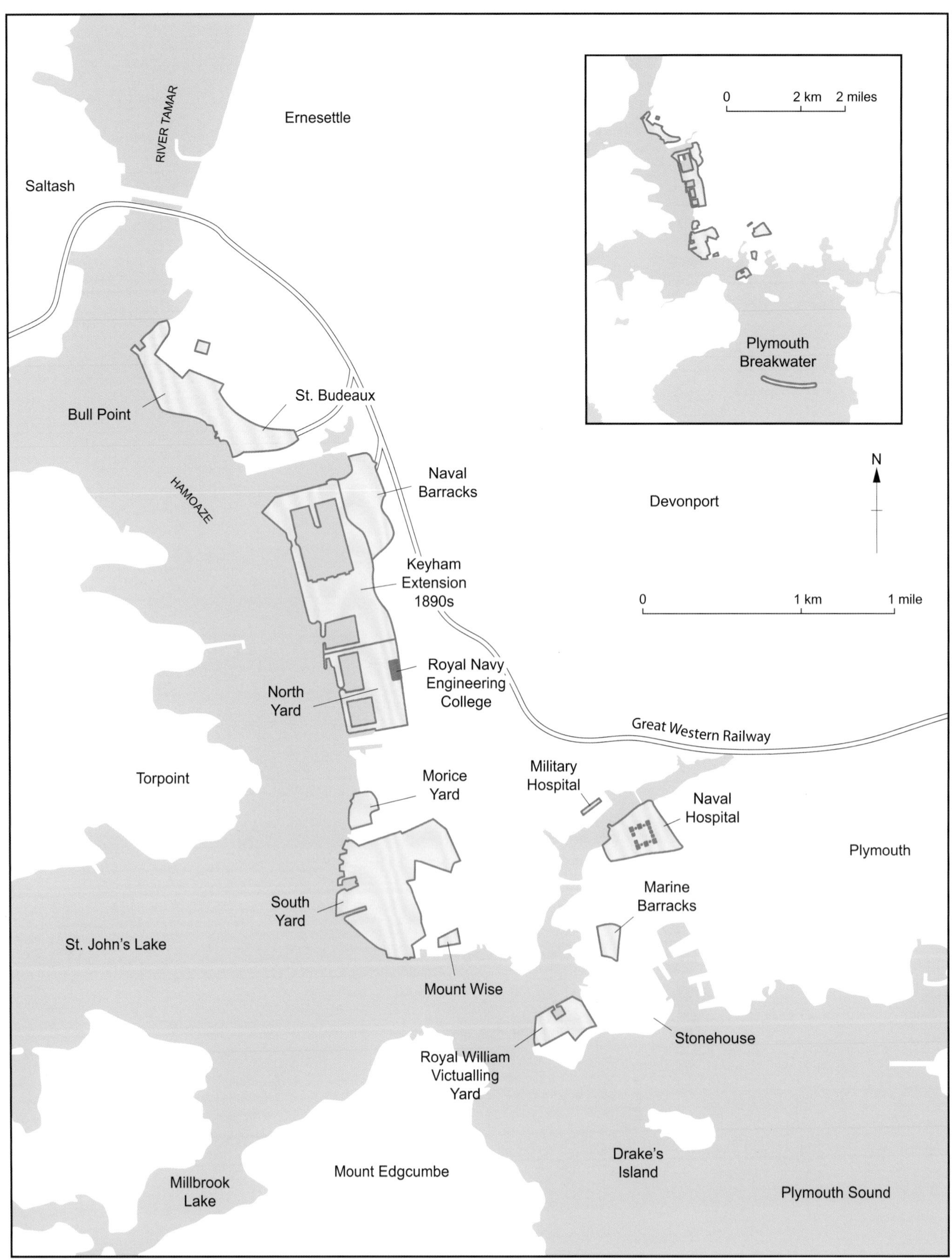

Naval installations at Plymouth and Devonport

INTRODUCTION

The Royal Navy is seldom thought of as a major patron of architecture and civil engineering, yet almost from inception as a permanent force early in the 16th century its royal dockyards developed as very significant industrial centres. Their focus on constructing, fitting out and maintaining warships of the Royal Navy led to the evolution of a variety of specialised and distinctive buildings. The growth of the fleet in the 18th century that culminated in its world-wide operations in the 19th and 20th centuries was mirrored in the expansion of naval bases both at home and increasingly overseas.

At their heart lay the dockyards with their associated victualling and ordnance yards. The more important of these dockyards were joined in the 18th century by naval hospitals and barracks for Royal Marines and in the 19th century by specialist training establishments and naval barracks. Huge engineering workshops and coaling stations became increasingly important as the fleet changed from sail to steam and from wood to iron and then steel. State finance, particularly from the early 18th century, allowed naval buildings and civil engineering works to be planned and constructed with a permanency and on a scale that until the 19th century could rarely be rivalled by commercial concerns.

This book aims to chart the broad history of the construction, establishment and evolution of these naval bases between 1700 and 1914. This period covers the Royal Navy's remarkable expansion in the 18th century, followed by its global dominance after the Napoleonic Wars. For most of the 19th century it had no serious rivals and exercised a world-wide influence using surprisingly slim resources.

The year 1700 is a convenient starting date for an architectural history, because only one or two 17th-century naval buildings survive. The year 1914 marks a watershed in more ways than one. By then Canada, Australia and New Zealand were establishing their own navies as their contribution to imperial defence, inheriting the Royal Navy's bases on their territories. The reduced post-1918 Royal Navy had little need for further shore establishments. With the sole exception of Singapore Dockyard, none was created in the years between the wars. In the existing bases the buildings and installations constructed in the great periods of expansion from 1760 to 1800 and from 1840 to 1914 generally were more than ample, and there were few major additions between 1918 and 1939. A century on, today's Royal Navy at Portsmouth and Devonport still uses many of the buildings, basins and docks constructed by the Victorian Admiralty Works Department and its Georgian predecessors.

Over the last half century a growing appreciation of the importance of the royal dockyards and their buildings in naval, industrial and national history has seen remarkable conservation achievements at former Royal Navy bases in Antigua, Bermuda, Sydney, Malta, Haulbowline and, perhaps above all, at Chatham, where almost the entire Georgian dockyard survives.

Naval buildings and engineering works cannot be understood in isolation, and an attempt is made to set them in the broader context of the fleet requirements, administrative practices and evolving technologies inside and outside the naval establishments. Until the Industrial Revolution in the 18th century, the royal dockyards can lay claim to being some of the most varied and versatile industrial centres in Britain. Constructing a warship was and remains one of the most complex of all tasks, requiring the input of a large number of trades and skills, nearly all of which were to be found in the dockyards and their immediate hinterlands. But from the latter part of the 18th century, the growth of industrial centres elsewhere in Britain offered the potential for innovations and improvements to be shared with the royal yards. These early links are explored, including those with the principal engineers, inventors, industrialists and contractors.

The steam engine was at work in the royal dockyards years before it went to sea in a warship, and at Portsmouth the world's first factory using steam-driven machine tools for mass-production was in operation in time for Nelson to inspect it immediately before he sailed for Trafalgar. In Edward Holl the late Georgian navy had probably the most experienced architect in the country in the employment of cast and wrought iron in construction. His work survives in many of the home bases, as well as in Bermuda and Port Royal. This expertise was continued and developed by the Royal Engineers in the Admiralty Works Department, beginning with the great expansions and modernisations of the royal yards from the 1840s, as wooden warships with broadside armament gave way to ever-larger, steam-driven armoured successors with turret guns.

In a number of instances creation of these major government establishments on green-field sites led directly to the creation of new communities, as at Portsea (now a suburb of Portsmouth), Plymouth Dock (the modern Devonport), Pembroke Dock, Rosyth, Bermuda and briefly Port Antonio. Although not directly financed by the Admiralty, these communities largely relied for their growth and existence on the wages paid in the dockyards, and to that extent their layout and architecture indirectly reflected Admiralty patronage.

This book is devoted to the dockyards and their associated facilities, rather than the great series of fortifications that by the end of the 19th century protected the major bases. The initial chapters describe in detail the dockyards at home and overseas. The later chapters discuss and set in context the facilities associated with the naval bases that were essential for the efficient functioning of the fleet and well-being of its sailors – the victualling and ordnance yards, the great naval hospitals, training establishments, barracks, coaling stations and protected harbours. With such an extensive canvas, there has had to be a degree of selectivity, with inevitable compressions and omissions. The guiding principle has been to try to cover the broad architectural and engineering history of the shore bases during the Royal Navy's global pre-eminence, illustrating this with many of the notable surviving elements.

Jonathan Coad
Salehurst, July 2012

1

The Royal Dockyards in Great Britain, 1700–1835

Establishment and location

In 1337 the *All Hallow's Cog* became the first royal ship known to have been armed with a primitive gun. Such weapons, probably more frightening psychologically than for any damage they might have inflicted on crews or ships, remained rare in the king's fleet. In the 15th century, out of Henry V's substantial navy of some 30 ships, only 15 carried a total of 42 guns. But as heavy ordnance improved, this changed and 'by 1485, a single royal ship could carry more guns, of various types, than Henry V's entire navy'.[1] Although gunports and gundecks do not seem to have been developed until the early 16th century, this growing weight of ordnance set the king's ships apart from their mercantile sisters.[2] More significantly, the early Tudor monarchs abandoned the practice of all their medieval predecessors who had created fleets for specific purposes, then disposed of the ships or simply let them rot. For Henry VII and especially Henry VIII, a permanent navy was a symbol of royal authority and an instrument of power that could be used in furtherance of political objectives in nearby Europe. Henry VIII himself took a keen personal interest in his ships and expanded and developed the small navy inherited from his father.[3]

One major consequence of the establishment of this permanent navy was the need to create shore facilities for support and maintenance. Medieval monarchs generally made temporary use of locations at Greenwich and elsewhere along the Thames as these were conveniently close to London. Early in the 15th century Southampton was briefly favoured as a base by Henry V when he was planning the reconquest of Normandy. In 1420 a forge and storehouse were established there, later supplemented by additional facilities on the River Hamble where three of Henry's great carracks were laid up.[4]

Portsmouth can claim to be the oldest naval base still in operation with the construction in 1492 of a crude forerunner of the modern dry dock, from which it differed in two principal ways. In design it must have had the appearance of a building slip, but perhaps extended further into the water and was protected by earth walls on either side. Ships entering it were apparently part-hauled out of the water, and the entrance was sealed by a coffer-dam construction – the 'inner and outer gates' – built across the dockhead. The space between these gates was then filled with clay and rubble. Constructing this dam apparently took some six months, with a further month to dismantle it when the ship was ready to leave. Such a protracted procedure inevitably ensured that the dock's usefulness was restricted to major hull repairs.[5] Nevertheless, the Portsmouth installation set two important precedents. Its high cost was to be echoed by its successors – dry docks remained probably the navy's most expensive capital equipment on shore until the advent of nuclear facilities in the latter part of the 20th century. Even more importantly, finding a suitable site for a dry dock determined the location of the whole dockyard. As its name implies, the dockyard was literally the yard that grew around the dock, and the name tended to be applied even if a new yard lacked a dock. Chatham did not acquire a dock until more than fifty years after its foundation in 1547. In 1694 Edmund Dummer maintains the distinction, referring to 'His Majesty's New Dock and Yard at Plymouth'.[6]

The Portsmouth dock was to be followed by a small clutch of yards downriver from London. Woolwich Dockyard developed following the decision in 1513 to construct the *Henry Grace de Dieu* (Fig 1.1), making the yard contemporary with its neighbour at Deptford. A further short-lived yard was established downstream at Erith the following year. It appears to have been abandoned in the 1540s as it lacked a secure anchorage and was prone to flooding.

Fig 1.1
The Henry Grace de Dieu, *the first warship to be constructed at the new dockyard of Woolwich c 1514, its tiers of guns clearly distinguishing it from most contemporary merchant ships. (© The Pepys Library 2991, Magdalene College, Cambridge)*

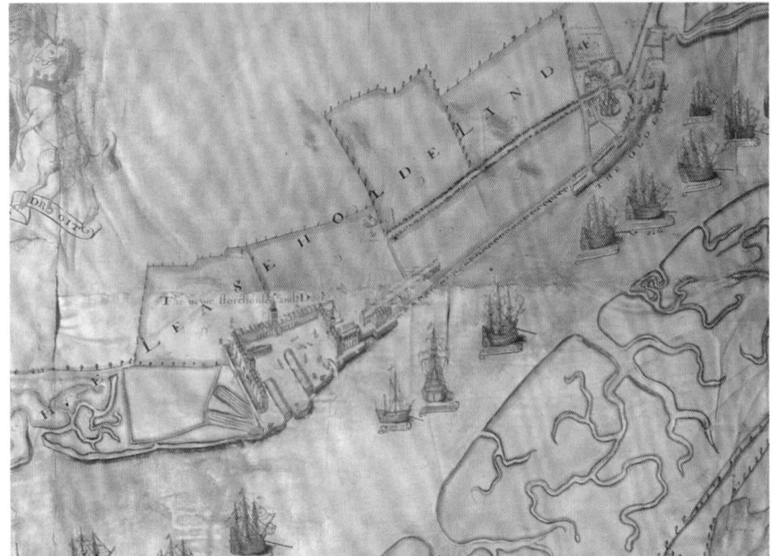

Fig 1.2 (below)
Chatham Dockyard c 1633, which had just been rebuilt on this site, one of the earliest-known views of a dockyard. In the centre are a double dock and single dock, with the storehouses, workshops and houses arranged round them. To the right is part of the ropery and to the left two building slips. Part of a painting in Alnwick Castle. (Collection of the Duke of Northumberland)

These new yards benefited from the shipbuilding expertise available along the Thames as well as access to supplies of all sorts in the London markets; they were also convenient to Henry VIII's palace at Greenwich. However, this concentration of dockyards ignored the wider strategic need to have bases convenient to likely theatres of operation. Later yards were sited to take account of this, their foundation dates tending to reflect contemporary requirements.

As the size of the Tudor navy grew, so did the attractions of the River Medway immediately below Rochester bridge as a safe and secure anchorage for laying up warships. What had probably begun as an informal arrangement in the 1540s was made official policy by the Privy Council in 1550, three years after a storehouse had been hired at Gillingham, marking the establishment of what was to grow into Chatham Dockyard (Fig 1.2).[7] In 1557 the Royal Navy reached a degree of maturity when the Privy Council secured it a peacetime budget, or ordinary, of £14,000 a year, giving it far greater financial security compared to its medieval predecessors. This in effect recognised that warships and their bases needed to be permanently maintained.[8]

Just under a century later, with the Commonwealth at war with the Dutch, a small dockyard was established at Harwich under the energetic direction of the Navy Board Commissioner, Nehemiah Bourne.[9] Although convenient for the North Sea, Harwich was to be supplemented and rapidly eclipsed by a new dockyard begun in 1665 at Sheerness at the mouth of the Medway.[10] Harwich closed in 1713, although naval forces were to be based there during most of Britain's subsequent European wars. In 1672 a naval storehouse was built at Deal in Kent for warships using the important Downs anchorage. From this grew a small naval yard of around five acres, extending north from the castle and including a victualling yard. This was the only naval base dependent on launching its necessarily small craft from the shingle beach. It was finally closed and the site sold in 1864.

By the end of the 17th century, England's maritime focus was shifting into the Atlantic and beyond, the greater distances leading to the gradual establishment of overseas bases (*see* Chapters 9 to 13). More immediately, this westward shift also made a new base imperative in south-west England. In September 1689, the Assistant Surveyor of the Navy, Edmund Dummer, was ordered to 'go to Dartmouth and Plymouth, and taking notice of all the parts thereunto, to represent what was found most suitable to the design and building one single dry dock'.[11] His choice of a site alongside the Hamoaze at Plymouth was fortunate, for the initial proposal to build a small base for the western squadron was rapidly transformed into the creation of a fully fledged dockyard (Fig 1.3). The deep water of the Hamoaze was to allow Plymouth to have a greater number of moorings for ships of the line than any other dockyard, something that would have been quite impossible at Dartmouth.[12]

In 1694 a cruiser base was also established at Kinsale in southern Ireland, but although a number of storehouses were constructed, the bar at the river mouth made it inaccessible to ships of the line, and it remained principally a supply base.[13] In 1795, at the request of the Victualling Board (*see* Fig 6.3), the architect Samuel Pepys Cockerell drew up plans for a substantial victualling base on Haulbowline Island in Cork (Cobh) Harbour to replace the storehouses at Kinsale. Nothing was done, but in 1806 the proposals were revised and expanded to include dockyard facilities which were completed in the early 1820s.[14]

Construction of Haulbowline overlapped with the building of the only royal dockyard in Wales. Pembroke Dockyard was begun in 1809 specifically as a warship-building yard and was equipped with a final total of 13 building slips and a graving dock laid out alongside Milford Haven.[15] It was sited to take advantage of largely untapped timber supplies and a reasonably plentiful workforce. These years also saw wartime supply bases being established at Falmouth and Great Yarmouth.[16] In Scotland there had been intermittent political pressures since the Act of Union to establish a naval base, with Leith considered a strong candidate. As there was no strategic imperative to do so before the early 20th century, the Admiralty (*see* Figs 6.1 and 6.4) had firmly resisted all such pressures. However, from time to time, stores were kept at Leith during the 18th century, and in the Napoleonic Wars a squadron, initially under Admiral Richard Bligh, was maintained

Fig 1.3
Plymouth Dockyard soon after 1695 when newly completed, in rural surroundings. This view by Kip shows the dry and wet docks in the centre, overlooked by the officers' terrace. To the rear are the first dwellings of what was to become the town of Plymouth Dock, renamed Devonport in 1824. To the right are the buildings of the ropery and the great quadrangle storehouse. Isolated on the bottom left is the smithery. The yard is set out on a more spacious scale than at Chatham 70 years earlier, with some room to expand.
(© The British Library Board. Add MS 9329 fol 180)

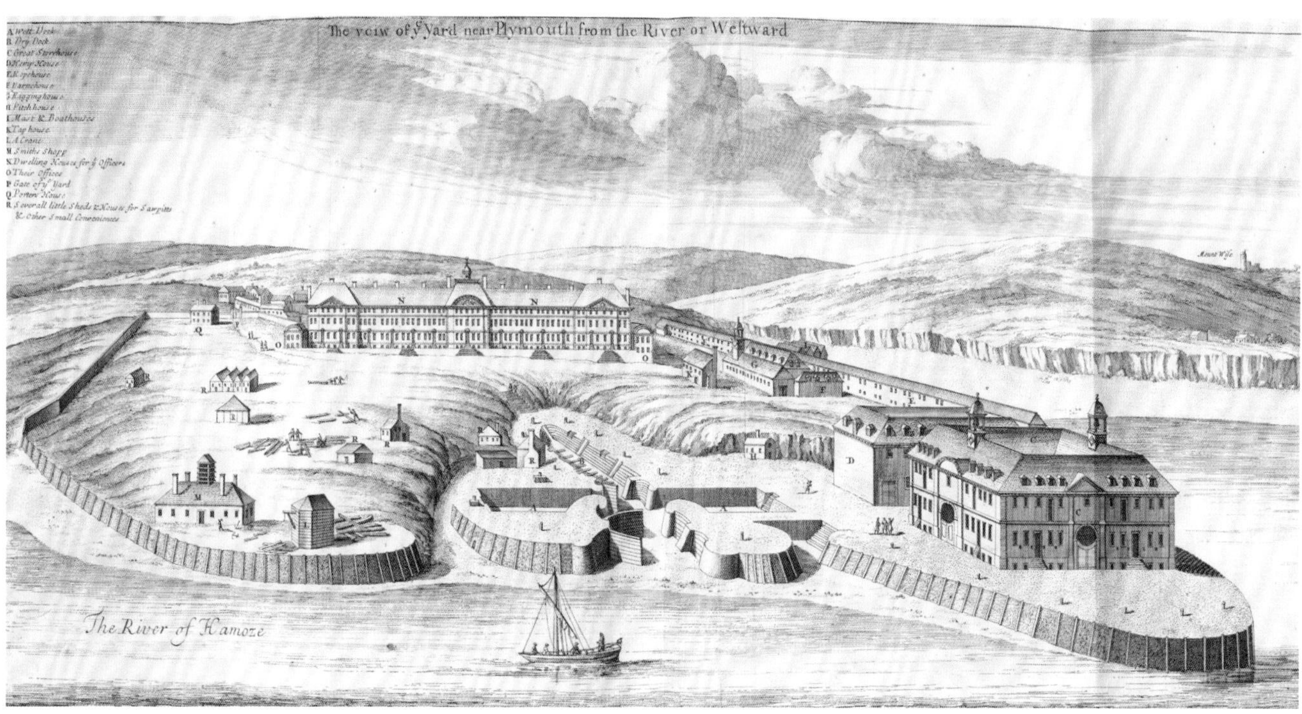

on station. By 1900 the emergence of Imperial Germany as a major naval power and challenger to the supremacy of the Royal Navy was rapidly altering British strategic considerations, leading to the establishment of a new dockyard at Rosyth on the Forth and later the development of protected anchorages at Cromarty Firth and more famously at Scapa Flow in Orkney.[17]

Although the Admiralty was in overall charge of the navy, responsibility for the dockyards between 1545 and 1832 rested with the Navy Board (*see* Figs 3.1 and 6.2). Inevitably, the relative importance of the dockyards varied over time. Location, changing strategic requirements, ease of access and ability to adapt and expand were all significant factors. For long, Woolwich and Deptford had retained their influence because of proximity to the capital, although they lacked sufficient secure anchorages for more than a few warships. In the first half of the 16th century, despite the extra costs of sending supplies from London and its distance from the Court, Portsmouth remained important largely on account of its sheltered harbour. But with the use of the Medway as a fleet anchorage and the subsequent establishment of Chatham Dockyard in 1547, Portsmouth declined sharply compared to its Thames and Medway rivals.[18] The Dutch wars in the latter part of the 17th century led to the growth and pre-eminence of Chatham and the establishment of Sheerness essentially as a forward base for the up-river yard. By 1700 rivalry with the Dutch had been replaced by conflict with France, favouring the renaissance of Portsmouth and the establishment and growth of a base, a few miles from the port of Plymouth. This yard and the new town that grew up alongside were known as Plymouth Dock until both were renamed Devonport in the following century (*see* Chapter 17).

Chatham, Portsmouth and Plymouth were all sited next to substantial and relatively safe anchorages, an advantage denied to the other home yards. This effectively ensured that for more than 250 years from the start of the 18th century, these three home dockyards consistently received the major share of government funding. Alongside them grew the buildings of the victualling and ordnance yards. These were to be joined by the principal naval hospitals, barracks for the Royal Marines and late in the 19th century and early years of the 20th century by the construction of proper naval barracks to replace the hulks then used as accommodation for sailors. Although these had become *de facto* naval bases by the time of the Napoleonic Wars, the term 'royal dockyard' remained in official use for their principal component until the late 1960s.

The Great Rebuilding: Portsmouth, Plymouth and Chatham, 1760–1808

During the 18th century the fleet expanded at an unprecedented rate in response to Britain's defence requirements and as the country's overseas commitments grew. In 1695 the Royal Navy possessed 112 line-of-battle ships and some 46 cruisers. By 1765 the fleet had more than doubled in number and, as warships were growing in size, had tripled in overall tonnage. Numbers were to peak in 1810 with 152 line-of-battle ships and an astonishing 183 cruisers.[19] This had important and ongoing consequences, especially for the dimensions of building slips, dry docks and the depth of water alongside the yards, as well as in the approaches to the up-river yards, particularly Chatham (Fig 1.4).

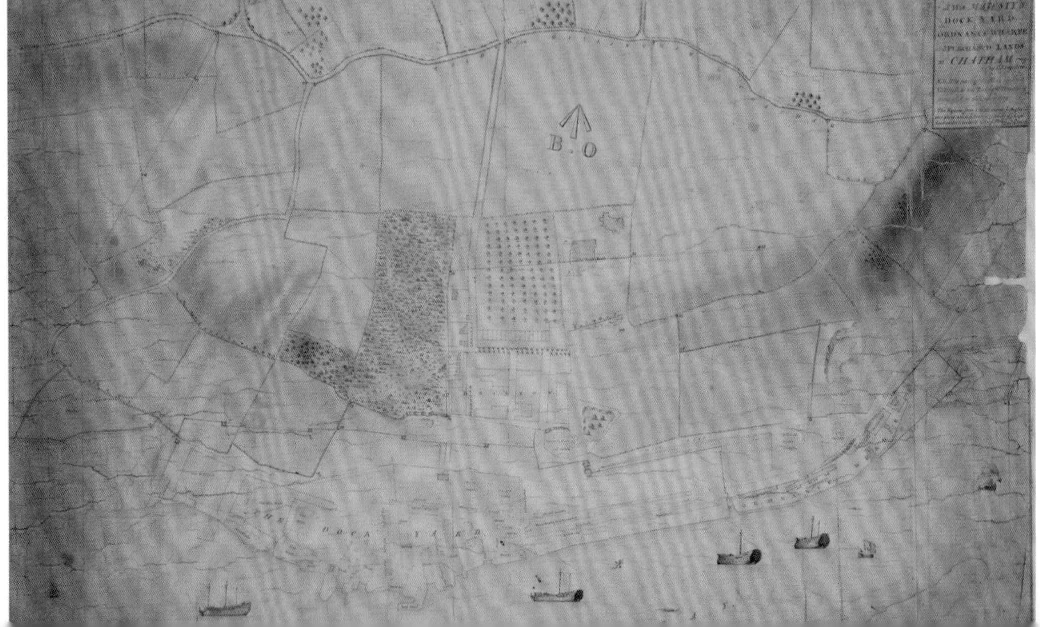

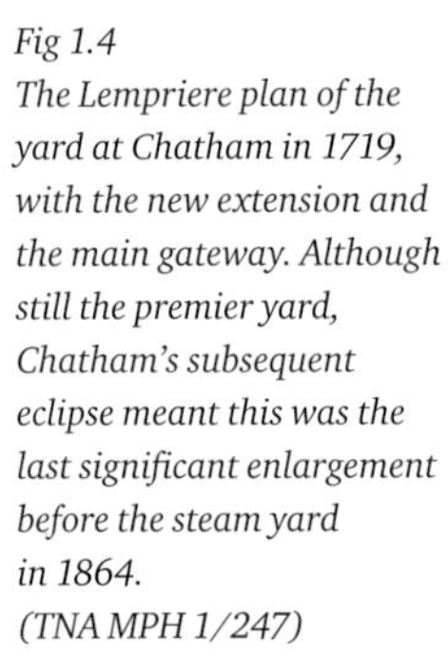

Fig 1.4
The Lempriere plan of the yard at Chatham in 1719, with the new extension and the main gateway. Although still the premier yard, Chatham's subsequent eclipse meant this was the last significant enlargement before the steam yard in 1864.
(TNA MPH 1/247)

The Spanish War of 1739–48 and more particularly the Seven Years' War of 1756–63 put immense pressures on the navy and its bases. Britain emerged victorious with an enlarged and different empire no longer based almost exclusively on trade and with a fleet that had shown itself capable of operating successfully on a virtually global scale. For nearly twenty years the dominating figure at the Admiralty was Admiral Lord Anson, First Lord for most of the last eleven years until his death in 1762. Credited with transforming naval power into a global asset and leaving a fleet 'well supplied with battle-winning officers, well-found ships, bases and funds',[20] Anson appreciated the vital importance of ensuring that the navy had the necessary finance and shore infrastructure. In this work he had a willing and able ally in the Earl of Sandwich, who had been appointed to the Admiralty on the same day in December 1744.

Sandwich was to precede and later succeed Anson as First Lord, becoming the most effective administrative head of the navy in the 18th century, finally relinquishing his post in 1782.[21] He took a close personal interest in the royal dockyards, pioneering regular tours of inspection by the Board from 1749 and acquiring an unrivalled knowledge of their workings. His long periods of office were important in giving continuity to the works begun in the 1760s. Sandwich maintained a close interest in the yards until he finally left office in April 1782, nearly forty years after his first tenure at the Admiralty. His knowledge, longevity in office and support for the navy also enabled him to maintain essential funding at times when the Government was seeking to reduce naval expenditure.[22] A third key figure was Lord Egmont, who succeeded Sandwich as First Lord for 3 years from September 1763 and supported Anson's and Sandwich's plans to modernise the royal dockyards at the crucial early stages of the work.

Between 1695 and 1765 numbers employed in the yards almost doubled, rising to 8,500 but still inadequate for the increasing workload (*see* Tables 1.1 and 1.2).[23] Investment in facilities also lagged well behind, while the strategic importance of two key dockyards had altered very substantially. The Seven Years' War, with its emphasis on operations in the Mediterranean and Atlantic, had diminished the importance of Chatham as a naval base, while raising that of Portsmouth and Plymouth. Anson had also systematically developed the Western Squadron into a powerful force to be stationed off Cape Ushant and Cape Finisterre, taking advantage of the prevailing south-westerly winds to protect merchant ships and intercept invasion fleets. This was to be 'the basis of British success in the French wars of the next seventy years' and was to emphasise the key role of Plymouth both in refitting and supplying the squadron. The French and Spanish had no deep-water bases within the Channel. The Plymouth dockyard would later be supplemented by the development of Haulbowline.[24]

By 1760 modernisation and enlargement of the principal yards were engaging both the Admiralty and the Navy Board. The huge sums of money involved led to prolonged debate as to the relative merits of Portsmouth and Plymouth, clearly summarised by Sandwich after the Board's 1771 visits. Portsmouth was felt to be more secure from attack, its central location and safe roadstead making it 'happily situated for facilitating a junction of our ships from Eastward and Westward'. But Plymouth was ideal for the cruising squadron, and the Hamoaze had a 'depth of water for laying up more large ships' even if the base was felt to be vulnerable to attack.[25] In truth, the boards knew that both yards were vital and both needed substantial investment.

Table 1.1 Numbers employed in home yards from 1711 to 1901. These figures, reflecting periods of war and peace, show a steady upward trend over two centuries, with remarkable surges during the Napoleonic Wars and again in the naval arms race at the end of the 19th century.

Year	*numbers employed*
1711	6,487
1730	9,618
1790	8,790
1805	10,000
1815	14,754
1820	12,725
1834	5,964
1840	7,965
1857	15,375
1870	14,980
1880	17,514
1890	20,663
1901	30,094

Figures for 1711 are from Merriman (1961, 373); those for 1730 and 1740 are from NMM ADM/BP/346. The remaining figures are from TNA ADM 49/181. The 1901 figures include for the first time Portland and Haulbowline.

Table 1.2 The very significant employment provided in the royal dockyards in the 18th century is apparent in these figures which also reflect the relative importance of the individual home yards.

Dockyard	*year*			
	1711	*1730*	*1790*	*1814*[a]
Chatham	1,309	1,722	1,695	2,474
Deptford	1,102	1,303	1,127	2,084
Harwich	89	–	–	–
Kinsale	35	–	–	–
Pembroke	–	–	–	4
Plymouth	736	2,464	2,141	3,914
Portsmouth	2,022	2,437	2,173	4,133
Sheerness	250	536	560	969
Woolwich	944	1,156	1,094	2,070
totals	**6,487**	**9,618**	**8,790**	**15,648**

a The 1711 figures come from Merriman (1961, 373–4), and the remaining figures from NMM ADM/BP/346, 12 Feb 1814. The Pembroke figure of 4 refers to the dockyard officers only; the workforce did not transfer here from the former private yard at Milford until March 1814.

In 1761 Thomas Slade, the Navy Board Surveyor, and Timothy Brett, then beginning his long reign as Controller of Treasurer's Accounts, were sent to Portsmouth and Plymouth to liaise with the commissioners and other senior officials and to draw up modernisation and expansion plans. When the Navy Board put their proposals for Plymouth to the Admiralty in November 1761, their accompanying letter clearly set out their thinking that this was a master plan 'to answer every purpose to be prosecuted as opportunity shall offer'.[26] This approach reflected the Admiralty's own views that such plans were to be 'settled with care and judgement, so that they may be proceeded on Year after Year in a regular and substantial manner'. New buildings and other works were 'to be fit and durable … instead of the Slight Provisions hitherto made in the said yards as expedients'. Almost above all, the Admiralty was keen to avoid 'the many inconveniences

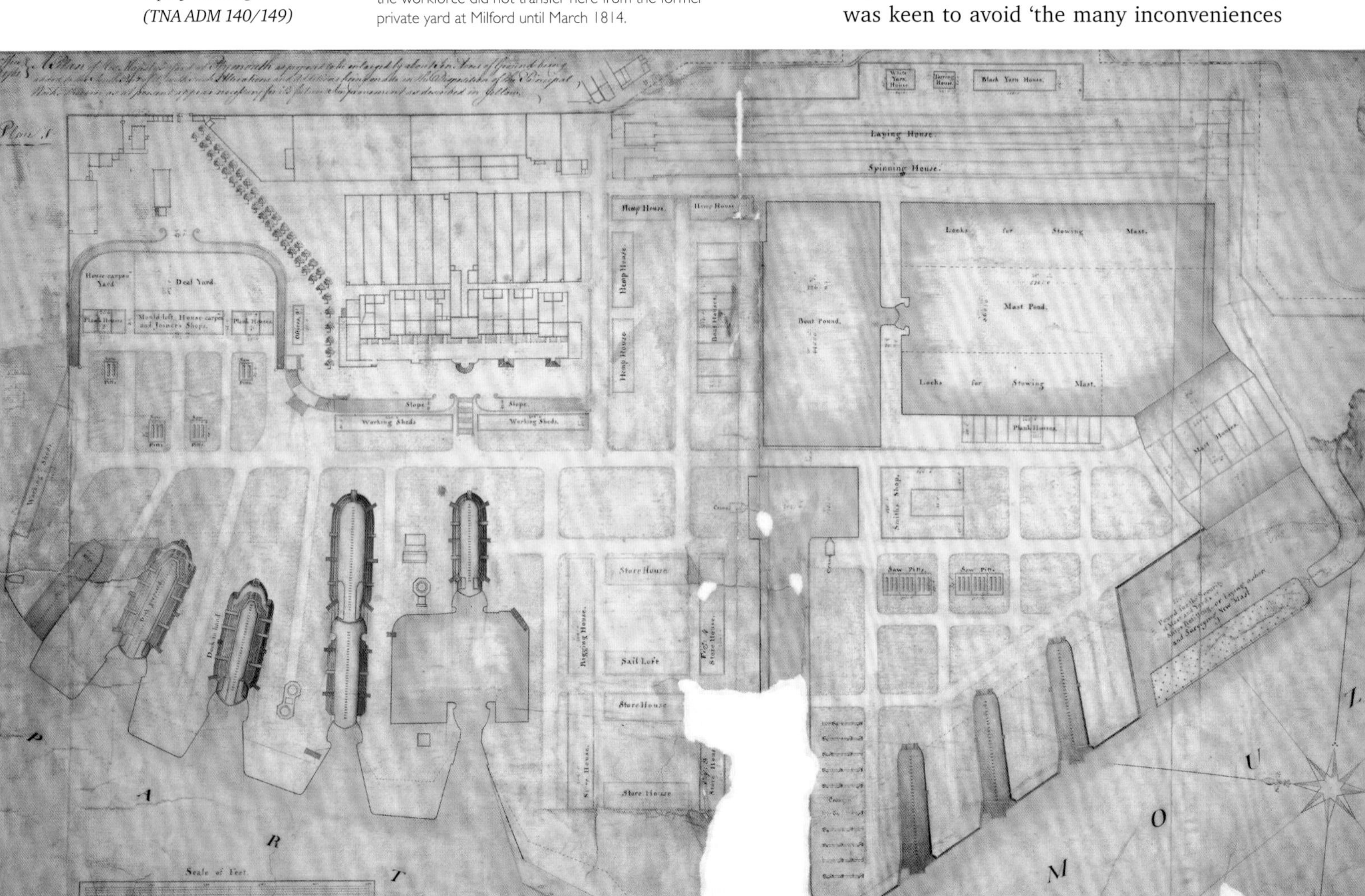

Fig 1.5
The plan of enlargement for Plymouth Dockyard dating to c 1769 and shown in yellow superimposed on the existing yard. These proposals were modified in the course of the work. Much depended on relocating the ropery buildings.
(TNA ADM 140/149)

attending the want of sufficient space and of proper Docks and Slips'.[27]

The estimates for the works at Portsmouth came to £352,240 4s 3d and at Plymouth to £379,170 1s 2d, though there is good reason to believe that the final bills were substantially higher.[28] This was the first time that major expansion and modernisation of the principal home yards had been undertaken on such a scale and with such clear objectives. The works were not to be completed until early in the 19th century, but they were sufficiently far advanced by the outbreak of war with revolutionary France to ensure that by then the Royal Navy had the best-equipped and most modern dockyards in Europe. The yard plans and many of the buildings and engineering works in the older parts of Portsmouth, Devonport and Chatham Historic Dockyard largely date from this extraordinarily far-sighted and sustained programme (*see* Figs 1.5 and 1.6).

At Portsmouth, dockyard expansion was only possible by reclaiming mudflats north of the existing yard, while at Plymouth extra space was gained by laboriously cutting down the rocky hillside south of the yard and using the rubble for reclaiming the adjacent mudflats and for new buildings.[29] As might be expected with projects spread over so many years, plans had to be revised, most notably at Portsmouth where two serious fires in the heart of the existing yard in 1760 and 1770 forced the Navy Board to rebuild the ropery on its existing inconvenient site, as land for its proposed location along the new northern boundary of the yard extension was not yet available (*see* Chapter 6).[30] Here too, debates between the yard officers, the Surveyor of the Navy and finally Samuel Bentham led to a whole series of proposals for extending the complex of dry docks round the Great Basin, the final layout not being agreed until 1795.

The modernisation of the two south coast yards also brought into sharp focus the future of Chatham yard. By then, its strategic value had diminished while the increase in warship sizes was causing acute problems of access. Shoaling of the Medway had led the Navy Board as early as 1680 to contract for a dredging engine, but this and subsequent attempts to maintain a navigable channel had limited effect. Well before the 1750s, larger vessels could only use the river during the few days of spring tides each month, provided these coincided with favourable winds. A 1771 survey of eight warships ordered to proceed from Sheerness to Chatham found that they took an average of 6 weeks to find the right combination of wind and water. The fastest succeeded in 1 month and 13 days, while the slowest, HMS *Magnificent,* needed 4 months and 3 days. Such problems made Chatham no longer viable as a fleet base, but closure of the yard was impossible, as the other yards did not have the capacities to take on Chatham's workload.

In 1773 Sandwich and his fellow members of the Admiralty Board visited the Chatham yard, praised its efficiency and recommended that its future should be for warship building and major repairs where speed of access was less crucial. They also noted that 'Everything appeared to be in good order except the buildings themselves, the chief of which are in a very ruinous state and must be rebuilt as soon as the other more necessary works [at the south coast yards] will admit'.[31] When funds were found, they were almost wholly concentrated on modernising the southern end of the dockyard, starting in 1778 with construction of the existing huge southern storehouse on Anchor Wharf. This building first appears as a proposal in outline on a plan of 1771, and an early version can be seen on the 1774 model of the yard now displayed in Chatham Historic Dockyard.[32] Following the 1773 Admiralty recommendations, the Chatham yard officers were also able to reconstruct the majority of the adjacent ropery buildings between 1786 and 1793, finishing with the Fitted Rigging House at the north end of Anchor Wharf, which was completed around 1805.[33] The last major investment linked by date to this phase of modernisation was Edward Holl's smithery in the centre of the yard. Planning for this started in 1805, and it was largely completed by 1808.[34] With the exception of the smithery, all these buildings remain largely unaltered internally, although the smithery still retains much early equipment. This limited but costly programme, combined with a lack of major investment in the rest of the yard, helped ensure that today Chatham has a higher proportion than any other dockyard of surviving buildings dating from throughout the 18th century (*see* Figs 1.7 and 1.8).

Although at the time the 'Great Rebuilding' between 1761 and 1808 had its critics, including Sandwich,[35] it was an extraordinary investment. It paid the country incalculable dividends in the wars at the end of the century and gave the navy some of its most attractive and functional buildings. These included three brand-new roperies, new workshops of all kinds, smitheries

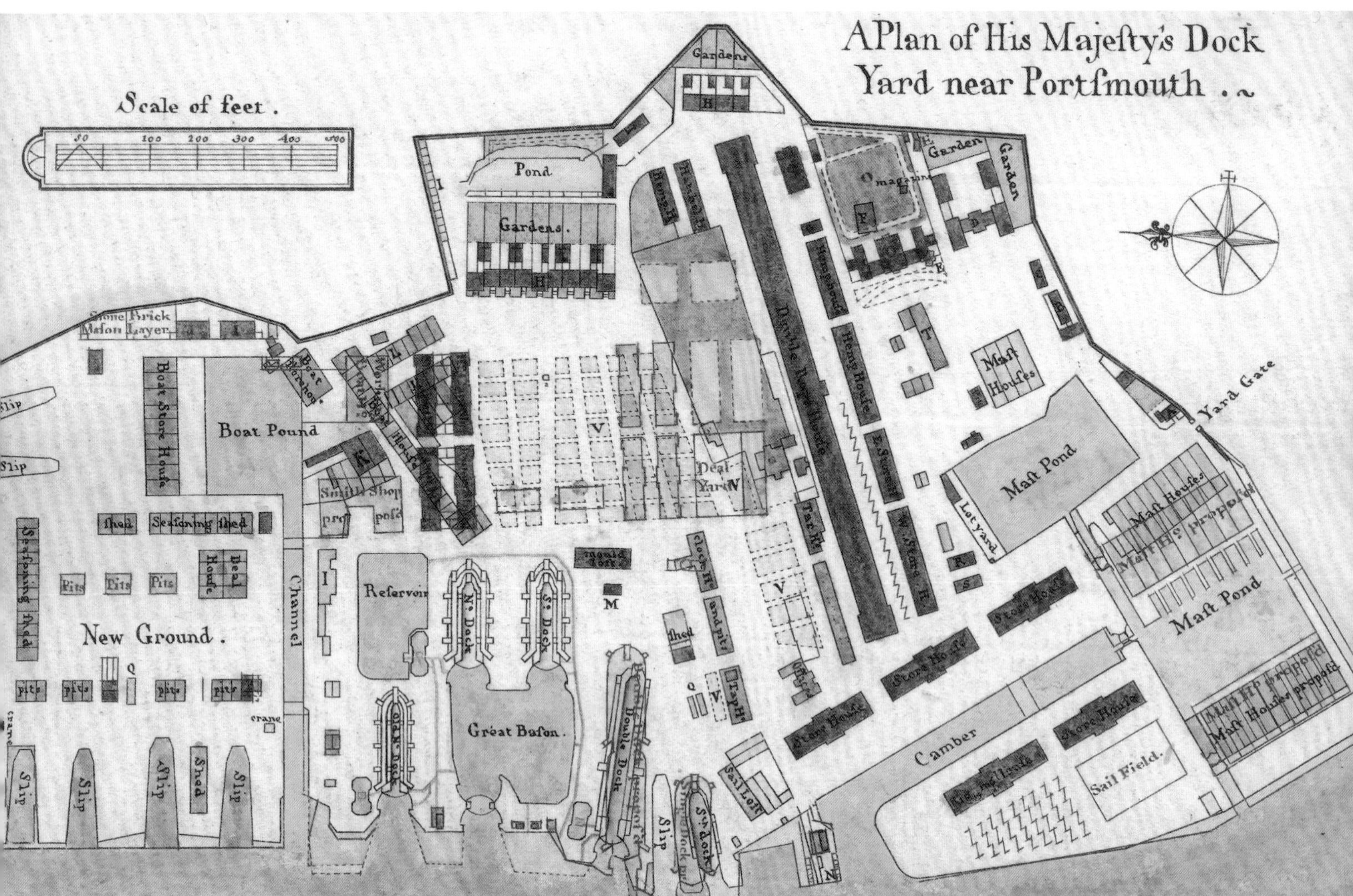

Fig 1.6
Portsmouth Dockyard c 1786. The new ropery buildings and storehouses are prominent to the right of centre. Buildings and docks not yet constructed are shown in yellow superimposed on existing facilities. (NMRN Plans of HM Dockyard, Portsmouth, c 1786, MS 1993/443)

and foundries, sawpits, suppling kilns, paint shops, a block mill and diverse other industrial buildings. Storehouses of every sort, boathouses, timber seasoning sheds and mast houses were laid out on a grand scale, and new houses provided for some of the yard officers. A substantial number of these survive and remain in use. Wherever possible, they were of brick or stone rather than timber clad and framed, both for durability and to lessen the spread of fire, both objects dear to Sandwich. Central also to his interests was the adequate provision of new slips and docks. In October 1775 he noted with some satisfaction that 'I have caused nine new slips to be made', adding that 'I do not believe it would have been done now, if I had not visited the yards, and pointed out where the slips were to be made'.[36]

By the end of the works, Portsmouth's two small slips had been replaced by three large ones on the reclaimed ground, and Plymouth's had risen from four to six. At Portsmouth, the number of dry docks was increased from three single and one double to eight single, while at Plymouth two new dry docks were added to the existing one single and one double.[37] Individual sizes of the new slips and docks also increased, although not by the quantum leaps seen in the late 19th century. However, nothing was done at Chatham in the late 18th century to modernise its shipbuilding and repair facilities. Three of its six slips were less than 150ft in length and suitable only for smaller warships, while the dry docks were still of all-timber construction. The figures emphasise just how important Portsmouth had become as a major repair base for the navy's ships and how much remained to be done at this Medway yard. Despite the obsolescence of some of the facilities at Chatham, the major royal dockyards appeared for the first time as substantial, carefully planned and well-constructed

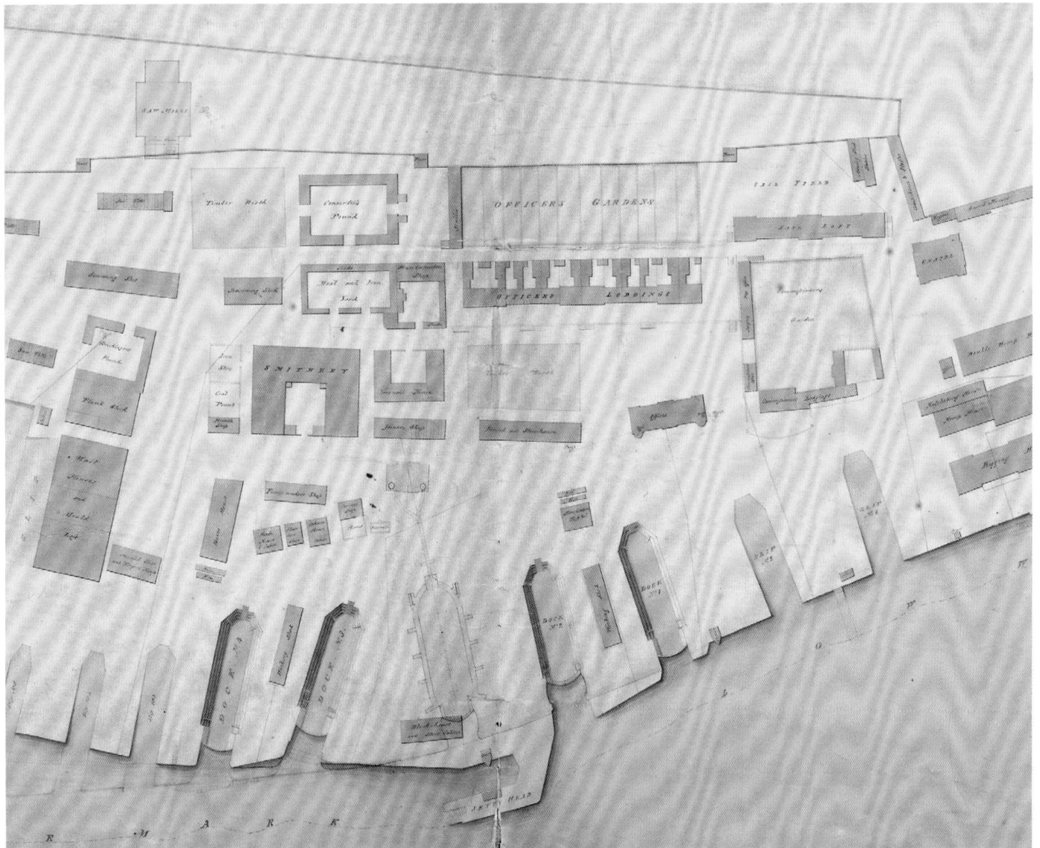

Fig 1.7 (above)
Joseph Farington's great painting of the yard at Chatham c 1794. The majority of the dockyard buildings shown here still exist. Combined with those subsequently added before the late 1850s, they make Chatham the finest example of a surviving dockyard of the great age of sail. To the rear of the dockyard are garrison barracks, the village of Brompton and the bastions of the Chatham Lines, constructed to protect against overland attack. (© National Maritime Museum, Greenwich, London, BHC1782)

Fig 1.8 (left)
Chatham in 1814, by when the buildings at the southern end had been largely reconstructed. The proposed new dry dock and Brunel's sawmill are shown in a pink tint. (TNA ADM 140/21)

Fig 1.9
Pocock's great painting of Plymouth Dock c 1800 is a vivid depiction of the industrial muscle that underpinned the Royal Navy.
(© National Maritime Museum, Greenwich, London, BHC1914)

manufacturing centres, the industrial might that underpinned the Royal Navy. The scale of the achievements in the three principal bases is abundantly clear in Pocock's great painting of Plymouth Dockyard after its modernisation (Fig 1.9).

The smaller home dockyards, 1808–1835

Although it may be convenient shorthand to refer to the 'Great Rebuilding' of the main yards and to mark its end with the completion of the smithery at Chatham in 1808, this was a phrase that would not have been recognised by contemporaries. The war with Napoleonic France was still far from over, and the Admiralty was continuing to invest heavily in its shore establishments. The capture of Malta in 1800 had brought with it the dockyard of the Knights that needed updating, and work was about to begin on the major fortified base at Bermuda. In the South Atlantic the capture of the Cape meant acquisition of facilities at Simon's Town, while in the Indian Ocean there were moves afoot to create a base at Trincomalee.

In Britain, the major investments needed in the Thames and Medway yards were waiting for decisions on their future, while in Wales the bankruptcy of a small warship-building yard established in 1797 on Milford Haven had forced the Admiralty to assume control of it.[38] Meanwhile, work was starting on a new base in southern Ireland on Haulbowline Island in Cork Harbour. The future of the Thames and Medway yards presented the most intractable problems. Investment had been largely channelled to Chatham in the last quarter of the 18th century, mainly because this was the largest and most important of the four, and closure would have seriously dislocated the navy's shipbuilding and repair programme. Sheerness at the mouth of the Medway was too small and was considered vulnerable to enemy attack. Its surrounding waters were also infested with the hull-boring *Teredo navalis* worm, while the mudflats and quicksands presented major engineering problems and expense for any extension. Woolwich had around £40,000 spent on its buildings between 1791 and 1793. Both Woolwich and Deptford occupied cramped locations, with the additional problems of shoaling and access. By the 1760s, warships were being delayed at Deptford for up to two months waiting for suitable winds. A little later, to lighten ships and reduce their draught, larger warships here had their stores and guns sent downriver on lighters for loading at Northfleet or Gravesend.[39] These inconveniences and problems remained largely insoluble until the advent of steam dredging. Significantly, the first time the navy used steam engines afloat was in two dredgers constructed in 1802 and 1807 for Portsmouth and Woolwich, an idea that is credited to Marc Brunel and the design of the machinery to Simon Goodrich.[40] In both cases, the steam engines powered the dredging machinery, not the vessels. By the mid-19th century, a better understanding of the causes of shoaling, regular use of more powerful steam dredgers and the creation of deep-water channels were largely eliminating the problems.

A radical solution, first seriously discussed in the 1760s when a site was briefly considered on the Isle of Grain, was to create a large yard at a new location to supersede all four Thames and Medway yards. Forty years on when the idea was revived, civil engineering was advancing rapidly, notably with the development of more efficient mercantile docks. In 1796 John Rennie senior (1761–1821) had given evidence to a Parliamentary Committee on the benefits of having wet docks and basins for the transhipment of cargoes rather than the common method of using lighters to load and unload ships anchored in the fairway. The Brunswick Dock at Blackwall, with its 8 acres of enclosed basins, had been finished in 1790, but it was the completion of the vast East and West India Docks downriver from London in 1806 that really demonstrated the strides made by civil engineering.[41] These had some 54 acres of enclosed basins accessible by fully laden ships, a figure way in excess of anything in the royal dockyards and one they could not rival for another half a century.

Samuel Bentham was quick to see the advantages of such a system for building and fitting out warships. At the time, the largest basin, and the only enclosed one, was at Portsmouth, now No. 1 Basin. This had only recently been extended to just over 2 acres, almost twice the size of the tidal basin at Plymouth. In 1800 Bentham proposed a new yard again on the Isle of Grain. Seven years later, John Rennie put forward a plan for one at Northfleet, and following an Order in Council in December 1808, some 543 acres were eventually purchased here. Rennie was thinking in terms of a basin to hold 70 ships of the line; the Commissioners of Revision even more ambitiously were considering basins for 300 warships.[42] In a variant on the theme, in 1814 Rennie followed up a suggestion by the master attendant at Chatham with a scheme for a new channel for the Medway that would allow the old loop of river to form the basis of a 243-acre wet dock alongside the dockyard.[43] The major stumbling block for all these was the likely cost, even with the use of convict labour, which was first being discussed in 1812. Although land was purchased at Northfleet, nothing came of any of these grandiose schemes.

Sheerness

The only financially viable option was to improve existing yards. In practice, this meant limited works to the Thames yards and Chatham, coupled with a far more ambitious expansion and modernisation of Sheerness (Fig 1.10). This was the only one of the four without a shoaling problem and was easily accessible by the largest warships. Well before 1800, the yard had occupied all available space, with a number of buildings located within the ramparts of the Garrison Point defences, which was a major inconvenience both to the garrison and the dockyard officials. The need to redevelop Sheerness was given added urgency following severe gale damage in January 1808. At the Admiralty's request, Bentham produced a comparatively modest plan for improvements centred on a new smithery and one or possibly two new docks opening off Mud Dock, which did inadequate duty as a basin (*see* Chapter 5).[44]

Something of the troubled relationship between Bentham and the Navy Board is apparent when the Board commissioned John

Fig 1.10
The cramped dockyard at Sheerness is portrayed in this 1774 model of the yard, with the numerous hulks that were used for storage and accommodation until the rebuilding of the yard after the Napoleonic Wars. (Author)

Rennie to produce an alternative modernisation plan. Rennie worked closely with Joseph Whidbey who had been master attendant at Sheerness from 1799 until his appointment to a similar post at Woolwich in 1804. In 1810 a delegation of senior officers of the Navy Board visited the yard to assess the rival proposals. The committee reported that superficially Bentham's and Rennie's plans look similar, 'but they differ very materially in regard to the more important works, such as the docks, basin and wharfs on which the efficiency of the dockyard principally depends'. Rennie and Whidbey proposed that the dockyard should be 'limited to the repair of frigates, sloops of war etc' and not ships of the line. The smaller vessels were widely used in the North Sea, but creating a dockyard capable of accommodating ships of the line would involve very expensive engineering works 'on account of the badness of the substrata'. Nevertheless, the committee came down in favour of Bentham's proposals, which included a dock capable of taking a 74-gun ship (Fig 1.11), and they also made other recommendations for new buildings.[45]

This endorsement of Bentham's so-far comparatively modest proposals seems to have unleashed in him something of a creative whirlwind to design a completely new and architecturally bold and astonishing dockyard. The concept was a vastly more elaborate version of a small factory he had developed when employed by Prince Potemkin to bring modern industrial techniques to the Ukraine. He and his older brother Jeremy, the utilitarian philosopher, developed this idea into his better-known Panopticon design for prisons as part of his philosophy of penal reform, but it was Samuel's Sheerness design that would have carried the concept to surely the ultimate limits. Highlights of his proposals were the six-storey hexagonal dockyard offices in the centre, with workshops and storehouses radiating from them. Forming an outer ring were two huge covered slips and four docks, which opened into an encircling basin approached from the Medway by locks at each end and capable of holding 12 first-rate warships.[46]

The buildings were conceived on a heroic scale, not least the covered slips, which were probably inspired by Bentham's earlier visit to see the one at Karlskrona in Sweden (*see* Chapter 5). With the exception of the central offices, all the major buildings were given a vertical emphasis, each bay of their fenestration contained in giant arcading the full height of the buildings. The drawing, finished in February 1812, is labelled as Bentham's proposals 'drawn under his supervision by Edmund Aiken, Architect'.[47] Aiken had been employed by Bentham since 1811 to help him on major projects 'which require some architectural skill ... to the giving them an appropriate beauty and grandeur of appearance'. Bentham estimated the total cost at a million pounds, a figure about which the Navy Board was almost certainly correct to be suspicious, though Bentham was more concerned that hostility from Rennie and Whidbey would lead to its rejection.[48]

In June 1812 a committee was appointed to look again at the future of Sheerness. Its members included the Controller of the Navy Board, the Surveyor of the Navy, the Chatham Commissioner, Josias Jessop, Joseph Huddart and James Watt. Watt was by then aged 76, and his attendance at what was to be his last such venture was due in large part to his friendship with Jessop and Huddart.[49] The plan they agreed on during their July visit, and which was approved by the Admiralty in August, owes much to Rennie's earlier work and included land reclamation and a substantial basin with a dry dock opening off it.[50] Bentham seems to have had little if any involvement before he was dismissed the following December, but Edward Holl continued to be the architect responsible for the buildings until his death in 1823.

With the exception of Bentham's 'Panopticon' proposals, all the rebuilding schemes

Fig 1.11
Samuel Bentham's revolutionary proposals for a totally new yard at Sheerness. (TNA ADM 140/1404)

at Sheerness, including that approved by the Admiralty in August 1812, failed to address the root problem of the cramped nature of the existing dockyard, its west side fronting the Medway but hemmed in on its north and eastern sides by its protective defences and to the south by the Ordnance Yard centred on Powder Monkey Bay. In 1810 the Navy Board had sought to obtain 'part of the Medway Battery', saying that 'We understand this can be done without material injury to the defence of the yard'.[51] Expansion south along the river bank, as envisaged in these early schemes, left the fortifications and the Ordnance Yard intact, but posed serious obstacles to yard expansion and communications. On Bentham's departure, Rennie assumed overall control, and in April 1813 he submitted what was described as an amendment to the plan agreed the previous August. In practice, Rennie was following Bentham's 1812 example and proposed a completely new yard, which reduced the extent of the fortifications, encroached on the housing of Blue Town and relocated the ordnance facilities to the north-west extremity of the site, well placed to serve both navy and garrison. This 1813 plan, inevitably slightly modified, is what shaped Sheerness until its closure in 1960 (*see* Fig 1.12).[52]

Although more than double the size of the existing 23-acre yard, Rennie's new yard remained comparatively small at around 56 acres, much of it on reclaimed land. Although some work started in 1813, little major work could be undertaken during wartime, especially as the work involved cooperation with the Board of Ordnance and the relocation of some of its facilities. In 1815 the dockyard closed and did not reopen until 1823, although works continued into the 1830s. The original contract for the modernisation works allowed £543,137 0s 7d for the engineering works and £310,964 2s 7d for the buildings, a total of £854,101 3s 2d, not so far short of Bentham's estimate of a million pounds for his own ambitious scheme. However, there is good reason to suppose that the final bill was different. Economies were sought, and in 1824 the estimated total cost was reduced to £795,101.[53]

The heart of the new yard formed a rectangle, its west side fronting the Medway, with a long triangular area running due east, occupying the site of the former defences and mostly used for timber storage and for officers' houses

(Fig 1.12). The dockyard church was located at the apex of the triangle, just inside the dockyard wall where it could be reached more easily by worshippers.[54] The principal buildings of the dockyard were grouped round three basins opening into the Medway, making this the first royal dockyard to be provided with a series of dedicated basins after the manner pioneered by the developing London dock system. The northern basin, the only tidal one, was for small boats and was shared with the Board of Ordnance. Opening from it was the yard's one building slip, a small graving dock and a slightly larger frigate dock. The central or Small Basin, used by supply craft, had the monumental Quadrangle Storehouse at its head (Fig 1.13) and a warehouse for the Victualling Board on the south side of the approach channel.[55]

The operational heart of the dockyard was centred on the southern or Great Basin, which had three dry docks along its eastern side. Round the latter were grouped the necessary sawpits, suppling boilers, hoop house, mould and sail lofts. The southern end of the yard was partly occupied by a mast pond with associated mast houses. The mast pond was connected to the river by a small channel with a series of locks. The civil engineering problems of building on these mud banks and quicksands were formidable, forcing Rennie senior to use a foundation system he had successfully pioneered in harbour works at Grimsby Docks in 1797. Behind a huge protective coffer-dam, its piles driven up to 30ft into the subsoil, thousands of further piles were positioned to support hollow wall foundations consisting of a series of inverted arches carrying the wharves, basins, docks and buildings.[56] These are clearly shown in the large-scale model of the yard ordered in 1825 by the Navy Board, probably as a detailed record of the complexities of this entire project (Fig 1.14).[57]

In 1813 Boulton and Watt had supplied three pumping engines to keep the excavations dry. The largest was of 45hp and with its pumps was estimated to cost £4,550; the two smaller ones were estimated at £4,170.[58] Samuel Smiles noted admiringly that 'the whole stood fast until the completion of the work, contrary to the expectations of many, who regarded it as altogether impracticable to construct coffer-dams of such magnitude in so exposed a situation, where the pressure to be resisted was so enormous'.[59] The two main contractors were Nicholson and Milton and Jolliffe and Banks. Convicts were used on a considerable scale for these works, possibly for the first time, perhaps indicative of difficulties recruiting labour to this bleak, isolated and unhealthy corner of Kent. The principal buildings are notable for their extensive use of cast and wrought iron, reflecting

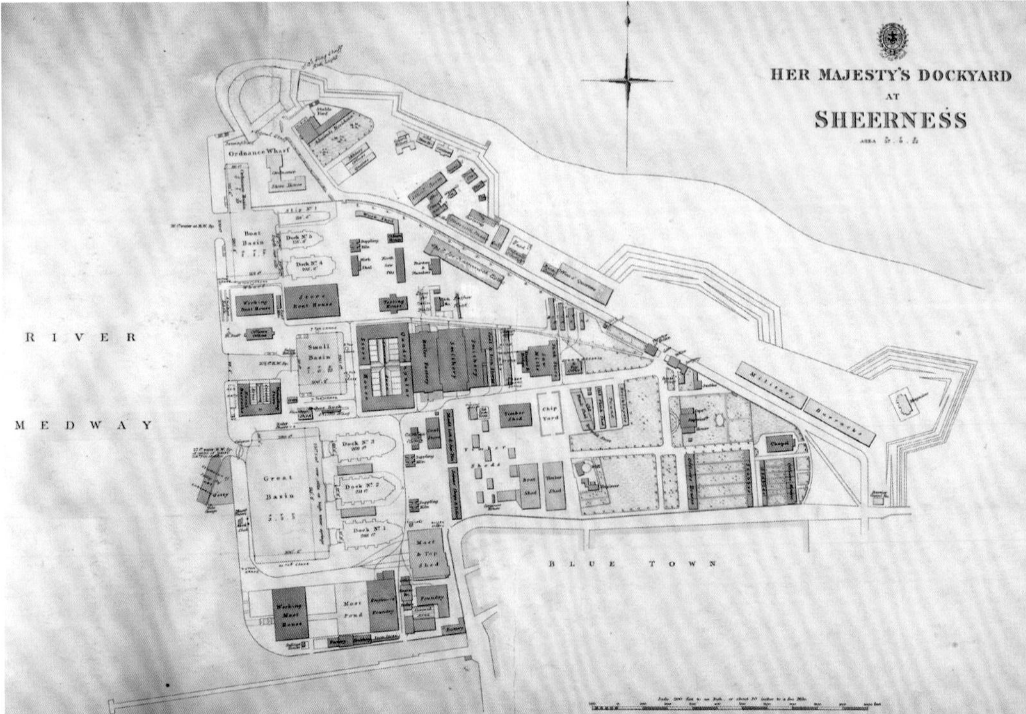

Fig 1.12
The dockyard at Sheerness in 1863. Except for a number of engineering facilities for steam warships, there were few significant additions following the great rebuilding after the Napoleonic Wars. (AdL 1863 Naval Establishments Da 02 fol 4)

Fig 1.13
The Quadrangle Storehouse at Sheerness shortly before demolition. (Author)

Fig 1.14
Part of the great model of Sheerness Dockyard, commissioned in 1825. It is on cast-iron stands because every structure is shown with its underlying piling. It is shown displayed in the boat store before closure of the dockyard. (AA59/00888)

Holl's influence. Rennie also used these materials for the first time in 1821, not long before his death, to construct iron gates rather than timber ones for the dry docks at Sheerness and Chatham. Contracts were awarded to the Bowling Ironworks of Sturges and Company of Bradford, who at that time was also providing the ironwork for the new naval hospital at Port Royal, Jamaica.[60] The completion of the Quadrangle Storehouse in late 1831 and the remainder of the senior officers' houses a couple of years later effectively marks the end of the great rebuilding of the yard, the last significant modernisation of any home yard before the impact of steam ships began to be felt.[61] In 1824 the future role of Sheerness was defined as a peacetime refitting base, leaving Chatham to concentrate on a warship-building role.[62]

Pembroke Dockyard

The founding of Pembroke Dockyard in 1809 was largely an accident of fate, stemming from an Admiralty decision in 1797 to award a contract for constructing new warships to a private shipyard at Milford Haven. The latter's subsequent bankruptcy forced the Admiralty to take control in 1800 to safeguard its order. Wartime pressures made all shipbuilding facilities valuable, and in 1809 an Order in Council regularised these arrangements, authorising the development of a new dockyard. This was sufficiently remote from existing government yards to lessen the Navy Board's fear that it would deprive them of skilled men and timber.[63] The earliest surviving plan at Milford for 1809 shows the original yard, its three slips and an excavation for a dock. To the rear are a scatter of small buildings, all apparently of timber save for the smithery. A sawpit is marked as being 'in ruins'.[64] Initial thoughts were to develop this site, and an elaborate design was drawn up in 1810 and signed by Sir William Rule, the senior Navy Board Surveyor. This envisaged two new dry docks alongside the three slips and the construction of a long range of buildings of assorted uses at the rear, overlooking the yard. Behind these, uniquely and optimistically for a home dockyard, an open-air ropewalk is shown running the full length inside the dockyard wall (Fig 1.15).[65] Milford, however, lacked deep water, and dredging was not considered feasible.[66] A report in 1810 recommended moving to a location at Pater Church adjacent to the fort. This was accomplished by the end of June 1814, when the few remaining items in the old yard, including the muster bell, were sold, mostly to the landowner.[67]

Over the next couple of decades the new base was developed, and in 1817 it was renamed Pembroke Dockyard at the request of Mr Humphreys, Mayor of Pembroke, and in deference to the town of Pembroke some 2 miles distant.[68] The navy had no strategic reason for

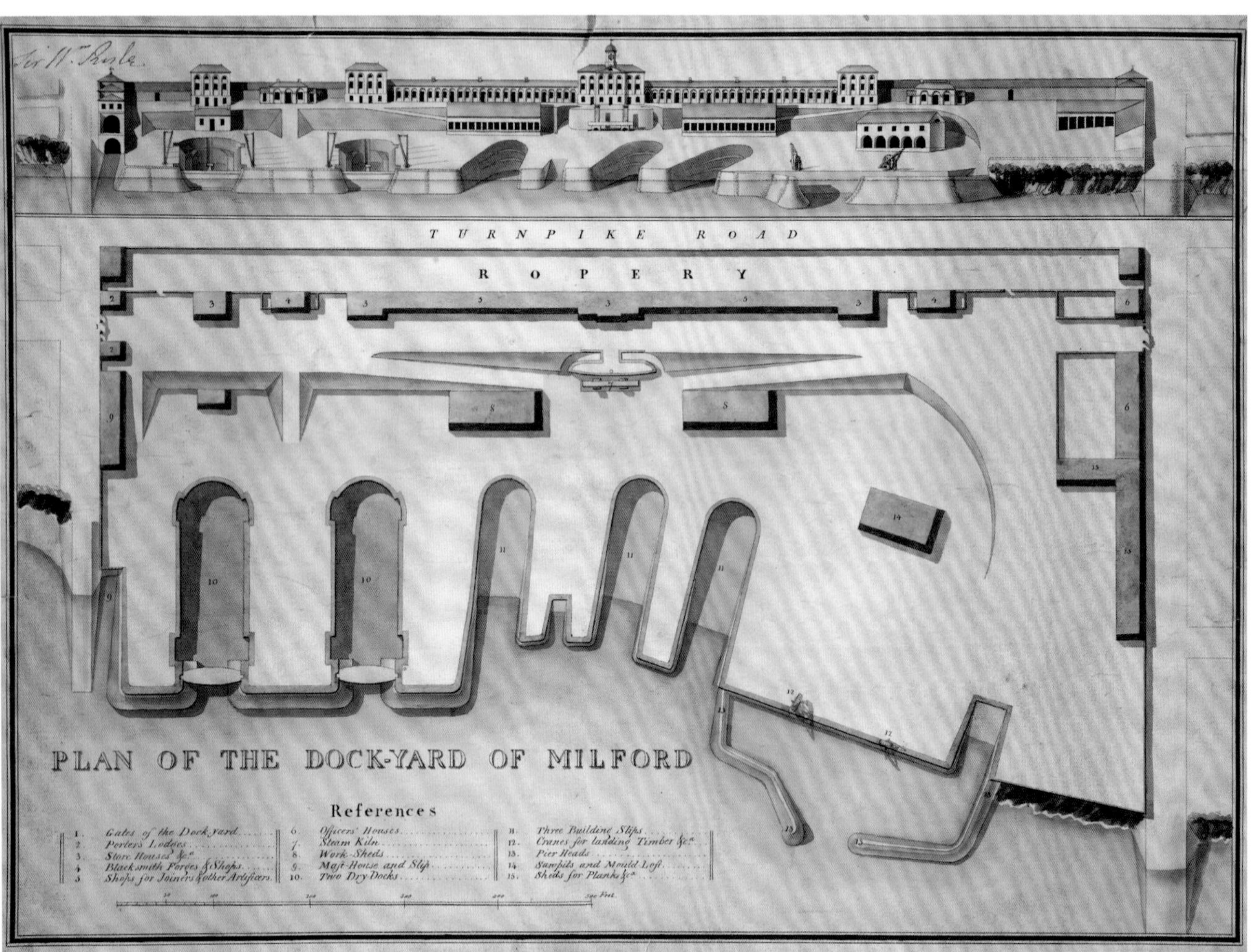

Fig 1.15
An early and unrealised 1810 plan for the new yard at Milford. The proportion of slips and dry docks suggests that it was the intention to create a 'general-purpose' yard rather than a specialist shipbuilding centre. (TNA ADM 140/492)

a base here, and throughout its life it never developed beyond being a specialist warship-building yard focused on its extensive slips.

The new yard occupied a substantial rectangular site sloping gently down to the shore on the south side of Milford Haven. Although early yard plans do not appear to survive, the civil engineering owed much to John Rennie and after his death to his son John, the design of the buildings to Edward Holl and the general yard layout a combination of the Rennies and Holl, no doubt with contributions from the yard officers and the Navy Board Surveyor.[69] However, before this yard could be formally laid out, sufficient temporary facilities had to be built to maintain production. Surviving records give glimpses of the practical and human side of creating the new yard in this comparatively remote location. In March 1814, shortly before the move from Milford, the yard officers told the Navy Board that they would need to enclose the new yard and construct sawpits, a smith's shop, a shed for iron and a porter's lodge. To this list a coal yard was subsequently added. Apart from the boundary wall, all these buildings were to be temporary, the yard officers assuring the Board that all the windows and doors would be reused in the permanent buildings 'and therefore no loss is likely to arise to the public'.[70] By May, Mr James Isaacs was at work on the boundary wall, reckoning he could complete it by the end of March 1815, provided he could open another quarry, presumably on site. He was also constructing the walls of the other temporary buildings.[71] By 1816 the main contractor, Hugh McIntosh, had won the contract for the dry dock and sea wall, the latter to take account of any building slips. This contract was extended to include levelling the site of the yard, stone slips and most of the first phase of yard buildings.[72] Although no slips are mentioned in the early years, at least one would have been essential. It may be these do not appear in the records, as they could have been constructed in timber by the yard shipwrights and later replaced by masonry.

For both the dockyard officers and the labour force, the transfer from Milford to Pater created considerable practical and personal difficulties due to the lack of local accommodation. Officers hired lodgings in Pembroke town, but cost ruled this out for most workers. There would also have been pressure on accommodation from McIntosh's workforce, which by the summer of 1818 numbered some 450 men.[73] In a report to the Navy Board, the officers noted that 'many of the men reside at a distance of eight or ten miles in the country', while others 'are at Milford, and so scattered along the banks of the haven as to require eighteen boats to carry them to the yard and back'.[74] Although the yard officers worried about the expense of all this ferrying, they were much more concerned that the men were already fatigued when they arrived for work. The Navy Board was asked to make 'immediate arrangements for building habitations on the government ground at the back of the yard'. In 1817 the Admiralty agreed terms for building leases, and within a few years developers were laying out a planned town outside the dockyard wall. Progress was slow until the Admiralty supported a petition for a market to be established. Initially, there were two separate developments, Pater Town and Melville Town, the latter in memory of Viscount Melville, First Lord of the Admiralty. Later, the community was renamed Pembroke Dock and on completion housed the majority of the dockyard employees.[75]

An 1819 plan proposed 10 building slips and a dock, all roofed, but by the early 1830s there were 8 slips and the single graving dock. The sea wall, stone slips and the dock were to designs and specifications by the Rennies. The specifications for the new dock opened with the cautionary words, 'The scite [site] of the intended dock is supposed to be principally of hard limestone rock, in some parts however this rock is supposed to be soft and slatey, and in others there is earth; out of these various strata the Dock is to be excavated'. John Rennie senior estimated the cost at £35,000, but the geological information proved faulty, and it proved impossible to form the altars 'out of the native rock'. The contractor hoped to complete by August 1817, but by then the estimated cost had risen to more than £60,000. Problems with the dock gates had still not been solved by the middle of 1823, by which time John Rennie junior had assumed responsibility for the work here.[76] A number of the slips initially were built of timber, replaced by stone later; by 1821, Slips 1 to 3 had roofs, and all were covered by 1832 (Fig 1.16), although some roofs were described as 'temporary'.[77] By then, four warships were under construction, including the 120-gun first-rate, the *Royal William*, and the 92-gun second-rate, *Rodney*. The latter, designed by Seppings, was the first British two-decker to carry 90 guns or more. *Rodney* spent 6 years on the stocks, the leisurely pace of construction reflecting the peacetime navy's limited need for such large ships.[78] Further slips were added, including two at the western side of the yard in the early 1840s that involved shifting the boundary wall; the same decade also saw the timber roofs being superseded by all-metal ones.

The 1853/4 estimates have a figure of £16,958 for two additional slips, the increasing size of mid-century warships reflected in the accompanying note that 'It is proposed to occupy the sites of three small and unserviceable slips with two new efficient ones'.[79] By the mid-1850s the yard at Pembroke had attained its maximum of no fewer than 12 slips (*see* Fig 1.17).[80] The dockyard never had a basin. Perhaps more surprisingly, until the nearby facilities at Hobbs Point were acquired a couple of decades after the yard had been founded, Pembroke had no alongside berths for fitting out new warships, resulting in many having to be completed at one of the south coast yards or at Chatham.[81] Slips 1 and 2, the dry dock and adjacent western camber are all that now remain of these facilities.

The middle belt of the Pembroke yard behind

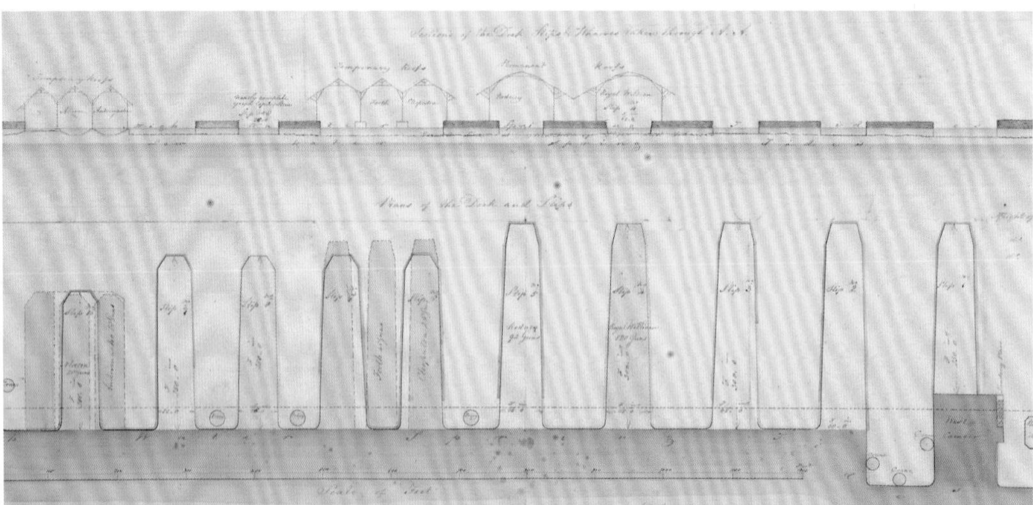

Fig 1.16
The line of covered slips at Pembroke in 1832.
(TNA ADM 140/429)

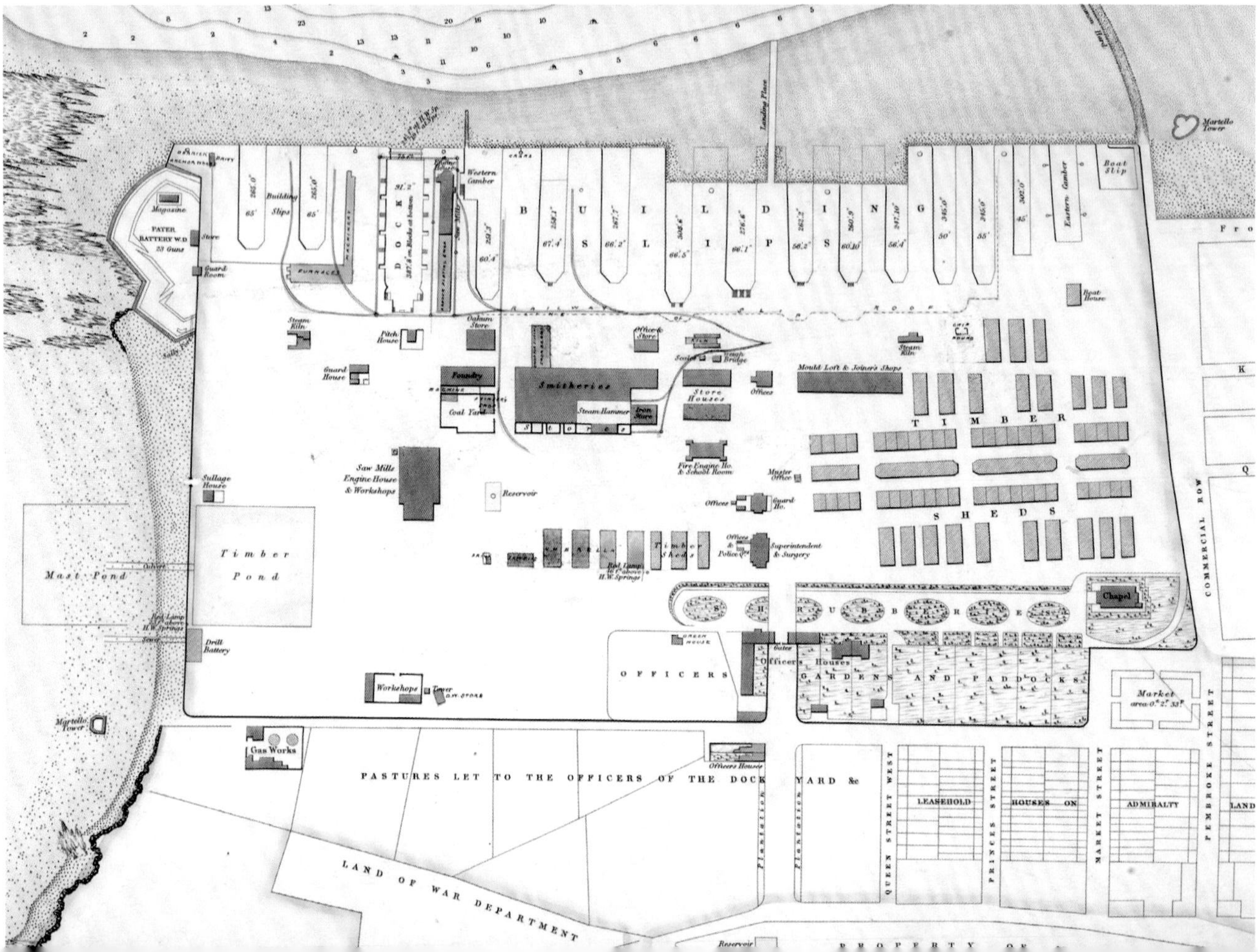

Fig 1.17
The plan of the developed warship-building yard at Pembroke in 1863.
(AdL Da02 fol 7)

the slips was laid out with the usual workshops, storehouses and offices, the western end terminated by a large mast pond. The first phase of buildings may be said to have been completed in the early 1840s by the construction of a military guardhouse and surgery and a building containing a set of sawpits.[82] The great majority of these early buildings were demolished after the closure of the dockyard. Two notable survivors are the former No. 1 Storehouse, a handsome two-storey pedimented building, one of two that sufficed for the yard. This may have been the one adapted as dockyard offices before completion in 1826.[83] Adjacent are the former Officer's Offices, which once overlooked Slips 7 and 8 in the centre of the yard. The mast pond also remains largely intact.

The southern strip of the yard on either side of the main gate was allocated for the residences and gardens of the senior officers, and the lack of local accommodation resulted in priority being given to their construction. As at Sheerness, this is now the best-preserved area. In 1817 Holl established the overall plan and designs for the buildings inside the gateway, which was approached by a short road bordered by the high walls of the adjacent officers' gardens. At the gate, colonnaded pedestrian entrances flank the carriageway and originally were intended to abut a pair of sizeable two-storey lodge houses, the western one later an adjunct to the Commissioner's House and the eastern one providing accommodation for the yard warden and space for a guardroom.[84]

East of the main gate, and breaking with the tradition of housing senior officers in a terrace, Holl designed two pairs of handsome, three-storey semi-detached houses with substantial walled gardens to their rear (Fig 1.18). Drawings were completed in November and December 1817, and by mid-1818 McIntosh had some 50 masons and 50 labourers working on these buildings. The civil guardhouse and the officer's houses were apparently completed by the end of 1819.[85] These houses are notable for Holl's employment of cast iron for roof trusses and for the principal floor beams, using designs clearly derived from his first major use of this material in the rebuilding of the spinning house at Plymouth some 4 years earlier. At Pembroke, strength, durability and possibly economy rather than fireproofing were the requirements, since the ceiling and floor joists were of timber. William Miller drew up plans for the basements and was responsible for the drawings of the decorative plaster cornices in the principal rooms.[86] Work on the yard gate may have taken rather longer, as it was not until April 1823 that McIntosh was submitting a bill for this as well as the adjacent colonnades.[87]

Fig 1.18
Edward Holl's design for two of the officers' houses at Pembroke.
(TNA ADM 140/448)

Fig 1.19
The officers' houses and main entrance at Pembroke today. (Author)

In 1833 Captain Henry John Savage of the Royal Engineers was posted to Pembroke to supervise all building contracts in the yard. He was well qualified 'in heavy works of masonry', having previous experience at Hobbs Point and at the Cobb at Lyme Regis.[88] His principal tasks would no doubt have centred on the building slips, but he also assisted Taylor in drawing up plans for an additional storey on both the gate lodges to provide extra accommodation for a surgeon and the police, together with further work on an adjacent house for the new Captain Superintendent who had replaced the Navy Board commissioner. This work seems to have been finally completed in 1835, giving this area much of its present appearance.[89] The officers' houses still overlook the narrow formal strip of wooded park whose eastern axis, sadly now bisected by the new main road into the dockyard, appropriately ends by framing G L Taylor's dockyard church, also completed in 1835 (*see* Fig 1.19).[90]

Haulbowline

In 1683 the Victualling Board's proposal to establish a Victualling Agent at Kinsale marks the first step to creating permanent naval facilities in southern Ireland.[91] Six years later, the time taken to repair Torrington's squadron at Portsmouth after the Battle of Bantry Bay, while the English Channel lay undefended, was a catalyst that forced the Admiralty to look for a far western location for a new dockyard. Plymouth was eventually selected, but not before Cork with its fine natural harbour and sheltered anchorage had been considered. In 1694 Kinsale became a cruiser base, although the bar on the River Bandon that prevented any ships of the line from entering ruled out any thoughts of a dockyard here.

In the 18th century more permanent depots were established at both Kinsale and later at Cork. Although these were primarily intended for victuals, ships' equipment was also kept, and there were links with local craftsmen able to undertake small repairs.[92] A plan of the Kinsale facilities around 1800 shows a walled establishment on the banks of the Bandon, with three ranges of storehouses round a courtyard fronting the river and a further open courtyard with, among other facilities, a mast pond, paint store and sailmakers' loft.[93] As late as 1813 Admiral Sir Edward Thornbrough was to comment disapprovingly about the amount of cordage and sails for third-rates that had been in store here for at least 20 years.[94] At Cork, premises were rented adjacent to one of the quays fronting the River Lee. An 1803 survey suggests a rather more substantial establishment than at Kinsale, but one that was also inconveniently sited and inadequate. The Victualling Agent was advocating moving to a 'wharf lately erected at the west end of the town' that was closer to the anchorage and had a better supply of fresh water. With his report he enclosed a plan for a new victualling yard there, 'fully adequate to the supply of 8,000 or 10,000 men for four months independent of a large supply of beef and pork'.[95]

By then, the limitations of both establishments were well appreciated, and as early as 1790 the Navy Board had recommended to the Admiralty that the Kinsale facilities should be relocated to the uninhabited Haulbowline Island in Cork Harbour. The island had been purchased by the Board of Ordnance from the Earl of Inchiquin around 1778 and would be well protected by new fortifications to be constructed on the adjacent Spike Island.[96] In 1795 Captain John Schank visited Haulbowline and produced a report and plan for a victualling yard 'containing such buildings as appear necessary for ... stores for the occasional supply of two ships of the line, ten frigates and four sloops, and provision for 3,000 men for four months'.[97] Based on this report, the architect S P Cockerell, Surveyor to the Victualling Office, designed a set of buildings that the Navy Board declared to be 'in our opinion equal to the service required, nor can we suggest any improvements'.[98] Cockerell's drawings do not appear to survive, but his proposals must have been relatively modest, although they apparently included a Great Storehouse. In 1804, nothing having happened in the meantime, Cockerell replied to a Navy Board question about the total cost, stating that he had estimated it at £19,705.[99]

By now, the renewal of war with Napoleonic France had led to fresh interest in Haulbowline. Lieutenant Colonel Sir Charles Holloway, Commanding Royal Engineer at Cork, recommended in November 1804 that the western half of the island should be occupied by the Board of Ordnance and the eastern half by the Victualling Board, further noting there was 'sufficient spare ground for a naval hospital'.[100] The hospital had been suggested by Admiral Gardner, then in command of the Irish station, who was also pressing his case with the Admiralty for a naval base and hospital, as well as victualling facilities, with 'storehouses adequate for ... stores for five ships of the line and as many frigates'.[101] On Admiralty instruction, Samuel Bentham sent out his assistant John Peake to draw up plans and an estimate. These were completed by March 1805,[102] and Bentham informed the Admiralty that 'I hope shortly to have it in my power to prepare the requisite plans'.[103] It is possible that he never produced these, for in July 1805 he departed to Russia to look into the possibilities of constructing ten 74-gun and ten 36-gun warships at St Petersburg and Archangel. He did not return until December 1807, leaving Simon Goodrich in charge of his department during his absence.[104]

In 1806 the navy obtained some 14 acres of Haulbowline, leaving the remaining 8 acres to the Board of Ordnance.[105] That December the Admiralty ordered work to go ahead, the Navy Board sending Goodrich 'the drawings which have been prepared for the same' and telling him to draw up a contract.[106] The absence of early plans and the paucity of documentary records make it difficult to follow progress in any detail during the early years. However, the Admiralty Terrier for Haulbowline records that from 1807 to 1818 the work of levelling much of the site produced sufficient spoil to add just over a further 4 acres to the island.[107] Building works clearly started as soon as was practical. As a supply base, the principal components of the new yard were two sets of three storehouses, one overlooking a sheltered camber on the north side of the island and the other overlooking a similar camber on the eastern side. To their rear was to be built a very substantial vaulted reservoir for rainwater and on top a cooperage for the victualling yard and stores.[108] The southern side of the island had a slip for two sets of mast houses and boathouses, while the western area was partly used for houses for the officers and terraces of cottages for the workforce (*see* Fig 1.20). Provision of the cottages reflected Haulbowline's remoteness from any civilian settlement.[109] Wherever possible, island

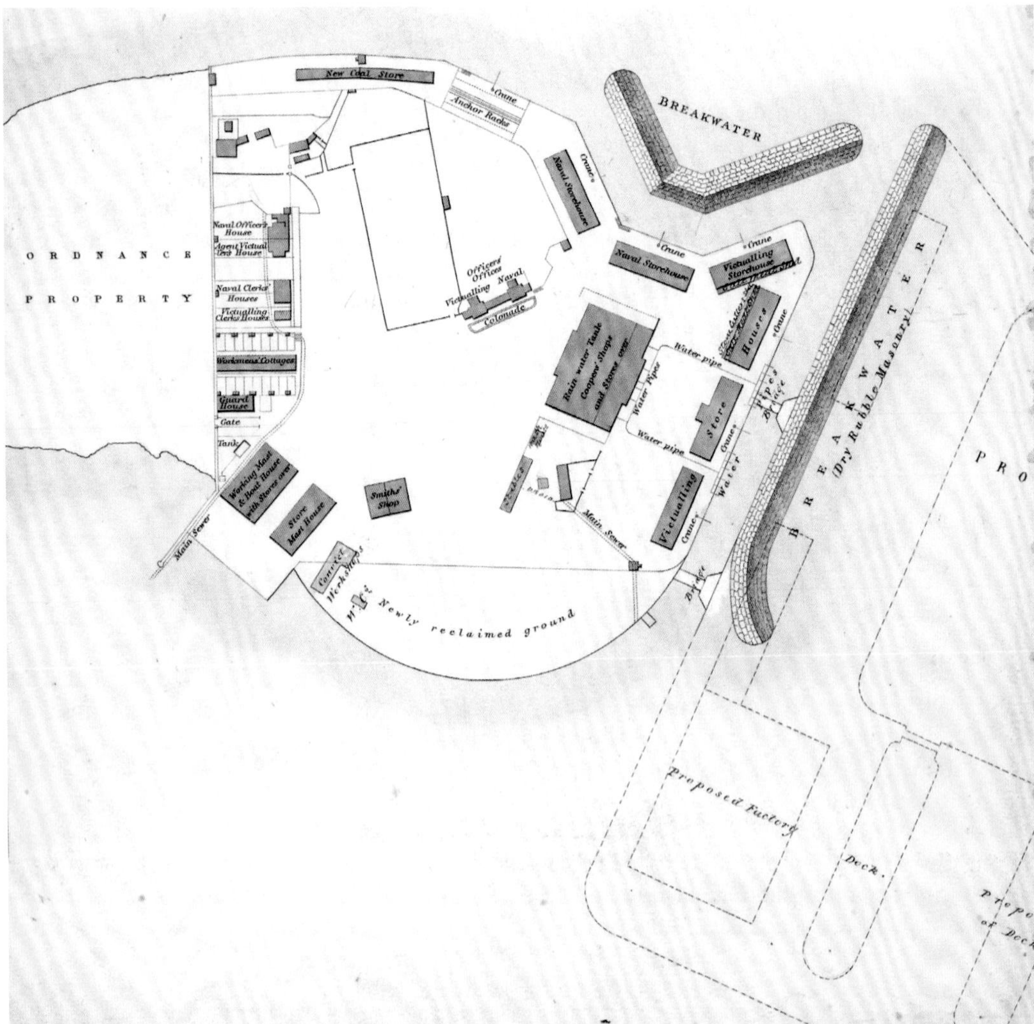

Fig 1.20
Haulbowline Dockyard in 1863, little changed since completion of the original works 40 years earlier. (AdL 1863 Naval Establishments Da 02 fol.8)

limestone was to be used in preference to brick, while the timberwork for the mast houses, boat-houses and storehouses was to be prepared and prefabricated in Plymouth Dockyard.

In January 1807 it was agreed that Edward Holl should go over to Haulbowline to superintend the works, but it is unlikely he stayed for long.[110] In 1810 and 1811 tenders were received for three houses for the naval officer and the two clerks and for cottages for six labourers. It is not clear whether these were then built. An 1815 report mentions a 'landing place in front of the existing storehouse', suggesting that only one storehouse was then complete, most probably the westernmost of the three northern ones.[111]

In 1814 an indication that Haulbowline's facilities were progressing comes with the appointment of George William Kingdom as Naval Storekeeper, a post he held until at least 1827.[112] The ending of the Napoleonic Wars led to an acceleration of construction work. Holl returned to the island in 1815, one of his tasks being to liaise with the contractor who was only allowed to quarry stone for the buildings in areas 'that may be pointed out ... as unobjectionable by the Surveyor of Buildings'.[113] In late July Holl was expecting tenders for several works, which included a smithery, mast houses and 12 cottages; two years later the contractor was estimating his spend for 1817 would be at least £25,000.[114] Local contractors were responsible for all the early works at Haulbowline, although it is not until 1815 that names occasionally appear in the records. In November 1815 'Mr Deane' is recorded as the contractor 'for the works about to be executed on this island'. Thomas Deane clearly ran a substantial business, undertaking £10,000 of work in 1817. In July that year 'the canal abreast of the new wharf' was completed; this is almost certainly the channel in front of the storehouses along the northern side of the yard protected by a massive stone breakwater. If Deane was the principal contractor, two others whose names survive in the records made significant contributions. In 1817 Urquhart completed this canal that was begun by 'Mr Hegarty the late contractor'. This was a considerable operation involving the removal of nearly 7,500 cubic yards of 'rock and rubbish' and probably the construction of the massive protective breakwater. By late November, work was under way on the foundations of a further wharf wall.[115]

The 1818 estimates are the first surviving ones to refer specifically to storehouses, when £15,000 was included 'towards erecting storehouses etc at this yard'. Deane's name is linked to the main storehouses, as well as the yard boundary wall and works on the admiral's residence at Cove. It is possible that he was also responsible for the substantial vaulted reservoir to the rear of the main storehouses; a drawing of the reservoir by William Miller is dated 1816. In April 1821, when there was clearly pressure to complete the works, between 100 and 130 men were engaged on it, a figure that rose to around 400 by July.[116]

By March 1819 the Victualling Agent was already using one of the new stores, and the ground floor of the central victualling store was almost ready for occupation.[117] An indication that the major works were nearing completion comes in a note in January 1821 that the Agent Victualler had acquired designs for lamps and lamp posts that differed from Holl's sketches. Holl's response was polite but firm: 'The Lamp Irons etc were simple in their form, economical in point of expense, require no posts to fix them to, and were applicable not only for the officers and clerks' houses but for all the storehouses and buildings upon the island'. He requested that 'with a view to uniformity' the naval officer should stick to the sketches.[118]

In 1822 the use of convict labour was suggested by George Kingdom, 'as I understand that convicts have been employed in England on various public works with the most beneficial effects'. In early April 1822 HMS *Trent*, a fifth-rate that had been used as a hospital and then a receiving ship, was to be fitted up for temporary reception for 100 convicts. Nothing apparently was done, and the ship was broken up at Haulbowline in 1823.[119] By 1824 the yard appears to have been substantially complete when William Miller reckoned that works valued at upwards of £180,000 had been undertaken.[120] In a final flourish in January 1824, Kingdom asked for a yard clock, with Miller supporting this request and undertaking to design a turret clock if authorised. This is probably the handsome clock turret on the central storehouse of the north range.[121]

Architecturally, the finest surviving buildings from this period are the six storehouses (Fig 1.21). Although the original drawings do not survive, they are almost certainly attributable to Edward Holl, most probably with assistance from his draughtsman Miller. The similarity of architectural details to Holl's

Fig 1.21
Three of the great storehouses at Haulbowline, almost certainly the work of Holl.
(Author)

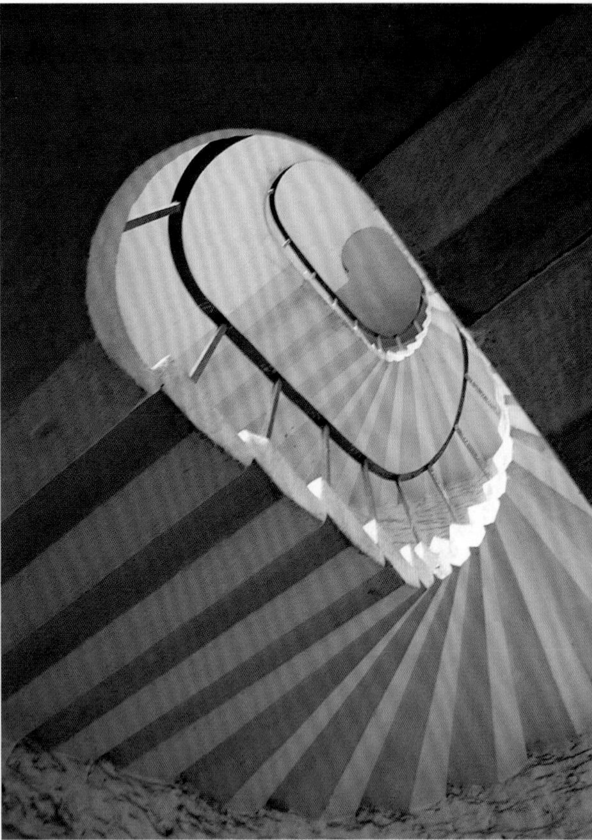

Fig 1.22 (above)
Detail of the internal ironwork at Haulbowline, very similar to that in the Royal William Yard. In both cases ironwork was used for its strength.
(Author)

Fig 1.23 (above right)
One of the elegant cantilevered stone staircases inside the storehouses at Haulbowline.
(Author)

work at Sheerness, Pembroke and at Stonehouse hospital is striking, while the extensive use of cast-iron columns and principal beams (Fig 1.22) are hallmarks of his work during his last 10 years. The interiors are also notable for the survival of a number of elegant cantilevered elliptical stone staircases (Fig 1.23), similar to surviving ones in the slightly later Melville Square Storehouse in the Royal William Victualling Yard at Stonehouse. As with other similar naval storehouses, those at Haulbowline proved readily adaptable to uses other than just naval stores and victuals.

In 1822 Holl approved a plan to convert part of one storehouse into a chapel for a congregation of between 70 and 100 island residents.[122] Admiral Gardner's wish for a naval hospital at Haulbowline was answered in part in 1820 when what were described as 'reporting rooms' were converted into a temporary hospital, to be followed in 1822 by the ground floor of one storehouse that was fitted up as a dispensary.[123] Not until much later in the 19th century was the southern of the three eastern storehouses, until then a victualling store, converted into a proper naval hospital, its western side softened by extensive new areas of lawn.[124]

By the mid-1820s, Haulbowline's original facilities were complete, and its future must have seemed assured. But only 6 years later, in April 1831 as part of naval economies, the yard was ordered to be closed and the stores returned to England. A naval storeship, only just arrived with fresh supplies from Plymouth, was turned round, after making room in her hold for 'the accommodation of 23 women and 10 children [presumably from a shipwreck] brought and left here by HM Ship *Windsor Castle*'. The run-down of Haulbowline was rapid, and in early September 1831 the last of the yard employees, an engineer, three storehousemen, an office messenger, eight watchmen, five boatmen and a lamplighter for Holl's 'economical' yard lamps were discharged. But a decade later, the yard reopened and was given a new lease of life.[125]

All these works ensured that by the 1820s in the aftermath of the Napoleonic Wars, the navy's home bases were unrivalled in terms of scale and facilities. The impetus for nearly all these late 18th- and early 19th-century improvements had been war or the threat of war. The next modernisation was to have its formative roots in changing technologies.

2

The Royal Dockyards in Great Britain, 1835–1914

For most of the century from the end of the Napoleonic Wars to the outbreak of the First World War, the Royal Navy had no serious rivals and was able to exercise a world-wide *Pax Britannica* with comparatively small resources, building on the feats of its Georgian predecessor and sustained by the technological developments of the Victorian era.

New technology and yard modernisation, 1835–1860

After unsuccessful experiments between 1795 and 1797 with the *Kent* and its novel method of steam propulsion, the Admiralty suspended further work with steam ships until after the Napoleonic Wars.[1] In 1816 the paddle-tug *Regent* was hired for trials, and the navy launched its first steam vessel, the *Congo,* at Deptford. As early as 1823, the First Lord of the Admiralty, Viscount Melville, in discussions with Sir Robert Seppings, Surveyor of the Navy, and in confidential correspondence with Vice-Admiral Sir Thomas Byam Martin, the Comptroller, was exploring the possibilities of constructing small steam-driven warships. The following year he wrote to the Duke of Wellington, telling him that 'if we are tolerably alert, with our command of machinery and fuel we ought to outsteam all Europe'.[2] However, the limitations of early steam engines, the vulnerability of paddle wheels to gunfire and the valuable broadside space they occupied meant that the navy would not adopt steam propulsion for its line of battle ships for another 30 years. However, it was well aware of the new technology, kept a watchful eye on its development and employed it where there were clear benefits, such as in the use of tugs and small craft.

In 1837 the navy gained further valuable experience as well as acquiring trained personnel when it became responsible for the 26 steam packets of the Post Office fleet.[3] The growing number of steam-assisted naval vessels had led in 1835 to the appointment of the first Chief Engineer and Inspector of Machinery, but acquisition of the Post Office fleet two years later led the Admiralty to create a Steam Department under the control of Captain Sir W E Parry.[4] By 1842, approximately one-fifth of naval ships in commission were steamers, including small paddle frigates and navy-operated Post Office steam packets (*see* Fig 11.1). The total by 1844 was 85 vessels, of which 39 were warships, described in a contemporary report as 'very weak, and having been built in the infancy of steam are very inferior'. In addition to these were a further 9 steamers employed in the surveying service, 26 steam packets and a miscellaneous assortment of tugs, river and harbour craft and the royal yacht.[5] The development of the screw propeller in the 1830s and the trial in 1845, when the sloop HMS *Rattler* convincingly demonstrated its superiority over her paddle wheel-driven sister ship HMS *Alecto,* marked a further step along the road to steam-powered battleships.

But if critics felt the Admiralty was too slow to adopt the technology in the main battlefleet, there were good reasons for the cautious approach. In June 1839 the Vice-Admiral at Halifax reported to the Admiralty that HMS *Columbia* had arrived on the 14th with her steam machinery 'in such a defective state as to be past repair on this station' and that consequently she had been ordered to sail to Spithead. 'I deem it right to draw to your lordships notice', he continued, '... that within the last two months [three similar vessels] have been ordered to England in the same defective state'. These unfortunate occurrences had caused problems maintaining the West Indies mail service.[6] A decade later, reliability remained an issue. Trials of a squadron of steam-assisted warships off Lisbon in 1850 reaffirmed that low-pressure boilers then in use consumed vast quantities of coal and the steam engines themselves were still far from trustworthy. Commodore Martin reported that after 5 days steaming, all the ships had some defects in their machinery. Nevertheless, it was clear by now that as technical problems were solved, steam power would play an ever-greater role, although it was not expected to replace sails totally.

But irrespective of steam technology, the navy's warships had also been changing. Initially, the spur had been the exigencies of the Napoleonic Wars and the unprecedented need to keep the fleet at sea throughout the year in all weathers to blockade the French navy. Vigilance in such conditions exposed structural weaknesses in hulls and wore out the ships. Between 1800 and 1814, Robert Seppings introduced a series of crucial technical developments in the design of hulls of warships (*see* Chapter 5). In 1804, Seppings had been appointed master shipwright at Chatham, and from 1813 to 1832 he was Surveyor of the Navy. His work allowed warships to be increased in size by over 50 per cent and to have sufficient resilience to bear in due course the weight and vibration of steam engines and boilers.

Seppings was succeeded as Surveyor of the Navy by Sir William Symonds, who held the post until 1847 and was greatly indebted to his assistant John Edye; between them (and building on Seppings's innovations) they designed and constructed the largest and most powerful sailing warships ever built. The structural developments that made these possible had in part been spurred by continuing rivalry with the navies of France and America, but they became crucial where additional space had to be found for machinery and coal bunkers. By 1849, the Admiralty felt sufficiently confident of the improving steam technology to suspend the construction of pure sailing warships and order the building of the 91-gun HMS *Agamemnon,* the first British battleship to be designed from the start to make use of steam power. Before *Agamemnon,* steam power had been added to existing sailing warships (Fig 2.1), frequently with disappointing results, not least to their sailing qualities. *Agamemnon* with her finer lines was to prove a great success both under sail and steam and was to influence the shape of the steam battlefleet evolving in the 1850s.[7]

Fig 2.1
HMS Victoria, *a steam-assisted first-rate launched in 1859, only a year ahead of HMS* Warrior, *the world's first all-metal armoured warship. This photograph shows* Victoria *serving with the Mediterranean fleet at Grand Harbour, Malta, c 1865.*
(© National Maritime Museum, Greenwich, London, 8949)

The Woolwich steam factory of 1839

The first phase of dockyard modernisation resulting from a growing accumulation of all these factors began in 1839 with the completion of the navy's first steam factory at Woolwich Dockyard (*see* Fig 2.2). Until then, the only boiler shops and metal mills were at Portsmouth and Plymouth. Their very limited capacity was focused on making small metal castings and repairing boilers and engines. They were wholly inadequate to cope with the scale of steam machinery then coming into use in the dockyards and the fleet. The navy was also becoming increasingly dissatisfied with the private firms who supplied these engines and boilers. There were frequent failures to deliver machinery on time to the dockyards, partly the result of poor labour relations in the industry.

In 1835 Peter Ewart was appointed as Chief Engineer and Inspector of Machinery at Woolwich Dockyard, where work was just finishing on enlarging and modernising its basin and was about to start on improving its dry docks. It was these modernised facilities that secured Woolwich's place as the lead yard for the major investment in the new mechanical engineering. Ewart was one of the most experienced engineers of the day who had worked for Boulton and Watt and assisted James Watt junior in planning the famous Soho Foundry where steam engines were first manufactured in-house rather than being mainly assembled from parts bought in from subcontractors. The estimates for the new steam factory at Woolwich, authorised in 1837, specifically mentioned that it was 'for the manufacture and repair of engines for steam vessels'. Although its cramped site and lack of deep water

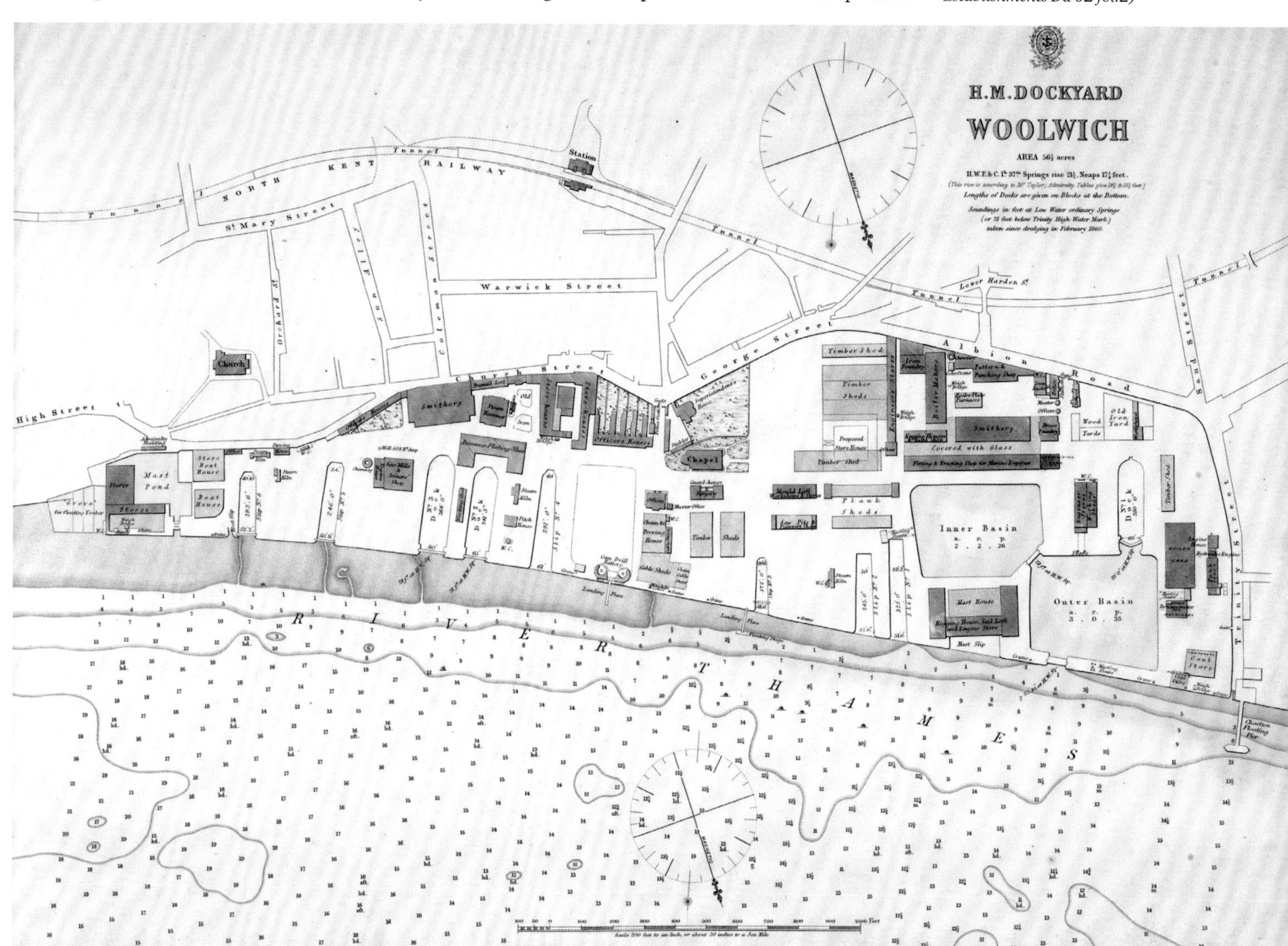

Fig 2.2
Woolwich Dockyard along the River Thames in 1863. The buildings of the steam yard are on the right side, with the Inner Basin on the site of a former mast pond. (AdL 1863 Naval Establishments Da 02 fol.2)

Fig 2.3
Part of the 19th-century pitch house and smithery excavated towards the south end of Woolwich Dockyard in 1972, showing the very substantial foundations necessary for these industrial buildings. (Author)

ultimately led to the yard's closure, Woolwich had the added advantage in being in the midst of the country's steamship builders and marine engine makers who were then concentrated along the Thames. The Admiralty, lacking adequate skilled staff of its own, depended heavily not just on the products of these firms but also on its ability to make use of their engineers and fitters.[8]

Building a steam warship involved new working, manufacturing and assembly processes that in turn were radically to influence the layouts of the dockyards. Hitherto, the main shipbuilding crafts and trades had been focused on the building slips and graving docks. But a steam vessel had engines and boilers installed only after her launch. These also had to be removed on occasion for repair or replacement. This meant that once afloat, the new vessel had to be secured alongside a quay equipped with heavy cranes or sheer-legs close to the new machine shops, preferably in a wet dock or, as it became known, a fitting out basin, where a constant water level could be maintained. The machine shops and boiler shops in turn required iron and brass foundries nearby to supply them with castings and material (*see* Fig 2.3).

In 1838 the site for the new Woolwich steam factory was chosen on land to the south of the mast pond, which was deepened and converted into a fitting out basin. The Fitting and Erecting Shop for Marine Engines was constructed along its south side, with the foundries and other buildings of the new metal trades forming an irregular quadrangle to the rear. The new fitting out or inner basin was then linked to the adjacent main outer basin.[9]

The Portsmouth steam basin of 1843

Lack of space to expand at Woolwich forced a series of compromises on the Royal Engineers involved in the modernisation project. By the mid-1840s, it was increasingly apparent that resources for a steam navy at the three principal

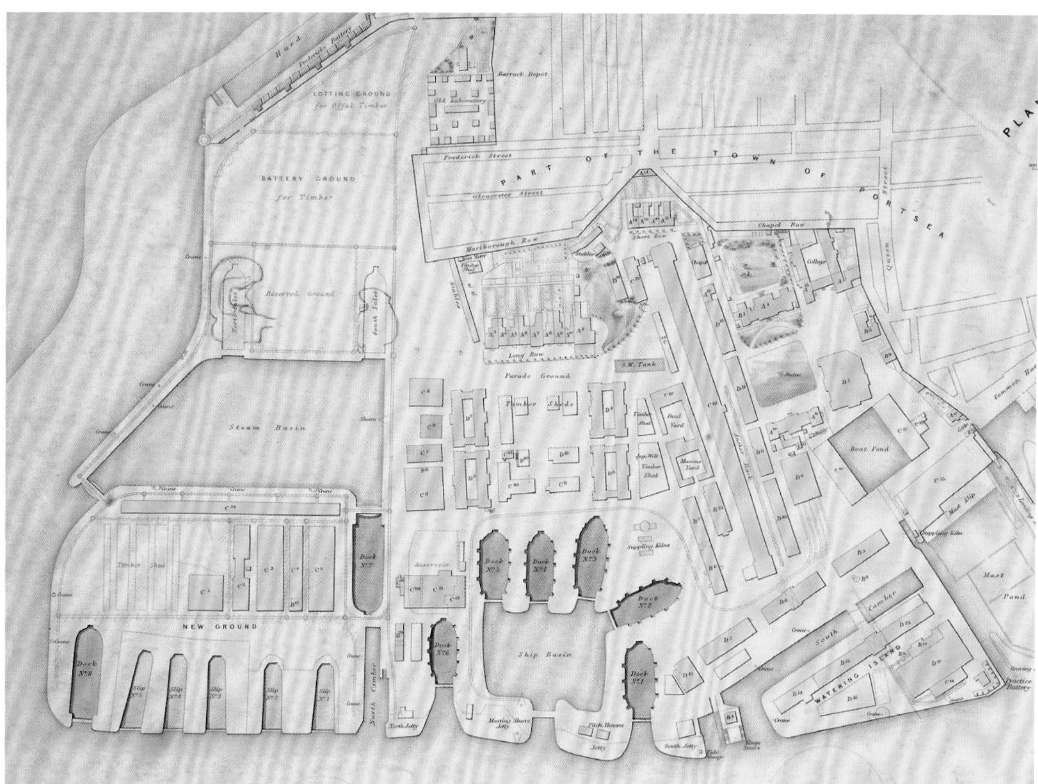

Fig 2.4
Portsmouth Dockyard in 1849. This plan shows the new steam basin and associated workshops grafted on to the northern end of the Georgian dockyard. (TNA ADM 140/555 fol 20)

dockyards of Chatham, Portsmouth and Plymouth Dockyard (renamed Devonport in 1843, following the earlier change of name of its town) would need to be on a massively larger scale to cope with the new warships and their machinery. These facilities would have to be provided without impairing the yards' abilities to look after the existing fleet. The solution adopted first at Portsmouth and Devonport and later at Chatham was to reclaim or acquire land and graft new steam yards on to the existing dockyards. The immediate spur for all this investment in the two south coast yards was the development of French naval bases at Cherbourg and Brest.

In 1843 reclamation work began in Portsmouth Harbour for a steam extension to be added to the northern boundary of the existing Georgian dockyard (Fig 2.4). At its heart was a new 7-acre steam basin. This was the focus of the associated workshops, the most notable being the former steam factory, or West Factory, now No. 2 Ship Shop. Designed by Captain Henry James RE, its length of over 600ft and its handsome elevations still dominate the western side of the basin.[10] Opening off the basin were three dry docks. The first to be ready in 1849 was No. 9 Dock. By the time the last one, No. 11 Dock, was completed in 1863 with enlarged dimensions, No. 9 had already been extensively rebuilt to accommodate the increasing sizes of warships. The reclaimed land also allowed space for the construction of five large building slips and an associated graving dock west of the steam factory buildings; by 1863 these too had all had to be enlarged, along with their roofs. The original estimated total costs for the building slips and their roofs came to £171,000 and the basin £240,000. The tally for five dry docks was some £447,000, including three iron caissons. The final costs remain unclear, but were almost certainly substantially greater than these figures, which are chiefly useful for comparative purposes with other dockyards.[11]

The Keyham Steam Yard, Devonport, of 1844

A few months after the start of work at Portsmouth, a similar but considerably more ambitious project was started at Devonport. Here, Morice Ordnance Yard prevented any immediate expansion of the existing yard along the riverfront. Instead, in February 1844 the Admiralty acquired the site of the Keyham powder magazines and purchased adjacent land fronting the Hamoaze immediately north of

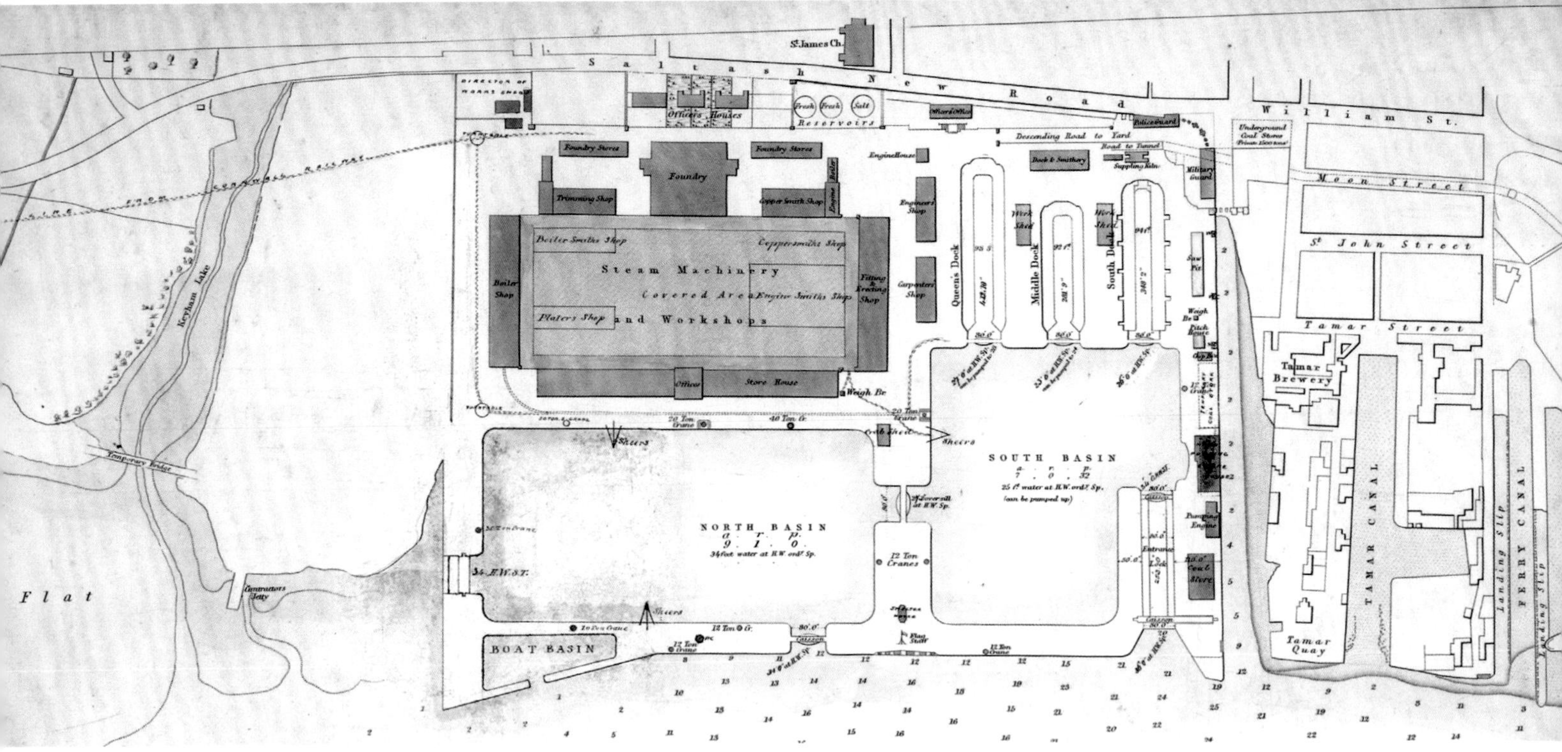

Fig 2.5
The separate Keyham Steam Yard at Devonport in 1863. The scale of the great Quadrangle of workshops and storehouses is readily apparent. (AdL 1863 Naval Establishments Da 02 fol 6)

Morice Yard to construct the wholly separate Keyham Steam Yard (Fig 2.5). Over the next decade, there were to be a number of alterations to the plans as originally agreed, but by the mid-1850s the major engineering works were complete. Fronting the Hamoaze were two linked basins with a third small one for minor craft. The 7-acre South Basin, approached through an entrance lock provided with the first sliding caisson, had three dry docks along its eastern side. The even larger 9-acre North Basin was eventually flanked on its eastern side by the monumental buildings of the steam factory.

On 7 October 1853 HMS *Queen* became the first warship to use the new dry docks. A note with the 1854/5 estimates records that 'the basins and docks have been brought into use', but that 'the buildings urgently required for the repair of the steam vessels and their machinery' had yet to be built.[12] Part of the delay in constructing the factory complex was the need to complete the new ordnance facilities at Bull Point further up the Tamar, so as to allow demolition of the powder magazine at Keyham. Construction finally started in 1853 to designs by William Scamp, then Deputy Director of Admiralty Works (1852–67), Colonel Godfrey Thomas Greene, the Director, and Charles Barry; it was completed by 1865. David Evans rightly describes it as 'the greatest single monument of the steam navy'.[13]

The disadvantages of the Keyham Steam Yard being physically separate from the existing dockyard were mitigated to an extent by the construction of a linking tunnel beneath the intervening Morice Ordnance Yard. This tunnel was authorised in 1854 when £35,000 was put in the annual estimates, and it was opened in 1857. Surprisingly, its original design apparently only allowed horse-drawn carts and foot traffic, and not until 1879 was it adapted to take a standard-gauge railway track. On completion, the Keyham Steam Yard was renamed Devonport North Yard, while the original Plymouth Dockyard was renamed as Devonport South Yard.[14]

Building slips were not constructed in Keyham Steam Yard, in part because they already existed in the main Georgian yard, although most of these had to be enlarged in the 1850s. More significantly, the Admiralty sought to maximise the use of its expensive investment in the new engineering facilities here to fit out and engine warships that were built at Pembroke Dockyard, along with many from private yards on the Mersey and the Clyde. These included the second ironclad, *Black Prince*, built by Napier and Son at Govan, launched in February 1861 and commissioned at Devonport 15 months later.[15]

Technical developments ashore and afloat, 1835–1860

The massive costs associated with these new steam yards, along with the timescale needed to implement the works, meant that the Admiralty had to phase the programme of major yard modernisations. The mobilisation of the fleet at the start of the Crimean War put a strain on resources and led to a hasty equipping of Sheerness with facilities to maintain and repair the fleet operating in the Baltic. It also prompted a modest but significant diversion of effort when the needs of the new flotillas of steam gunboats led to the construction of Haslar Gunboat Yard at Gosport between 1856 and 1859. Much more significantly, during the nearly two decades it had taken to construct and equip Keyham Yard, the growing pace of technological change had effected a revolution in the navy's warships.

The steam yards at Portsmouth and Devonport had been designed in the early 1840s in response to the increasing use of steam engines and the growth in warship sizes resulting from improved hull designs. Although it was appreciated that steam engines would have a significant role, they generally were still seen as an auxiliary method of propulsion. There was no great reason to assume that the main battlefleet would not continue for some time to be predominantly a sailing navy, its warships constructed of timber and largely equipped with smooth-bore broadside armament. This view was not the result of conservatism and inertia on the part of the Admiralty, but more a reflection of current practicalities. Steam had its uses, manoeuvring warships in and out of confined spaces in harbours and, it was thought, helping to form a battle line. But problems of mechanical reliability and the logistics and expense of buying and then supplying coal in vast quantities to far-flung fleets or flotillas favoured the continuing use of sails.

A similarly cautious but not blinkered approach can be detected in the Admiralty's views on metal hulls. Iron hulls potentially had the merit of strength and durability, with the added bonus of freeing the navy from its dependence on timber. One major drawback was that the dockyards had neither the machinery nor the skills to build or repair such ships. A second obstacle to iron-hulled, ocean-going ships was magnetic compass error, a problem that had engaged the Admiralty for some time and was only partially solved in 1838 by the Astronomer Royal, Sir George Airy. Following this breakthrough, in 1839 the Admiralty ordered its first iron vessel, the mail packet *Dover.* Two years later, the Niger River Expedition was equipped with three small iron steam vessels, which acquitted themselves creditably and whose lighter hulls gave them an advantage in shallow rivers over wooden ships of similar size. Further small iron vessels followed, including the Royal Yacht, HMY *Fairy.* In 1845 in a bold step, the Admiralty ordered four substantial iron frigates, the largest, HMS *Simoom*, almost the size of Brunel's SS *Great Britain* launched 2 years earlier.

But concern about the impact of iron shot on wrought-iron hulls led to a series of firing trials at Woolwich Arsenal, where it was found that these hulls could be vulnerable. In certain circumstances iron shot caused jagged holes that were difficult to repair and, more importantly, generated showers of lethal iron splinters. The Admiralty, perhaps over hastily, converted the frigates to troop ships, of which the most famous was HMS *Birkenhead.* David Brown suggests that the Admiralty was needlessly panicked into this decision to convert the frigates, but a former Surveyor of the Navy, Sir William Symonds, writing to the Earl of Minto in October 1847, had little doubt about their unsuitability, and not just because of the effects of shot: 'Twenty iron vessels built and building unfit for war purposes from the fatal effect of shot on them, and if sent abroad they soon lose their speed from their great tendency to engender weeds etc.'[16] As so often, war was to provide the catalyst for further advances.

The impact of the steam battlefleet, 1860–1895

The devastating effects of shells fired against wooden warships were cruelly demonstrated when a Turkish squadron anchored in the Black Sea port of Sinope was annihilated by a Russian squadron using shell guns in the opening moves of the Crimean War (1854–5). Faced with the need to bombard fortifications, the Anglo-French response was to design floating batteries protected by thick armour plate, some of which were used at the final bombardment of Kinburn at the end of the war. From these, it was a logical step to building an armoured warship. The French navy led the way with the launch of the *Gloire* in 1859, a single-decked ship with

Fig 2.6
HMS Warrior, *permanently berthed at Portsmouth after restoration.*
The seismic effect of her design, technology and materials on the world's navies was only equalled by the impact on the royal dockyards, where new skills, materials, facilities and equipment had to be introduced to build and maintain such warships.
(Author)

a 4½-in thick carapace of iron attached to her hull. Limitations of French industry had forced Dupuy de Lôme, *Gloire*'s designer, to construct the latter of timber. The vastly greater industrial resources available to the British Admiralty enabled the naval architect Isaac Watts to design the world's first iron-hulled armoured warship, HMS *Warrior* (Fig 2.6), launched a year later.

With the arrival of these two ships, Admiral Ballard was later to write with a measure of hyperbole, 'all war values had to be reckoned on a perfectly clean slate. Old, long-established standards simply ceased to count, and the top-gallant masts of the three-decker were due to disappear over the horizon for the last time'.[17] These two warships with their armoured protection and shell guns in theory made every other major warship obsolete, while the change-over to metal hulls freed naval architects from the limitations of timber and enabled them to design ships of ever increasing dimensions. For some 10 years, HMS *Warrior*'s growing fleet of iron sisters with their broadside armaments – known collectively as the Black Battlefleet from the colour of their hulls – were provided with full sailing rig, retaining something of the feel of the sailing navy. But developments in naval ordnance were leading to fewer and more powerful weapons, to the end of the broadside armament and to its replacement with gun turrets with their vastly greater arcs of fire. Attempts to combine gun turrets with full sailing rig on HMS *Captain* led to disaster in September 1870 when the ship capsized in a storm off Cape Finisterre.

But with the launch at Portsmouth in July 1871 of HMS *Devastation* (Fig 2.7), the Royal Navy arguably acquired its first recognisably modern capital ship, the battleship successor to the ship of the line as the most important type of warship in the fleet. *Devastation* had her main armament in twin turrets on her centreline and relied entirely on her engines for propulsion. All sailing rig had been dispensed with, while her broader beam aided stability and provided space for coal bunkers, giving her a range of up to 4,700 miles at 10 knots. Although the Royal Navy was to retain small operational sailing warships with auxiliary engines into the early 20th century, such sloops were largely limited to policing duties in the further-flung and quieter reaches of the empire. For the main battlefleet the future lay with *Devastation* and her ever-larger and more powerful successors.[18] Less than 20 years separates her from HMS *Agamemnon*. The astonishing changes in the Royal Navy's

Fig 2.7
HMS Devastation *launched at Portsmouth Dockyard in 1871.*
(© Imperial War Museums (Q 21155))

warships were reflected in the equally revolutionary developments required in the royal dockyards to support the new fleet.

Between 1850 and 1870, the ships of the Royal Navy underwent their most profound change since the invention of the gunport and introduction of broadside armament around the start of the 16th century. Given the rapidity of these developments, the difficulties of forecasting future warship sizes and the lead-in time for major engineering works in the dockyards, it is not surprising that the dockyards were in a state of almost constant expansion and remodelling into the early years of the 20th century. Planning, financing, building and commissioning dockyards took several years, longer if land first had to be purchased or reclaimed. Building adequate, large dry docks had been a difficulty in the mid-18th century, but then the growth in warship sizes was modest, restricted by limitations in timber technology. Georgian dockyard officers were not faced with the sort of unknown quantum leaps in warship sizes that confronted their Victorian successors, who also had to cope with more intensive uses of dry docks.

Screw-driven vessels needed regular docking for glands around the screw shafts to be checked. Metal hulls also proved highly attractive to marine growths, which needed to be regularly removed. The old system of careening a ship – hauling her down on each side in turn to allow the exposed hull to be worked on – had always been a risky undertaking, but the installation of heavy machinery and boilers that could break loose within the hull put an end to this practice, adding further pressure on the use of dry docks. In 1861 the home dockyards had a total of 33 dry

Table 2.1 Dimensions of some of the Royal Navy's largest warships, built between 1682 and 1913. Note the marked differences between HMS *Victoria*, the last of the wooden battleships, and HMS *Warrior*, the first armoured all-metal Royal Navy ship.

Warship	*date launched*	*length overall (ft)*	*maximum breadth (ft)*	*draught*	*tons*[a]
Britannia	1682	146	47	19	1,708
Victory	1765	186	52	21½	2,142
Victoria	1859	260	60	25½	6,959
Warrior	1860	380	58½	26	9,210
Devastation	1871	285	62	26½	9,378
Majestic	1895	421	75	26½	14,900
Dreadnought	1906	527	82	26½	17,900
Warspite	1913	644	90½	29½	27,000

a Tonnage up to 1873 is Builder's Measurement, based on capacity; after 1873 it is Displacement Tonnage. These figures are from Archibald 1968, Ballard 1980, Colledge and Warlow 2006, Lambert 1984, Lambert 1987.

docks complete or being built. However, only two of these could accommodate HMS *Warrior*, and then only at certain states of the tide. In 1864 a parliamentary select committee drew attention to the problems caused by the growth in size of the fleet, but felt, somewhat unhelpfully, that they had not 'had sufficient evidence to justify themselves in expressing any opinion as to the accommodation which an armour-plated steam navy might require in time of war'.[19] A major acceleration occurred in dimensions and tonnage with the change to all-metal construction, beginning with HMS *Warrior* (*see* Table 2.1 and 2.2).

This rapid growth in warship sizes also had repercussions on the building slips, wharves and basins, all of which likewise had to be increased in capacity. Along with these went the provision of the necessary foundries and engineering workshops that largely supplanted the working mast houses, sail lofts and roperies which were so essential to the sailing navy. In the case of the Thames yards, these requirements posed insoluble problems. After the Napoleonic Wars, Deptford was closed between 1830 and 1844, although it remained in use for ship-breaking. It then reopened, and limited sums were spent upgrading five slips 'devoted principally to the building of steam vessels', but it did not enjoy the degree of investment channelled to Woolwich with its new steam facilities 'for the repair of steam machinery'. Neither yard had expansion space to cope with the era of ironclads inaugurated by HMS *Warrior*, and both yards were closed in 1869.[20]

The rapid pace of warship design in the 1850s meant that even before the Portsmouth steam extension was completed, two of the docks had to be increased in size. Elsewhere in the 1850s, the Admiralty was forced to expend further money upgrading and enlarging dry docks and slips at Chatham, Sheerness, Devonport South Yard and Pembroke. At Pembroke, slips and their recently completed roofs had to be lengthened and the graving dock widened.[21] These substantial engineering works went on in tandem with the extensions at Portsmouth and Devonport.

Table 2.2 Average numbers employed in home and overseas yards in 1865/6. Home figures are from TNA ADM 49/181 and overseas figures from TNA ADM 181/77.

Home yards	*numbers employed*
Deptford	845
Woolwich	2,449
Chatham	3,348
Sheerness	2,020
Portsmouth	4,740
Devonport	3,660
Pembroke	1,261
total	**18,323**
Overseas yards	
Gibraltar	35
Malta	315
Halifax	37
Bermuda	197
Antigua	12
Port Royal	9
Ascension	11
Sierra Leone	6
Cape of Good Hope	5
Trincomalee	2
Hong Kong	24
Esquimalt	3
total	**656**
overall total	**18,979**

In 1848, in a separate development as part of a modest programme of penal reform, the concept of public-works prisons was introduced, in which convicts were to provide manpower for major public projects as part of their rehabilitation. Dockyard expansion programmes involving excavations, earth shifting, brick-making and construction on a huge scale were thought to be ideally suited, with the added bonus of promised financial savings over using contractors. These savings did not always materialise. In 1861 the Director of Works noted that at Chatham it had been necessary to 'employ free labour to a much greater extent than originally intended, chiefly in consequence of a large portion of the work requiring to be done when the tides are favourable and when convicts are not permitted to work'.[22] Convict labour, which was not always available in the numbers required, was found to be of marginal benefit since machinery was increasingly employed. In 1863 convicts at Bermuda were replaced by Royal Marines who could earn extra pay,[23] and the system was phased out in the dockyards after the Chatham extension and replaced entirely by contractors' labour.

Chatham steam yard 1864–1885

The last of the principal home yards to be equipped for the steam navy was Chatham. This yard had long lost the pre-eminence it had enjoyed in the 17th century. For much of the 18th century, increasingly plagued by access problems caused by the shoaling of the River Medway, Chatham had been in slow decline, eclipsed by what were rapidly becoming the strategically more important yards at Portsmouth and Plymouth. Only from the 1770s was Chatham found a new role as a yard for shipbuilding and major repairs. Limited funds were spent over the next 30 years, principally rebuilding the ropery and constructing the adjacent storehouses, but then modernisation largely ceased as the future of all the existing Thames and Medway dockyards was put in doubt.

At the beginning of the 19th century the Admiralty began to consider seriously the possibilities of replacing these with a new and spacious dockyard with much improved access (*see* Chapter 1). Unsurprisingly in a period of post-Napoleonic Wars retrenchment, such schemes remained only an idea. However, in a tacit abandonment of any idea of constructing a new yard on the Isle of Grain, the Admiralty did start buying land on St Mary's Island, just down-stream and separated from Chatham Dockyard by St Mary's Creek, completing the purchase of the remaining parts of the island in 1854.[24] By then, despite the provision of five new covered slips at the north end of the yard between 1836 and 1851, Chatham was woefully out of date and ill equipped.

From 1850 to the early 1860s, a number of expansion and modernisation schemes were proposed for Chatham by Colonel G T Greene, Director of the Admiralty Works Department, and his chief assistant, William Scamp. These all centred on extending the existing yard to incorporate St Mary's Island and forming three basins on the site of its creek. But mindful of the rate at which warship developments were making even new dockyard facilities insufficient, the Admiralty was in no hurry to endorse a proposal for Chatham that might quite probably also turn out to be inadequate.

In 1853, in anticipation of works, it was decided to construct a prison next to the dockyard for 1,135 convicts. This was completed in 1856, although indecision about the future of Chatham is still apparent in the records. The estimates for that year noted that construction of the river wall had been suspended 'pending the decision of the general requirements of this yard'. By 1858 it was recorded that only £6,303 had been expended on convict labour.[25] But events elsewhere were to force the pace. The Crimean War and operations in the Baltic dramatically emphasised the need for a modern dockyard on the eastern side of Britain. Chatham had no repairing basin, and to cope with the Baltic fleet Scamp hastily had to construct a factory fitted with modern machine tools at Sheerness, together with sawmills at Deptford. These sawmills were partially equipped with machinery 'nearly complete for the Russian government, when it was taken possession of as a Droit of the Crown'.

By the late 1850s, rapid developments in accurate long-range ordnance were making coastal yards such as Sheerness, Portsmouth and Devonport seemingly vulnerable to bombardment by warships. Chatham, by contrast, was sufficiently far up-river to be out of range and could in any event be given added protection by the proposed ring fortresses. These were recommended for all the principal home and overseas yards by the Royal Commission on the Defence of the United Kingdom, set up in 1859 in response to widespread public concern about French intentions. In 1861, a Parliamentary Committee strongly urged the Admiralty to proceed with the Chatham extension works.[26] Despite this, it was to be late

1864 before works got under way (Fig 2.8), initially under the Director of Works, Sir Andrew Clarke, and they were not completed until 1885. The Royal Engineer Charles Pasley was appointed in October 1865 as resident engineer in charge of the project as well as of works at Sheerness, continuing in this post until 1873 when he was promoted as Director of Admiralty Works.

The scale of the works at Chatham dwarfed everything that had gone before. St Mary's Island and St Mary's Creek added a further 380 acres to the northern end of the existing 97-acre yard. At the heart of this extension were three great basins excavated along the site of the creek, through which vessels could pass and join the Medway through locks at both the Upnor and Gillingham Reach ends. The 21-acre Repairing Basin (3 Basin) at the western end had a depth of 33ft and was equipped with four dry docks on its southern side. It was completed in 1871, and the last of the four docks (No. 7) was finished in January 1873. Next to be completed was the Factory Basin of 7 acres (2 Basin) and finally, in 1883, the enormous 30½-acre Fitting Out Basin (1 Basin). The juxtaposition of these to the group of five modern building slips at the northern end of the existing yard gave Chatham

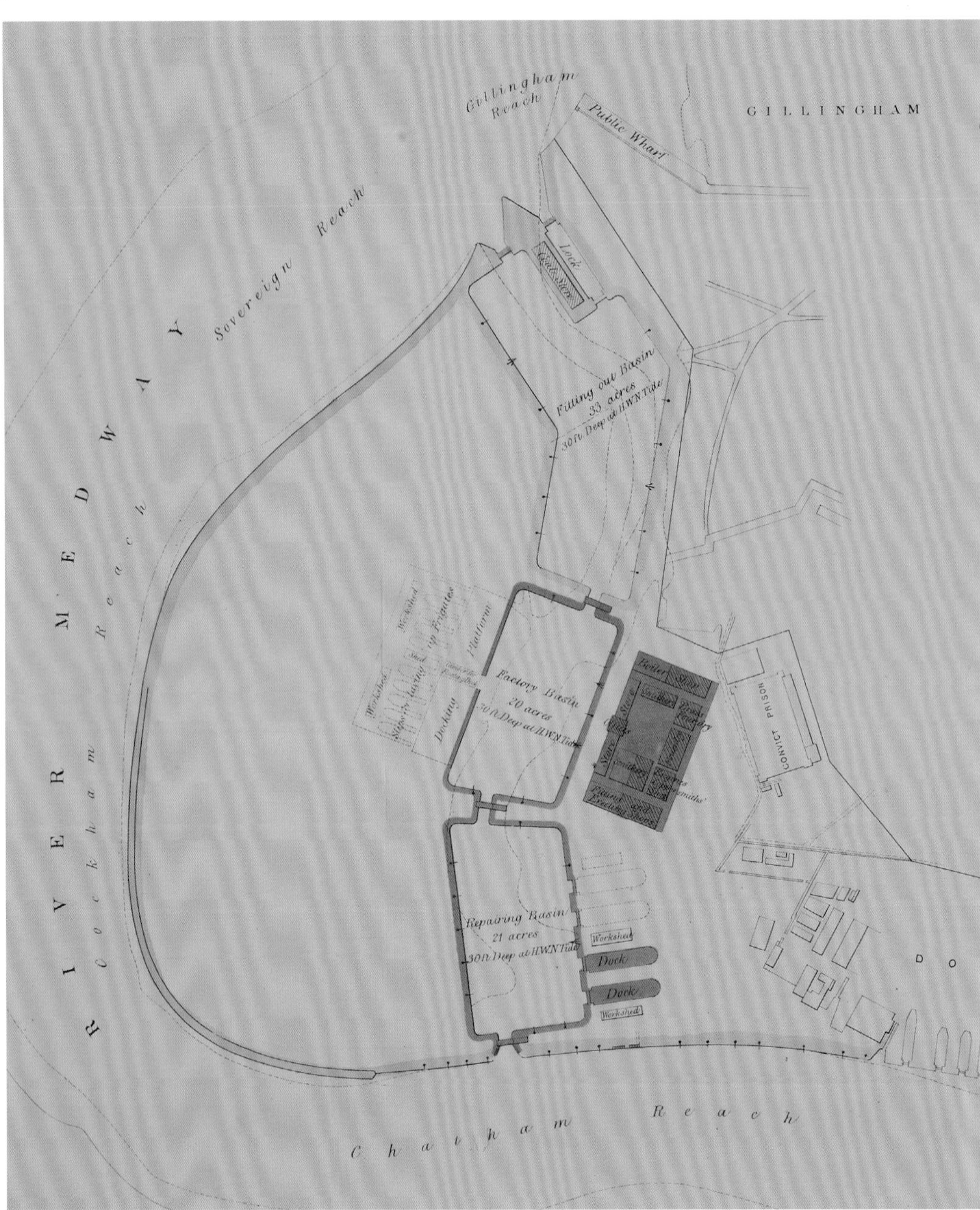

Fig 2.8
The northern end of the extended Chatham Dockyard in 1865, showing work under way on the new steam yard. At that stage, a factory complex similar to that at the Keyham Yard was planned.
(TNA ADM 1/5939)

a unique warship production line. A newly launched hull could be easily towed to the Repairing Basin for minor problems to be sorted, before being moved to the Factory Basin for installation of engines and boilers, and then on to the Fitting Out Basin to be rigged, have its guns mounted and take on coal and stores.[27]

The bulk of the site levelling and the excavation and construction of the basins were done by convict labour, which also was responsible for brickmaking on the adjacent brickfields. Although the superintending Civil Engineer, E A Bernays, was pleased with the quality of their work, a serious lack of convicts led to problems, even though the convict prison had been enlarged in 1866 and again in 1869 to cater for extra numbers. By 1870, only 700 were available compared to the 2,000 needed, and by 1871 these had to be supplemented by contractors' labour. In the opinion of many engineers, convict labour was highly inefficient, and in 1864 John Coode, in charge of the works at Portland, reckoned that the convicts had taken 12½ years to do work that contractors would have done in 5.[28] Despite the Chatham extension having been planned on a generous scale, extra funds had to be found by 1875 for 'alterations in the work consequent on increased width of ships'. Although not specified in the annual estimates, this probably involved alterations to the widths of dry dock entrances as well as the basin locks. By 1880 work was under way for the dock pumping engines, and by 1885 the steam yard was very largely complete (Fig 2.9).[29]

As finished, the Chatham extension differed

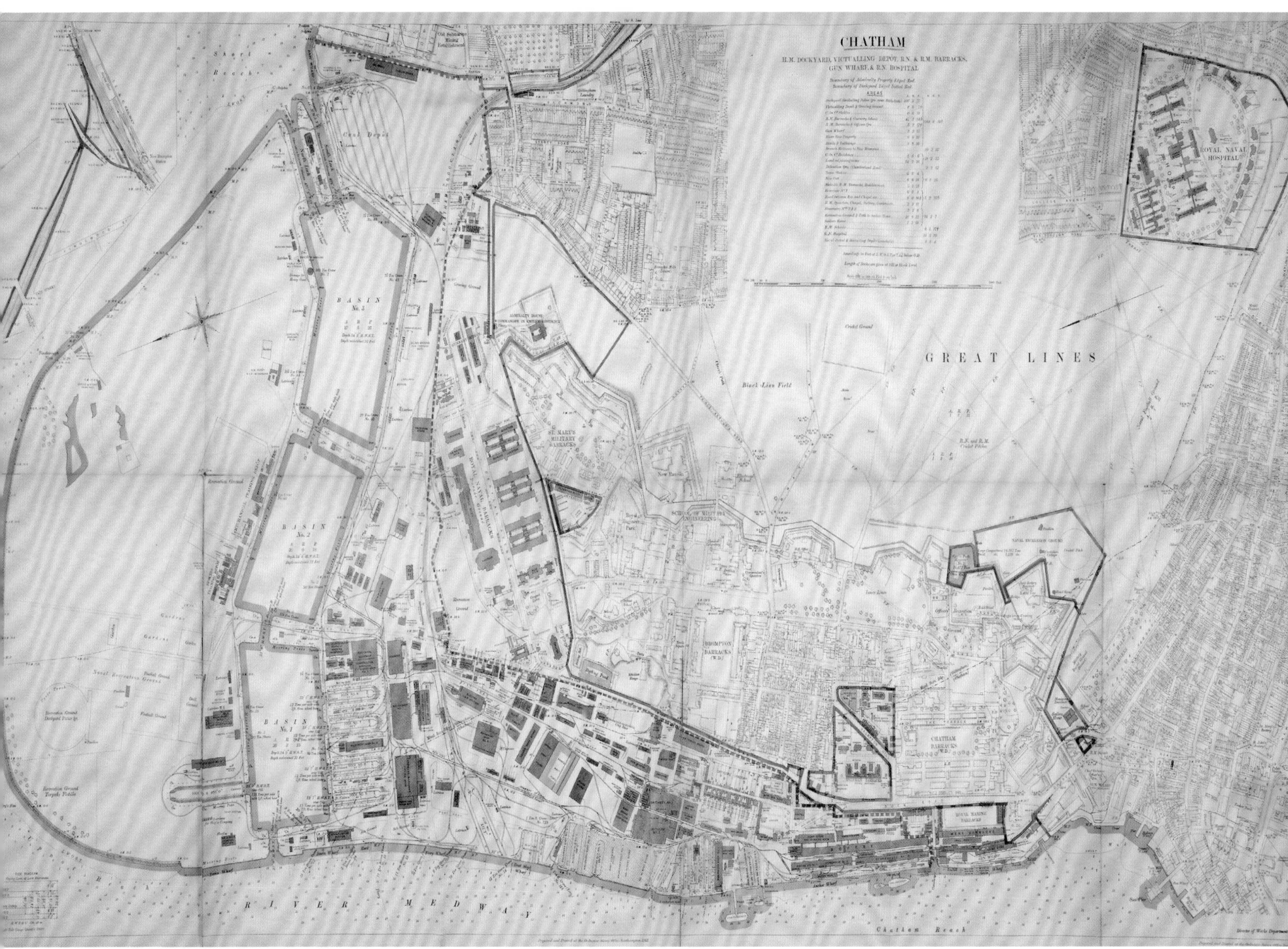

Fig 2.9 (below and in an enlarged scale on the following page) Chatham Steam Yard as developed by 1914. (TNA ADM 140/1484–5)

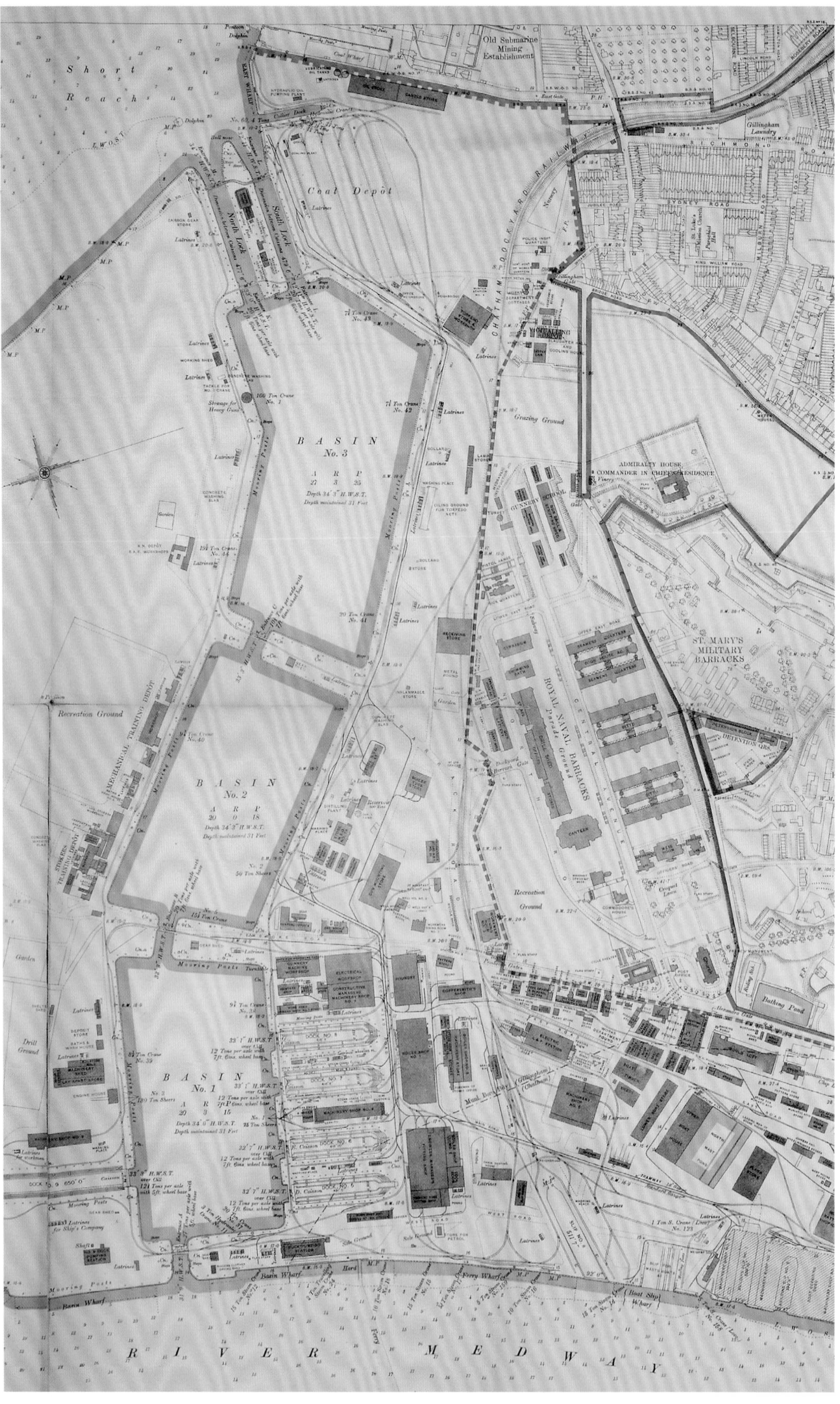
Old Submarine Mining Establishment
Short Reach
Coal Depot
North Lock
Gillingham Laundry
BASIN No. 3
Grazing Ground
ADMIRALTY HOUSE
COMMANDER IN CHIEF'S RESIDENCE
GUNNERY SCHOOL
ST. MARY'S MILITARY BARRACKS
Recreation Ground
ROYAL NAVAL BARRACKS
BASIN No. 2
Recreation Ground
BASIN No. 1
Bathing Pond
Drill Ground
Basin Wharf
Ferry Wharf
RIVER MEDWAY

in two major respects from the proposals of Scamp, Greene and his successor, Colonel Sir Andrew Clarke. In 1849 Scamp had put forward a proposal to haul warships out of the water and store them ashore. This was rejected by the Admiralty in 1852, but in modified form was agreed for smaller vessels at Haslar in 1856 and revived by Scamp for Chatham the following year. He proposed to construct on St Mary's Island a far larger version of the Haslar Gunboat Yard then taking shape on the Gosport peninsula. His scheme would have had a traverser capable of lifting and transporting ships of the line to dry berths able to store up to 25 of these in ordinary. Even with the boundless self-confidence of the Victorians, this might have been stretching technology beyond contemporary limits, and nothing came of the proposal, although modified versions were still being considered in 1863.[30]

On the opposite, southern side of the Factory Basin it was intended to have a quadrangular set of workshops, foundries, offices and stores of a similar scale and layout to the Keyham Quadrangle factory. Although some foundations were begun, it was never built. Instead, the closure of Woolwich Dockyard in 1869 allowed the Admiralty to save substantial sums of money by dismantling the recently constructed metal-framed slip roofs and re-erecting them at the head of the new docks at Chatham. Slip roof 4 was resited at the head of 7 and 8 Docks and became a machine shop, later the Boilermakers' Shop and Machinery Workshop, while the former 5 Slip roof was re-erected at the head of 5 and 6 Docks and became the Fitting Shop. If these lacked the architectural grandeur and formal grouping of the Keyham factory, their clean functional lines, flexibility resulting from ample headroom and absence of internal load-bearing walls and the extensive use of corrugated iron were to be more typical of a number of subsequent factory buildings.[31]

By the turn of the 20th century and only some 15 years after completion of the Chatham extension, docking facilities were already becoming inadequate for the new generation of battleships. In 1904 ambitious plans were drawn up by Colonel Edward Raban RE, Director of Works, and Mr T Sims, Assistant Director, in conjunction with the yard officers to create a fourth basin of some 57 acres, taking up most of the undeveloped area of St Mary's Island. This was to be approached by twin locks from the Medway, and on its western side were to be three new dry docks, the largest of which was to be 800ft long and the other two 600ft and 630ft. The cost was estimated at £4,676,265, but by then the Government's priority was the creation of a new dockyard at Rosyth, and nothing came of the proposal.[32]

Expansion at Portsmouth in 1867

The pace of changes in warship designs and sizes ensured that well before the completion of Chatham, the earlier schemes at Portsmouth and Devonport were becoming inadequate for the navy's needs. By the late 1850s, Portsmouth required more basin facilities, further wharf space for warships, larger dry docks and a new iron foundry. The only possible site was an area of Portsmouth Harbour north of the existing dockyard. In 1862 William Scamp produced a noteworthy plan even more ambitious in scale than his contemporary proposals for Chatham. At Portsmouth he envisaged dredging 103½ acres to provide three basins and deep-water berthing. A further 244 acres were to be reclaimed from the harbour for workshops and other facilities, including generous space for a timber ground, a surprising provision just as the navy was moving towards all-metal warships. Remarkably, given that work had just started on the Royal Commission's ring forts to protect Portsmouth, he proposed fortifying the extension within a bastioned and musket-looped trace.[33]

Sir Andrew Clarke drew up the extension scheme, which was eventually submitted to Parliament in 1864 and begun in 1867. Although more modest than Scamp's, it was still ambitious because approximately half the total of nearly two hundred acres had to be reclaimed from the harbour, while there were also encroachments on Portsea town. As at Chatham, three interlinked basins formed its heart, allowing warships being completed, repaired or simply fitted out to progress logically from stage to stage. The three controlled basins and the 9-acre tidal basin were arranged as a block of four, with the tidal basin in the south-west quadrant. Warships in the tidal basin were taken on an anti-clockwise circuit, first entering the 22-acre repairing basin through one of two huge parallel locks, each nearly 460ft long, so constructed that they had 41½ft of water at high water springs and could be entered at any stage of the tide. Warships then went to the 14-acre rigging basin before being taken to the identically sized fitting out basin. From there, they completed their circuit and returned to the tidal basin, where they could take on coal from the adjacent coal yard (Figs 2.10 and 2.11). Between basins and locks was a mix of conventional floating caissons and sliding ones.[34]

In 1865 the estimated cost for Portsmouth's Great Extension was the suspiciously exact sum of £1,500,000. The contract for much of the work was awarded to the firm of Leather Smith & Co, but as at Chatham, convicts provided a significant proportion of the manual labour on the excavations and in the brickworks. A prison

Fig 2.10
Part of Portsmouth Dockyard as it had developed by the end of 1887. The coaling point is bottom left, the Georgian dockyard bottom right. (AdL Da 0121 fol 1)

Fig 2.11
The coaling point with its cranes and elevators beside the tidal basin, later part of the enlarged 3 Basin. This photograph was taken in 1908, when the site was being cleared in preparation for the construction of C and D Locks. (Author's collection)

to hold 1,020 men had been constructed just outside the dockyard between 1850 and 1853. By 1870, revised estimates put the cost of the Great Extension at £2,250,000 if done solely by contractors, with a saving of a million pounds if assisted by 2,500 convicts. Using 700 convicts, apparently the maximum generally available, the estimated cost was £2,207,000. Six years later, a further £143,000 was added to allow for alterations 'consequent on the increased width of ships'. The final cost was almost certainly comfortably in excess of this revised sum. Very commendably Clarke found funds to save the 1778 Unicorn Gateway, once part of Portsea's defences at the end of North Street, and rebuilt it as the principal gateway in the extended dockyard wall of 1870.[35]

Steam power was employed on a very considerable scale for the first time to assist the work at Portsmouth, where there were formidable engineering problems owing to the soft harbour mud. Mass application of steam power and human muscles completed the tidal basin, the repairing basin and their associated locks by 1876; the remaining two basins were finished in 1881. Three dry docks, varying in lengths from 410ft to 417ft, were also built, with space left for further additions. Until a new steam factory was completed in the south-east corner of the site in 1905, the Great Extension lacked major workshops near the basins. Instead, it had to rely on a web of dockyard railways bringing materials and equipment from workshops and stores that were mostly in the older part of the yard. Colonel Clarke's work has, however, stood the test of time. Despite later increases that he could not have foreseen in the size of the navy and its capital ships, Portsmouth Dockyard has not been enlarged since, although there have been significant modifications within his Great Extension.[36]

Protected harbours

In the middle of the 19th century, a small number of protected harbours was built at strategic locations around the British Isles, largely at the instigation of the Admiralty in parallel with the expansion and modernisation of the royal dockyards. The harbours' main and most expensive components were generally the massive breakwaters and, where provided, the less obvious defences paid for by the War Office. Construction of Plymouth Breakwater, begun in 1811, was only then nearing completion (*see* Chapter 5). It demonstrated all too clearly the costs and physical challenges involved in building these massive engineering works in such hostile environments. The contractors at Portland and especially at Alderney were to be faced with equally great problems, and even with the steam machinery increasingly available, the task of construction ran on for decades. At Alderney, where the breakwater enclosed a harbour of some 150 acres (Fig 2.12), the severity of winter storms precluded masonry

Fig 2.12
Alderney Breakwater providing a harbour of refuge during a storm in 1895. Land fortifications further protected the harbour.
(TNA ADM 195/1 fol 13)

work except in the summer season. Such harbours generally lacked significant naval installations save for coaling facilities at Portland and Alderney.

A combination of factors lay behind the decision to construct these 'harbours of refuge'. As their name suggests, they were partly designed to offer safe havens for both merchant ships and warships caught off otherwise harbourless coasts during stormy weather or when mechanical failure threatened. As steam vessels of all kinds grew in size over this period, and the cost of warships in particular increased enormously, many of the smaller, older ports and harbours were no longer accessible in emergency. Although altruism and its responsibility for the Post Office mail packet service played a part in the Admiralty's early deliberations, notably with the construction of a harbour of refuge at Holyhead from the late 1840s, the main driving force behind the creation of most of them was the strategic factor. Unlike their sailing predecessors, early steam fleets had very limited endurance before their coal bunkers had to be replenished and their machinery maintained. This demanded quick

Fig 2.13
Peterhead harbour of refuge under construction c 1909.
(TNA ADM 140/1484 fol 60)

Fig 2.14 (opposite top)
Portland Harbour with breakwaters in c 1909, with the coaling facilities at the southern end.
(TNA ADM 140/1484 fol 31)

Fig 2.15 (opposite bottom)
Portland Harbour with the Channel Fleet c 1895.
(TNA ADM 195/78 fol 13b)

access to a secure base where, if necessary, emergency repairs could also be undertaken.

The modernisation of the great French naval base at Cherbourg was seen as a major threat, leading directly to the establishment of a protected harbour at Portland and a similar 'forward base' in the Channel Islands at Alderney, work on both beginning in the late 1840s. In a minute of May 1858 the Surveyor of the Navy, Rear-Admiral Sir Baldwin Walker, noted that if there was war with France,

> the necessity of providing an easy and safe means of coaling a fleet with despatch would in my opinion direct attention more immediately to Portland which ... would necessarily be the head-quarters and rendezvous of our Channel Fleet. Moreover ... if an electric wire were laid down from Portland to Alderney, a fleet might remain quietly in the former port with the certainty of being made aware of all the movements of the enemy's fleet by means of the wire and with the aid of a look-out or inshore squadron ... it may be said that such a place would be little less than tantamount to drawing a chain across the Channel.[37]

This view on the importance of Portland and Alderney generally held sway as long as France was considered the main threat. Similar thinking lay behind the creation of the Admiralty harbour at Dover, under construction in phases from 1847 to 1905 and likewise fortified because of its proximity to France.[38] As Germany replaced France as the principal threat, concern grew for the vulnerability of the north-east coast, leading in the years just before the First World War to the construction of two massive breakwaters to form a new harbour of refuge in the bay on the southern side of Peterhead (Fig 2.13).[39]

Portland saw the greatest continuing Admiralty investment, because of its location midway between Portsmouth and Devonport. In the late 1850s a plan was put forward to create a small dockyard with three dry docks, three building slips, a small basin and associated buildings. Portland was seen as a valuable coaling and watering location for warships steaming between Portsmouth and Devonport, an indication of the very limited endurance of early steamers when planning for Portland began in 1847.[40] Nothing came of the proposal, and for the rest of the 19th century a succession of more elaborate coaling facilities was installed and the breakwaters gradually extended to enclose a greater area (Figs 2.14 and 2.15). The last breakwater was completed *c* 1905.[41]

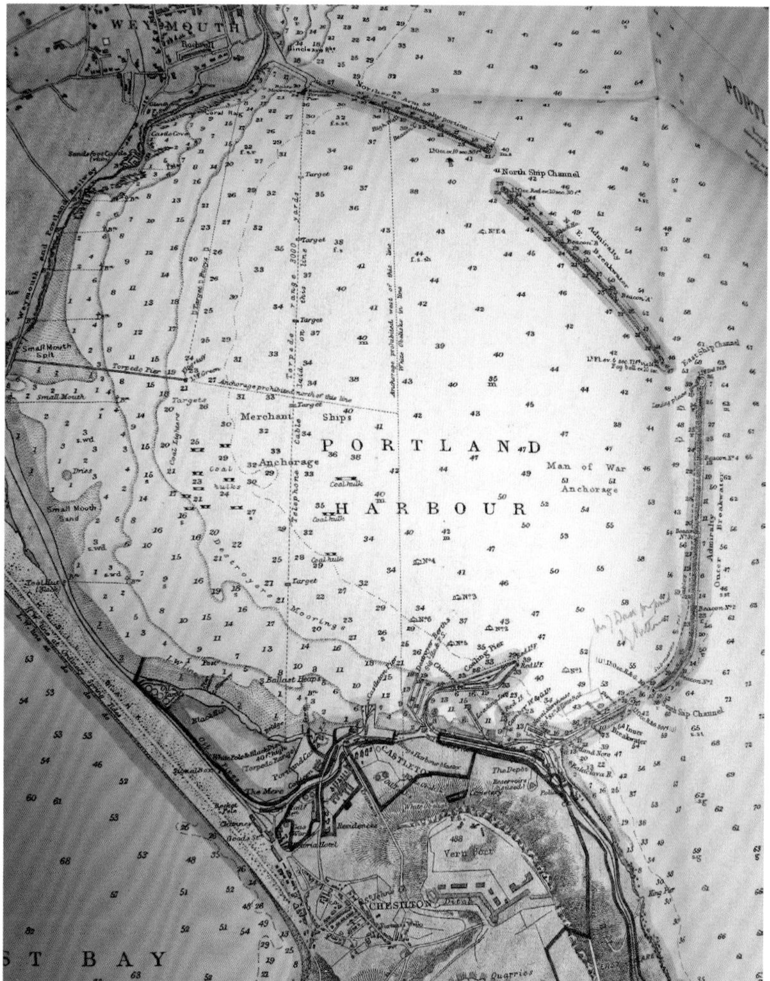

Fig 2.16
The 14,150 ton battleship HMS Royal Sovereign, *designed by William White and undocked at Portsmouth in 1891. Name ship of a famous class, her high freeboard enabled her to operate her guns in nearly all weathers. Over forty warships were based on this design.*
(© National Maritime Museum, Greenwich, London, N00432)

Berths for torpedo boat destroyers were under construction in 1903–4, and the last and most elaborate of the coaling plants was completed in 1906.[42] New shore facilities included three residences and a canteen, to be followed shortly afterwards by a naval hospital and a power station. Its ample sheltered moorings and convenient location saw Portland being used for most of the 20th century in peacetime principally as a base for the training squadron. The base finally closed in 1995, and the naval helicopter station shut in 1999.

The 1895 Naval Works Act

In 1885 William White, one of the most able warship designers of the 19th century, was appointed as Director of Naval Construction. An almost inevitable result of a quarter of a century of rapid evolution in warship design had been the creation of a fleet of disparate and increasingly obsolete vessels. In 1887 White recommended scrapping 72 such ships and replacing them at a cost of £9 million. These proposals were subsumed in the Naval Defence Act of 1889, which authorised the construction of 70 battleships and cruisers in the next 5 years at a cost of £21.5 million. Central to this programme were new battleships, of which White's *Royal Sovereign* and *Majestic* classes were the most famous (Fig 2.16), the *Majestic* the first to be built using armoured steel in place of iron. Such a programme had repercussions on the main yards, as its principal requirement was for more and larger dry docks as well as space in the basins, while the building yards in addition needed enlarged slips (*see* Table 2.1).

To address these needs, the Naval Works Act of 1895 inaugurated what was to be the last modernisation programme largely driven by rivalry with France. Money was provided for work at Chatham, Portsmouth, Devonport, Haulbowline and Gibraltar,[43] and extensive works were then authorised at the dockyard at Simon's Town. A common requirement was for a dry dock of sufficient size for the largest new warships of White's programme to be available at every major base. The one exception was Portland, as damaged ships in the Channel were expected to make for Portsmouth or Devonport. At Portland the pressing needs were for a new breakwater and berths for torpedo boat destroyers.[44] The problem facing the Admiralty was the familiar one, set out in a draft memo to the Treasury in October 1895:

> The question of the length of Docks has been under consideration during the last two years in connection with the possible increased lengths of certain types of future men-of-war. The cruisers *Powerful* and *Terrible*, now under construction greatly exceed in length any of the vessels in the Navy, and the necessity for additional speed

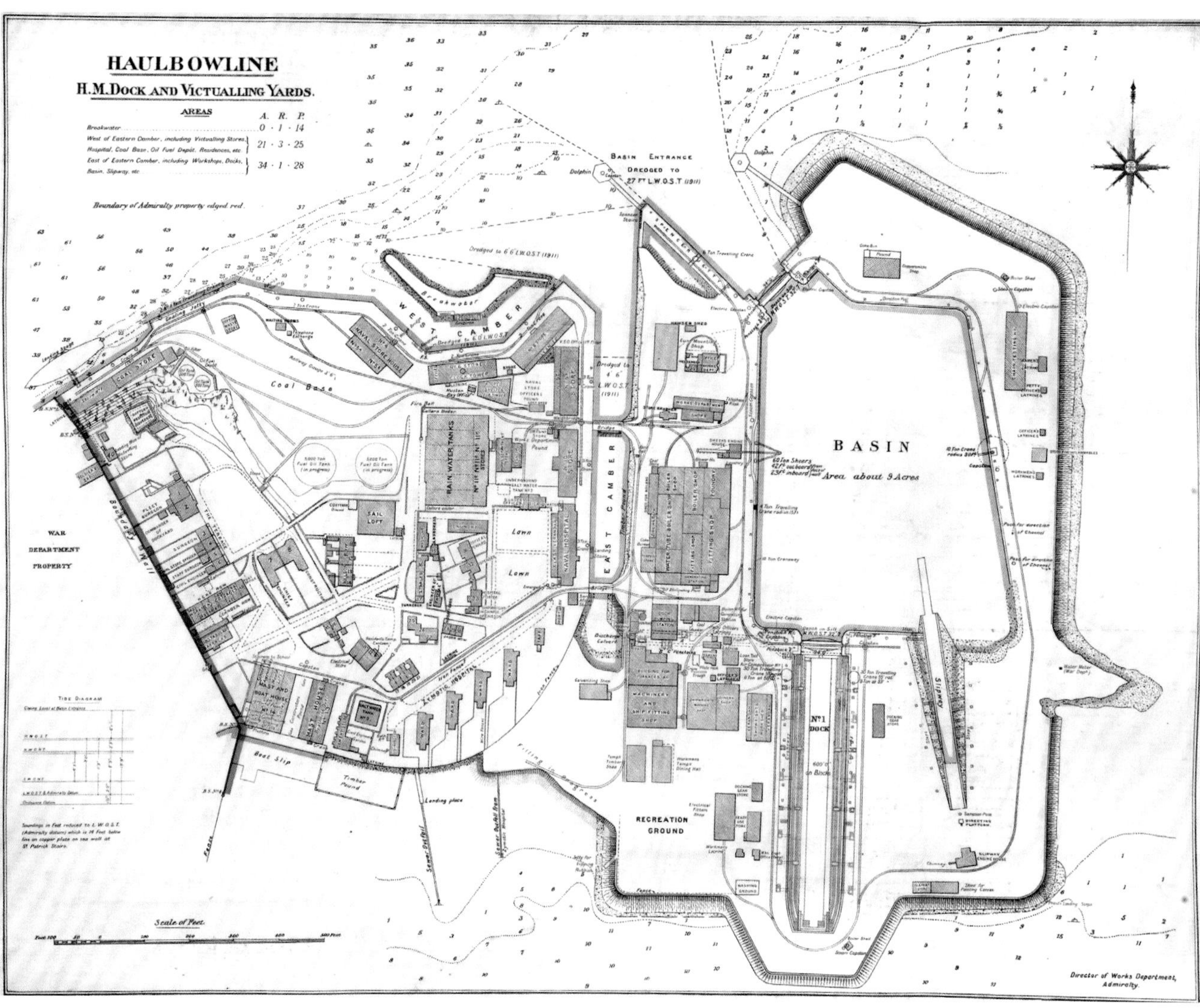

Fig 2.17
Haulbowline Dockyard with the new basin and extended dry dock, completed shortly before the First World War. (AdL Vz 14/72)

points to a still greater length in vessels which may be designed in the near future. There is also a tendency in the Merchant Marine to increase the length of their fastest and most powerful vessels such as would be used as armed cruisers in case of war and which might have to be docked in the Royal Dockyards ... Devonport ... would probably be the first point reached in time of war by battleships injured in action ... and as the value of a single battleship approaches a million, it is necessary that every arrangement should be made to provide proper docking for them.[45]

At the time, Devonport had only one dry dock capable of accommodating a first-class battleship.[46] *Powerful* and *Terrible*, each 538ft long with beams of 71ft, were briefly the longest warships in the world. There was no foolproof solution to catering for future warships of unknown dimensions; all that could reasonably be done was build the largest dry docks that space, technology and finance would allow. At Chatham a new 650ft dry dock was authorised on the northern side of the repairing basin, opposite the four existing smaller ones; this was nearing completion in 1903.[47] At Haulbowline the single basin was too small to incorporate a second dry dock, so the existing one was increased in length from 408ft to 600ft. As this involved reclaiming part of Cork Harbour to house the lengthened head of the dock, permission was sought and obtained from the Harbour Board in January 1907, and the work was completed shortly before the outbreak of the First World War (Fig 2.17).[48]

At Portsmouth modifications and additions were made within the overall perimeter of Colonel Clarke's earlier works, and improvements continued almost unabated to the outbreak of war in 1914. Clarke's scheme had allocated space for two further dry docks to be built on the southern side of the repairing basin. Numbered 14 and 15, they were completed by the contractor J Price & Co and were in use by 1896. Both were 563½ft long. No. 15 was 94ft wide, some 12ft more than No. 14, and was more square in section to allow for the bilge keels then being fitted to warships to aid stability and assist gunnery accuracy. Even these sizes, along with the similar 13 Dock, proved inadequate. The length of No. 13 was increased by 1905, and 2 years later No. 15 was extended. In 1914 No. 14 Dock was rebuilt to the remarkable length of 720ft and width of 100ft. With dry docks of these sizes in the repairing basin, it was necessary to provide similar or larger-sized locks from the harbour, as the existing north and south locks were just under 460ft in length.

The only possible solution was to construct two more huge locks immediately north of the south locks. Numbered C and D (Fig 2.18), these too were completed in 1914 by Morrison and Mason, contractors from Glasgow. Both locks were 850ft long and 110ft wide and have proved adequate ever since.[49] To make way for these locks, the coaling point had to be cleared, as well as a substantial part of the fitting out basin (*see* Figs 2.10 and 2.11). To give manoeuvring room for the great warships, the internal quay walls dividing the three basins were mostly removed, and the resultant single basin was renamed No. 3 Basin. In 1905 the Factory was completed just to the south-east, the largest engineering workshop built in the yard up to that date. Measuring some 580ft by 280ft, its massive gables still dominate this part of the base, witness to the growing number and complexities of warships in the last years of Edwardian peace.[50]

At Devonport, the dockyard had had very little significant modernisation since the completion of Keyham Yard some 30 years earlier, and the most innovative developments had taken place outside the dockyard. In 1879 work had started on the first major naval barracks to be built in Britain. In 1880 the need for more and better-trained engineer officers for the navy's ships led to the construction of the Royal Naval Engineering College just outside the dockyard wall from the Keyham Factory where the cadets would spend most of their time.[51] In the dockyard work had begun in Devonport South Yard in 1860 to replace No. 2 Dock with a substantially larger one known, somewhat unimaginatively as Long Dock. Its length of just over 461ft was the most that could be achieved in the restricted space, and it was in use by 1866. Next to it work began in 1876 on what was described as a 'first class dry dock'. This was 3 Dock, completed some 6 years later. Space restricted its length to just over 416ft, and it was

Fig 2.18
The 26,500-ton battlecruiser HMS Queen Mary *entering the new D Lock at Portsmouth in April 1914. The ship was to be sunk at Jutland two years later.*
(Author's collection)

abundantly apparent that no more dry docks could be fitted into South Yard. At intervals, various modernisation proposals were put forward for Devonport, but nothing was settled.[52]

The Keyham extension, Devonport, 1896

Following the 1889 warship programme, the Director of Works in 1891 drew up plans for a major expansion of the dockyard. These were referred to the President of the Institution of Civil Engineers, Sir John Coode, who had earlier worked at Portland. Modifications were accepted in July 1893, and the revised plans were implemented following the passing of the Naval Works Act 2 year later. These plans were the responsibility of Major Sir Henry Pilkington, Engineer-in-Chief until 1906.[53] Seven firms tendered for the project, which was estimated to cost approximately £3 million, and the contract was awarded to the civil engineering firm of Sir John Jackson, who began site works in February 1896.[54]

The Keyham extension added a further 112 acres along the Hamoaze on the north side of the existing Keyham Yard (Fig 2.19). At its heart was the 35½-acre No. 5 closed basin (Figs 2.20 and 2.21), with the 10-acre No. 4 tidal basin at its southern end. Between these were three dry docks, of which No. 8, the smallest, could only be entered from the closed basin. No. 8 proved to be too small in the age of the *Dreadnought* and was lengthened twice, in 1906 and again in 1910, by which time it was almost as long as its neighbours. These, 9 and 10 Docks, 715ft and 711ft in length respectively, linked the two basins and had sliding caissons at both ends (*see* Fig 2.22), enabling them to double as locks and dry docks. There was also direct access to the closed basin from the Hamoaze and a second access through a 730ft entrance lock at an oblique angle next to 10 Dock. This second entrance, known as the North Lock, could also be used as a dry dock. The northern arm of the closed basin was largely devoted to a huge coaling facility, and the area east of the tidal basin was used for workshops and stores. Most importantly, the extension provided much valuable deep-water wharf space for the fleet.

In its engineering complexity and extent, the Keyham extension scheme rivalled Clarke's

Fig 2.19 (below top)
The two basins, 4 and 5, formed the heart of the 112-acre Keyham Extension at Devonport Dockyard, begun in 1896. The new naval barracks overlook 5 Basin.
(TNA ADM 140/1484 fol 36)

Fig 2.20 (below bottom)
Work beginning in April 1896 on the site of 5 Basin in Devonport's Keyham extension. Beyond are the buildings of the Steam Yard.
(TNA ADM 195/61 fol 6)

Fig 2.21
Excavating the site of 5 Basin and the dry docks in Devonport's Keyham extension in October 1899. By then, mechanical plant was used extensively. The solitary locomotive (centre) is dwarfed by the scale of works. (TNA ADM 195/61 fol 48)

Fig 2.22
The housing for the sliding caisson at the inner end of the North Lock can be seen in this 1901 photograph of works in progress at Devonport Dockyard's Keyham extension. Note the size of the culvert. (TNA ADM 195/61 fol 83)

Fig 2.23
Excavated material at the Keyham extension was hauled up the timber slide and transferred to railway wagons running on temporary timber viaducts. A photograph taken in July 1898.
(TNA ADM 195/61 fol 40)

earlier works at Portsmouth. Part of it was on land formed by rubble from excavations for the earlier steam yard, but 78 acres had to be won from the muddy foreshore. Work went on protected by a 7,600ft coffer-dam along the river frontage. Some 80 acres were excavated to a depth of 40ft to allow a sufficient depth of water by the wharves and in the basins and docks and to enable these to have their foundations set on the underlying rock. As before at Portsmouth, steam pumps, cranes, cable ways and railways aided the army of navvies in excavating and shifting over 1¼ million cubic yards of rock and 4¼ million cubic yards of mud (Fig 2.23), the latter dumped at sea. Much of the engineering works were constructed using Cornish granite, supplemented by supplies from Norway (Fig 2.24). By 1904 the new pumping station and its equipment were in place, the docks and locks were well on the way to completion, and 1,950ft of wharf wall had been finished. In February 1907, the Prince and Princess of Wales formally opened the extension. By 1914, Devonport was the largest naval base in western Europe, a position it maintains a century later.[55]

Fig 2.24
No. 5 Dock at Devonport's Keyham extension was well on the way to completion by July 1903, the date of this photograph. The scale of the engineering works and high quality of the masonry are evident.
(TNA ADM 195/61 fol 101)

Construction of Rosyth Dockyard

The expansion programme funded by the 1895 Naval Works Act had hardly started before events unfolding across the North Sea in Germany began to have a profound impact on British naval planning. In 1897 Admiral Tirpitz was appointed as minister of marine; two years later, with the Kaiser's approval, the Navy Law was passed to create a powerful German navy. The navy's ultimate purpose was unclear, but its potential threat and Germany's expansionist foreign policy could not be ignored. Most immediately, it demonstrated the need for a modern base for the Royal Navy in the north of the United Kingdom, with good access to the North Sea.

A naval base in Scotland, with its implications for employment, the economy and security had been an intermittent dream since the 1707 Act of Union, but until now the Admiralty had resisted such demands, arguing with reason that there was no strategic need for a northern base.[56] By 1900 this position was changing, driven in part by the rising numbers of capital ships causing overcrowding in the southern dockyards and a strain on their maintenance facilities. The mechanical, ordnance and other complexities of the warships of the late Victorian navy, along with their fuel needs, required

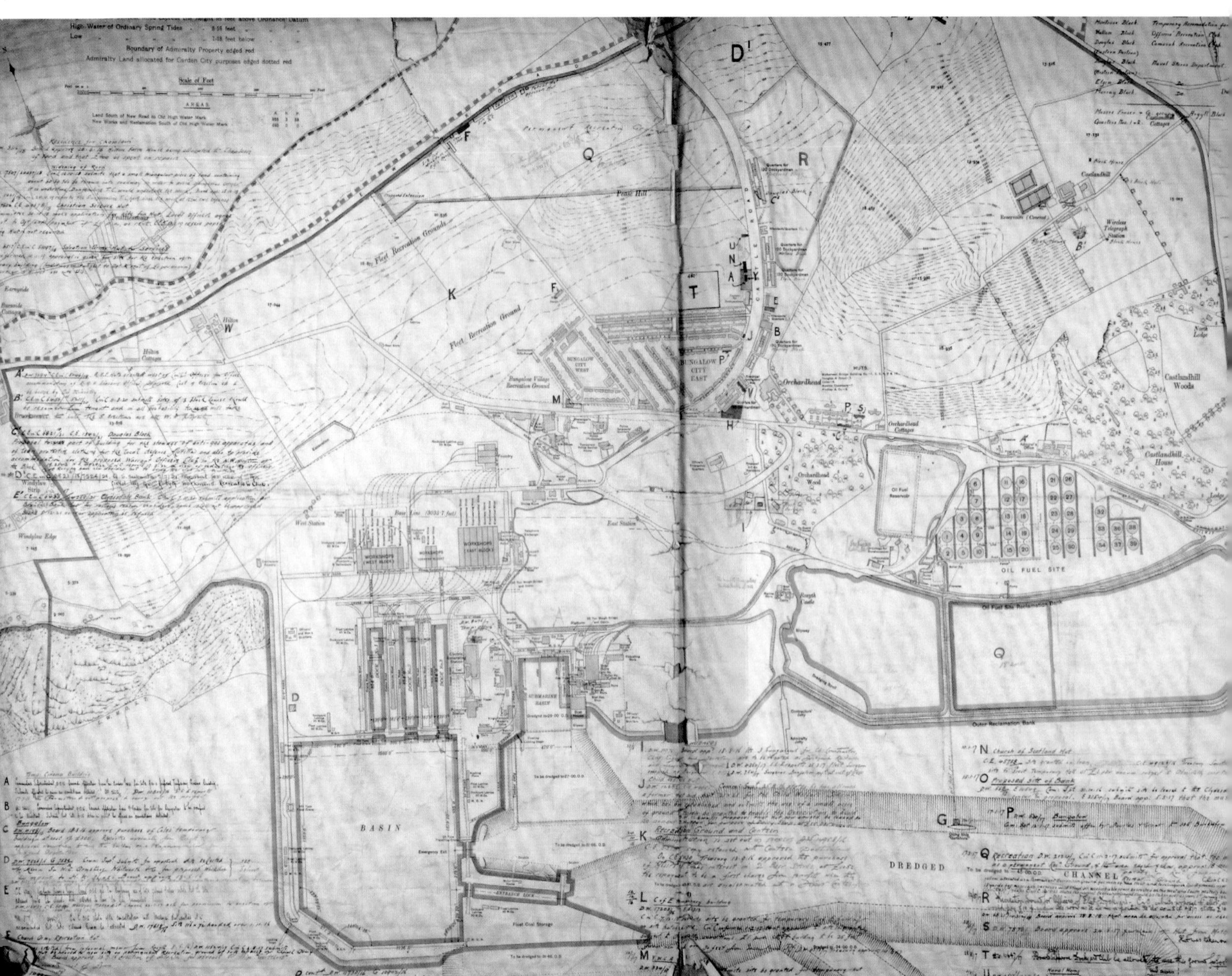

Fig 2.25
Rosyth Dockyard in 1918 shortly after its initial completion. Outside the yard lies Bungalow City East and Bungalow City West, built to house yard workers. (AdL Vz 14/145)

a regularity and frequency of re-supply and dockyard attention that had been largely unknown in the sailing navy. In a detailed report presented in January 1902, Admiral Sir William Wharton, the Hydrographer of the Navy, firmly recommended that a new base be established on the north-east bank of the Forth, just above the famous railway bridge. The extensive anchorage here at St Margaret's Hope was, he considered, the best on the east coast, with the deep-water approach making it accessible for the largest warships at all states of the tide. Rail communications were good, and effective defences already existed lower down the Forth, making attack difficult. The dockyard itself would need to be created partly on reclaimed land and partly on the adjacent farmland. In February 1903, Lord Selborne, First Lord of the Admiralty, announced the Government's intention to establish what he described as a 'fourth naval base and depot in the United Kingdom'.[57]

Shortly afterwards, the Admiralty purchased some 1,470 acres of farmland and foreshore around the ruins of Rosyth Castle. Ambitious plans to create a manning base complete with naval barracks, on the same scale as Chatham, Portsmouth and Devonport, were drawn up. These proved unsustainable at a time when Admiral Sir John Fisher, appointed First Sea Lord on 21 October 1904, was pushing through his Dreadnought building programme, concentrating the Royal Navy's strength in home waters, and also scrapping obsolete warships and closing overseas bases to try to cut naval expenditure. Not until March 1908 did the government decide to proceed with Rosyth, at an estimated cost of £3 million and with a projected completion date of 1918. The main contractor, Easton Gibb and Sons, signed the contract on 1 March 1909.[58]

The revised plans abandoned any idea of Rosyth being a manning base, thus removing the need to construct naval barracks and associated facilities. Proposals for the dockyard were also scaled back to that of a repair and maintenance base, with the possibility of later expansion to include warship construction. The 1909 plan centred on a rectangular closed basin of some 56 acres (Fig 2.25), approached from downriver on the south-eastern side either through an entrance lock at any stage of the tide or directly through adjacent gates at high tide. On the northern side of the closed basin, the 1909 plan had a solitary dry dock, but this was later more realistically increased to three dry docks, each 854ft in length and with gate widths of 110ft, able to cope with the largest capital ships. Space was left for a further two dry docks if needed. East of the closed basin was a tidal basin. Set back at right angles from the heads of the dry docks were three sets of workshops. The eastern group contained the engineering shops, coppersmiths' shops, electrical shops and gunnery store. The smaller central workshops specialised in boiler repairs. The western set contained the smithery, shipwrights' shops, electrical fitters' shop and the woodworkers.[59]

Fig 2.26
Rosyth Dockyard under construction in 1912. The chimneys belong to the dock pumping station on the left and the electricity generating station to the right. (Dunfermline Carnegie Library)

Fig 2.27
A hazy aerial view of Rosyth between January 1919 and May 1921. On the right is the main entrance lock to the basin. Alongside the quay in the foreground are the Battle cruisers Courageous *and* Glorious. *Further along the quay to the left lie the depot ships* Sutlej *and* Crescent. *In the central dry dock, and harbinger of a changing navy, is the aircraft carrier* Furious; *in the dock to her left is a seaplane carrier, possibly the* Pegasus. *Beyond the three dry docks are the engineering workshops. The battleship alongside the quay on the right is possibly one of the four super-dreadnoughts of the Iron Duke class. (RCAHMS)*

By the time these buildings came to be constructed, the country was at war, and the need was for economy and efficiency. All were simple brick-clad, steel-framed industrial workshops with glazed top lighting, and the last was completed in May 1918.

On the outbreak of war in August 1914, Rosyth was far from operational. Two dry docks were ready, but were useless until the basin was completed, excavation of which was not finished until September 1915. Not until the following March were the basin, entrance lock and docks operational, just in time to receive casualties from the Battle of Jutland. By then, decisions in 1912 to create 'a floating second-class naval base and war anchorage' at Cromarty Firth and its small port of Invergordon and in 1913 to develop Scapa Flow in Orkney as a wartime base for the Grand Fleet meant that the Royal Navy was rapidly acquiring the northern facilities it needed to counter the German High Seas Fleet. Rosyth did not have a sheltered, adequate or safe wartime fleet anchorage, as the one below the Forth Bridge was vulnerable to torpedo attack and mines.[60]

Closure

Rosyth Dockyard rounds off the architectural history of British naval bases at a time when the Royal Navy was at the zenith of its power. It was not the last naval base to be established for the fleet. In the 1930s, money was poured into creating a powerful naval base at Singapore. This was still incomplete at the outbreak of the Second World War. In the 1960s and 1970s there was major government investment building the Clyde submarine base at Faslane, first for Polaris then for Trident boats.

In the last half century a numerically shrinking fleet and warships needing less frequent maintenance have resulted in the 21st-century Royal Navy operating from the three bases of Portsmouth, Devonport and Faslane. The first home dockyard to be closed in the 20th century was the building yard of Pembroke Dockyard. Its life depended on the continuance of a substantial fleet and a lack of building capacity in other naval and merchant yards. Following the reduction in the size of the Royal Navy after the Washington Treaty of 1922, Pembroke's days were numbered, and it effectively closed in 1926, although the Royal Maritime Auxiliary Service maintained a limited presence in part of the yard until early 2008. Haulbowline remained as a Treaty Port after the establishment of the Irish Free State in 1921, but was transferred to the Irish Government 2 years later and today is the principal base for the Irish Navy.[61]

The rate of closures accelerated after the Second World War. Bermuda Dockyard was axed in 1951, and Sheerness was closed in 1960, to be followed by Malta, Gibraltar and the great base at Chatham in 1983. Along with these went the supporting facilities, once run by sister boards to the Admiralty, but long since subsumed beneath the Admiralty's umbrella. The Royal Victoria Yard at Deptford, oldest of all the victualling yards, had been shut in 1961. Changing methods of food production and distribution led to the closure some 30 years later of its sister yards, the Royal Clarence at Gosport, the Royal William at Stonehouse and the tiny Georgian yard at Gibraltar. The end of Chatham Dockyard in 1983 also signalled the end of HMS *Pembroke*, the associated naval barracks, as well as extensive ordnance facilities on the opposite side of the Medway. Haslar, begun in 1746 and the last and most famous of all naval hospitals, was relinquished by the Ministry of Defence in 2007.[62]

3

Planning and Building the Royal Dockyards to 1795

Tradition and Evolution, 1700–1760

The royal dockyards had been the responsibility of the Navy Board since the 16th century. Their management system had gradually evolved, largely driven by custom, but since 1662 incorporating instructions laid down by the Duke of York.[1] Working with the commissioners of the Navy Board at their offices in Seething Lane near the Tower of London (Fig 3.1) was a core of professional staff, notably the Surveyor, together with a growing number of clerks. By 1700 there were generally agreed procedures in place for the design, construction, maintenance and repair of buildings and engineering works in the home dockyards. In broad terms, this largely 17th-century system remained mostly untouched throughout the 18th century as the fleet and yards expanded.

In 1786 the Navy Board moved to more spacious accommodation in the newly completed Somerset House in the Strand (*see* Chapter 6). Significant change in their working arrangements with the royal dockyards was to follow, with Samuel Bentham's appointment as Inspector General of Naval Works in 1795, followed by the more radical reforms of 1832. For the overseas yards, remoteness from the Navy Board and slow communications inevitably led to greater local initiatives and somewhat looser arrangements. When Admiral Sir John Jennings arrived on station in the spring of 1711, he promptly activated earlier orders from the Sick and Hurt Board and ordered construction of the navy's first purpose-built hospital in the Mediterranean, siting it on the Isla del Ray in Mahon Harbour for security and to prevent desertions (Fig 3.2).[2] Jennings arranged for Captain Robert Latham, the Royal Engineer officer attached to the island garrison, to supervise the construction of the naval hospital (*see* Chapter 16), financing it by a loan secured by a whip-round of the ships' officers. He only sought permission for the works some months after it had started and sorted out the resultant repayment row when he returned to England.[3] This is one of the earliest examples of Royal Engineer involvement in naval works, but not the only instance at an overseas base of a naval officer instigating a major project before obtaining full agreement from London.[4]

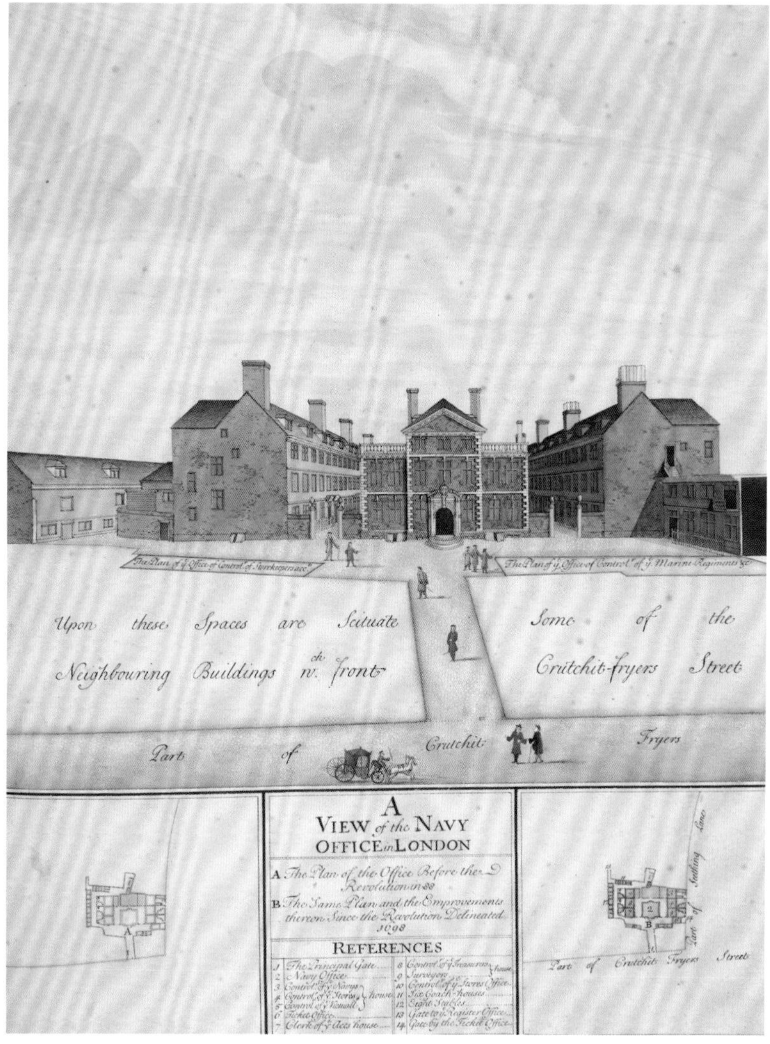

Fig 3.1
The Navy Board's offices in Seething Lane, London, in 1698. Like the Admiralty, this building provided office space and housing for members of the Navy Board and senior administrative staff.
(© The British Library Board. Kings MS 43 fol 147)

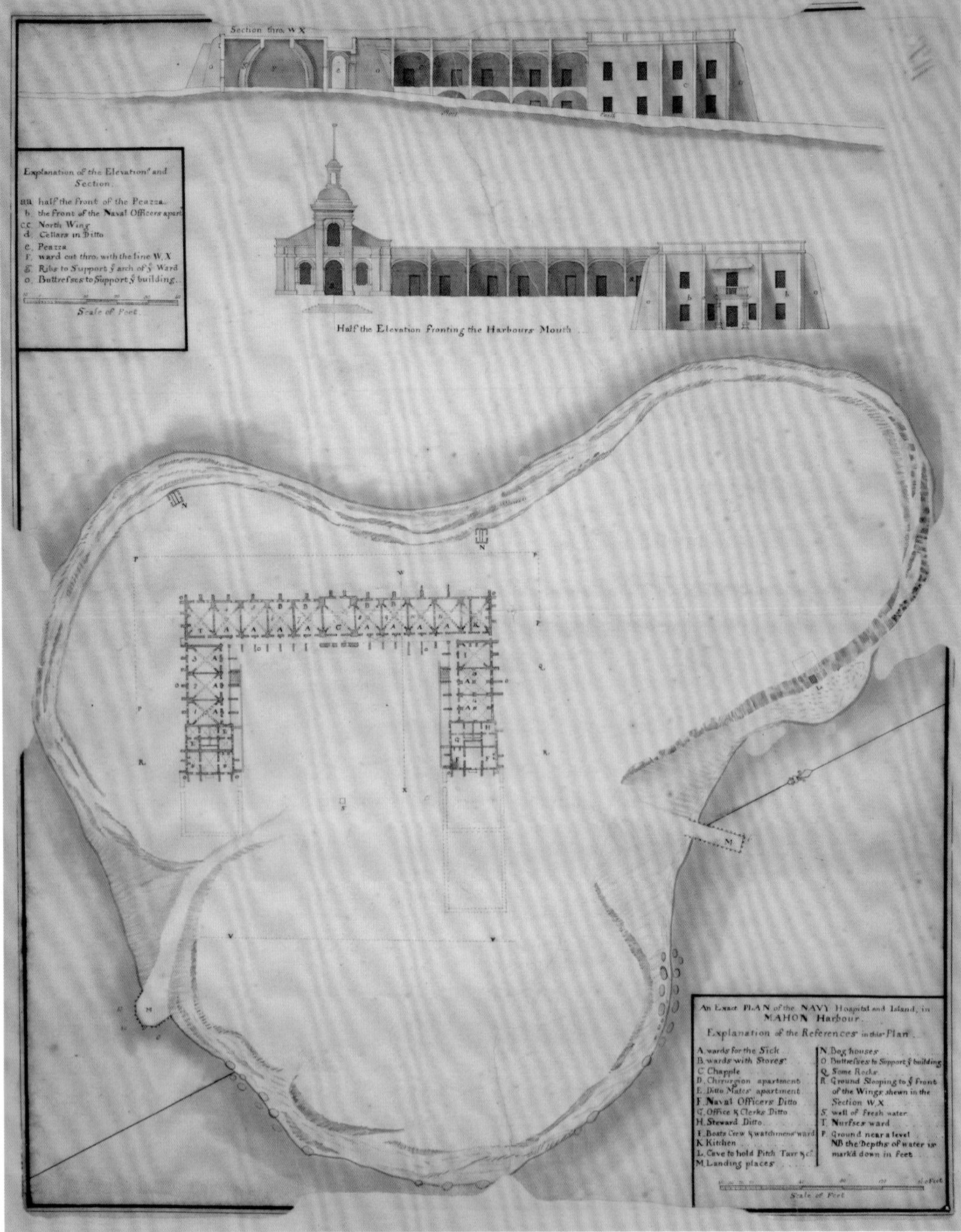

Fig 3.2
A plan and elevation drawing of the naval hospital at Minorca, on its island in Port Mahon harbour, as constructed in 1711.
(TNA ADM 140/1321)

The principal dockyards were in the immediate charge of outstationed commissioners. In the 1780s, there were 11 commissioners, of whom 7 were based in London and 4 outstationed at Chatham, Portsmouth, Plymouth and Halifax, Nova Scotia. Numbers tended to grow, and at the end of the Napoleonic Wars there were commissioners at Deptford, Woolwich, Sheerness, Chatham, Portsmouth, Plymouth, Quebec, Port Royal, Antigua, Malta, Cape of Good Hope, Madras and Bombay.[5] Although owing their allegiance to the main Board, they were powerful figures able to exercise considerable independent command in their own yards and frequently able to get their own way if it suited their interests. In 1704, when George St Lo transferred from being commissioner at Plymouth to Chatham, he insisted that a new house be built for him at Chatham. Nearly eighty years later, Commissioner Henry Martin at Portsmouth successfully overruled John Marquand, the temporary Building Surveyor, who reported that the Commissioner's House was quite capable of being repaired. Martin simply employed Samuel Wyatt, who obligingly produced a report stating exactly the opposite, tendering his designs for the new house at the same time. The Navy Board accepted Wyatt's recommendation.[6]

The independence exercised by the more strong-minded commissioners was always a factor in any dealings between Navy Board officials and the senior officers of the dockyards. Among the former, the Surveyor of the Navy had more occasion than most to be in regular contact with the yards. His main task was to keep accounts of all naval material, including the condition of ships and buildings. However, in 1672 Pepys arranged the appointment of Sir John Tippetts, the first master shipwright to be Surveyor, his brief specifically extended to include responsibility for shipbuilding. Such was felt to be the sense in this arrangement that senior shipwrights monopolised the post for the next 160 years. In this role, one of their main tasks was to standardise classes of ships, although initially not to common designs, because the draughts of individual ships remained the preserve of the master shipwrights concerned.[7] This extra work, coinciding with the sustained growth of the fleet, almost certainly limited the time that most surveyors could devote to the dockyards. Given the size, complexity and scattered nature of the naval estate, most could do little more than exercise a broad control from London over the planning of the yards and over the disposition, general form and choice of construction materials of the more important buildings. Virtually all the detailed design work, along with the supervision of construction, maintenance or repairs, was delegated to the men on the spot – the outstationed commissioners and senior resident dockyard officers.

The outstationed commissioners were generally naval officers of ability, while the senior resident dockyard officers – especially the master shipwright who in modern parlance was more of a general manager – were almost invariably educated men of considerable experience, at or near the peak of their professions. Together they were responsible for the design, building, fitting out, repair and maintenance of warships, which were among the most complex of all human constructions. These officials would have considered themselves quite capable of designing the great majority of whatever dockyard buildings were needed and would have seen absolutely no need to seek outside professional assistance. In pre-Industrial Revolution Britain, the dockyards in any event had the greatest concentration of specialist trades and skills, and away from London it would not have been immediately obvious where to turn for outside help.

Only in rare instances before 1800 were naval buildings designed by outside architects rather than by the Surveyor or dockyard officers. These few exceptions were invariably the grander or more specialised buildings, such as the naval hospitals at Haslar and Stonehouse and Wyatt's 1784 Commissioner's House at Portsmouth, which owed more to the commissioner's determination to outmanoeuvre the Surveyor and have a new house rather than the need to employ an outside architect. Nevertheless, when there were tasks requiring skills not immediately available in a particular yard, the Navy Board knew whom to ask in London. In May 1693, wanting a detailed report and survey of the works under way at the new yard at Plymouth, the Board warned the master shipwright there to receive 'two workmen, Ephraim Beacham and Thomas Webb ... who have been recommended to us by Sir Christopher Wren'.[8] Busy rebuilding St Paul's Cathedral and Kensington Palace, Wren was becoming involved with proposals for the Royal Naval Hospital at Greenwich. A century later, Bentham was to involve many of the leading engineers and men of science in modernising the yards.

From 1692 to 1699, the Surveyor of the Navy was Edmund Dummer, one of the most able and talented men to hold the post. He numbered Pepys and John Evelyn among his circle and had played a notable part as an assistant to Sir John Tippetts in the unprecedented 1677 programme of laying down 30 ships of the line. Dummer sought to apply the principles of reason and science to his work, rather than relying on the traditional surveyor's skills learnt through apprenticeship and practical working experience. In 1684 his skills as a draughtsman caused Pepys at the king's orders to send him to the Mediterranean, where he made meticulous sketches of vessels, arsenals and fortifications.[9]

When Dummer was appointed Surveyor in 1692, the country had been at war for 3 years. In 1690, galvanised by the humiliation of defeat at the Battle of Beachy Head, the Government began an expansion of the navy that over the next quarter of a century was to see the construction of 159 ships of the line and 113 cruisers. Such a programme would have taxed most surveyors, but Dummer had the added responsibility of the parallel drive to modernise the dockyards.[10] Despite all this, he found time to compile an extraordinarily detailed and meticulously drawn survey of all the royal dockyards, illustrating every building, its value and the cost and particulars of improvements carried out in each yard between 1688 and 1698 (*see* Fig 3.3).[11] He estimated that the total sum spent was £166,799, giving a combined value of the yards in 1698 as £291,124 2s 8¾d. This survey vividly illustrates the complexities and extent of the royal yards and was probably intended to serve as a reference work in the Navy Board offices.

Dummer was clearly capable and industrious, but his tenure as Surveyor is instructive in showing the extent and limitations of his ability to employ 'elements of mathematical calculation and meticulously honed standards of empirical observation ... to introduce a more rational, planned approach to ... building ships and dockyards'.[12] His most significant contributions to the dockyards were his introduction of the first recognisably modern dry docks at Portsmouth and Plymouth. Having selected Plymouth as the location for a western dockyard in 1689, he was responsible for its overall planning. He arranged the buildings logically, which were focused on the dry dock and wet dock (Fig 3.4). He put the great central storehouse conveniently adjacent to the wet dock, while the smithery was isolated on the far side because of its fire risk. Along the eastern boundary Dummer placed the ropery, where its great length would cause least obstruction to yard traffic. Finally, he located the officers' terrace and yard offices on high ground, from where the occupants could overlook the whole yard and keep an eye on activities (*see* Fig 7.2; *see also* Chapter 7).

In his pursuit of clear planning, logic, efficiency and control, Celina Fox compares him with his contemporary, the great French military engineer Vauban.[13] Celia Fiennes, who passed by the new dockyard in 1698, was clearly impressed:

> there is a great deale of buildings ... a very good house for the Masters and severall lesser ones and house for their cordage and makeing ropes, and all sorts of things required in building or refitting ships; it lookes like a little town the buildings are so many, and all of marble with fine slate on the roofs, and at a little distance it makes all the houses shew as if they were cover'd with snow and glisters in the sunn which adds to their beauty.[14]

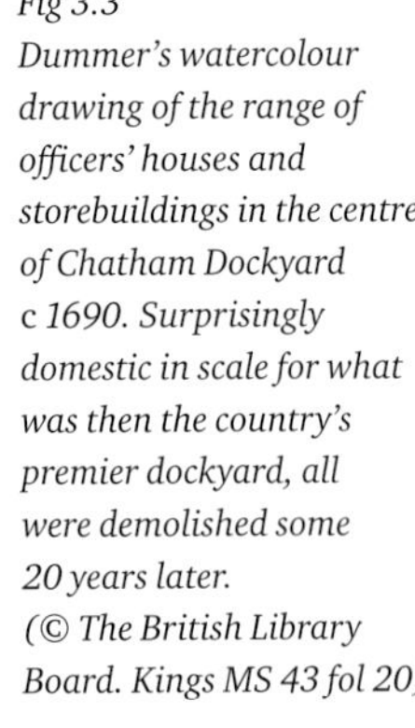

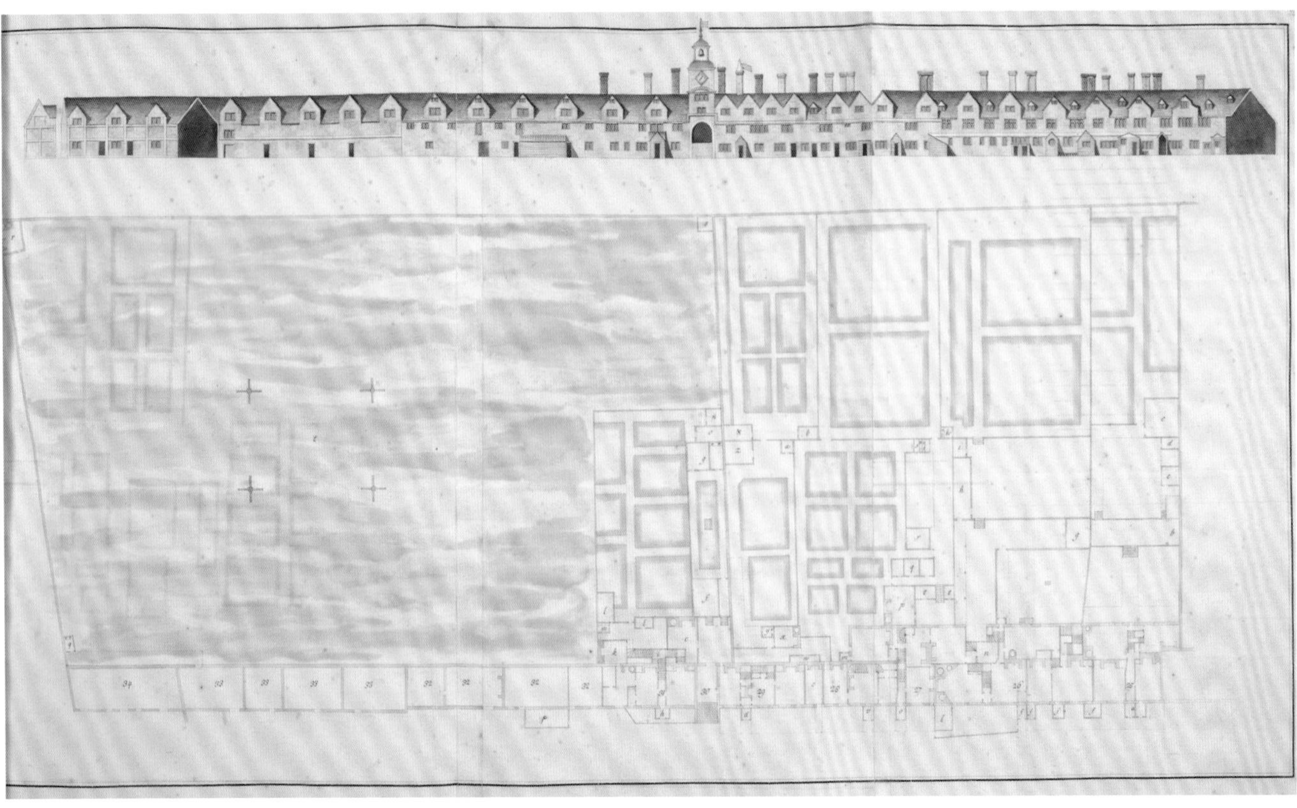

Fig 3.3
Dummer's watercolour drawing of the range of officers' houses and storebuildings in the centre of Chatham Dockyard c 1690. Surprisingly domestic in scale for what was then the country's premier dockyard, all were demolished some 20 years later.
(© The British Library Board. Kings MS 43 fol 20)

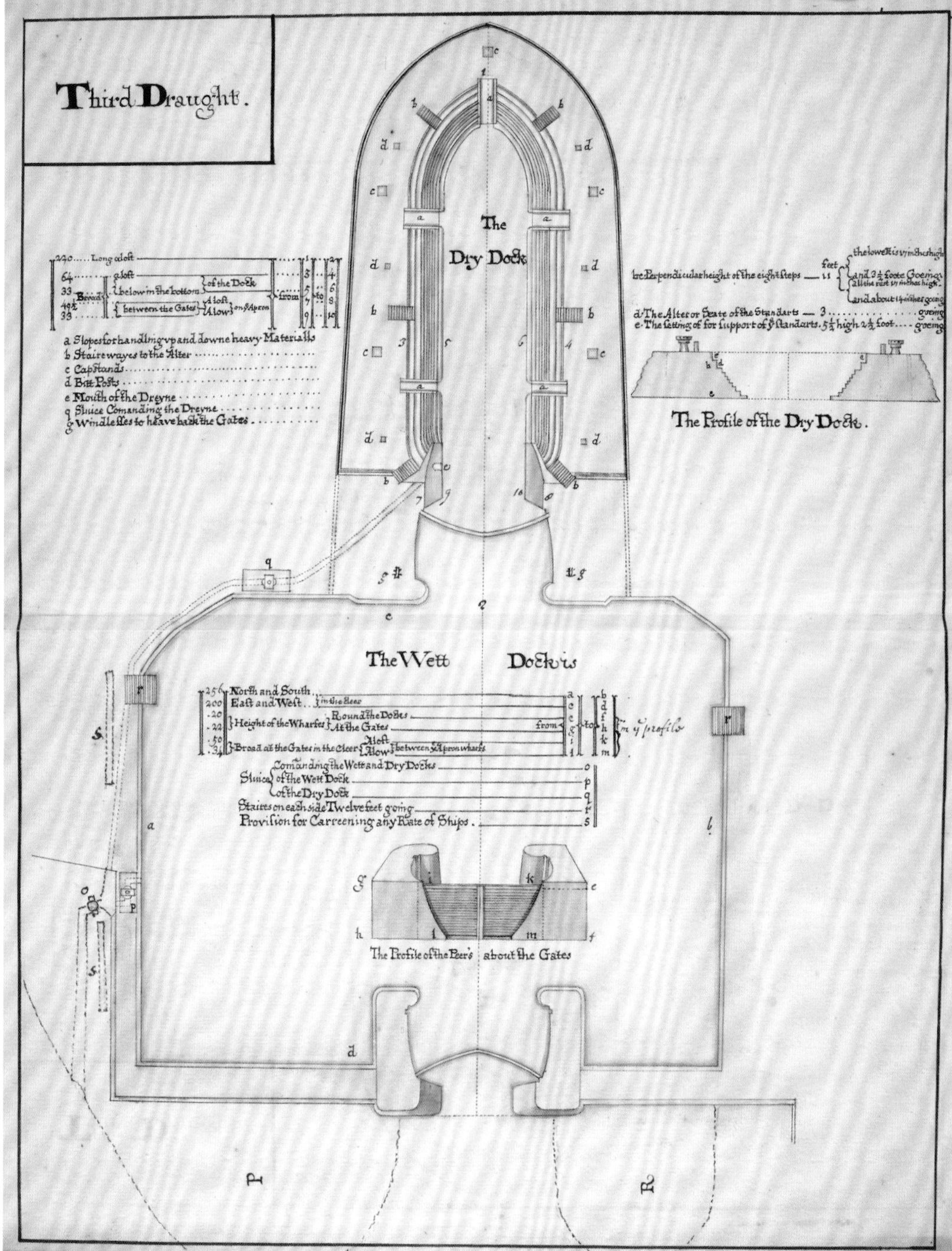

Fig 3.4
Dummer's 1696 drawings of his dry dock and wet dock in the new yard at Plymouth. (© The British Library Board. Lansdowne MS 847 fol 45)

Dummer's tenure as Surveyor ended abruptly in August 1699 when he was dismissed, almost certainly unfairly, amidst a welter of lawsuits and accusations of bribery that were eventually decided in his favour. These largely stemmed from an earlier row with John Fitch, one of the main contractors for the dockyard buildings at Plymouth, who was also responsible for the dry dock and two wet docks at Portsmouth where there were problems with foundations and accusations of shoddy workmanship.[15] In part, Dummer's dismissal was probably the result of entrenched opposition to his approach to his post. As Fox has noted, 'He knew how to employ the language of the Royal Society … for promotional purposes, yet in order to achieve anything on the ground he had to operate in a world of mechanical arts whose operators used other, more pragmatic disciplines and forms of communication'.[16]

At Plymouth, Dummer's clarity of purpose had been helped by his instructions and the advantages of a new site. A quarter of a century later, when extra land was acquired at Chatham to expand the yard, the picture suggests that a much more piecemeal approach was the norm. No overall plan seems to have been agreed at the outset, and the yard officers rather than the Surveyor took the lead. In 1716 the Navy Board had instructed the yard officers to enclose the new land with the present dockyard wall. This was well advanced by early 1719, but only in March that year did they suggest that it might be extended to include the extensive buildings of the ropery 'which now lye naked and [liable] to the ill designs of every desperate sly villain and the bolder attempts of the giddy rabble and unruly mob, whenever spirited up by ill-designing men, or it may be by the secret and sudden attempts of desperados hired by a foreign enemy'. It comes as no surprise that the grandest and most expensive building in the extended yard at Chatham was the new terrace for the yard officers (*see* Fig 7.7).[17]

In the absence of long-term guidance from the Navy Board and its officials, piecemeal developments initiated largely by the yard officers were the norm. Only 70 years after the founding of Plymouth Dockyard, a 1761 report by the Navy Board was scathing about its state:

> the several magazines for stores and other buildings of various kinds ... are not nearly sufficient ... and the greatest part of them are improperly placed, some of the principal ones still remaining on the surface of the original rock, others standing upon the part that has been levelled more than 30 feet below them, with many temporary additions, so that the whole is crowded and very inconvenient ... the whole by any accident of fire would be in danger of being destroyed.[18]

At its best, the system could produce good, robust industrial and domestic architecture and engineering works, as surviving examples demonstrate. Where funds were tight, the dockyards were equally adept at constructing timber-framed buildings, some of which survive. The system was at its weakest when it came to the long-term planning and efficient layout of individual yards. Successful outcomes also depended heavily on good personal relationships rather than clear, defined chains of command. Radical or novel proposals were liable to be met with entrenched opposition, especially from dockyard officers if they felt their interests threatened. The lack of accurate financial control caused confusion and facilitated corruption. These problems could be exacerbated where the Surveyor appointed the major building contractors, but for the more distant yards the Surveyor inevitably had to leave the day-to-day supervision of the contract and maintenance of standards to the dockyard officers. Normally, this would be the responsibility of the master shipwright or the master house carpenter and their more experienced staff, but resident commissioners could also become deeply and sometimes minutely involved in major projects, as at Portsmouth where Commissioner Richard Hughes kept a general oversight on the construction of the huge naval hospital at Haslar in the mid-18th century (*see* Chapter 16). In December 1752, for example, his letter to the Navy Board on the progress of work included recommendations on what should be done with the spare brick clamps, scaffolding and the houses and suttling places for the workmen if building works were to be stopped. He wrote that he had organised coals from the dockyard smithery to air the hospital, appointing a man to undertake this task, and recommended three more watchmen to prevent vandalism and theft. His close attention to detail included reporting that the holes in the 'bogs' (latrines) were too small, to what effect is not recorded.[19]

Unsurprisingly, not everyone had the necessary skills to match the scale of some tasks. Construction projects were rarely straightforward, because the location of naval bases on the vulnerable interface between land and deep water gave them unique problems. Here, waterside structures were exposed to gales, and wharves, docks and slips sometimes had to withstand strong currents as well as the remorseless suck and surge of tides. Deep water rarely coincided with a conveniently flat foreshore with good stable subsoil, and with detailed geological knowledge in its infancy problems almost invariably arose as soon as excavations were begun for foundations. The new dockyard at Plymouth was largely built on solid rock. Elsewhere, extensive use of timber piles was necessary for the majority of buildings, while docks and wharf walls were further stabilised with horizontal ground anchors secured into the subsoil to their rear (Fig 3.5). If the dockyards in 1700 enjoyed a degree of insularity and autonomy from their unique position as the country's most complex industrial

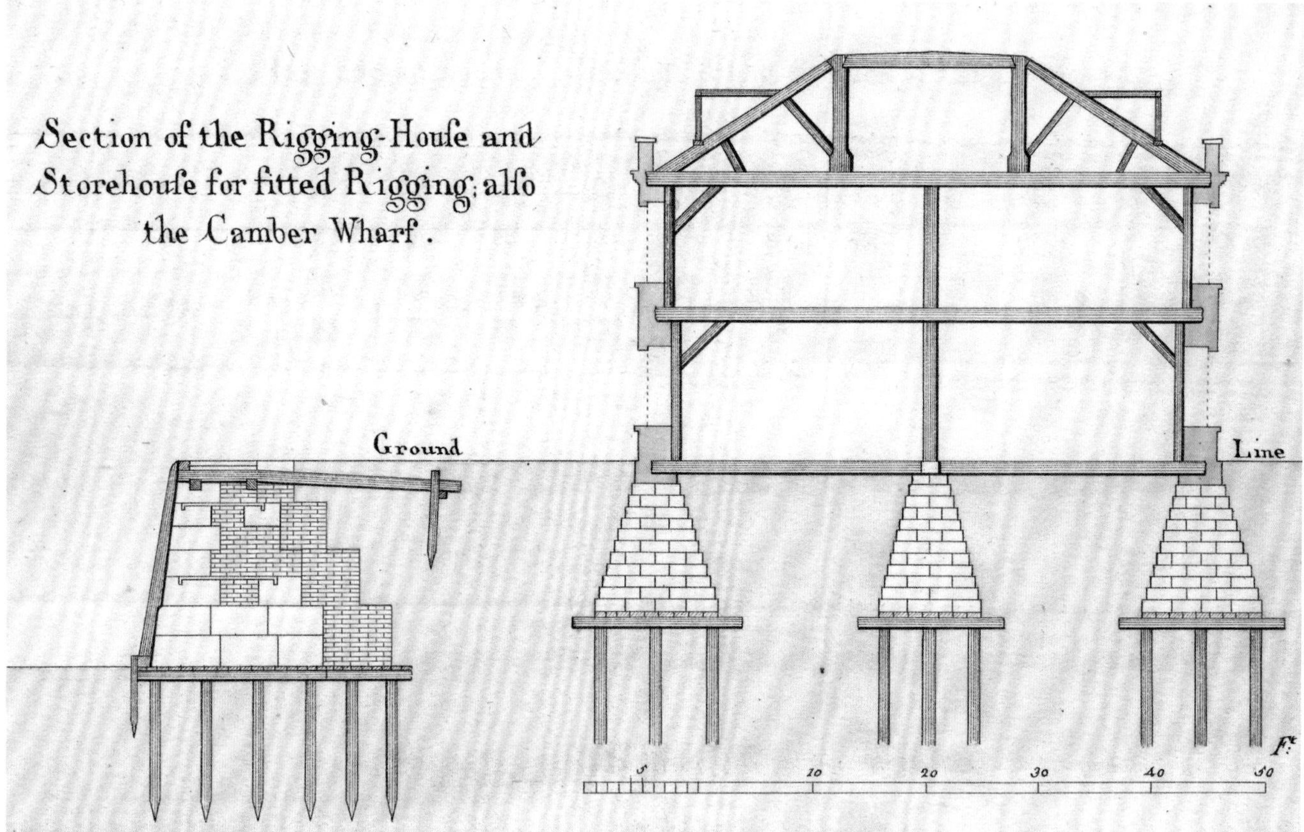

Fig 3.5
A 1786 cross-section of the Rigging House on Camber Wharf at Portsmouth, showing the extensive piling and foundations needed in this yard. (NMRN Plans of HM Dockyard, Portsmouth, c 1786, 1993/443)

centres, this was challenged as the century wore on, the navy expanded and industrialisation with its widening skills and innovations gathered pace from the 1760s elsewhere in the country.[20]

The Great Rebuilding of 1760–1785

While not changing the system, the unprecedented scale of the modernisation and expansion of Portsmouth and Plymouth that was begun in the mid-18th century did attempt to remedy a principal weakness. For the first time, master plans for both yards were drawn up at the start. In a letter to the Admiralty about the Plymouth programme, the Navy Board explained that 'we thought it much the most advisable to lay down one general plan to answer every purpose, to be prosecuted as opportunity shall offer, constant experience showing us the advantages that would have attended designs of the same kind had they been laid down for the rest of His Majesty's Yards'.[21] Given their scale, such programmes inevitably took many years to complete, a prospect that would have daunted earlier generations of officials when long-term financing was more difficult to obtain and sustain.

By the mid-18th century, the Royal Navy was in a far stronger position, a direct result of sustained government investment in expanding the fleet to counter war and the threat of war and to ensure protection for Britain's growing overseas trade and commerce. The need for dockyard modernisation was further driven by shipbuilding reforms introduced by the Surveyor, Sir Thomas Slade, later famous as the designer of *Victory* (Fig 3.6). Slade's new 74s were significantly larger than their 70-gun predecessors, as were his 90s compared to their immediate precursors. They were also appreciably stronger, and after HMS *Bellona*'s capture of the French *Courageux* in August 1761, 'it would be taken for granted that a British ship could beat a French one of up to fifty per cent greater gun power'.[22] These larger vessels and their successors needed slips, docks and other facilities to match; it was fortunate that Slade had some practical experience of dockyard works gained in the 1740s when surveying the harbour at Sandwich and helping to draw up plans to improve Sheerness yard.[23] He was also in post at a time when Anson's years at the Admiralty had reformed, reinvigorated and immeasurably strengthened the Royal Navy.

Fig 3.6
HMS Victory, *laid down at Chatham in 1759, vividly demonstrates the multiplicity of skills and resources required to build, fit out and maintain these great sailing warships. Her construction coincided with the start of the sustained expansion and modernisation of the Royal Navy's principal home dockyards. HMS* Victory *remains in commission as flagship of the First Sea Lord at Portsmouth.*
(Country Life *Will Pryce 023464)*

Anson had worked closely with the Earl of Sandwich, who developed a keen and informed interest in the royal dockyards, which had hitherto been the preserve of the Navy Board. Sandwich's actions were to ensure that both boards were to gain a far better understanding of them.[24] When Lord Egmont succeeded Sandwich between 1763 and 1766, he continued with his active approach to the dockyards, appreciating the need to modernise Portsmouth and Plymouth and securing funds at a crucial period in the infancy of these works.[25]

The master plans for the south coast yards were drawn up in conjunction with the yard officers, who were sent general instructions by the Surveyor. In practice, room for manoeuvre was fairly circumscribed. Topography and available space largely dictated the location of existing and proposed dry docks and slips, and it was logical to group with these the workshops and stores needed by the shipwrights and other trades. The greatest scope for improved planning lay in relocating the immensely long buildings of the ropeyards on new ground at these two yards. At both Portsmouth and Plymouth, the master plans had these sited immediately adjacent and parallel to new boundaries, away from the centres where they were serious obstacles to yard traffic. Inevitably, given that land reclamation and construction work took the best part of 40 years, there were modifications and refinements to the original proposals.[26] At Plymouth these were comparatively minor, but serious fires at Portsmouth forced the rebuilding of the ropeyard on its existing site rather than on the northern boundary of the reclaimed ground (*see* Chapter 6), while debates about the location of new dry docks around the great basin were only finally settled by Bentham's intervention in 1795.

It would have been taxing for most members of the Navy Board to keep abreast of all this rebuilding and expansion, as well as the normal Board correspondence and works of maintenance and renewal in the other home yards. They could read letters from the yard officers, hear reports from the surveyors and see the various plans in the Navy Board office, but their only other significant source of information was what they learnt on the so-called annual tours of inspection (which tended to be at irregular intervals). In their 1771 visit to Plymouth they noted with enthusiasm 'a very ingenious model of the whole yard carved in wood by the foreman of the yard' (Fig 3.7), and it seems this was the inspiration for the Board to order models of all the dockyards as a way of making them familiar with their size and complexities.[27] In January 1772 the Board ordered the Chatham and Portsmouth officers to find 'proper persons' to make models of their yards to the same scale of 1:40 as the Plymouth model.

At Chatham, the model makers were housed in the extant middle tower that was once used as a powder magazine on the dockyard boundary wall. By August 1773, the Navy Board was telling the Chatham and Portsmouth officers that their models were 'very much wanted', and the following March they were again urging completion and ordered the models be sent to the Navy Board offices. By 1774 models of all the home dockyards (*see* Fig 3.8) were displayed there, the Board also having required each yard to place these in 'a neat mahogany case, the top to be of glass, to open in the middle and turn back on the hinges, distinguishing the several buildings and works, whether of stone, brick or wood, by proper colours'. The cases were to be identical to the mahogany case containing the Deptford model, clearly already completed. The Plymouth model (Fig 3.7) remains the most elaborate, with sections that can be swapped to show different proposals.[28]

The design of individual buildings in these major redevelopments remained largely the responsibility of the dockyard officers, with detailed guidance from the then Surveyor, Thomas Slade, or possibly William Bately, his deputy and co-surveyor until 1765. For Plymouth, Slade instructed that the double quadrangle of the principal storehouses 'as a guard against fire are not to join at the angles; whose fronts are to be uniform, to be three stories in height, with arched cellars under them, built of stone and rubble work, plain

Fig 3.7
Part of the 1770s model of Plymouth Dockyard, showing the complexity of a major Georgian dockyard, in the process of expansion and redevelopment. The long brick building (centre left) is the original ropery. At the back, on the right, are the long stone buildings of the new ropeyard that replaced it. The smithery (which survives, though substantially altered) is on the left (centre). (Author)

Fig 3.8
Part of the model of Chatham Dockyard in 1774. Among the surviving buildings are the Clocktower Storehouse (centre) and the officers' terrace behind. The two dry docks still have the cumbersome and inefficient triple-leaf gates. (Author)

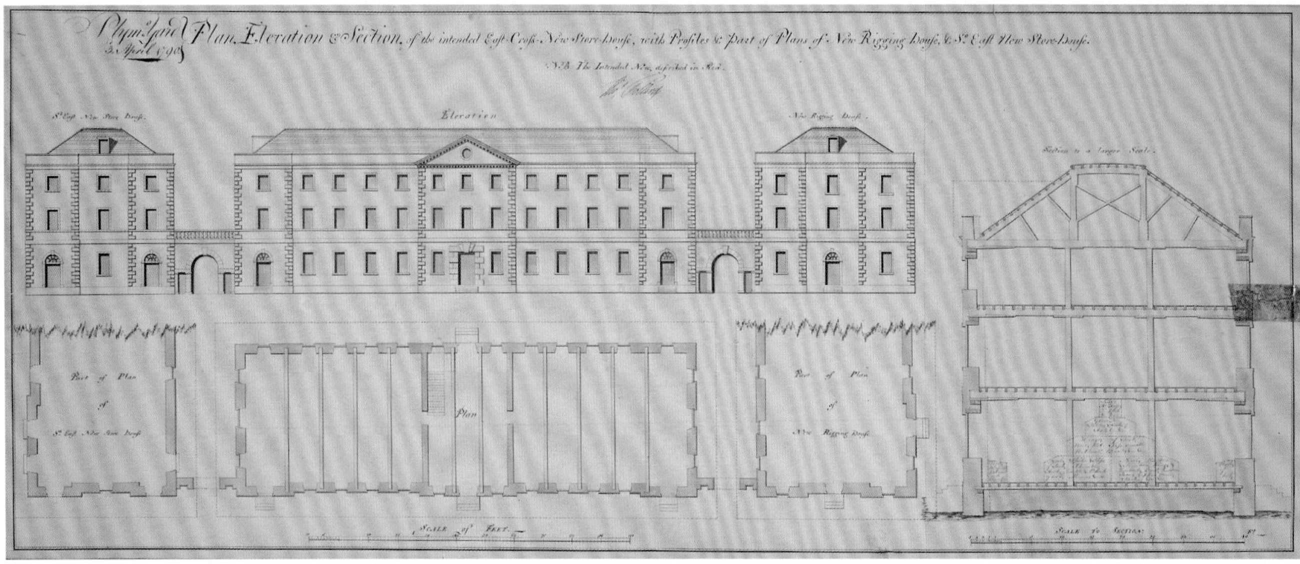

Fig 3.9
Drawing of the double quadrangle of storehouses proposed for Plymouth Dockyard in 1761. These were destroyed by wartime bombing. (TNA ADM 140/270)

strong and convenient, of which you are to send us a design, with plans etc of the floors'.[29] From this guidance, the officers drew up the detailed designs and estimates for approval in London (Fig 3.9). These handsome buildings were burnt out in the blitz and subsequently demolished. It is unclear if Slade and Bately divided the work of writing instructions to the yards between them. Little is known about Bately and whether he had much experience of building and yard planning.

At Portsmouth the handsome range of three storehouses (*see* Figs 3.10 and 3.11) flanking the approach to HMS *Victory* and the *Mary Rose*, and now in part the home of the National Museum of the Royal Navy, has an unusually

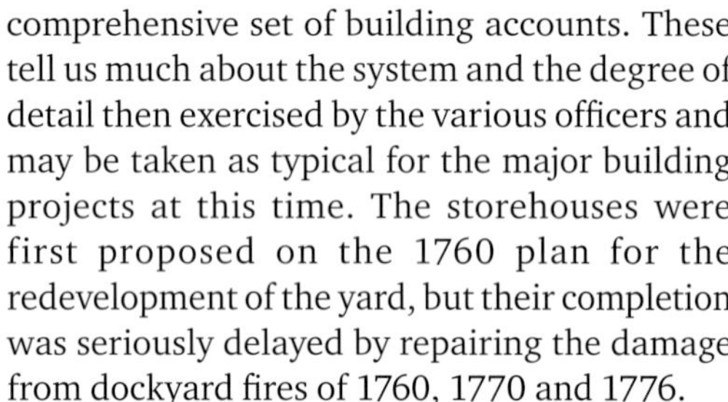

comprehensive set of building accounts. These tell us much about the system and the degree of detail then exercised by the various officers and may be taken as typical for the major building projects at this time. The storehouses were first proposed on the 1760 plan for the redevelopment of the yard, but their completion was seriously delayed by repairing the damage from dockyard fires of 1760, 1770 and 1776.

In October 1763 the Navy Board asked the Portsmouth officers for a design and to put money into the following year's estimates for the Present Use Store at the northern end of the range. The Board agreed the estimate of £7,598 the following month, and a warrant was issued on 23 November. A surviving drawing of the proposed building – noted on its reverse as 'a copy of this sent to Portsmouth for building a storehouse ordered by ye board on 24 November 1763' – was presumably the one drawn up by the yard officers following the Board's October request.[30] The Board was content to let the yard officers decide whether to go out to contract or to employ dockyard labour in its construction, but by the following March a contract had been awarded to 'James Templer of Rotherhithe ... and George Collard of Crutched Fryers, London, House Carpenters', who were then building the east and west storehouses at Plymouth. The contract sets out in great detail very precise specifications for the various dimensions of the building, including the diminishing thickness of the exterior walls: 'the foundation to the exterior sides and ends ... to be five bricks thick, and from thence to the first floor four and a half bricks thick', finally

Fig 3.10
The three great storehouses built at Portsmouth between 1764 and 1785. A view from the south. (Author)

reducing to three and a half bricks 'from the attic floor to the upper side of the plate of the roof'.[31] All the timberwork was described in similar detail, with precise dimensions given. Sash windows were carefully specified, their jambs boxed for double weights. An appreciation of the potential for rot is apparent in the instruction that the 13in by 15in main girders or floor beams should have arches over their ends within the walls 'for a free circulation of air'.

As was normal with such building contracts, the dockyard would supply all the carpenters' material, either from new stock in the yard or where possible from buildings or warships being dismantled. All other materials were to be found and provided by the contractor, 'all the walls of the said storehouse to be sound hard brick', mortar was 'to be well tempered, beat and wrought, and made with fresh water and the best lime' with 50 bushels of lime to 2 loads of sand. The roof was to be covered with 'the best and largest slates taken from Delibole or other quarries in Cornwall', and stonework for steps, plinths and architectural details was to be Portland or 'moorstone'.[32]

In further correspondence as work was starting, the contractors asked if they could obtain lime from the dockyard lime kiln, not so much for reasons of convenience, but principally because this was producing the more durable 'stone lime' rather than lime from chalk. They also successfully obtained the services of 'Daniel Lye a bricklayer and George Braine a house carpenter', both employed in Portsmouth Dockyard, to act as foremen on the new storehouse. The last arrangement must also have suited the dockyard officers and Surveyor, as it put two of their own employees in key positions to ensure good workmanship.[33] It seems to have been quite a common practice – at Pembroke in 1826 'John Mills, first leading hand of the masons' was loaned to McIntosh the contractor, then building a storehouse in that yard. Mills had come from Plymouth where he had helped build the new chapel and rebuild the burnt spinning house.[34]

Fig 3.11
The original drawing of 1776 for the Middle Storehouse at Portsmouth, signed by Edward Hunt, the yard's master shipwright. (TNA ADM 140/522 pt 2)

In the light of their Plymouth experience, James Templer also queried the specification to use moorstone granite, 'having further observed since my contract for the new storehouses at Plymouth that where Moore Stone is introduced for ornament with marble (Portland or Purbeck stone) that it lessens rather than heightens the lustre of such buildings by reason that Moor Stone is formed of rough open dark pointed particles, which catches and retains every tinge of dirty matter that flies'. Templer's careful observations and evident desire to construct a building that would reflect well on his firm, as well as being an ornament to the dockyard, appear to have been noted, because stone detailing is almost wholly in Portland stone. The contract specified that the Present Use Storehouse should be 'wholly completed by or before Midsummer 1765'. It would seem likely this target was missed by about nine months, as in January 1766 the contractor was finishing laying the floors and busy lining the internal walls with 'planed, grooved and tongued deal'.[35]

Ten years were to pass before work on the second of the three storehouses at Portsmouth (the Middle Storehouse, more recently 10 Store) was to start, following completion of a further stretch of wharf wall along the eastern side of the adjacent Camber wharf. Again, detailed records give a similar picture of considerable care in the planning and execution of the work, following a Navy Board directive to the yard officers in May 1776 to produce a drawing of the proposed building. This time, the Surveyor asked that the building should include 'a proper archway for the convenience of taking in cordage from the ropehouse', whose west end was across the road directly opposite the proposed storehouse. Comparatively rarely for one produced in a dockyard, this subsequent drawing, dated 19 June 1776, has the signature of Edward Hunt (Fig 3.11). He was then the yard's master shipwright, previously a master boat builder, but soon was to bring these architectural skills to London as one of the joint surveyors. With its clocktower, cupola and well-proportioned central archway, Hunt's Middle Store forms a fitting centrepiece to this fine range of buildings.[36]

Initially, the Navy Board had proposed to employ yard workmen supplemented by 6 additional bricklayers and 12 bricklayers' labourers. In the event, the dockyard labour force was instructed to build the foundations and 'raise the groins [vaults] to receive the first [ground] floor'. A contract for the rest of the building was awarded to what had, after 10 years of huge Navy Board contracts including the adjacent Camber wharf, become 'James Templer of Acton ... Thomas Parlby of Plymouth Dock ... and William Templer of Gosport ... Builders'. The Middle Storehouse was completed and bills submitted in November 1779, by which time the firm was simply referred to in Navy Board correspondence as Templar and Parlby, though the spelling Templer is more common in the records. By the early 1780s Templer and Parlby appear to have grown to a size where they could handle all the contracts.[37] The final South Storehouse was not started until 1782 and was completed some 3 years later in 1785.[38] Construction seems to have been done entirely by contract.

It is clear from these accounts that much responsibility remained with the yard officers, but the Surveyors were playing more active roles and remained key figures, agreeing or modifying building proposals. This trend to a greater involvement in details of the largest projects is also apparent in a letter to the Chatham officers in 1787, which warns them to expect that working drawings for the new double ropehouse 'will be sent to you by the Brompton Coach in a day or two', suggesting that the Surveyors were not content in every case to leave final details to the yard officers.[39] Of particular interest is the Navy Board's pragmatic approach to the actual construction of the three Portsmouth storehouses. The yard bricklayers and carpenters, who generally concentrated on maintenance and repair tasks and minor building works, would have been stretched to undertake works on this scale, yet in 1763 the Board left this option open, while in 1776 it positively encouraged the building of Middle Storehouse with yard and extra labour.

The Navy Board's favouring of direct labour is probably best explained either from a feeling that the contractors were already at capacity, or by a desire to provide an element of competition and cost-comparison. The works at Plymouth and Portsmouth at this time were almost exclusively in the hands of contractors, in practice Templer and Parlby who enjoyed a near monopoly of works in both yards in the last 40 years of the 18th century.[40] In 1777, in an attempt to ensure that building contracts were well executed and valuations accurate, the Navy Board appointed John Marquand as a building surveyor, but his post was abolished in 1786. He was retained on a temporary basis until 1787, and in 1798 Bentham was to express a strong preference for yard labour at Plymouth to be government employees, not contractors .[41]

The impact of the Industrial Revolution: unease and change 1780–1795

In general, these arrangements produced handsome, well-constructed dockyard buildings, as the surviving storehouses and workshops demonstrate. However, there was still much leeway in a system that allowed yard officers scope for significant variations in the size and design of major buildings. Some are readily explicable: the two huge monolithic storehouses on Anchor Wharf at Chatham, the longest ever built by the navy, stemmed from the need to cram the maximum storage space into a narrow restricted site (Fig 3.12). Less explicable, except possibly in terms of yard pride, are the different lengths of the roperies built as part of this modernisation. The most ambitious ropery was that built at Plymouth between 1766 and 1773, its twin spinning and laying houses each some 1,200ft long (*see* Chapter 6). In August 1770, following the serious fire at Portsmouth, Sir Thomas Slade and Timothy Brett recommended rebuilding the ropeyard on its existing site.[42] For reasons of space, the separate spinning and laying houses were amalgamated into one building, with the spinners on the upper floors. This double ropehouse was 1,030ft in length and formed the model for the one built at Chatham between 1787 and 1792. At Chatham, however, the double ropehouse was constructed to a length of 1,040ft.

No naval cordage-manufacturing requirement accounts for these different sizes of building, although a few private ones exceeded these lengths.[43] In 1774 the Earl of Sandwich had noted after the official inspection of Plymouth that

Fig 3.12
The Anchor Wharf storehouses at Chatham. These were the largest linear storehouses built in a royal dockyard, their size designed to maximise the space in a long narrow site. This 1968 photograph shows the buildings still in use. (Author)

one of the new Ropehouses ... is now out of use, and will probably not be constantly wanted even in time of war, as the work that can be done in one of the houses is more than sufficient at present for the service of the yard; were the two house employed, they could work seventeen [spinning] wheels, whereas at Portsmouth where there are double the ships in ordinary, and a much greater resort of ships in commission, only nine [spinning] wheels are now used which effectively answer every purpose.[44]

Even as this report was being written, the new ropehouse at Portsmouth was being completed and its capacity increased to 12 spinning wheels.

Given the immense size and cost of these buildings, it is surprising that there were apparently no attempts to estimate the overall cordage needs of the fleet as a basis for a central decision on the size and number of ropeyards required. There could also be extensive procrastination when it came to agreeing new works. At Portsmouth, some 10 years were spent from 1785 arguing the merits of retaining a double dock in the yard. These had their champions, but unless there was very strict planning in their use, a warship at the inner end could remain trapped, awaiting the completion of works on the second ship occupying the outer half of the dock. Little progress could be made while the arguments ebbed and flowed between the yard officers, the Navy Board and an external committee that had been called in to adjudicate; it was only Bentham's arrival that cut this particular knot.[45]

Fig 3.13
A 1972 photograph of part of the surviving Hartley fireproofing system using iron sheets. These were installed in three Portsmouth storehouses, now partly occupied by the National Museum of the Royal Navy.
(Author)

In the overall context of a dockyard expansion and modernisation programme that was giving Britain the best-equipped and most modern dockyards in Europe at a crucial time in her history, these were perhaps comparatively minor points. They were, however, symptomatic of an organisational conservatism that in an earlier age might have gone unremarked. But the modernisation of the yards almost exactly coincided with the onset of the technological revolution that was to transform Britain into the modern world's first industrial nation. Much of the early progress centred on iron and textile production and had little apparent relevance to dockyards, where wooden warship building and maintenance demanded a high degree of craft skills. The early development of steam power also had little to offer to the yards. Until the invention of the rotary motion for steam engines in the early 1780s, steam power was largely limited to pumping water out of mines. In these, its continuous operation justified installation and running costs, whereas intermittent use emptying a dry dock in a royal dockyard did not. Here, the use of horse gins for pumps allowed deployment of the horsepower to other tasks when not required on the gins. Even with a rotary motion, a steam engine had limited economic use unless it could provide continuous power for machinery designed for simple repetitive tasks. Such tasks were not immediately apparent outside the textile and other mills.

Nevertheless, as the transformation of the industrial landscape of Britain gathered pace, there was concern that, largely through ignorance, the Government's own industrial enterprises were not reaping any benefits from the new technology. Such criticism was not always well informed, as there are examples of Navy Board officials being fully aware of developments outside the walls of the royal yards. In 1773 the MP David Hartley[46] patented his system of fire protection using thin, rolled, wrought-iron sheets attached to the undersides of floorboards and joists. In the lack of anything better, the plates were widely used over the next quarter of a century, notably by Henry Holland when rebuilding the Theatre Royal in Drury Lane between 1791 and 1794, where the sheets were also used to construct a safety curtain.[47] The Navy Board was quick to adopt the system, using it when rebuilding the fire-gutted ropery at Portsmouth in 1777, as well as incorporating the plates in the new storehouses nearby. These plates can still be seen in the storehouses (Fig 3.13).[48]

Naval demand could also stimulate the commercial application of inventions that had a major impact on the Industrial Revolution, perhaps most notably as a result of Portsmouth Dockyard's need for high-quality iron chains for moorings. These and other iron stores had long been supplied by the small ironworks at Funtley, a few miles north-west of the head of Portsmouth Harbour on the River Meon. Unable to meet growing demand for its products in the late 1770s, the new owner, Henry Cort, introduced two new methods of manufacture. He replaced the tilt hammers used to fashion the bar iron with grooved iron rollers to shape the bars, and he introduced the puddling process for refining cast iron into wrought iron. The gains in quality and productivity were immediate, for the first time allowing the large-scale production of wrought iron and transforming the British iron industry.[49] There is an argument that the dockyards as a whole needed to be more aware of developments in the outside world, but almost the greater need was for there to be a management system in place that could exploit these developments in an efficient way for the benefit of the navy and the State.

The greatest impact on the royal dockyards from the first phase of the Industrial Revolution came directly from the massive canal building programme following the successful completion in 1761 of the Bridgewater canal between Worsley and Manchester. Over the next 30 years some 850 miles of canals were completed, the resultant opening up of trade leading to improvement in roads, bridges and harbours and the development of major commercial docks, notably at London, Liverpool and Hull.[50] This massive investment in new infrastructure spurred the growth of the profession of the civil as distinct from the military engineer. Until the mid-17th century, the term 'engineer' applied exclusively to military engineering. Increasingly used in relation to civil projects, it was not until 1763 that the term 'civil engineer' first appears in a London directory. The year 1771 saw the founding of the Society of Civil Engineers, an association with many members whose interests and skills also encompassed mechanical engineering and architecture.[51] A significant number of those later involved with Admiralty projects learnt their skills constructing the early canals. Thomas Telford (Fig 3.14), Clerk of Works for Samuel Wyatt's Commissioner's House at Portsmouth, went on to supervise construction of the Ellesmere Canal, including the astonishing Pontcysyllte aqueduct with its channel of cast iron. He later employed James Meadows Rendel, first as a road surveyor and then as a draughtsman in his London office. Rendel was later to design the great breakwater for Portland Harbour.[52]

Fig 3.14
Thomas Telford (1757–1834) as a young man, probably painted soon after he left Portsmouth Dockyard.
(Courtesy of Shropshire Museums, SHYMS: FA/1991/109)

Fig 3.15
John Rennie (1761–1821); a pencil sketch of 1818 by Francis Leggatt Chantrey. (© National Portrait Gallery, London, 316a[183])

John Rennie senior (Fig 3.15), perhaps best known for his work on London docks, earlier worked with Boulton and Watt before developing his engineering business and undertaking a stream of river improvements, fen drainage schemes and canals, beginning with the Kennet and Avon. Later he was to work closely and harmoniously with Joseph Whidbey, a noted surveyor who had worked with George Vancouver (1757–98) in his great surveying voyages along the north-west coast of North America from 1792 to 1794. Whidbey was later appointed master attendant at Woolwich before collaborating with both Rennies on the massive breakwater at Plymouth (*see* Chapter 5).

William Jessop was apprenticed to John Smeaton, gaining valuable experience of civil engineering projects. His own father, Josias Jessop, was a dockyard officer at Plymouth and had helped Smeaton reconstruct the Eddystone lighthouse. Smeaton himself embraced both civil and mechanical engineering, becoming consulting engineer to the Carron Ironworks at Falkirk, where one of his major contributions was the development of cast-iron parts for machinery. By the 1790s William Jessop's experience of constructing canals and improving harbours and ports led many to see him as 'the first engineer of the kingdom'. Four of his sons also became engineers, notably Josias who was sent by the Admiralty to Bermuda in 1819 to check on the progress of the new dockyard and to recommend improvements (*see* Chapter 12).[53]

In some ways the least known but among the most remarkable was Hugh McIntosh (1768–1840),[54] whose engineering knowledge was considerable but who made his name as a contractor. McIntosh started as a navvy on the Forth and Clyde canal and gradually built up one of the largest civil engineering companies in the country, moving seamlessly from canal construction to docks, harbours, Buckingham Palace and ultimately railway building. He undertook work at Portsmouth and Plymouth following the demise of Templer and Parlby, notably constructing the Royal William Victualling Yard, and was responsible for nearly all the building and engineering work at the new yard at Pembroke.[55] Although some of his men would have been local, the majority were probably navvies – a term then including skilled men as well as those who just excavated canals and docks – from other McIntosh contracts. His successful tender in 1823 for completing the Gloucester and Berkeley canal at a cost of £111,493 15s 11d is an indication of the scale of his operations by then.[56]

Even at the end of the 18th century this embryonic civil engineering world was still a comparatively small one, where most of the main practitioners knew each other. They also knew the important ironmasters and their products, such as John Wilkinson at the Bersham and Bradley ironworks, the Darby dynasty at Coalbrookdale and the owners of the new and expanding ironworks at Blaenavon in south Wales. There were also close links with the principal engine builders Boulton and Watt, with their famous Soho works, and Fenton, Murray and Co at their Round Foundry works at Holbeck near Leeds. To these were added the machine makers, perhaps the most famous being Henry Maudslay (Fig 3.16) and the equally skilled if less well-known Matthew Murray, who was a friend of Bentham's mechanist, Simon Goodrich. Both Maudslay and Murray were to supply the first machine tools to Portsmouth Dockyard in the early 19th century – Maudslay all the block-making machinery, Murray a horizontal boring mill.[57] Most of these manufacturing concerns were still comparatively small. A notable exception was the Blaenavon Ironworks that by 1798, some ten years after its establishment, employed around 350 people.

Fig 3.16
Henry Maudslay (1771–1831), the machine tool maker responsible for constructing Brunel's block-making machinery. Maudslay's 1811 ropemaking machinery is still in use in Chatham ropery. (© National Portrait Gallery, London, D1378)

In 1802 the Soho foundry employed 54 men and boys, while the Carron Works in 1814 was considered remarkable in having a workforce of some 200 compared to the average Scottish foundry with its 20 workers, a figure only slightly smaller than among English counterparts. [58]

The growing numbers of civil and mechanical engineers had the potential to provide invaluable new resources for the Admiralty and Navy Boards, supplementing the assistance they already received on occasions from the Royal Engineers. Such expertise was also a source of enlightenment for Parliament, with engineers well used to giving evidence before committees, and it added to a sense of concern both there and outside Westminster at the cost and effectiveness of the royal dockyards and whether or not they were keeping up with this new technology. In 1791 the Society for the Improvement of Naval Architecture was formed, adding its voice to the general criticisms. The public tended to have very different perceptions of the Royal Navy and the royal dockyards, although the two were totally interdependent, generally giving the navy wide approbation and regarding the dockyards, not always fairly, as inefficient, expensive, probably corrupt and for ever in need of reform. These widely held views of the royal yards were to be succinctly summed up a little later by the President of the Royal Society, Sir Joseph Banks, in an appeal to a reluctant James Watt in 1812 to join the delegation being asked to comment on the proposed works at Sheerness and, as he wrote, to 'help subdue the dragon of the Dock Yards'.[59]

Such was the general background of unease that led Parliament in 1785 to set up the Commission on Fees to look into abuses in the dockyards and other government departments. Although primarily concerned with financial matters, its fifth report examined the organisation of building operations in the yards and made a number of important recommendations.[60] It expressed considerable concern that building contracts were 'entirely under the superintendence, management and direction of the shipwright officers', without any outside financial checks. Concluding, the Commission wrote, 'We allow the shipwright officers every merit for their ability in their professional line, but we conceive that to be Naval not Civil architecture; and we must express our surprise that it has never yet been thought necessary to appoint a Surveyor of Civil Architecture to the Navy Office, where such extensive works are continually carrying on.' In the Commission's view 'a regular Surveyor of Civil Architecture is absolutely necessary'.[61]

The Victualling Board, with a very much smaller estate to manage, but one lacking the resource skills of the royal dockyards, had reached a broadly similar conclusion in the 1730s, appointing an Inspector of Repairs who also undertook limited work for the Navy Board. Benjamin Glanville held the post from 1731 to 1774 and was then succeeeded by James Arrow, who was followed by the architect Samuel Pepys Cockerell in 1785 (Fig 3.17). The office was abolished in 1800.[62] Given the huge scale of the principal dockyards, the wide geographical spread of naval bases with their extensive civil engineering and architectural works, the Commission's recommendations for a post of Surveyor of Civil Architecture was in many ways the minimum possible response.

Fig 3.17
The architect Samuel Pepys Cockerell (1754–1827) in c 1793 when he was employed by the Victualling Board as their surveyor.
(© National Portrait Gallery, London, D12191)

4

Planning and Building the Royal Dockyards, 1795–1914

Samuel Bentham and the royal dockyards' Industrial Revolution, 1795–1832

The fifth report of the Commission on Fees was not published until 1806, but by then many of its recommendations had been implemented, spurred on from a different quarter. The key figure and catalyst responsible for inaugurating the navy's own Industrial Revolution, establishing an embryonic but lasting organisation that included architects, mechanical engineers and scientists and meshing these into the new industrial world outside the royal yards, was Samuel Bentham (Fig 4.1).

As a boy, Samuel was keenly interested in mechanical contrivances and shipbuilding, and at the age of 14 had been apprenticed to the master shipwright at Woolwich, moving to Chatham and then completing his 7-year apprenticeship at the Naval Academy at Portsmouth. After gaining sea experience in Lord Keppel's fleet, he travelled to northern Europe to study naval architecture. Between 1780 and 1791 he stayed in Russia, gaining a knighthood and rising to the rank of Brigadier General in the Empress Catherine II's service. He travelled to the Chinese frontier and later commanded a Russian flotilla against the Turks. For much of the time he was based at Krichev in the centre of Prince Potemkin's estates, where he helped establish manufacturing industries, including sailcloth and ropemaking as part of a drive to modernise the Russian navy. During this time, he invented a number of woodworking machines that he patented in Britain, but his 1786 proposal to maintain better discipline and industry by constructing a series of workshops radiating out from a central supervisory hub was never realised, because Prince Potemkin sold his Krichev estate the following year.[1]

Back in England from 1791, Samuel helped his brother Jeremy develop this Panopticon design as the basis for a model prison (*see* Chapter 1) and continued to invent and patent woodworking machines.[2] These were installed in a workshop at Jeremy's house in Westminster and led Samuel to be described later as 'the father' of woodworking machinery. The fame of the workshop attracted many notable visitors, including Henry Dundas, Secretary of State for War, who praised the machinery in speeches in

Fig 4.1
Samuel Bentham (1757–1831), depicted in a miniature by Henry Edridge. (© National Portrait Gallery, London, 3069)

Parliament.[3] Earl Spencer, who was appointed First Lord of the Admiralty in 1794, was equally impressed, visiting the workshop accompanied by his fellow commissioners. In 1795, then aged 37, Bentham approached the Admiralty and offered to assist in modernising and mechanising the dockyards.[4] He chose his timing well. Sir Charles Middleton, later Lord Barham, had recently joined the Board of Admiralty and, like Earl Spencer, was keen on reform. Bentham also had support from his half-brother Charles Abbot, who entered Parliament that year, rising rapidly to become Speaker in 1802.

In Samuel Bentham's papers are a series of undated Admiralty drafts addressed to the king, outlining the need for a new department to modernise warship construction and improve dockyard efficiency. Bentham clearly influenced these drafts, which are among the earliest attempts to apply scientific principles to the work of the royal yards. The proposals were accepted with the clear intent that Bentham should head this new department. Although his office was not formally established until the Admiralty Order in Council of 23 March 1796, he had begun work the previous year, as outlined by the Admiralty to the Navy Board in April 1795, in which the former expressed concern that

> how little advantage appears to have hitherto been taken of a variety of improvements, particularly in the application of mechanical powers that modern discoveries have brought to light, and having taken a view of a system of machinery combined and carried into practice by Brigadier General Bentham, which appears to be capable of being adapted with peculiar advantage to various works carried on in the said dockyards, we are induced to … procure to His Majesty's service the benefits of Brigadier General Bentham's ingenuity and experience … in the different branches of the Naval Art … we have authorised the said Brigadier General Bentham to visit the several dockyards … for that purpose, and have desired him to report to us such observations as may occur to him, and suggest such improvements in the said branches as they may appear to be susceptible of; We do therefore desire and direct you to give the necessary directions to your several officers for permitting … Bentham to have free access to the said dockyards at all reasonable times.[5]

This letter, with its overt criticism of the Navy Board's stewardship of the dockyards, was not one calculated to win friends in the yards or make Bentham's task any easier. From the Navy Board's viewpoint, worse was speedily to follow.

Bentham's first visit took him to Portsmouth to assess the vexed problem of the proposed new dry docks. Within weeks he had produced a plan radically altering their layout and design and had it approved by the Admiralty. In early June 1795 the Admiralty sent the plan to the Navy Board, ordering all potentially abortive work at Portsmouth to cease and somewhat abruptly telling the Board that 'the nature [of the plan] the General will explain to you at any time you may appoint'.[6] Not surprisingly, Bentham's subsequent formal establishment as Inspector General of Naval Works responsible to the Admiralty was to lead to much friction, ultimately contributing to the abolition of his post in 1812.[7]

To have any hope of fulfilling his brief, Bentham needed not only to work with talented officers such as Joseph Whidbey and Robert Seppings, but also to establish a small team of specialist staff to help him and who would introduce skills largely new to the dockyards. They would report directly to Bentham, which would increase his central control of projects. His team included the first salaried Civil Architect, who was also expected to have some knowledge of what would later be defined as structural engineering,[8] as well as the first mechanical engineer, then called a mechanist. To these Bentham added a post of chemist, a modest title which said little about the intended scope of the job. Bentham's own interests and experience crossed all these boundaries and early on also included the construction of experimental vessels at Hobbs and Hellyer's shipyard at Redbridge near Southampton.[9]

The first Civil Architect, appointed in 1796, was Samuel Bunce, a former pupil of the architect James Wyatt and friend of the sculptor John Flaxman who he first met in Italy. Perhaps surprisingly, Bunce was able to continue with private commissions after his appointment. The most notable, undertaken with Jeremy Bentham, was his design for the 'Panopticon House of Industry' or workhouse, based on Samuel's proposals at Krichev. This unrealised workhouse was, remarkably, designed almost entirely of iron and glass, lit by a continuous band of windows like a modern factory.[10] In his 6 years with the Inspector General, Bunce probably spent most of his time vetting building proposals drawn up by the dockyard officers. He was involved in constructing the vaults over the reservoir at Portsmouth and with the initial work on Bentham's wood mills above them, as well as rebuilding the Clocktower Storehouse at Chatham in 1802. In a letter to Bentham in 1801 he also refers to the Governor's House at Haslar Hospital, 'built under my direction'. This is the centre of a distinctive terrace range of nine houses constructed between 1796 and 1799, almost certainly Bunce's most ambitious architectural work in a naval base.[11] In October 1802, Samuel Bunce died at the early age of 37, to be succeeded soon after by Edward Holl.

In 1796 Bentham had appointed the chemist of the team. James Sadler (Fig 4.2) was then 43 years old and had enjoyed a varied career, most spectacularly by becoming the first English aeronaut in 1784 when he ascended from Oxford in a balloon of his design and making. For a time he worked in the university chemical laboratory, where a contemporary called him 'a clever, practical, and experimental manipulator in chemistry and as such ... patronised ... by the few scientific men then at the University'.[12] Another contact there, Thomas Beddoes, who had links with Coalbrookdale, encouraged Sadler to develop his self-contained direct-acting steam engine, a number of which were built in London and Coalbrookdale between 1792 and 1799. It was a Sadler engine of this design that became the first to be used in a royal dockyard when it started work at Portsmouth in March 1799.[13] In 1795 Sadler had become barrack master at Portsmouth before being recruited by Bentham the following year. In his role as chemist he had an impossibly wide brief. This included ordnance experiments, distillation of sea water and seasoning of timber, but principally he was charged with an examination of 'the causes of decay in all bodies and the means of preventing it [and] ... to devise means of securing ships from fire'.[14] The unhappy relationship he apparently had with Bentham before the latter dismissed him in 1809 may reflect the impossibility of Sadler producing solutions for more than a small proportion of these problems.

In many ways the most important member of the team was the mechanical engineer, for as the Admiralty had mentioned to the Navy Board when informing them of Bentham's arrival, they were interested 'particularly in the application of mechanical powers that modern discoveries have brought to light'. Bentham's first mechanist or mechanical engineer was the little-known Samuel Rehe, a shadowy figure, who had been apprenticed to the scientific instrument maker Jesse Ramsden and had supplied parts and material for Bentham's woodworking machinery before Bentham became Inspector General.[15] Rehe played a major part in erecting the Sadler engine along with its attendant salt-water pump in the Portsmouth wood mills, but died later in 1799. Three years earlier, Simon Goodrich had been recruited as his draughtsman, and on Rehe's death Bentham appointed Goodrich as his successor.

Fig 4.2
James Sadler in 1820, some years after he had left Bentham's team.
(© National Portrait Gallery, London, 4955)

At the age of 29, Goodrich found himself the sole mechanical engineer employed by the Admiralty. Although talented, clearly well educated and highly literate, his work as Rehe's draughtsman, probably mostly at Portsmouth, would not have given him many opportunities to see at first hand the burgeoning new industrial world. Bentham would have been aware of this, and almost immediately after Goodrich's promotion he armed him with letters of introduction and sent him on what was clearly an educational tour of the principal industrial centres in England. Goodrich's letters and sketches to Bentham describing his journey between 14 November and 14 December 1799 reflect an eager and inquisitive intellect at work. They give a vivid insight into a world well known to Bentham and one with which he knew his immediate staff would have to become equally familiar if the navy was to benefit from new industrial processes and inventions. No doubt he also wished the industrialists to be equally aware that changes were afoot in the royal dockyards.

By stage-coach, canal barge and on foot, Goodrich journeyed through midland England, staying in inns and private houses, the vicissitudes and hardships of the road never blunting his enthusiasm to see the new industrial Britain and to carefully record its salient points. At Derby, where he spent some days, he was taken by William Strutt round his cotton mill, and noted the Boulton and Watt engine at work and the ingenious stretching pulley with its weighted frame, which kept the endless rope drive to the machinery properly tensioned. His sketch of the pulley arrangement shows it to be almost identical to later ones that still perform this function on the laying floor of Chatham ropery. He was deeply impressed with the fireproof construction of the mill – 'The Building of Mr Strutt's Cotton Manufactory has not less merit than the machinery' – and carefully noted how the cast-iron and wrought-iron components were interconnected.

Here and in the other cotton mills he visited, Goodrich paid particular attention to the machinery. Near Derby he sketched a water-powered reciprocating saw frame containing six or eight saws used for cutting the local marble, noting that it 'might be advantageously applied in the stone masons yards about London'. Both Bentham and later Brunel were to develop such multiple saws for cutting timber in Portsmouth and Chatham; whether this sketch influenced Bentham is unknown. At Belper, George Strutt conducted Goodrich round another of his family's fireproof cotton mills, where he noted an ingenious hot-air heating system. Nearby he visited Mr Outram, who 'received me very politely and showed me everything in his foundry, which is newly constructed'. Goodrich was particularly interested in his boring mill. At Sheffield he was taken to 'Mr Huntsmans the cast steel maker where I examined the method of melting the steel in pots and casting it into ingots'. Nearby he went round Attercliff Colliery, examining the 'large atmospheric steam engines' used for pumping the mine.

From Sheffield Goodrich walked 22 miles to the Peak Forest canal to see the inclined plane, the heavy descending wagons drawing up the empty ones by an endless chain, and connecting the canal to limestone quarries above Chapel-en-le-Frith – 'I got into one of the empty wagons ... I never travelled so fast before up so steep a hill'. At the head of the canal he found a 'steam engine work'd without a beam by a crank under the cylinder exactly in the manner of Mr Sadler's', and after walking to Stockport, he caught a coach and arrived at Manchester 'much pleased with my day's journey'. His days here were spent looking at canals, especially their locks, and at a number of factories and workshops. Although he did not visit it, he also learnt that 'Mr Sharrat a Founder and Millwright of this place is building a cotton manufactory with the beams and joists of the floors of cast iron, supported by cast iron pillars, for the purpose of resisting fire'.

On Sunday 1 December Goodrich took a passenger boat along the Bridgewater canal and sketched a small stern-wheeler steam paddle tug, 'which from appearances and from what we learnt, did not answer its intended purpose'. Nothing daunted, he wrote a careful description of the craft and its apparent method of operation. The following Thursday he was at William Reynolds's ironworks at Ketley near Ironbridge, noting and sketching a horizontal drive shaft that transmitted power from a steam engine to work a pump some 200yd away.[16] Just over a year later this visit bore fruit at Portsmouth Dockyard, where the pump for a new freshwater well 274ft deep was connected by an identical system to the steam plant in the wood mills some 400ft distant.[17]

For Goodrich, an undoubted highlight of his travels was his visit to the famous Iron Bridge in the Severn Gorge, a mecca for sightseers since its completion some 20 years earlier. He stayed at the Tontine Inn at its foot and 'examined the Iron bridge as soon as it was daylight', before visiting the clutch of iron works centred on Coalbrookdale, famous for the Darby dynasty's earlier development of the use of coke rather than charcoal for iron smelting. He inspected 'Mr Brodie's Cannon Foundry' with its 'extensive apparatus for turning and boring cannon'. Alexander Brodie is perhaps better known for his ships' stoves, patented in 1764. Brodie's Calcutt's works then had no fewer than 11 steam-powered horizontal boring mills, which must have then been one of the largest such concentrations in the country. They had begun to supply the Board of Ordnance with four different types of guns in 1795, but did not survive for long after the end of the Napoleonic Wars.[18] Goodrich's attention was also attracted to the three inclined planes for tub-boats on the nearby Shropshire Canal, which linked it to a basin at river level at Coalport.[19] He made a careful note of their method of operation, illustrating it with two meticulous sketches. These planes had come into use in 1793, following the success of the pioneer installation constructed by William Reynolds in 1788 for the Ketley Canal.[20]

Bentham's letters of introduction to owners were almost invariably passports to the most significant industrial firms of the day, and it is clear that the Inspector General was already a widely respected figure. Near Wolverhampton, such a letter gained Goodrich a guided tour of John Wilkinson's Bradley Ironworks, where after seeing the furnaces he was shown 'a stupendous apparatus for converting ... pig iron into wrought iron without the use of hammers, the work ... is here effected by rollers. Part of this apparatus was upon a new plan and had only been set going a fortnight'. Perhaps aware that he was treading a fine line between that of interested visitor and industrial spy, he prefaced his next paragraph, 'As much as I could superficially learn of their process of making wrought iron is as follows', before launching into a detailed three-page report. He also noted the production of plate-iron boilers and canal boats.[21] On his way there he had observed 'many [canal] boats ... made entirely of plate iron, used for carrying coals or limestone'.

At Birmingham, a letter of introduction secured Goodrich the help of William Whitmore, the engineer and iron founder, who accommodated him and advised him what to see.[22] Not all his visits here involved heavy engineering, but included a 'whip manufactory where there was a very simple machine for platting the gut round the whip handles'. Of possibly more significance for the future, he saw Mr Bolton's button manufactory, where there were 'several pairs of rollers worked by a water wheel for rolling the ingots of copper into sheets of various thickness which were for making buttons'. A copper furnace and rolling mill would be established in Portsmouth in 1803 (*see* Chapter 5). Goodrich passed by Boulton and Watt's new foundry, noting that 'No strangers are admitted into this manufactory'. He added tartly, 'but it does not seem that their superiority to others renders this precaution necessary', recording that 'they still get some of their best castings from the [nearby] Eagle Foundry' – which Goodrich did see.[23] He did, however, call at the Boulton and Watt counting house and obtained estimates for 10hp, 12hp and 30hp steam engines, respectively £491, £525 and £1,050, for 'all the metal materials including one iron boiler, but excepting the ironwork for screwing the framing and cisterns together'.

For the final visits before returning to London, Whitmore's 12-year-old son acted as his guide. Together they looked round a Japanned Paper Manufactory, the Union Flour Mill and then Whitmore's own factory, which was powered by a waterwheel that drove turning and boring machines, as well as 'a machine for cutting large screws and several machines for grinding rollers cylindrical, besides some steel-polishing, button-making and thimble-making machinery'. Goodrich noted that 'Mr Whitmore is a very clever man, and seems to be the properest person to apply to, for any large quantity of wrought iron work'. By the evening of Saturday 14 December 1799, Goodrich was back in London, 'highly satisfied with my journey in the course of which I had nothing to complain of but the shortness of the days which prevented me from seeing so much as I otherwise should'.[24]

Goodrich's report has been quoted at length as it is a milestone, evidence of a conscious move to end the sometimes introverted stance of the royal dockyards and to reap benefits for the navy by integrating them with the products and skills of a burgeoning industrial Britain. His letters provide a vivid portrait of a commercial and still-agrarian country in a state of change and reinvention. Before Bentham's appointment, it is highly doubtful if the initiative for such a journey of learning and discovery would have been forthcoming from within the navy's organisation, while nobody else then in either the dockyards or the boards had the contacts and knowledge to suggest an itinerary or to provide the very necessary letters of introduction. Goodrich himself, like Bentham, was to maintain such links by copious letters and further visits. By the time of Bentham's dismissal in 1812, it had become unthinkable not to consult with the leading engineers of the day and, where appropriate, to harness products of industrial Britain.

Bentham must have been well pleased with his young protégé's reports of his travels, and he and the navy were to be well rewarded. In Goodrich, whose career with the navy was to span some 35 years,[25] Bentham 'had someone who was able to bridge the gap between scientific principles and mechanical practice'. His professional reputation was to be rapidly made in his collaboration with Bentham and slightly later with Marc Brunel in the establishment of the Portsmouth Wood Mills and Metal Mills. It was not just supervising the construction of the buildings and the installation of the machinery at these Portsmouth mills that were important, but also his skills in draughtsmanship in providing informative plans and drawings when Boulton and Watt needed additional information.[26] To Goodrich also fell the tasks of recruiting and training men to be engineers, boilermen, founders, millwrights and machine operators, none of which skills and trades existed in the dockyards before 1799. It is a mark of Bentham's respect for Goodrich's abilities – 'a person on whose intelligence and probity I can have full reliance' – that he asked for Goodrich to be appointed as his deputy during his absence in Russia between July 1805 and December 1807.[27] In 1820, 2 years after its founding, Goodrich was elected a member of the Institution of Civil Engineers.

Fig 4.3
Marc Brunel (1769–1849). To his left in the portrait of c 1812 is a mortising machine constructed as part of the Portsmouth block-making machinery. (© National Portrait Gallery, London, 978)

Bentham himself was something of an engineering polymath. He was equally at home with woodworking machinery and civil engineering, developing the inverted arch form of dock design which secured the rigidity of the gate piers of dry and wet docks by linking them with an inverted masonry arch under the dock floor (*see* Chapter 5). An important element of Bentham's skills lay in his ability to recognise the potential in other people's inventions and products, allied to a willingness to champion these even when they were possible rivals to machinery he was developing. Nowhere was this more important than in his support of Marc Brunel (Fig 4.3), when he was approached by him early in 1802 with his revolutionary scheme to manufacture ships' blocks using steam-powered machine tools (*see* Chapter 6). Success here catapulted the Royal Navy to the vanguard of the Industrial Revolution with the world's first mass-production line using machine tools.[28] The fame of the Block Mills, as the Wood Mills became known, established beyond all doubt the value to the navy of linking the royal yards with the mainstream of industrial and engineering practitioners and developments in the outside world.

The small department created by Bentham was to achieve further successes, notably with the metal mills at Portsmouth and with Marc Brunel's steam sawmill at Chatham (*see* Chapter 6).[29] However, opportunities were strictly limited for this sort of dramatic innovation. As Dummer had found a century earlier at Plymouth, while it was possible to design and construct on a virgin site a new dockyard laid out on rational lines to optimise production flow and supervision, it was far more difficult to introduce such radical changes in working practices or to introduce yard planning to existing yards.[30] For Bentham, appointed towards the end of a massive investment programme in the principal yards, opportunities for grand and innovative designs were even fewer, while the circumstances of his appointment, together with his own somewhat intransigent personality, did not make for harmony with the Navy Board and senior dockyard officers.

In truth, some of his schemes were neither practical, nor timely nor well received. In 1811, when the Rennie-Whidbey plans for the Plymouth Breakwater were already agreed (*see* Chapter 5), Bentham championed as an alternative plan a series of pyramidal triangular timber frames filled with rocks to form wave-calming obstructions in Plymouth Sound, despite the known failure of a similar scheme tried and abandoned at Cherbourg. This caused considerable friction between the Admiralty and Bentham, with Whidbey reporting to Rennie that 'they think him to be mad and he thinks them to be fools'.[31] In 1808, against Bentham's wishes, he and his small department had been transferred to the Navy Board, becoming the department of the Civil Architect and Engineer. In 1812 his office was abolished, and he was dismissed.[32] Had he managed to have his extraordinary Panopticon design successfully implemented at Sheerness, Bentham would be remembered as an engineering visionary on a par with William Jessop, David Hartley and the Rennies. Perhaps Bentham's greatest legacy to the Royal Navy was establishing lasting links between the dockyards and the wider world of an industrialising Britain and, as a matter of course, consulting and employing the leading engineers. Innovation was encouraged, notably with steam power, improvements in dock design and the processing of materials.

On the death of Samuel Bunce in 1802, Edward Holl had become Civil Architect under Bentham, remaining in service until his own early death at the age of 58 in 1823.[33] Holl's origins are obscure, but he apparently held the post of Inspector of Works at Deptford immediately prior to this new appointment.[34] After Bentham's departure in 1812, Holl continued in post and remained very busy. At Pembroke and Sheerness he worked closely with Sir Thomas Thompson, the Controller of the Navy, and with both Rennies drawing up plans for the yards and being responsible for designing the buildings. After a reorganisation in the Navy Board in 1796, the Controller now had 'a general superintending and directing power, for the regular management of the business, and controlling the expense in every branch of the Office'. Thompson held this post for 10 years from June 1806.[35] Holl was also responsible for much of the works at Haulbowline during this period, making a number of visits. From time to time assistants were provided to help with such a geographically diverse workload. In 1806 Samuel Hobbs was 'employed under the Inspector General on the superintendence of architectural works',[36] including works at Sheerness and the new Royal Marines Barracks at Chatham. From 1809 Holl was increasingly helped by his draughtsman, William Miller.[37]

In 1812, after Bentham left, Holl's title of Civil Architect was changed to Surveyor of Buildings, reverting to Civil Architect in 1832 after the next post-holder, G L Taylor, reasonably complained that it caused confusion with the Surveyor of the Navy.[38] The employment of architects and the increasing use of outside consultants such as the Rennies did not immediately end the involvement of the Surveyor of the Navy or his subordinates in shore establishments, especially when they had specialist skills to offer. Joseph Whidbey made a very successful transition in 1812 from master attendant at Woolwich to resident engineer for the Plymouth Breakwater project. Seppings's design in 1814 for long-span canopies over building slips and docks meant, in James Sutherland's opinion, that from then until 1850 'the thinking on long-span building structures was more advanced in the naval dockyards than in almost any other field and more advanced in Britain than in any other country'.[39]

In the home yards Holl had largely taken over from dockyard officers the responsibility for architectural design of all but the most minor structures. He maintained the yards' tradition of constructing handsome, well-proportioned buildings, and numerous examples of his work survive at Chatham, Sheerness, Plymouth, Pembroke, Haulbowline, Port Royal and Bermuda. Exerting his authority in the overseas bases could be more of a problem for him, for although Bentham's writ included these, senior officers overseas wielded considerable power and most probably reckoned themselves perfectly capable of designing buildings. As they were also responsible for obtaining tenders for building plans and specifications sent out from London, this gave them further reasons to intervene. In Barbados Admiral Sir Alexander Cochrane had built a naval hospital to his own design, constructed of 'timber lathed and plastered'. Later, in command of the North America station, he was unimpressed with Holl's designs for a 250-bed naval hospital at Bermuda, which had been approved by the Board of

Admiralty in 1813. Cochrane preferred to build a replica of his Barbadian hospital and complained to the Admiralty that Holl had simply produced a copy of Haslar Hospital, which prompted a reply from Holl, written with some feeling, that 'I can only observe that the Admiral must be but very imperfectly acquainted with Haslar Hospital or he would have not made such comparisons for there is not the least similarity between the two buildings'. Holl also pointed out that Cochrane's hospital cost on a per-bed basis £367 10s 2½d per patient compared to £264 13s 4d per patient for his own design.[40] The upshot was a temporary stalemate, the navy continuing to use rented accommodation on the island, supplemented by the hulk of the fifth-rate *Romulus*, a troopship since 1799, which was moored off Spanish Point as a hospital for ratings. The *Romulus* was broken up at Bermuda in November 1816.[41] Not until June 1818 was a purpose-designed and much smaller naval hospital opened on Ireland Island, initially with accommodation for 80 patients in 4 wards.[42]

Holl was a noteworthy early exponent of the structural use of cast and wrought iron. The earliest example of cast iron used as such in a dockyard building is in his 1806 church at Chatham, where slim, fluted, cast-iron columns support the gallery (*see* Chapter 5). After the 1,200ft-long spinning house at Plymouth ropery was gutted by fire in 1812, Holl modified and restored the building using only fireproof materials, adding an extra floor. The floors are stone slab, the two upper floors carried on inverted cast-iron tee beams and joists supported by a central row of iron columns. The simple truss roof employs wrought-iron tie-rods bolted to cast-iron principals. The cast-iron purlins are held in their sockets by cast-iron wedges, similar to the system used at the Iron Bridge across the Severn Gorge (at present-day Ironbridge) in 1777. Iron shutters secured the window openings, and the window frames themselves are of cast iron. Gill Bray and Hornbrook supplied the ironwork.[43] As Holl's first essay in fire-retardant construction, this is something of a tour-de-force, demonstrating his full awareness of contemporary developments in the outside world. He was probably also well aware of Major-General John Evelegh's use of cast-iron columns to support heavy floor loadings in the Grand Storehouse at the New Gunwharf at Portsmouth, under construction since 1811, though not designed to be fireproof (*see* Chapter 15). The same combination of elements is apparent in Holl's fireproof Lead and Paint Mills at Chatham, which have remained largely unaltered since completion in 1819. A slightly later example, completed after his death, is the former No. 1 Storehouse in Pembroke, its hipped roof carried on a series of queen-post metal trusses spanning a remarkable 40ft.[44]

Iron also offered Holl exciting possibilities for prefabrication, particularly at the overseas bases where materials and labour were frequently scarce and expensive and timber was prone to rapid decay and insect attack. Following his abortive proposals at Bermuda in 1814, he designed a new hospital for the Sick and Hurt Board at Port Royal, Jamaica, which was built between 1818 and 1822.[45] Holl followed this with a house for the commissioner at Bermuda, based on the same principles of a masonry core under an iron-framed roof and further protected by verandas (*see* Chapter 12). His original design of 1822 would be completed by his successor, G L Taylor. In this instance, not just ironwork and masonry but also joinery came from England.[46] The wisdom of using these materials is evident from the survival of both buildings, each of which has withstood hurricanes and long periods of neglect. Holl did not push out the structural boundaries in his use of iron in the way that his contemporary Thomas Rickman did with his Liverpool 'iron churches' of St George's Everton (1813–14) and St Michael in the Hamlet (1814–15),[47] and as his successors were to achieve with the great slip roofs in the 1840s, but he showed himself fully alive to its benefits as a strong, durable, fire-resistant material that lent itself to prefabrication. By the time of his death Holl probably had wider experience of using structural ironwork than any other architect in Britain.

Following Bentham's departure, his small organisation had undergone a number of changes, including the abolition of Simon Goodrich's post. Desperate not to lose his skills, the Portsmouth officers arranged a series of short-term contracts for him until sense prevailed. In March 1814 he was formally appointed as Engineer and Mechanist, confirmed by an Order in Council of 21 April, to be based at Portsmouth, and, as he noted with pleasure in his diary, 'upon the same salary and footing as Mr Holl'.[48] The salary was £600 a year, and his new rank also entitled him to a draughtsman and a clerk. As part of the same reorganisation, the masters of the Wood and Metal Mills and the millwrights were given salaries of £250, and each was allowed a foreman and a cabin keeper. In formalising these appointments, the seeds of the later mechanical engineering and production departments in the royal dockyards can be seen.[49]

In 1832 further and much more widespread structural reorganisations were to follow when the Navy Board and the Victualling Board were abolished, and instead individual Admiralty commissioners became responsible for the running of these departments.[50] In the dockyards the most immediate and noticeable impact of this later reform was the combining of the posts of dockyard commissioner and Port Admiral into the new post of yard superintendent, renamed Admiral Superintendents in the 1870s and Port Admirals in the 1970s.

On Holl's death in 1823, the architect George Ledwell Taylor (1788–1873) was appointed as Surveyor of Buildings. Taylor's fellowships of the Society of Antiquaries, the Institution of Civil Engineers and the Royal Institute of British Architects reflect his wide interests and considerable experience.[51] He completed a number of Holl's unfinished projects at Sheerness, Pembroke and Bermuda and was also responsible for constructing Melville Hospital at Chatham, rebuilding the Royal Clarence Victualling Yard at Gosport and modernising a number of dry docks. He experimented with the use of concrete in the yards, notably underpinning one of the great storehouses on Anchor Wharf at Chatham in 1834 'with concrete compressed and forced by steam'.[52] This appears to have been more successful than his collaboration with William Ranger, when he used Ranger's concrete blocks for wharf walls at Chatham and Woolwich, works that were later condemned by Pasley. It was not until Sir Andrew Clarke's tenure as Director of Works (1864–7) that he and Scamp introduced Portland cement on a large scale in the new works at Chatham and Portsmouth.[53] In 1837 Taylor was accused of authorising extra work at Woolwich without permission, but by then the Admiralty was looking to obtain architectural and engineering advice for the royal dockyards more economically. Taylor was pensioned off and his post abolished.[54] In its place a new Department of Architecture and Civil Engineering was established, which soon changed its name to the Works Department or Admiralty Works Department. This was in the charge of a Director of Works, sometimes known as Director of Admiralty Works or by his full title, which for a time was Director of Engineering and Architectural Works. Captain Henry Brandreth, a Royal Engineer, was appointed as its first Director.[55]

The Admiralty Works Department, 1837–1914

By 1837 the involvement of military engineers in naval bases had a long history, comfortably predating the formation of the Royal Regiment of Artillery and the Corps of Engineers in 1716. Such co-operation was natural, given the frequently close proximity of the two services. Virtually every naval base, no matter how small, had its artillery defences, while the more important ones had resident garrisons that usually included military engineers. One of the most remarkable was Christian Lilly, who surveyed Port Royal at Jamaica after the great earthquake of 1692 and designed and laid out the new town of Kingston across the harbour. After returning to England and being posted as the senior officer for the Plymouth district, he was responsible for choosing the site and the general layout of Morice Ordnance Yard adjacent to the new dockyard.[56] Towards the end of a distinguished career, Lilly was back in Jamaica in early 1729 for a third time as chief engineer to work on the defences and settlement for the new naval base at Port Antonio (*see* Chapter 12).[57]

In 1711, faced with the problems of designing and building a naval hospital at Port Mahon in Minorca, Admiral Sir John Jennings sought the help of Captain Robert Latham, a military engineer working with the army garrison on the island. The first hospital here was almost certainly designed by Latham (*see* Chapter 16).[58] At the end of the 18th century, the Royal Engineer William Twiss, responsible for the Portsmouth defences, was also active in the Hampshire yard advising on works to dry docks. A little later, in 1804, the Royal Engineer Robert Pilkington started work on the remarkable arsenal constructed in Palladian style at Weedon in Northamptonshire.[59] In the 1820s the young Royal Engineers Richard Nelson and Charles Pasley began their careers in Bermuda, principally constructing the defences round the new dockyard, but also working in the dockyard.[60] A couple of decades later, in April

Fig 4.4
Francis Fowke (1823–65), a Royal Engineer who began his career in Bermuda. (© National Portrait Gallery, London, D2361)

1845, the 22-year-old Lieutenant Francis Fowke (Fig 4.4) arrived on the island at the start of his career as a military engineer, designing a small shell store and the major powder magazine in Keep Yard at the dockyard. These were possibly his earliest buildings in a career that was to culminate in his appointment in 1856 as Architect and Engineer to the Department of Art and Science.[61] Similar examples of such help can be found in other yards, frequently arranged at local level on an *ad hoc* basis following some problem or crisis, but normally with the eventual knowledge of the Surveyor and later the Director of Works in London.

In 1741 the Royal Military Academy had been founded at Woolwich to provide formal training for the Corps of Military Engineers, in 1787 renamed the Royal Engineers. There they benefited from 'exposure to some of the finest mathematicians and scientists of the day in Britain',[62] and from 1812 furthered their practical education at the new Royal Engineers Establishment at Chatham, renamed the School of Military Engineering after 1869. The mathematician and scientist Peter Barlow, appointed to the staff of the Royal Military Academy in 1801, installed a testing machine of his own design in Woolwich Dockyard that enabled him to publish in 1817 *An Essay on the Strength and Stress of Timber*, the first major work on the strength of materials in Britain.[63]

The Royal Engineers also had close links with the military engineers employed by the East India Company, and a number of the Bengal Engineers were to be appointed to senior positions in the Works Department. Although use of Royal Engineers outside the army by the Government was certainly motivated by thoughts of economy, an equally compelling reason well into the 19th century lay in them being the only 'organised body of scientifically trained persons' available to the State.[64] Their skills were valued not just by the Admiralty, but also by the Board of Trade, the Home Office and the Office of Works, notably in the Railways Inspectorate and the prison service. In 1853, following the Great Exhibition, the Science and Art Department was established, later with the Royal Engineers Francis Fowke and then Henry Scott as architect and engineer to the Department, responsible for the major museum, educational and public works at South Kensington. Fowke prepared drawings for the Royal Albert Hall, but died before he could supervise the work; the proposals were modified and executed by his successor, Henry Scott.[65]

The Royal Engineer Captain Henry Brandreth was 43 years old when appointed as the first Director of Naval Works in 1837. Commissioned in 1813, he had seen extensive service in the West Indies before carrying out in 1829 a detailed survey and a report on the island of Ascension and its military and victualling establishments.[66] He arrived at his new Admiralty post at Somerset House as the first facilities for the steam navy were under construction at Woolwich Dockyard. His remit was responsibility for 'all engineering and architectural works not connected with the construction of ships of war, manufacture of stores or conversion of materials for shipbuilding' throughout the navy's dockyards and victualling establishments.[67] In essence, it was a variant on Bentham's instructions from the Admiralty nearly half a century earlier, but with one crucial difference. Bentham's appointment had to an extent been experimental, to explore among other things the possibilities of new technology within the dockyards; his department remained very small and was never fully accepted in all quarters.

By the 1830s steam was well established ashore and at sea, warships were starting to grow in size to accommodate the new machinery, and it was increasingly apparent that works on a larger scale than those at Woolwich would be needed at the other major home and overseas yards. The Admiralty had accepted the implications for the royal dockyards, and as a consequence Brandreth's new department was soon organised along rather more generous lines. The abolition of the Navy Board in 1832 had lessened the damaging rivalry with which Bentham was forced to contend,[68] and Brandreth was able to appoint Royal Engineer officers as superintendents in a number of the dockyards and provide them with civilian support staff. These dockyard superintendent engineer posts were generally linked to major modernisation and expansion schemes, but civilian staff became permanent and valued both in London and in the engineers' organisation in the yards. The top posts were never the exclusive preserve of military engineers, and in 1864 Henry Wood, a qualified civil engineer, was appointed as Superintending Civil Engineer at Portsmouth.[69] In 1843 the Admiralty decreed that 'the title of the Civil Architect is in future to be the "Director of Engineering and Architecture" and he may in common use be styled "Director of Works"'.[70]

The proportion of Royal Engineers holding senior posts had become significantly reduced by the early 20th century, with civilian engineers playing an increasing role from the start. In the same year that Brandreth was appointed as Director of Naval Works, in 1837, the 36-year-old William Scamp became assistant engineer at Woolwich Dockyard. Scamp was a self-taught architect and engineer who at the age of 19 had won a competition to design Assembly Rooms for Ilfracombe, before being recruited by Sir Jeffrey Wyatt, becoming his clerk of works for 13 years during the extensive rebuilding of Windsor Castle. Scamp was to work closely if perhaps not always harmoniously with Brandreth and was to rise to become Deputy Director to Colonel G T Greene. In 1860 Godfrey Greene wrote of Scamp that 'The present Admiralty establishments at Malta, Gibraltar and Bermuda, are almost entirely projected by him. Deptford, Woolwich, Sheerness, Portsmouth and Pembroke owe many of their best buildings to his professional talent. Keyham is almost entirely his own, from first to last.'[71] Brandreth and his successors reported directly to the Civil Lord of the Admiralty. They communicated with their staff in the dockyards using the established channels through the Captain Superintendents, who occasionally offered opinions, but did not apparently take the sort of proactive roles favoured by some 18th-century dockyard commissioners, a reflection of the increasingly professional role of architects and engineers in the 19th century.

The Works Department effectively took over the architectural and engineering tasks that had once fallen to the Surveyor of the Navy and then to Bentham's department, to Holl and to his successor, Taylor. With more resources now available, directors were able to centralise yard planning and design to a considerably greater degree. However, old habits died hard, especially in overseas bases. In 1842 Sir John Barrow, the long-serving Admiralty Secretary, sent a circular to these overseas bases, telling them that 'The Master General of the Ordnance has represented that serious inconvenience arises from the frequent references made from the Naval and other departments to the Commanding Engineer Officers in the colonies for assistance in forming plans and estimates and superintending naval and other works.' In future, the overseas yards were not to make such requests 'until reference has been made to their Lordships and the assent of the Board of Ordnance obtained by them, except in any such pressing cases of emergency'.[72] This does seem to have had some effect, and references to Royal Engineers become less frequent, but until the spread of the telegraph system there must have been a temptation in the more remote bases to turn a blind eye rather than wait months for permissions.

Until the 1850s an important exception to the centralisation of individual building and engineering design was the provision of major metal-framed structures such as slip roofs; these were generally designed by engineering contractors who had been carefully selected to tender on the basis of their skills. Similarly, very large civil engineering projects, such as the construction of Portland Breakwater from 1849 to 1872 and later its associated naval facilities or the extensions at Simon's Town,[73] were put out to tender by the Admiralty. Most of the design and supervision of these works were awarded to firms of consulting engineers, and possibly the best known in the latter half of the 19th century was that of Sir John Coode (1816–92). He began his career articled to James Meadows Rendel, one of the most prolific harbour engineers of the second quarter of the 19th century. Coode worked initially as resident engineer under Rendel on the construction of Portland Harbour breakwater. On Rendel's death, Coode took over as Engineer-in-Chief and was knighted on completion of the project in 1872. By then he had launched a hugely successful civil engineering firm, building, modernising and extending harbours throughout most of the Empire.[74]

Increasing centralisation did not signal the end of the use of local architects, particularly in more remote bases. At Esquimalt in the 1880 and 1890s, John Teague designed the main buildings of the naval hospital and the residence of the naval storekeeper, now Admiral's House. He was an architect with an extensive practice and had his own construction firm in Victoria BC, where he was responsible for designing and constructing many of the city's commercial buildings in the 1870s and 1880s. Nelson and Oliver (1982) credit Teague with having a monopoly of construction work at the base for 'at least fifteen years'.[75] Similarly, much of the new base on Garden Island in Sydney Harbour was laid out in the 1880s and early 1890s to designs by James Barnet, the prolific designer of public buildings during his long tenure as the Colonial Architect for New South Wales from 1865 to 1890, when the post was reorganised. He was assisted by a Mr Fishenden, an experienced engineer sent out by the Admiralty in late 1883, whose task would have been to ensure that the local designs matched Admiralty standards of fitness for purpose. However, he would almost certainly have left architectural style and ornament to Barnet, who spent time in the summer of 1885 inspecting works in Chatham, Portsmouth and Devonport.[76]

Godfrey T Greene held the post of Director of Naval Works from 1850 to 1864. His 7 Slip roof of 1852 at Chatham brought the great metal slip roofs to a significant level of maturity. Gone are the curved ribs of its immediate predecessors, to be replaced by a rigid frame of H-section, cast-iron columns braced by open trellis-type cast-iron girders, which were probably adapted from similar ones first used at the Crystal Palace in 1851. These columns also carried rails for overhead cranes, running the length of the slip and side aisles. The 82ft-wide roof was formed from wrought-iron triangular trusses.[77] The emphasis here on lateral stability was to come to fruition in Greene's famous multi-storey Sheerness Boat Store of 1858.

As dockyard projects grew in scale and complexity and the staff of the Director of Works expanded, it becomes both more difficult and increasingly meaningless to ascribe to any one person complete responsibility for the design of any single work. As Susan Hots noted, when considering the work of Major-General Charles Pasley, Director of Works from 1873 to 1882, he had inherited projects from his two predecessors, as well as benefiting from the work of colleagues such as Scamp and employees of the calibre of E A Bernays.[78]

During Greene's tenure as Director, the management system for the yards may be said to have come of age and was to survive in most essentials well into the 20th century. Superficially, it reflected in part the earlier arrangements of the Georgian Navy Board where individual yards initially put forward requests for works, together with preliminary designs, to the Surveyor of the Navy. But there the similarities largely ended. Now, the Director of Works generally instigated and invariably assessed proposals; if these were large or contentious, he would visit in person, as did Major-General Percy Smith, Director of Works 1882–90, in order to decide on the location for Hamilton Dock at Malta.[79] If the Director had accepted a proposal originating from yard officers, they could then formally submit their scheme to the Board of Admiralty for approval in principle. If this was granted, the Director and his immediate staff took a leading role in the design process, sometimes entirely remodelling the yard submission, at other times accepting it wholly or with modifications. His staff also prepared the estimates, and once Parliament had approved them, the Director assumed almost total control of major projects, preparing instructions for the calling of tenders, making ready the contracts and being ultimately responsible for the satisfactory execution of the works. However, the local yard officers, as earlier, provided day-to-day supervision in those instances where consulting engineers had not been commissioned. Greene and his successors also had the immense advantage not available to their Georgian predecessors of the development of swift and reliable communications. The growth of railways and steamships, the consequent improvement of postal services and the invention of the telegraph, the telegram and later the telephone allowed for a far more effective central control of the Admiralty's widespread empire.

Greene's enthusiasm for centralisation was not always shared by the yards. At the time, not all yards had Royal Engineers based in them, and there were complaints that some of the projects did not suit the operational needs of the yard concerned. In this there are echoes of the tensions between Bentham and the yard officers half a century earlier. Such a system gave the Director huge powers and responsibilities, as he did not have to seek Admiralty Board approval for design and contracting details and had sole responsibility for the actual construction works.[80]

In addition to their main construction and maintenance duties, the Admiralty Works Department staff also had to evaluate new building technologies and materials, especially the increased use of structural metal and reinforced concrete. Common services were introduced, initially water supplies and yard drainage, and new sources of power were assessed as they became available, being adopted where appropriate. Bentham had pioneered the introduction of water mains for fresh water and firefighting at Portsmouth in the first years of the 19th century, and in 1811 he proposed a similar scheme at Chatham.[81] Piped water with proper sewerage and drainage systems were gradually introduced elsewhere by his successors, who also ensured that gas lighting largely replaced oil lamps in the dockyards by the mid-19th century.[82]

Sometimes the Director of Works was asked to consider schemes that would more properly seem to be within the remit of the Chief Constructor of the Navy, as when in 1862 Scamp was asked to consider whether gas lighting could be used on board warships instead of candles. Cautiously, he replied that 'the ... subject needs to be treated with more than ordinary care', but promised that Mr Stevens the Gas Inspector who was going to Plymouth to see if the naval barracks could be gas-lit would also report 'on the most perfect method of supplying gas to ships'.[83] Perhaps unsurprisingly, nothing more was heard of this proposal. Hydraulic power, first used on a substantial scale in the London docks in the 1850s, was subsequently introduced, along with its necessary generating equipment and accumulators, in a number of the main dockyards and victualling yards at home and overseas to power cranes and capstans. William Armstrong had demonstrated hydraulic cranes in 1846 at Newcastle, but it needed the introduction of the weight-loaded accumulator in 1850, enabling hydraulic power to be stored, before this technology became widespread. Small cast-iron accumulators remain within Chatham Historic Dockyard.[84] The early 20th century saw a massive investment in the generation and distribution of electric power throughout the home and major overseas yards. Its introduction marked the end of the supremacy of the steam engine as a source of motive power in dockyard and victualling yard factories and workshops and its replacement by the more flexible electric motors.[85]

The Director of Works and his staff also had to solve the more fundamental problems of transport within the yards, which until the 1850s remained largely unchanged and traditional, relying heavily on human labour and horse teams on roads that were mostly unmetalled and at the mercy of bad weather. Paving seems to have been largely limited to the immediate surroundings of some of the dry docks, presumably to provide a better working surface for the shipwrights and to lessen the likelihood of gravel from roads getting into the docks and blocking culverts and sluice gates. Far heavier loads needed to be transported following the introduction of steam machinery into warships and the substitution of metal and armour plate for timber hulls. Improvements were therefore imperative.

In the early 1840s part of the works at Woolwich associated with the new steam factory included an estimate for 'forming a railroad to the masting sheers' from the factory; if it was ever constructed, then this would represent the first railway to have been installed in a royal yard. This was more than a century after the Board of Ordnance had installed a timber railway in its new storehouses at Morice Yard (*see* Chapter 15).[86] Coincidently, the Board of Trade was just setting up the Railways Inspectorate to examine and report on all new lines before they could be opened to the public and also to investigate the causes of railway accidents. The Inspectorate was to be exclusively staffed by Royal Engineers, once more broadening the Corps's practical experience in an area of benefit to the Admiralty.[87] In 1848 the Admiralty created its own Harbours and Railway Department, initially under the command of Captain C R Drinkwater RN and Captain James Vetch RE, but this had a comparatively short independent existence before it was relieved of its main statutory duties outside the dockyards.[88]

Although in the rest of Britain steam railways were becoming well established and were spreading all over the country, railway systems were not easy to fit into the confined layouts of most existing yards. Numerous turntables were necessary where spaces were too restrictive for the radius necessary for a railway line, hampering the efficient movement of locomotives and trains of wagons.[89] As late as 1849 stone and cast-iron wagon ways relying on human or horse power were seen as more flexible solutions within the dockyards. Rectangular granite blocks or heavy cast-iron plates to form the running surfaces for the dockyard carts and wagons were set flush with the road surfaces, allowing confined spaces to be more easily shared with other users and enabling the numerous existing horse teams and wagons to continue to operate. In 1849 'tram roads' were included in the Woolwich estimates to link the wharf with the timber yard and the factory to the sheer-legs. Stone wagon ways were also proposed for Portsmouth and Chatham. At Portsmouth a dual system of 'rails and tramways' (wagon ways) was planned, while at Chatham the wagon way was to link the wharf with the timber sheds, where it was noted that 'this improvement may be gradually extended to other parts of the yard'.[90] The following year, additional monies were allocated for these lines, which allowed completion of the 'granite tramway from the mast houses to the docks and basin' at Portsmouth. This was a less ambitious scheme than the railway planned for the more spacious new area of the dockyard and was designed to link 'the slips, factory building, the new timber ground and coal stores'.

In 1851 granite wagon ways were proposed for Sheerness and possibly Gibraltar.[91] That year the Admiralty also allocated £820 to pay the South Western Railway Company to build a short extension into the Royal Clarence Victualling Yard from its branch, which since 1842 had connected Gosport to London. This extension initially ended at 'Her Majesty's new landing place', providing a direct and altogether more seemly link than a granite wagon way for the Queen and Prince Albert on their journeys to Osborne House on the Isle of Wight. This first connection between a naval establishment and the main railway system may have been spurred by the holiday habits of the royal family, but the benefits of also being able to run trainloads of wagons into the heart of a yard were not lost on the Admiralty and its Works Department.[92] The 1857 estimates for Portsmouth included the substantial sum of £5,330 to link the yard's growing railway system with the terminus of the South Western Railway in the town; that year the yard already had 3 miles of track in use.[93] At Devonport and at the new steam yard at Keyham, William Scamp was planning an extensive railway system.[94] By the end of the 1850s it had become apparent that granite wagon ways were not able to cope with the loads now being transported, and the future in most cases lay with proper dockyard railway systems using steam locomotives.[95] Lengths of the granite tram roads remain visible at Portsmouth and within Chatham Historic Dockyard.

At Chatham progress was slower, and the stone wagon ways (Fig 4.5) remained in use until the early 1870s and the construction of the new steam yard under the immediate direction of Charles Pasley. In the mid-1850s he had gained first-hand experience of railway engineering when he had been appointed a trustee of the Melbourne and Mount Alexander Railway while on secondment in Australia.[96] At Chatham he championed the economies and flexibility of a narrow-gauge steam railway with an 18in gauge similar to one he had observed in the Crewe Railway Works. This was successfully introduced at Chatham in 1868 using cast-iron tram plates, the narrow gauge allowing for very tight curves which enabled most parts of the existing yard and the whole of the extension to be served (Fig 4.6).[97] In 1873 a link was proposed with the London, Chatham and Dover Railway's main line, which was completed in 1877. Initially, the new line led only to No. 2 Basin and an open space by the river north of 7 Slip intended as a huge coal yard. By 1914 it had been extended to most parts of the dockyard, duplicating much of the narrow-gauge system, except its ability to operate in more confined spaces and smaller buildings.[98] By the end of the 1870s all the home yards and the new base at Portland had been provided with extensive rail networks that were linked to the main railway

Fig 4.5
Surviving lengths of granite 'wagon way' c 1850 at Chatham Dockyard and the narrow-gauge railway lines installed from 1868. (Author)

Fig 4.6
A working party of sailors in 1902 with a locomotive and wagon of Chatham Dockyard's narrow-gauge railway outside Storehouse 12, now the Clocktower Building.
*(*Navy and Army Illustrated *5 Apr 1902, 62)*

system, and the use of railways was spreading to all but the smallest overseas bases.[99]

Keeping abreast of technological innovations and making use of these in the series of dockyard expansion programmes from the mid-19th century to the eve of the First World War kept the staff of the Admiralty Works Department fully occupied. To these tasks were added the naval barracks programme begun in 1879 and the extra commitments following the Naval Works Act of 1895. The work resulting from this Act led Major Sir Henry Pilkington, Director of Works, to suggest that he himself should be appointed Engineer-in-Chief with a separate staff for the Loan Works only, and that Major Edward Raban, then Superintending Engineer at Portsmouth, should be appointed as a new Director of Works. These suggestions were approved and implemented. At the same time Austen Chamberlain, the young Civil Lord of the Admiralty, set up a committee to look at the operation of the Works Department. Its recommendations included appointing an assistant to the Director of Works, giving the responsibility for the engineering branch to the Superintending Civil Engineer and ensuring that members of staff were moved around to gain experience.[100]

The increasing workload in the architectural and engineering aspects of the royal dockyards in the 70 years before the outbreak of war in 1914 is evident in the growth of the professional staff responsible for them (Table 4.1). In 1795 the Inspector General of Naval Works was allocated just six staff. By 1838 this had hardly grown, even though the need for such a department was generally accepted. Brandreth started with a staff of two draughtsmen, two messengers, two housekeepers and a porter. In 1914 the headquarters staff under Mr T Sims, the Director of Works and Civil Engineer-in-Chief, comprised two assistant directors, two superintending engineers, three civil engineers, a chief surveyor, a surveyor of lands and two assistants, five surveyors, seven Assistant Surveyors and a registry clerk.[101] These managed outstationed staff wherever there were significant works in progress or where maintenance and repairs presented particular problems. By 1886, the Admiralty Works Department had 150 officers, including 99 at home and overseas who were described as 'temporary'.[102] Despite this growth, the Admiralty Works Department retained to a considerable extent the structure it had developed by the time of Greene's departure in 1864.

Table 4.1 Distribution of the 150 officers of the Director of the Admiralty Works Department in 1886, just before the major dockyard expansions from the 1890s (TNA ADM 181/96 fol 22).

Location	*head of branch*	*superintendent civil engineer*	*assistant civil engineer*	*clerk of works*	*draughtsmen, clerks etc*	*temporary assistant civil engineers and clerk of works*	*temporary draughtsmen, clerks*	*temporary foremen*
London	4				17		8	
Greenwich			1				2	
Chatham		1	1		3		5	1
Sheerness				1	1		1	1
Portsmouth and Eastney		1	1	1	4	2	10	4
Devonport and Keyham		1		1	2	1	8	2
Pembroke		1			1		2	1
Portland			1				2	1
Gibraltar						1	2	1
Malta		1				1	10	3
Bermuda			1				2	1
Gosport			1		1		1	1
Plymouth				1	1		1	2
Haulbowline		1				2	3	
Walmer				1				
Deptford								1
Plymouth Breakwater						1	1	1
Alderney Breakwater						1		1
Yarmouth						1		
Halifax and Jamaica						1	1	
Cape of Good Hope						1	1	
coastguard								4
naval reserve batteries								2
totals	**4**	**6**	**6**	**5**	**30**	**12**	**60**	**27**

5

Engineering Works of the Sailing Navy, 1700–1835

By 1700 the royal dockyards in England had evolved well-established roles building and maintaining the fleet. Variations of scale and purpose between yards reflected their relative strategic importance and whether or not they served a fleet anchorage. Looking after large numbers of warships in an anchorage, preparing them to be laid up or put in ordinary and subsequently readying them for sea generally ensured a steady and relatively constant workload for the dockyards involved. In turn, this was reflected in their facilities and size of workforce. But a powerful influence in shaping the individual yards, apart from their topography, was the engineering works necessary not just for their smooth running but for their continued existence in what could be a hostile environment at the junction of land and water. In any significant harbour establishment, there has always been a fine line between engineering and architecture, and the royal yards were no exception. Much of the civil and structural engineering may go unseen and unremarked in the form of massive foundations where the subsoil was treacherous and later on in the extensive use of iron for structural or fireproof purposes, which would only be apparent inside a building.

Until Samuel Bentham's department was established in 1795, the Navy Board's Surveyor was nominally responsible for dockyard planning and for the buildings and engineering works. This was no sinecure. Instead, it was a considerable imposition on a man whose primary task was designing and overseeing the provision of warships and whose training and experience had normally been as a shipwright before rising to the rank of master shipwright in one or more of the royal dockyards. 'Plain, strong and convenient' sums up the majority of industrial works in the Georgian dockyards built under the Surveyor's sometimes nominal supervision. Most of the buildings have a strong family resemblance, differing principally in the use of construction materials. Before the rise of the professional architect and even without guidance from the Surveyor in London, dockyard officers would have considered themselves well able to provide designs for whatever structures were required in their yards. This remained broadly true, especially in the overseas bases where distance from London made close supervision impracticable. Even if the base was small and in the sole charge of a storekeeper, there was quite often an engineer officer attached to the local garrison who was able to help. This devolution of the final designs to the yard officers means that in the majority of cases earlier than the early 19th century, the designer of a wharf wall, dock or storehouse generally remains unknown.

Among the greatest challenges facing dockyard officials were the substantial civil engineering works involved in building wharf walls and the closely associated dry and wet docks and slips. Sheltered river yards, as at Chatham or along the Thames, presented fewer problems, especially when low water allowed access to the whole of the river frontage for building work and maintenance, a luxury not generally available at dockyards, particularly in the tideless Mediterranean. At Minorca in 1715 Vice-Admiral Baker reported that crews of naval ships drafted to help construct the wharves of the new naval yard worked 'above half their depth in ye water, both in slinging stones that are taken up along the shores of the harbour, as well as placing them when they come to the wharf'. These stones weighed between 2 and 6 tons.[1] Elsewhere, conditions could be harsh, with exposed yards such as Sheerness vulnerable to damage from heavy seas and the Caribbean yards of Port Royal and English Harbour at the mercy of hurricanes. English Harbour at Antigua was reputed to be hurricane-proof, but this did not make it immune to occasional damage.

As established yards expanded, surveyors frequently had to contend with alluvial subsoil, which made firm footings difficult to establish. This was a particular problem in the 18th century at Portsmouth as the yard expanded up-harbour, while faulty or inadequate geological information could be a further hazard, as at Pembroke where unexpected problems added considerably to the costs of the wharves and slips, despite Rennie carrying out a series of trial borings at the site of the yard in 1813.[2] At Sheerness that same year he introduced for the first time enormous coffer-dams and steam pumps to enable construction of the massive piled foundations for the rebuilding of the yard. Engineering equipment on a huge scale was to become a feature of most subsequent dockyard expansion operations.

Well into the 18th century some yards still had timber-faced wharves, but by the 1840s these had been generally replaced by brick or stone. Later expansion schemes have meant that nearly all wharf walls predating 1800 have been swept away or buried by land reclamation, but good examples remain along the riverfronts at Deptford and Chatham Historic Dockyard and at Portsmouth at the South Camber. Overseas, at Port Mahon the wharves enclosing Saffron Island mostly date from the late 1760s and are matched by similar ones at English Harbour at Antigua.

Construction problems associated with wharves could be minor compared to those facing the builders of docks. Dry docks, as their name implies, could be drained to allow the construction or repair of vessels within them. By contrast, wet docks – or basins as they were generally termed – were designed to retain their water at a constant level. At Plymouth the tidal range, as Dummer noted, uniquely allowed the wet dock to be drained by gravity if necessary.[3] Basins provided secure berths for warships, but perhaps more importantly the constant water level made repair, maintenance or fitting out work much easier on warships secured alongside the quays. This became especially important from the mid-19th century as heavy engines, boilers and later complete gun turrets were fitted after the launch of a warship. Originally, double sets of inward- and outward-opening gates were needed to resist changing tidal water pressures and retain the impounded water in the basin, but the success of Bentham's caisson, replacing the double gates at the entrance to the Great Basin at Portsmouth in 1802 (*see* p 94), led to its widespread adoption for basins and dry docks.[4]

Dry docks were generally the most expensive of all dockyard installations; as a consequence, not every yard was provided with them from the start, while minor yards like Harwich never possessed them. Not until the late 1840s did Malta become the first overseas base to be equipped with one. The origins of dry docks can be traced back to 1495 when Henry VII ordered the construction at his new base at Portsmouth of what was probably a crude prototype. The little that is known about this early timber-lined dock and its few successors indicates that they relied on gravity drainage and were secured by specially constructed temporary earth and stone dams rather than gates. Over the next century and a half, timber-lined dry docks were constructed at the royal yards at Woolwich, Deptford and Chatham, together with one for the East India Company at Blackwall on the Thames and for private merchants at Bristol. By the 17th century a number of these had alters or steps, typically 4–5ft wide and planked, but not on the number and scale that Edmund Dummer was to introduce in the 1690s.[5]

The first dry dock on mainland Europe did not become operational until 1671, when it was completed at the new French naval base at Rochefort on a pattern 'à l'anglaise'. Initially, this was of timber construction, but a lack of stability led François Le Vau, the engineer, to rebuild the walls in stone, their stepped sides still apparently primarily designed to counter the thrust of the surrounding soil and only incidentally being found useful as working platforms for the shipwrights. Although altered, Rochefort remains the oldest extant dry dock. In 1681 work began on a dry dock at Copenhagen, but technical difficulties caused abandonment of the project until 1739. The first dry dock in the Baltic was begun at Karlskrona in 1716 and became operational in 1724.[6] In England, although their design had improved by the end of the 17th century with the development of dock gates, dry docks remained crude and inefficient, their sheer timber sides prone to distortion and decay, while the lack of structural stability at their entrances led to ill-fitting gates and consequent leakages.[7] Nevertheless, dry docks became the focal point for every yard so equipped, determining its development. Their central importance was publicly recognised as part of a yard's official title until the late 1960s, when 'dockyard' was replaced by the more encompassing term of 'naval base'.

Radical change in the construction and hence the efficiency of dry docks in England came with Dummer's innovative design and extensive engineering works in the 1690s at Portsmouth and at the brand new yard of Plymouth Dock, where he had carefully selected the site on the Hamoaze (*see* Chapter 1). Here he could locate the dry dock, centrepiece of the new yard, in a shallow valley opening on to deep water. Though the underlying rock made excavation difficult, it provided a firm foundation for the works. This was probably the very first dock deliberately designed with stepped stone sides or alters for practical convenience, rather than just structural reasons. Alters allowed the use of shorter timbers to support vessels in the dock, provided working platforms for the shipwrights and reduced the volume of water required in the dock. It may well be that the Admiralty knew sufficient of Le Vau's work to enable Dummer to refine and develop the concept, but this could equally be a case where two intelligent men working independently arrived at the same solution.

At the Plymouth dry dock there were integrated stone steps and chutes at regular intervals along the alters to aid the movement of men and materials. Drainage was by gravity, a culvert with sluice gates connecting the dry dock with the foreshore, and instead of the cumbersome triple-leaf dock gates then in use, Dummer substituted twin gates that required far fewer men to operate. These rapidly became standard, although as late as 1816 one of the dry docks at Chatham was still secured with the old method using three great timber panels held firm by stanchions.[8] As finally constructed, the Plymouth dry dock was 230ft long, with a width at the gates of 49ft and a depth of 22ft. The dock opened directly into a basin 220ft by 256ft.[9] Although Dummer reported that the basin and dock were completed by December 1694, problems with the fit of gates and especially with the stonework persisted and do not seem to have been wholly solved before 1700.[10]

At Portsmouth, Dummer's original 1690 brief was to design and build a single dry dock capable of accommodating the largest first-rates.

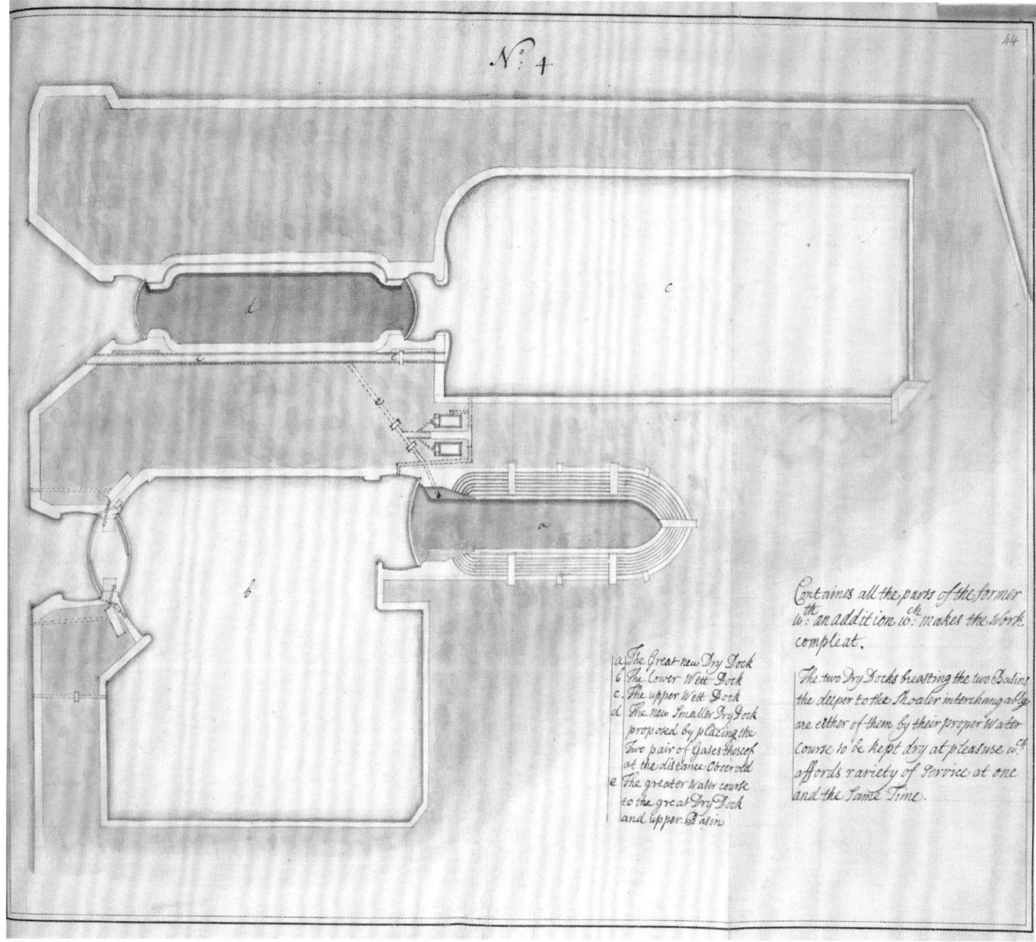

Fig 5.1
Edmund Dummer's 1698 plan of his new stepped dry dock (centre) at Portsmouth, with its pair of single gates opening off what is now 1 Basin (bottom left), with its opposing sets of gates into Portsmouth Harbour. What originally was planned as a channel to the Upper Wet Dock (top right), with a single set of gates to impound water, was converted into a second dock ('North Stone Dock') by the addition in 1699 of a second set of gates.
(© The British Library Board. Harley MS 4318 fol 44)

The Portsmouth dock was smaller than that at Plymouth, with a length of 190ft and a width at the gates of 51ft; it was rebuilt and enlarged in 1769 and is now 5 Dock.[11] In October 1691 the project was substantially expanded to include two wet docks. As at Plymouth, the dry dock opened into one of these wet docks, now No. 1 Basin, while the second, known as the Upper Wet Dock, lay immediately to the north and was approached from the harbour by a long channel closed by a set of gates. In 1699 the Admiralty ordered the addition of a second set of gates at the opposite end of the channel, effectively creating another stone dry dock, albeit one lacking stepped sides. This was named North Stone Dock (now 6 Dock) and was to be enlarged and rebuilt with alters to take first-rates in 1737, at an estimated cost of £15,694 (Fig 5.1).[12]

The tidal range at Portsmouth meant that Dummer had to provide chain pumps for his original dock. Uniquely and ingeniously, he powered these by a waterwheel that worked on the tide mill principle, taking its water through a culvert from water penned in the Upper Wet Dock and discharging it into the harbour. As this could only work towards the end of an ebb tide, he also linked the pumps to a horse gin to allow for continuous operation (Fig 5.2), possibly the first use of a gin in a royal yard. In 1698 he claimed that the dock could be largely emptied on the ebb tide, and the remaining six feet of water could be pumped out in one night.[13] All these new works were sited at the northern end of the existing yard on land reclaimed from the harbour, giving rise to substantial problems with unstable foundations and settlement, which still caused problems in 1702.[14] As at

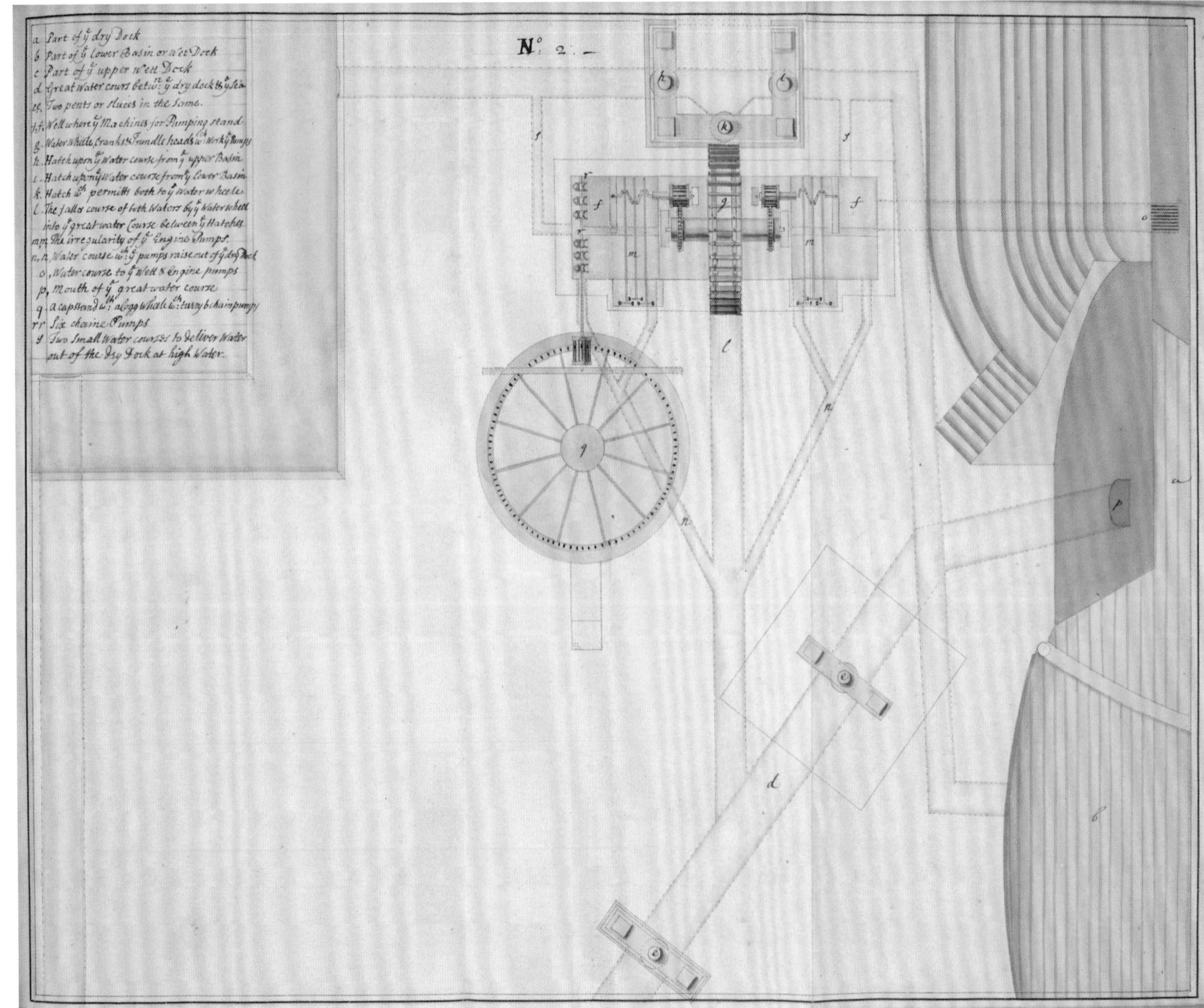

Fig 5.2
Dummer's remarkable arrangement of the 1690s for emptying his new dry dock at Portsmouth, part of which is seen on the right. At low tide the chain pumps were driven by the waterwheel turned by water piped from the wet dock, part of which is obscured by the key (top left). At other times the horse gin drove the pumps.
(© The British Library Board. Harley MS 4318 fol 42)

Plymouth, where there were similar complaints about poor workmanship, much of the construction work was the responsibility of the contractor John Fitch. The bitter recriminations and accusations about workmanship were instrumental in leading to Dummer's dismissal in August 1699.[15]

On 28 June 1698 the *Royal William* became the first warship to enter the new dry dock at Portsmouth. Despite the construction difficulties and the expense of building in stone and brick rather than wood, it was clear that the future lay with these potentially far more durable structures, although it was to be over a century and a half before the last of the timber dry docks was replaced.[16] Importantly, these two new docks could accommodate first-rates and second-rates, removing the need to send them to Woolwich or Chatham for major hull repairs and giving a crucial boost to the utility and importance of the south coast yards. For dimensions and details of dry docks, *see* Table 8.1

Dummer's work in the 1690s set many of the standards for the design, materials and construction of dry docks for the sailing navy. However, at Portsmouth and Plymouth teething problems highlighted that there were still design weaknesses leading to problems with foundations, with the relationships of walls to dock floors and in the fit of the dock gates. The new stepped stone or brick and masonry docks and wharf walls were massively heavier structures compared to their timber predecessors. This was not a problem where they were built on firm bedrock as at Plymouth, but the softer subsoils of Portsmouth Harbour caused repeated problems. In 1716 a coffer-dam had to be constructed outside the Great Basin so that it could be drained for bricklayers to work on the walls. In the mid-1760s further repairs were needed, and the opportunity was taken to award a substantial contract to James Templer to deepen the basin, lowering its foundations and resetting the sills to allow larger warships to enter. This was part of a major modernisation scheme involving the enlarging of what are now 4 and 5 Docks. To the very end of the 19th century engineers continued to experience problems stemming from inadequate foundations in this part of the dockyard.[17]

The walls of dry docks and basins until the middle of the 18th century seem generally to have been constructed on top of timber rafts laid along the bottom of the foundation trenches, a technique probably first used in Britain by the Romans with their chain of Saxon Shore forts.[18] However, not until the start of South Dock, now 4 Dock, at Portsmouth in 1767 does it appear that piles were systematically used under both dock walls and floor in addition to the rafts (Fig 5.3). These piles gave added stability to the

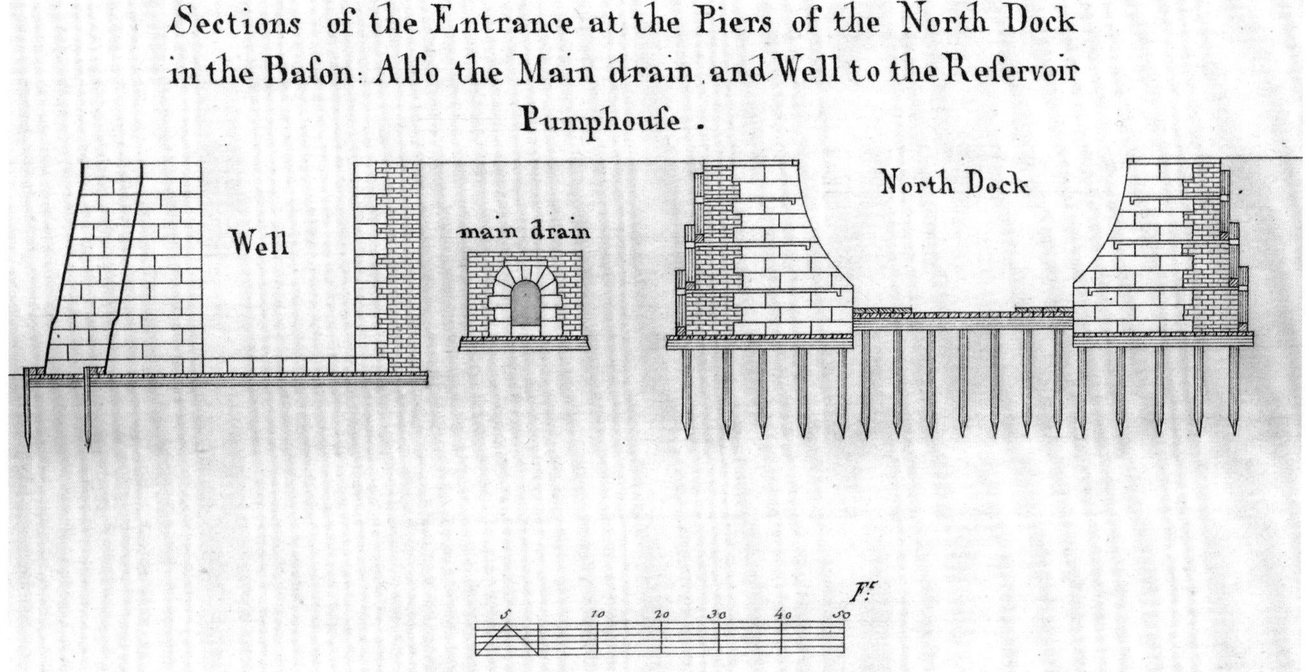

Fig 5.3
A drawing of the later 18th century showing part of the dock system and its foundations at Portsmouth. The relationship between the dock's timber floor and masonry walls is clearly shown.
(NMRN Plans of HM Dockyard, Portsmouth, c 1786, MS 1993/443)

walls, which were sometimes further secured by horizontal timber ground anchors, tying their tops back into the adjacent subsoil.[19]

With the exception of Plymouth, the floors of the dry docks seem generally to have been constructed using substantial balks of timber until the late 18th century. Although these were almost invariably laid on piles to cope better with the weight of warships, the timber floors remained independent and untied to the surrounding walls, although their principal timbers were wedged under the latter.[20] The fit of the dock gates depended very largely on the relationships between the two opposite sides of the dock entrance and on the timber dock floor remaining absolute and immovable. In practice this was difficult to achieve, especially at Portsmouth where even now the levels of some of the 18th-century docks can move imperceptibly with the tide. Throughout the 18th century, successive surveyors and master shipwrights wrestled with the problems of keeping dry docks operational and reasonably watertight, usually by adding further piled foundations to strengthen the entrances.

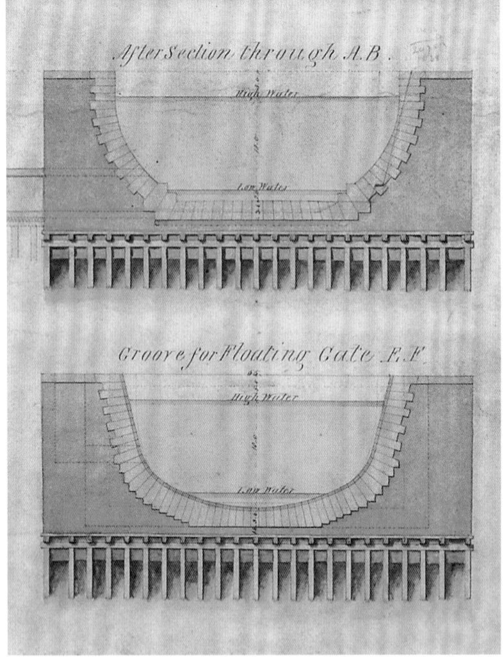

Fig 5.4
Cross-section of the 1824 Frigate Dock at Sheerness Dockyard, showing its inverted arch construction that gave the whole structure absolute rigidity. The drawing is signed by G and J Rennie, an instance of John Rennie junior being assisted by his brother George.
(TNA ADM 140/777)

The first major advance in the design of dry docks where there were problems of subsoil pressure or instability was the introduction of an inverted masonry arch beneath the dock floor, binding the sides and especially the gate piers together. This was pioneered by Samuel Bentham at Portsmouth, where the lack of firm subsoil had led to endless problems that resulted in ill-fitting dock gates and consequent leakages.[21] His proposal in 1798 was agreed by the Admiralty in October the following year, after considerable opposition from the Navy Board. In instructing the yard officers to proceed with the work, the Board was careful to distance themselves from the design, writing that the work was 'to be carried on in the manner General Bentham has proposed, as it is concluded he has sufficiently informed himself on the advantages of the inverted arch of masonry for the bottom of the dock without the use of piles or woodwork'.[22]

Although plans showing the inverted arch do not appear to have survived, a contemporary letter from the Navy Board to the Portsmouth officers advised them that 'Messrs Thomas and John Parlby having stated to us that they have received orders to prepare and set the stones for the inverted arch between the piers and at the bottom of the new parallel Dock in the Basin of your yard'. This makes it clear that the intention was to have the inverted arch running the length

Fig 5.5
Contemporary model of the Victualling Storehouse and later naval barracks at Sheerness Dockyard. This clearly shows the combination of inverted masonry arches carried on massive piles that had to be used by John Rennie senior and John Rennie junior to underpin all their works at this dockyard.
(Country Life)

of the new dock.[23] Works on the dock, now 2 Dock and appropriately the home of HMS *Victory* since 1922, and on its immediate neighbour in the basin were largely complete by 1802. It is unclear whether or not in these instances Bentham dispensed with piles entirely; given the problems with the yard subsoil, it would have been a bold decision. In similar circumstances 20 years later, Rennie senior was certainly using piles in combination with inverted arches at Sheerness (Figs 5.4 and 5.5).[24]

Bentham's championing of masonry for the floors of dry docks was one shared by Rennie, but provision of brick, masonry or, later on, reinforced concrete floors rather than timber did not become standard practice until some way into the 19th century. As late as 1815 the Admiralty was unsuccessfully urging the Rennies to use timber for the floor of No. 3 Dock at Chatham (Fig 5.6) on the grounds of economy, ignoring the benefits of masonry and the fact that the plans had been agreed with Holl.[25] The Board remained unconvinced in 1818, noting in their report that 'we inspected the works ... and could not but be forcibly struck with the inutility of a foundation of nearly twelve feet thick, which has occasioned an additional expense of several thousand pounds, as well as great delay in the work'.[26] Not for the first time, the Admiralty was finding that well-executed civil engineering was expensive, but Rennie's insistence on high standards ensured that nearly two hundred years later the dry dock remains in use and in virtually its original state (*see also* Chapter 6).

Fig 5.6
No. 3 Dock at Chatham designed by the Rennies, occupied by HMS Bellerophon, *laid down on 28 December 1863, 5 days after the launch of HMS* Achilles, *the first armoured metal warship to be built at the yard. This photograph may have been taken shortly before* Bellerophon's *commissioning in March 1866. The dock remains little altered.*
(Author's collection)

Bentham's second important introduction was the development of an effective caisson to replace dock gates. What was probably the first caisson had been built for one of the dry docks at Rochefort in the mid-1680s when it was described as 'a new and little known invention'.[27] A few years later Commissioner St Lo at Chatham claimed to have designed what seems to have been a similar device. In 1703 the Admiralty ordered an evaluation of his 'floating gates', which the dockyard officers said were 'preferable either to hanging or wicket gates'. Despite St Lo offering to meet the £500 estimated cost of construction if it failed to work, nothing more was heard of it.[28] In 1798 Bentham revived the concept with what he called 'a hollow floating dam', and one was successfully installed at the entrance of the Great Basin (now No. 1 Basin) at Portsmouth in 1802. Bentham's caisson was boat shaped and largely constructed of timber, but had all the essential features of its modern successors (Fig 5.7). Once towed into position, cisterns deep inside its body were flooded, causing it to settle against stone flanges or grooves in the basin or dock entrance, where it was held by the pressure of water against its outer face. Removing it simply involved a reversal of this sequence. The term 'ship-caisson' is convenient shorthand to identify a caisson that was towed or winched into position rather than sliding into a recess as was to become standard practice for new docks later in the century. Caissons had fewer joints, with their potential for leaks, compared to a pair of dock gates, and as they were not physically joined to basin or dock entrances, stresses transmitted into the masonry by gate hinges were eliminated.

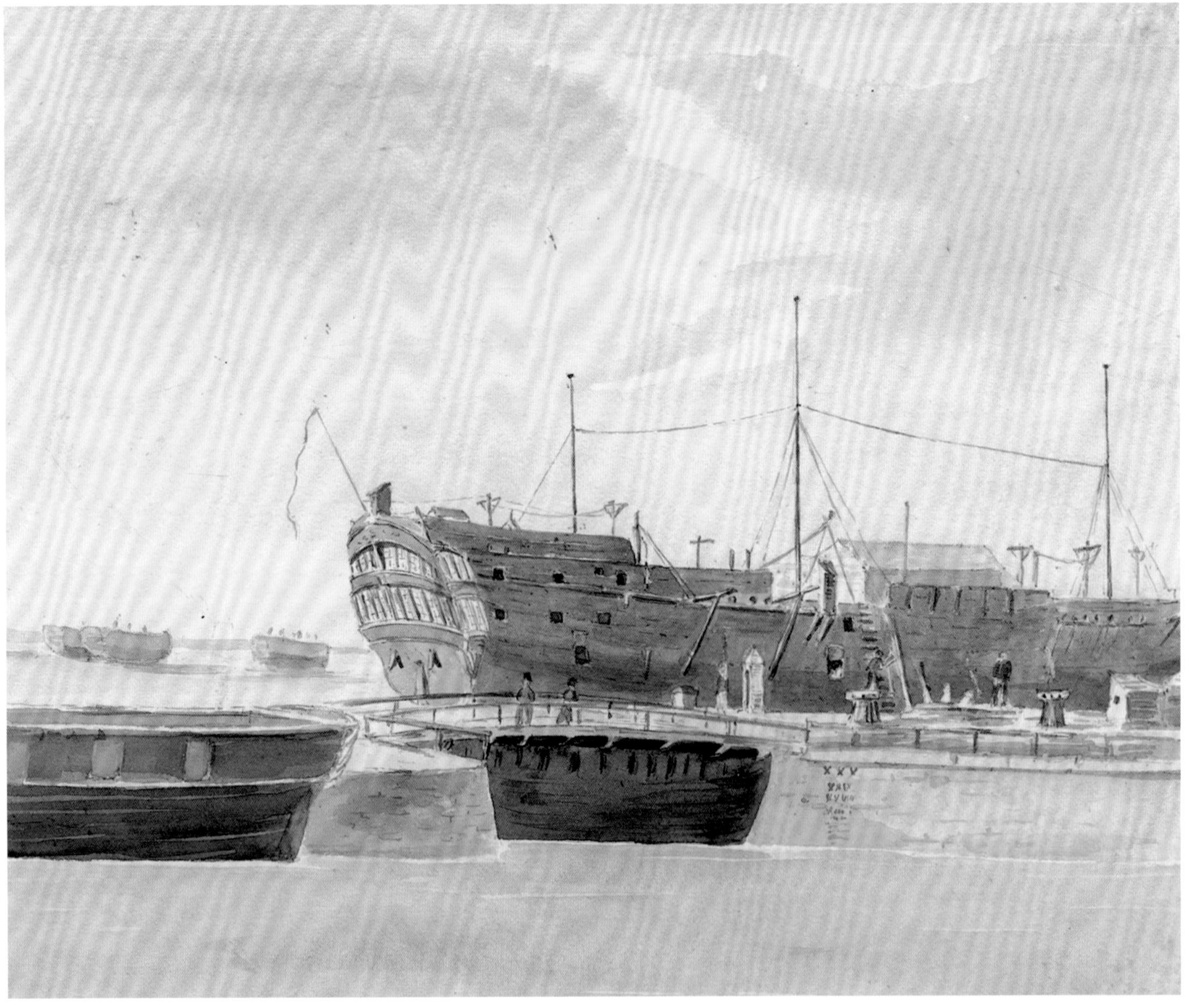

Fig 5.7
A rare watercolour of Bentham's new boat-shaped caisson with its roadway above at the entrance to No. 1 Basin at Portsmouth. The vessel in the harbour alongside the wharf is possibly a victualling hulk. Captain Durrant, a militia officer, painted a number of Portsmouth scenes while stationed here, guarding prisoners-of-war between 1802 and 1813. (Hampshire Museums Durrant collection FA1990.23.118.1. DPAAQF23)

A further practical benefit lay in the broad 'deck' of the caisson that could be used as a roadway, sometime saving long detours for dockyard traffic, as at the entrance to the Great Basin at Portsmouth. For repairs or maintenance, a caisson could simply be placed in a dry dock like any other vessel.[29] However, despite these advantages, sealing the entrances of docks remained a problem, and it is notable that the Rennies used a caisson with an inner set of gates at their dock at Chatham. By then, they had also pioneered the replacement of timber gates by iron ones with superior durability, strength and rigidity.[30] Iron caissons seem to have made their first appearance in the 1840s (*see* Chapter 8).

Until the last year of the 18th century, all the Royal Navy's dry docks depended on manual or horse-powered chain pumps to remove water that could not drain by gravity. Dummer's introduction of an auxiliary waterwheel at Portsmouth in the 1690s remained an exception. Elsewhere in Europe, other forms of power were being tried. By the mid-18th century, the Swedish navy was using windmills at Karlskrona, and at Sveaborg a large windmill powered a sawmill and grist mill as well as a dock pump. [31] At Copenhagen two pumping engines for dock drainage were in use by 1774, the same year that the Spanish navy installed two for a similar purpose at Cartagena, followed later by ones at Cadiz and Ferrol.[32] All these seem to have been atmospheric engines of the type invented by Newcomen in 1712. Such engines were very inefficient and could be used only for pumping as they lacked any rotary motion. Watt's invention of rotary motion transformed the potential of steam power, and when the navy's first steam engine started work at Portsmouth in 1799, it powered woodworking machinery and drained the adjacent dry docks. James Sadler (*see* Chapter 4) designed both the engine and the lift-pump. Lift-pumps gradually replaced the chain pumps as steam power spread to the other yards.[33] However, the system of using one steam engine for a variety of disparate tasks was not always satisfactory; later dock pumps usually had dedicated engines, although at Plymouth in 1835 it was proposed to make the planned new steam engine 'applicable to various other purposes' as well.[34] At Chatham in 1815 Rennie had looked to future expansion when working on his new 3 Dock and installed twin engines on either side of a central pump house, which was completed in 1822 (*see* Chapter 6).[35] In due course, new docks were linked to this.

At the rebuilding of Sheerness in the 1820s, John Rennie junior was able to achieve immediate economies of scale by linking the four new docks by a single culvert to a substantial steam pump house near the southern boundary of the yard.[36] Installation of further steam pumps at other home yards was slow. Although one had first been proposed in the yard in 1816, Plymouth relied on horse gins until well into the 1830s. Woolwich had a single pump by 1848, probably associated with its new dry dock, while Deptford's solitary double dock was so shallow that apparently it could drain entirely by gravity.[37]

By the 1820s, dry docks had largely achieved their modern form, with most technical problems overcome. Developments later in the 19th and early 20th centuries were generally ones of scale and shape, reflecting the quantum leaps in warship sizes, tonnage and design. Foundations had to be more massive, and this period also saw the introduction of reinforced concrete, refinements to the design of gates and caissons, which were now constructed of steel, and the introduction of more efficient pumping systems.

Wet docks or basins along with the larger timber and mast ponds shared many of the construction problems and engineering solutions associated with dry docks and wharf walls. Before the 19th century, only Deptford, Portsmouth and Plymouth had wet docks. Sheerness could muster only the aptly named tidal Mud Dock into which opened two dry docks and a slip. In 1808 Bentham proposed to close it with a caisson, but nothing was done before it was replaced in the post-war rebuilding of the yard.[38] As the navy changed to steam propulsion, the need for wet docks, or basins, grew since they allowed newly launched warships to be tied alongside to be fitted with engines and other heavy equipment. Woolwich had shown the way in the 1830s, and by the end of the 19th century every dockyard in the British Isles, with one exception, had been equipped with basins; ironically, the exception was the specialist shipbuilding yard at Pembroke.

Slips presented few engineering problems, and as long as they were built of timber, they were well within the construction capabilities of the dockyard labour forces, a factor possibly accounting for the comparative paucity of detailed documentary records. Their prime requirement was to open directly into deep water, with sufficient space to secure warships

Fig 5.8
A typical 18th-century timber slip with the supports used by shipwrights when working on the hull of a vessel under construction. The 100-gun first-rate Royal George *was launched from this slip at Chatham Dockyard in 1788.*
(© The British Library Board. Kings Top. XVI 42i)

after launching. This generally meant placing slips along the dockyard waterfronts facing into the harbour or river (Fig 5.8). In the 18th century, Portsmouth, Sheerness and Deptford had a small number of slips opening into their wet docks, but this severely restricted the size of vessels that could be launched from them, and only Deptford retained this arrangement until its closure.[39]

In the 17th and 18th centuries most slips were simple timber platforms, built on a slope of 1:20, strengthened by cross-timbers and secured by piles.[40] Warships were built on keel blocks laid on the slips, their hulls braced during construction by temporary scaffolding that also supported platforms from which the shipwrights worked. Such slips were comparatively cheap and easy to build and adapt as warship sizes changed (Fig 5.9).[41] By the second half of the 18th century more durable and expensive stone slips were being constructed, although when Pembroke yard was laid out a number of the slips apparently were first built of timber, to be replaced by stone a few years later. This was probably done for speed so that warship building could commence quickly and employ shipwrights (*see* Chapter 1). No. 1 Slip at Devonport, built in 1774–5, is the only 18th-century one to remain largely unaltered (Fig 5.10), its survival attributable to its later adaptation as a patent slip allowing small craft to be hauled out of the water for repairs.[42] Their prime waterfront locations meant that few slips survived once they ceased to be used. Most were infilled, and a number remain buried along the riverfronts, notably at Chatham Historic Dockyard.

The numbers of slips varied considerably over time, in size and between yards, influenced by a variety of factors. By the 18th century, the royal yards were concentrating on constructing the larger ships of the line, leaving the bulk of the fleet to be built by private firms. It was always regarded as essential to maintain shipbuilding skills in the dockyards, and there was a general assumption within the navy that ships built there were better constructed and more durable than those from merchant yards. In the royal yards master shipwrights by the 18th century tended to prefer dry docks for shipbuilding, as it was easier to float out a completed warship than launch her down a slip. This had drawbacks as shipwrights' priorities were the repair and maintenance of the fleet, but warship construction could take several years, blocking dry docks and affecting the yards' repair capacities. Master shipwrights probably agreed with Bentham's later view that floating a new ship out of a dock avoided possible distortion to her frame caused by a slip launch. However, in 1764 the Admiralty forbade the practice of using the dry docks, ordering that 'no ships be built in the future but on slips, that the docks may be always free for ships wanting

Fig 5.9
HMS Vindictive *a 74-gun third-rate, under construction at Portsmouth soon before her launch in November 1813. Captain Durrant's sketch emphasises the insubstantial nature of a timber slip and scaffolding used by the shipwrights working on the exterior of the hull. A timber ramp along the port side was the principal access to the interior for men and materials. (Hampshire Museums Durrant collection FA1990.23.116, DPAAQF19)*

Fig 5.10
No. 1 Slip at Devonport Dockyard, constructed in 1774–5 and the only surviving 18th-century slip to remain intact in a royal dockyard. The roof is later, as are the rails for a patent slip. (Author)

repair'.[43] This ban coincided with the modernisation and expansion of the principal yards, enabling the Earl of Sandwich a decade later to claim that he had 'caused nine new slips to be made'.[44] What he omitted to say was that this had given the Navy Board the opportunity to group together the slips in more convenient locations. At Portsmouth five new building slips were gradually constructed on reclaimed ground at the north end of the yard, and a similar concentration took place at Plymouth. Much later at Chatham there was a virtually identical reorganisation after additional land was acquired at the north end of the yard in the 1830s, allowing five roofed slips to be completed only just before the change to metal warship construction.[45]

In 1700 Plymouth had possessed no slips, Portsmouth had one and Chatham had two.[46] A century later Plymouth had four, Portsmouth five and Chatham six slips, the last reflecting the Medway yard's changed role to a shipbuilding and major repair yard.[47] Cramped Sheerness at the mouth of the river had only two small slips.[48] As might be expected with the Thames, which was then the country's shipbuilding centre, Deptford and Woolwich by 1800 had a concentration of slips, the former with five and the latter with four. The Harwich yard had been officially closed in 1713, but remained a supply base, and two small slips survived here into the 1840s.[49] Numbers alone do not tell the whole story, for Woolwich had only one slip that could accommodate a first-rate warship, Deptford could build nothing larger than a 74-gun third-rate, and Sheerness reached building capacity with 38-gun frigates. By contrast, Plymouth and Chatham each had three slips capable of accommodating first-rates. Portsmouth had a single slip for first-rates, but two that could take 74s, arguably a more useful combination.[50]

The drive in the 1770s to lessen dry rot by trying to ensure that the royal yards used only seasoned timber for warship construction was unlikely to succeed as long as ships were built on slips exposed to all weathers. For a warship to be on the stocks for 5 years was not uncommon, with the hull soaking up water until the main deck was finally planked and the ship caulked. Occasional references to 'portable housings' for ships under construction or repair occur in the records,[51] showing an awareness of the problem, but details are largely unknown, and at best they can only have been partial palliatives. Curing rot had been one of the ambitious targets set for Bentham when he was appointed. By then, a very small number of covered slips and docks were in use in Sweden, Spain and France.[52] In Britain, early roofing initiatives seem to have come first from officials at Plymouth Dockyard, with the Navy Board later noting that 'The placing of roofs over Slips and Docks was recommended as long back as 1806 by Mr Sumpter, a Quarterman ...whose plan was presented to the First Lord of the Admiralty by the Right Honourable R P Carew'.[53] The following year Bentham visited the Swedish naval base at Karlskrona to see its covered slip. Although totally enclosed now, this was then apparently an open-sided structure, its roof carried on six pairs of massive masonry piers (Fig 5.11). The resultant draughts were reported as being uncomfortable for the shipwrights and caused timbers to split and warp.

Fig 5.11
The 18th-century covered slip at Karlskrona Dockyard, Sweden, visited by Bentham in 1807. The great stone piers that support the roof are prominent.
(Author)

According to his widow, Bentham looked to covering docks rather than slips, and he avoided the Swedish faults by designing the housings to be 'enclosed as to resemble the best workshops ... perfectly lighted, ventilated and warmed'. He agreed with both Rennie senior and Thompson that docks were preferable to slips for warship building.[54] Nothing came of these proposals, like many defence projects probably killed on grounds of over-elaboration and cost. However, in February 1812 Bentham was in Portsmouth, still pursuing 'the contrivance of covered docks, combined with various accommodations subservient to the building of ships within them'. His unrealised plans for Sheerness that same year show four-storey, gas-lit, centrally heated workshops and covered slips, which clearly illustrate what he intended.[55] Also that year, and apparently without reference to Bentham or the Surveyor, the Plymouth officers built a roof over South Dock, which was still extant in 1821. Its design is not known, but roofs for docks not intended for masted ships did not need the height required for building slips and for that reason were simpler and cheaper to construct.

The year 1814 saw a rapid increase in proposals for covering docks and slips, sums of £6,000 being entered in the estimates for Chatham, Portsmouth and Plymouth for roofing a dock in each yard.[56] The Plymouth officers proposed 'roofs without buttresses but resting on standards'. An accompanying cross-section drawing, noted 'as proposed by the Plymouth Yard officers to the Navy Board in a letter dated 1 January 1814', shows a rather spindly timber housing, its pillars supporting a wall plate carrying a simple king-post timber roof of standard design.[57] A larger and taller version of this, its roof oversailing the pillars and with additional braces, was built over No. 1 Slip (later renamed 4 Slip) in 1814, its design credited to Richard Pering, the clerk of the cheque at Plymouth (Fig 5.12).[58] The Navy Board had considerable doubts about Pering's method of framing, later noting that 'on its being carried into execution it was judged advisable from the effects produced by gales ... to lower the roof, by taking eleven feet from its apex'. It would appear from the evidence that the Plymouth officers, perhaps taking advantage of their distance from London, were undertaking quite substantial works without always keeping Edward Holl informed.

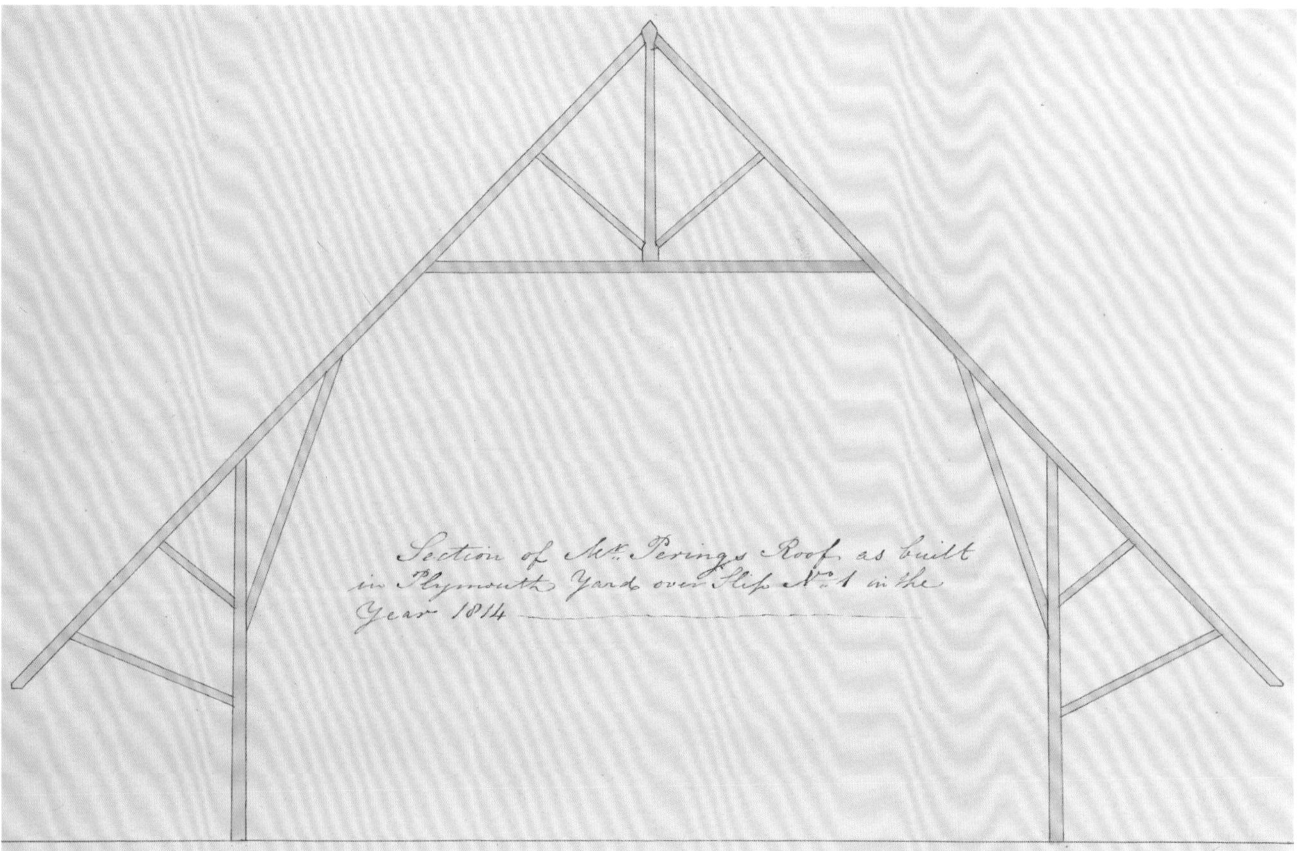

Fig 5.12
Richard Pering's 1814 roof over No. 1 Slip at Plymouth Dockyard. Its overall design is clearly derived from vernacular buildings such as large barns.
(© National Maritime Museum, Greenwich, London, ADM/BP/41b)

In parallel with Pering's work, two slip roofs were also constructed at Deptford and Woolwich yards. The one at Woolwich was almost certainly the first to be designed by Seppings, newly appointed as Surveyor of the Navy, and it has the elaborately braced trusses oversailing their supporting pillars that were to be the hallmark of his slip roofs (Fig 5.13). The Deptford example is merely noted as 'proposed by an architect and built at Deptford Yard in 1814' (Fig 5.14). This is a much less assured design, with simple strutted trusses through which the supporting pillars project and oversailing roofs that are not continuous with the main roof span.[59] Despite the promise of Seppings's design, Holl remained strongly opposed, and when later that year a Mr Lukin wrote to the Admiralty recommending simple timber roofs over slips,[60] his reaction was unequivocally hostile: 'the material of the shed being wood is exceedingly objectionable on account of its inflammability', while its employment would run counter to the aim of 'discontinuing the use of this material in any building to be erected in future in a Dock Yard'. Holl was also concerned that 'no light is admitted ... but through apertures, closed it is true by wooden shutters'. He felt that if the shutters were open, the workmen and the warship would be 'exposed to the injury experienced from currents of air', and if they were shut, there would be insufficient light for safety.[61]

The Admiralty and Navy Boards had to weigh

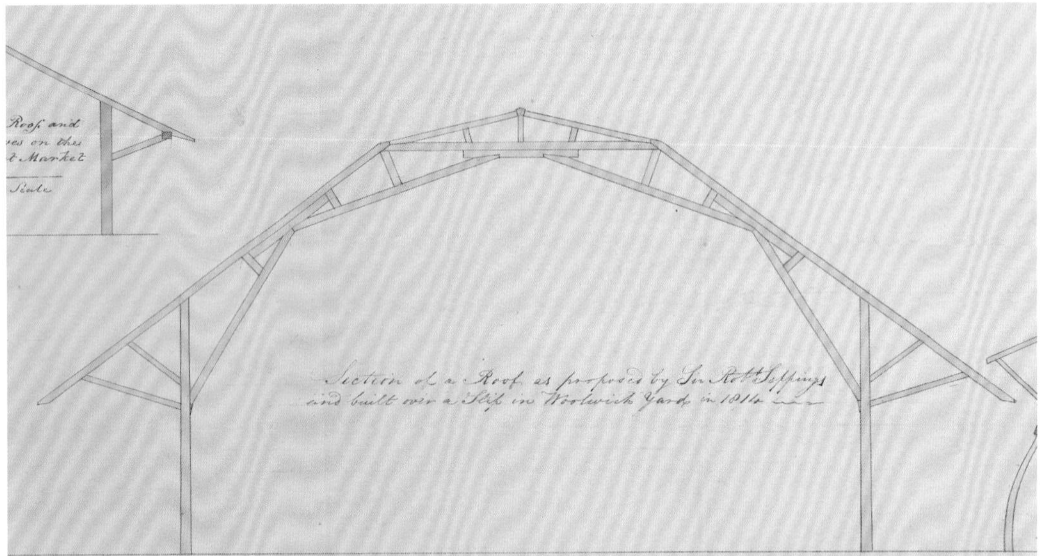

Fig 5.13
An 1817 drawing of a proposed slip roof at Woolwich Dockyard. The elaborately braced oversailing trusses are a hallmark of Seppings's designs. A similar roof was also proposed for 2 Slip at Chatham in 1817. (© National Maritime Museum, Greenwich, London, ADM/BP/41b)

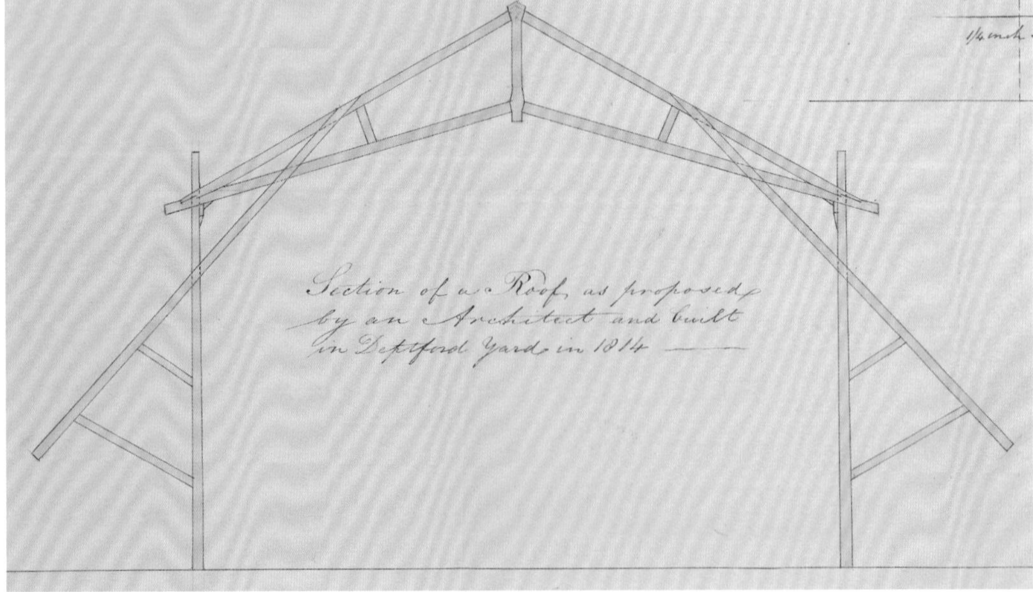

Fig 5.14
An 1814 design for a slip roof constructed at Deptford Dockyard by an unnamed architect. (© National Maritime Museum, Greenwich, London, ADM/BP/41b)

Holl's concerns for fire and safety against the pressing need for a more durable fleet. In the event, John Rennie was consulted and asked to consider a number of proposals, coming down firmly in favour of the Surveyor of the Navy's design. Seppings was highly talented and had already made a name for himself as master shipwright at Chatham. There he had developed an innovative system of warship construction using longitudinal trussing, diagonal bracing and other measures that significantly increased the strength and rigidity of hulls, reducing any tendency for them to hog. A ship is said to hog when its ends droop relative to the middle section, a serious problem with larger warships. Seppings had already won the Society of Arts' Gold Medal in 1803 for his invention of the 'Seppings's blocks', a triple set of adjustable wedges that made it easier to lift ships in dry dock, reducing the labour required from 500 to 20 men.[62] His knowledge of the properties of timber would have been invaluable in designing a workable timber cover building for a slip or dock where the high span required for protecting a first-rate warship was pushing contemporary timber technology to its limits.

Confidence gained from completion of the Woolwich slip roof is reflected in the 1815 estimates, where money was allocated for slip and dock roofs for all the yards, with £6,200 allowed to cover a dock and slip at Chatham, £15,600 for two docks and three slips at Deptford, £3,200 for one slip at Woolwich, £9,200 for a slip and two docks at Portsmouth, £2,000 for a dock at Sheerness and £6,200 for a slip and a dock at Plymouth.[63] Progress was rapid, and by December 1815 the Portsmouth yard officers were being ordered by the Navy Board, who carefully left the method to local initiative, to remove snow 'as speedily as possible from the roofs over the docks and slips'. If the Chatham evidence is typical, responsibility for constructing the roofs lay with the master house carpenters, for in June 1815, following an order to construct roofs over the first slip and the first dock there, the Navy Board authorised the Chatham master house carpenter to 'proceed to Woolwich to examine the roof that has been erected there, and to obtain any information respecting it that may be necessary'. The Woolwich slip roof was the one designed in 1814 by Seppings.[64]

In 1817, after visiting Portsmouth and Plymouth, the Admiralty felt that the benefits of building warships under cover were so great that they urged that all slips and such docks as were not required to accommodate masted warships should have cover buildings: 'So much importance do we attach to this measure that we think it should take precedence over all other objects because there is none that can compare with it as so immediately and permanently affecting the public purse'.[65] Two years later, the Navy Board Controller, Sir Thomas Byam Martin, was writing in similar vein to Lord Melville, the First Lord, reckoning that 'if we are at peace for a few years and the work goes on, the ships will be gradually brought into such a state by building and repairing under cover and using only choice materials, and giving them full seasoning in the progress of repair, that we shall have *for the first time* a really sound and desirable fleet'.[66]

The timber housings or canopies constructed between 1814 and the late 1830s demonstrated remarkable boldness. At a time when there were few timber roof spans in Britain greater than 40ft, the largest of these structures had spans of nearly 100ft, the roofs set at high levels to clear the warships beneath them. Unlike the slip at Karlskrona with its massive stone piers (*see* Fig 5.11), British versions were supported on tall, slender, compound wooden pillars, with surviving examples set in substantial stone or cast-iron shoes set flush with the slip surround. Each elaborately braced truss acted as a balanced cantilever, oversailing its supporting pillars to aid stability in the absence of external buttressing, while also helping to provide more covered space. The sides initially seem to have been left open. Roofs had glazed skylights and at first were covered in a variety of materials, including tarred paper, slates and tiles. The 1817 estimates allowed slates for roofs at Deptford and Woolwich. None of these materials was satisfactory, and after some years zinc or copper sheets were adopted as standard.The 1818 estimates allowed for copper sheets over the roof of the first slip at Chatham, possibly the first use of this material for a slip roof.[67]

Three of these graceful canopies remain, all constructed on the Seppings's principles, two of which are in South Yard at Devonport. The smallest covers No. 1 Slip and is almost certainly the oldest extant example, probably dating from 1815; it is also the only timber one still covering an intact and visible slip. A second and much larger canopy over the former 1 Slip must have replaced Richard Pering's 1814 slip housing, which he constructed to cover the

Fig 5.15
No. 3 Slip roof constructed in 1837–9 at Chatham Dockyard. This 1855 photograph includes the new wagon ways laid in the yard and a typical wagon of the period.
(Royal Engineers Library, Brompton Barracks)

Fig 5.16
The interior of No. 3 Slip roof at Chatham Dockyard after conservation in the 1990s, showing the immense span. Photographed from the later mezzanine floor.
(Author)

Fig 5.17
Slips 3–7 at Chatham Dockyard in 2007 after completion of major conservation work. This view from upstream shows (from right to left) the all-timber 3 Slip of 1837, the all-metal 4–6 Slips of 1847 and Greene's 7 Slip of 1852. (Author)

Britannia. Documentary references are largely lacking, but there is an absence of any money in the Plymouth estimates after 1821 for slip roofs. Early on, the Navy Board had expressed doubts about the strength of Pering's design, but until the *Britannia* had been launched in October 1820, little could have been done.[68] When warship building ceased on this slip in the latter part of the 19th century, the slip was floored over to form a vast scrieve board. Chatham Historic Dockyard has the third example, built in 1837–9 and carefully conserved in the late 1990s (Figs 5.15 and 5.16).[69] After warship building ceased here, it also had its slip infilled; around 1900 a metal mezzanine floor was inserted, and the space used for storing ships' boats. This was almost the last timber canopy to be constructed before the Royal Engineers introduced all-metal ones in the early 1840s.[70] At Chatham four of these later metal slip roofs stand immediately adjacent (Fig 5.17), providing a vivid demonstration of advancing technology, but one then still employed for constructing sailing warships. For these later slips, *see* Chapter 8.

Although the early 19th-century civil engineering works at Sheerness, Pembroke, Bermuda and the Royal William Victualling Yard at Stonehouse were both extensive and expensive, no single naval engineering project at that time came close to rivalling the construction of the great breakwater in Plymouth Sound, described as 'one of the greatest engineering achievements of nineteenth century Britain'.[71] The need for a 'spacious, safe roadstead ... for great fleets in times of war' in order to 'avoid the crookedness and intricacy of the entrance of the harbour' – the approach from the Sound to the Hamoaze and Plymouth Dockyard – had been noted by the Admiralty in 1771.[72] Plymouth Sound offered no protection from westerly gales, forcing any fleet to shelter in Torbay. The spur to action was St Vincent's re-appointment to command the Channel fleet in 1806 and his fear that it could be wrecked if caught unprotected in the Sound.

In 1806 John Rennie and Joseph Whidbey met at Plymouth to draw up plans for a detached breakwater across the centre of the Sound (Fig 5.18).[73] Its central section was to be 3,000ft

Fig 5.18
Part of the original plan for a breakwater at Plymouth Sound, drawn up in April 1806 by Rennie senior, Henmans and Whidbey.
(TNA ADM 140/369 pt 1)

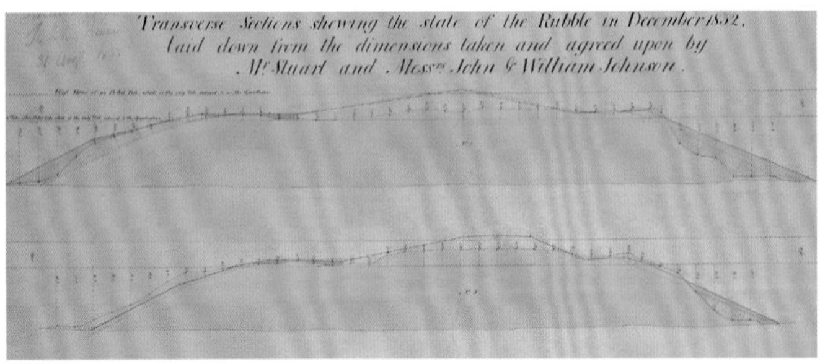

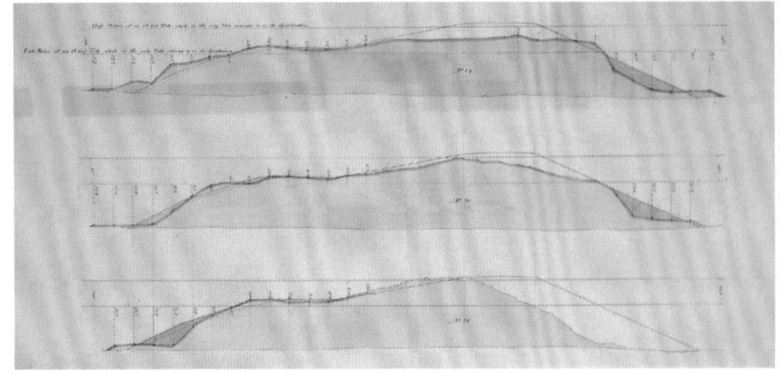

Fig 5.19
Cross-sections of Plymouth Breakwater showing the extent of the rubble and dressed stone.
(TNA ADM 140/377)

long with 1,050ft arms at each end, inclined inwards at an angle of 160 degrees. The footings beneath low-water level were to be formed of blocks of rubble weighing up to 5 tons, which were to be tipped, allowing wave action to dictate their angle of repose. Above low water the breakwater was to be constructed from granite and limestone masonry, carefully jointed and dovetailed together (Fig 5.19).

The magnitude of the project at a time of financial stringency meant it was not until January 1811 that the Admiralty felt able to authorise the scheme. Good limestone supplies were secured by the purchase of 25 acres for a quarry at Oreston, just over a mile up the River Plym where there was also a deep-water loading place.[74] A railway linked the quarry to the quay and to a fleet of 80-ton sailing vessels, 10 in number, probably designed jointly by Whidbey and Rennie. These vessels were possibly the first ever roll-on roll-off ships, and they had two railed decks equipped with retractable ramps to load the sturdy iron quarry trucks (Figs 5.20 and 5.21). Once at the site, they discharged their 5-ton stones over the stern. A further fleet of up to 45 smaller vessels transported smaller stones. By the summer of 1812, Whidbey had relinquished his post as master attendant at Woolwich and moved to Plymouth, where he was to remain for the rest of his career as resident engineer of the breakwater, retiring in 1830 at the age of 75.[75]

On 8 August 1812, the Prince Regent's birthday, the first stone was tipped amidst great ceremony. This was a mammoth undertaking in deep water exposed to storms and rough seas that could halt work for weeks on end. In 1812 the project was estimated to require 2 million tons of stone and to need 6 to 10 years to complete. Three years from the start, the nascent structure was already providing a degree of protection for ships in the Sound and was admired among others by Napoleon on his way to exile in St Helena. In 1819 the project employed 765 people, 398 in the quarries, 265 in the vessels and 102 on the breakwater. Serious storms in 1817 and especially in 1824 caused considerable structural damage, forcing

Fig 5.20 (below top) Drawing of one of the vessels specially built to transport stone from the quarry to the site of Plymouth Breakwater. (TNA ADM 140/387 pt 4)

Fig 5.21 (below bottom) Detail of the rail tracks on the deck of the stone vessel, showing arrangements for tipping the stone over the stern. (TNA ADM 140/387 pt 1)

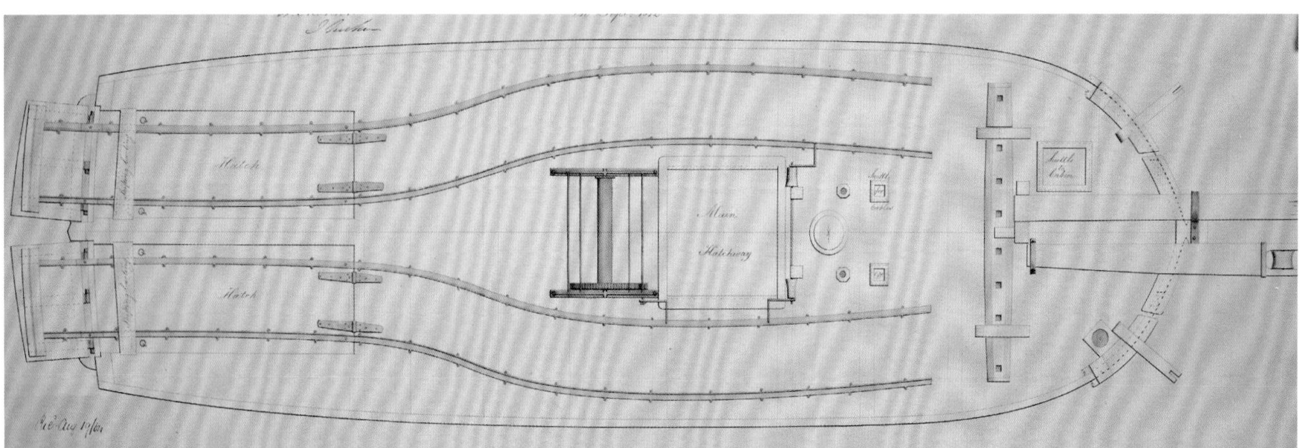

modifications to the original design, which in 1825 led to the need for an extra half a million tons of rock. In all, it took 53 years and some 4 million tons of stone to complete the breakwater, and it still requires continuous maintenance on account of its exposed position.[76]

In 1812 it had been estimated that Plymouth Breakwater would cost £1,051,000. By 1847, when the bulk of the work had been finished and its original scope considerably extended, it was reckoned that some £1,446,963 had been expended. Actual costs turned out to be less than had been later allowed for. This was a remarkable achievement, which shows the care with which the original contracts were drawn up by Rennie and his fellow engineers for quarrying and transporting the stone.[77] The breakwater transformed the usefulness of this western naval base. For the first time the fleet had an easily accessible, capacious and secure anchorage close to the dockyard. Samuel Smiles, writing as the project was almost complete, probably reflected a widespread sentiment: 'As forming a convenient and secure haven of refuge for merchant ships ... as a capacious harbour for vessels of war, wherein fifty ships of the line, besides frigates and smaller vessels, can at all times find safe anchorage – Plymouth Breakwater may in all respects be regarded as a magnificent work, worthy of a great maritime nation.'[78]

Expertise gained working in the hostile environment of Plymouth Sound was to be put to use, notably with the breakwaters at Alderney and Portland, and at the end of the 19th century with additional harbours of refuge and the naval bases at Gibraltar and Simon's Town. At this southern African base, a breakwater had to be thrust boldly into the Indian Ocean to enclose a massive dockyard extension, while at Gibraltar the works included a large, new commercial harbour.

6

Buildings of the Sailing Navy

The London headquarters and the telegraph system

The Admiralty and its subsidiary boards ran their widely scattered empire from a variety of buildings in London. By 1700, the Lords Commissioners of the Admiralty were established in Whitehall in newly completed premises. However, problems with the foundations led to their replacement by the present building, constructed between 1723 and 1726 to a design by Thomas Ripley who was to succeed Sir John Vanbrugh as Comptroller of the Works.[1] Ripley's design, with its ill-proportioned Ionic portico, attracted much criticism, although the general effect was improved by the addition in 1760–1 of Robert Adam's screen enclosing the courtyard and fronting Whitehall (Fig 6.1). In 1786 a new house for the First Lord was attached on the southern side, overlooking Whitehall and St James's Park to a design by S P Cockerell, newly appointed to the post of Inspector of Repairs.[2]

The Navy Board since 1654 had occupied

Fig 6.1
A late 19th-century photograph of Ripley's 1723 Admiralty in Whitehall, London, which replaced the first Admiralty building of 1695 on the same site. Both provided a combination of offices and official residence. The Adam screen was added in 1760–1. (BB67/08245)

Fig 6.2
The Strand elevation of Somerset House in London. The Navy Board moved here on completion of the offices in 1786, and they remained in Admiralty use until the late 19th century.
(BB69/04539)

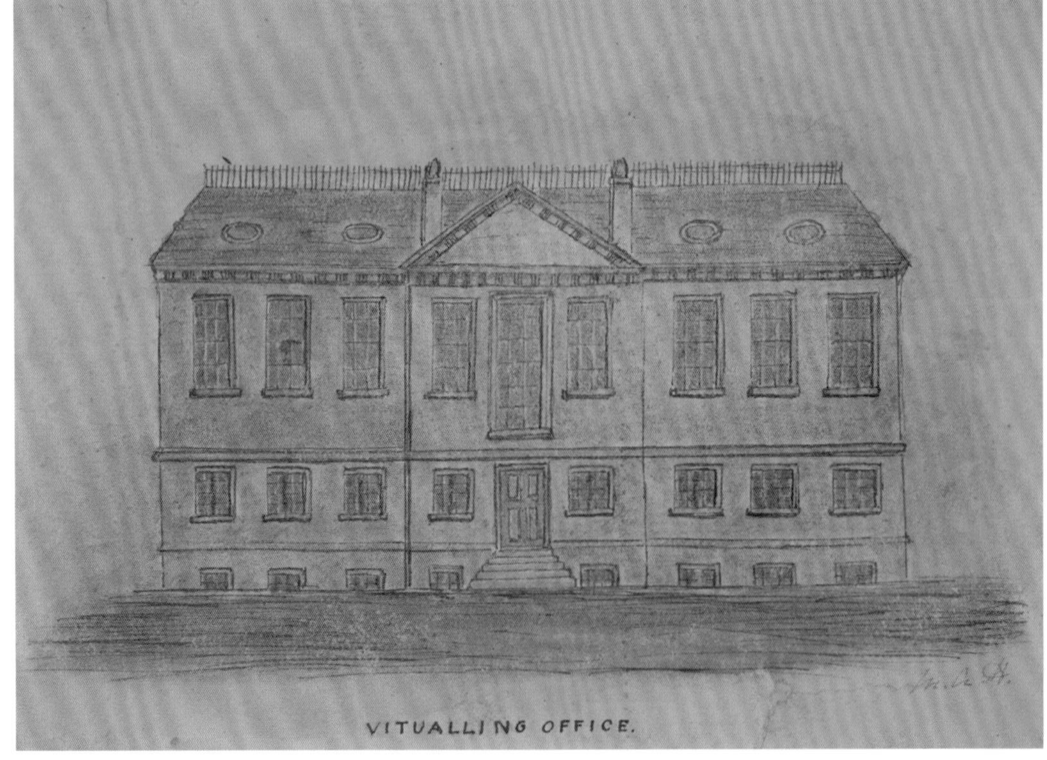

Fig 6.3
The Victualling Board headquarters on Tower Hill, London, was a comparatively modest building constructed in the 1720s. By 1800, the time of this watercolour by Mary Ann Hedger, the Board was operating at the Deptford victualling yard.
(City of London, London Metropolitan Archives)

premises in the city in Seething Lane, close to the Tower of London (*see* Fig 3.1). In 1786 it moved to Somerset House (Fig 6.2), which was designed by Sir William Chambers, following the 1775 Act of Parliament, to house a number of official and academic bodies in what was hoped would be mutually beneficial close proximity. The Victualling Board was based at its victualling yard on Tower Hill. During its latter years there, its office was a modest pedimented building, constructed between 1720 and 1726 (Fig 6.3).[3] From the mid-1740s it was based at new premises at the Royal Victoria Victualling Yard at Deptford (*see* Chapter 4). All these separate establishments provided living accommodation for the senior officials and their families, along with boardrooms for meetings (Fig 6.4). The exception was Somerset House, which was designed specifically as offices and meeting rooms.

After the administrative reorganisations of 1832, the offices at both Somerset House and the Royal Victoria Victualling Yard continued to function. The specialised nature of the work at the latter allowed it a more autonomous existence, but the former Navy Board operations at Somerset House required daily liaison and supervision from the Admiralty. This was perfectly possible, although inconvenient, but in 1868 the decision was taken to centralise operations in Whitehall. This meant converting what had essentially been a series of residences for the Lords Commissioners into something of a rabbit warren of offices.[4] These became steadily more crowded and less satisfactory as the work of the Admiralty grew in the latter part of the 19th century, and the Admiralty Works Department had many of its staff located

Fig 6.4
The Admiralty boardroom in London in 1894. The panelling here may have come from the earlier Admiralty building. Above the fireplace is the famous wind-direction indicator. (BL12810/007)

elsewhere in London. A series of proposals which included a variety of extensions and amalgamation in huge new premises with the War Office were proposed over the next decades, but came to nothing. Finally, in 1887, Leeming Brothers, the Halifax architects responsible for the abortive 1883 designs for a new Admiralty and War Office building, were authorised to construct an economical extension to the existing Admiralty. In the event, this turned out to be anything but economical, but the three great blocks constructed over the next 18 years round a courtyard to the rear of the Admiralty remain much as complete (Fig 6.5). Their design and use of red brick rather than stone attracted a similar degree of odium to that directed at Ripley's building nearly two centuries earlier.[5]

Communications between the London headquarters and the principal yards, fleet bases and anchorages were to be transformed at the end of the 18th century by the introduction of the semaphore telegraph system. In 1793 Claude Chappe's system had come into operation in France. The necessarily prominent locations of its apparatus meant that secrecy was impossible, and it was not long before details reached the Duke of York, Commander-in-Chief of the army, who passed them to the Admiralty. Their importance was immediately recognised, and after brief experiments the Admiralty in September 1795 authorised construction of two lines of shutter telegraphs (Fig 6.6) to link the Admiralty to Portsmouth and the Spithead anchorage and to Deal with its anchorage in the Downs. A spur line branching off near Faversham reached Sheerness. These were in operation by 1797, and in 1805 work was authorised to extend the Portsmouth line to Plymouth; two years later a new line was begun to link Great Yarmouth and its important roadstead, which was ready by June 1808. The responsibility for surveying the routes, setting up the 60 four-shutter

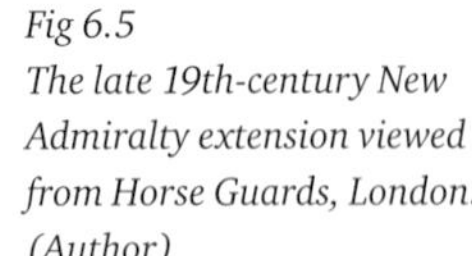

Fig 6.5
The late 19th-century New Admiralty extension viewed from Horse Guards, London. (Author)

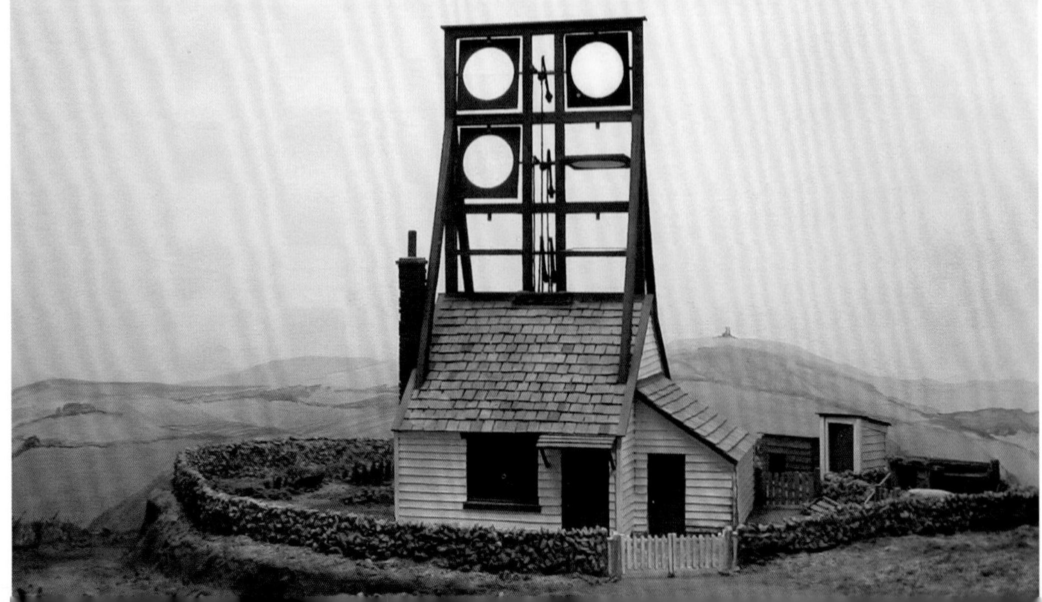

Fig 6.6
Model of one of the original shutter telegraph stations showing the temporary nature of the installations. (The Royal Signals Museum)

stations and ensuring their smooth operation fell to George Roebuck, appointed by the Admiralty as Inspector of Telegraphs, a post he was to hold until its abolition in 1816.[6]

Although the Admiralty had intended that the shutter telegraphs should be a wartime arrangement using temporary structures and had closed the system in 1814, their value was demonstrably important, enabling messages to pass between London and Portsmouth in about 15 minutes.[7] In 1815 a decision was taken to create a permanent system, this time using the more adaptable and distinguishable semaphore telegraphs and a signalling system derived from one largely devised and refined by Admiral Sir Home Popham, originally for use between warships. An experimental line was authorised in November 1815 from London to Chatham, from where semaphores mounted on ships in the Medway linked it to Sheerness.[8] Its success led to the construction of a permanent line to Portsmouth, later extended to Plymouth, and a second line linking the Admiralty to Chatham, Sheerness and Deal. A projected extension from Deal to Dover was not implemented, and a new line to Great Yarmouth was not even considered.

The semaphore stations were robustly constructed, their heights varying according to their location (Fig 6.7). The semaphore apparatus was constructed at Henry Maudslay's London factory, and Dollands supplied the telescopes. Numbers of these later telegraph towers remain, but the only one to retain its semaphore machinery is at Chatley Heath near Cobham on the London–Portsmouth line. The system remained in use until the end of 1847, when it was superseded by the electric telegraph, the wires mostly laid alongside the railways that now linked the capital with the coasts.[9]

Fig 6.7
Chatley Heath semaphore tower on the London–Portsmouth line. This line of semaphore towers superseded the earlier line of shutter telegraphs and was completed in 1822. This tower was restored by Surrey County Council and uniquely retains the original operating mechanism. The mast, with its pair of semaphore arms housed within it when not operating, is a modern replacement. (Author)

Dockyard buildings

Dockyards serving the sailing navy employed a multiplicity of trades and skills, which have left their mark in the surviving buildings associated with building, fitting out, maintaining and supplying the fleet. Along with all the industrial structures were the naval stores and the official houses and other buildings associated with the small resident yard populations during this period. By 1835, steam power, machine tools and other specialised processes, especially those involving the metal-working trades, had become well established, but their impact on dockyard landscapes was to remain relatively insignificant until a steam-driven fleet became a reality and metal replaced timber in warship construction. When King William IV died in 1837, such developments were largely in the future, and the dockyards retained their predominantly late 18th-century appearance. Dockyard manufacturing facilities until the late 1850s were principally geared to four principal materials used in the construction, fitting out and maintenance of sailing warships.

Timber – mainly oak, but also elm and pine – was purchased in vast quantities. The 2,162 tons of the hull of a first-rate such as HMS *Victory*, laid down in 1759, required timber from around 3,000 trees, the bulk arriving at the yards as whole trunks.[10] Finding and purchasing such quantities of timber was a perpetual task. Oak and elm were predominantly home grown, but between 1801 and 1812 the dockyards' annual requirements rose from 36,000 to 74,000 loads under the exigencies of war, and the Navy Board was increasingly forced to import hull timbers. Processing this timber employed 901 sawyers, because with the very limited exception of timber from the wood mills at Portsmouth, all timbers still had to be sawn by hand. Sawpits remained prominent features of the yards, though by 1812 Brunel's steam sawmill at Chatham was under construction.[11] Fir for masts and spars came from the Baltic countries and increasingly from North America and even New Zealand.[12] On the infrequent occasions when the Navy Board achieved its aim to hold a 3-year stock of timber to allow for proper seasoning ahead of use, every vacant space in the dockyards was filled with piles of tree trunks awaiting the sawyers.

Iron was needed in surprisingly large quantities for nails, hinges, mast hoops, galley fittings and as the component parts of equipment, varying from buckets to rudders and anchors. Its use increased steadily as warships became larger and when iron knees and straps were introduced on a regular basis from early in the 19th century. This increase is mirrored in the size of the dockyard smitheries, which by 1812 employed some 755 smiths and their servants. The Navy Board purchased the metal in a semi-processed state as wrought iron, but with warships being supplied with iron ballast 'pigs' at least as early as 1729, the purchase of cast iron was also growing in importance.[13]

Canvas was the third of the principal materials. As with timber, much of this was imported, at the start of the 18th century principally from the Low Countries, France and the German states, although from the reign of Henry VIII successive governments had encouraged home production of flax. The 'house for flax combers' recorded with the ropery buildings at Chatham in 1698 indicates that at least some of this was being used in cordage manufacture.[14] Much later, towards the end of the Napoleonic Wars, the navy was purchasing canvas from factories in Calcutta.[15] Initially the navy had contracted with private manufacturers to provide all its sails, but this was never an entirely satisfactory arrangement, and as early as 1608 there were widespread complaints about the quality of the canvas as well as suspicions about the honesty of some contractors.[16] In the 17th century, dockyard sail lofts were used for limited manufacturing, but it seems that most of the sailmakers' work involved repairing sails and maintaining those from ships in ordinary.

In 1716 the Admiralty finally lost patience with private sailmakers and ordered that the Navy Board 'should be directed to cause the sails for the ships of the Royal Navy to be made in His Majesty's yards for the future as hath been proposed, in regard the same may not only be much better performed, but as cheap also or cheaper'.[17] Following this decision, sail lofts in all the dockyards were improved. By 1722, Portsmouth employed 26 sailmakers, and by the end of the decade the Navy Board was commenting favourably on the better quality not just of the purchased canvas, but also of the sailmakers' workmanship. As a consequence, the Board felt able to recommend that the number of spare sails carried by warships could be reduced.[18]

Well before the end of the 18th century, sail production for the navy was closely regulated, from the quality of the bolts of canvas – each 38yd long and 2ft wide – to the strength of twine used for sewing the canvas and the number of stitches per yard.[19] The importance of sailmakers can be gauged by the size of a set of sails required by the first-rate *Royal George* of 1788. These weighed nearly 10 tons and in aggregate were said to cover an area of more than 2 acres.[20] By the late 18th century, Royal Navy ships generally carried a minimum of two suits of sails. Although the great majority of canvas went into sails, significant quantities were also used for hammocks, awnings, below-deck screens, waterproof coverings and the shutes, known as windsails, used to channel fresh air to the lower decks. In 1801, the Navy Board estimated its annual consumption of canvas exceeded 95,500 bolts, and by 1812 the 291 sailmakers in the home yards had long formed a significant proportion of the skilled workforce.[21]

The fourth material, also imported, was hemp for the standing and running rigging, the bolt ropes and head ropes for the sails, the guns' tackle, anchor cables and other miscellaneous uses. As with canvas, the navy's needs were enormous. A 74-gun third-rate warship at the end of the 18th century required cordage in 28 different circumferences, from ¾in to 18½in. It also required a considerable variety of lengths, ranging from 72ft long with a circumference of 14in to 26,718ft long with a circumference of 3½in. The largest cordage manufactured in the dockyard roperies was 25½in for the anchor cables of first-rate warships.[22] The spinning and laying stages of manufacturing the rope needed immensely long spaces; commercial ropemakers with limited capital generally carried out these processes in open-air ropewalks that were subject to the vagaries of the weather. The navy, crucially dependent on reliable supplies and with far greater financial resources, manufactured its cordage in buildings, although at some of the overseas yards there were small open-air ropewalks, and one was proposed at the new yard at Pembroke. The whole process was very labour intensive, with 1,465 ropemakers employed in the home yards in 1812 and additional dockyard workers needed for laying the largest cables.[23] The expense of such enormous buildings and difficulty accommodating them within the confines of a dockyard meant that only the home yards at Woolwich, Chatham, Portsmouth and Plymouth had roperies.[24]

Other materials used in significant amounts included lead, brass and copper, the last in greatly increased quantities following the decision in 1779 to sheath the underwater areas of the hulls of the entire fleet.[25] These materials generally arrived at the dockyards in sheet form for final cutting and trimming, as no royal dockyard was equipped with smelting furnaces or rolling machinery before the early 19th century. Tar or pitch and the ingredients for paint and varnish similarly needed further processing and mixing before use.

Before the spread of canals in the latter part of the 18th century and then railways in the second quarter of the 19th century, overland transport for heavy and bulky goods remained very slow and expensive. Defoe in the 1720s recorded that roads in the heavily wooded clay lands of the Kent and Sussex Weald were impassable in wet seasons for teams of oxen drawing a tug or cart laden with a tree trunk and noted that 'sometimes 'tis two or three years before it gets to Chatham'.[26] Faced with the need to be able to react quickly to unexpected demands for repairing vessels or mobilising and equipping warships, the Navy Board not surprisingly endeavoured to stockpile significant reserves of stores and materials in every dockyard.

Naval storehouses

Maintaining quantities of stores required substantial warehousing, especially at fleet bases. Apart from unsawn timber and later on iron anchors that could also be kept in the open, everything needed to be secured under cover, not least to minimise pilfering. A substantial number of brick and stone naval storehouses survive from the 18th century and are among the most handsome of dockyard buildings. Most were designed to be general purpose. It was rare for them to hold only one particular type of item, although one or more rooms inside might be appropriated for such a specific purpose. At dockyards with warships in ordinary, a number were designated as 'lay-apart stores', where equipment from decommissioned warships was kept, laid apart and separate, usually in secure timber-latticed spaces to await return to their particular ships. Other storehouses, designated as 'present use', housed the myriad of items of equipment needed by warships being commissioned for service. Increasingly, these buildings were located close to where vessels were fitted out, in the same way

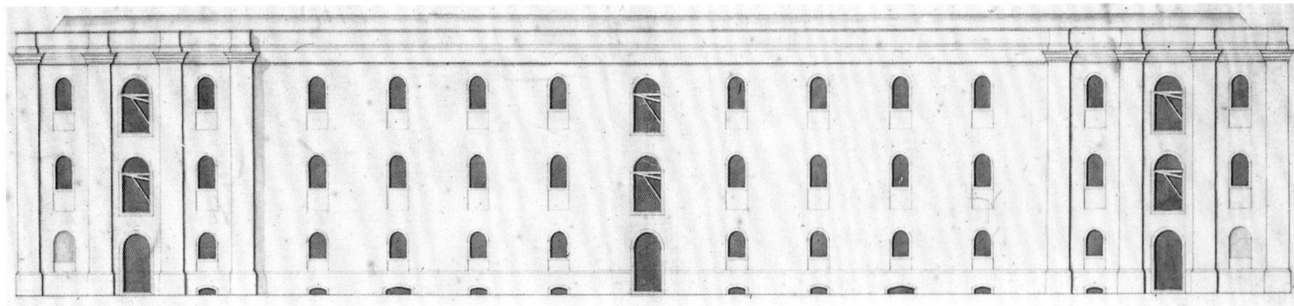

Fig 6.8
The 1718 cordage and tar storehouse on Anchor Wharf at Chatham Dockyard, the first naval storehouse to be designed with a view to ease of stores' handling in mind. (DoE)

that iron stores tended to be close to the dockyard smitheries.

Naval storehouses of the 17th century appear to have been designed with little thought for the storekeepers. The only access was through doors that were frequently approached up steps, while the interiors were subdivided into what must have been inconveniently small rooms. It was little wonder that stores were often reported in disarray and spoilt. The first recognisably modern naval storehouse was a cordage and tar storehouse built next to the ropery at Chatham in 1718 (Fig 6.8). Ground-floor access was on the level, the floors were open plan, and there were loading bays with wall cranes at regular intervals. This was closely paralleled by two contemporary and surviving ordnance storehouses at Morice Yard, Plymouth Dock, that had wooden railways to help shift ordnance within the buildings.[27] These features became standard in nearly every subsequent dockyard general storehouse, although interiors tended to be divided into large spaces by cross-walls, later provided with fireproof iron doors.

Only with the Anchor Wharf stores of the late 18th century at Chatham did naval storehouses rival the scale of some of the largest of the warehouses of the commercial docks, such as George Gwilt's slightly younger North Quay warehouses in the West India Docks in east London.[28] The generous provision of new storehouses in the dockyards between 1760 and the completion of works in Sheerness some 60 years later meant that very few were subsequently built for the navy. Storehouses that survived air raids in the Second World War generally remained in use into the 1970s, when changing working practices made the majority redundant.

A multiplicity of specialised storehouses was also developed over the years for materials such as hemp, which needed cool, dry conditions, and flammable substances like tar, train oil and some paints, which were increasingly kept in brick-vaulted rooms to lessen the spread of fire. As late as 1912, Chatham had a substantial storehouse just for candles; wisely, this was placed alongside the oil store at some remove from any other building.[29]

Specialised stores for planks and masts were to be found in every yard. With few exceptions, these were single-storey, timber-framed and weatherboarded buildings filled with racking. To save dockyard space, they were sometimes built partly over the associated mast ponds which stored the pine timbers waiting shaping into masts and spars. To prevent the timbers from drying out and splitting, they were kept in ponds, held in racks fixed into two or more lines of submerged brick arches. When the timbers were needed, they were hauled up slips into the adjacent working mast houses. The majority of mast ponds were filled in and built over once the navy changed to steam propulsion; uniquely, Chatham retains its original two mast ponds (Fig 6.9). The south mast pond was excavated in the second half of the 17th century; it was filled in during the latter part of the 19th century and used for open storage. The north mast pond, dug in 1702, is still largely intact and remains water filled.[30]

Fig 6.9
Part of the 1774 model of Chatham Dockyard showing the two mast ponds with their timber racks. In the foreground are the 1753 masthouses and mould loft. The model is now in Chatham Historic Dockyard. (Author)

Buildings of the timber trades

The bulk of the materials flowing into the dockyards were for warship building, refitting or repairing. Constructing a sailing warship remained very much a craft industry, with few individual timbers or items of equipment being replicated in large numbers to identical sizes. Shipwrights generally were by far and away the largest group of workers in the home yards. Towards the end of 1812, the 4,214 shipwrights on the home dockyard payrolls formed nearly 30 per cent of dockyard employees.[31] Once a warship's plans had been drawn out by the master shipwright and agreed by the Navy Board, the shipbuilding process itself began on the floor of the dockyard mould loft. This was described in the late 17th century as being 'laid very smooth and even, and to render the Marks, which among shipwrights are generally of Chalk, the more conspicuous, the Floor is wash'd over with black size'.[32] On this mould loft floor, under the supervision of the master shipwright, the cross-sections of a new warship were drawn out full-size with chalk from his scale drawings. Later shipwrights tended to scribe lines on the mould floor with a scrieve hook rather than use chalk. Fir boards or battens ¾in thick were then joined and shaped to match the outlines of each of the timbers forming the principal frames, and these moulds were carefully taken to the sawyers to act as templates for cutting the timbers for the shipwrights.

Apart from being smooth and even, a mould floor needed to be as large as possible and completely free of obstructions such as pillars. These requirements were most easily met on the upper floors of dockyard buildings, but the growing size of 18th-century warships in turn forced the construction of larger mould floors, very few of which now remain. Scribed lines of part of a ship from what may be the earliest surviving mould floor remain on the top floor of the 1723 storehouse at Chatham, now the Clocktower Storehouse.[33] At Portsmouth, part of 25 Storehouse, one of a handsome set of four storehouses and workshops that framed the view of the dry docks from the officers' terrace, was used in part as a mould loft after its completion in the 1780s. Others are known only from records or illustrations, such as the handsome arcaded mould loft incorporated in the plank houses at the inner mast pond at Plymouth (Fig 6.10).

The change to metal warships in the 1860s saw their forms continuing to be laid off in the same way on the mould floors, with the shape of every rib carefully delineated. But now the lines were copied on to 'scrive' or scrieve' boards, which were taken to the perforated slabs in the smitheries to guide the teams of smiths preparing to bend the new warship's frame angles to the correct profiles.[34] As metal warships grew ever larger, new scrieve floors had to be provided. At South Yard, Devonport, a new mould floor above the sawmills was included in

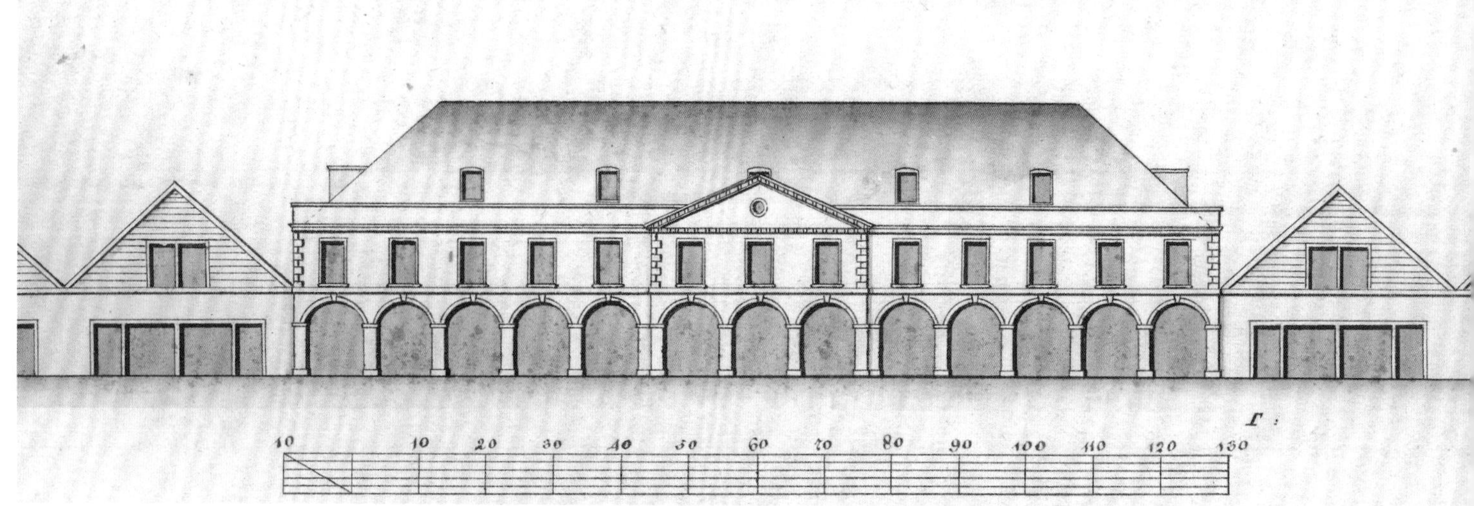

Fig 6.10
The mould loft at Plymouth Dockyard, constructed between 1773 and 1782, its design perhaps reflecting the pride of the master shipwright. As at Chatham, this was a timber-framed building, but its ground floor was a boat store. (NMRN Plans of HM Dockyard, Portsmouth, c 1786, MS 1993/443)

the 1859/60 estimates, and when this proved inadequate a few years later, Slip 5, roofed and conveniently adjacent to the smithery, was floored over and turned into what was probably the largest of all dockyard scrieve floors.[35]

The absence of other surviving 18th-century examples of mould lofts is compensated by the survival at Chatham of a remarkable timber-framed mould loft. In the summer of 1753 the yard began construction of a set of eight single-storey, timber-framed and timber-clad working mast houses adjacent to the south mast pond (Fig 6.11). In October the master shipwright petitioned to be allowed to build a mould loft over the central two mast houses, because the existing mould loft was too small. This was agreed, and the building seems to have been completed within a year. The new mould floor, some 119ft long and 55ft wide, was possibly the largest in any royal dockyard at that time. The roof over the mould floor was carried on 13 tie-beams, which were 57ft long. Running across the top of these tie-beams from a small drawing office in the roof space was a narrow walkway to allow the master shipwright to overlook the floor below. The only significant alteration to the building since its completion was the modification of the two adjacent mast house roofs in 1833 to provide additional space for storing boards and moulds. Two years later, the present mould floor was laid over the original one.

By the time the mould loft went out of use in 1888, a roll-call of both wooden and iron-clad warships had had their lines drawn out here.[36] By far and away the most famous, although documentary proof is lacking, is HMS *Victory*. A new first-rate warship would have needed the largest available mould floor, and there can be little doubt that when the keel of HMS *Victory* was laid down in No. 2 Dock on 23 July 1759, her lines would have been drawn out and her moulds prepared in this new building. In due course, her first masts and yards were almost certainly formed in the ground-floor mast houses. Working mast houses, as the name implies, were where masts were fashioned by the mast makers before being stored in ordinary mast houses. Initially, only the lower masts were fitted to *Victory*, because, once floated out, she was placed in ordinary, and her first sailing trials did not take place until 1769. In 1973, during work on the mould loft, a timber was found stating that the lines of 19 warships and their names remained on the original mould floor sealed over in 1835.[37]

Timbers for a warship's hull would be sawn to size by saw teams at the sawpits in the dockyard and then trimmed to their final fit by the shipwrights constructing the vessel on the building slip or, before the practice was banned in 1764, possibly in a dry dock. Sawing was a labour-intensive and exhausting occupation, especially for the pitman. In 1812 the Navy

Fig 6.11
The 1753 mast houses and mould loft at Chatham Dockyard after conservation in the late 1980s.
(Author)

Board had 901 sawyers on the payroll; Portsmouth with 240 employed the largest number and Sheerness with 55 the fewest. Sawpits were frequently arranged in batches of a dozen or more in the larger building yards, while even a small yard like Sheerness was provided with around 24 sawpits during its rebuilding in the early 1820s, some years after steam sawing had been introduced up-river at Chatham.[38] For convenience, such sawpits were located as close as possible to the dry docks and building slips. In comparison, a small overseas base such as English Harbour in Antigua was equipped with only a pair of pits, sufficient for minor repairs to warships.

In the home yards, most of the sawyers' output went to the shipwrights who were building or repairing vessels, but from the 1770s a deliberate policy of careful seasoning was introduced, and a significant element of their work was cutting timber for seasoning under cover in new sheds. The use of unseasoned timber in warship construction had long been identified as a prime cause of dry rot, but with funds always tight in peacetime, the Navy Board rarely had the opportunity to acquire sufficient stocks of timber to ensure a supply of seasoned wood when war led to an accelerated shipbuilding programme. In the early 1770s the Earl of Sandwich had identified this as a major problem, complaining in 1773 of 'the enormous expense in renewing … [warships] six or seven years after they have been built'.[39] In 1771 he had inspected HMS *Ardent,* a third-rate of 64 guns completed at Hull in 1764 at a cost of £23,000 and laid up at Chatham, where Sandwich found that rot had occasioned repairs estimated at £17,000.[40] That spring, a standing order was issued to all the yards on the proper use of seasoned timber and was backed by funding for the purchase of more adequate stocks. A modular design was produced for timber seasoning sheds that were 45ft deep (*see* Fig 6.12), and it was originally estimated that sheds with a total run of 7,470ft would be needed to hold a 3-year supply of timber.[41] This was reduced to 2,990ft, which was still a sizeable total to fit into yards where space was at a premium. The last two groups of seasoning sheds to survive are at Chatham Historic Dockyard (Fig 6.13), where they were built between 1771 and 1775 as part of two batches of six groups totalling 600ft ordered for this yard.[42] These sheds were the first dockyard structures to be built to a common design, and although architecturally humble, they helped improve the longevity of the navy's ships in advance of the Napoleonic Wars.

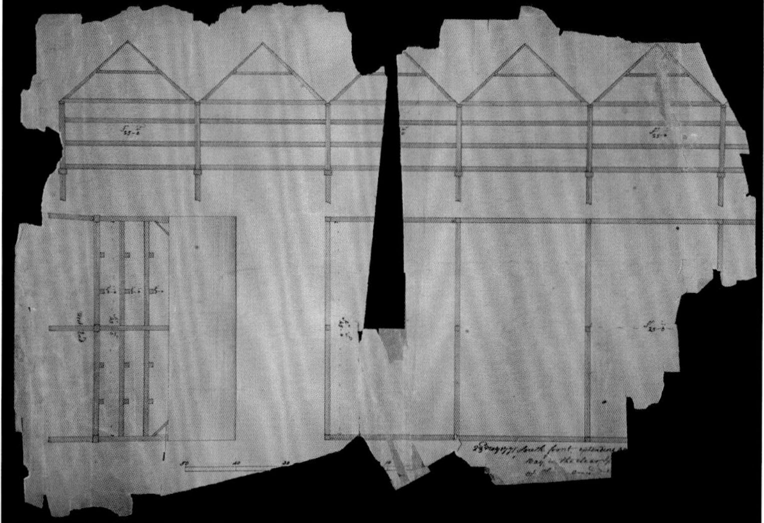

Fig 6.12
A 1771 drawing of the proposed timber seasoning sheds, the first industrial structures built to a common design in the royal dockyards. (TNA ADM 140/538)

Fig 6.13
The last two surviving groups of timber seasoning sheds at Chatham Dockyard. (Author)

Fig 6.14
The handsome workshop at Devonport Dockyard was occupied by the house carpenters, joiners and other woodworking trades. This design resembled contemporary storehouses, but the interiors of such buildings were usually subdivided to accommodate different crafts and trades. This example, like most of the officers' terrace to the rear, did not survive the Second World War.
(Navy and Army Illustrated *2 Nov 1901, 167)*

Timber from the sheds went to the shipwrights and also to the house carpenters and joiners, two other woodworking trades present in significant numbers, with 718 carpenters and 405 joiners on yard payrolls in 1812.[43] The distinction between these two trades is not always clear, and there was probably a good deal of overlap, but the house carpenters concentrated on building and maintaining dockyard buildings and the joiners on providing fixtures and fittings for the warships. At Chatham in 1740, where money was especially short, a new timber-framed building was proposed to house both trades, but in 1742 it was more expensively constructed in bricks, matching those of the adjacent officers' terrace. This building still stands, though disfigured by modern alterations.[44] A combined workshop and storehouse was built at Portsmouth in 1786, where it still remains (*see also* Fig 6.14). Originally it was divided between storerooms, offices and small workshops housing wheelwrights, blockmakers and capstan makers, trades normally represented by a couple of men in each yard.

A few skills were so specialised that they were limited to particular yards. In 1812, oar makers were only to be found in the Thames and Medway yards, with one apiece, while carvers were represented by two at Chatham and a single one at Deptford.[45] The architectural and archaeological evidence for these varied occupations is usually lacking, and we are generally dependent for knowledge of their location on the survival of dockyard records.

The small steam-powered Wood Mills built at Portsmouth in 1799 with its specialist machinery was the forerunner of the huge workshops of 50 years later with their power-driven machine tools (*see* Chapter 2). These made possible the Victorian navy's steam-driven metal warships, at the same time replacing many of the older craft skills with new ones in the metal trades.

Dockyard buildings of the metal trades

In a Georgian dockyard, specialised and architecturally distinct manufactories were comparatively few in type. Dockyard smitheries were most easily identified by the smoke of their forges and noise of metal working and almost certainly formed component parts of every royal dockyard from the start. When laying out the new dockyard at Plymouth in the 1690s, the smithery was located well away from other buildings because of its fire risk. However, such isolation was not always possible or convenient, and in most yards they were located near to the slips and docks where the shipwrights worked. Until the early 19th century, their fixed equipment was mostly limited to numbers of manually operated cranes for heavy lifting and

Fig 6.15
The anchor smiths' shop at Portsmouth c 1803. Captain Durrant's sketch appears to show the fluke of an anchor being heated in one of the forges. Note the manually powered bellows and the substantial wooden crane with its chain supporting the anchor's shank.
(Hampshire Museums Durrant collection FA1990.23.119, DPAAQF16)

a series of hand-operated forges for working the wrought iron, each with its own chimney.

Dockyard smitheries generally undertook all types of ferrous work, and as the iron industry developed and reliable supplies of quality bar iron became more abundant and consequently cheaper, the range of uses on warships grew. In the 1780s Gabriel Snodgrass, the East India Company Surveyor, had introduced into new Company ships the use of iron knees, riders and braces. In May 1805 the Navy Board followed suit, additionally allowing their use in ships under repair – many of those to be seen on HMS *Victory* date from her 'great repair' of 1814–16.[46] This considerably extended the work of the dockyard smitheries, already under growing pressure as warships grew in size and required larger anchors. Apart from a ship's guns, which were the responsibility of the Board of Ordnance, anchors were the largest iron items on a warship, and at a number of the major yards in the 18th century anchor smiths developed as a distinctive and specialised group, equipped with very large forges and lifting tackle (Fig 6.15). The completion by 1806 of an iron furnace at Portsmouth beside the smithery allowed the smiths to experiment with cast-iron anchors, and in 1819 the Navy Board ordered trials on HMS *Spartan* of a 'mixed metal anchor ... cast after a plan suggested by Mr Kingston, Master Millwright at Portsmouth'.[47]

Between 1700 and 1835 the smitheries in every dockyard were rebuilt and expanded to keep up with demand, and no unaltered examples from this period now survive. However, the South Smithery at Devonport, greatly extended in the mid-1850s, does incorporate part of the 'smiths' shop and coal yard', which was built in 1776 and in turn had replaced the original late 17th-century building.[48] At Portsmouth, the smithery was possibly rebuilt or enlarged three times in the

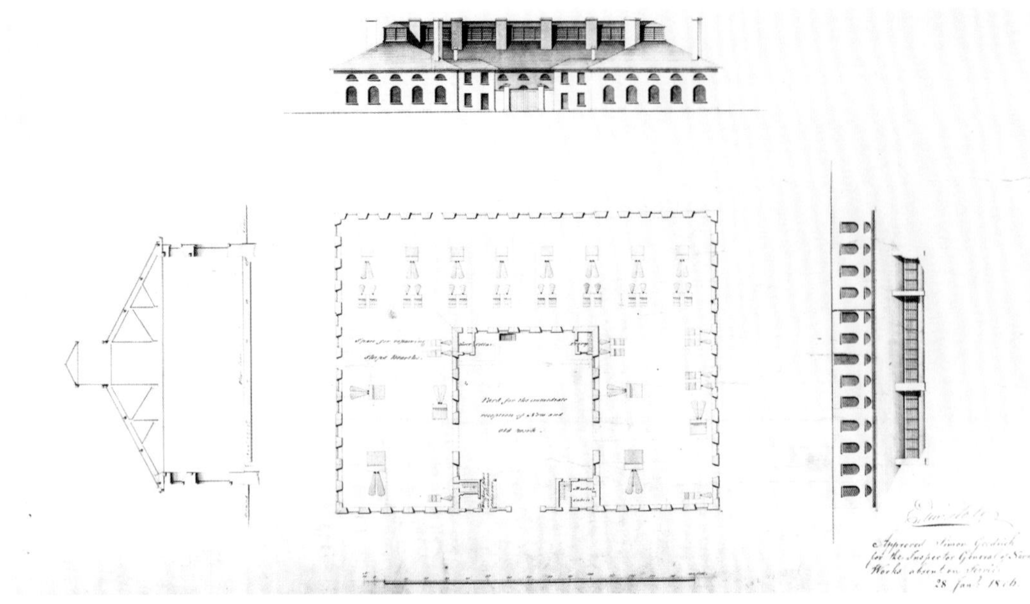

Fig 6.16
Holl's 1806 drawing for the new smithery at Chatham Dockyard. This survives as the core of No. 1 Smithery, along with much of ts equipment.
(© National Maritime Museum, Greenwich, London, neg. C7520D)

Fig 6.17
Steam hammers from No. 1 Smithery at Chatham Dockyard photographed in 1982 after their relocation to the Victorian dockyard. They are now in the care of the Chatham Historic Dockyard Trust.
(Author)

18th century, before a different site was selected on the reclaimed 'new ground' at the north end of the yard. In 1794 the new smithery was nearing completion,[49] and its three ranges grouped round an enclosed courtyard closely mirror the plan adopted a decade later by Holl at Chatham.

The most complete of the Georgian smitheries, although later considerably altered and extended, is the former No. 1 Smithery at Chatham. This was the first to be built after the appointment of the Inspector General of Naval Works. Both Bentham and John Rennie senior were involved in its construction and equipping after the dockyard officers had put forward initial proposals for a new building in September 1805, at an estimated cost of £16,305.[50] The following January Edward Holl, clearly working closely with Simon Goodrich, drew up the spacious quadrangular design that was completed by July 1809 (Fig 6.16).[51] Perhaps surprisingly, on the recommendation of Rennie, the forges were traditionally equipped with individual bellows rather than a steam-driven 'blowing engine' favoured by Bentham.[52] Three years after its completion, 106 smiths worked here out of the total of 755 smiths and assistants then employed in the dockyards.[53] The building was later extended and re-equipped on several occasions, and it remained in use until 1974, in later years playing a major part in the submarine building programme at this Medway yard. Much of its equipment survives (*see* Fig 6.17), and part of the building now houses the national collection of ship models.[54]

Early steam power in the royal dockyards

One of Bentham's prime aims as Inspector General had been to introduce mechanical power into the royal yards to drive machinery, improve efficiency, reduce labour costs and allow the introduction of new manufacturing processes. By the time of his departure, steam power was playing a significant and expanding role, while the machinery and mass-production methods of the Block Mills had made the Royal Navy in this instance a world leader in industrialisation. Key buildings and, in a number of important instances, their machinery remain from this pioneering phase of mechanisation.

When Bentham took up his post, the dockyards were almost totally reliant on human muscles. A century earlier, Edmund Dummer had installed at Portsmouth a horse gin to power a set of chain pumps that emptied his new dry dock, which could also be driven by a waterwheel (*see* Chapter 5).[55] At the time, the Portsmouth dry dock was the only one requiring such mechanical assistance; the few other dry docks were sufficiently shallow to allow water to drain out by gravity at low tides. As new dry docks were constructed in the course of the 18th century, or existing ones enlarged, further horse gins were added at Portsmouth and Plymouth. By 1761 Plymouth had a double and a single horse gin,[56] while the concentration of dry docks at Portsmouth by 1796 required three double horse gins.[57] A horse gin consisted of a large, geared wheel set above the height of a horse on a vertical axle. One or more horses was harnessed to the perimeter. Walking round a circular track beneath the wheel, their motion was transmitted to the chain pumps from the geared wheel by a horizontal shaft and bevel gears. A double gin had two horse wheels on opposite sides of the sets of chain pumps. Such devices were common on large farms by the early 19th century for driving threshing machinery. None of the Thames or Medway yards needed pumped drainage for dry docks before the 19th century, when they made the transition directly to steam pumping. The only other places where horse gins were to be found were in tarring houses attached to the roperies at Chatham and Plymouth and at the double ropehouse at Portsmouth, where its precise use remains unknown. Bentham early on had investigated the possibility of using a huge overshot waterwheel, supplied by a long leet, to power machinery in the carpenters' and joiners' shop at Plymouth, but nothing came of the proposal.[58]

Portsmouth Dockyard offered the best opportunities for the introduction of steam power, with its extensive refitting and maintenance work on the fleet and its concentration of modern dry docks, which had a partly linked system of culverts combining gravity and mechanical drainage. In 1797 Bentham noted that two further dry docks then under construction, together with the deepening of the reservoir – the former North Basin now used as the sump into which the docks drained – would be beyond the capacity of the great battery of 16 horse-driven chain pumps that emptied the reservoir. At the time, the Inspector General was hoping to introduce some of his powered woodworking machinery at Hobbs and Hellyer's shipyard near Southampton, where two of his experimental vessels were then under construction. Various delays and problems caused this proposal to be abandoned. Instead, in April 1798 Bentham obtained Admiralty approval to switch the machinery, including a small steam engine designed by James Sadler (Fig 6.18), to Portsmouth Dockyard. The steam engine and a pump were installed alongside the existing chain pumps at the reservoir, partly replacing one of the horse gins. It was planned to use the steam engine to work the pump at night and to power the sawing machinery during the day.[59] Although a 1797 plan proposed

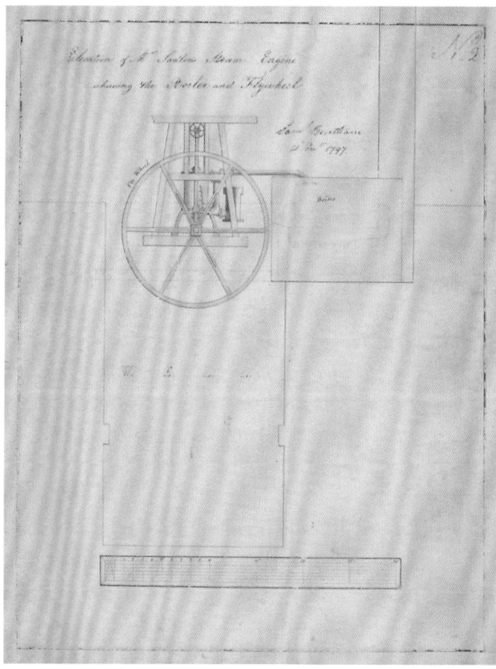

Fig 6.18
'Elevation of Mr Sadler's Steam Engine showing the Boiler and Flywheel'. This drawing, signed by Bentham on 21 December 1797, ushered in the age of steam power in the royal dockyards.
(TNA ADM 140/496 pt 2)

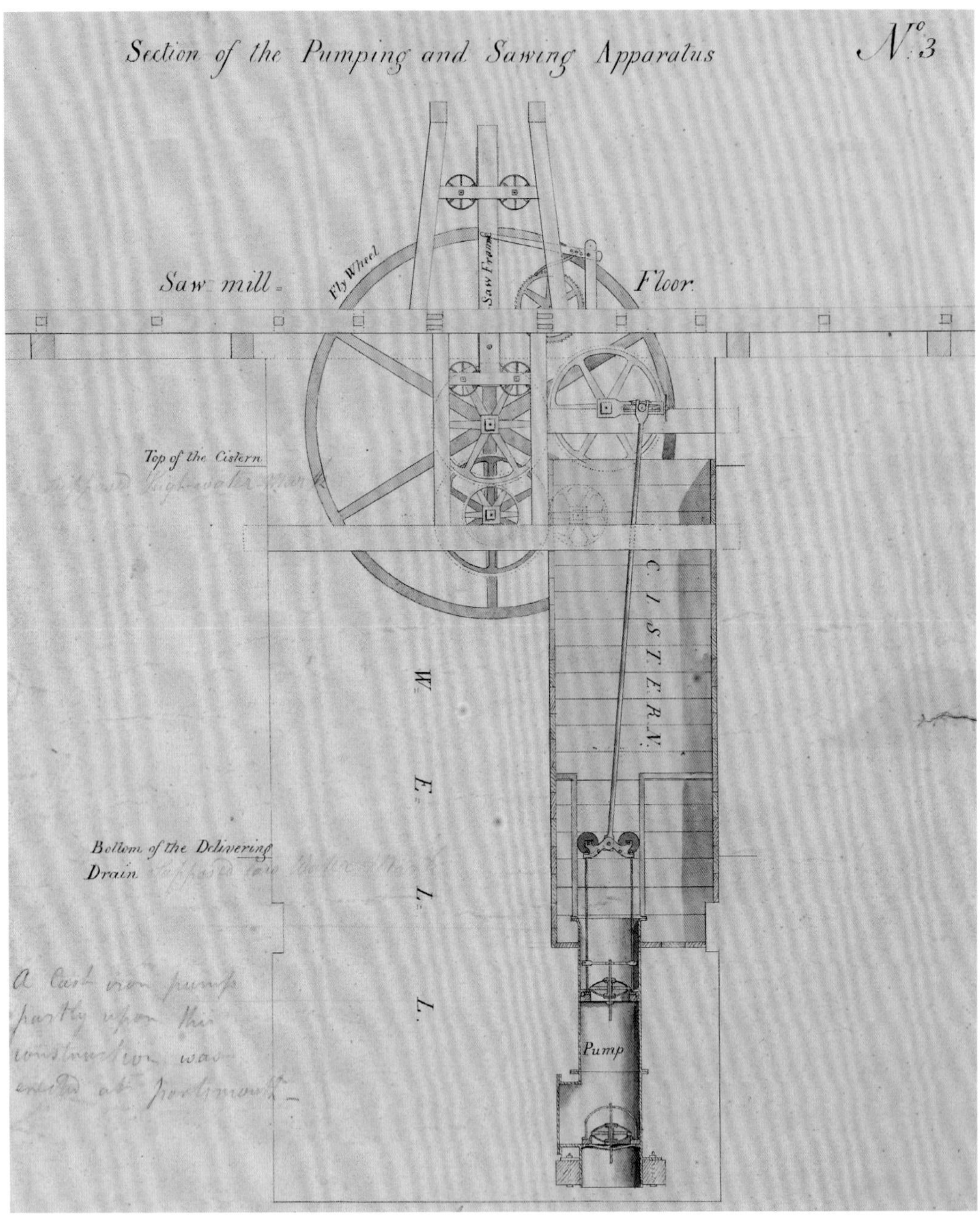

Fig 6.19
A 1797 drawing of the reservoir pump at Portsmouth Dockyard. There is no evidence that the sawmill machinery, illustrated here, was constructed. (TNA ADM 140/496 pt 3)

a sawmill above the horse gins, there is some doubt whether this part of the scheme was implemented (Fig 6.19).

The Royal Navy's steam age can be said to have begun in March 1799, when Sadler's table engine was first put to work pumping the reservoir.[60] The walls of the engine house still exist within the south range of the subsequent wood mills designed by Bentham early in 1802. Six months later, he revived in a more elaborate form an earlier proposal by Samuel Wyatt to cover in the adjacent reservoir. Bentham's scheme had two tiers of brick vaults, the lower space to continue as a sump for the adjacent docks, while the upper tier he optimistically assumed could be used for storage, though this proved too damp.[61] Construction of the vaults began in the spring of 1800, their top at ground level providing a substantial area on which Bentham could build his wood mills.

The success of the Sadler engine enabled Bentham to persuade the Admiralty early in 1800 to order a double-acting beam engine with a 21ft flywheel from Boulton and Watt. This was partly to provide an alternative source of power when the Sadler engine was inoperative, but mainly to increase the power available for woodworking machinery. The parts of the Boulton and Watt engine arrived at Portsmouth by sea from Bristol in the autumn, by which time the typical Boulton and Watt narrow, three-storey engine house must have been well under construction. This was located to the west of the existing Sadler engine house, on the opposite side of the chain pumps. The shell of this building and the frame of the engine also remain embedded in the existing south range of the wood mills.[62]

Construction of the two parallel ranges of the wood mills began in April 1802, as soon as the new vaults were sufficiently advanced to provide a base. The buildings were substantially complete by May 1803 when war was renewed with Napoleonic France. Bentham's woodworking machinery, largely for sawing, was concentrated in the northern building, with power transmitted by line shafting from the engines in the south range. The flat roofs of both ranges carried large water tanks that supplied a fire main laid around the yard as well as within the wood mills; in 1806 a trial of this system showed that a jet of water could be thrown as high as a two-storey building.[63] Although Bentham's woodworking machinery marked a significant evolution in mechanical sawing, any fame it might have achieved was to be eclipsed by the new block-making machinery, the first set of which arrived here in the spring of 1803. This was barely a year after Bentham had taken the inventor, Marc Brunel, to see the Admiralty Board to secure their backing for his invention.

For Bentham to realise his aims of increasing productivity and efficiency by using mechanical power in the dockyards, he needed simple repetitive tasks capable of being powered by steam engines. But warship building had always been very much a craft skill, with very few such opportunities. Dock pumping and limited steam sawing had more or less exhausted contemporary possibilities. When Brunel had put his ideas to Bentham for manufacturing ships' blocks entirely by machinery, he immediately appreciated the significance of the proposals. Ships' blocks were among comparatively few items needed by the navy in very large quantities in a series of standard sizes for standing and running rigging and for warships' gun carriages. A first-rate such as HMS *Victory* required around 1,700 blocks, while the navy as a whole consumed around 100,000 a year, mostly bought from private contractors.

Brunel's genius lay in breaking down the methods of manufacturing the blocks into some 15 separate and distinct operations, and then designing simple, accurate and robust machinery for each stage of the process, while ensuring the machinery could be operated by relatively unskilled workmen. This last point was important, as skilled labour was expensive and in short supply, and it chimed with Bentham's own views honed by his earlier experiences setting up factories in Russia.[64] Brunel had the good fortune early on to establish contact with Henry Maudslay, probably the finest mechanical engineer of the day. Maudslay collaborated closely with Brunel, modifying and improving his designs and possibly suggesting that the frames should be of metal rather than wood, so increasing their strength and precision and thus allowing faster and more accurate operation. Maudslay's workshop initially made the set of models used to demonstrate the proposals to the Board of Admiralty, now in the National Maritime Museum, and then made the three sets of 45 full-size machines that were delivered to Portsmouth between 1803 and March 1805. This was a considerable capital investment by the navy, and the total cost just of the block-making machinery came to £36,798 14s 1d. Of this sum, just under a third was for materials and the rest was workmanship.[65]

The machines were mostly located in a new single-storey building linking the two ranges of the wood mills (Fig 6.20), with a number also placed in the north range of the mills. The fame of the machines soon resulted in the entire group being known as the Block Mills. The machinery was driven from overhead line shafts powered by the engines in the south range (Fig 6.21). Installation was the responsibility of Bentham's small team, especially Simon Goodrich who was also busy with the adjacent metal mills, which have long been demolished. By 1808 the Block Mills were achieving an annual output of some 130,000 blocks, this pioneering factory allowing the navy to manufacture its total requirements (Figs 6.22 and 6.23).[66] In 1911 electric motors replaced the steam engines, and production continued on an increasingly limited scale into the mid-1960s (Fig 6.24). A number of the original machines along with the overhead line shafts remain in the building, and a set is in the Science Museum at London. The building itself was immaculately conserved in 2006 (Fig 6.25).

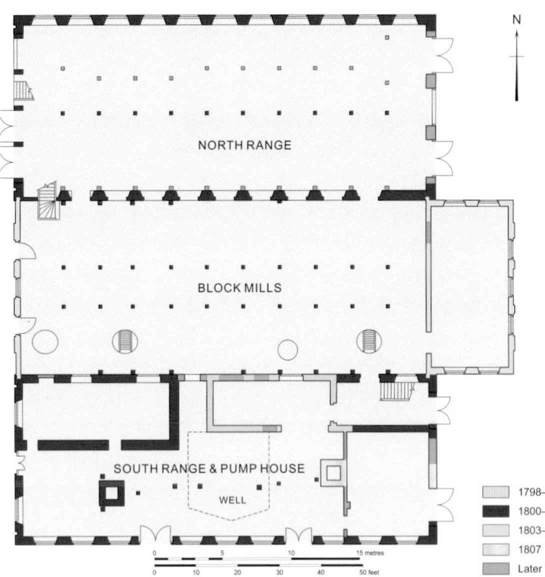

Fig 6.20 (right)
Plan of the Block Mills at Portsmouth Dockyard showing the evolution of the building.
(EH)

Fig 6.21 (far right)
The interior of the central range of Portsmouth Dockyard Block Mills in 2005, looking east. This shows the handsome turned wooden columns and the overhead line shafts, a mid-19th-century replacement for a similar system devised by Bentham, Brunel and Goodrich in 1805.
(Author)

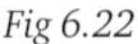

Fig 6.22
A rare photograph taken in October 1897 showing the Block Mills at Portsmouth Dockyard to the left of the two covered docks. This is the only known photograph to show the building with its boiler chimneys. To the left of the Block Mills is Greene's huge smithery of 1852–5. Its four corner chimneys and large central one graphically illustrate the growing scale of 19th-century industrial buildings in the royal yards.
(© National Maritime Museum, Greenwich, London, neg. N11569)

Fig 6.23
A shaping machine in operation in the 1890s at Portsmouth Dockyard Block Mills, with a partly formed block visible.
(Roland 1899, 52)

Fig 6.24
A scoring machine cutting a groove for a rope. This was photographed in 1965, the last year of block production in the building. (DoE-Author)

Fig 6.25
The Block Mills at Portsmouth Dockyard in 2009. One of the culverts of the dock drainage system is clearly visible in the north wall of No. 1 Basin. (Author)

The Block Mills were used in part as a test bed that eventually and indirectly led to Marc Brunel's only other major collaborative project with the Admiralty. Brunel had used some of his time at Portsmouth in 1805–6, during the installation and bedding-down of the block-making machinery, to experiment there with mechanical saws of his own invention.[67] Some of this work was to bear fruit a little later in his Battersea sawmills, and the further experience gained here led him in 1811 to propose that a number of sawmills should be installed in the principal dockyards. Brunel calculated that the daily output of the 300 pairs of hand sawyers employed in the dockyards amounted to some 66,000ft of timber, of which he reckoned that 40,000ft could be cut more economically and efficiently by machinery. To do this, he offered to supply the Admiralty with four identical sawmills, each equipped with a 24hp steam engine, a wrought-iron boiler and cast-iron machinery for eight saw frames.[68] Each mill was to cost £11,400, replace 46 pairs of sawyers and produce annual savings of £3,600. In 1812 sawmills were briefly considered for Deptford, Woolwich, Sheerness, Chatham, Portsmouth and Plymouth (Fig 6.26), but not, surprisingly, for the warship-building yard then being established at Pembroke.[69] Probably for reasons of economy as well as a desire to see if the estimated savings did materialise, the choice was narrowed to a single mill either for Woolwich or Chatham.[70]

Chatham as the principal warship-building yard was the obvious choice, but lack of available space in the yard necessitated the purchase of part of the high ground at the northern end adjoining its eastern boundary.[71] To ensure that the timber arrived at the mill free of stones and mud after being dragged through the yard, Brunel proposed a narrow canal from the southern mast pond. The last part of the canal was in a tunnel ending in an elliptical shaft 90ft by 72ft in diameter, immediately north-east of the mill (Fig 6.27). Timbers were floated along the canal tunnel to the shaft where an elevator, guided by two cast-iron standards, raised them to the surface some 40ft above. The elevator worked on a counterpoise system 'with extraordinary velocity', according to an observer in 1838,[72] and it used a tank capable of holding up to 10 tons of condenser water from the sawmill's beam engine. At the bottom of the shaft, the water was discharged into a small reservoir for recycling, allowing the empty platform of the elevator to descend for the next load of timber.

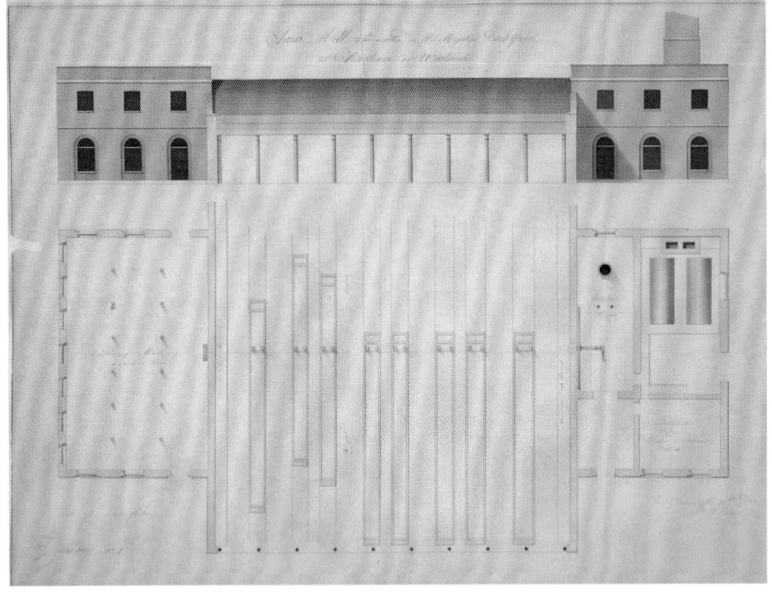

Fig 6.26
An 1812 drawing of Brunel's sawmills proposed for Woolwich or Chatham. (TNA ADM 140/98 pt 1)

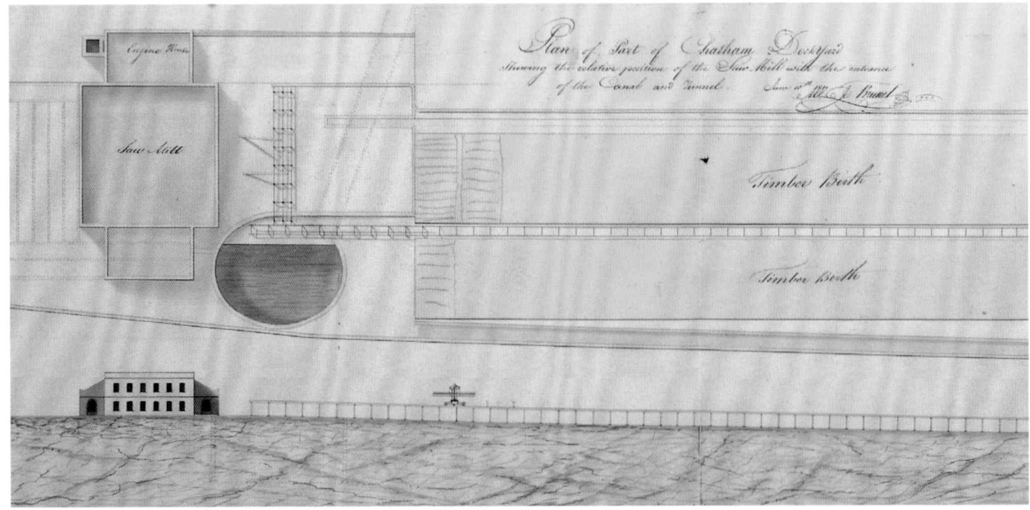

Fig 6.27
An 1817 drawing showing the layout of the sawmills at Chatham Dockyard, with the elliptical shaft linked to the canal tunnel below. The sawmills are shown in elevation at the base of the drawing, together with the overhead railway and travelling crane. (TNA ADM 140/99 pt 28)

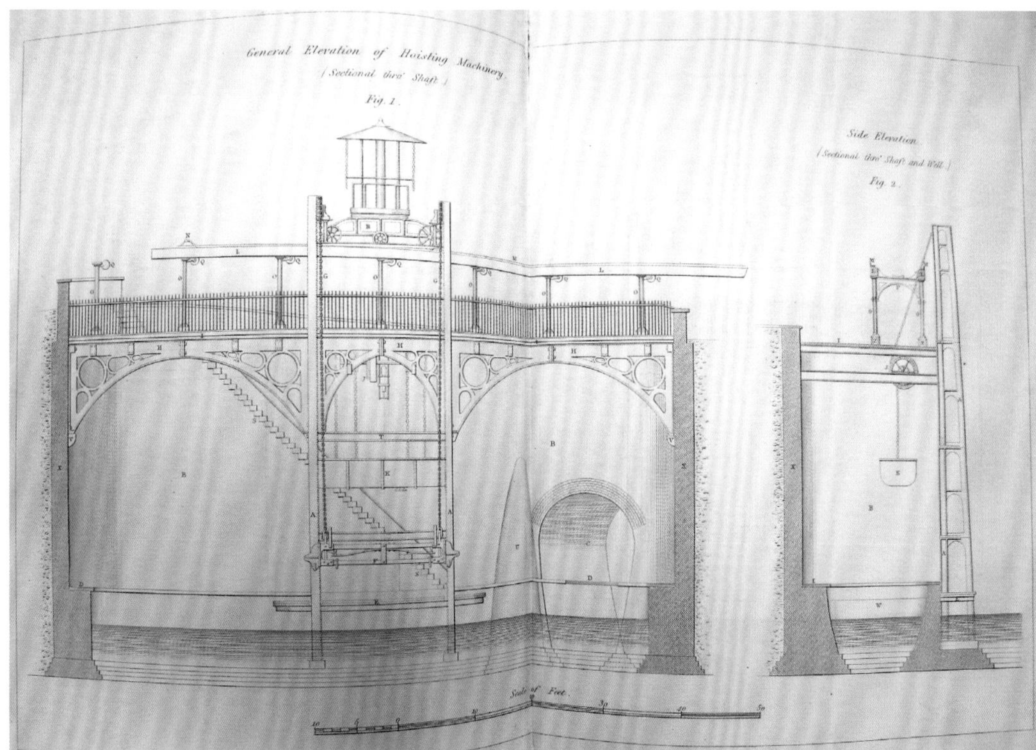

Fig 6.28
An 1842 drawing of the Chatham Dockyard sawmills with cross-section of the vertical shaft next to the sawmills. At the base is the elliptical canal tunnel and towpath linking the mast pond and River Medway.
In the centre of the shaft are the cast-iron standards for the platform that lifted the timber. Beyond the iron railings at the head of the shaft is the overhead railway and travelling crane.
To the right is a further cross-section showing more clearly the overhead crane supports. Note the elaborate cast-iron spandrels.
(Dempsey 1843, pl 19)

At the top of the shaft, timber was picked up by a small crane on an overhead railway supported by triple rows of cast-iron columns and with its rails secured to longitudinal timbers (Fig 6.28), a fixing system later adopted by Marc Brunel's son, Isambard Kingdom Brunel, when laying the Great Western Railway. The overhead railway, which ran for a distance of some 840ft to the north of the shaft, was laid on an incline, allowing the crane to run from the head of the shaft by gravity while it stacked timbers on either side of the track. On its return journey with timber for the mill, it was hauled by a chain wound on a drum driven by the sawmill beam engine. One man worked this entire operation. Although the canal tunnel survives, the shaft has long been infilled, and few traces survive of the overhead railway.

The sawmill building does remain much as completed in 1814. Its central section contained eight sets of cast-iron saw frames for rigidity and accuracy. These were bolted to the cellar floor and extended the full height of the ground floor. A shaft running the length of the cellar from the engine house at the western end transmitted power to each saw frame, which had a cranked drive shaft driving a vertical rod connected to the reciprocating saw frame on the floor above. Each of the saw frames could accommodate between three and seven vertical blades, depending on the timber thicknesses required.

Wide doorways on both sides of the building allowed the timber to be fed in from the north by the crane, which had a short length of transverse track so it could align its load with a particular frame. Doors on the south side, from 1868 connecting directly with the narrow-gauge railway, allowed the sawn timber to be distributed round the yard. The main mill building was flanked at either end by two wings. At the west end was the beam engine and boiler house, while the eastern wing contained further woodworking machinery. Apart from a room with a stoneflagged floor above the boiler house, the building was not designed to be fireproof. Its interior was largely reconstructed after a serious fire in 1854, when much of the machinery appears to have been replaced, although the system of power transmission was retained.[73]

Extensive surviving drawings suggest close collaboration between Brunel and Holl, but disentangling individual contributions is not always straightforward. Holl clearly spent time at Chatham during the construction phase, as some of Brunel's drawings for the engine and boilers are marked as being 'sent to Mr H at Chatham' in May 1813.[74] The final design of the mill building reflects Holl's experience and architectural input, as does the extensive use of cast iron for structural columns and principal

Fig 6.29
Detail of the metal shoes used in place of traditional joints in the roof trusses at Chatham Dockyard sawmills.
(TNA ADM 140/99 pt 9)

joists. Their design closely matches his contemporary use of these elements in his reconstruction of the spinning house at Plymouth.[75] However, 1812 designs for the composite roof trusses are signed by Brunel and are notable for the use of cast-iron shoes to secure the rafters to the tie-beams, eliminating the need for mortise-and-tenon joints and greatly simplifying construction (Fig 6.29).[76] The mechanical plant and the engineering works such as the canal tunnel, shaft and railway were clearly the preserve of Brunel. He was probably also responsible for the design of the structural ironwork at the top of the shaft with its elaborate spandrels, as well as the travelling crane with its quirky conical iron roof. The ironwork here is considerably more florid than the more functional designs of Holl.[77]

Portsmouth may have been the pioneer yard for steam power, but Chatham retains more surviving examples of its early use than any other dockyard. A year after the sawmills were completed, Rennie senior submitted an estimate to the Navy Board for an urgently needed new dock. It is a measure of how outdated were some of Chatham's facilities then that docks were still of timber and so shallow that they mostly drained by gravity.[78] The dock, now No. 3 Dock and begun in March 1816 to designs by John Rennie junior, overcame all these disadvantages. To allow for the largest warships, its floor was set 4ft below the level of low water at ordinary spring tides, ensuring for the first time here that efficient mechanical pumping would be necessary.[79] Perhaps influenced by the early 18th-century castellated architecture found on some of the Chatham buildings, the Rennies designed a splendidly ornate pump house (Fig 6.30).[80] Perhaps regrettably, more sober considerations prevailed, and the surviving stock-brick building clearly owes much to Holl's influence, although the Rennies are credited with the design (Fig 6.31).[81] The opportunity was also taken to introduce a pumped water supply throughout the yard for firefighting purposes, modelled on the earlier system at Portsmouth.[82] In 1822 Boulton and Watt were paid £4,027 for an engine and pumps; part of the beam engine frame remains in the building.[83]

In 1817, following a suggestion from Mr Weekes, the leading man of plumbers at Chatham, the Navy Board approved the establishment of a factory to produce milled and sheet lead and paint, combining it with a proposed new painters' shop. Initial thoughts were to locate this alongside the Chatham sawmill, so that it could power the factory's machinery. This proved impracticable, and a new factory was designed by Holl and located at the southern end of the yard (Fig 6.32).[84] Construction was authorised in September 1817, the contract was won by Thomas and George Marshall, and the building was apparently in production by the end of 1819. This facility concentrated the production of refined lead and paint at Chatham. The single-storey southern end of the long rectangular building housed the beam engine and boiler, along with a lead smelting furnace, a casting area and rolling mill and a room for boiling oil. The two-storey northern half of the building contained further oil tanks set below the floor level and a set of mills for pigment grinding and paint mixing; adjacent was space

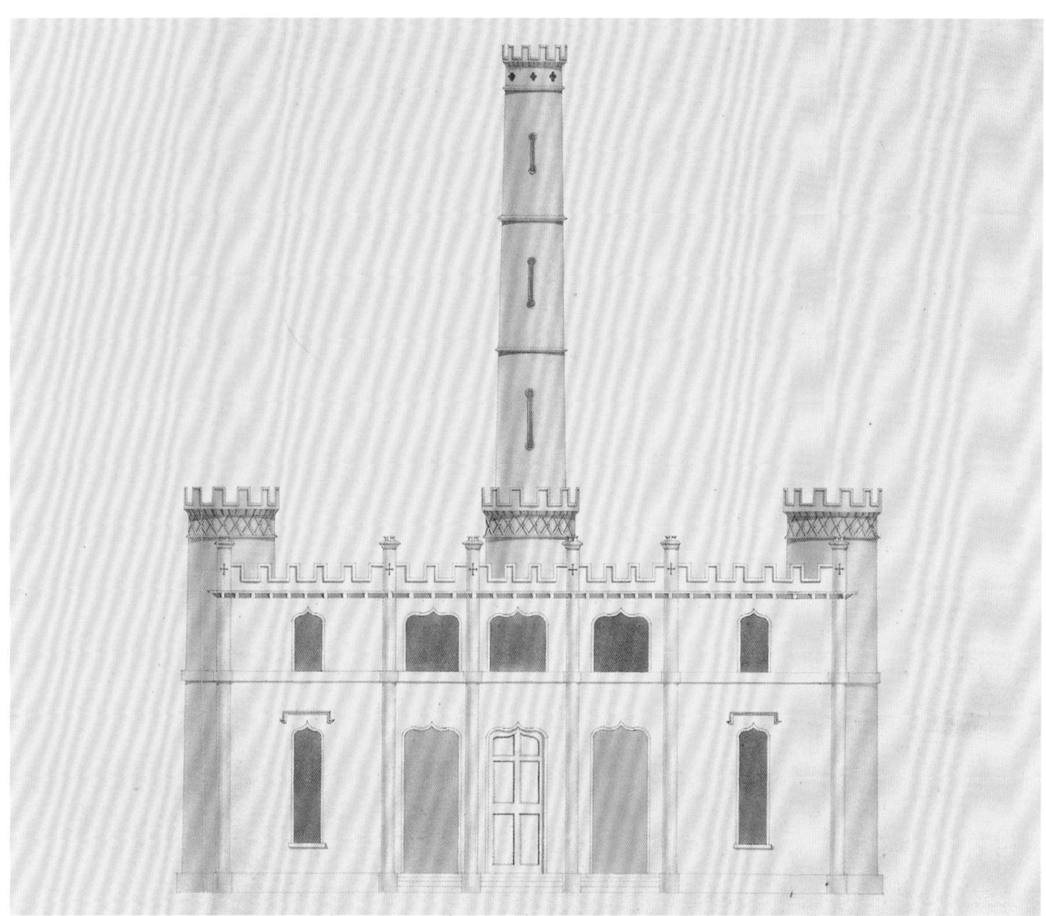

Fig 6.30
An early but unbuilt design for the new pump house for 3 Dock of the Rennies at Chatham. This Gothick extravaganza, perhaps inspired by Wyatt's works at Ashridge and Fonthill Abbey, did not pass muster with the Navy Board.
(TNA ADM 140/96 pt 1)

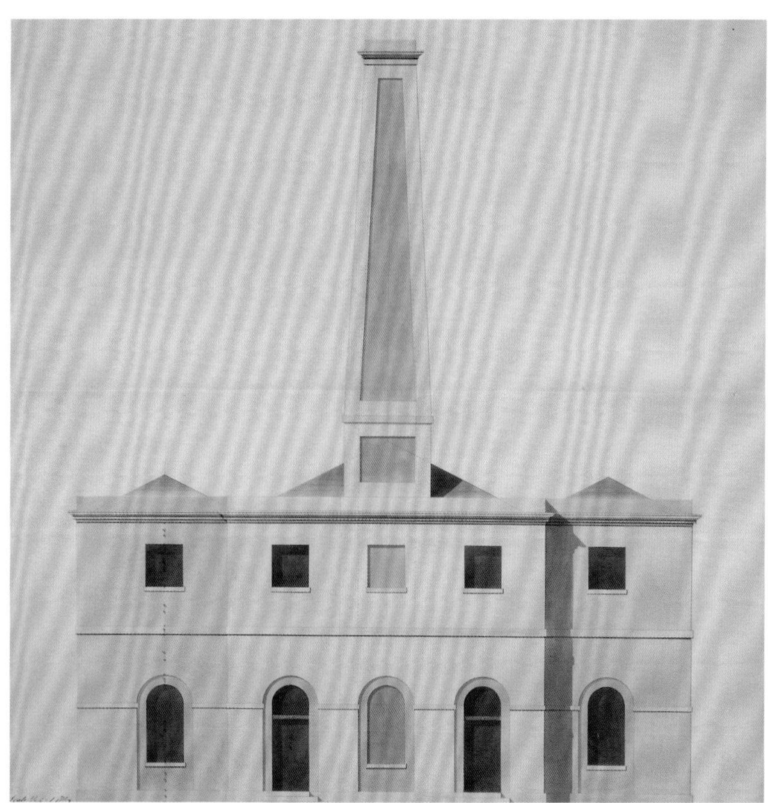

Fig 6.31
Rennie's design for the pump house for 3 Dock at Chatham, influenced by Holl and built between 1816 and 1822.
(TNA ADM 140/97 pt 6)

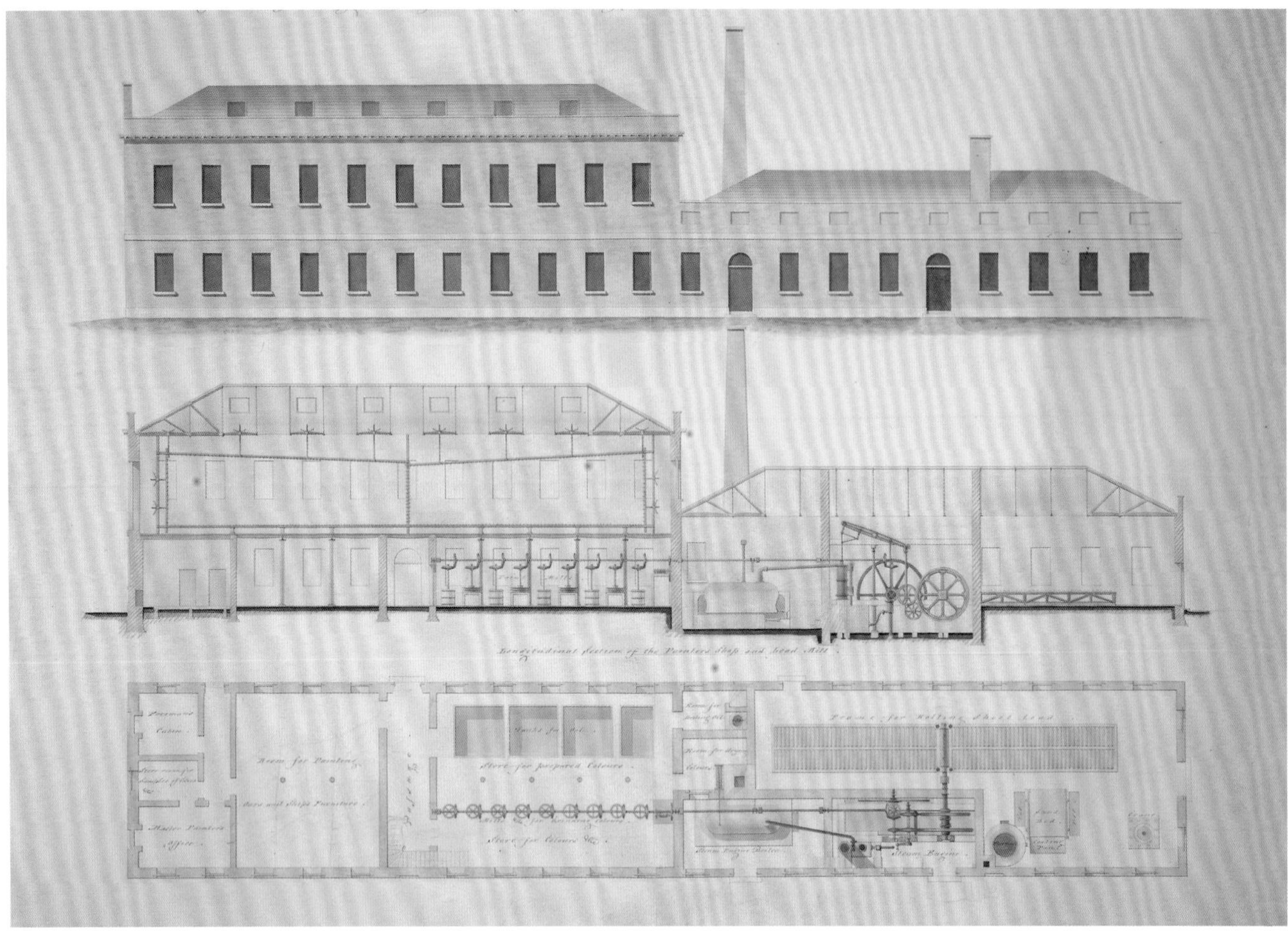

Fig 6.32
Holl's 1817 drawing for the Lead and Paint Mills at Chatham Dockyard.
(TNA ADM 140/107 fol 3)

for painting oars and ships' furniture, while the first floor had a series of adjustable metal frames on which canvas could be stretched before painting. None of the machinery survives, although its marks are still visible in places, but the adjustable frames remain on the first floor. Given the potent mix of materials, products and processes in the building, it is no surprise that Holl designed it to be fireproof, using the same combination of metal columns, joists and roof members, along with cast-iron window frames and doors and stone floors, as he had employed at the Plymouth spinning house. As added security, brick cross-walls further subdivided the building.[85]

Nearly twenty years were to pass after the completion of the Lead and Paint Mills before Chatham acquired its fourth steam engine. In 1837 John Penn of Greenwich supplied the boilers and Boulton and Watt provided a 14hp beam engine to power the ropery. The frame of this engine and some of the drive shafts and gears remain in the engine house at the northern end of the ropery.

Cordage manufacture: the naval roperies

Manufacture of cordage led to some of the most distinctive of dockyard buildings, while their immense length meant that only the four principal southern yards were fully equipped with ropeyards. Rope was being produced at Woolwich by 1612 and at Chatham by 1620; in both cases the size of the roperies led them to be sited outside the dockyards.[86] Woolwich ropeyard always remained detached, but Chatham ropeyard was incorporated within the main yard when it was being expanded early in the 18th century. By then, the spinning and laying houses were over 1,000ft long, with those later built at Plymouth in the 1760s reaching an astonishing 1,200ft, allowing the manufacture of unspliced ropes and cables in the longest footages required by the fleet. To economise on yard space, ropeyards at Portsmouth and Chatham, rebuilt after 1760, incorporated the spinners on the upper floors of the laying houses. These combined buildings were known as double ropehouses, while twin ropehouses had separate and parallel spinning and laying houses.

Fitting a ropeyard into an existing dockyard, as happened at Portsmouth in the mid-17th century, resulted in the spinning and laying houses being sited across the heart of the yard, where they remained a serious obstruction to circulation. When ropemaking ceased in this yard in the mid-19th century, no time was lost in cutting carriage and pedestrian arches through the centre of the double ropehouse. In the 1690s Plymouth became the only home dockyard to have a ropery from the start, enabling it to be sited alongside the southern boundary, where it would cause least inconvenience to other yard activities.[87]

Even with these four yards, naval requirements during the Napoleonic Wars meant that commercial ropemakers also supplied the navy, while production was supplemented from time to time by much smaller naval ropeyards elsewhere, which have left little trace. Sheerness in 1800 had what was described as a 'Rope Ground', implying an open-air ropewalk, although the plan suggests a building. In 1810 this was described as taking up too much space and was recommended for closure. It was not replaced when the yard was rebuilt.[88] At Milford, shortly to be superseded by the creation of Pembroke Dockyard, an open-air ropewalk was proposed in 1810.[89] The base at Port Mahon certainly had one towards the mid-18th century, and a ropery was constructed at Malta in 1806. By the 1840s, Port Royal had a ropehouse lying against the southern boundary of the yard. These facilities generally lacked the full range of ancillary buildings such as hatchel houses, and the ropehouses and open-air ropewalks were considerably shorter. Port Royal was 410ft long and 19ft wide; exceptionally, the one at Malta was 800ft in length. Their principal use seems to have been to rework damaged or worn cordage from ships on station.[90]

By the mid-18th century, the principal naval ropeyards were carefully laid out to suit the well-established manufacturing sequence.[91] Bales of hemp, mostly from southern Russia but later also from Italy and India, were stored in dedicated hemp houses, usually single-storey brick buildings with board-lined interiors and shuttered windows to keep the interiors dry and cool. From these, the hemp was taken to the hatchelling house where the bales were opened up and the hemp fibres straightened by being pulled across hatchel boards densely covered in rows of small iron spikes. The hemp was then spun into yarns on the adjacent spinning floors, where typically each spinner would be given 65lb to process in a day's work. Two pounds were allowed for waste, and from the remaining 63lb the spinner would produce 18 threads, each 1,020ft long and weighing 3½lb apiece.[92] To do this, he attached the required number of fibres for the yarn on to a revolving hook on a manually turned spinning frame at one end of the spinning floor. Walking backwards from the frame he would feed the emerging yarn from a bundle of fibres wrapped round his waist (Fig 6.33).

Fig 6.33
A spinner walking backwards from a manually turned spinning frame, with a bundle of fibres round his waist being formed into yarns. This method was used in all naval roperies until the introduction of mechanical spinning in the 1860s. Photographed at Ofir, Portugal, in 1961. (Author)

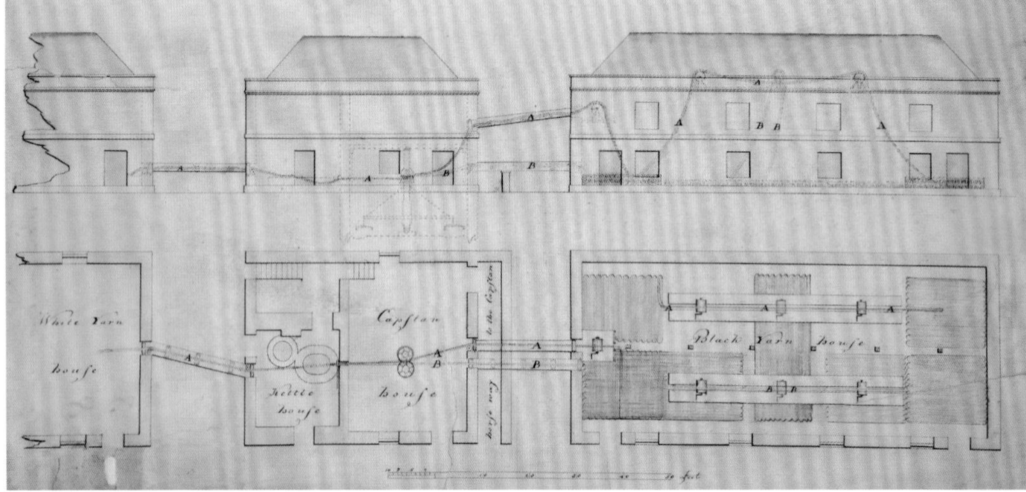

Fig 6.34
A 1799 drawing showing the progress of yarns in the white and black yarn houses of the Chatham Dockyard ropery. These buildings remain largely intact. (TNA ADM 140/110)

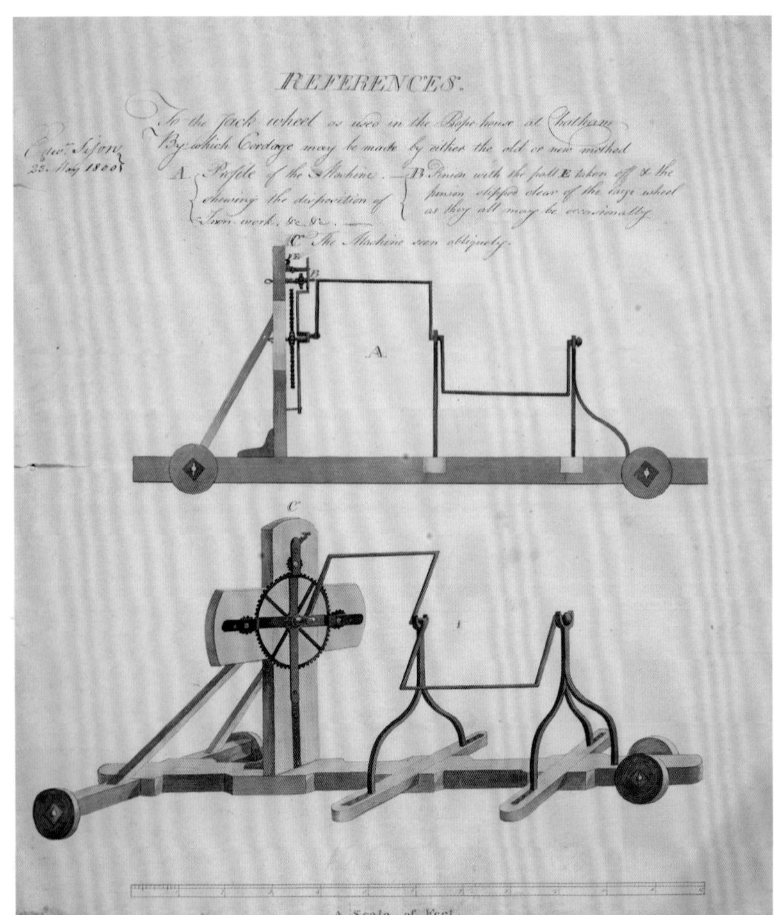

Fig 6.35
One of the ropery laying machines at Chatham used in conjunction with stationary winches at the ends of the laying floor to form ropes and cables. These laying machines were largely superseded by Maudslay's 1811 forming machines. (TNA ADM 140/111 pt10)

The white yarns were then taken in bundles or 'hauls' to the white yarn house, from where they were fed on rollers by a capstan into the tar kettle in the adjacent tarring house. Further rollers fed the tarred or black yarns into the black yarn house. Here they were hung in hauls to dry, before the yarns were wound on to bobbins and arranged at one end of the laying floor for the final stages of forming the yarns into strands and laying the strands up into ropes and cables of different diameters, using forming and laying machines (Figs 6.34 and 6.35). The flammable nature of the principal materials – hemp, tar, tallow and whale oil – was made vastly more dangerous by the amount of hemp dust generated by the spinning and laying processes. To help reduce the dust, window openings on spinning and laying floors were unglazed and provided with shutters that had to remain open when the buildings were in use. Despite such precautions, there were destructive fires in the roperies at Portsmouth in 1760 and 1770, at Malta in 1809 and at Plymouth in 1812. Portsmouth ropehouse was again gutted in 1776, but this was an arson attack.[93]

Ropemaking was highly labour intensive, skilled and very physical work, relying almost exclusively on human muscles. The men were divided into gangs or wheels, each gang with all the skills necessary for the entire manufacturing process. In 1812 Chatham ropeyard employed 415 people, including 174 spinners, a greater number than in any other naval ropeworks, while Woolwich employed 273, Portsmouth 382 and Plymouth 395.[94] The final stages of producing an anchor cable with a circumference of 24in demanded some 220 men, 59 turning the giant winches at the end of the laying floor (*see* Fig 6.37).

Not surprisingly, the application of steam power to replace manual labour and to obtain a greater consistency of quality had been suggested at intervals from the 1790s, and commercial ropeworks were some years ahead of naval ones in its use. John Grimshaw ordered a 16hp engine from Boulton and Watt for his patent ropery near Sunderland in 1795, and the Gourock Ropeworks Company had an engine in operation by 1808.[95] Meanwhile in the dockyards, horse gins powering the capstans winding the yarns through the tar kettles provided limited help, and at Portsmouth the rebuilt double ropehouse of 1777 is shown as having a 'wheel house' at the western end of the building by the early 1790s. This may indicate a horse gin linked to the manual winches at the end of the laying floor, but if so, it was shortlived. However, the Portsmouth ropery was the first naval one to have steam power, since a steam engine powering the tarring process is recorded in use in 1823.[96] It was not until 1837 that Chatham ropery became the first naval one to have its main machinery steam powered. Although fear of fire was clearly a consideration in its late application, other factors included the cost and the need for robust ropemaking machinery that could be power driven.

By 1800, Woolwich was the only naval ropery not to have been rebuilt and modernised in the previous 40 years. On New Year's Day 1803, following an Admiralty request to relocate cordage manufacture within Woolwich Dockyard, Samuel Bentham set out on a tour of a number of commercial rope manufacturers in northern England to see if there were improved methods of production that could be adopted in the proposed new ropeyard. He was particularly impressed with Grimshaw, Webster and Co's works near Sunderland, described as 'probably the world's earliest factory for machine-made rope'. Here, steam power was used for the entire process, from hatchelling to laying, and 'the necessity for a long ropehouse is entirely done away' thanks to new machines of Grimshaw's invention.[97]

In January 1804, working in conjunction with John Grimshaw, Bentham produced proposals for a five-storey quadrangular fireproof ropeworks at Woolwich, its internal courtyard measuring 304ft by 60ft. The building was to be centrally heated, provided with an internal water main for firefighting, and its machinery was to be driven by two 100hp engines linked to some 3,000ft of line shafting. This factory was to be substantially larger than the one in Sunderland, which was initially powered by a single 16hp Boulton and Watt engine and in 1804 produced some 800 tons of cordage. Bentham calculated that the factory planned for Woolwich 'working day and night' could produce some 10,000 tons of cordage annually.[98] He calculated that the construction costs saved by 'the adoption of this compact ropery instead of the long buildings hitherto necessary' would be some £75,000. Unfortunately, Grimshaw's machinery for Woolwich was also estimated at £75,000, so there were no capital savings, and the proposals for the new ropeworks were abandoned. Grimshaw's method of manufacture meant that none of the existing machinery at Woolwich could have been used in the new process. Doubtless for this reason, as well as having new ropeyards in all the other dockyards, the Navy Board and its successors retained the old roperies, eventually introducing spinning machines, but retaining the existing forming and laying processes.[99]

Woolwich ropeyard remained a separate entity outside the dockyard until its closure in the mid-1830s.[100] Despite its lack of investment, Woolwich's annual cordage production over the three years of 1804 to 1806 averaged 1,180 tons, compared to 1,570 tons at Portsmouth, 2,387 tons at Plymouth and 2,394 tons at Chatham. Thirty years earlier, Sandwich had expressed concern at the scale of the new ropery at Plymouth, remarking that even in wartime only one of the twin ropehouses here would be required.[101] By 1804, even with all four substantial naval roperies in full operation manufacturing an annual average of 7,115 tons of cordage, the demands of the fleet in the opening years of the Napoleonic Wars were such that the Navy Board still had to purchase over the same period an annual average of 6,834 tons from private contractors.[102]

Early in 1808 the Navy Board raised the possibility of installing a steam engine at Chatham ropery, asking the Admiralty to request Bentham to prepare drawings and an estimate. This was not to be used for the spinning process, but was to be of a power 'sufficient for the formation of strands for cables and hawsers'. This would have been Chatham's first steam engine and the first outside Portsmouth Dockyard, its novelty leading the Navy Board to wonder to the Admiralty 'whether the power of the said engine might be applied to some other purpose besides those of ropemaking ... perhaps constantly or occasionally to many other purposes which we do not immediately forsee'.[103] Bentham's mechanist, Simon Goodrich, was sent to Chatham, where he compiled detailed notes on the operation of the ropery, together with careful sketches of the machinery being used.

Nothing came then of the steam proposal, probably because all the wooden forming and laying machinery was not sufficiently robust to withstand steam operation. However, in November 1810 and probably as a direct result of this visit, the Navy Board did order a set of four all-metal forming machines from Maudslay's ironworks. They were delivered the following year and remain in daily use at Chatham (Fig 6.36). These machines were considerably stronger and technologically far more advanced than their predecessors. An endless rope running the length of the building moved each forming machine along the laying floor and powered a pulley wheel on the machine linked to bevel gears that rotated the set of hooks to which the yarns from the bobbin banks at the end of the laying floor were attached. The diameter of the pulley wheel could be adjusted so that the hooks would revolve for a set number of turns per foot travelled, enabling the machines to produce different diameters of cordage to a more uniform standard than was possible from the manually turned hooks on the older machines. Used in conjunction with Huddart's recently installed register plates and forcing tubes, through which the yarns were fed from the bobbin banks, these new machines transformed the production of naval cordage, giving it a consistency of strength and quality largely unknown before.

The designer of these forming machines is not known with certainty. In 1803 when considering the new ropery at Woolwich, Bentham had

Fig 6.36
One of the four Maudslay forming machines ordered in 1810 and still in use at Chatham Dockyard. (Author)

noted that 'for Chatham and any other dockyards, where the expense of long buildings is already incurred … it may be advisable to adopt great part of the laying apparatus used by Messrs Chapman near Newcastle'. However, there is no further reference in the Bentham papers. It seems more likely that Goodrich's detailed sketches of the existing Top Carts and other machinery at Chatham in 1808 formed the basis for developing the Maudslay machines, their design perhaps a collaborative effort between engineer and machine tool maker.[104] For the first 35 years of their life, these new forming machines must have been manually operated, using the great winches at each end of the Chatham laying floor (Fig 6.37).

Finally, in 1836 Chatham became the first ropery to have a steam engine installed for operating the main ropemaking machinery, when engine and boiler houses to a design by G L Taylor were completed at the northern end of the double ropehouse.[105] Boulton and Watt supplied the 14hp engine for £1,052 and John Penn of Greenwich manufactured the boilers for £280. A Mr Parsons provided the four cast-iron capstans for the endless rope drives. These capstans, together with their drive shafts from the beam engine and the frame of the engine, remain in place.[106]

Although a similar installation was suggested for Plymouth in 1838 and again in 1849, there is no evidence that this ropery was provided with steam power before the mid-1860s following the installation of mechanical spinning machinery, apparently at one end of the spinning house. The engine house was placed between the spinning and laying houses at one end and had a detached boiler house across the road; part of this building, which largely survives, was used as a dining room. This was possibly the

Fig 6.37
One of a pair of huge winches at the end of the laying floor at Chatham Dockyard. These remained in use until steam power was introduced in 1836. (TNA ADM 140/111 pt 7)

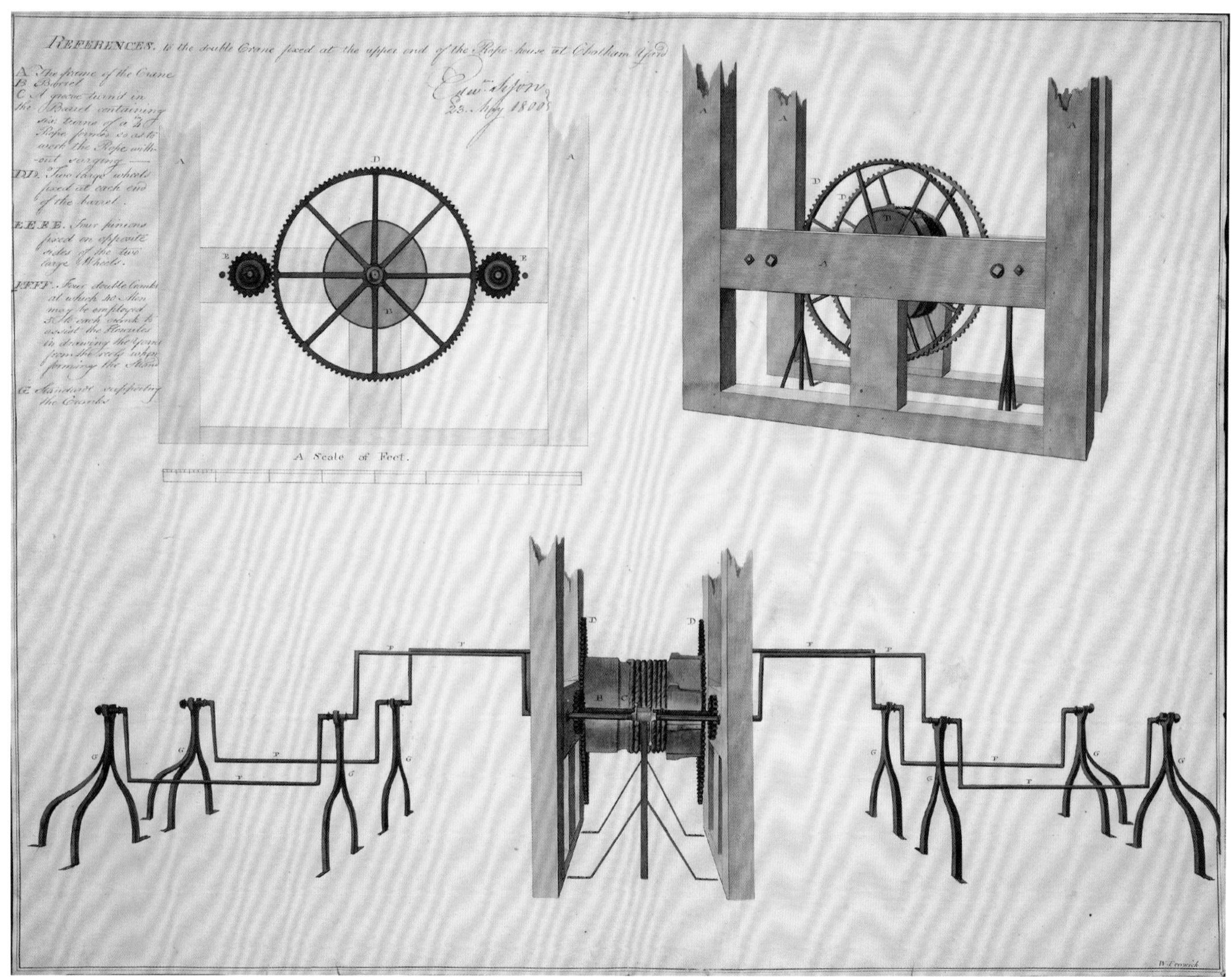

Fig 6.38
The line of yarn houses on the left showing their relationship to the spinning house on the right. All were constructed at Devonport Dockyard between 1766 and 1773.
(Author)

Fig 6.39
The sole surviving set of winding drums in the 1766 white yarn houses at Devonport Dockyard.
(DoE)

'dining room for workwomen' specified in records of the Director of Works. This spinning machinery led to women being employed for the first time for skilled jobs in the dockyards.[107] The steam engine proposed for Plymouth in 1838 was apparently diverted to Deptford, probably for installation at Woolwich ropeyard, which no longer survives. Apart from the tarring process, Portsmouth ropeyard seems to have remained manually operated until its closure in 1868.[108]

The modernisation and expansion of Portsmouth, Plymouth and Chatham yards in the latter part of the 18th century included the rebuilding of their ropeyards.[109] At Plymouth the existing ropery would have bisected the enlarged yard. Instead, new buildings were constructed on a north–south axis alongside the new eastern boundary wall, where the ropery could 'give no interruption to the other works, or communicate any danger of fire to the rest of the yard'.[110] The new ropeyard, with its twin 1,200ft spinning and laying houses, built in the local stone by contractors between 1766 and 1773 (Fig 6.38). In 1812, the spinning house was gutted by fire, but was restored over the next 5 years by Edward Holl, who added an extra floor and used fireproof materials for the floors and roof structure (*see* Chapter 4). This ropery remained in production until severely damaged by bombing in 1941. However, two-thirds of the spinning house remains, along with a repaired hemp store, the former house of the master ropemaker and the handsome group of white and black yarn houses separated by the tarring house, where the rollers were powered by the horse gin. The tarring house, uniquely, is linked by wooden rollers at gable height to the yarn houses, and the wooden winding drums survive in the roof spaces of the white yarn houses for shifting the hauls of yarn (Fig 6.39).

At Portsmouth, the 1760s expansion plans were also seen as a golden opportunity to relocate the ropeyard away from the crowded centre of the yard. These plans involved reclaiming an extensive area of the harbour abutting the northern end of the existing dockyard. Here the new ropeyard could be constructed along the new northern boundary, its twin 1,200ft spinning and laying houses matching those shortly to be built at Plymouth. The area of the old ropeyard would be partly used for storehouses and the road system improved.[111] As cordage production had to be maintained, the existing ropery would remain in use until the new buildings were complete and equipped; it was anticipated this would be in 1778. In July 1760 a fire had caused serious but not irreparable damage in the largely timber-built ropery. In anticipation of the eventual move, this was repaired at minimal cost to maintain production.

But almost exactly 10 years later a far more devastating fire destroyed much of the heart of the dockyard, including most of the ropery buildings. With the need to resume production as quickly as possible and the proposed new site still not available, the Surveyor of the Navy, Sir Thomas Slade, had little option but to report that 'we are obliged to restore the laying and spinning houses upon the same spot'.[112] It made no economic sense to build temporary buildings, and with two fires in 10 years neither the Admiralty nor the Navy Board would have been willing to see a timber ropery reconstructed here. It was better to perpetuate the inconvenience of a major factory astride the centre of the dockyard. To save space, a brick double ropehouse and associated buildings were planned and were largely completed and in operation by 1775. The wisdom of building in brick was amply demonstrated the following year when the double ropehouse was set on fire by the arsonist James Aitken.[113] Although the interior was gutted, the walls prevented the fire spreading, and the building was repaired.

In its reconstruction between 1771 and 1782, Portsmouth ropeyard followed the general layout of naval roperies. Its spine was the great three-storey double ropehouse, at 1,030ft probably the maximum length that could be constructed without causing insufferable problems to yard traffic. Its twin lofts were used for spinning fishing lines, the finest of all and the preserve of the most experienced spinners. Here, too, apprentices were trained. The two floors below were for spinning, and the ground floor was for laying up the ropes and cables. As with all naval roperies, bays at each end were wider to accommodate the huge winches used for hauling the forming and laying machines along the ground floor. Parallel to the double ropehouse on the south side stood a range of four subtantial storehouses, two of which contained hemp for the ropemakers, while the other two were for general naval stores. On the north side at the eastern end stood the hatchelling house and parallel to this a smaller hemp store. The hatchelled hemp was taken to the spinners on the first floor of the ropehouse along a handsome arched passageway above the road. At the opposite end on the north side was the tarring house. After ropemaking ceased here in 1868, the ropery buildings became storehouses. By the early 1960s the buildings were in poor repair, their timbers riddled with rot. With the exception of the former hatchelling house, they were converted into open-plan stores.[114] The hatchelling house and its associated hemp store still retain much of their original interiors, and the tarring house survives, though much altered. The buildings continue to dominate the old centre of Portsmouth Dockyard, a vivid reminder of how a serious fire upset Georgian replanning nearly 250 years ago.

Only at Chatham Historic Dockyard is it possible to see an almost totally unaltered 18th-century naval ropery still in operation, laying ropes and cables using a combination of machinery installed here during the Napoleonic and Crimean Wars. It is one of the most important industrial monuments in Europe, occupying a site used for naval ropemaking since at least 1620.[115] The 17th-century ropeyard was added to and altered over the years, and with the exception of the hemp houses, all the buildings appear to have been timber. Cramped conditions here are apparent in a 1753 report, which said that the laying house was too short to lay up four 130-fathom cables for the 'Dutch Yacht'. [116] The solution was to shift the dockyard gate at the south-west end of the yard 'opening on the gravel walk near the new stairs leading to the church', so that it was opposite the doors at the end of the laying house, allowing the rope-makers to extend their manufacturing into the open. With the exception of the hemp stores, all these buildings were replaced between 1787 and 1791.

The 1787 rebuilding was prompted in part by the Navy Board's acute awareness of the fire risk of timber buildings in the wake of the Portsmouth disasters. Chatham ropery itself had a narrow escape in September 1768 when the tar kettle in the tarring house caught fire and the flames spread to the adjacent yarn house.[117] In 1786 the Board ordered that the double ropehouse should be 'built upon the plan of that at Portsmouth', and as there was slightly more space at Chatham, its length was increased by 10ft to 1,040ft. Along with the huge adjacent storehouse nearing completion on Anchor Wharf and the proposed fitted rigging house of similar size to be built at one end of it, this major investment marked the start of a renaissance of Chatham's fortunes and its shift in emphasis to a yard for warship building and major repairs.[118]

The contract for the great double ropehouse was awarded to the London contractor, Nicholson and Son, Baker and Martyr, but the dockyard bricklayers and house carpenters were apparently responsible for the hatchelling house, the black and white yarn houses and the tarring house (Fig 6.40). In 1787 the yard was allowed to recruit two extra bricklayers and labourers to ensure these smaller works were completed by the end of the year.[119] Reconstruction was clearly phased to ensure that as far as possible cordage production never entirely ceased. As the new double ropehouse was to occupy the site of the existing spinning house, the Navy Board was very specific that the old laying house – which could do double-duty as a spinning house – should not be demolished until the double ropehouse had been completed. Construction of the ropehouse was largely finished by early 1791, differing slightly from that at Portsmouth, because the Medway yard's sloping site allowed a series of brick-arched cellars to be incorporated beneath its northern end (Fig 6.41).[120] The tar barrels stored here could be taken in a tunnel beneath the ropery to steps leading to the tarring house on the eastern side of the building.

Internally, the ropery remains largely unaltered with its limewashed brick walls and most of its original timber floors. Production is now concentrated on the great laying floor (Figs 6.42 and 6.43), its astonishing length brought

Fig 6.40
The Anchor Wharf storehouses with the buildings of the Chatham ropery to their rear. The enormous size of these Georgian buildings is clearly shown in this 2003 aerial photograph of the southern end of Chatham Historic Dockyard. To the left is the commissioner's house with the sail loft overlooking the garden.
(NMR 23186/08 4 Aug 2003)

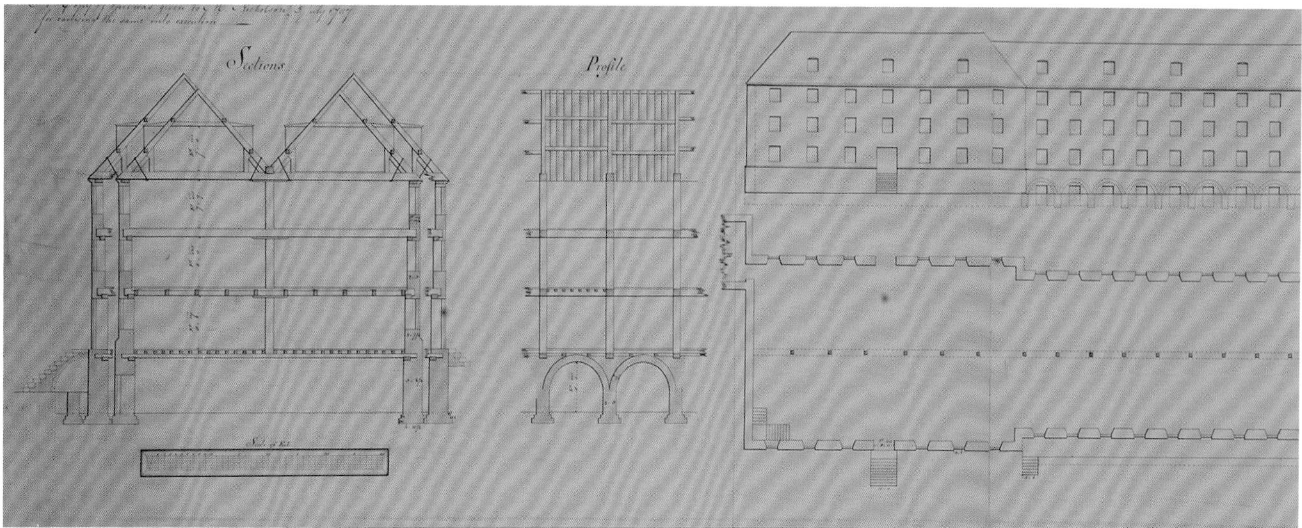

Fig 6.41
An original plan and elevation of part of the double ropehouse at Chatham Dockyard. (TNA ADM 140/104 pt 4)

alive by the sounds and vibrations from the massive cast-iron Georgian and Victorian forming and laying machines, as they whirr and rumble from one end to the other, driven by endless ropes from capstans once powered by the 1836 beam engine (Fig 6.44). Externally, the double ropehouse is notable for the quality of its deep red brickwork with its pattern of grey brick headers. To help disperse hemp dust and hence reduce fire risk, the lower two floors of the ropery had no glass in the windows until the late 1940s. Still to be seen are a number of shutters that were closed only when the ropery was not working. Many of the ground-floor window openings retain their massive wrought-iron security bars as a deterrent to pilfering. The top floor and the twin lofts used exclusively by spinners had their windows glazed earlier than the rest of the building, once mechanical spinning had been introduced on the first floor of the hemp house in the 1860s. An extensive programme of conservation in the early 1980s included replacing the corrugated asbestos on the roofs with peg tiles. A painstaking paint

Fig 6.42
A view down the ropery laying floor at Chatham Dockyard, with Maudslay machines in the middle distance. The rails were installed in the 1850s for heavier laying machines introduced then. (Author)

Fig 6.43
Bobbin banks at the end of the ropery laying floor at Chatham Dockyard. Yarns from the banks in the foreground are being fed into the register plates and on to hooks on the laying machines for forming into ropes.
(Author)

Fig 6.44
Capstans at the far end of the laying floor from the bobbin banks at Chatham Dockyard. Endless ropes from these power the laying machines. Now electrically driven, these capstans were originally powered by the 1836 beam engine.
(Author)

analysis has enabled the external joinery to be repainted in the late Georgian colour scheme of stone and rich brown.

Projecting from the north-eastern corner of the double ropehouse is the tall narrow hatchelling house, positioned so that the combed fibres could be taken directly to the spinners on the upper floors of the ropehouse. For now unknown reasons, the hatchelling house was aligned on the axis of the previous spinning house, and as a result stands at a slight angle to the double ropehouse. Its interior remains largely intact, with few traces of its original use. For most of the 20th century, its lower floors were used as a fitters' shop for maintaining the ropery machinery. Immediately at the north end of the double ropehouse is the former engine house, little altered and with its characteristic round-headed windows; adjacent is the boiler house with its tall brick chimney. Abutting the north end of the boiler house is a substantial two-storey brick building, its upper floor well lit by large rectangular windows and provided with a loading door and wall crane at its northern end. Details of its construction have not been found, but it must have been built between 1837 and 1840 when it was in use as a receiving room and additional hatchelling house. The need for manual hatchelling in this building would have ended with the introduction of mechanical hatchelling and spinning in the 1860s.[121]

Parallel to the double ropehouse on its east side stand the white and black yarn houses and the tarring house. These were located to allow a steady flow of yarns from the white yarn house to pass on rollers through the tar kettle in the tarring house and on into the black yarn house. The single-storey, double-height yarn houses had manually operated capstans in their roof spaces to manoeuvre the hauls of yarns to where they would be coiled on the floor below. Between these buildings stood the tarring house where the yarns were passed through the tar kettle over rollers driven by a horse wheel or gin operated in the cellar below. By 1840, the white yarn house had been doubled in width, with part being used by the hatchellers, but both uses had lapsed by the end of the century, and the buildings had been joined to each other to form a series of large storehouses and miscellaneous workshops.[122] Little survives within the buildings to indicate their original uses, apart from the board linings.

Immediately north of the yarn houses, and still very much in use for its original purpose, is the surviving hemp house (Fig 6.45), which was extended at intervals between 1728 and 1840. It was the first significant brick building in the ropeyard, a crucial reason why it was not replaced in the 1787 rebuilding. The first hemp store, which occupied the site of some of the officers' gardens, was a single-storey building with tar cellars below. Its exterior was decorated with brick pilasters and attractive Dutch gables above wide doorways, and the board-lined interior was lit by unglazed, shuttered window openings. In 1743 it was doubled in width, and the extension was given the same architectural motifs. The exigencies of the Napoleonic Wars put further pressure on storage space in the hemp store, and in 1812 the dockyard officers received permission to add a first floor with a broad, pitched slate roof, necessarily removing the Dutch gables in the process.[123]

Fig 6.45
The hemp house at Chatham Dockyard, the different-coloured bricks indicative of its various extensions. Alongside is a well-preserved length of wagon way. (Author)

By 1840, the building had been extended to the south, again employing matching brickwork and details.[124] By the middle of the 1860s, the upper floor and roof were adapted to their present configuration to house the new mechanical hemp combing and spinning machinery that superseded the old line spinning methods.[125] The new machinery was powered from overhead line shafts by a mill engine located in a new engine house attached to the south end of the building.[126] The local newspaper noted that 'It is still undecided whether to employ young women or lads to take charge of the machinery, but as a certain delicacy of touch as well as nimble fingers is required, it is probable that the Admiralty will break through the rule hitherto observed, and will introduce girls for employment in Chatham Dockyard'.[127] The Admiralty did indeed introduce women and girls, and for most of the 20th century priority was given to naval and dockyard widows. Limited spinning is still carried on here, and bales of hemp are stored on the ground floor.

Boat building and sailmaking

As might be expected when most craftsmen used simple hand tools, the external appearance of many dockyard buildings gives no hint of the quite substantial trades, such as boat building, that were once carried on inside. Although ships' boats could be purchased from private yards, most of the dockyards from the 18th century built, maintained and stored such craft. Every warship carried ships' boats, the number and size of which varied according to its rating. By the end of the Napoleonic Wars, these craft came in a bewildering variety of types and sizes, including launches, pinnaces, cutters, yawls and gigs. There were 17 different lengths of launches, from 16ft to 34ft, 6 sizes of gigs from18ft to 26ft and 17 varieties of cutters from 12ft to 34ft.[128] Constructing ships' boats required no special facilities beyond adequate working space, access to a slip and wide doorways. By the 18th century boathouses were generally timber-framed and weatherboarded buildings that could be of considerable size. Nos 5 and 7 boathouses at Portsmouth, built as late as 1875 and 1882, are late examples of this type (*see* Fig 8.46). Most of these buildings seem to have been used not just for building and repairing ships' boats, but also as boat stores.[129]

The craft of sailmaking created no readily identifiable style of architecture. By the mid-18th century, sailmakers tended to be given space in the new storehouses then gradually being built as part of the dockyard modernisation programmes. Often they shared premises with flag makers. At Plymouth they were accommodated in one of the ranges of the now-vanished great double quadrangle of storehouses and workshops constructed in the latter part of the 18th century, and a similar arrangement is apparent in the contemporary storehouses at Portsmouth. At Sheerness in the 1820s, sailmakers were among the crafts accommodated in the Quadrangle Store.[130] The Devonport buildings were destroyed by Second World War bombing; the Sheerness Quadrangle was demolished by the Medway Ports Authority.

Chatham is unique in having an early purpose-built sail loft, which replaced one described in 1698 as 'ye Sailmakers' Room' that was located above a tar storehouse and four other stores.[131] The new sail loft was constructed in 1723, almost certainly as a result of the Admiralty decision in 1716 that the dockyards should manufacture the navy's sails. An early design shows it with two wings at the front, which would have taken up a substantial part of the commissioner's garden, so it is no surprise that they were not built (Fig 6.46).[132] To the rear was the sail field, where completed sails could be spread out and thoroughly dried before being folded for storage. From the outside, the three-storey building looks like any other large naval storehouse (Fig 6.47), with its provision of loading bays and small wall cranes for hoisting in the bolts of canvas and dispatching the completed sails.

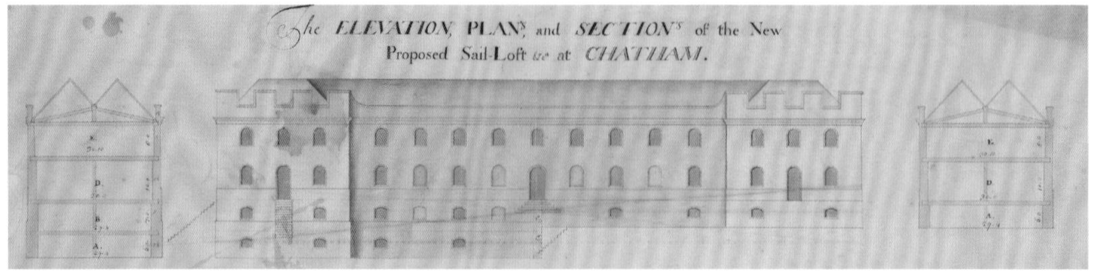

Fig 6.46
The proposed sail loft. This early drawing of the existing building at Chatham Dockyard shows the two unbuilt wings. The top floor of the main range has omitted the central timber pillars to give an open floor area for the sailmakers. (© National Maritime Museum, Greenwich, London, ADM/Y/C/29)

The building's distinguishing feature inside is the very large working area. This had to be free of any structural supports to allow the sailmakers to spread out the canvas when working on the great mainsails and fore topsails. Such space was most easily provided on the top floor, where structural columns to support floors were not required – hence the term 'sail loft' (Fig 6.48). In the latter part of the 20th century, this floor found a new use as space for manufacturing inflatable life rafts for warships. The lower floors were used for canvas and sail storage, as well as by flag makers who probably occupied this building without a break for more than 275 years, from its completion until October 2001. The wooden pillars supporting the lower floors are reused ribs from a 17th-century warship. Despite the oft-repeated instructions of the Navy Board to dockyard officers to 'make use of ships being taken down', this is a comparatively rare surviving example of such recycling.

Fig 6.47
The sail loft today at Chatham Dockyard. The render is a 19th-century addition. (Author)

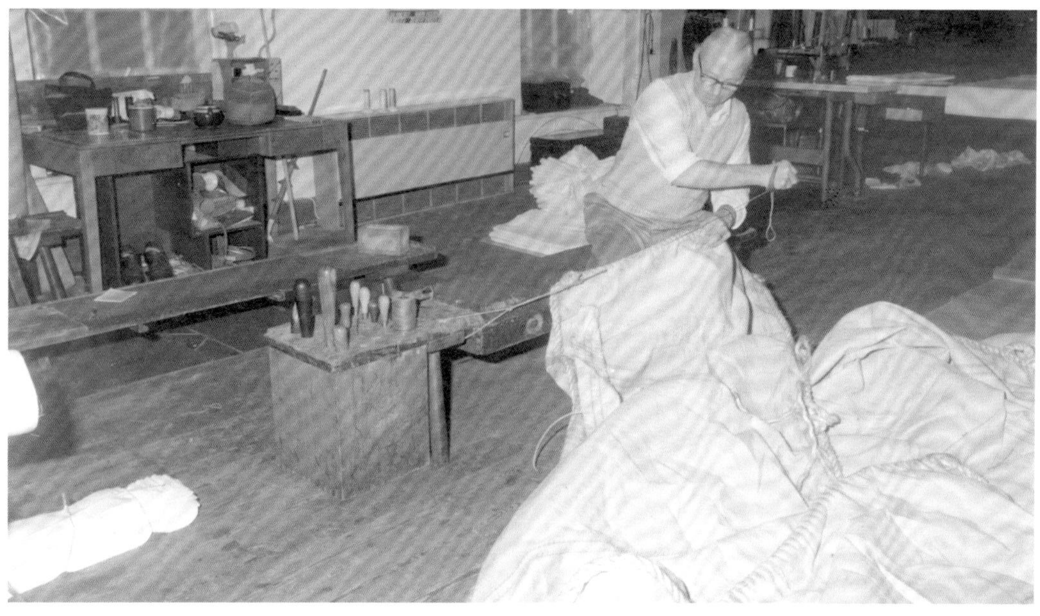

Fig 6.48
A sailmaker's bench in use in the Sail Loft at Chatham Dockyard in 1981. (DoE)

Fig 6.49
Taylor's 1829 pitch house at Sheerness Dockyard. This is a rare drawing of such a structure. (TNA ADM 140/1030)

Minor industrial buildings

All dockyards possessed an accumulation of small buildings that were used for a variety of industrial purposes but no longer survive and are known to us only from records, drawings and occasionally models. Three types that were closely associated with wooden shipbuilding and repairing, with fire central to the process, were the pitch houses, hoop houses and timber-bending kilns.

Pitch was principally used for caulking, so the pitch houses had to be located within reach of the building slips and dry docks. In 1709 the Navy Board ordered an additional pitch house for Portsmouth to be sited between the recently completed Great Basin and the stone dock. It had a brick-vaulted interior some 27ft long and 19ft 6in wide.[133] Heating flammable material such as pitch was inviting trouble, as in 1736 when the 'old pitch house' at Chatham was destroyed by fire. By then, these buildings were generally brick vaulted to contain the spread of fire, and this design was followed in Chatham's replacement building.[134] A solitary example of a 19th-century pitch house survived at Pembroke Dockyard as late as 1973. At Sheerness in 1829 G L Taylor designed an attractive pedimented pitch house containing six pitch kettles, three on either side of a common stokehole, each with its cowled metal ventilator above (Fig 6.49).[135]

Soon afterwards, experiments were begun to lessen the fire hazard by heating pitch using steam. When Chatham ropery had a steam engine installed in 1836, its boiler provided steam to heat tar for tarring the yarns on the spinning floor, a place where the fire risk would have made it impossible to locate a conventional pitch boiler.[136] In 1839 a Mr Perkins invented another way of melting 'pitch resin' by steam, and the Admiralty agreed to erect the necessary machinery at Woolwich at a cost of £40.[137] There is no evidence that such methods were widely adopted before all-metal warships dramatically reduced the need for this product.

Hoop houses, used for heating iron hoops before they were shrunk on to masts, were small, single-cell buildings located close to the working mast houses. One designed for Chatham in 1795 was a rectangular brick-vaulted building with a fire hearth at one end. This had a large iron grid on which the hoop was placed for heating. At Plymouth in 1830 the hoop house was combined with the pitch house, reducing the number of hearths.[138] From an early date the direct heat of a fire in a kiln was used to help bend timbers to fit the curved areas of a warship's hull. In the 1720s, Captain Cumberland working at Deptford Dockyard advocated heating planks in hot, damp sand. Although apparently an improvement on the kilns, this was not entirely satisfactory, and in 1744 the Admiralty ordered that planks should be made supple in 'boiling troughs'. As a result, boiling troughs or suppling boilers were to be found in some numbers in all the yards. Timbers were immersed in the boiling water, allowing an hour for every inch of thickness until they became pliable.

Although no troughs survive, they clearly developed into substantial structures. In 1762 the copper trough of one ordered for Chatham weighed 56cwt 13qr 9lb. In 1823 two pairs of suppling boilers to go between the heads of the Great Basin dry docks at Sheerness were designed by Holl's assistant William Miller (Figs 6.50 and 6.51). Each had two parallel boiling troughs, with furnaces under each end.

Fig 6.50
The suppling boilers at Sheerness Dockyard, designed by William Miller in 1823.
(TNA ADM 140/1036)

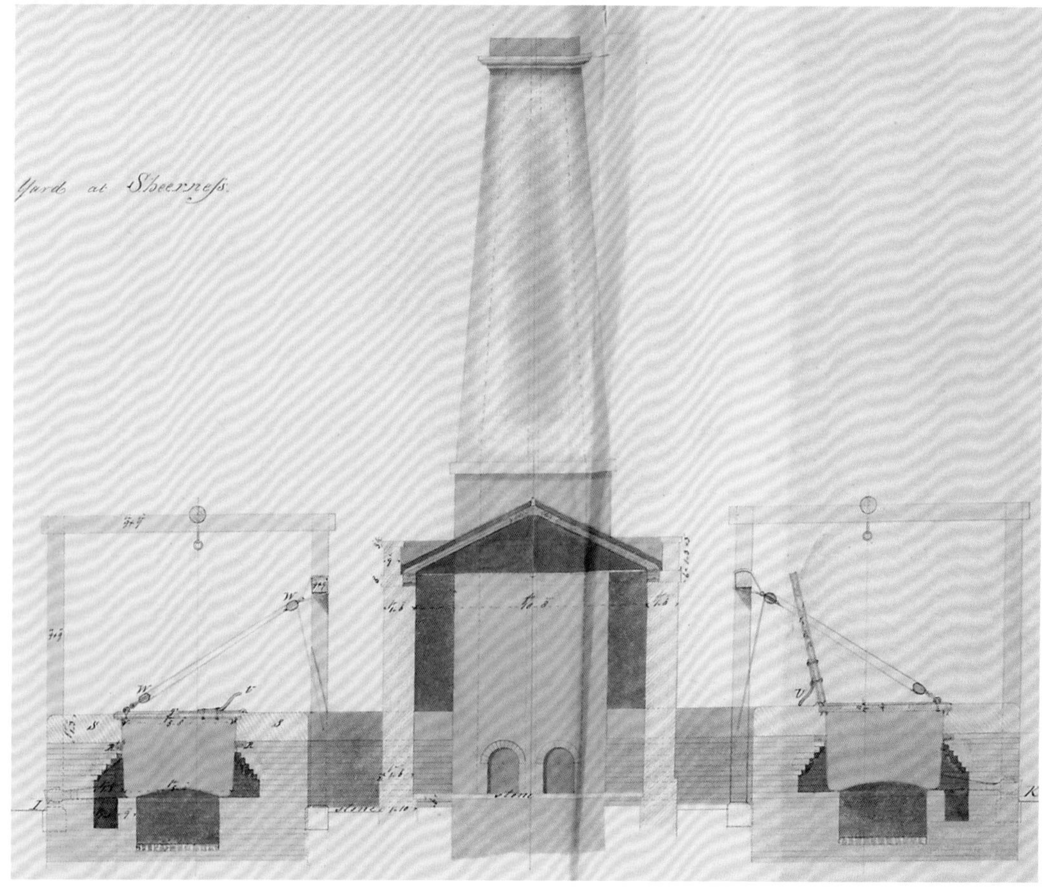

Fig 6.51
Cross-section of the suppling boilers at Sheerness, showing the pair of copper troughs for the timbers and the blocks and tackle used to raise their lids.
(TNA ADM 140/1036)

The troughs were 40ft long and 3ft 8in wide at the ends. They were angled out on their external sides to a maximum width of 5ft. Wooden frames above each trough had blocks and tackle for lifting the pairs of hinged lids and loading and unloading the timbers. Between these parallel troughs was a pair of substantial brick-built stores for keeping the fuel dry. The furnace flues were arranged in a common chimney in the centre after apparently providing some heat for the wood stores.[139] By the 1830s the use of boiling troughs was gradually superseded by steam kilns for the smaller dimensions of timbers that were used in boat building.[140]

With plentiful materials to hand and labour readily available, it is safe to assume that numbers of small additions were made to the yards without reference to higher authority and quite possibly without even the prior knowledge of the resident commissioner. A survey of Chatham Dockyard in 1698 lists numerous small buildings, including sheds that were used for a variety of purposes, by pump makers to lime stores. There were also a number of cabins, which in reality were small offices or mess rooms, the equivalent of today's ubiquitous site offices, as well as a painters' shop, butchers' shop and an open shed 'for Joyners to work under'.[141] All dockyards over the centuries have accumulated such structures; these no doubt made life easier for those using them, but have rarely left any physical trace or made any significant architectural contribution.

7

Dockyard Housing, Offices and Chapels

Housing the senior officers

Houses and offices for the senior yard staff are among the most handsome of dockyard buildings. By 1700 all except the minor yards were generally in the overall charge of an out-stationed Navy Board commissioner. He and the senior civilian staff, who in the largest yards could number a dozen or more, were provided with accommodation, usually strictly graded according to rank. Among these was the master shipwright, the storekeeper, the master attendant, the master caulker, the clerk of the cheque, the clerk of the survey and one or two of their senior assistants. The list tended to vary slightly over the years, depending on the yard's importance, the availability of housing inside and outside the yard and the needs of the particular office holder. Yard surgeons, master ropemakers, sailmakers and, from the latter part of the 18th century, chaplains were others who were normally found official accommodation.[1]

As befitted their status, commissioners and their successors occupied the grandest residences with the largest gardens, generally detached houses by the 18th century. Fine examples remain at Chatham (1704), Gibraltar (1783), Portsmouth (1784), English Harbour, Antigua (1787), Bermuda (1823) and Sheerness (1824).[2]

Before the 1690s housing in the yards had generally developed in a piecemeal way. The mid-17th-century red brick Commissioner's House at Portsmouth, with its Dutch gables (Fig 7.1), was set in a large garden. Its belvedere and balcony on top of its staircase tower were suggestive of watching the chase rather than for overlooking the king's ships in harbour and might have been built for a prosperous country squire. Houses for the less senior yard officers at that time, although usually provided with substantial gardens to their rear, tended to be in rows of lodgings, which reflected the local artisan vernacular.

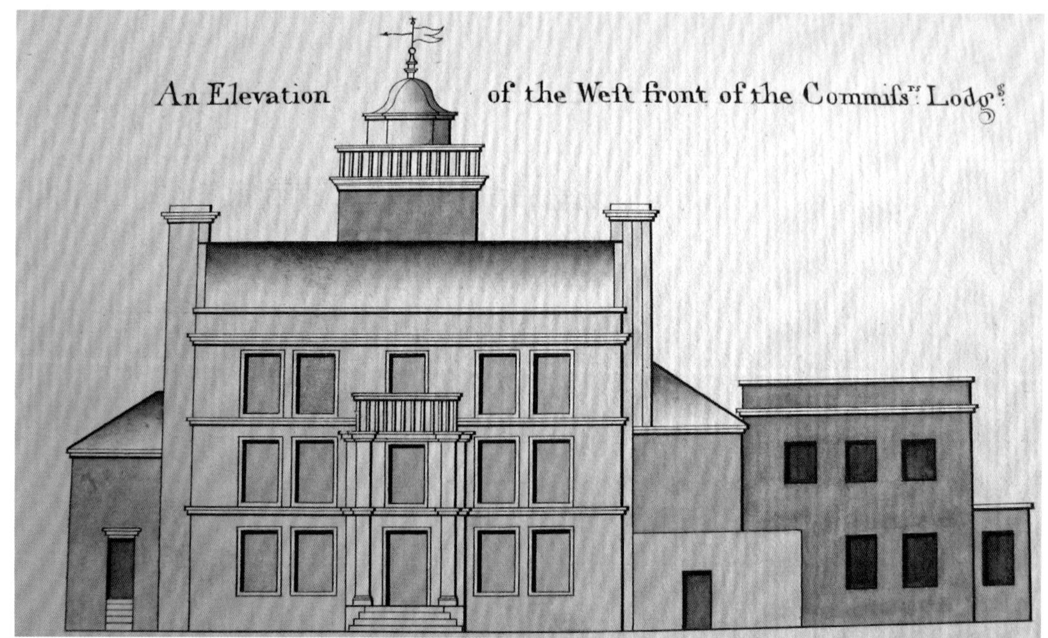

Fig 7.1
The 17th-century Commissioner's House at Portsmouth Dockyard, predecessor of the present Admiralty House. (NMRN Plans of HM Dockyard, Portsmouth, c 1786, MS 1993/443)

All this was to change in the 18th century following the precedent set by the new dockyard at Plymouth. There Dummer had the advantage of a virgin site, which allowed him to plan the layout of the yard with a view to improving working efficiency and supervision. His monumental range of houses for the commissioner and 12 other officers dominated the centre (Fig 7.2). At its ends were modest two-storey offices. This remarkably early essay unifying a group of terrace houses behind a long palace front may well owe much to Robert Hooke's Bethlehem Hospital at Moorfields in London or to Les Invalides in Paris. However, the terrace's final design, especially the addition of a third storey against Dummer's advice, was done at the behest of the yard officers and, in particular, the first commissioner, Captain Greenhill.[3] Even though Dummer had the advantage of a virgin site at Plymouth, it is significant that he did not always get his own way, complaining bitterly that the yard officers 'may thank themselves for ye upper storey (of their new terrace); it was done against my opinion'.[4] Terrace residences not only saved valuable space in a dockyard, they brought the officers together, optimistically encouraging harmony, closer working and better communications. Dummer deliberately chose the location to allow the officers a good view over the yard activities, in some ways anticipating Bentham's desire a century later to encourage individual responsibility. It was also a way of spotting abuses, which, as Dummer said, were 'too many to be named, and some too subtle to be discovered'.[5] Embellishing the pediments of the terrace with the arms and trophies of the king and of the Admiralty and Navy Boards was a final flourish, perhaps in part intended to emphasise the authority of the Crown over a city which 50 years earlier had been solidly Parliamentarian.

The Plymouth terrace, completed early in 1695, set new standards of accommodation as well as emphasising the importance of the occupants, notably the commissioner living in the centre of the range.[6] His house mirrored the earlier Commissioner's House in Portsmouth in its provision of a roof-top balcony, a feature which became a characteristic over the next 80 years on houses for commissioners at Chatham, Portsmouth and Halifax. At Port Royal, the commodore's house (by 1900 renamed the Captain's House) had a tall functional look-out tower, as did the main storehouse, both probably necessities in an area famed for privateers (Fig 7.3).[7]

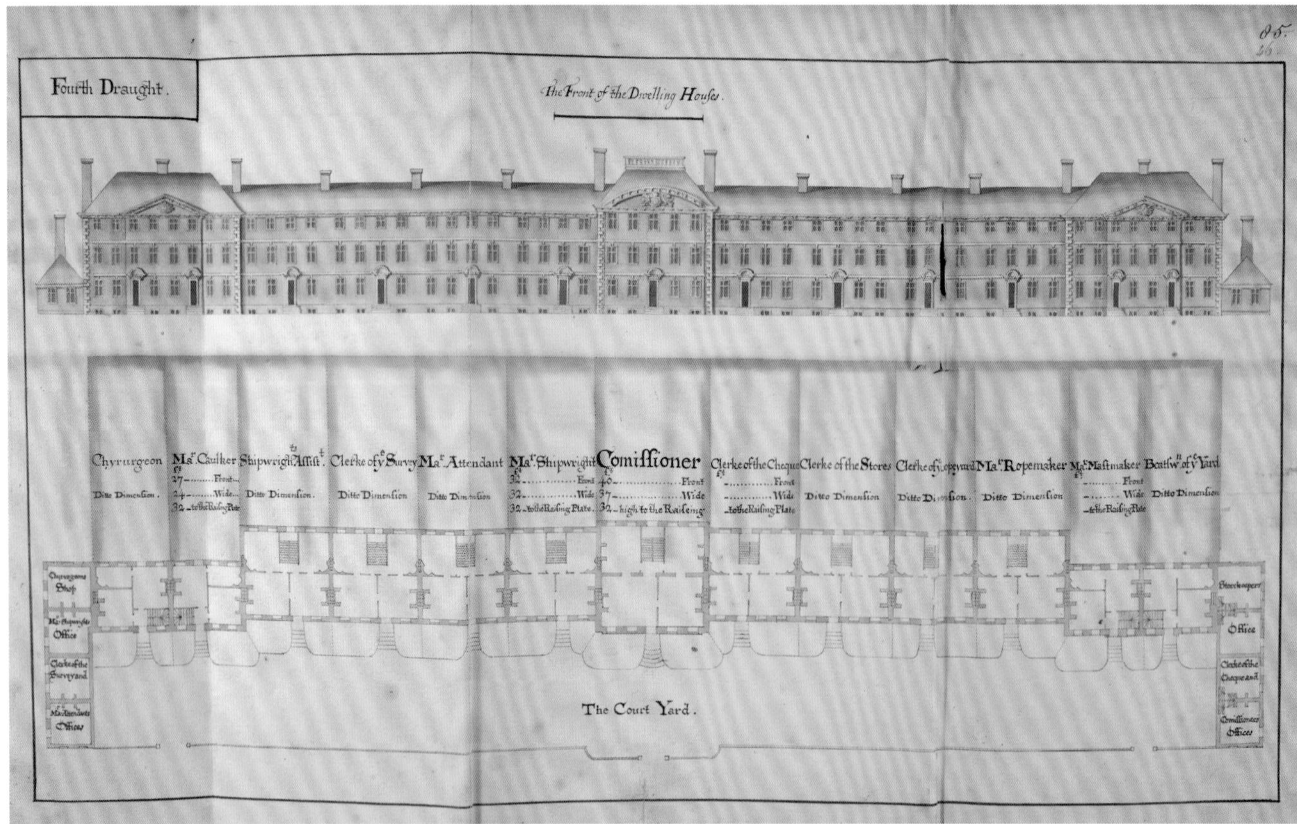

Fig 7.2
Dummer's officers' terrace at Devonport Dockyard, one of the earliest palace-fronted terraces in Britain. The dockyard commissioner had the central residence as well as the largest garden to the rear of the building.
(© The British Library Board. Lansdowne 847 fol 46)

Fig 7.3
A late 19th-century photograph of the commodore's house at Port Royal, its tall tower matched by a similar one on the nearby storehouse. By then its principal use was as a signal station, but both were also used as watchtowers. (TNA ADM 195/49 fol 34)

Holl's design for the Commissioner's House (*see* Chapter 12) that was begun on the headland of Ireland Island at Bermuda in 1822 and completed in 1831 needed no roof-top balcony, but the building was provided with deep verandas on three sides (Fig 7.4). In the aftermath of the brief war with the United States, Commissioner John Lewis, who had already noted that the Americans were watching the growth of this naval base 'with an evil and enquiring eye', unsuccessfully petitioned the Navy Board to have the verandas extended 'round the end of the house which fronts to the westward, as an uninterrupted lookout in the quarter from which we may expect our American visitors is indispensable'.[8] This is the only reference found giving a military reason for these features. In the home dockyards in particular, although no doubt justified as allowing the commissioner or naval officer to keep an eye on yard activities, they became more of a highly visible status symbol.

Fig 7.4
Holl's Commissioner's House, Bermuda Dockyard. (Author)

Not surprisingly, officers in other dockyards soon wished for something comparable to the Plymouth terrace, although commissioners and later on Port Admirals seem to have preferred the greater prestige and privacy of substantial detached houses. The first commissioner to live in the new Plymouth terrace, Captain George St Lo, set the precedent when in 1703 he was subsequently appointed commissioner at Chatham. Being the premier yard, this was a considerable career advancement. However, the existing residence was not to St Lo's liking and, as the Navy Board noted in a letter to the

Admiralty, 'not only before he came to Chatham, but since having desired to have the house the Commissioner lived in pulled down and a new one built in its place'. St Lo's persistence paid off, and the house he demanded is now the oldest intact dockyard building (Figs 7.5 and 7.6).[9]

In 1715 work started at Portsmouth on a terrace for eight of the senior officers; this had to be supplemented in the late 1770s by a terrace for a further four. Around 1722 a terrace for 12 officers was begun at Chatham (Fig 7.7).[10] In the course of the next century, every home yard was provided with similar housing, with the exception of Harwich, which was too small,

Fig 7.5
The Commissioner's House of 1704 at Chatham, the oldest intact dockyard building. The wing to the right was built later in the 18th century to provide more accommodation and a larger kitchen. (Author)

Fig 7.6
The painted ceiling at the head of the main staircase in the Commissioner's House at Chatham Dockyard. This assembly of the gods, painted by Thornhill, was originally intended for the great cabin of HMS Royal Sovereign. *(Author)*

and Pembroke, where Holl designed pairs of spacious semi-detached residences (*see* Figs 1.18 and 1.19), begun in 1817 and remarkable for their use of iron structural members (*see* Chapter 1).[11] A few years later, Sheerness became the last dockyard to have terrace housing provided for the yard officers. In 1824 construction of a substantial terrace for the 'five principal officers' was authorised here by the Navy Board to plans drawn up by Holl three years earlier.[12] Construction was supervised by Holl's successor, G L Taylor, who also designed a rather less commodious terrace of seven houses 'for the inferior officers' on a site immediately south of the dockyard church (Fig 7.8). These were begun in 1829, when a seventh house was added at the south end for the senior victualling officer.[13]

Fig 7.7
The 1720s Officers' Terrace at Chatham Dockyard. Most of the 12 houses have been little altered internally since construction. All have service wings and long detached gardens to the rear. (Author)

Fig 7.8
G L Taylor's terrace of seven houses for the 'inferior officers' at Sheerness Dockyard, adjacent to the dockyard church in the distance. A separate gate allowed access to the town. (Author)

None of the terraces were given grand palace façades following the Plymouth precedent; nearly all were plain and functional and could have been lifted from any Georgian street in London. The one exception was the Chatham terrace, which was embellished with the handsome flowing crenellations that characterised buildings constructed in the Medway yard at that time (Fig 7.9). Its warren of rooms and awkwardly placed staircases are evidence for it being designed locally by yard officers unversed in domestic spatial planning and more concerned to present a grand façade to the world.

From the early 18th century Port Admirals had been appointed according to need at the main fleet bases and at the Nore.[14] They played an increasingly important administrative role, providing extra links and continuity between the Admiralty, the dockyard commissioners and the local squadron commanders.[15] For long they were generally provided with accommodation afloat, perhaps on a guard ship or hulk, but from late in the 18th century they were gradually given shore accommodation. At Portsmouth a house in town was rented until 1832 when a suitably grand residence was added to the end of the officers' terrace of 1715. At Plymouth a house at Mutton Cove was rented, but with space in the dockyard at a premium, a new house was completed outside in 1809, close to Government House and probably to a design by Holl (Fig 7.10). Its major drawbacks lay in its position overlooking the garrison parade ground and the lack of any view of the dockyard or fleet. This was remedied in 1934 when the Admiralty acquired Government House (built between 1789 and 1798 for the military commander of the Western District) from the army in exchange for the former Port Admiral's residence. Cuts in the defence budget in the 1980s led to the disposal of the property.

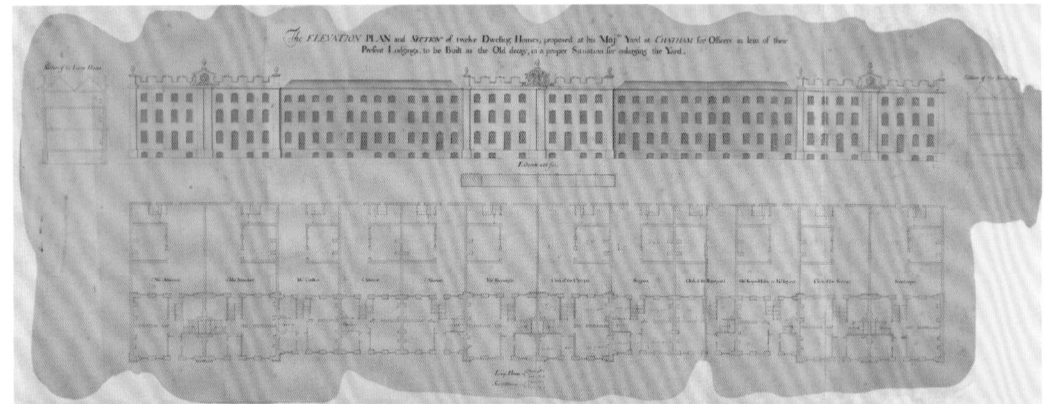

Fig 7.9
One of a number of drawings prepared for the proposed terrace at Chatham Dockyard, the nearest to what was actually constructed. (© National Maritime Museum, Greenwich, London, ADM/Y/C/22)

Fig 7.10
The Port Admiral's House at Devonport, completed in 1809. (Author)

At Deal in February 1812 'the house of Mr May' was purchased for the Port Admiral.[16] This was a wartime appointment, and the house was presumably sold after 1815. In 1810 at Sheerness it had been recommended that 'the long-delayed house for the Port Admiral' should be built to allow him to give up his quarters on the *Vindictive* hulk moored alongside the mast pond, but it was to be another 23 years before the house was completed (Fig 7.11).[17] As at Plymouth, yard space at Sheerness was at a premium, and little progress was made until May 1827 when the Duke of Clarence, in one of his first acts after being invested in the long-defunct title of Lord High Admiral, partly as a way of keeping him out of mischief, ordered the construction of the residence on land to be purchased from the Board of Ordnance.[18] The royal command had immediate effects. By August work on the new house was under way on the site of the Three Tuns Inn. What prompted the Duke's involvement is unclear, but he may have intended using it when at the Nore. G L Taylor, who was then investigating the use of concrete as a material for civil engineering works such as dock floors, apparently used the material for the foundations of this house. Vice-Admiral Sir John Beresford, who held the Nore command from 1830 to 1833 and was its first occupant, was so pleased with the new residence that he presented Taylor, who had a large and growing family, with a calf from their house cow, which was duly shipped round to Woolwich.[19] The house was demolished in the 1960s after the yard closed.

Fig 7.11
The Port Admiral's House at Sheerness, authorised by the Duke of Clarence in 1827. A 1948 photograph. (AA59/00811)

Fig 7.12
Admiralty House at Halifax Dockyard. It was begun in 1816 and was constructed of the local stone. On top of the roof was originally a balcony look-out. (Author)

Fig 7.13
The late 18th-century terrace for three officers at Halifax Dockyard. Like many buildings here, this was timber framed using the ample local supplies of wood. It no longer survives. (TNA ADM 195/49 fol 3b)

Apart from the official residences of the Port Admirals that survive at Devonport and Portsmouth, a solitary example completed in 1819 also remains at Halifax (Fig 7.12). There, a Port Admiral was first appointed in 1813, combining the role with that of flag officer for the North America squadron. As the squadron by the end of the Napoleonic Wars was based in Bermuda, where a new Admiralty House had also been constructed in 1816, the Halifax house was little used for its intended purpose.[20]

Overseas bases had few senior staff before the middle of the 19th century, so the demand for official housing was correspondingly less, and only two terraces are known. At Halifax in 1793,

following complaints about the high cost of renting housing in the town, the Admiralty authorised a commodious pedimented terrace of three weatherboarded houses in the dockyard, its multiplicity of chimney stacks indicative of the harsh local winters (Fig 7.13). Like the majority of the dockyard terraces, these houses had large enclosed porches with classical details, in this case very close in design to the surviving ones at Chatham and Portsmouth.[21] The terrace was damaged in 1917 and demolished in 1930. In Malta in 1843 the Admiralty acquired a terrace of three houses built in the 18th century in Senglea, overlooking Dockyard Creek (*see* Fig 11.15). Originally constructed for the Knights' galley captains, they were converted into accommodation for six senior dockyard officers (*see* Chapter 11).[22]

The interiors of dockyard houses tended to reflect the rank of the occupants, with the grandest living in some considerable style. Among others, the commissioners' houses at Chatham, Portsmouth and Plymouth all had ballrooms, generally added or adapted from existing rooms in the 19th century, while the Port Admiral's house under construction at Sheerness in 1829 was provided with a 'grapery' and had the ceilings of its principal rooms prepared for chandeliers. The Navy Board was happy to pay for these, but the differing priorities of Regency England are apparent in their refusal at the same time to provide a bath for the occupants. Such facilities were introduced only in the latter part of the 19th century, probably spurred on by improvements in naval hospitals.[23]

All the houses for the senior dockyard officers had substantial walled gardens, generally stretching to the rear of the properties. Occasionally, where space was at a premium, some gardens were located elsewhere in the dockyard, as at Chatham in 1719, where three gardens are shown next to the ropery.[24] The earliest examples to retain their original boundary walls largely intact are those finished at Portsmouth in 1719 and at Chatham in 1731, while other complete sets of gardens survive to the rear of the 1770s terrace at Portsmouth and the 1829 terrace at Sheerness (Fig 7.14).[25] The Sheerness and Chatham gardens also retain the associated contemporary ranges of stables for the officers' horses. Uniquely, one range at Chatham incorporates a coach house, provided when the commissioner also had responsibility for Sheerness. As might be expected, the gardens of the commissioners' detached houses were the largest. At Portsmouth, the former Commissioner's House of 1784, now Admiralty House, retains its equally spacious gardens laid out to its rear. This is now the only former Commissioner's House that is still a residence and in Royal Navy ownership.

At most of the overseas bases where land was cheap or free and where the Surveyor of the Navy was unlikely to visit, local officials could be adept at interpreting rules, and so houses for the senior officers tended to be more commodious and surrounded by extensive grounds. Late in 1743 the newly arrived military engineer-in-ordinary at Minorca, James Montresor, drew up plans for three spacious detached houses with

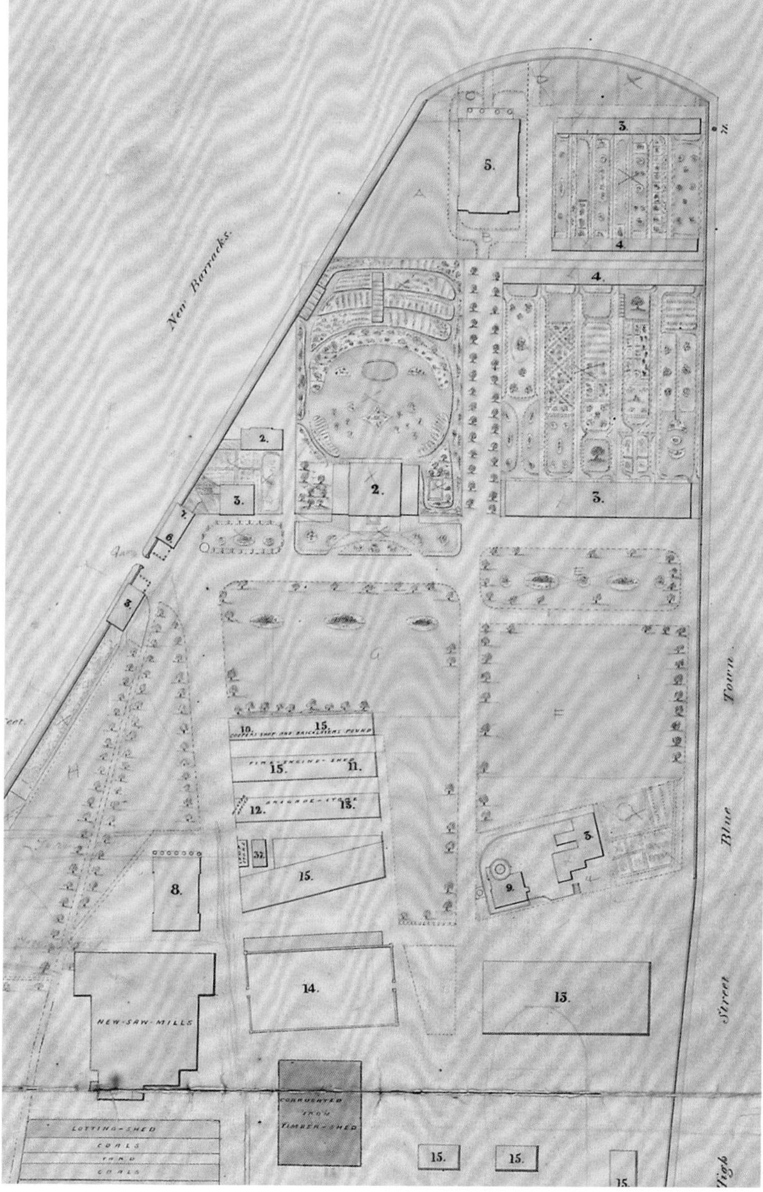

Fig 7.14
The eastern end of Sheerness Dockyard in 1850, with its spacious grounds and gardens around the terraces of the senior dockyard officers, the former Commissioner's House and dockyard chapel. Although the individual planting schemes are not known, there is no reason to doubt the garden layouts shown here.
(TNA ADM 140/701)

gardens for the commissioner and senior officers. These were on high ground overlooking the dockyard, but it is not clear whether they were ever built.[26] Some of the grandest of all naval residences were those constructed from the end of the 18th century for the flag officers on foreign stations, many of whom would have been used to substantial mansions of their own. In 1819, the new Admiralty House at Halifax with just over 17 acres of gardens and grounds comfortably eclipsed the total area of the dockyard; in 1810 Admiralty House at Trincomalee enjoyed no less than 25 acres, while Admiralty House at Bermuda had some 9 acres of gardens and just over a further 8 acres described as 'kitchen gardens and paddock'.[27]

In 1793 the Navy Board rented for their new Gibraltar dockyard commissioner the house reconstructed for his retirement by Lieutenant-Colonel Sir William Green, the senior Royal Engineer who played such a distinguished role in the Great Siege of 1779–83. The Board acquired the freehold in 1799. The Mount, described in 1805 by Mrs Middleton, wife of the then commissioner, as 'like a good comfortable large farmhouse', was to be altered and extended later in the 19th century. If it lacked the grandeur of the commissioners' houses at Portsmouth and Devonport, its views across the Straits of Gibraltar are stunning, with the house and garden located high on the western slope of the Rock (Fig 7.15). It has one of the largest gardens on the Rock. The well-wooded and fertile garden originally covered some 11 acres, compared to the 4 acres of the dockyard at that time. It remains one of the largest on the Rock, and the house and gardens were acquired by the Gibraltar government when the Ministry of Defence closed the base.[28] At Bermuda, the Commissioner's House, begun in 1822, likewise enjoyed sweeping views across Great Sound, but the exposed location and the barren rock would have defeated even the most determined gardener.

Dockyard residents might stay in their official accommodation for a decade or more, although most tenancies were for shorter periods, especially from the early 20th century. Such transient populations might be thought to have taken little interest in their gardens, while only the most senior officers were provided with gardeners, ensuring regular maintenance and providing continuity between tenures. There is, however, good evidence that the majority of senior dockyard officials – educated men at the tops of their professions and trades, many well travelled and having contacts with leading figures in society – were generally proud of their yards and keen to show them to best advantage. Thus in September 1719 the occupants of the recently completed officers' terrace at Portsmouth wrote to the Navy Board requesting that a double row of 36 lime trees should be planted in front, where they 'would not only be

Fig 7.15
The Commissioner's House at Gibraltar in 1971. This is no longer used by the Royal Navy. (Author)

a means to break off the weather from the houses, but a very great ornament to the building'.[29] Their request was granted; nearly 300 years later descendants of these trees are still fulfilling the dual roles originally envisaged. Similar formal tree plantings exist in other naval establishments, notably at Pembroke, Chatham Historic Dockyard and in the former naval hospitals at Haslar and Stonehouse, all indicative of continuing interest by generations of resident officers. It is reasonable to assume that such people would have had a similar regard for the private gardens attached to their official residences.

In 1663 John Evelyn had been much impressed at Chatham where the commissioner, Peter Pett, had created a 'pretty garden, banqueting house, potts, statues, cypresses, resembling some villas about Rome'.[30] As befitted the country's then premier naval base, the commissioner's garden at Chatham was the most elaborate of those recorded by Dummer some 35 years later. His survey included some of the features remarked on by Evelyn, such as the banqueting house and the three terraces. The lowest of these by then had a shortlived Dutch-style water garden with four narrow canals and a central brick fountain (Fig 7.16), probably the work of Edward Gregory, commissioner here from 1689 to 1703.[31] This terraced landscaping still remains, as does what may be the late 17th-century banqueting house.

There are very few documentary sources relating to life in naval houses and gardens, although such records may well survive in the private correspondence of tenants and their visitors.[32] Our best evidence to date comes from the dockyard plans and 18th-century models, a number of which indicate the arrangements of flowerbeds, lawns, paths and trees. Unusually, the gardens of the officers' terrace at Chatham and those at Short Row, Portsmouth, are separated from their houses by narrow service roads, as were all except the commissioner's garden at the Plymouth terrace. At Chatham this allows for a small paved courtyard to the rear of each house, while the main gardens additionally are terraced into the hillside, each garden approached by covered steps cut into the hillside.

Fig 7.16
The garden of the Commissioner's House at Chatham, photographed in 1856. This is the oldest of the dockyard gardens and was unique in having a fountain, here with Captain Superintendent George Goldsmith and his wife.
(DoE)

Long, narrow gardens tended to dictate an axial design for each garden, with a central path generally flanked by two paths close to the side walls and linked by cross-paths at intervals. At Chatham the gardens had a series of parterres for flowers, while the walls had fruit trees trained along them. Only three houses had small areas of lawn. All appear to have had small and rather charming timber garden rooms at the lower end, built above the rear of the access stairs; remarkably, one of these survives in a good state of preservation. Its gothick windows overlooking the garden and its delicate Chinese Chippendale trellis decoration suggest a late 18th-century date.[33] Such timber structures were well within the capabilities of the dockyard joiners and are unlikely to appear in the written records; similar garden buildings almost certainly existed in other yards.

The dockyard plans and models suggest that the Chatham officers' gardens may have been the most elaborate of these 18th-century terrace gardens, but this may simply reflect more detailed records. However, the Chatham gardens are the only ones to have had limited research and archaeological investigations in the late 1980s. Among other discoveries were a number of 'hot walls', probably predating 1816, as evidence for the growing of tender fruits.[34] Significantly, the excavations indicate that the gardens on the 1774 yard model are an accurate representation and that much of the 18th-century layout of these survives today (Fig 7.17).

Less is known about the gardens and grounds at the various overseas bases, since detailed records are fewer. The smallest establishments such as English Harbour, Antigua, and Esquimalt on the coast of British Columbia were generally in the charge of storekeepers. Their accommodation usually reflected their lower status, though the storekeeper at Trincomalee lived in a vast Regency house larger than most of the commissioners' houses in the home dockyards.[35] At Antigua, where space was at a premium, there were only a couple of modest gardens in the dockyard itself, but when a new house was built on a hill on the other side of the harbour in the late 1780s, it was surrounded by more extensive grounds. It was constructed for the young Prince William Henry, later Duke of Clarence and King William IV, when he was on station here with Nelson. Clearly something of a white elephant after the prince's departure, little attempt seems to have been made to develop a formal garden when it was in Admiralty ownership. It is now known as Clarence House (*see* Chapter 12).[36] As might be expected, some of the most luxuriant gardens were to be found in bases such as Port Royal and Trincomalee, where a combination of generally

Fig 7.17
The gardens to the rear of the officers' terrace at Chatham Dockyard shown on the 1774 model.
(© National Maritime Museum, Greenwich, London, L2712-013)

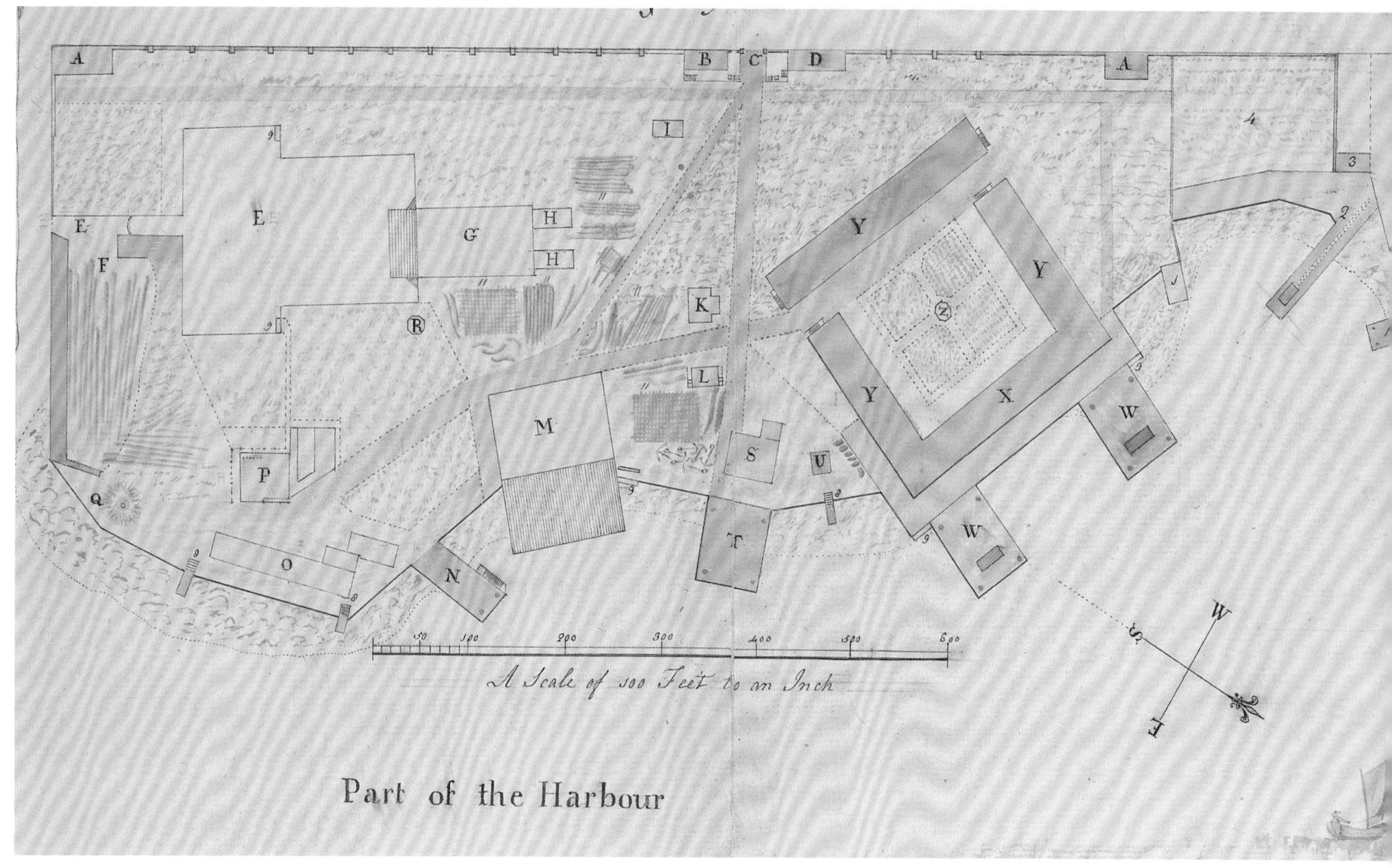

Fig 7.18
A 1771 plan of Halifax Dockyard inscribed to 'the Hon. Hugh Palliser', then Comptroller of the Navy but formerly Governor and Commander-in-Chief at Newfoundland.
(© National Maritime Museum, Greenwich, London, Lad 11/51)

benign climates, fertile soils and availability of labour allowed yard and naval staff and their wives ample scope for horticultural enthusiasms. Late 19th-century photographs of these and other houses show what must have been richly colourful flower gardens close to the houses, while the larger establishments had sweeping lawns used for croquet and receptions, with paddocks and less formal areas of trees and shrubs beyond. Tennis courts were common features, while the mid-19th century Admiralty House at Halifax also possessed a quoit ground.[37]

Outside the residences it is also apparent that those officials stationed overseas, like their home counterparts, took some care to soften the industrial landscapes of the yards. By the mid-19th century, Port Royal and Trincomalee were notable for their profusion of palm trees, and by the end of the century Esquimalt's open spaces had a variety of native trees, most of which probably predated the dockyard.[38] At Halifax by the 1770s a formal garden unusually had been laid out within the quadrangle formed by the capstan house and the storehouses, a contemporary plan showing what may have been lawns intersected by a grid of paths with a sundial in the centre (Fig 7.18). Such a feature in the often harsh climate would no doubt have been welcomed in the summers by the seamen quartered here. Nearby, the officers' houses, adapted from the Commissioner's House of 1785, also overlooked an oval of grass with a few trees.[39]

Ascension Island, with its bleak volcanic landscape and almost total lack of water, proved the most intractable for keen gardeners (Fig 7.19). Only around the hospital above the cloud line on the top of Green Mountain, where there was vegetation and some rainfall, was it possible to grow limited crops. The scattering of buildings forming the naval station on the coast at Georgetown had to make do with growing plants in half-barrels and stone troughs outside the houses and workshops, using ingenuity, perseverance and imported soil. By 1900 there was a tennis court to the rear of the officers' cottages, and although this is described on some maps as a *lawn* tennis court, photographs suggest this may have been the interpretation of an optimistic cartographer.[40]

Fig 7.19
Gardening enthusiasts on Ascension Island had to use their ingenuity on this barren outpost. The resident engineer's quarters in 1895 was typical in its limited employment of half-barrels, generally filled with imported soil.
(AdL Da 032)

Gates and lodge houses

The only other employees whose jobs required them to be housed on site were the yard porters and occasionally the yard boatswain, who were provided with small residences inside the main entrances. Such buildings have been especially vulnerable when entrances have been widened. At Portsmouth the early 18th-century Porter's Lodge, although altered, remains in use as offices just inside the old main gateway. It is the oldest such building. The most impressive are the crenellated and machicolated twin towers of the 1718 main gateway to Chatham Dockyard that once housed the yard porter and the boatswain, along with their families. The contemporary dockyard wall once had half a dozen small towers along it at intervals, like a town wall. As with the main gate, these towers were for show rather than strength, and they had a variety of uses. The two surviving ones have long been used as small houses (Fig 7.20). Chatham is also unique in having just inside the main gate the marine guardhouse, constructed in 1764 when marines replaced civilian watchmen in an effort to reduce pilfering by the yard workers. The handsome colonnade was added in 1813. The marine guard would have been quartered in the nearby marine barracks, then in the course of construction.[41]

Fig 7.20
One of the two surviving wall towers of 1718 at Chatham Dockyard, later adapted as a house. The contemporary dockyard wall beyond forms the end of the officers' gardens (see Fig 7.17).
(Author)

At Pembroke and Sheerness considerable care was taken in the 1820s with the design of the main gates and their associated guardhouses to ensure they formed handsome entrances to the yards, if not perhaps as grandiose as their contemporaries at the victualling yards at Plymouth and Gosport. At both dockyards the main gates were flanked by monumental stone walls with pedestrian entrances leading to short colonnades fronting the pairs of guardhouses (Fig 7.21). The construction of the main gate and guardhouses at Sheerness was authorised in 1827, but the design of the houses and their colonnades is clearly based on Holl's 1817 Pembroke design, although his successor Taylor emphasised the massy nature of the whole enterprise in his employment of smoothly rusticated ashlar blocks for the main wall.[42] The Pembroke entrance remains intact;

Fig 7.21
The main gate of Sheerness Dockyard photographed in 1958.
(Author)

Fig 7.22
The simple main gateway of c 1770 at English Harbour, Antigua, is typical of many of the smaller naval bases. It has a guardhouse just inside.
(Author)

regrettably, the needs of modern traffic have led to the demolition of the Sheerness gateway and the colonnaded porticoes, although the two houses still stand.

In the overseas yards good examples of guardhouses and porters' residences survive at the former yards at English Harbour, Antigua (Fig 7.22), and at Kingston, Ontario. The single-storey porter's residence with its colonnaded elevation at English Harbour probably dates from the 1770s, while at Kingston the colonnaded porter's lodge lies just inside the former dockyard gateway, with a separate, small, single-storey guardhouse adjacent.[43]

Dockyard offices

Until the 19th century, offices for senior dockyard staff were comparatively modest, both in scale and number. In general, before the invention of the typewriter and telephone, these all functioned in much the same way. They were work places for the officers and provided space for clerks writing, copying and filing the interminable correspondence generated by such large industrial complexes. Master shipwrights, who used their offices for drawing plans of warships and for storing their models, tended to occupy the largest and best-lit rooms. In the roof spaceof the 1754 Chatham mould loft, overlooking the mould floor beneath, is a small drawing office, possibly for last-minute alterations to plans drawn in the main office. In Dummer's fourth draught of 1694 for the Plymouth terrace, he incorporated two single-storey ranges, each with four small offices of identical size at opposite ends of the terrace. Surprisingly, given his interest in efficiency, these offices were not linked internally, and their entrance doors and windows faced away from the 400ft terrace walk. This was not a desire to preserve the privacy of the occupants of the houses, for Dummer saw the terrace walk as an open-air – and, one assumes, fair-weather – focal point, 'where the said officers may meet and confer together for the due understanding of one another in the general despatch of the service'.[44] Dummer's 1694 design was clearly seen as inadequate, for on construction the offices were increased to two storeys, with their front rooms overlooking the dockyard.[45] The northern of the two ranges survived the 1941 air raids, and although altered internally, it is the only surviving example of a late 17th-century dockyard office.

Evidence of the original absence of internal communication is apparent in the surviving range of 18th-century offices that gradually accumulated along the outside of the northern wall of the commissioner's garden at Chatham. Piecemeal development may have contributed to this, but when the dockyard came to build a new centralised office in the yard in 1750, the planning showed only a moderate advance on Dummer. The handsome two-storey pedimented range had seven external doors giving direct access to offices, some of which were paired together with internal doors, but with no common corridor on the ground floor (Fig 7.23). Eight staircases rising from within these offices suggest better vertical than lateral integration. As would be expected, the master shipwright had the largest office in the centre of the range, while at one end a tap-house may have been used for informal meetings.[46] These offices were demolished in 1808.

Apart from the small offices built against the commissioner's garden wall at Chatham, only

Fig 7.23
The 1750 offices at Chatham Dockyard. Each department had its own space, with no lateral internal communications.
(© National Maritime Museum, Greenwich, London, ADM/Y/C/10)

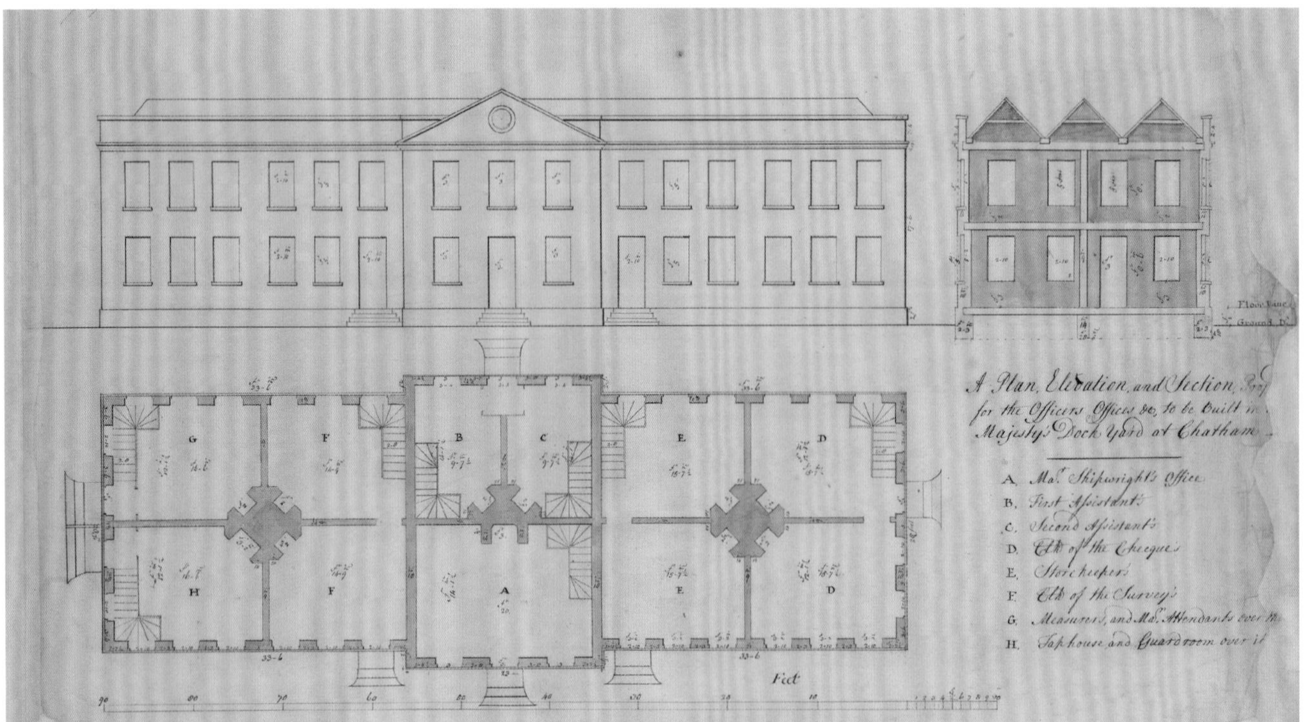

two Georgian office blocks remain in the home dockyards. The oldest of these, and the earliest surviving purpose-built office to have spine corridors on each floor for internal communication, is the South Office Block of 1786–9 facing HMS *Victory* in Portsmouth (Fig 7.24). Many of its ground-floor offices, however, still retained their own external doors, probably for reasons of status as much as convenience. At Chatham in 1808, when Edward Holl replaced the 1750 offices, he carried internal planning to its logical conclusion, not only providing spine corridors but also reducing the number of external doorways to three (Fig 7.25). Similar offices existed in other yards, but fell victim to wartime bombs or subsequent redevelopment.

In 1789 the Portsmouth officers, concerned to maintain the architectural balance and with it the dignity of the centre of their dockyard, insisted that a new storehouse to be built adjacent to their new offices should match the latter in size and external appearance. Some half century later, as the demands for office space grew, it was a simple matter to link the two buildings with a handsome archway block, so forming the present South Office Block. This enlightened and sensitive conversion was emulated some years later when the 1820s boiler shop and smithery at Portsmouth had become obsolete. Rather than demolish the building, the dockyard carefully converted it into offices, a use it still retains.[47]

Fig 7.24
The original 1786 offices at Portsmouth Dockyard. The central archway block was added when the storehouses beyond were adapted as offices. (Author)

Fig 7.25
Holl's 1808 offices at Chatham Dockyard. (Author)

In the 19th century, major naval developments tended to incorporate offices within complexes of buildings, rather than have them freestanding. The Melville Square Storehouse, begun in 1829, was the showpiece centre of John Rennie junior's Royal William Victualling Yard at Stonehouse (*see* Chapter 14) and included offices within its central entrance range. Across the Hamoaze a quarter of a century later, the main offices were incorporated in the centre of the western range of storehouses, part of the huge steam factory in the new North Yard at Devonport.[48]

Among the more specialised, small administrative buildings to be found in every yard were the pay offices, not just for the dockyard workers, but also for the crews of naval ships in harbour. These buildings housed the pay clerks, the cashier and a secure room containing the money for wages. In 1744 the Navy Board approved a new pay office at Portsmouth in the south part of the yard that 'will be very convenient, as the Commissioner will be free of the noise and disturbance that generally happens at the payment of ships'. Ships' muster and pay books were also frequently lodged in these pay offices before being sent to the Navy Board in London. In wartime, seamen in the 18th century were generally paid just before their ship sailed and again at the end of a commission, as soon as the pay books had been made up. On such occasions, the commissioner of the dockyard and his pay clerks usually went on board with the cash.[49]

Pay offices could hold considerable sums of money, and when Bentham put forward proposals for a new pay office in Portsmouth in 1808, he was mindful to make it 'more secure against such depredations as that which was effected through the ceiling of the cash room at Plymouth'. To this end, he proposed that a fireproof first floor should be carried on brick groin vaults supported by cast-iron columns. The record room and adjacent cash room on this floor were similarly to be vaulted, and there were to be double iron doors and iron shutters to secure the windows against both fire and intruders.[50] A wartime air raid destroyed the upper storey, but the ground floor – originally used as a guardhouse – survives, with its brick vaulting and fluted iron columns, cast at Bentham's suggestion in the new metal mills in the yard (Fig 7.26). This is the earliest naval building to use cast iron as a major part of its fireproof structure.

Fig 7.26
The ground floor of the former pay office of 1808 at Portsmouth Dockyard showing the cast-iron columns supporting the brick vaults. Photographed in 1981, when the building was used by the naval film unit.
(DoE)

In the great rebuilding of Sheerness Dockyard after the Napoleonic Wars, a pay office of similar appearance was constructed, which was completed by March 1829; as at Portsmouth it was combined with a military guardhouse, but was not fireproofed.[51] The new yard at Pembroke, perhaps due to its small size and remote location, had a pay office inside the new office building. The room was simply protected by cast-iron doors, and the officers asked for 'one of Mr Chubb's patent detector locks' to be fitted.[52] At Chatham the 18th-century pay office was built adjacent to the room housing the Chatham Chest, against the north side of the commissioner's garden wall. In 1814 the Chatham Chest funds were amalgamated with those of Greenwich Royal Hospital, allowing the pay office to expand. In 1822 an extra floor was added; inside, only the windowless strong room marked it as anything out of the ordinary.[53] Although the cashiers worked in this building, by the 1840s the yard employees were paid their wages in a room at the nearby marine guardhouse at the main gate.[54]

Dockyard chapels

Chaplains were at sea with the fleet by the latter part of the 16th century, and 100 years later were to be found in most of the buildings then used as naval hospitals during wartime. However, not until the 1700s did purpose-designed chapels appear in naval establishments.[55] The earliest of these formed part of Christopher Wren's plans for the Royal Hospital at Greenwich, founded by Queen Mary in 1694 as a thank-offering for victory at La Hogue 2 years earlier. Modelled on the Royal Hospital at Chelsea, this was to house elderly, infirm and indigent sailors. Its chapel was atypical, because its size and decoration reflected the scale and magnificence of the whole foundation.

What was almost certainly the first purpose-built chapel in an active naval base formed the central element of the new naval hospital of 1711 at Minorca. The chapel, with its classical orders, dome and cupola, has echoes of its Greenwich contemporary, though on a considerably more modest scale. This suggests that Captain Latham, who designed the hospital at Minorca, was probably aware of the Greenwich chapel. The hospital still survives in modified form (*see* Chapter 16).[56] Later, when navy-built and navy-run hospitals were constructed in England, first at Haslar in the 1740s and then at Plymouth a decade later, chapels were included in their original plans. In this they may simply have been emulating arrangements in the two famous London hospitals of St Bartholomew's and St Thomas's, long used by the navy for its sick and injured in wartime.[57] However, the case for chapels in the dockyards was not so apparent, as relatively few people lived within their boundaries, and most yards were sited in towns close to parish churches.

The first dockyard chapel stemmed from a petition in 1703 to the Lord High Admiral from the 'officers, clerks, artificers and all others of every rank and quality belonging to Her Majesty's Dockyard' at Portsmouth. The dockyard lay isolated from the town of Portsmouth, outside Bernard de Gomme's new bastioned defences, beyond the substantial mill pond and across a common.[58] The settlement of Portsea was developing immediately outside the dockyard for its workers, but the nearest churches lay in Portsmouth or Kingston. As the petitioners complained, the 'extreme badness of the roads', especially in winter, frequently prevented them from attending. Their modest request was for a piece of land within the dockyard on which 'to erect at their own proper cost and charges, a chapel'. This was approved by the Admiralty. A similar arrangement was later agreed at the new Plymouth Dockyard, which lay equally distant from its town.[59]

The 1774 model of Portsmouth Dockyard shows this first chapel to have been a handsome brick building, its pitched roof surmounted by a cupola. Its height allowed the subsequent insertion of a gallery for students from the nearby Naval Academy opened in 1733; quite properly, the Navy Board paid for this alteration. The 1774 Plymouth Dockyard model shows its chapel to have been an ambitious stone building, with a substantial bell tower at its west end. In 1767 the Reverend Robert Hughes, chaplain of the ordinary and evidently a man of means, had written to the Admiralty asking permission to add another aisle at his own expense.[60] The Navy Board, never one to miss an opportunity, supported the request and promised to supply scaffolding and 'unserviceable materials towards making the roof', on condition that 'an additional gallery for their use and a pew for the officers in the guard-ships be reserved in the new building'. In such cases, 'unserviceable materials' were generally sound but not of suitable dimensions for use on

Fig 7.27
Holl's 1814 proposal for the dockyard church at Devonport. (TNA ADM 140/234 pt 2)

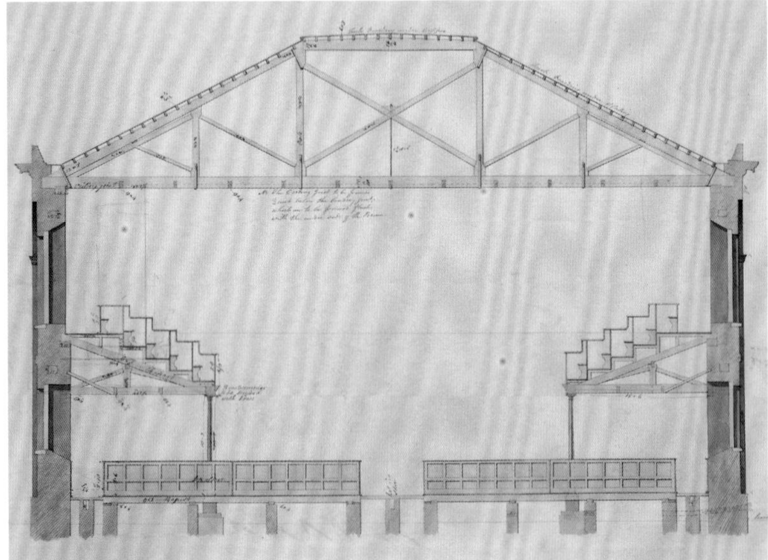

Fig 7.28
A cross-section of Holl's dockyard church at Devonport. (TNA ADM 140/234 pt 6)

warships. Despite this extension to the chapel, it soon proved inadequate, and in 1797 an Act of Parliament was obtained for a new building, although war prevented this being achieved for nearly two decades.[61] In May 1814, Edward Holl drew up plans for a new church, which apparently held 2,000 worshippers and remained in use until destroyed by bombing in the Second World War (Figs 7.27 and 7.28).

By the latter part of the 18th century the Navy Board was prepared to be more financially supportive towards places of worship for the yards. At Chatham, the dockyard lay close to the parish church of St Mary, where the commissioner at least had a pew,[62] but in 1755 the Board provided the hulk *Russell*, later replaced by the *Revenge*, as a floating chapel. By the 1770s the chapel at Plymouth was receiving £10 a year towards its maintenance, and in 1781 the Navy Board authorised £489 towards repairing Portsmouth chapel, only 4 years before it had to be demolished to make way for the commissioner's new house. Understandably, its replacement, the present St Ann's church, was wholly funded by the Navy Board;[63] by then it seems to have been tacitly accepted that the construction, maintenance and staffing of dockyard churches were the responsibility of the navy, although it seems that worshippers still had to pay pew rents.[64] Pembroke Dock did not have a purpose-built chapel until 1835 (*see* below), but by 1818 there was a yard chaplain, and by the following year a temporary chapel had been established. This was in such a parlous state by 1825 that shores had to be inserted under the floor 'to enable the congregation to assemble with any degree of safety'.[65]

A combination of circumstances probably contributed to this gradual change of heart. The Navy Board may have been influenced in part by the example of the Sick and Hurt Board, who with generally less-ambulant inmates provided chapels in their new hospitals at Gosport and Stonehouse.[66] But at its root lay an element of paternalism on the part of the Navy Board towards its workforce. Allied to this was greater pressure on existing places of worship resulting from the growth and modernisation of the fleet and expansion of the principal yards. But behind these considerations also lay the rise of nonconformity and evangelism, with the perceived threats of subversion to the established order.[67] Both the Admiralty and the Navy Board would not have wanted their very large industrial workforce to be led astray by open-air lay preachers and others. One obvious way to counter this was to ensure that their workers had easy access to dockyard churches staffed by approved chaplains.[68]

Four dockyard churches built under the auspices of the Navy Board still remain in varying degrees of preservation. The earliest of these, and the only one still in naval use, is St Ann's church at Portsmouth, designed by John Marquand, the Navy Board's Surveyor of Buildings, following a visit to the yard in December 1784.[69] The sum of £,1850 was allowed in the 1785 estimates for the new building, which had to be completed under the auspices of the Surveyor within a year by the contractors, Thomas Parlby Senior and Thomas Parlby Junior. The detailed contract specified that the balusters, presumably either for the altar rails or the stairs to the gallery, were to be 'turned by the people of the yard', but everything else was the responsibility of the contractor. Fittings from the interior of the old chapel were to be reused, but the pulpit at least was new. The chaplain, the Reverend Mr Brown, prudently selected a design for the pulpit to 'give the greatest scope to the voice'.[70] St Ann's suffered war damage in 1941, and its west end was rebuilt in shortened form in 1956 (Fig 7.29).

Fig 7.29
The west front of St Ann's Church at Portsmouth Dockyard, shortened by two bays after wartime damage. (Author)

Fig 7.30 (right)
Holl's 1805 drawing of his proposed church for Chatham Dockyard.
(TNA ADM 140/68 pt 4)

Fig 7.31 (below top)
The west end of Holl's church at Chatham Dockyard.
(Author)

Fig 7.32 (below bottom)
The interior of Holl's church at Chatham Dockyard.
(Author)

Chatham Dockyard's first and only church was not authorised until 1804, and Holl's plans were not approved until October the following year (Fig 7.30). Building started in 1806, and the church was in use by the summer of 1810. It is one of Holl's first buildings after his appointment as architect on Bentham's staff, and the first dockyard building to use cast-iron columns as structural members, in this case to support the church gallery.[71] Unusually, the church was mostly constructed using dockyard labour rather than by contract, although specialist plasterers and a local artist were employed. The pulpit was constructed from the casings of ships' pumps sent from Plymouth in 1806. Sadly, this no longer survives. Chatham Dockyard church remained in naval use until Christmas Eve 1981 (Fig 7.31) and is the least altered of the four surviving buildings, still retaining its original plasterwork and early tiered gallery seating (Fig 7.32).

At Sheerness, the community that had grown outside the dockyard following its founding suffered from the same problems as at Portsea, with the nearest parish church some 4 miles distant at Minster. The provision of a church for Sheerness proved to be less straightforward, since the cramped nature of the yard meant there was no space to construct a church within its boundaries. The garrison had a small chapel over the gatehouse to the fortifications, but its size ruled out a more general use, although it seems likely that dockyard officers were able to worship there.[72] For the dockyard labour force, concentrated in the two Sheerness communities of Mile Town and Blue Town outside the defences, the only alternative to a long walk to Minster was to attend local nonconformist private meeting houses and chapels. By 1800 nonconformity was well established here, with the master mastmaker, William Shrubsole, playing a leading role. In 1810 the dockyard officers, concerned that the military chaplain was about to be posted to Portugal, petitioned the Navy Board for a proper chapel, and Holl was ordered to draw up plans.[73] Ongoing discussions on the expansion and modernisation of Sheerness made the Navy Board reluctant to proceed, but in 1812, apparently at Admiralty insistence, building was started on a site shown to be vacant on the plan drawn up for the yard's modernisation by the delegation led by the Controller of the Navy who had visited in June (*see* Chapter 1). This lay outside the then boundaries of the yard and its defences, west of the New Road and the well with its steam pumping house, recently constructed for the dockyard.[74]

The church, very similar in size and design to Holl's new one at Chatham, was completed by late 1814.[75] It was to have the shortest life of any dockyard church, for the modified plans produced by Rennie senior for Sheerness left it inconveniently in the heart of the expanded new yard. In 1824, bowing to the inevitable, the Admiralty agreed to a new building, to be placed on or outside the yard boundary to make it readily accessible to the dockyard town.[76] G L Taylor's design of January 1826 was considered inadequate by the Navy Board, and he was asked to enlarge the building to seat a further 400 people. In May 1826, the contractors Jolliffe, Banks and Nicholson were allowed to demolish the existing church, so that the materials could be reused in the new building, but it seems that the Board of Ordnance did not hand over the land needed for its construction until early 1827. The second new church was ready for its first service in mid-September 1828, and the following month the final touches were done when the Navy Board requested Thwaites and Reed to send 'a proper person to the yard to put up the clock in the chapel'.[77] The new building was sited at the eastern apex of the expanded yard, convenient for the adjoining officers' houses, the new main gateway and the town (Fig 7.33).[78] After the closure of the dockyard, nearly all the fittings of the church were removed, and after a long period of dereliction the building was gutted by fire in 2002.[79]

Fig 7.33
A contemporary model of G L Taylor's church at Sheerness Dockyard. The 1825 model of the dockyard is in the care of English Heritage. (Author)

The last of the four surviving churches stands at Pembroke Dockyard, where it was finally completed in 1835, also to designs by G L Taylor. The 1829/30 estimates had allowed £7,944 for its construction, but the Controller of the Navy Board subsequently reduced that figure to £4,000. This may account for the church's rendered finish rather than the fine ashlar that hitherto had been used for important buildings here.[80] It was clearly popular with the yard workforce and their families, for within a year of its opening, a further sum of £3,500 was put in the estimates 'for constructing galleries required for the accommodation of the increased numbers and for making an additional entrance to the chapel'. Four cast-iron columns to support the galleries were to come from Deptford Dockyard.[81] After a long period of neglect, the church was acquired by the local authority shortly after the millennium and carefully restored (Fig 7.34).

These surviving dockyard churches share a number of common features. Their rectangular plans, similar to many nonconformist chapels, were carefully designed to accommodate large numbers of worshippers within a comparatively

Fig 7.34
Taylor's recently restored church at Pembroke Dockyard.
(Author)

small area and at comparatively modest cost. More capacity was achieved by incorporating galleries, and costs were kept down generally by building in brick and reducing architectural embellishment to a minimum. For Marquand's church at Portsmouth and Holl's somewhat larger church at Chatham, architectural ornamentation was largely confined to the handsome pedimented western elevations, surmounted by modest bellcotes. Interest was added at Chatham by Holl's skilful articulation of the external wall surfaces. By the time Taylor came to design chapels for Sheerness and Pembroke, the great surge of 'Commissioner's Churches', under way following the 1818 Church Buildings Act, possibly influenced his ideas and account for the more expensive ornamentation.[82] At Sheerness a two-stage tower and a handsome portico supported on Ionic columns distinguished the west front, while inside, the church was noted for its fine plasterwork and its barrel-vaulted nave. At Pembroke, the last dockyard to have a purpose-built church, there is a slightly less elaborate west porch and domed tower, a reflection of its reduced funding.

Less attention was paid to the provision of places of worship at the overseas bases where staff numbers were far smaller than in the home yards. When chaplains were to be found at overseas yards, their primary duties were to the crews of ships on station or, as at Bermuda, with caring for convicts working on the naval and military installations. Bermuda had a chaplain long before the dockyard had a church. Uniquely, and a poignant reminder of the price paid by so many sailors on distant stations, Esquimalt had a naval cemetery complete with a small, immaculately maintained chapel, which were established in 1867 and served the Pacific Squadron years before the dockyard was established.[83] Admiral Charles Knowles's hugely ambitious 1748 plan to develop Port Royal into a powerful fortified base, even larger than the one created later on Bermuda, did include a substantial cruciform church in the centre, but the scheme remained firmly on paper.[84]

At Haulbowline, developed at the same time as Pembroke, the Admiralty allowed the conversion of one floor of a new storehouse into a chapel for between 70 and 100 people in 1822, establishing a precedent that was to be followed in a number of overseas yards.[85] At Bermuda in 1852 the first floor of No. 2 Victualling Store was opened as a chapel, and by the end of the 19th century similar arrangements existed at Simon's Town and Garden Island, Sydney. At both bases the chapels were accommodated in the sailmakers' lofts. By then, personnel at Trincomalee appear to have used the nearby military church of St Mary.[86] Yards such as English Harbour, Antigua, or Esquimalt were too small to justify their own places of worship. In the case of Esquimalt and at Halifax and Gibraltar, there were nearby churches in the local communities. The Anglicans in Malta Dockyard, finding themselves in a sea of devout Roman Catholics, established a chapel in an existing building, described in 1843 as being on an 'unsuitable site'.[87] Little more is heard of this, and it seems likely that the small number of Anglicans in the dockyard probably migrated to the magnificent Anglican Cathedral then being built in Valletta under the supervision of William Scamp.[88]

8

Buildings and Engineering Works of the Steam Navy, 1835–1914

The history of the development of the home yards for the steam navy up to the outbreak of the First World War was outlined in Chapter 2. This chapter considers the principal buildings and engineering works that survive from this period and sets them in context.

Much of the Victorian work in the royal dockyards was on a vastly greater scale than what had gone before, while the involvement of the Royal Engineers in the design and construction of both the engineering works such as the docks and slips and the great factory buildings makes it sensible to consider these together, rather than in separate chapters. The majority of new steam facilities were almost invariably grafted on to existing yards on new land. At Plymouth the Keyham Steam Yard, renamed Devonport North Yard, was separated by Morice Ordnance Yard from the existing yard, renamed Devonport South Yard. All three have long formed a single unit. However, where space was limited and proposed additions were comparatively minor, yards were partially redeveloped, as at Woolwich, Sheerness and Pembroke. After 1835 the only wholly separate new establishments constructed were Haslar Gunboat Yard and the protected harbours at Portland, Alderney, Dover and Peterhead. These were joined in the early years of the 20th century by Rosyth, the last new dockyard to be built in Britain.[1]

Nothing had a greater impact on the landscapes of the dockyards or illustrates the changing requirements of the navy more clearly than the provision of basins and dry docks. These were central features of the new steam yards, their vastly greater scale reflecting the step change in major warship sizes following the introduction of all-metal armoured hulls in 1860. Grouped alongside these installations for convenience of operation were the huge foundries, factories and machine shops of the metal-working trades. The steam yards focused almost exclusively on the processing of metal in one form or another for hulls and machinery; most other materials and the multitude of smaller items required to fit out a warship were generally supplied from existing workshops and storehouses in the older adjacent parts of the yards.

Basins and dry docks

At the end of the Napoleonic Wars in 1815, Portsmouth, Plymouth and Deptford were the only yards with basins; each had a single wet dock giving them a combined total of just over 4 acres of enclosed water. Just under a century later on the eve of the First World War, the three fleet bases of Chatham, Portsmouth and Devonport had 11 basins impounding some 163 acres of water. Sheerness had two small basins enclosing just over 4 acres, and there was a 9-acre basin at Haulbowline, while at Rosyth a single huge 56-acre basin was nearing completion.[2] The same growth is seen in the provision of dry docks at the three fleet bases. In 1815 Chatham had four, Portsmouth six and Devonport three, along with and a double dock. The figures for 1914 are respectively 8, 15 (plus a floating dock) and 11. Table 8.1 illustrates how the sizes of individual dry docks increased over this same period.

By any standard these basins and docks are impressive achievements, and it is not to belittle the work of the Royal Engineers and other engineering consultants involved to say that they benefited from the earlier work of engineers like the Rennies, the Jessops, Whidbey and Bentham. These pioneers had to overcome the difficulties of poor subsoils, employing substantial coffer-dams and diving bells while constructing harbours, dockyards and engineering works in hostile coastal environments at places like Grimsby, Sheerness and Plymouth Sound. The ongoing construction and modernisation of commercial docks and basins in London, Liverpool, Bristol and elsewhere in the 19th century also added to the sum of engineering expertise, as well as the number of practitioners, a trend accelerated from the 1830s with the rapid spread of railways and their related civil engineering needs.

In engineering terms, the design of docks and basins built from the 1840s onwards by the Admiralty may be said to be mainly evolutionary rather than revolutionary. The engineers in charge had the assurance of relatively secure government funding and a growing wealth of experience on which to draw. Construction always relied heavily on manual labour, at first usually a mix of convicts and contractors (Figs 8.1 and 8.2), but steam power was also increasingly used. In 1813 John Rennie had pioneered extensive coffer-dams and steam pumps to keep the excavations dry for his enlargement of Sheerness (*see also* Figs 8.3 and 8.4), but otherwise had relied on human and horse power. Basin and dock walls were almost invariably set on extensive piles, whose positioning was immensely speeded up by James Nasmyth's 1845 invention of the steam-driven pile driver that found immediate application in the construction of Keyham Yard (*see* Fig 8.5).[3]

At Sheerness, the unstable subsoil with its quicksand had led Rennie to employ a system of

Fig 8.1
Excavating one of the basins in the steam extension at Chatham Dockyard using convict labour. Although the introduction of steam power was enormously important, manual labour remained crucial, whether convict or contractor.
*(*The Graphic *608, 23 Dec 1871)*

Fig 8.2 (right)
Convicts at Chatham Dockyard transporting building stone under the watchful eye of a warder.
*(*The Graphic *608, 23 Dec 1871)*

Fig 8.3 (far right)
The Keyham extension of Devonport Dockyard under construction in the late 1890s. Massive timber coffer-dams and steam pumps kept the workings dry, a combination pioneered by Rennie senior at Sheerness from 1813.
(TNA ADM 195/61 fol 33)

Fig 8.4
A temporary steam pump positioned within the coffer-dam protecting work on the steam yard extension at Chatham Dockyard. (Royal Engineers Library, from Evans 2004, 205)

Fig 8.5
Pile-driving in progress on the steam yard extension at Chatham Dockyard in the 1860s. (Royal Engineers Library, from Evans 2004, 205)

inverted arch foundations and piling to counteract this (*see* Figs 5.4 and 5.5). At Keyham in the 1890s, where similar conditions were encountered, rather than dig through some 50ft of mud with the aid of extensive shuttering, the engineers used columns of triune cylinders of concrete. This was a system that had been successful on the Clyde from the early 1870s to provide foundations for quay walls. The three hollow cylinders, made from interlocking rings some 2ft 6in thick, were assembled in position and weighted down by kentledge or iron ballast, which could in some circumstances weigh up to 800 tons. Once the weight had caused the columns to sink to a firm footing, the mud inside the three shafts was excavated and replaced by concrete.[4] A variant of this system was later to be used for foundations for the basin walls at Rosyth. Here some 120 square-section monoliths, each with four shafts, were sunk in position (Fig 8.6), and timber shuttering allowed concrete to be added at the top of each monolith as the structure sank through the loose substrata. Progress was aided by workers at the bottom of the four shafts excavating spoil that was winched to the surface; sometimes small blasting charges were used, the concussion vibrating the structures and speeding up the sinking.[5]

The massive expansion programme begun at Portsmouth in 1867 to an overall design by Colonel Sir Andrew Clarke, Director of Admiralty Works, and largely undertaken by the contractor Messrs Smith and Co, established the precedent for all subsequent similar Admiralty projects in its extensive use of plant and steam machinery. Some 9 miles of timber viaducts carried temporary road and railway tracks over the site. Trains of wagons on the railway tracks were fed mud from huge steam shovels and dredgers before being hauled by locomotives across Fountain Lake on a temporary viaduct to discharge their loads to form the present Whale Island (*see* Figs 8.7 and 8.8). Four miles of track were laid for huge self-propelled steam gantry cranes, which were principally used to position the massive granite blocks brought to the site by the railways for the dock and wharf walls. The excavations were kept drained by steam

Fig 8.6
The top of one of the monoliths used extensively for foundations at Rosyth. (Dunfermline Carnegie Library)

pumps, and at the peak around eighty steam engines were at work. It was optimistically hoped to complete most of the project in 5 years.[6]

In many ways, the biggest imponderable faced by the engineers was designing basins, docks and slips that would still be of sufficient size to meet the requirements of the navy when they were completed (*see* Table 8.1). Over-large docks merely increased working costs by requiring greater volumes of water to be pumped out and the provision of extra-long shores to secure warships using them.[7] In practice, even the most ambitiously planned dock or lock did not remain adequate for long in the half century before 1914, and the majority had to be enlarged or otherwise modified.[8]

Fig 8.7
Steam excavators loading spoil into temporary railways laid along the top of the wall of 5 Basin at the Keyham extension at Devonport Dockyard.
(TNA ADM 195/61 fol 55)

Fig 8.8
Work under way in 1904 on 15 Dock at Portsmouth. Beyond lies 5 Basin. The alluvial subsoil underlying most of the dockyard (clearly visible) made excavation comparatively easy here, but added to problems of constructing stable foundations.
(Author's collection)

Table 8.1 Dry docks of the Royal Navy. This table gives details of the number, location and size of dry docks owned by the Royal Navy between 1690 and 1914 which either remain in use or have been infilled and are thought to survive in whole or in part as buried structures. Also included are overseas dry docks to which the British Government contributed funds in the latter part of the 19th century to help pay for construction. Where a dock was enlarged, the dimensions given are the final ones. Overall lengths are quoted as floor lengths; coping head lengths normally are significantly longer. In addition, a dock closed with a caisson could gain up to a further 10ft in length from the figures quoted here, if the caisson could be secured against an outer stop. The dimensions are taken from a variety of sources and need to be treated with some caution; in a number of cases contemporary sources give slightly different figures, but they are useful for their comparative value. While the growing number, size and geographical distribution of dry docks are listed, this table can only hint at the technical advances that lay behind them.

Place	*dock*	*start date*	*significant alterations up to 1914*	*length*	*width*	*depth*[a]
Auckland	Calliope*	1888		521ft	80ft	20ft[b]
Bermuda	Floating Dock	1869	replaced 1902	380ft	124ft[c]	
Chatham	2 Dock	1823	1855	404ft 3in	63ft 7in	23ft 7in[d]
	3 Dock	1816	1855	336ft 5in	63ft 2in	23ft 5in[e]
	4 Dock	1836		331ft 10in	62ft 2in	23ft 5in
	5 Dock	1864		491ft 5in	80ft	32ft 7in
	6 Dock	1864		416ft 10in	80ft	32ft 7in
	7 Dock	1864		416ft 8in	82ft 3in	33ft 1in
	8 Dock	1864		416ft 8in	82ft	33ft 1in
	9 Dock	1895		650ft	84ft	33ft 3in[f]
	North Lock	1864		477ft 6in	94ft	33ft[g]
	South Lock	1864		479ft 6in	84ft	32ft 11in
	Entrance A	1864		single caisson	79ft 7in	31ft
Deptford[h]	Single Dock[i]	1716				
	Double Dock[j]	pre-1800	c 1840 gates modified	head 167ft 6½in stern 196ft	head 46ft 10in stern 54ft 1in	15ft 3½in
Devonport South Yard	Shallow Dock	1909		294ft	58ft[k]	
	1 Dock	1690	1776	303ft 7in	65ft	27ft 8in[l]
	2 Dock	1860	1897	461ft 2in	73ft	31ft 10in[m]
	3 Dock	1876	1890, 1898	424ft 4in	94ft	34ft 9in[n]
	4 Dock	1783	1839	263ft	64ft 5in	19ft[o]
Devonport North Yard	5 Dock	1844	1858	347ft 2in	80ft	25ft 6in[p]
	6 Dock	1844		295ft 2in	80ft	22ft 6in
	7 Dock	1844		413ft 6in	80ft	26ft 6in
	8 Dock	1896	1906, 1910	650ft	95ft	36ft
	9 Dock♥	1896		745ft	95ft	36ft
	10 Dock	1896	1937	741ft	95ft	47ft 6in[q]
	North Lock	1896		730ft	95ft	47ft 6in[r]
Esquimalt	Government Dock*	1887		481ft	65ft	26ft 6in
Gibraltar	Dock 1♥	1900		851ft 9in	95ft	38ft 6in†
	Dock 2	1900		552ft	95ft	38ft 6in
	Dock 3	1900		450ft	95ft	38ft 6in
Halifax, Novia Scotia	Government Dock*	1886		546ft	89ft 3in	29ft 6in[s]
Haulbowline	Dock 1	1865		600ft	94ft	32ft 7in[t]
Hong Kong	Dock 1	1903		554ft 9in	95ft	not stated[u]
Malta	1♥	1855		281ft	82ft	25ft[v]
	2♥	1844	1862	253ft 7in	90ft	25ft[w]
	3 Somerset Dock	1865		448ft	80ft	33ft 6in[x]
	4 Hamilton Dock	1888		520ft	94ft	33ft 8in
	5 Dock♥	1899		440ft	95ft	34ft 3in
	6 Dock♥	1899		336ft 6in	95ft	36ft 9in
	7 Dock	1899		550ft	95ft	34ft 3in
Pembroke	1 Dock	1816	1855	387ft 8in	75ft	24ft 8in[y]
Portsmouth	1 Dock	1789	1859	228ft 4in	57ft	19ft 10in[z]
	2 Dock	1799		222ft 4in	63ft 6in	23ft 5in
	3 Dock	1799	1859	275ft 5in	67ft 5in	26ft 1in[aa]
	4 Dock	1767	1859, 1863	278ft 2in	67ft 3in	26ft 10in[bb]
	5 Dock	1690	1769	257ft 7in	55ft 5in	19ft 9in[cc]

Place	dock	start date	significant alterations up to 1914	length	width	depth[a]
	6 Dock[dd]	1699	1737	196ft	32ft 8in	19ft 5in
	7 and 10					
	Double Dock[ee]	1797	1858	615ft	88ft 11in at west end, 90ft 5in at east end	27ft 8in
	8 Dock	1850↕	1862	307ft	68ft 9in	22ft 8in[ff]
	9 Dock	1850↕	infilled by 1900	268ft	64ft 11in	21ft 9in[gg]
	11 Dock	1863↕		401ft 3in	68ft 9in	27ft 9in
	12 Dock	1867	1903	496ft 9in	80ft	33ft 3in
	13 Dock	1867	1905	559ft 9in	82ft	34ft
	14 Dock	1896↕	1914	720ft	100ft	34ft
	15 Dock	1896↕	1907	610ft 11in	93ft 11in	34ft 1in
	Deep Dock	1867		435ft 5in	81ft 9in	41ft 5in
	South Lock	1867		458ft 8in	81ft 9in	41ft 7in
	North Lock	1867		458ft 8in	81ft 9in	42ft 9in
	C Lock	1914↕		850ft	110ft	
	D Lock	1914↕		110ft	110ft	
	Floating Dock	1912	scrapped 1984	lifting capacity 32,000 tons		
Rosyth	Docks 1, 2, 3	1909		854ft	114ft	basin depth 40ft 8in[hh]
	Entrance Lock	1909		850ft	110ft	38ft[ii]
Sheerness	Dock 1	1819	1854	225ft	63ft	25ft[jj]
	Dock 2	1819		225ft	63ft	25ft 2in
	Dock 3	1819	1854	225ft	63ft	25ft 5in[kk]
	Dock 4	1819	1903	287ft 1in	50ft 3in	19ft 8in[ll]
	Dock 5	1819	1825, 1903	288ft	64ft 8in	14ft 6in[mm]
Simon's Town	Dock 1♥	1904		745ft	95ft 1in	36ft 3in[nn]
Sydney	Fitzroy Dock	1847	1870, 1880	284ft		
	Sutherland Dock	1880	1911, 1928	638ft	84ft	32ft[oo]
Trincomalee (Colombo)	Dock	1896		708ft	85ft	32ft[pp]
Woolwich[qq]	Dock 1[rr]	1839		250ft	65ft	22ft
	Dock 2[ss]	1835		241ft 3in	65ft	21ft
	Dock 3[tt]	1845		264ft	80ft	21ft

* dry dock partly funded by the Admiralty.

♥ dry docks, sometimes extended, with a third set of caissons or gates set part way along, enabling use as a double dock.

† normal tide levels in Mediterranean.

↕ completion date.

a At high water spring tide. TNA ADM116/536 is a comprehensive world-wide list of dry docks, Admiralty, commercial and government-owned, that were operational in 1899. This list gives dimensions for that date.

b New Zealand Government. AdL Da 0 36 fol 83.

c TNA ADM 181/78 estimates. The dimensions are from Stranack (1990, 54) and TNA ADM 116/536. The dry dock was replaced in 1902 by a second one measuring 545ft long and with an internal beam of 100ft. Built by Swan Hunter, this was then the largest in the world (Stranack 1990, 56).

d MacDougall 2009, 54; TNA ADM 106/1829, 18 Dec 1824, suggests the work was well under way. No. 1 Dock was infilled in 1860 to provide a level space for workshops connected with the construction of HMS *Achilles*, the first ironclad to be built in a royal yard (MacDougall 2009, 55). TNA Work 41/80 notes the rebuild of No. 2 dock in 1855 and gives the dimensions as 300ft by 57ft and 'present entrance to remain'. MacDougall (2009, 98) gives slightly different dimensions.

e TNA ADM 181/66 estimates; MacDougall 2009, 53–4.

f The repairing basin was completed in May 1871 along with Nos 5 and 6 Docks. Dock 8 was completed in Oct 1872 and 7 Dock in early 1873. The 1903–4 Admiralty Review notes that 9 Dock was nearly complete (TNA ADM 181/99).

g TNA ADM 140/1484. The depth of water on the river side of the dock was 34ft 8in.

h This yard is included for completeness, although both docks were filled in after the yard closed in 1869. Archaeological investigation in 2010 and 2011 indicates that some of the double dock probably remains intact.

i Oppenheim 1926, 367.

j Dimensions from an Admiralty plan of 1862 in Ad Lib Da 02 fol 25. For 1840s modifications, principally to the entrance, see TNA ADM 181/49 estimates. Evidence for this was found in the 2010 trial excavations.

k Converted from 2 Slip to form a dry dock capable of accommodating two torpedo boats (Burns 1984, 76–7; Ad Lib Da 0 36 fol 36). The internal width of the dock was 80ft.

l The original dimensions were 170ft long, with a width of 46ft at the gates. During construction in 1690 the dock was increased to 230ft long and the width at the gates to 49ft. At the same time, the depth was reduced by 2ft to 22ft. See Coad 1989, 94.

m Money for lengthening first appears in the 1860/1 estimates (TNA ADM 181/71). *See also* the 1875/6 estimates (TNA ADM 181/86). This was built on the site of the double dock constructed in the 1720s (Coad 1983, 351). For the 1897 lengthening, *see* Burns 1984, 65. Final dimensions from TNA ADM 116/636.

n TNA ADM 181/87 estimates. This replaced a dock constructed in 1758 (Coad 1983, 352). For the 1890s, *see* Burns 1984, 65. Final dimensions from TNA ADM 116/636.

o Coad 1983, 361. For the 1839 alterations, *see* TNA ADM 181/50, ADM 116/636 and Burns 1994, 37. For money for altering the entrance, *see* the 1875/6 estimates, TNA ADM 181/86.

p TNA ADM 181/69 estimates.

q The 1937–9 work widened the dock by 35ft and increased its length by 20ft. It could then accommodate any RN ship except HMS *Hood* (Burns 1984, 95).

r The 1871 agreement was for the Imperial and Dominion Governments each to contribute $250,000 towards the cost (Nelson and Oliver 1982, 48). A solitary Admiralty contribution of £10,000 first appears in the 1887/8 estimates, TNA ADM 181/98. Tenders for the dock had first been sought in 1872, but it was not until 1887 that the dock was finally opened (12 May 1887, TNA ADM 116/744; Nelson and Oliver 1982, 48–52).

s *See* 1905 Admiralty report on Canadian yards, TNA ADM 116/993. The original agreement of 9 March 1886 involved the Admiralty contributing $200,000 in $10,000 (£2,050) annual instalments.

t £150,000 first appears in 1865 estimates, TNA ADM 181/76. The 1886 estimates allow £18,000 for caissons for the new dock (TNA ADM 181/96).

u The Admiralty contribution (not quantified) to the Hong Kong and Whampoa Dock Company, in aid of the construction of a new dock at Kowloon, is included in the 1887/8 estimates, TNA ADM 181/98. By 1904, the naval dock was nearly completed (TNA ADM 181/99).

v TNA ADM 181/96 fol 70. Dimensions are from the 1863 plan of the yard in Ad Lib Naval Establishments 1863 Da 02.

w TNA ADM 181/53. Confusingly, Dock 2 at Malta is older than Dock 1. For the 1862 alterations to the entrance, *see* TNA ADM 181/73. Dimensions are from the 1863 plan of the yard in Ad Lib Naval Establishments 1863 Da 02.

x TNA ADM 181/74. Extra money was inserted in the estimates in 1869 for enlarging this before completion – *see* TNA ADM 181/80. The entrance was widened again in 1879 – *see* TNA ADM 181/90. Dimensions are from TNA ADM 174/363.

y TNA ADM 181/66 estimates; TNA ADM 1/5697, 22 Nov 1858, refers to work widening the dock.

z TNA ADM 181/70 estimates. Unless otherwise noted, the dimensions for the Portsmouth docks are taken from a plan of *c* 1909 in Ad Lib Da 0 36 fol 16.

aa TNA ADM 181/68 estimates 1859; *see* TNA ADM 181/74 for the 1863 project for lowering the dock floor.

bb TNA ADM 181/69 estimates.

cc The original 1690 dimensions were 190ft by 66ft with a 51ft entrance. *See* NMM ADM/A/1770 15 Dec 1690.

dd This was originally the North Stone Dock, created in the North Basin channel by the addition of dock gates. It was completely rebuilt in 1737. *See* NMM Por/A2, 19 May 1699; Por/A10, 5 Aug 1737.

ee Coad 1989, 104. These were originally built by Bentham, converting the North Camber Channel.

ff For the 1862 extension, *see* TNA ADM 181/73.

gg Riley 1985, 16. Dimensions are from an 1887 plan in Ad Lib Da 021. An uncatalogued plan there of 1900 shows that the dock had been infilled to provide space for materials adjacent to the huge 5 Slip.

hh At high water spring tide. Dimensions taken from an uncatalogued plan of 1918 in Ad Lib.

ii At low water spring tide.

jj Contract with Jolliffe, Banks and Nicholson – *see* TNA ADM 106/2750, 12 Jan 1819; ADM 140/688; and ADM 181/66 estimates. Obtaining accurate dimensions for the sizes of individual docks at particular dates is hazardous. Rennie's original dimensions for Docks 1–3 at Sheerness were 225ft long and 63ft clear at the gates (Sargent 2008, 93). The annual estimates for 1854/5 and 1855/6 contain sums for lengthening Docks 1 and 3. An 1863 plan of the yard, Ad Lib Da 02 fol 30, gives the dimensions for 1 Dock as 268ft by 57ft 7in wide at the gates, 2 Dock as 251ft by 57ft 7in and 3 Dock as 268ft by 63ft 6in. TNA ADM 140/1484 shows that by 1909 the lengths of 1–3 Docks were 241ft, 234ft and 268ft 10in. Docks 1–3 have been filled in with sand, along with the Great and Small Basins, but are included for the sake of completeness.

kk TNA ADM 181/65.

ll The 1903–4 Admiralty Review notes that the land needed for the extension to this and 5 Dock is being cleared – *see* TNA ADM 181/99. At the time, 4 Dock was 177ft long and 5 Dock 176ft. The outline of their final extensions is shown on an undated plan in Ad Lib; these figures accord with Ad Lib Da 0 36 fol 13, a yard plan dated between 1909 and 1912.

mm In 1825 Rennie converts this frigate dock to a graving dock – *see* TNA ADM 106/2160, 16 Apr 1825, and ADM 140/678.

nn Plan of dockyard 1909–12, Ad Lib uncatalogued. The length represents the dock being used as a single dock. Uniquely, this could be divided into three separate compartments.

oo Jeremy 2005, 12–15. Both these docks and the naval facilities that developed around them on Cockatoo Island were the responsibility of the Government of New South Wales.

pp TNA ADM275/17 p123. This is dated 1938.

qq Woolwich Dockyard was closed in 1869 and is included here for the sake of completeness. The three docks listed here are those extant at the time of the yard's closure. They replaced the one single and one double dock that existed in 1800. See Oppenheim 1926, 384. The docks have long been filled in.

rr TNA ADM 1/3502, 22 Nov 1838. This opened off the new Outer Basin and replaced an incomplete project for a concrete dock on the river front apparently proposed by G L Taylor.

ss In TNA ADM 1/3502, 18 Dec 1836, Taylor agreed a quotation of £8,603 to construct a granite invert for the dock at Woolwich. TNA ADM 181/45 estimates for 1834/5 first mention work on the dry docks when a sum of £35,000 was estimated for 'repair of the existing docks no longer fit for use and straightening the river wall'. Repairs were clearly impracticable when facilities of a larger size were required. TNA ADM 181/46 estimates for 1835/6 note that a new graving dock was constructed in lieu of the patent slip that had been proposed in 1833. Denison (1842, 224) gives a fuller account.

tt TNA ADM 181/58 estimates for 1847/8 include a sum of £31,600 to complete the dock, estimated to cost in total £92,061.

At Portsmouth the newly completed No. 2 Dock had a length of 222ft and an entrance width of 63ft, and it was capable of accommodating capital ships of the Georgian navy. Up-harbour just over a century later in 1914, No. 14 dock was extended to 720ft in length and some 100ft wide to take the navy's newest battleships, such as the 27,000-ton HMS *Warspite.*[9] No. 14 Dock was to be comfortably exceeded by the three huge new docks completed at Rosyth a couple of years later, each 854ft by 114ft, and by the strategically sited 851ft by 95ft No. 1 Dock at Gibraltar and the 745ft by 95ft dock at Simon's Town (*see* Fig 13.13).

This vast increase in scale was necessarily accompanied by a corresponding robustness in the strength of the dry docks. Bentham had championed the replacement of their timber floors with masonry, but the Admiralty was still unconvinced in 1818, complaining bitterly of the expense and delays with the 12ft-thick floor of the Rennies' new 3 Dock at Chatham (*see* Chapters 5 and 6) and forcing the abandonment of similar proposals for Sheerness.[10] The massively heavier capital ships from the 1860s ensured that dry docks had to have correspondingly substantial foundations and dock floors, and piles continued to be used where there was an absence of firm underlying strata. The three dry docks constructed as part of the Keyham extension at the end of the 19th century still had 14ft-thick concrete foundations, although built off the underlying bedrock more than 40ft below the surface; their walls were correspondingly massive, matching the adjacent 55ft-high basin walls with their 30ft-wide bases (Figs 8.9 and 8.10).[11]

Fig 8.9 (left)
No. 5 Dock in the Keyham extension under construction in 1900 at Devonport. Although the underlying rock could prove difficult to quarry, it helped provide solid footings.
(TNA ADM 195/61 fol 62)

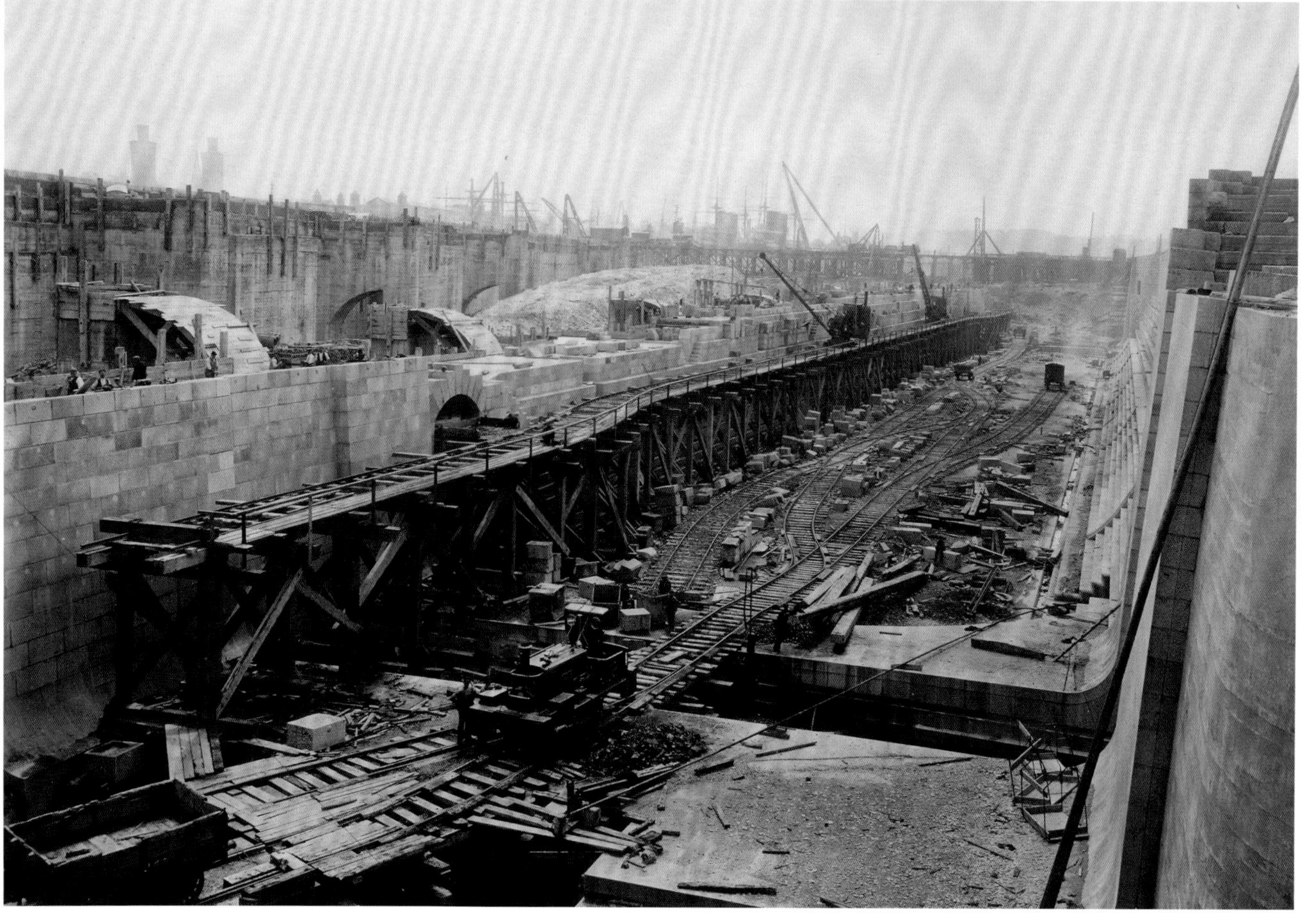

Fig 8.10 (below)
The massive North Lock under construction in the Keyham extension at Devonport Dockyard. The quality of the masonry is evident.
(TNA ADM 195/61 fol 99)

Docks and basins were generally faced with granite, Portland stone or bricks backed by masonry rubble and concrete (Fig 8.11), and it was not until the Chatham steam yard begun in 1867 and the contemporary expansion of Portsmouth that Clarke, Scamp and Bernays pioneered the gradual introduction of concrete facing blocks and the extensive use of Portland cement, the latter proving superior to the varieties of concretes and mortars then in use (Fig 8.12).[12] Concrete facing blocks were only used below water level, with brickwork above to match earlier work. The tidal basin wall at Portsmouth, part of the works begun in 1867, did make use of mass concrete, but Sir Andrew Clarke, unsure of the strength of a wholly concrete wall, insisted on including reinforcing bands of brickwork. Without exception, the basins and docks built after 1800 in the royal dockyards were constructed to the highest standards, their materials especially selected for durability, the masonry carefully laid and the detail robust. Much of the engineering works, such as the culverts, remains unseen, and the rest is best viewed at low water or when the dry docks are empty and the craftsmanship readily apparent. A century on, the Royal Navy still relies almost exclusively on docks and basins constructed between 1850 and 1916.[13]

Apart from their scale, the most noticeable

Fig 8.11
Dockyard extensions consumed construction materials in prodigious quantities. Suitable building stone had to be located from sometimes distant quarries, but brick was generally produced locally.
This brickfield was set up on St Mary's Island for the Chatham steam extension and covered 21½ acres.
It was largely worked by convicts, as seen in the foreground, and by 1868 was estimated to have an annual output of 15 million bricks.
*(*Illus London News *385, 20 Apr 1867)*

Fig 8.12
By the end of the 19th century concrete blocks were used extensively in dock, basin and breakwater construction. Contractors set up their own block-making yards, as here in Gibraltar at Devil's Tower, photographed in April 1899.
(Author's collection)

difference between 19th-century dry docks and their Georgian predecessors were their entrances. At Chatham and Sheerness Rennie senior had pioneered the use of iron dock gates in place of timber.[14] These had cast-iron and wrought-iron frames to which iron plates forming the faces of the gate were bolted. Each gate was operated by an iron chain attached to an underground windlass connected to a capstan on the dockside above. Only the former frigate dock and its original iron gates remain visible at Sheerness today (Fig 8.13).[15] Although the strength, rigidity and durability of iron were obvious attractions for the Navy Board, dock gates remained fairly cumbersome pieces of equipment, and the future lay with the ship-caisson, first developed as a practicable proposition by Bentham at the entrance to the Portsmouth Basin in 1802 (*see* Chapter 5).

Fig 8.13
A set of Rennie senior's iron gates at 4 Dock at Sheerness Dockyard, photographed 2011.
(Author)

Fig 8.14
A 19th-century iron caisson on display in the old naval base at Suomenlinna, Finland. The boat-shaped lower part is similar in design to early iron ones used in the royal dockyards.
(Author)

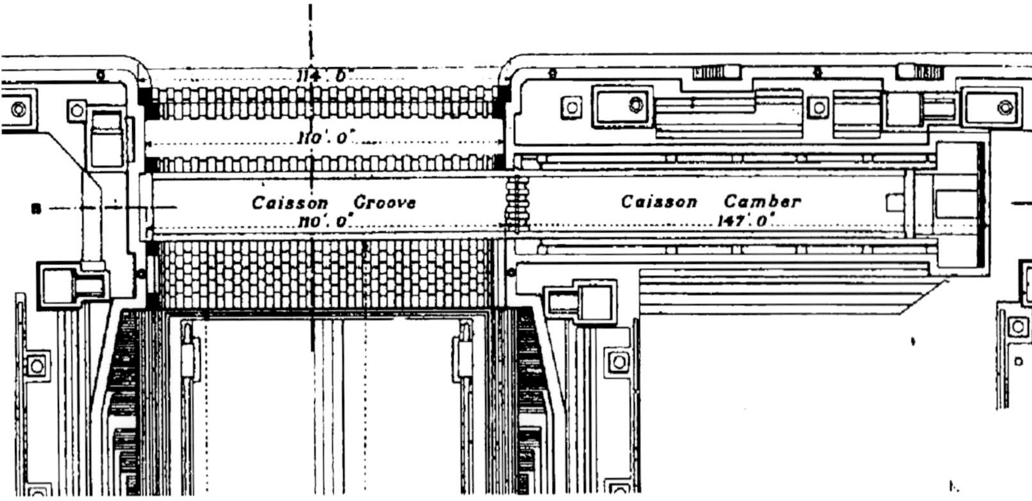

Fig 8.15
A drawing of the housing for one of the sliding caissons at Rosyth Dockyard. This shows some of the complexities involved in civil engineering works in the royal dockyards. (Crown copyright: RCAHMS)

At Sheerness, the Rennies closed the Great Basin with a copper-sheathed timber caisson, probably not dissimilar to Bentham's earlier Portsmouth one. In 1833 James Mitchell, foreman millwright and later civil engineer at Sheerness, introduced an important modification, apparently inserting a separate upper ballast tank above the flotation level. Except when there was a requirement to move the caisson at high tide, when pumping remained necessary, this allowed sufficient water in the upper ballast tank to drain by gravity through valves, rather than as hitherto having to be pumped to give flotation to the caisson. This greatly reduced the manpower and time for the operation. Mitchell went on to modify the actual design of the caisson, giving it more of a box-like cross-section rather than the boat-shaped profiles of the first two caissons, and significantly strengthening the vulnerable ends by housing the end timbers more securely into the main body of the caisson. This simplified design, first employed to seal the graving dock at Sheerness, dramatically reduced the cost here from £7,840 to £2,272.[16]

Caissons were installed in the new steam basin at Portsmouth in the 1840s, when the basin entrance and the new No. 7 dry dock were provided with metal ones manufactured at William Fairbairn's Millwall Iron Works. These followed Bentham's double-ended boat-shaped design with a cantilevered deck carrying the road and rail track, rather than the modified design pioneered by Mitchell that may have been thought to be less stable in the more open waters here.[17] At the new Keyham Steam Yard at Devonport, six similar caissons were employed exclusively in preference to dock gates to seal the three dry docks and the locks and entrances to the interlinked North and South Basins.[18] A seventh installed at the outer entrance to the lock leading to the new basin was the first sliding caisson to be installed in a royal dockyard. It had a rectangular cross-section, and in operation sufficient water ballast was drained to give it minimal buoyancy, allowing it to rise about 4in. It was then towed into a recess beneath the adjacent quay by chains worked by winches. The installation was largely impervious to wind and tide, presented minimal hazard in a tideway and took less than half the time and effort required to manoeuvre a conventional caisson. It was invented by Scamp, and with it the design of caissons may be said to have come of age (*see* Fig 8.15).

From that point onwards, the Admiralty specified caissons and not gates for all new docks and basins in the home and overseas yards (Fig 8.16). Wherever space permitted, these were of the sliding variety, later variants rolling on wheels on rails, an innovation possibly attributable to Sir Andrew Clarke.[19] Manual operation was replaced by hydraulic power and then by electric motors.[20] Elsewhere in the yards some existing dry docks had their gates replaced by ship-caissons; where this was not practical, as in the old Great Basin at Portsmouth, timber gates were gradually replaced by metal ones. Apart from the one set of gates at Sheerness, three of the dry docks associated with No. 1 Basin at Portsmouth are the only naval ones to retain dock gates. Docks 2 and 3 at Portsmouth were sealed with permanent dams when they became respectively the homes of HMS *Victory* and the *Mary Rose*.

As dry docks grew in size, pumping systems

Fig 8.16
Hamilton Dock at Malta, begun in 1888 and showing the standard late 19th-century pattern of Admiralty sliding caisson. The metal plates covering the caisson chamber could be removed for access. (Author)

had to keep pace. Well before the end of the 18th century horse-driven chain pumps were reaching the limits of their ability as docks were enlarged and deepened. Following its successful introduction at Portsmouth in 1799, steam pumping gradually spread to other yards as dry docks were modernised. Where possible, groups of docks were linked by culverts for economies of scale in the use of steam plant. The Portsmouth experiment using steam engines for a variety of purposes and for dock pumping was not repeated; later engine houses here and in the other home yards were all dedicated structures, with the possible exception of Pembroke.[21] The earliest to survive is the Rennies' handsome pump house completed at Chatham in 1822 and ultimately linked to Docks 2–4 (*see* Fig 6.31). Good later examples remain in the other principal bases. At South Yard at Devonport the stone pump house drains Docks 1–4 and dates from the construction of Nos 2 and 3 Docks between 1860 and 1876 (Fig 8.17).[22]

The Keyham extension at the end of the 19th century was equipped with a larger pumping station responsible for the North Lock and Docks 8–10. The great steam yard extension at Chatham originally relied on three pump houses. The solitary 650ft 9 Dock on the north side of No. 1 Basin was provided with one (demolished after the closure of the naval base), as were the North and South Locks at the entrance to 3 Basin. The pump house located between the locks also supplied hydraulic power for the sliding caissons and capstans there.[23] A third on

Fig 8.17
The later 19th-century pumping station for Docks 1–4 at Devonport. The tower contained the engine and pumps, with the boiler house adjacent. (Author)

the south side of No. 1 Basin was responsible for Docks 5–8; completed in 1874, it is architecturally the most exuberant of the three pump houses with its extensive use of polychromatic brickwork. Sadly, it lacks its chimney and most of its machinery, although the pumps are still in position.[24]

At Portsmouth, No. 1 Basin and its four dry docks still drain into the reservoir beneath the Block Mills.[25] Architecturally the most distinguished, least altered externally and largest of the surviving pumping stations is No. 1, constructed at the south-west corner of what was to become 3 Basin at Portsmouth (Fig 8.18). The drainage culverts from all the docks in the post-1860s extensions were linked to this. Rightly described by Evans as 'a temple of power', this was originally designed in the mid-1870s, probably by Colonel Charles Pasley,[26] but work on site did not apparently start until the early 1880s, with completion a few years later.[27] The monumental brick engine house, flanked on its eastern side by the single-storey boiler house with its handsome central chimney, originally contained dock-pumping machinery of 1,000hp, with two pairs of 120hp engines. The smaller engines powered the dockyard fire main, helped with dock drainage and drove air-compressors that Pasley's predecessor, Sir Andrew Clarke, had championed in preference to a hydraulic system to provide power for dockyard cranes, capstans, caissons and other machinery.[28] Dock pumping stations, distinguished by their tall chimneys, formed notable additions to Gibraltar and Simon's Town dockyards following the construction of their new dry docks at the start of the 20th century (Fig 8.19). Unlike the larger pumping stations in the home yards, these did not provide power for hydraulic or compressed air mains.

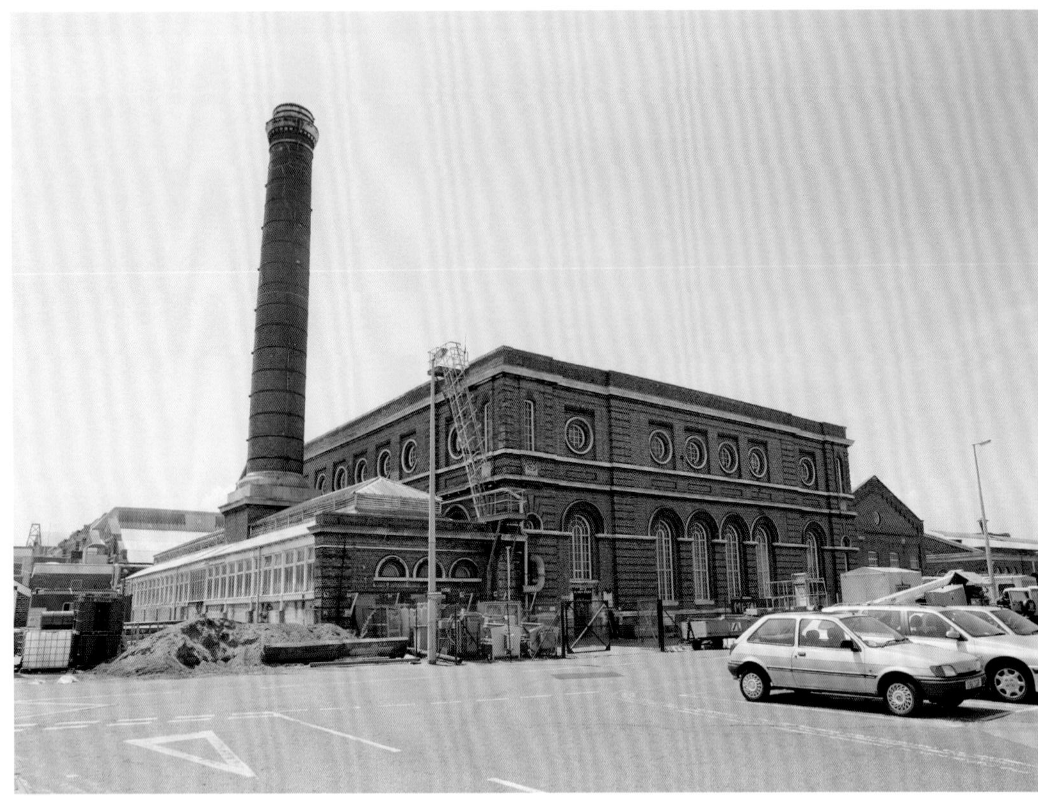

Fig 8.18
The impressive No. 1 pumping station at Portsmouth constructed in the 1880s to provide centralised drainage for all the post-1860 dry docks. (AA045931)

Fig 8.19 (below)
Construction under way in 1909 on the handsome steam pumping station for the new dry dock at Simon's Town. By then, pumps increasingly were electrically powered. (TNA ADM 195/98 fol 25)

Building slips

The new steam extensions were primarily for the maintenance, fitting out and repair of the steam fleet. None ever had building slips, which remained in the older, more crowded areas of the yards (*see* Chapter 5), almost inevitably giving rise to problems when later they needed to be enlarged. The royal dockyards, however, never built more than a percentage of the fleet, and steam-driven metal warships and a growing navy tended to accelerate a trend to a greater reliance on commercial warship construction. Warship building largely continued in the royal yards to ensure continuity of employment in peacetime, keep up with evolving technology, preserve valuable skills and serve as benchmarks for quality and cost. Until well into the 20th century, the principal dockyards generally concentrated on the largest warships, usually constructing the name ship of a new class, such as Dreadnought at Portsmouth in 1906.

These various developments meant that by the start of the 20th century the principal yards had a combined total of only four major slips and a medium-sized one in use. At Chatham, where only one of the seven slips (No. 6 Slip) constructed for wooden warships before 1850 remained usable by 1900, the slips were too small for the new capital ships, varying between 211ft and 251ft in length and 53ft and 60ft in width. By then 7 Slip, completed in 1852, had had its original length extended from 325ft to 510ft (Fig 8.20). In 1904 No. 8 Slip, of similar length but at 92ft some 15ft wider, was completed to the north and laid diagonally to the river to maximise use of scarce yard space and to allow longer vessels to be safely launched into the Medway.[29] The following year Chatham's last battleship, the pre-Dreadnought *Africa,* was launched from it.[30] Slips 1 and 2 were infilled, but their entrances can be seen in the river wall. The covered 3–6 Slips remain beneath later surfaces that were laid when they became stores and workshops in the 1900s; Slip 7 remains intact; and Slip 8 has been mostly destroyed.

The same pattern is apparent at Portsmouth, where only 1 and 2 Slips retained their original dimensions and timber roofs dating from just after the Napoleonic Wars. No. 3 slip was rebuilt in the mid-1840s when 4 and 5 Slips were constructed alongside, replacing the two northern slips demolished to make way for the new steam basin. By 1900 No. 1 Slip was a boat store for warships forming part of the steam reserve, 2 and 3 Slips remained intact but apparently largely disused, and 5 Slip, stripped of its metal roof, had been rebuilt on a vastly

Fig 8.20
The 15,000-ton battleship Prince of Wales *at Chatham Dockyard, ready for her launch on 25 March 1902. No. 7 Slip had been specially extended to accommodate her hull, graphically illustrating how the Edwardian navy had outgrown mid-Victorian dockyard shipbuilding facilities.*
(© National Maritime Museum, Greenwich, London, neg. N18718)

Fig 8.21
A photograph of c 1910 looking across the Steam Basin at Portsmouth Dockyard. Behind No. 2 Ship Shop can be seen the covered slips, by now disused for warship building. No. 5 Slip, to the right of the covered slips and distinguished by an array of timber pillars and struts, had been enlarged and its roof removed to enable it to cope with Dreadnoughts. (Author's collection)

greater scale to cope with the new sizes of capital ships (Fig 8.21). Probably at this time the adjacent Slip 4 was infilled, its roofed space becoming 3 Ship Shop, while 3 Slip was about to be floored and used as a scrieve board.[31]

At Devonport the five slips existing in 1850, all less than 200ft long, had similar chequered careers.[32] In 1900 No. 1 Slip of 1774 remained in use, but would shortly be converted to a patent slip for repairing small craft, 2 Slip was to be redeveloped by 1912 as a shallow dock, and a totally new 3 Slip was constructed across the sites of the inner and outer mast ponds following the Naval Works Act of 1895. This was of a similar size to the new 5 Slip in Portsmouth, dwarfing all the other slips at Devonport. On completion it measured 520ft by 53ft, but was extended to 752ft by 90ft by 1912, in time for the laying down of HMS *Warspite*, constructed in parallel with HMS *Queen Elizabeth* then being built on 5 Slip at Portsmouth and name-ship of this famous class of super-Dreadnoughts.[33] The remaining three slips at Devonport, all laid out in the mid-18th century, were modified and rebuilt at intervals in the mid-19th century, but their cramped sites precluded extensive lengthening. After the construction of the new 3 Slip, the original 3, 4 and 5 Slips were renumbered 4, 5 and 6, and in 1850 they were 197ft, 156ft and 174ft long respectively. By 1909 No. 4 Slip had been enlarged to 460ft by 80ft (Fig 8.22), but it was

Fig 8.22
No. 4 Slip in South Yard, Devonport. Mid-18th century in origin, this slip was rebuilt and enlarged at intervals in the second half of the 19th century. On its right is the former 5 Slip, its roof concealing a scrieve board laid over the slip. (Author)

not possible to extend 5 and 6 Slips beyond some 260ft.[34] No. 5 Slip was floored over, probably in the 1870s, and turned into a scrieve board that remained in use into the 1960s. No. 6 Slip was unused by 1900 and later had a building constructed across it.[35]

The specialist building yard at Pembroke never lived up to its potential, because the Admiralty failed to make investments necessary to re-equip it to serve the steam fleet. By 1914 only one slip here exceeded 500ft in length; the majority were between 250ft and 350ft and essentially obsolete for all but minor warships. Lacking a fitting out basin and sufficient engineering workshops, most new warships had to be towed round to Devonport for completion. The only other yard to retain a building slip in 1900 was Sheerness. In the 1820s it had been re-equipped with a single 200ft slip on which it built a succession of the smaller warships for the Victorian navy. These included the composite screw sloop *Gannet*, launched in 1878 and now preserved at Chatham Historic Dockyard.

As warship sizes and tonnage increased over this period, the construction of slips had to become correspondingly robust, but the design essentials remained largely unaltered. Slips with timber floors laid directly on the subsoil pegged to timber holdfasts and with timber sides remained common, but the durability of masonry led to its increasing employment, notably at Plymouth during the rebuilding of the yard in the last four decades of the 18th century. In 1811 Bentham proposed that the all-timber 1 Slip at Chatham should be rebuilt with a timber floor, but with masonry sides.[36] By the 1840s, the need for strong foundations was fully appreciated, and in 1843 Nos 4, 5 and 6 Slips at Chatham had stepped stone sides, similar to dry docks, and concrete and masonry slip floors; all were underpinned and secured by extensive piling.[37] Greene's 7 Slip of 1852 likewise had its masonry floor set on piled concrete foundations. This proved adequate for the vastly heavier metal warships constructed on it, starting with the 7,842-ton ironclad *Lord Warden* in 1863 and

Fig 8.23
The launch of Okanagan *for the Royal Canadian Navy at Chatham's 7 Slip on 17 Sept 1966. Her launch marked the end of some 60 years of submarine building on this slip, a record unequalled by any other royal dockyard. (Author's collection)*

ending with the considerably lighter 'O' class submarine *Okanagan* for the Canadian navy in 1966 (Fig 8.23).

Slips continued to be provided with roofs until all-metal warships made them largely unnecessary. The existing timber roof of 1838 over 3 Slip at Chatham was followed by two at Pembroke in 1841. These were the last timber ones to be constructed, and they no longer exist.[38] Such roofs required considerable maintenance, were prone to rot and, as Holl had forcibly pointed out when first they had been suggested, entailed huge fire risks. By the early 1840s and spurred by these problems, Captain Henry Brandreth, the Director of Works, was looking at the possibilities of all-metal slip roofs. He would also have been aware of the improved durability of corrugated iron invented by Henry Palmer in 1829 and its pioneer use to roof the new Turpentine Shed in the London docks. A contemporary observer was moved to enthuse that 'It is, we should think, the lightest and strongest roof (for its weight), that has been constructed by man, since the days of Adam'.[39] But however strong when new, the sheeting remained highly vulnerable to corrosion, especially in industrial atmospheres, and it was only the invention of hot-dip galvanising that gave corrugated iron the necessary durability to make it attractive from the early 1840s as a cheap and strong material for roofing and cladding.[40]

In 1842 the Admiralty, no doubt advised by Brandreth, felt sufficiently confident to decide that all future slip roofs should be metal, and in consultation with the master shipwrights a set of standard dimensions was agreed for the span over the slips and the distance between supporting pillars.[41] Surviving records are incomplete and by no means clear, but it would seem that Brandreth sent sketch proposals for two metal slips to the yard officers at Pembroke in September 1842, and these may have formed the basis of the winning design submitted by the firm of Fox Henderson who were involved in designing and building iron structures, particularly for railway companies. The two slip roofs were begun in 1844, the overall design of cantilevered roof clearly derived from Seppings's timber progenitor, but with the size of individual members refined, reduced in cross-section and tailored to the different properties and strengths of iron in tension and compression. Corrugated iron sheeting helped to lighten the structure, removing the need for timber purlins and board linings that had supported the various waterproof coverings previously used.

Although Fox Henderson was first in the field, the substantial contractors George Baker and Son were to be more successful, erecting 11 roofs compared to Fox Henderson's 5. Baker was responsible for three metal roofs at Portsmouth over the new 3, 4 and 5 Slips, which first appear in the 1843/4 estimates.[42] The roof over 5 Slip

Fig 8.24
Original drawing for Slips 4–6 at Chatham Dockyard. (TNA ADM 140/60 pt 7)

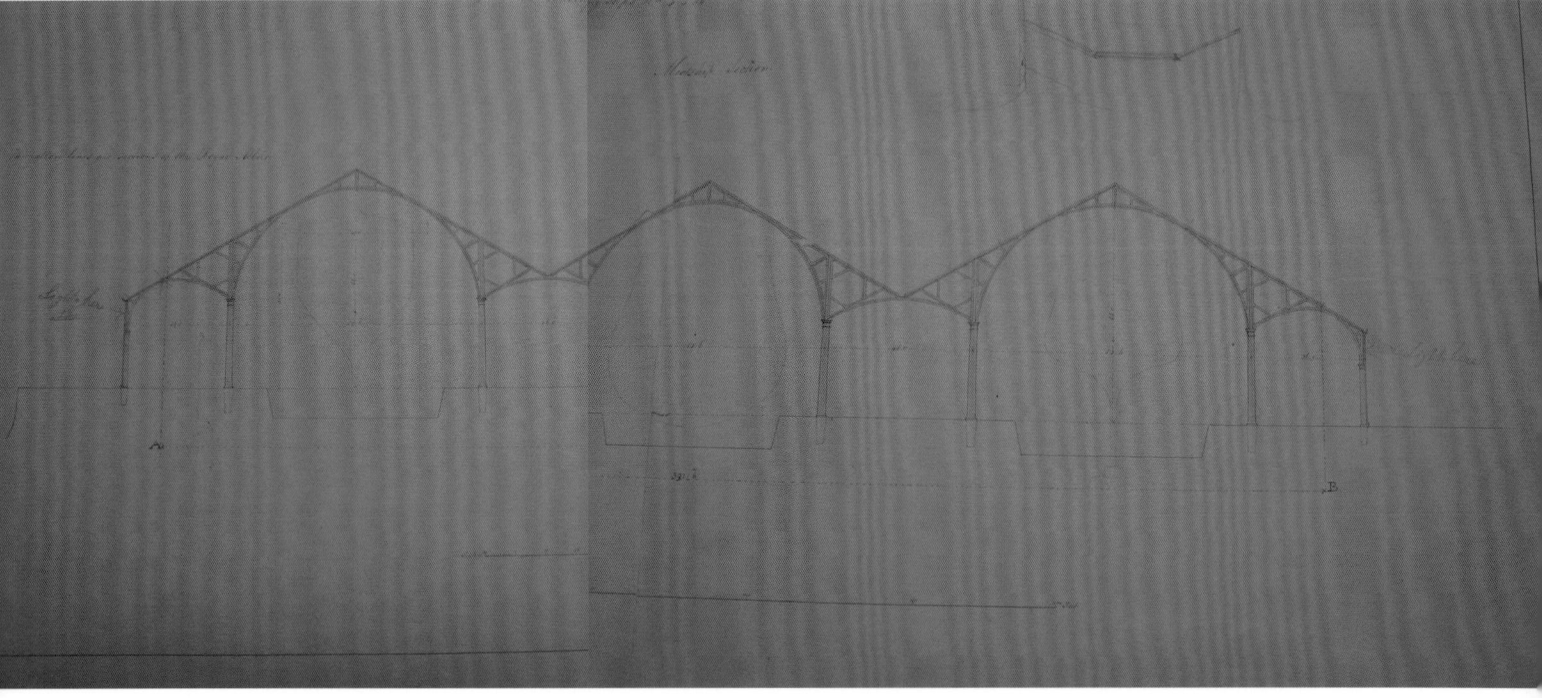

was demolished later in the 19th century, presumably ahead of the lengthening of the slip; the remaining two roofs were demolished in the early 1970s. These Portsmouth roofs were followed by three much more modest roofs for the smaller slips at Deptford, erected between 1845 and 1847.[43] The size of these Deptford roofs is reflected in their estimated cost of £20,000, compared to the contract cost in September 1847 of £32,590 for three surviving roofs over 4–6 Slips at Chatham.[44] The Baker pattern followed the earlier Fox Henderson design in having cantilevered aisles on either side of the slips, but by the time the Chatham roofs were constructed, they were significantly strengthened by wrought-iron T-sections, notably ones providing tensile ties along the cantilevers. Their distinctive arched ribs were constructed of wrought iron, with cast iron employed for the standards and most other parts of the framing. A more obvious advance, and one especially helpful to the shipwrights working under them, was Baker's more than doubling of the spacing of the frames and their supporting pillars to nearly 30ft, an achievement helped by the use of light trussed purlins to transmit the weight of the corrugated iron roof to the frames (Fig 8.24).[45] The Chatham metal roofs, sited immediately adjacent to the timber-roofed 3 Slip of 1838, were first proposed in January 1843,[46] but completion of the slips delayed their construction. Captain Thomas Mould, the superintending Royal Engineer at Chatham, seems to have played an active part in their design, working closely with Rivers, the clerk of works, and George Baker (Fig 8.25).[47]

Although the completion of 3–6 Slips and their roofs greatly enhanced the shipbuilding facilities of the Chatham yard, more capacity was needed, and a further slip at the north end of this range was authorised in 1851.[48] By then, G T Greene was an actively involved Director of Works with a keen interest in metal-framed buildings, and the resultant design is generally attributed to him, although he was clearly influenced by Fox Henderson's 4 Slip roof at Woolwich.[49] The growing size of warships is reflected in the 325ft length of the new slip compared to the 251ft of each of its three neighbours, with widths the same at 59ft, but experience gained from using existing iron-roofed slips also played a part in the eventual design. Until then, the roofs had been there simply to protect vessels and workmen from the elements, and the iron roofs in particular were lightly constructed and not designed to carry additional loads. The temptation to sling pulleys over convenient beams or to attach hoists to lift ships' timbers into position had already resulted in an official but not entirely successful prohibition of these practices in 1846. Construction of a new slip offered an opportunity to strengthen the structure and to 'design out' the problem of misuse

Fig 8.25
The landward elevations of the five slips at Chatham Dockyard, from left to right, the all-timber 3 Slip of 1837, the all-metal 4–6 Slips of 1847 and, in the distance, Greene's 7 Slip of 1852. The curved framework of Slips 4–6 is clearly visible. (Author)

Fig 8.28 (opposite) Looking up 7 Slip from the river end at Chatham Dockyard. (Author)

by incorporating overhead travelling cranes, already used in heavy industry such as locomotive works and recently incorporated into James's new steam factory at Portsmouth.[50] The contemporary 5 Slip at Woolwich was similarly equipped.[51]

In September 1852 the contract for 7 Slip roof was awarded to Henry Grissell's Regent's Canal Ironworks that had supplied much of the extensive structural ironwork used in the new Houses of Parliament. It was to be 1857 before all work was finally finished after the landward end of the slip was extended and an additional roof bay was added over it. Completion brought the great metal slip roofs to a significant level of maturity. Gone are the curved ribs of the immediate predecessors, to be replaced by a rigid frame of H-section, cast-iron columns braced by open trellis-type cast-iron girders, the latter probably adapted from a design first used at the Crystal Palace in 1851. These columns supported the 82ft-wide roof formed from wrought-iron triangular trusses, and they also carried the tracks for the overhead cranes that run the length of the slip and the side aisles (Figs 8.26, 8.27 and 8.28).[52] Half a century later, in 1902, the 15,000-ton battleship *Prince of Wales* became the last capital ship launched from this slip. Her 431ft length had meant removing the landward end bay of the roof and temporarily extending the slip across the dockyard railway and further into the yard.

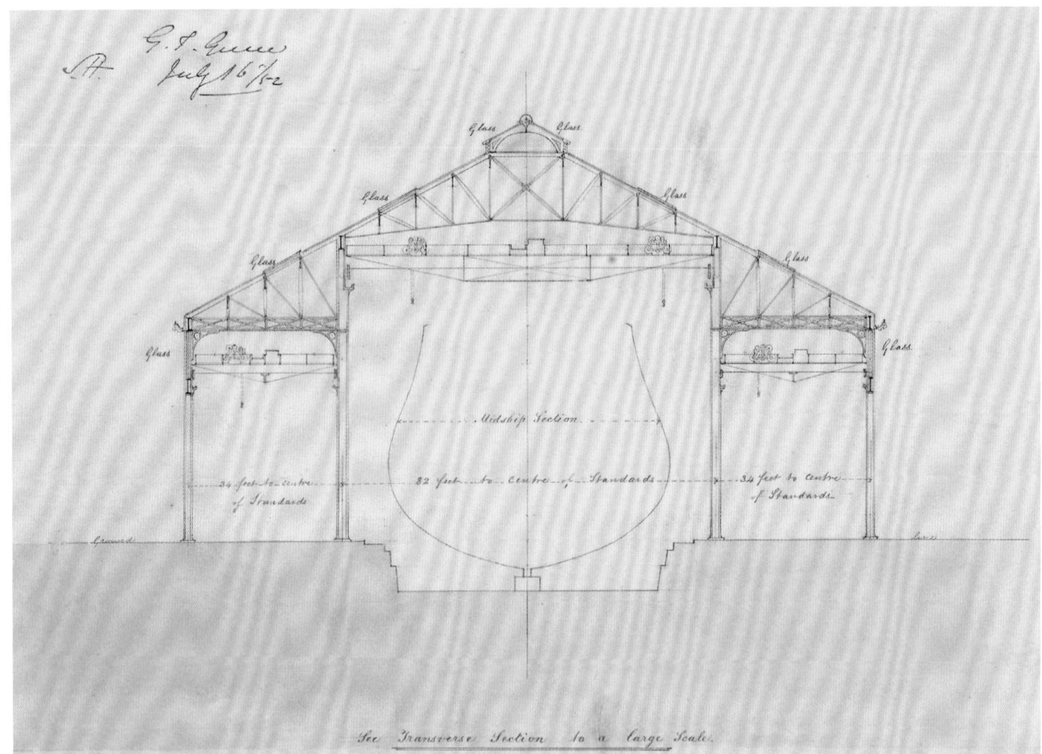

Fig 8.26 A cross-section of Greene's design for 7 Slip at Chatham Dockyard. This marks the coming-of-age of the design of these great metal housings with their overhead travelling cranes. (TNA ADM 140/66 pt 7)

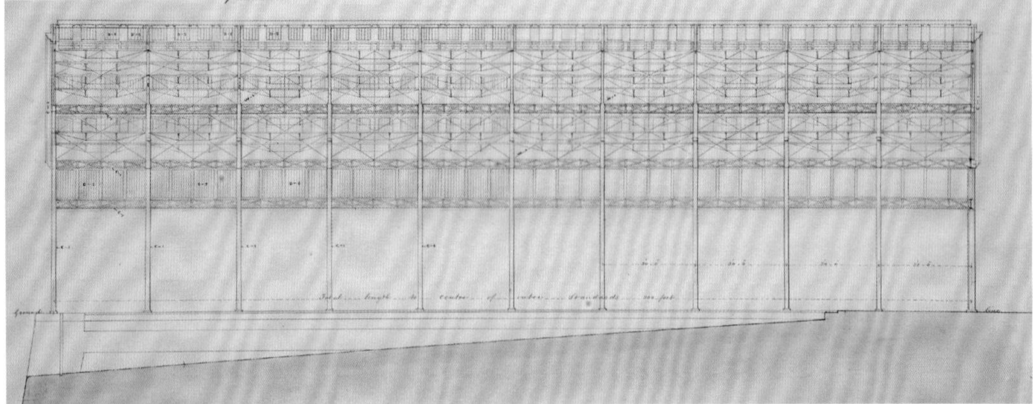

Fig 8.27 A longitudinal section of Greene's 7 Slip at Chatham Dockyard. (TNA ADM 140/66 pt 6)

Three years later the 453ft *Africa* of 16,350 tons was launched from the adjacent new 8 Slip, but within a year the launch of the 17,900-ton *Dreadnought* at Portsmouth signalled the end of battleship construction at Chatham, unable any longer to keep up with the naval monsters then joining the fleet.[53] In 1907 No. 7 Slip at Chatham found a new role when submarine C17 was built on it; a further 57 submarines were to follow, ending with *Okanagan* in 1966 (*see* Fig 8.23). This tally was more than any other royal dockyard, helping to ensure the survival of these covered slips sufficiently long for their historic importance to be fully appreciated.[54] Carefully conserved in the 1990s by the Chatham Historic Dockyard Trust, this remarkable range of slip roofs continue to dominate this part of the Medway valley, iconic symbols of naval shipbuilding here.

By a quirk of fate, the metal roofs constructed over Slips 4 and 5 at Woolwich were dismantled after the yard closed in 1869 and were re-erected a few years later in the Chatham steam yard at the head of 5–8 Docks (Figs 8.29 and 8.30). No. 4 Slip roof, originally constructed in 1847–8 by Fox Henderson and probably designed by Edward Cowper, became the boiler shop.[55] In 1856–7 No. 5 Slip at Woolwich became the

Fig 8.29
The former 4 Slip housing from Woolwich being re-erected at Chatham Dockyard as the boiler shop. (TNA ADM 195/7 plate 86)

Fig 8.30
An 1896 photograph of the Empress of India *in dock at Chatham. Beyond her is the former 5 Slip housing from Woolwich, re-erected as a fitting shop.*
*(*Navy and Army Illustrated *20 March 1896)*

last slip in a royal yard to have a metal roof, its design very similar to the slightly earlier 7 Slip at Chatham and almost certainly attributable to Greene's team. At Chatham it was re-erected, extended and adapted as the principal fitting shop.

The steam factories

Central to the operation of the steam yards were the associated foundries, forges and engineering workshops sited close to the fitting out basins. Initially these maintained and in some cases built the mechanical plant required by the new steam vessels. From the 1860s, as the principal dockyards started to build the navy's armour-plated, metal-hulled warships, they also had to be able to cut, drill, finish and bend increasing sizes, weights and thicknesses of metal plates. Such heavy engineering work depended on the application of steam power, which was most economically provided from a single engine house and transmitted by overhead or underground line shafts. These in turn dictated a centralised layout for the workshops and their machine tools, and the gradual introduction of hydraulic or compressed air mains, which powered some machinery from the 1860s, gave a small degree of freedom in their location and layout. It was only the introduction of mains electricity and increasingly powerful electric motors from the end of the 19th century that allowed the flexibility of planning which derives from a wholly decentralised power supply.

Buildings of the metal-working trades in the pre-1800 dockyards were limited to the smiths, split between general ironwork and the more arduous forging of anchors. Although by then increasing use of iron in warships for such items as ships' knees was leading to a growth in the size of dockyard smitheries, as with Holl's 1806 No. 1 Smithery at Chatham, these did not dominate the yards and were diminutive in scale compared to their Victorian successors. Little remains of the pioneering steam factory at Woolwich, but its immediate successor – now known as 2 Ship Shop – remains in use at Portsmouth. Originally called the West or Steam Factory, 2 Ship Shop was designed by Captain Henry James, whose first 20 years as a Royal Engineer officer had been spent with the Ordnance Survey, before being appointed in 1846 as superintendent at Portsmouth.[56] James sited his new building on the west side of 2 Basin, which was then nearing completion (Fig 8.31). Its length of 687ft was exceeded only by the dockyard roperies; its width of 39ft was probably dictated by the optimum length for the massive cast-iron beams carrying the upper floor. The generous height of the ground-floor workshops reflected their use. Half the space was used as boiler shops, with the remaining area divided into heavy turning and punching shops and shearing shops, all served by overhead travelling cranes, probably the first such installations in a royal dockyard. The first floor, carried on a fireproof jack-arch construction, originally housed the millwrights' shop, a light turning and fitting shop and the pattern makers and their stores. The monumental brick exterior with its stone detailing, handsome pedimented bays and giant windows, which reflect the internal floor levels, is an immensely confident statement of the new technology, still dominating this part of the dockyard more than a century and a half after completion in 1848. A separate and long-vanished engine house to the west provided power for the factory.[57]

Although James's new Portsmouth factory

Fig 8.31
The Steam Factory at Portsmouth Dockyard, later known as 2 Ship Shop, next to 2 Basin. It was designed by Captain Henry James and completed in 1848. The Ship Shop and basin remain in use.
(Author)

brought together a number of the new trades, it was in no sense an integrated facility covering all the manufacturing processes for the steam navy. Most conspicuously, it had no provision for foundries or smiths' workshops; these remained housed in increasingly outmoded buildings. In late 1846 James designed a combined iron and brass foundry on the south side of the steam basin, its exterior design similar but on a much reduced scale to his steam factory. Within 10 years demand for iron exceeded the capacity of the foundry, although it remained in use as a brass foundry into the 20th century, and the building still stands.[58] As a short-term solution, James also designed a highly successful temporary smithery, clad in corrugated iron, using the cast-iron columns and girders salvaged from Taylor's cask sheds that were demolished at Royal Clarence Yard in 1844.

In 1849 James drew up plans for a permanent smithery to the west of his factory at Portsmouth, but in 1850 he returned to the Ordnance Survey,[59] the same year that Godfrey T Greene became Director of Admiralty Works. Greene was to be responsible for the construction of the large new smithery on the same site and to the same plan as that drawn up by James. Work began in January 1852, and the building was in use by September 1855. This was the first major permanent workshop in a dockyard, apart from the iron slip roofs, to exploit the combination of an iron frame with corrugated iron exterior cladding. With its dominant louvred roof and clerestory, handsome brick chimneys at each corner and a massive central stack, this was a hugely imposing addition to the dockyard; even now, used for a different purpose, shorn of its chimneys and with part of its structural ironwork renewed, it remains a distinctive building (*see* Fig 6.22). As only a ground plan signed by James survives, it is not clear how much the eventual building owes to him or to Greene.[60]

This design was to be repeated by Greene in a smaller version at Devonport, where it had become imperative to update the existing smithery of 1776, which apparently lacked any machinery and still relied on a manually operated Hercules or drop hammer, requiring up to 60 men on the ropes when forging anchors.[61] In effect, the old smithery remained in production, and Greene completed a new one to the east by 1858.[62] This was a metal-framed structure, and the wall spaces between the external pillars were banded with stone lower sections and continuous glazing and louvres above (Fig 8.32). Unlike Portsmouth, there was no great central chimney, but the smithery was provided with a chimneys at each of its four corners, though they have since been demolished to eaves level. Although long disused, this Plymouth smithery retains more of its original structural ironwork than its larger stable mate at Portsmouth.[63]

Fig 8.32
Greene's new Devonport Dockyard smithery of 1858 (in the middle distance), distinguished by its generous glazing. The bases of the corner chimneys are visible, and the older smithery lies to its right.
(Author)

In September 1855 Greene was authorised to proceed with a new and substantial iron foundry at Portsmouth on the vacant land between the newly completed South Inlet Dock (8 Dock) and the north end of Long Row, the officers' terrace.[64] Work began in 1857 when the contract was awarded to Edmund Smith, and the building was operational from late 1861. It remains one of the most handsome of all mid-19th-century dockyard industrial buildings (Fig 8.33). Originally L-shaped in plan and built round an off-centre open courtyard, the principal north and west ranges echo James's factory in their use of red brick with stone detailing and iron-framed windows and main doorways recessed within monumental blind arcading. The western range is surmounted by a cast-iron freshwater tank. The interiors of these ranges are of fireproof construction, with the various industrial processes carefully compartmentalised. The building is notable for incorporating from the start rail tracks linked to the new dockyard railway. Later in the century, the stables belonging to the adjacent officers' terrace were demolished to make way for an extension.[65]

The somewhat piecemeal nature of dockyard expansion at Portsmouth in this period did not provide the occasion for a grand formal layout of the associated new buildings. By contrast, Keyham Yard was effectively a self-contained steam yard on a virgin site. In 1857 it was linked by a tunnel to South Yard, through which a railway line was laid in 1879 (*see* Chapter 2). The construction of Keyham Yard gave the Director of Works a unique opportunity to consolidate all the new workshops, foundry and stores into one single, central and, it was hoped, more efficient complex of buildings. Constructing these on a grand scale and to a unified design that reflected the navy's standing in the nation and the world was an added incentive. In 1847 Captain George

Fig 8.33
Greene's iron foundry of 1855 at Portsmouth Dockyard. (AA 045930)

Burgmann, the Royal Engineer in charge at Keyham, had prepared drawings for a factory, but these did not meet with approval, even though they were forwarded to the architect Charles Barry to design suitably grand façades. Barry's proposals in a modified form were to be used, but the eventual layout and design of this huge complex, known as the Quadrangle, were almost entirely the work of William Scamp, working closely with the Director, Colonel G T Greene. In 1852, with the basins and docks approaching completion, the need for the Quadrangle was becoming increasingly urgent. Construction started the following year and was completed in 1865.

Behind Barry's imperial façades, the new factories, workshops, storehouses and offices were arranged in a formal quadrangular

Fig 8.34
A 2009 aerial view of the Quadrangle at Devonport Dockyard, the vast integrated engineering complex built to support the new steam navy. The external ranges housed stores, a sail loft, a boiler shop, and a fitting and turning shop. The internal quadrangle was home to the plate shop, a smithery, a shipwrights' shop and the coppersmiths. By the end of the nineteenth century it also housed a gun-mounting store and teaching space for the engineer students from the adjacent Royal Naval Engineering College. To the rear stands the foundry with its massive chimneys. (NMR 26406/015)

Fig 8.35
The interior of the foundry at Devonport Dockyard, now used as engineering workshops and stores. (Author)

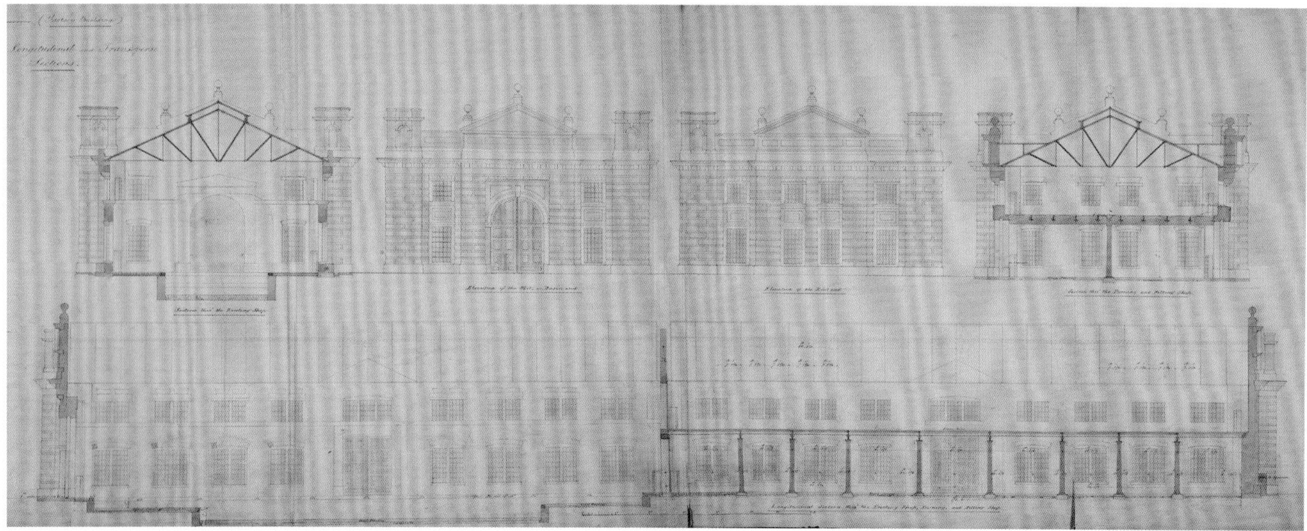

Fig 8.36
One of the preliminary elevation drawings for the Quadrangle at Devonport Dockyard, with cross-sections showing the extensive use of structural ironwork. (TNA ADM 140/364)

pattern round a huge central courtyard, dominated on its western side by a foundry flanked by its two massive chimneys (Figs 8.34 and 8.35). Experience gained from quickly equipping Sheerness with extra workshops for its Crimean War role by roofing over spaces between buildings was put to good use at the Quadrangle. The central courtyard was given a partly glazed metal roof carried on a grid of metal columns, carefully designed for maximum flexibility in the space below (Fig 8.36). Buildings within this courtyard, shielded from the outside world by the main limestone-clad ranges, were largely constructed of brick. There have been no significant additions since 1865, a testament to the wisdom of building on a monumental scale and to the adaptability of the design. The Quadrangle remains the heart of Devonport's engineering and fleet support workshops almost a century and a half after its completion.[66]

The skills and numbers employed in the navy's four steam factories in 1868 soon after the completion of the Quadrangle and a year before the closure of Woolwich are given in Table 8.2. Chatham is notably absent from this list, as it would lack a steam yard for another decade and a half, despite its warship-building role that included the first of the new armoured warships constructed in a royal yard.[67] Sheerness owed its hasty equipping with engineering workshops precisely because of the lack of such facilities and a basin at Chatham.

Well before the completion of the last of the

Table 8.2 Numbers and trades employed in the steam factories in 1868/9 (TNA ADM 181/79).

Description of workmen etc	*Woolwich*	*Sheerness*	*Portsmouth*	*Devonport (Keyham)*	*totals*
draughtsmen and writers	9	0	10	9	28
assistant timekeepers and recorders of work	4	4	5	4	17
leading men of stores	1	1	1	1	4
store ports, messengers and boys	5	5	5	5	20
engine keepers	6	8	11	11	36
pattern makers, including leading men, assistants and boys	16	14	25	19	74
fitters and erectors, assistants and boys	175	140	250	198	763
millwrights etc, including those formerly under the master shipwright	12	18	89	59	178
boiler makers, assistants and rivet boys	191	142	199	213	745
engine smiths and hammermen	43	27	34	42	146
founders	31	21	49	33	134
coppersmiths	22	26	26	17	91
painters	2	1	4	3	10
labourers	142	87	112	178	519
total numbers	**659**	**494**	**820**	**792**	**2,765**
total wages (£)	**£40,530**	**£31,277**	**£54,781**	**£46,414**	**£173,002**

Fig 8.37
The western elevation of the metal mills at Chatham Dockyard in 1975 after they had ceased to be used. The covered slips are on the far left.
(DoE)

Fig 8.38
The interior of the metal mills at Chatham Dockyard in 1975. The structural ironwork matches that in the 1843 drawings.
(DoE)

five new slips in 1857, the Admiralty had been forced to modernise Chatham's metalworking facilities. Holl's smithery (completed in 1809) had been reaching capacity by the early 1840s, when it was gradually equipped with new steam-powered machinery including tilt hammers, rolling machinery, a Hercules and cranes for the heavy anchor forging.[68] Over the next 40 years a series of piecemeal extensions was added to the northern end of the building to accommodate new processes, including small iron and brass foundries, while the courtyard was roofed over in 1865 to provide extra space.[69] The lack of adequate iron foundry capacity was a prime reason for the authorisation of new metal mills at Chatham in 1844 when a contract was signed in March with the contractors, Joseph and Charles Rigby of Hawarden Iron Works. Although the exterior of the brick building was conservatively styled, the metal roof trusses showed an awareness of current developments.[70] The building was estimated at £7,000, with a further £7,600 for steam engine machinery, much of it supplied by Boulton and Watt early in 1845, shortly before completion.[71]

One of the prime purposes of the furnaces was the reprocessing of old iron and the production of strip iron with a rolling mill.[72] As with Holl's smithery, it was not long before the metal mills proved inadequate to their task and were extended and re-equipped in piecemeal fashion at intervals over the next half century.[73] By 1879 the original façades were obscured by a series of extensions, economically constructed using metal frames with brick and corrugated iron panels, and before the end of the 19th century Holl's smithery was renamed No. 1 Smithery and the metal mills became No. 2 Smithery.[74] Both remained the centre of metal working at Chatham until closure in 1975, when No. 2 Smithery was demolished shortly afterwards, largely because of its dilapidated state. Historic equipment and machinery were salvaged and are now in the care of the Chatham Historic Dockyard Trust (Figs 8.37 and 8.38).

Fig 8.39
The dark hull of HMS Achilles *nearing completion in 2 Dock at Chatham only 2 months before her launch in December 1863. To the right is the pioneering iron shipbuilding shop which, like 2 Dock, still survives in modified form. Below, a line of washing flies on an accommodation hulk moored in the Medway.* (Illus London News *24 Oct 1863)*

In 1861 the decision to build *Achilles* in 2 Dock at Chatham led to construction of the first iron shipbuilding shop to provide working space and housing for some of the elaborate plant and machine tools for the new iron-armoured warships (Fig 8.39). Chatham yard was selected to build *Achilles* partly because of the availability of a suitable dock and partly because of proximity to the ironworking skills along the Thames. Two plate furnaces and two angle-iron furnaces were installed, along with levelling slabs and hydraulic machinery with rams and pumps for bending the keel and armour plates. Punching, shearing, slotting and planning machines also contributed to this hot, noisy working space, a world away from the hand tools used for constructing wooden warships. The single-storey, iron-framed and iron-clad shipbuilding shop had the widest span of any roof in the yard and was designed by G T Greene, manufactured by Grissell's and erected alongside 2 Dock under the supervision of Rivers, the clerk of works.[75] Its completion marked Chatham's entry to the iron-clad construction era; although modest, it helped make Chatham for a time better equipped for metal warship building than any other royal dockyard. Remarkably, this pioneer building still exists.

In drawing up plans for the steam yard that was eventually begun at Chatham in 1864, Greene and Scamp included a factory complex of a similar scale and layout to the Keyham Quadrangle.[76] However, the expense of the Quadrangle and the availability of redundant slip roofs following the closure of Woolwich in 1869 resulted in an Admiralty decision to reuse and adapt two of these as fitting and boiler shops at Chatham. Initially, no foundry seems to have been included in these revised plans. Nos 1 and 2 smitheries were conveniently located for supplying the building slips, and it may have been thought that they could also supply the requirements of the steam yard. If this was ever so, it was no longer the case by the time the steam yard was nearing completion. In 1886 money was put in the estimates for a new foundry and a coppersmiths' shop in the steam yard adjacent to the boiler shop.[77] These supplemented but never replaced the two smitheries, which remained in production in the older part of the yard until 1975.

Haslar Gunboat Yard

In comparison to the great steam extensions or even the modernisation of Chatham's shipbuilding facilities between 1840 and 1860, Haslar Gunboat Yard was something of a sideshow. However, its construction perfectly demonstrates Victorian ingenuity applied to solving a particular problem, while the yard, even in its neglected state, remains unique.

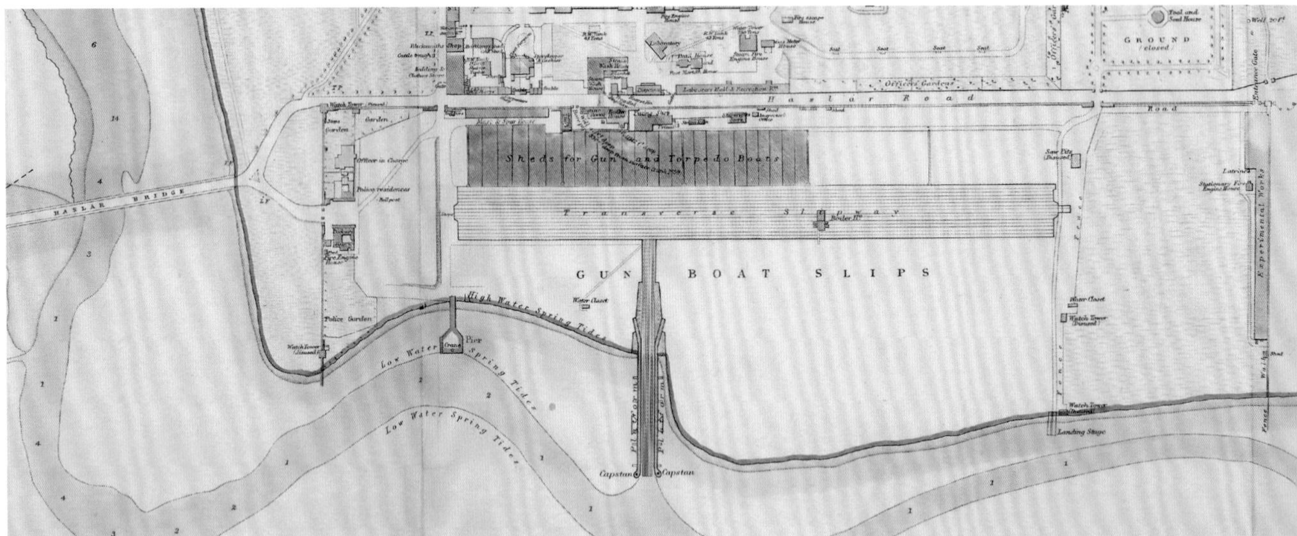

Fig 8.40 (above top) HMS Magnet*, one of the first generation of wooden gunboats. Such frail craft required careful storage when in reserve. (© National Maritime Museum, Greenwich, London, G02086)*

Fig 8.41 (above bottom) A 1909 plan of Gosport, showing Haslar Gunboat Yard's location between the Royal Naval Hospital and Gosport Creek. (TNA ADM 140/1484/25)

The Russian War of 1854–6 led to a sudden demand for large numbers of small gun vessels able to operate in the shallow waters of the Baltic and off the Crimea. Following the bombardment of Sveaborg in August 1855, Admiralty orders led to the construction of some 120 gunboats (Fig 8.40), many built in haste using unseasoned wood.[78] Together with their lightweight hulls and rust-prone engines and boilers, this meant that at the end of the war retaining them afloat 'in ordinary' or reserve was not practical.[79] In February 1856 William Scamp resurrected in a much-reduced scale his unsuccessful 1849 scheme for hauling ashore at Chatham the largest warships for storage (*see* Chapter 2). This was approved by the Admiralty, and four sites were considered before opting for one at Haslar adjacent to the naval hospital and opposite the gunboats' operational base at Portsmouth.[80] Construction was authorised by the Treasury in September 1856, and the yard was completed some 3 years later (Fig 8.41).[81]

The heart of Haslar Gunboat Yard was a patent slip enabling a vessel to float on to a cradle, which was then hauled ashore on rails by a steam engine and on to a traverser.[82] This ran on further rails sunk in a large rectangular pit set at right angles between the slip and a row of metal-framed and metal-clad boat sheds. The steam-powered traverser then

Fig 8.42
The sheds with the traverser at Haslar Gunboat Yard, photographed in 1974. The chimney belongs to the boiler house. To its right is the hospital water tower. (DoE)

Fig 8.43
The house provided for the officer in charge of Haslar Gunboat Yard, photographed in 1974. It has since been demolished. (DoE)

delivered gunboats to individual sheds (Fig 8.42). There they could remain on their railway-mounted cradles and be repaired, maintained, stored and readied for further service. A number of small workshops were provided for the shipwrights and engineers. The complex, surrounded by a handsome brick wall with miniature watchtowers and two guardhouses at the main gates, was completed by a house for the senior officer[83] and a small barracks for a police detachment (Fig 8.43).[84]

By 1861 there were 40 sheds in use, with

a further 10 proposed, along with new sawpits, a pitch house and shipwrights' store.[85] Although the yard had a promising start, by 1868 it was considered surplus to requirements, and it was proposed that the yard be rented out; over the next few years a number of the sheds were relocated to the dockyard, but Haslar apparently remained in being for repairing and storing small craft.[86] A revival in its fortunes is evident from the western range of boat sheds built to cope with larger vessels and probably to be identified with the 'new iron gunboat sheds' estimated at £7,000 in the 1886/7 estimates.[87] In the 20th century, the yard continued with its designed purpose, storing and repairing harbour craft and fast motor launches, motor torpedo boats and motor gunboats, lineal descendants of the mid-Victorian gunboats (Fig 8.44). It remained in use until construction of the present Haslar road bridge forced its closure in 1974. Since then, the site has been partly redeveloped.[88]

Individual projects

Inevitably, an architectural history of the principal dockyards in the 60 years before the First World War tends to focus on the great set-piece programmes of redevelopments and expansions associated with the steam yards. This might suggest that there was little further construction work in these steam yards or in the older areas of the yards. While this is broadly true, there remains a significant number of noteworthy buildings constructed under the aegis of successive Directors of Admiralty Works. These may be remarkable for advances in construction techniques and use of materials, for innovations in the processes they housed or for the new technology they contained.

Under Bentham and especially Holl, increasing use was made of structural ironwork. By the early 1820s its durability, strength, resistance to harsh environments and the ease with which ironwork could be prefabricated

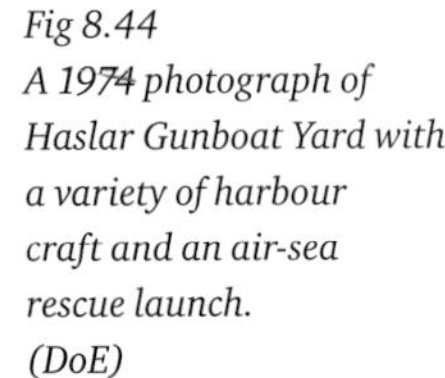

Fig 8.44
A 1974 photograph of Haslar Gunboat Yard with a variety of harbour craft and an air-sea rescue launch.
(DoE)

were demonstrated by Holl in his use of the material for the naval hospital at Port Royal and the Commissioner's House at Bermuda. By the 1830s its use was widespread, supporting floors and roofs in new buildings at Sheerness and Pembroke, while its compressive strength made it ideal for floor loadings in the great mills and bakeries at the Royal Clarence and Royal William Victualling Yards. A decade later it was being used, perhaps most spectacularly, in the immense and graceful roofs over building slips.

Three surviving buildings constructed as individual projects between 1840 and 1860 reflect different approaches to the use of structural ironwork and the experimental nature of the material. At Portsmouth the 27-year-old Lieutenant Roger Beatson had been appointed superintendent for the Admiralty Works Department in 1839, a post he was to hold until transferred to Woolwich in 1845.[89] His two most striking works at Portsmouth are 6 Boathouse and a substantial iron framework for a water tank. The tank served the dockyard fire main, which was originally installed by Bentham early in the 19th century, probably *c* 1806.[90] The new tank, supplementing and partly replacing two earlier header tanks on the roofs of the Block Mills (*see* Chapter 6), was carried on a rectangular grid of cast-iron columns, further braced by cross-struts. The £4,900 'for constructing a reservoir for water' in the 1842/3 estimates almost certainly relates to this structure.[91] The space beneath was originally used to season timber and then as the home of the dockyard fire service (Fig 8.45). The tank has long gone, as has the dockyard fire service.

Also at Portsmouth, Beatson designed in 1840 a single-storey weatherboarded boat store of traditional design, similar to the later 5 and 7 Boathouses that replaced earlier ones on this site and still survive.[92] Such buildings were greedy of yard space, even when they were constructed partly over boat and mast ponds, like the 5 and 7 Boathouses, and his proposal was abandoned. Instead, he designed a three-storey boathouse – now 6 Boathouse – to provide working space

Fig 8.45
The Portsmouth Dockyard fire brigade photographed c 1900 outside their headquarters beneath the water tank for the dockyard fire main. The tank, since removed, was constructed c 1843 to supplement tanks on the roofs of the block mills.
(Author's collection)

as well as storage (Fig 8.46).[93] Behind its conservative brick exterior, the building is notable for its dramatic use of cast-iron columns and enormous under-trussed iron girders carrying the floor joists (Fig 8.47).[94] Each of the girders bears the cast legend, 'The load on this girder should not exceed 40 tons equally distributed over its length', which was way in excess of anything likely to be stored. This suggests that the young Beatson either grossly overengineered the building, at needless extra expense, or he still lacked experience calculating structural strengths. The building seems to have been completed in 1845.[95] Inside, a central well enabled boats to be hoisted to the upper floors, but its narrow shape made it awkward to use, leading the Deputy Director of Works in 1857 to criticise the building for its expense and for being 'totally unsuited either for a working boathouse or a boat store', although both uses were to continue into the early 1980s.[96]

However impressive its internal spaces,

Fig 8.46
The three-storey 6 Boathouse of 1845 at Portsmouth Dockyard, with the late 19th-century timber-framed 5 and 7 Boathouses on either side of the boat and spar pond. (Author)

Fig 8.47
The ground-floor interior of Boathouse 6 at Portsmouth Dockyard, showing the striking iron framework. Part of the small central well for hoisting craft to the upper floors can be seen at the top of the photograph. (DoE)

Beatson's Portsmouth boathouse was something of a structural engineering blind alley. It stands in complete contrast to the third notable building to use iron, also a multi-storey boathouse, erected at Sheerness in 1858. This was designed by Greene and constructed by Henry Grissell & Co, the same combination responsible for the roof over 7 Slip at Chatham. Famed as one of the earliest multi-storey, iron-frame buildings, Sheerness boatstore is the precursor of a style of construction to be seen in factories and warehouses all over the world. The four-storey building was clad in corrugated iron and had ample fenestration (Fig 8.48). Unlike its Portsmouth predecessor, it was equipped with a spacious central well with travelling cranes and could handle the largest ships' boats of 42ft in length (Fig 8.49). It remains an icon in construction history.[97]

In the 1850s Greene also oversaw a major modernisation of timber processing in what was to prove to be for the royal dockyards the last

Fig 8.48
Greene's 1858 Boatstore at Sheerness Dockyard, photographed in 1974. The Small Basin in front has since been filled in. (Author)

Fig 8.49
The interior of the boatstore at Sheerness Dockyard in 1901, when it was still used for its designed purpose. This photograph includes part of the large central well with its traversers for hoisting and manoeuvring the boats.
(Navy and Army Illustrated 30 Nov 1901)

decade where timber shipbuilding reigned supreme. The modernisation was stimulated in part by a serious fire at Brunel's Chatham sawmills in 1854 (*see* Chapter 6), but mainly by a realisation that dockyards were still using sawpits and that the limited mechanical plant was generally woefully out of date. A decision was taken to repair the Chatham mill and to ensure that new sawmills were built to fireproof designs and incorporated the latest machinery.[98] New sawmills were proposed for Sheerness, Devonport South Yard and Pembroke, their rectangular layouts similar to those at Chatham and Woolwich, with the engine and boiler to one side, separated by fireproof walls, and the saw frames occupying the centre of the building. External walls were load bearing, but ironwork was used internally, cast-iron columns supporting the upper floors and the composite roof frames a mix of cast-iron struts and wrought-iron trusses. The Devonport sawmills are the least altered, remaining in production into the 1970s (Fig 8.50), but Pembroke sawmill has been demolished and only the carcass of the Sheerness one remains.

Concomitant with this programme was a drive to improve woodworking methods, introducing new machinery and modernising in particular the joiners' shops. The effect of this is best seen in the fine surviving joiners' shop at Chatham, which began life late in the Napoleonic Wars as a substantial brick treenail house built round three sides of an open courtyard to the south of Holl's new smithery.[99] In the late 1840s it was extensively rebuilt, and its first floor probably dates from this time. In 1855 its courtyard was roofed, and finally in 1863 a first floor was inserted in the former courtyard, lit by a distinctive strip of continuous glazing along its east side. During these later alterations, it was provided with a steam engine, traces of which remain in the north-east corner of the building.[100]

The new first floor of the joiners' shop at Chatham had probably just been completed, when less than a hundred yards away, on 23 December 1863, the new ironclad HMS *Achilles* was floated out for the first time from 2 Dock. Although the dockyard construction programmes for building and maintaining these

Fig 8.50
Greene's sawmills at Devonport Dockyard, still in use in the 1970s. Beyond is his contemporary smithery. (Author)

Fig 8.51
Work in progress in 1913 extending the gun-mounting workshop at Portsmouth. (Author's collection)

armoured warships centred on new basins, docks and metal-working facilities, by the 1880s they also included more specialised gun-mounting workshops of considerable size. Sailing warships with broadside armament had been issued with their guns and wooden truck carriages from the ordnance yards adjacent to the dockyards, hoisted on board before sailing and returned to the ordnance yards before a ship went into refit or was placed in ordinary. The 1860s saw the rapid evolution of new and heavier weapons, the introduction of breech-loading guns, traversing carriages, central battery ships and finally, with the launch of HMS *Devastation* in 1871, ocean-going turret ships. Their heavy armoured gun turrets had sizeable traversing and elevating mechanisms and complicated loading and firing systems.[101] Power assistance, whether steam, hydraulic or later electric, was incorporated from an early date. It was soon realised that the only practical method was to build the turrets as complete units in a specialised workshop and then hoist them aboard when the warship was alongside in the fitting out basin after her launch. At Devonport, a gun-mounting workshop was created within the Quadrangle, but Portsmouth alone retains a separate gun-mounting workshop and store. This is a substantial building with carefully detailed brickwork and was constructed to the west of 15 Dock in 1885. It was subsequently much altered and enlarged on at least two occasions, the last on the eve of the First World War (Fig 8.51).[102]

Another type of specialist workshop introduced during this decade was the torpedo workshop. At Portsmouth 'fireproof torpedo stores, workshops etc' were estimated at £40,000 and were accommodated in a large brick building, its four wings arranged round a central quadrangle (Fig 8.52). This was extensively damaged in World War II, but still retains one of its handsome, pedimented entrances with 'VR 1886' in its tympanum. Even more expensive than the building was the construction of a torpedo range for testing the weapons; £70,000 was allowed for its construction at the head of Portsmouth Harbour on Horsea Island.[103] A smaller sum was allocated for a similar workshop at Devonport in Keyham Yard, and a torpedo test range was planned for Malta Harbour.

Fig 8.52
The north end of the dockyard at Portsmouth. This pre-1914 photograph shows the New Factory beyond the dry docks. To its right are the torpedo workshops and stores. The large corrugated iron-clad building on the right is the boiler shop. (Author's collection)

Portsmouth also has the last of the great workshops built for the steam navy and the largest constructed in this dockyard. By the turn of the 20th century, the original Steam Factory of the late 1840s alongside 2 Basin was at some remove from the heart of fitting out operations then around 5 Basin and its huge new docks. The naval arms race with Germany was gathering momentum, and part of government funding was being allocated to improving and expanding shore facilities to keep pace.[104] In 1905 what was simply known as the New Factory was completed east of 13 Dock; this is a vast, single-storey building five times the size of the Steam Factory (*see* Fig 8.52). Behind its brick exterior the multi-gabled roofs over its cavernous spaces were carried on a steel framework that would have been the envy of Holl and Taylor 80 years earlier as they worked within the limitations and weight of cast and wrought iron.[105] The estimates for 1905/6 included a sum for 'transfer of existing machinery from old to new factory', where among its first tasks would almost certainly have been work fitting out HMS *Dreadnought*.[106]

In 1903 Parliament sanctioned a loan to pay for the construction of dockyard power stations and the installation of electricity throughout the home dockyards and initially overseas at Malta and Simon's Town.[107] By 1906, Portsmouth's power station was in operation, initially with a capacity for generating 9,800kw, expanded by a further 2,400kw in 1912 (Fig 8.53).[108] This was to be one of the more visually subtle modernisations, for the power stations were rarely given the architectural grandeur accorded to some of the 19th-century pumping stations, although the one at Portsmouth had a 200ft chimney. However, once electricity could be harnessed to power individual machine tools, they no longer had to be positioned to take their power by belts from central drive shafts, and factory design could be more flexible and decentralised. The manufacturing areas of 19th-century dockyards, like industry in general, had been characterised by a multitude of tall smoking chimneys and engine houses. As these engine houses were gradually closed down, dockyard skylines altered once their chimneys were demolished or foreshortened, usually to the architectural detriment of the building concerned. The Portsmouth power station building largely survives, but probably the only 19th-century dockyard engine house still to retain its chimney to its full original height is the one at the Chatham ropery.

Fig 8.53
The Portsmouth Dockyard power station in 1913 when its capacity was being expanded.
(TNA ADM 195/84 fol 13)

9

Growth of Empire: The Overseas Bases of the Sailing Navy, 1700–1835

Sir Robert Mansell's expedition against the Barbary corsairs in 1620 was the navy's first taste of distant water operations. In 1655 the capture of Jamaica marked the effective start of regular naval operations in the Caribbean. By1700 the navy had gained considerable experience and was an important instrument of national policy overseas, projecting Britain's growing power, protecting the country's overseas trade with the Mediterranean, the West Indies and North America and providing support and reassurance to colonists along America's eastern seaboard. These commissions where ships and men could be regularly at sea for months posed all sorts of new problems for an Admiralty more used to fleet operations in home waters. In an age when nutrition was imperfectly understood, when food preservation was extremely limited and when medical facilities were rudimentary or non-existent, the effect of longer voyages could be disastrous for crews. Scurvy was an ever-present hazard, while in warmer climates ships' companies faced new diseases, leading to soaring illness and mortality rates. The ships themselves needed routine maintenance, while storms and heavy seas could shred sails and splinter masts and spars. In warm seas ships were slowed by marine growths furring their hulls, while in the West Indies especially, the wood-boring *Teredo navalis* could wreak havoc on a ship's strength and seaworthiness.

Mansell's expedition had demonstrated the problems involved in supplying a fleet far from home, and as early as 1625, when Britain was at war with Spain, it had been suggested that Gibraltar should be captured and used as a base.[1] Later, the unexpected acquisition of Tangier, part of Catherine of Braganza's dowry on her marriage to Charles II, briefly was thought to offer a possible solution, and some £400,000 was spent improving the mole and establishing a naval stores depot. But the roadstead was too shallow and exposed, and after Tangier was abandoned in 1683, stores were moved first to Lisbon and then Gibraltar, where Admiral Herbert had arranged with the Spanish authorities to use the Rock as a base against the corsairs.[2] In the 1670s, after negotiating its use with Spain, an Agent Victualler was established at Port Mahon in Minorca, and the fleet under Admiral Sir Thomas Allin, Commander-in-Chief of the Mediterranean Squadron 1664–5 and 1668–70, and then Admiral Sir Edward Spragge, Commander-in-Chief 1670–2, used it as a careening, repair and stores base.[3] While temporary access to a foreign harbour was important, shifting European alliances meant that such use could only ever be short term, and facilities were generally limited to what was available and what could be rented. As a consequence, in the 17th century the navy's presence in the Mediterranean remained on a summer-time only basis.

Experience gained that century undoubtedly played a part in Admiralty thinking that long-term naval influence in a region was best aided by the establishment of strategically situated permanent bases. There seems to have been surprisingly little debate in official circles about the need for overseas bases for the navy. For the Admiralty, the advantage lay in an ability to keep ships on station for long periods, lessening the number of voyages to and from the home dockyards and consequently reducing the total number of ships required. There was also a valid point that crews long on station would be more familiar with a region than fresh squadrons sent out on an annual basis, with perhaps a less valid supposition that such crews would gradually acclimatise and be more resistant to local diseases. For the crews, the greatest benefit of such bases, apart from the possibilities for fresh provisions, was the opportunity for their sick and wounded to be cared for ashore. Hospital ships were introduced to the fleet following a suggestion by James Pearse, appointed Surgeon-General of the Navy in 1665, and in 1681 a hospital for military and naval use was established at Tangier. Significantly, in 1701 Admiral John Benbow ahead of his expedition to the West Indies sought and obtained permission not only for a hospital ship to accompany his squadron, but also a 'boarded house' or timber hospital, possibly prefabricated, to be erected in Jamaica, both to be served by appropriate medical staff.[4]

For the warships themselves, crucial elements of these overseas bases were careening wharves, storehouses for supplies and sufficient workshops capable of coping with minor repairs or of patching a warship sufficiently to enable it to sail to a home dockyard for a full repair (*see* Figs 9.1 and 9.2). One further and important consideration was that a base should be capable of being defended by permanent fortifications. With a very few exceptions, the overseas bases did not build warships, and it was not until the mid-1840s that Malta became the first overseas base to have a dry dock. However, the East India Company's Bombay Dockyard completed its first dry dock capable of being used by a 50-gun ship in 1750. Now known as Upper Old Bombay Dock, it is 209ft long, 47ft wide and 15ft deep. By 1765 a further two dry docks were completed, the last one at the urging of Admiral Sir Samuel Cornish, concerned about docking facilities for the British squadron.[5]

Fig 9.1 (below top)
A warship being careened at English Harbour in 1789. This involved much labour and was always a risky operation for a ship and its crew.
(© National Maritime Museum, Greenwich, London, L5911)

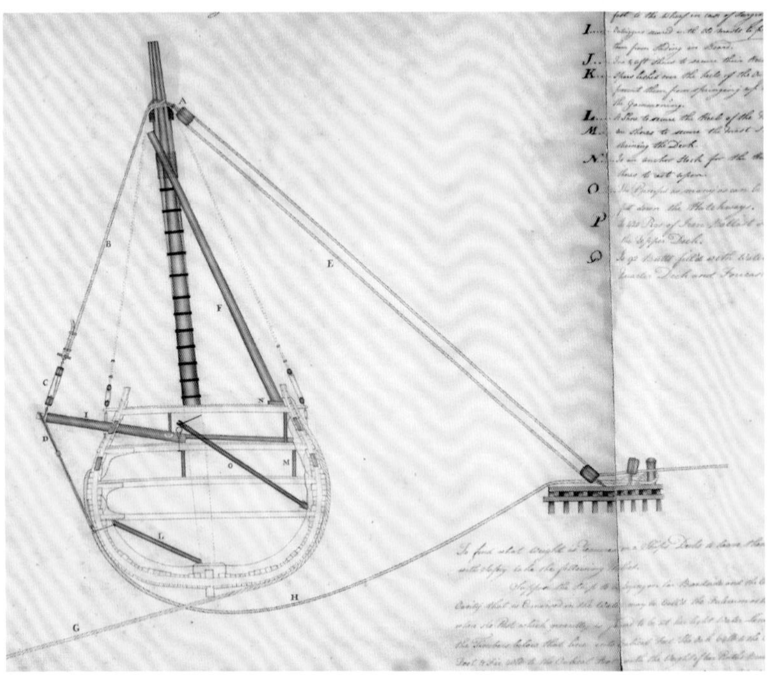

Fig 9.2 (below bottom)
A cross-section of the 47-gun HMS Blenheim *at English Harbour, Antigua, probably in the 1820s, showing the elaborate system of blocks, spars and tackle needed to haul a warship over to clean her hull at a careening wharf.*
(TNA ADM 140/1201)

By 1700 the Royal Navy was on the threshold of its eventual global expansion. Four years later it acquired its first overseas base when an Anglo-Dutch expedition captured Gibraltar. Although one of the world's great natural fortresses and strategically sited to monitor the Straits linking the Mediterranean to the Atlantic, it possessed only a short mole. Although this was later extended, it was to be two centuries before the Admiralty constructed a harbour of sufficient size to accommodate fleets operating here (*see* Chapter 11). In the 18th century, Britain's principal Mediterranean base was on Minorca at Port Mahon, captured in 1708 (*see* Fig 11.9). Minorca was then lost between 1756 and 1763, lost again in 1782 and briefly reoccupied 1798–1802.

In the West Indies, Port Royal had been used as a base at intervals since the capture of Jamaica, but the Admiralty limited itself to hiring storehouses and making use of commercial careening wharfs until the great earthquake of 1692 shattered the town.[6] Naval facilities at Port Royal and Port Antonio were to be provided in the late 1720s and 1730s (*see* Fig 12.1), at much the same time as English Harbour at Antigua was being developed (Fig 9.3).[7] In the Indian Ocean the navy was able to make use of the East India Company's dockyard at Bombay,[8] while along the eastern seaboard of North America warships used commercial facilities at, among other ports, Rhode Island, New York and especially Boston, where until the 1740s there was a dry dock capable of holding a 50-gun warship.[9] It was not until the outbreak of the Seven Years' War in 1755 and Anglo-French rivalry in this theatre that a naval base was founded at Halifax in Nova Scotia (Fig 9.4), and during this conflict small locally constructed warships were in operation on the Great Lakes.[10]

By now, growing experience and confidence,

along with better supplies and equipment, allowed the Admiralty to deploy warships overseas on a year-round basis, with much of their peacetime work foreshadowing the sort of policing role for which the Royal Navy was better known in the 19th century.[11] In January 1757 there were 7 ships on station in the East Indies, 30 guarding the Plantations (West Indies and eastern seaboard of North America), 27 in the Mediterranean and a further 82 on convoy work or patrolling. Manning these 146 warships were 39,730 sailors. These figures compare with the 184 warships and 48,985 sailors the following 1 July.[12] The organisation underpinning these figures should not be underestimated and reflects very considerable credit on the Victualling and Ordnance Boards as well as the Admiralty and Navy Boards.

The new-found strategic importance of Bermuda following the War of American Independence was not lost on an Admiralty also keen to replace facilities that were no longer accessible on the eastern seaboard of America. In 1783 Captain Thomas Hurd was ordered to survey the waters around Bermuda to find a passage through the surrounding reefs. By 1795 a small base was established at the capital, St George. These facilities were relocated to Ireland Island in 1809, when construction began on the great fortified dockyard. As relations deteriorated with the United States, attention was again focused on the need to control the Great Lakes to protect the remaining British colonies.[13] Small naval bases were established on Lakes Ontario, Erie, Huron and Champlain. As shoals and rapids on the St Lawrence river above Montreal prevented ships reaching Lake Ontario, those used on the Lakes had to be constructed locally, uniquely forming a separate, self-contained navy. A number were of considerable size: among the last to be built was HMS *St Lawrence*, a 102-gun first-rate launched at the Kingston yard in 1814 and the largest warship on this freshwater station.[14]

Elsewhere, the Revolutionary and Napoleonic Wars saw further naval bases established in

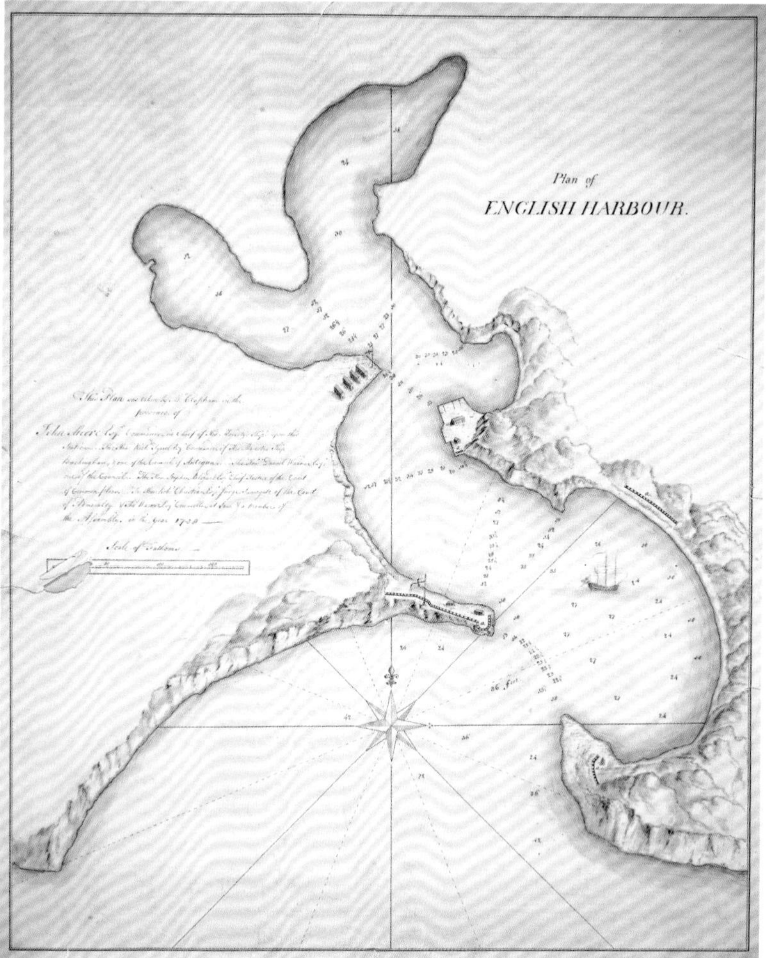

Fig 9.3
This 1750 plan shows Fort Berkeley guarding the crooked entrance to English Harbour, Antigua. On opposite sides of the harbour are a collection of storehouses and a careening wharf. (TNA ADM 140/1177)

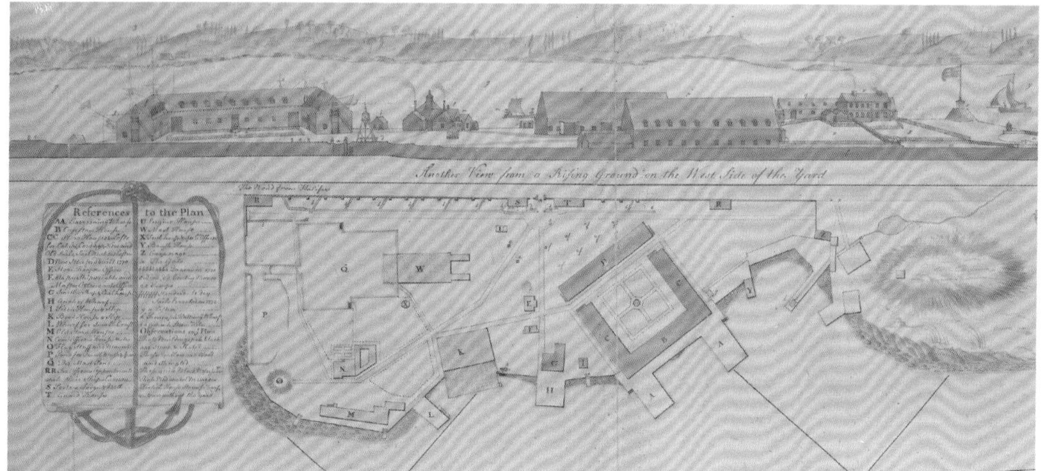

Fig 9.4
Halifax Dockyard c 1771, some 15 years after it was established. The political situation in North America ensured that the yard developed rapidly in its early years. (© National Maritime Museum, Greenwich, London, Lad11/52, Halifax Yard)

1796 at the Cape of Good Hope, later relocated to Simon's Town,[15] and at Madras. In 1800 Malta was captured, so lessening Minorca's importance, and in 1807 facilities were established at Barbados. Following operations in the Indian Ocean in 1809, bases were set up at Bombay in 1811 and at Trincomalee in Ceylon a couple of years later. At Rio de Janeiro the navy rented storage for supplies for its South Atlantic squadron.[16] By December 1814 at least 2,373 people were employed in the overseas yards (see Table 9.1).

Table 9.1 Numbers employed in the overseas yards in 1780 and in December 1814, showing their relative importance by the end of the Napoleonic Wars.

Base	*year*	
	1780	*1814*[a]
Halifax	175	246
Quebec	–	6
Bermuda	–	51
Jamaica	115	314
Antigua	137	332
Barbados	1	128
Gibraltar	31	175
Malta	–	383
Cape of Good Hope	–	97
Madras	–	520
Bombay	–	104
Rio de Janeiro	–	17
totals	**459**	**2,373**

a NMM ADM/BP/34B, 14 Dec 1814. These figures exclude Trincomalee, which was not yet operational; Minorca in 1780, where the figures are not recorded; and the yards on the Great Lakes. Bombay and Madras Dockyards, owned by the East India Company, had been repairing Royal Navy ships from the late 18th century and also constructing them from 1799 (Wadia 1957, 158, 185–6). At Rio de Janeiro, the Admiralty rented facilities.

In theory, with the exception of the established East India Company yards that undertook contract work for the Royal Navy, every overseas base operated under the same general rules governing home yards. Each was the overall responsibility of the Navy Board, and the senior officer in charge was expected to submit proposals for new works for approval in London. In practice, this was rarely possible before steamships and, much later, telegraphs shortened the time for communications. Local officials had to exercise their initiative, much less seems to have been referred to the Navy Board or its surveyors, and local record keeping remained patchy.[17] This was especially the case at the smaller yards during peacetime, when the storekeepers were frequently the senior resident figures. Their comparatively humble rank made it inevitable that for most of the 18th century they came under the authority of the senior naval officer on station. Admirals, with justifiable concern for their ships and their men, were not averse to instigating quite major building projects. This understandable but at times somewhat cavalier attitude was gradually tamed, particularly after professional architects joined the staff of the Admiralty and Navy Boards. In 1711 Admiral Jennings had authorised the design and construction of the first naval hospital at Minorca (*see* Chapters 13 and 16). A century later in 1813, when Admiral Sir Alexander Cochrane tried to impose his design for a new hospital at Bermuda in preference to the one proposed by Holl, he was firmly rebuffed. The result was a stalemate for 5 years, by which time the peacetime needs of the station resulted in a smaller hospital (*see* Chapter 4).

This process of gradually regularising the running of the overseas yards was helped during the long wars with France at the end of the 18th century when the Navy Board appointed commissioners at Quebec, Halifax, Jamaica, Antigua, Madras, Bombay, Cape of Good Hope, Malta and Gibraltar, though these posts largely went once peace was restored. The commissioners were expected to exercise better control of the bases than had been possible with transient naval officers, although one immediate result was the need for further official accommodation, most notably exemplified by the grandiose house built for the Bermuda commissioner.[18] Nevertheless, the new system appears to have been observed, at any rate by the latter stages of the Napoleonic Wars. When a decision was taken in 1813 to close down the naval establishment at Madras and create a new base at Trincomalee on the eastern side of Ceylon, plans for buildings at Trincomalee were prepared at the commissioner's office in Madras. The commissioner recorded in a letter to the Admiralty that 'as there was no person in this Establishment who could copy the plans and drawings ... I was under the necessity of employing the Master of the Free School at this Presidency for that purpose at the rate of 15 pagodas for each sheet when completed'. The proposed buildings included a careening house, wharf and jetty, store and canvas room, timber sheds and a house for the commissioner. Two sets of the drawings were sent to London and one retained at Madras.[19] What is not known is whether or not the commissioner waited for London's approval before starting construction.

The final choice of a site for an overseas base was largely the responsibility of the senior naval officers on station, although other factors inevitably played a part. At Malta and the Cape of Good Hope, the navy inherited and developed existing bases. Gibraltar, despite lacking facilities, had obvious strategic value, while Minorca had strategic value as well as a fine natural harbour at Port Mahon. In the West Indies especially, where rival European powers had colonised sometimes closely adjacent islands, colonial legislatures positively welcomed the establishment of a naval base and with it the comforting promise of the presence of warships. At Antigua in 1728, the island legislature purchased land for the navy at English Harbour, and the cost of the first careening wharf and a fort to guard the harbour entrance was paid for locally (*see* Chapter 12). Private landowners, however, were not always so helpful, as Admiral Edward Vernon found at Port Royal after his arrival there in 1739. Exorbitant sums were demanded for additional land for the dockyard and in the end a jury had to be assembled to agree a fair valuation, followed by an Act of the Assembly to convey the land to the navy.[20]

At Halifax, only established as a settlement 10 years earlier, Commodore Philip Durell in 1759 selected the site for the new base, the Admiralty acquired and purchased the land, and contracts were awarded. The new dockyard was welcome recognition of Halifax's new status as capital of the Province of Nova Scotia and helped the building boom then being enjoyed by the embryonic town.[21] In the 1730s and 1740s Sir Charles Knowles was stationed in the West Indies and played a crucial role in the development of English Harbour in the Leeward Islands and the two bases on Jamaica at Port Royal and Port Antonio. The devastating earthquake that had destroyed Port Royal in 1692 made the Admiralty understandably reluctant to invest here, but Knowles's alternative choice of the undeveloped Port Antonio on the north coast ended in failure because of the unhealthy climate and high mortality rates.[22]

In the largely virgin and empty territory of the North American mainland around the Great Lakes, communications depended heavily on rivers and lakes, naval staff were very few in number, and individual responsibility was high. Selecting the site for a new base and setting it up in such a vast region could involve considerable physical hardship. Probably typical of many such journeys undertaken there by naval staff was one made in the late summer of 1829 when Commodore Robert Barrie with a Royal Engineer officer and a surveyor embarked in a birch canoe and descended the Severn river from Lake Simcoe to select a site for a naval arsenal at Penetanguishene Bay. The site had been little developed, although it had already been used some years earlier to construct three small naval schooners, the *Bee, Wasp* and *Mosquito*, names no doubt reflecting the shipwrights' views on the summer-time discomforts of the area.[23]

Constructing a new base or extending an established one presented further problems when labour and materials were scarce. It was common practice for ships' captains to make use of their crews, as at Minorca in 1715 when they undertook the very heavy manual labour building much of the careening wharf, but this tended to be unpopular work even with extra pay, and there were limits. At Port Royal in the early 1740s crews were thinly stretched, maintaining their own ships, building a wharf and constructing the new naval hospital.[24] A century later it was proposed to use the Royal Marine garrison on Ascension Island to construct a hospital for cases of contagious infection, using materials shipped from England.[25] In Jamaica and later at Bermuda the navy early on had made use of slaves to supplement dockyard workmen, the Navy Board recommending to the Admiralty in 1730 that at Jamaica 'negro boys may be purchased and assigned to some of the most deserving shipwrights and caulkers to be instructed by them in the service of caulking and shipwrights' work'.[26] As Admiral Charles Stewart noted in a letter to the Admiralty Secretary in January that year, 'it has been the common practice for the gentlemen on this station to buy negroes to have them taught to caulk, and the government to pay ten shillings a day for their hire'.[27] Jamaica and Bermuda seem to have been exceptional in this respect, although in the 19th century the navy on Ascension Island was to employ liberated slaves.

On Ceylon, acquired from the Dutch at the same time as the Cape, a slightly different problem confronted Commissioner Peter Puget at Trincomalee in the early summer of 1813 when he arrived to find the area deserted by its inhabitants, since 'it appeared on enquiry that starvation to a very great degree had driven the Ceylonese from that district'. Fear of a repetition of the famine and attendant mortality meant that nobody was willing to return. A recruiting drive in southern India at Negapatam and Pondicherry eventually produced 30 local carpenters, 30 local bricklayers, 5 local blacksmiths and 200 coolies to form the new dockyard labour force. One of the ships' carpenters was transferred to supervise carpentry and joinery work.[28] The new yard was established along the side of a sheltered inlet between the main and inner harbours at Trincomalee, where beyond a narrow strip of jungle it was protected by the guns of the former Dutch Fort Ostenberg. Unlike the Cape where the navy acquired two established bases from the Dutch, there seems to have been little here. The first priority was a storehouse for stores already on the way from Madras sufficient 'for the refitment of three frigates and as many sloops'. In 1816 these were joined by 'all stores except those required for shipbuilding' from Bombay. There were also plans for a capstan house 'capable of holding the officers and crew of a 74-gun ship', clearly similar to the 19th-century one at Port Royal with accommodation on a floor above the capstans.[29] In 1820 works included the wharf, stores for rice and iron and a house for the commissioner.

Not everything at Trincomalee had to be constructed, because local accommodation was available outside the base. The Admiral on station was the fortunate tenant of a magnificent colonnaded and stuccoed mansion, shaded by deep verandas, and set in some 25 acres of grounds a little further up the inlet. This had been purchased at an auction by an army captain who re-sold it to the Admiralty in 1814 (Fig 9.5).[30] The palatial house was later to move one naval correspondent to flights of fancy, musing on 'How the Commander-in-Chief must revel in his pyjamas on the cool verandah, after the official business of the day is over and he can enjoy the *dolce far niente* undisturbed'.[31] Its magnificence was outclassed by the even more sumptuous house of the storekeeper, though it is doubtful if the Admiralty was aware its size when first acquired.[32]

It is not known how much of the Trincomalee yard had been completed when work was postponed in 1822 as part of the post-war economies, but by 1840 the yard had the range of buildings and facilities to be expected at an overseas base supporting a small squadron. In 1896 the Admiralty contributed to the cost of a dry dock at Colombo. The availability of repair facilities here probably held back the development of Trincomalee, which remained a quiet backwater and little modernised until the fall of Singapore in 1942, when it became the main base for the eastern fleet of the Royal Navy. The Royal Navy continued to use the base until 1957. None of the early buildings are known to survive.[33]

Craftsmen and labour for building and maintaining the bases were generally not a problem where there were existing communities, as at Malta, the Cape of Good Hope and to a lesser extent Minorca, where in the early years of British occupation the labour for major projects tended to be seasonal and to consist of Catalan and Majorcan workers.[34] At Halifax, despite the newness of the settlement, the storekeeper Joseph Gerrish apparently had no difficulty in finding three main contractors to blast the rock to form a mast pond, shift up to 24,000 cubic yards of soil to level the site and construct the buildings, slips and careening wharves of the new yard in 1759.[35] Problems of a different nature could arise in wartime. At Gibraltar in 1800, John

Fig 9.5
Admiralty House, Trincomalee, c 1900. There can have been few more agreeable official residences. (AdL Da 038)

Maria Boschetti, an enterprising local contractor who was constructing a new victualling yard that he had designed, including a huge brick-lined reservoir, tried and failed to obtain the bricks from Malaga 'in vessels under Moorish colours'. It seems that most of the million bricks had to be sent from England, occasioning a considerable delay.[36]

The greatest problems arose on the smaller islands where suitable building materials did not always exist and where labour, when available, was generally dear. This was one factor in the Navy Board's complaint in 1818 that 'all works [of ship repair and maintenance] in the colonial yards are found to be exceedingly expensive', and by the 1830s it was reckoned that the cost of labour in Bermuda was 10 times the home rate.[37] Early on, prefabrication of timber buildings was tried as one way to reduce costs and to ensure that local staff did not undertake grandiose construction projects. It is possible that the 'boarded house' required in 1701 for a hospital at Jamaica by Admiral Benbow was an early example of a prefabricated building shipped to an overseas base. Certainly by 1729 such a system was in use, because that year the Navy Board determined that two store buildings for Antigua should be 'prepared and framed in England and sent over on freight'. The following year a batch of three large timber buildings were sent to Port Antonio to be used as storehouse, mast house and smiths' shop, the largest of which was 150ft long, 19ft wide and 9ft high.[38] By the 1740s the system was sufficiently sophisticated for the Navy Board to be able to arrange for buildings to be prefabricated in New England and sent as freight to the West Indies, as in 1743 when a substantial two-storey timber building was expected at Antigua for use as a capstan house, the upper floor to be used as accommodation for the crew of the vessel being careened.[39]

The two substantial drawbacks of timber construction in tropical and subtropical climates were its vulnerability to wood-boring insects and rot-inducing fungus attack; consequently, maintenance requirements were high if such buildings were to last any length of time. Where suitable building stone was available, this could be substituted, but in the Caribbean yards extensive use was also made of brick, much of it imported from Britain as ballast, but a significant amount purchased locally. Replacing timber with iron as a structural material in buildings in the overseas bases offered significant advantages of prefabrication, durability and strength. Edward Holl was to exploit these at the naval hospital of 1818 at Port Royal and the Commissioner's House at Bermuda of 1822. These were to be the first and in many ways the most distinguished of numerous naval buildings overseas to employ structural iron. Holl's buildings paralleled the work by Royal Engineers, notably Brandreth, in the use of iron for barracks and other military buildings overseas.[40]

Some of the most intractable problems associated with establishing and maintaining a base followed the British Government's decision in 1815 to hold the Emperor Napoleon in exile on St Helena in the South Atlantic. The Admiralty had no problem acquiring land for a store depot and houses for the small number of shore staff stationed on the island, as it had been occupied and settled by the East India Company as a victualling station since 1659.[41] A far greater challenge was presented by Ascension Island. A naval presence was established here in 1816, as the island was seen by the British Government as a possible base for a French rescue of Napoleon. After his death in 1821, Ascension played a vital role for much of the rest of the 19th century, both as a victualling and supply station supporting the Royal Navy's anti-slavery patrols along the west coast of Africa and providing hospital facilities for sailors and liberated slaves struck down by sickness and disease (*see* Chapter 13).

The sheer ingenuity of the Royal Navy has seldom been better demonstrated than with its early 'colonisation' of Ascension. Apart from the volcanic tufa that could be used as building stone, everything had to be imported, the storeships lying off shore and materials landed from long boats; only later was a short mole or pier head formed and equipped with a hand crane.[42] By the late 1820s the small settlement of Georgetown had been established nearby, built by naval and marine labour. The only surviving building from this pioneer phase is the victualling storehouse with two storeys and a cellar, completed by December 1827, its rather crude appearance suggesting it was designed by the resident victualling officer and built by unskilled naval labour.[43] By then, it had been found that the upper slopes of Green Mountain, watered almost daily by showers, could be cultivated and used for a market garden and small farm to provide fresh food for the hospital and the settlement, and by 1822 the Victualling

Board was regularly sending out seed.[44] The resident victualling officer had no authority to purchase supplies from passing ships, but the plentiful Ascension turtles were valuable for bartering, 300 being exchanged in February 1829 for 55 'fine wether sheep' from the *Unity* barque of Bristol. In November that year the victualling officer reported with evident satisfaction to his Board that 'we have vegetables in abundance and have sown within the last fortnight eight acres of turnips and four with different grass seeds, grain etc'.[45]

In early June 1829 the Royal Engineer Lieutenant Henry Brandreth arrived on Ascension to spend some weeks surveying the island in order to design improvements in the facilities and defences. His visit was probably prompted by a report the previous year on the poor state of Ascension's buildings.[46] Apart from the top of Green Mountain where there was vegetation, Brandreth noted that the rest of the volcanic island was all covered in 'ashes, cinders and small masses of lava'. His proposals included barracks, officers' quarters, a hospital and a remarkable square musketry blockhouse forming the rear of Fort Cockburn, sited to protect the pier and Georgetown (Fig 9.6).[47] Brandreth's most lasting contribution to the island was to lay a piped water supply from Green Mountain to large cast-iron cisterns in the settlement, with a spur pipe down to the mole for supplying ships (*see* Fig 10.5).

Much of his next 2 years Brandreth spent in England, partly visiting ironworks in Birmingham and overseeing the production of cast-iron cisterns, air valves and pipes for the water supply, as well as iron girders, joists, shoes and other fittings for the barracks and hospital. In late 1830 Brandreth returned to Ascension to supervise the installation of the water supply and the start of work on the buildings and fortifications.[48] His work went some way to provide the island with the essential infrastructure required for the Preventive Squadron and its anti-slavery patrols. The magnitude and cost of their task are often forgotten, with 160,000 slaves freed in the 60 years of the squadron's existence at a cost of the lives of 17,000 naval personnel through disease, battle or accident.[49] By the early 1840s these patrols were being provided with small steam warships that were proving ideal in coastal waters and for steaming up the great rivers of West Africa.[50] By 1851 the number of steam vessels on the station had eclipsed the sailing warships, which by 1861 had dwindled to a tiny minority. This was the first sustained operational use of these vessels, resulting in this most remote of all overseas bases becoming one of the earliest to be equipped to maintain and supply them. For further details on Ascension, *see* Chapter 13.

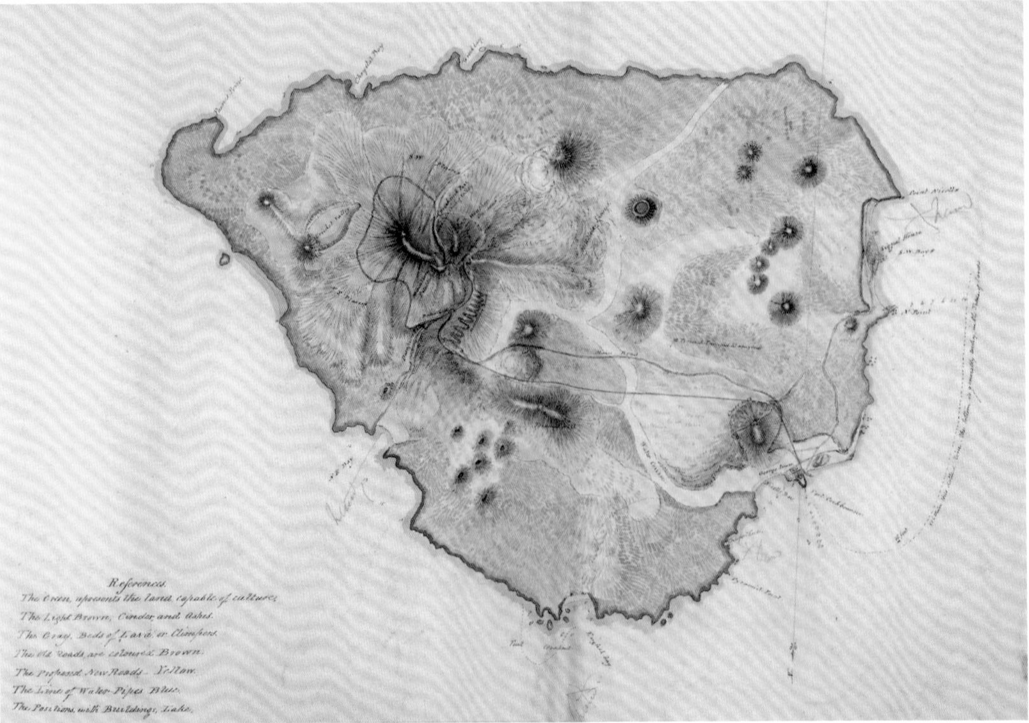

Fig 9.6
Brandreth's map of Ascension Island, accompanying his 1829 report on the island. (TNA MR 1/1771 fol 1)

10

Heyday of Empire: The Overseas Bases, 1835–1914

For more than half a century after the defeat of Napoleon, the Royal Navy had no serious rivals. Its overseas operations concentrated primarily on protecting Great Britain's trade routes and fishing grounds and maintaining a colonial presence to reassure settlers and merchants.[1] Although protection of the colonies was always seen as a primary task, much of the navy's time in colonial waters was spent helping the civil authorities, transporting local civilian and military officials, providing supplies and aid in emergencies and surveying coastal waters. In the absence of any major naval threats, the Royal Navy was able to undertake this largely policing role with an assortment of smaller warships, where economy and endurance rather than firepower were the primary considerations. Their use enforcing the Pax Britannica helped coin the phrase 'Send a gunboat!', with its pejorative connotations to a post-imperial world. But in so defining much of this era, the phrase more accurately reflects the limited naval forces needed to keep trade routes safe and further Great Britain's diplomatic and political objectives.[2]

By the start of the 19th century, the navy's overseas operations had long been organised on a series of stations, each with their squadron of warships. At the start of the French wars at the end of the 18th century, the four existing stations were Halifax, Mediterranean, East Indies and West Indies. They were joined by West Africa, created after the passing in 1807 of the Anti-slave Trade Act, and by Cape of Good Hope and South America. From 1832 the West Africa station was combined with the Cape station, and in 1837 the South American station was divided into separate squadrons for the Pacific and South Atlantic coasts of South America. The locations of the navy's overseas bases broadly matched these stations, but their relative importance was changing.

The capture of Malta in 1800 had given the navy priceless assets of a magnificent harbour and an existing small dockyard in the centre of the Mediterranean. The island's strategic worth was to be underlined by the Syrian crisis of 1839–41 that led to the British Government appreciating the benefits of having a substantial naval presence, effectively a small fleet, including steamers, permanently based in the Mediterranean. At the time, neither Gibraltar nor Malta was equipped to look after such a force on a permanent basis. For many years it formed the principal naval force readily available to the Government in any emergency. Warships based here had to be capable of meeting any challenges from other European naval powers. As a result, the scale of investment in Malta's naval facilities from the 1840s onwards came second to that of the principal home yards during the latter part of the 19th century, and this was clearly demonstrated when Malta became the first overseas base in 1847 to have a dry dock (Fig 10.1). In 1897 there were 10 first-class battleships stationed at Malta; three

Fig 10.1
By the 1880s the scale and facilities of Malta Dockyard rivalled the major home yards. To help employment when the Mediterranean fleet was absent, the Admiralty agreed in 1883 to the construction of a composite screw sloop, HMS Melita*, photographed in March 1888 during her launch from a specially constructed slip alongside the new Iron Ship Repairing Shop. The shipbuilding experiment was not repeated, and the slip was largely demolished about 20 years later.*
(© National Maritime Museum, Greenwich, London, P39574)

years later the *Navy and Army Illustrated* was able to assure its readers that 'our superb Mediterranean Squadron ... not only is ... the finest but the largest fleet afloat in the world under one command, for, exclusive of the port-guard ships at Gibraltar and Alexandria, Sir John Fisher has in his splendid command two battleships, nine cruisers, seven gun-boats [and] fifteen destroyers'.[3]

Elsewhere, the value of the West Indies bases declined as trade with the Caribbean lessened, while those on trade routes to the Far East became increasingly important. In 1812 the small port of Trincomalee was first used as a small stores depot. The following year the Admiralty decided to shift the naval establishment at Madras to Trincomalee to take advantage of the healthier climate, and by 1816 the new base was operational (*see* Chapter 9).[4] Nothing now remains of the small base at Madras. In 1841 a small naval base was established in Hong Kong as the base for the new China station, carved out of the existing East Indies station; the appointment here of a Naval Storekeeper and Agent Victualler in March 1842 indicated its principal role as a supply depot. Initially, a number of temporary timber buildings were used,[5] reflecting in part the shortage of funding for a peacetime navy and the resultant need to concentrate resources on only the most essential projects such as at Malta and Ascension Island. Hong Kong was to be supplemented by a small base further north at Wei Hai Wei on the Yellow Sea, leased between 1898 and 1930 from the Chinese government. The milder climate here made the latter a popular summer base.

In 1859 a separate station was established to cover Australia and New Zealand (*see* Chapter 13). In Sydney Harbour the New South Wales government provided land and facilities on Garden Island and Cockatoo Island, and the Admiralty funded most of the construction of an ordnance depot on Spectacle Island (*see* Chapter 15).[6] In 1908 plans to establish an Australian navy led to their transfer in 1913 to the Commonwealth of Australia and the establishment of the first dockyard for the Royal Australian Navy.[7] Land for a naval base in New Zealand had been set aside in 1869 in the Borough of Devonport, adjacent to Auckland on North Island, but was not developed. It was subsequently swapped in 1892 for land adjacent to the Calliope dry dock.[8] Within a few years a small number of timber buildings had been constructed, forming the nucleus of what would later develop into Devonport Dockyard after the 1913 Naval Defence Act authorising the establishment of the New Zealand Naval Forces.[9]

In the 1830s arrival of steam-driven warships on overseas stations meant they had to be equipped with suitable maintenance facilities, usually centred on existing smitheries. In February 1839 the first resident engineer was appointed to Port Royal, and a year later the Admiralty approved the suggestion that the yard should be equipped 'for the repair of steam machinery', subsequently sending out a boiler maker and an 'Engine Smith'.[10] By later standards the early facilities were comparatively simple. When HMS *Highflyer*, a wood screw frigate, visited Port Royal in 1852, G Aitchison her engineer compiled a list of machinery needed in the dockyard. In his report, he wrote that 'I consider the smithery sufficiently large for any general repair that may be required.' However, he found that in the fitting shop there was a need for 'two additional lathes with back motion, self-acting, capable of cutting screws 6in. diameter, one slotting machine, one driving machine large enough to bore out a brass of 18in. diameter, one smaller [driving machine] for common purposes ... [and] a complete set of Whitworth's taps and dies'. He felt that the boiler shop required 'two small forges, one furnace for heating plates, one driving machine sufficiently large for boring tube plates and also one smaller for general use'. To drive all this plant, he recommended a 10hp steam engine and boiler.[11] A similar variety and scale of equipment were probably to be found at the smaller bases at Ascension Island, Simon's Town, Hong Kong, Trincomalee and Esquimalt well into the 1890s.

A more intractable problem was to ensure adequate supplies of coal for warships' boilers. In areas lacking bases and where it was not possible or where it was considered too risky to make arrangements with commercial suppliers in neutral ports, specialist coaling depots had to be set up. In the more remote foreign stations, it was not reactionary conservatism that led the navy to employ sailing ships, or steam-assisted sailing ships, long after they had gone from the main battlefleets, but rather an appreciation of their adequacy as warships for policing tasks undertaken where there were no maintenance facilities and where fuel was expensive and hard to find. The problems posed by steam warships were well summarised by Colonel Sir William Jervois in 1875:

> Naval yards for victualling and refitting our squadrons were maintained at many foreign stations when our Navy consisted solely of sailing ships. Before the introduction of steam, however, vessels could keep to sea for considerable periods without going into any harbour. Many repairs were effected with the resources the ships carried with them and no coal was required. The man-of-war of the present day cannot keep the sea without frequent supplies of coal and occasional repairs.[12]

The vastness of the Pacific presented the greatest problems of maintenance and supply. From the early 19th century, what became the Pacific Squadron was based at Valparaiso, relying on a succession of stores ships and a rented magazine ashore. In 1855 distant ripples from the Crimean War led to the tiny settlement of Esquimalt near the southern tip of Vancouver Island off the mainland of British Columbia being used as a temporary base when a hospital was established here. This was followed 4 years later by construction of a coaling depot on Thetis Island in the harbour. Finally, in 1870, Esquimalt became the headquarters of the North Pacific Squadron, superseding Valparaiso.[13] The yard was not to develop significantly (Fig 10.2) until completion of a dry dock more than 20 years later, and Thetis Island was subsequently joined to the mainland by rubble excavated from the dry dock. One thousand pounds for 'additional buildings' appears in its first annual estimates, but by 1869 the only figure was £100 for maintenance. Throughout its life to 1905 as a Royal Navy base, development was jointly financed. The dockyard was funded by the imperial government, the protective batteries by the Dominion Government and the promised dry dock, after a number of false starts and a deal of wrangling, largely by the Dominion Government aided by an Admiralty subsidy.[14]

Esquimalt had the advantage of a deep-water anchorage, limitless supplies of mast and spar timbers in the virgin forests and suitable coal from the mines of Nanaimo 60 miles up the coast.[15] In the wake of the 1846 Oregon Boundary Treaty, establishing a base at the southern end of a largely uninhabited Vancouver Island also sent a clear message to any Americans still tempted at further territorial expansion. The potential importance of the base increased considerably following British Columbia joining the Canadian Confederation in 1871, in return for which the Dominion Government promised to construct a transcontinental railway line within 10 years. The eventual completion of the Canadian Pacific Railway in 1885 allowed troops and supplies to be rushed across the continent from Halifax should the need arise. Two years

Fig 10.2
Where facilities such as dry docks did not exist, the navy had to fall back on its own resources. Here the bow of the Chatham-built wood screw corvette HMS Charybdis *is under repair in Esquimalt harbour in May 1870. The ship is heavily ballasted at her stern to raise the bow, which is protected by a timber coffer-dam. Hulls of metal warships were not so easily repaired.*
(© National Maritime Museum, Greenwich, London, L5702)

Table 10.1 Proposed distribution of the overseas squadrons in 1869 (Hattendorf et al 1993, 593–5), excluding the Mediterranean.

Foreign stations in 1869	*ships*	*numbers of men*	*bases*
China	25	2,700–2,800	Hong Kong
East Indies	6	1,000	Bombay, Trincomalee
Cape of Good Hope	3	500	Simon's Town
west coast of Africa	11	1,000	Ascension, Fernando Po
south-east coast of South America	5	500–600	store ship at Rio de Janeiro
Pacific	10	2,000	Esquimalt
Australia	4	700–800	Sydney
totals	**64**	**8,400–8,700**	

later, the dry dock was completed.[16] *See also* Chapter 12 for the development of Esquimalt.

In the second half of the 19th century the relative importance of the overseas bases was reflected in the 1869 reorganisation of the overseas squadrons by Hugh Childers, First Lord of the Admiralty. His moves mirrored Edward Cardwell's army reforms that withdrew nearly 28,000 soldiers from imperial duties. Childers proposed to withdraw 14 ships and around 2,700 men from the foreign stations, leaving 64 ships and up to 8,700 men (Table 10.1) .[17] The majority of these vessels were sloops, corvettes and gunboats, but the China and Pacific stations each included '1 ironclad for the flag'. This reorganisation effectively marked the demise of the West Indies bases, although Childers envisaged an ability of the Admiralty 'to send a cruising squadron of frigates and corvettes to visit the stations from time to time'.[18] English Harbour closed in 1882 and Port Royal followed in 1905 (*see* Chapter 12).[19]

The impact of these naval and military reforms, together with the opening of the Suez Canal in 1869, brought into sharper focus the debate on the best ways of securing the sea routes vital to Britain's overseas trade and the security of the Empire. From these discussions evolved the concept of imperial fortresses, which were officially identified as Halifax, Bermuda, Gibraltar, Malta and the Cape of Good Hope (Simon's Town).[20] The more immediate impact of this reassessment was seen in the attention paid to their fortifications, but it was to be naval

Fig 10.3
The timber housing and slipways at Esquimalt for the small torpedo boats used for local defence in the 1890s.
(AdL Da 039)

developments elsewhere that caused a dramatic expansion of these bases, with the exception of Halifax, at the end of the century. By the 1880s the Royal Navy's comfortable ascendancy was being challenged. The French navy, unable to match the size of the British fleet and probably noting the success of the Confederate ship *Alabama* during the American Civil War, built a number of large armoured cruisers whose great endurance was clearly intended to allow their use as commerce raiders in distant waters.[21] The Americans themselves were expanding their navy from the 1880s, as were the French, the Russians, the Japanese and the Germans. By then advances in torpedo technology since its pioneering development by Robert Whitehead in the late 1860s were concerning the Admiralty.[22] Extensive moles and breakwaters to protect warships in harbours, especially at vulnerable locations like Gibraltar and Malta, were the principal passive defensive measure. To cope with any raiders, many of the overseas bases such as Esquimalt, Port Royal and Simon's Town were equipped not just with coastal gun batteries, but for a brief time in the 1890s with torpedo boats as well, which were capable of more offensive action. These frail craft could not be left permanently afloat, so were kept ashore in timber boathouses, ready to be launched from slipways (Figs 10.3 and 10.4). These buildings were comparatively ephemeral additions to the bases, and most had gone before 1914.

The Naval Defence Act of 1889 authorised the construction of 70 battleships and cruisers and effectively marked Britain's entry into the naval arms race that continued to the First World War. Although the focus was on the great fleets and possible confrontations in European waters, it was becoming clear that 'send a gunboat' would no longer be an adequate response to threats elsewhere to Britain's overseas possessions or to commercial and imperial sea routes. The introduction of fast, long-range merchant steamships in the 1870s in any event had outclassed the speed of most warships in the overseas squadrons. Now, the new generations of steel-hulled warships with larger coal bunkers, more economical triple expansion engines, higher speeds and much greater cruising ranges posed a growing threat in distant waters and one that the Royal Navy could only counter with warships of the same or greater calibre. As Admiral Sir John Fisher was to note in 1902 when proposing a further reorganisation of the distribution of the fleet, 'It will be a terrible anxiety to an admiral on the outbreak of war to get [gunboats such as the] *Partridges, Magpies, Redbreasts* and *Pygmys* into a place of safety, for they can neither fight nor run away'.[23]

As with the home dockyards, the main overseas bases needed substantial upgrading, principally of their foundries, engineering workshops and dry docks, if they were to service the new warships with their complex gun turrets

Fig 10.4
The twin torpedo boat slips installed in the 1890s at Port Royal. They were never roofed and still remain in the former dockyard. (TNA ADM 195/ 49 fol 48)

Fig 10.5 (above top)
The commercial dry dock at Hong Kong in 1899, occupied by HMS Powerful. (Navy and Army Illustrated *397, 7 March 1899)*

Fig 10.6 (above)
The floating dock at Bermuda in 1894, with the depot ship HMS Urgent *undergoing maintenance. (TNA ADM 195/5 plate 31)*

and other increasingly sophisticated equipment. With the cost of capital ships approaching one million pounds, access to dry docks for maintenance or to repair battle damage was crucial. The Royal Navy had long been aware of the need for strategically sited dry docks for its operations outside European waters. Metal warships added urgency to this requirement, for their hulls tended quickly to attract marine growths, while early propeller shaft glands required regular attention that was only possible in a dry dock, and it was not unknown for propellers to drop off. Groundings were also more common when much of the world still lacked adequate charts, despite the best work of the hydrographic department.

At Hong Kong and the Cape of Good Hope the navy was fortunate to be able to use commercial dry docks from the 1860s (Fig 10.5), but although such facilities became far more widespread in the latter half of the nineteenth century, very few could accommodate the growing sizes of the largest warships [24]. At Bermuda, where the porosity of the Ireland Island stone made construction of a dry dock almost impossible, the pressing needs of the new ironclads were met in 1869 when the base was equipped with a floating dock (Fig 10.6). Constructed on the Thames, this was capable of lifting a 10,000-ton ship; it was replaced in 1902 by an even larger one with a lifting capacity of 15,000 tons, at the same time as the dockyard's capacity was augmented by the construction of the south breakwater and south basin.[25]

At the majority of overseas bases, constructing an expensive dry dock for what would normally be only occasional use was clearly uneconomic; a much cheaper alternative was to enter into partnership with the host administration or with a commercial dock company if one existed.

Fig 10.7.
HMS Galatea, *an 1859 Woolwich-built wood screw frigate, in the government dry dock on Cockatoo Island, Sydney, in October 1870.*
(Mitchell Library, State Library of NSW – PXD 524)

This policy was endorsed by the Carnarvon Commission in 1882, by which time the Admiralty had some experience of these arrangements.[26] Such partnerships were pioneered in 1845 at Sydney, New South Wales, when the Legislative Council supported a proposition to the Governor, asking him 'to represent to Her Majesty's Government the advantages, which would accrue to this colony and to the Empire at large, were a Dry Dock to be constructed at Sydney for Men of War.' Although the Admiralty agreed with the sentiment, initially they declined to contribute, only relenting when the work was pressed ahead anyway, and contributing £3,094 towards a cost optimistically estimated at £4,085. The stipulation attached to this grant, and one that was broadly similar to all subsequent agreements, was 'on condition that it [the dock] is of such dimensions as will be sufficient for a large frigate or steamer, and that Her Majesty's ships have preference when required for its use' (Fig 10.7).[27] At Malta in the early 1860s, the colonial government contributed financially both to the dredging of Grand Harbour and to the construction of the Royal Navy's third dry dock, the Somerset Dock, where it promised £10,830 towards the estimated cost of some £50,000 (*see* Chapter 11).[28] Given the naval activity here, it seems unlikely that merchant ships would have been frequent users of this facility.

In 1865 to encourage the development of dry docks in the Empire, the British Government passed the Colonial Dock Loan Act. This enabled contributions to be made by the Government towards the construction of dry docks, provided that they were of a sufficient size to accommodate the largest British warship and that the Royal Navy had precedence in emergency. Not wishing to miss out on such an opportunity, the Falmouth Dock Company in Cornwall was the first, though unsuccessful, applicant.[29] However, in 1872 tenders were sought for a dry dock adjacent to the naval base at Esquimalt (*see* Chapter 12).[30] Ten years later work began on a second, larger dry dock at Sydney, authorised by the New South Wales Parliament and named the Sutherland Dock. This was built on Cockatoo Island in Sydney Harbour, and when completed in 1890 it was briefly the largest single dock in the world; its original dimension were 638ft long, 84ft wide at the entrance and with a maximum depth of water over the sill of 32ft.[31] At the same time, a dry dock was built just outside the dockyard boundary at Halifax, Nova Scotia, where the 1886 agreement involved the Admiralty contributing $200,000 in $10,000 annual instalments.[32]

At Sydney, Esquimalt and Halifax the dry docks were sustained by commercial use, but this was not always the case. In New Zealand, the Auckland Harbour Board at its own expense built the Calliope dry dock, which came into use in 1888 (Figs 10.8 and 10.9). In 1892, no doubt in a bid to make greater use of the dry dock, land held since 1869 by the Admiralty was swapped for land adjacent to the dry dock. This was not immediately developed, and by 1896 the dry dock had become a commercial failure. Rather than see it fall into disrepair, the British Treasury agreed to pay £59,350 towards fully equipping it, and the Admiralty made annual payments of £5,000 until 1903, when the New Zealand government took these over.[33] In 1896 the Treasury agreed to pay up to £159,000 of the £318,000 estimated as the cost of a new dry dock

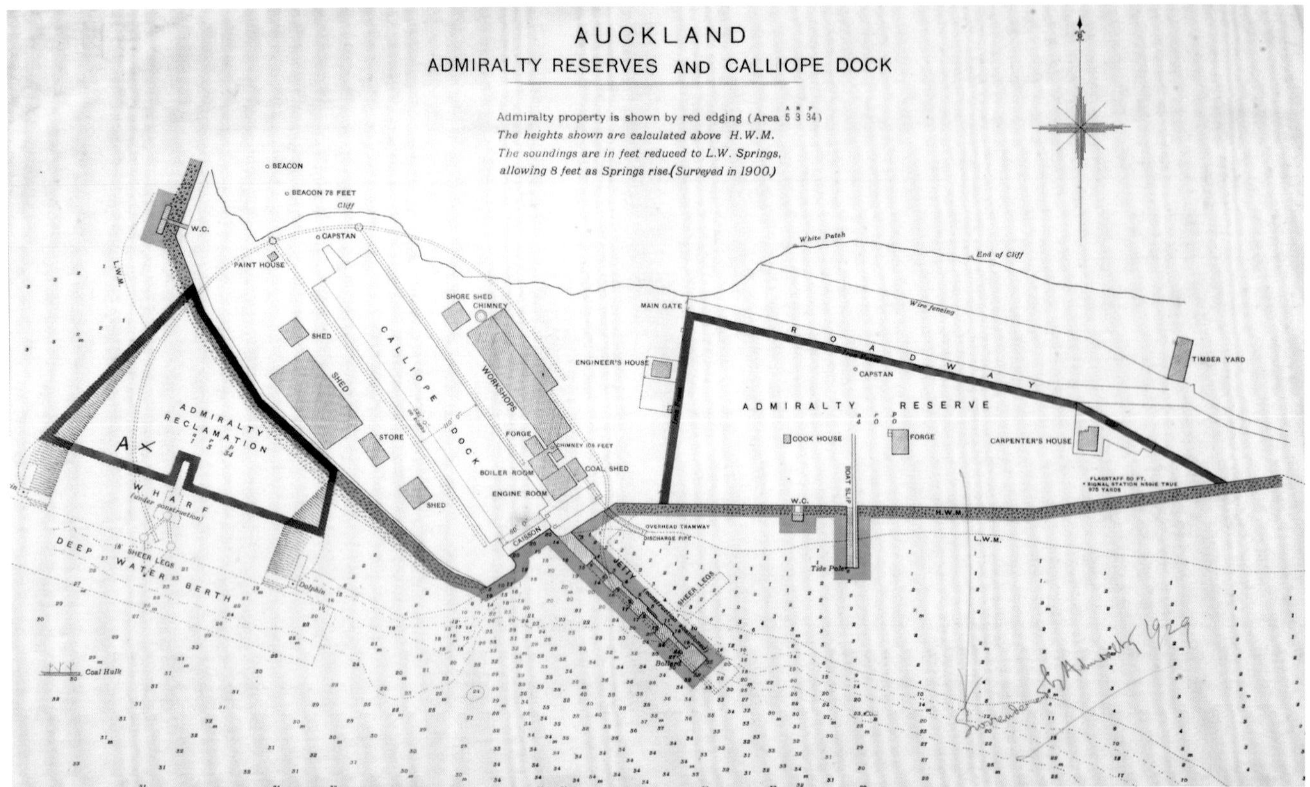

Fig 10.8
A 1900 plan of the Calliope dry dock and the adjacent land reserved for the Admiralty base at Auckland.
(AdL Vz 15/12)

Fig 10.9
The Calliope dry dock in the early 1930s. The clusters of adjacent workshops, store sheds and pumping station are little altered from those shown on the 1900 plan.
(© National Maritime Museum, Greenwich, London, neg. N44136)

at Trincomalee. This was perhaps the least convenient of these joint-use arrangements, because the dry dock was sited at Mutual Point, in the commercial port of Colombo, which was on the opposite side of the island from the naval base.[34]

By the 1890s these various arrangements meant that the only major overseas bases that did not have modern dry docks and where alternative ones were not readily available were Gibraltar and Simon's Town. Both these yards in any event required substantial modernisation of their repair facilities. Gibraltar was included in the 1895 Naval Works Act, which was principally concerned with the home dockyards; shortly afterwards money was allocated for Simon's Town. In 1897 the Admiralty considered providing a dry dock at Port Royal, but in 1899 the Government dismissed the idea, noting that a new floating dock for Bermuda was being 'sanctioned on condition of the Admiralty not pressing for the Jamaica dock'.

In the opening decade of the 20th century, the strain of meeting the challenge posed by imperial Germany, as well as the sheer cost of the naval arms programme, forced retrenchment on the Admiralty. Admiral Fisher's reforms concentrating the Royal Navy in European waters led directly to the closure of Port Royal, Esquimalt and Halifax in 1905 and the threatened closure of Trincomalee.[35] The naval base at Port Royal was later used in part as a Royal Naval air station and remained in British Government hands until 1955. It was then handed to the Jamaican government, who, perhaps mindful of the pioneering conservation works then under way at the former dockyard at English Harbour, agreed to provide 'an annual allotment of £250 towards the upkeep of the naval historical buildings etc'.[36] The Canadian yards were placed on a care and maintenance basis, their machinery 'to be painted and greased, boilers to be thoroughly dried internally, made air-tight and to have pans of dried lime placed inside them'. In 1910 both yards were transferred to the Dominion Government on the creation of the Royal Canadian Navy.[37]

Coaling stations

The increasing deployment of steam warships on overseas stations raised unwelcome issues related to the supply and cost of coal and its security.[38] These problems were not peculiar to the navy, and the issues of supply and cost were only partly mitigated by the development of the more economical compound engines from the 1860s.[39] The Peninsula and Orient shipping company (P&O), closest to the navy in terms of the scale of its overseas services, had done much pioneering work, early on arranging coal supplies to be held in a combination of storehouses and hulks at 14 locations from Gibraltar to Yokohama. By 1866 it was employing 170 chartered vessels, mainly colliers, to supply these locations, and within a few years was purchasing coal from Australia, India, China and Japan.[40] Unlike P&O which ran regular services along fixed routes, the Royal Navy had to plan for the unexpected. Where there were no existing bases or commercial coaling facilities, sites had to be acquired and coal purchased and stockpiled.

Coal itself varied widely in quality, and not all was suitable as boiler fuel. From early on, whenever opportunity offered, the Admiralty experimented with coal from different sources at home and overseas and also purchased patent fuels, although these were generally more expensive. In 1841 it went so far as to propose to manufacture 'Mr Grant's patent fuel', a mixture of coal dust and coal tar pitch said to burn well with less clinker and dust: 'The sum of £900 is provided for apparatus for preparing this fuel which is to be worked by the convicts at Portsmouth and Plymouth'.[41] Welsh steam coal was generally considered the best, as it burned cleanly, but it was more expensive than North Country coal. However, the ready availability of supplies was of crucial importance and a major factor in the Admiralty purchase of North Country coal during the Baltic campaign of 1854. This was the first occasion the navy had used a large fleet of steam vessels in war, and the well-developed east coast collier trade was able to supply temporary depots in the Baltic. But as Vice-Admiral Sir Charles Napier found in the Baltic campaign,[42] the volume and density of smoke from this coal meant that whenever the fleet raised steam, a huge pall of smoke betrayed its position and potentially made flag signals difficult or impossible to read. Welsh coal was specified for the steam fleet's review in 1856 so as to prevent smoke from obscuring the Queen's view, but as Table 10.2 shows, despite the huge growth in the Welsh coal trade, North Country coal was still much used by the navy in the mid-1870s.[43] Despite its drawbacks, North Country coal for long remained a mainstay

Table 10.2 The operational foreign coaling stations in 1876 (from TNA ADM 181/88). Esquimalt did not feature in this survey, although by then it had a coal depot; possibly it was disused at the time of the survey.

Location	*tonnage in stock, March 1876*	*source of coal*
Gibraltar	6,628	Welsh, North Country
Malta	9,000	Welsh, North Country
Sierra Leone	2,122	Welsh, North Country
Fernando Po	747	Welsh, North Country
Ascension	1,845	Welsh, North Country
Cape of Good Hope	5,571	Welsh, North Country
Zanzibar[a]	2,466	Welsh, North Country. Unsatisfactory contract with Messrs Cory
Trincomalee	2,355	Welsh, North Country
Singapore	5,334	Bulli and Newcastle (Australia); Welsh from contractor
Hong Kong	4,578	Welsh and Newcastle (Australia)
Shanghai	2,257	Welsh, Bulli, Newcastle and Wallsend
Nagasaki	2,883	Welsh
Hiogo	1,003	Welsh, Wallsend (Australia)
Halifax	3,114	Welsh, local Picton coal
Bermuda	4,055	North Country
Jamaica	4,440	North Country
Antigua	617	North Country
Barbados	707	North Country

a Operated by contractor

of Admiralty coal depots, increasingly supplemented by Welsh steam coal, patent fuels and coal from other regions. Practical experience revealed that in climates such as at Jamaica, Fernando Po and Zanzibar, 'coal deteriorated very rapidly' and patent fuels were found to be superior.[44]

The size of fuel stockpiles, especially in the more remote locations, was the subject of considerable debate; too little might be insufficient for a squadron in an emergency, and too much could deteriorate before the occasional visiting warships could consume it. By the late 1860s, as it became abundantly clear that the future lay with steam warships, the Admiralty for the first time became concerned about adequate coal supplies at its overseas bases. Such concerns lay behind the decision in 1874 by members of the Admiralty Board to continue favouring sail in the more remote foreign stations. That year, the Government gave the War Office responsibility for the protection of coaling stations and overseas bases, a division of responsibility that was not helped by the general lack of army-navy co-operation.[45] In 1880 the Admiralty decided that

> for Depots a long distance from England, there shall at no time be less than six or nine months' stock on hand, having reference to the time that must necessarily elapse before supplies can get out from this country. At Gibraltar or Malta where coal can be delivered by steam colliers within a few days of the date of shipment, it has been considered that the stocks can safely be reduced.[46]

A couple of years later the Carnarvon Commission, which had made it a priority to consider imperial trade routes, recommended two classes of coaling station to ensure security of supplies for the fleet. What were described as 'Refitting stations and harbours of refuge, in which coal is stored in large quantities' were to be heavily protected by large garrisons, while smaller coaling stations were those where coal should always be available, 'but for which it is unnecessary to provide an extensive system of defence'.[47] These heavily defended bases such as Halifax, Bermuda and Malta were increasingly regarded as 'imperial fortresses', although it was to be a couple of decades before Gibraltar and Simon's Town were sufficiently modernised fully to meet these criteria. Defences of the smaller coaling stations were at best barely adequate and at worst non-existent. The debates engendered between the British and Dominion Governments, the Admiralty and the War Office over the problems of location, supply and protection of coaling stations has led Donald Schurman to conclude that coaling station defence 'was the first problem that involved the empire as a whole in the age of the "new" imperialism', and that it led directly to the formation of the Committee of Imperial Defence in 1904.[48]

The small gunboats, sloops and corvettes that formed the bulk of the overseas squadrons in the latter part of the 19th century had bunkers which on average held considerably less than 100 tons of fuel. In sharp contrast in 1860 HMS

Warrior's bunkers could hold 700 tons. Half a century later, the *Indefatigable* class battle-cruiser HMS *New Zealand*, launched in 1911 and one of the last coal-burning Royal Navy warships, had bunkers for 3,170 tons of coal; steaming at 16 knots, this was consumed at the rate of around 217 tons a day.[49] Naval coaling depots had to reflect these changing realities, more especially once it became apparent late in the 19th century that capital ships would be augmenting or replacing the smaller warships on even the more distant stations.

From the late 1830s coal stocks, initially amounting to only a few hundred tons, were held at an increasing number of overseas bases and were stored as close as possible to wharf edges to reduce the amount of handling. In special circumstances larger amounts were held, as at English Harbour where it was proposed to increase coal stocks to some 3,500 tons in 1838, when the steam packet service was planning to change its coaling point from Barbados to Antigua. A factor in this move may have been the cost of coaling. An 1853 report on coaling at Antigua noted that it cost 8d per ton for discharging coal into the coal yard and then loading it into the bunkers of 'one of Her Majesty's steamers', compared to 'about 1/- per ton' at Port Royal, where the facilities were less convenient to the wharf (Fig 10.10).[50] At English Harbour in the early 1860s, 'the eastern capstan house, upper part used as seamen's quarters' was converted into a coal store, as was a nearby galley building used to feed ships' crews.[51] At Simon's Town in 1860 the coaling shed held 692 tons, while at Nassau in the Bahamas in 1863 the 'Old Naval Yard', disused since the end of the Napoleonic Wars, was largely occupied by two sheds, one for 90 tons of coal, the other for 300 tons (Fig 10.11).[52] As late as 1895 a storage capacity of 2,673 tons of coal was considered adequate at Esquimalt.[53] In comparison, Malta was then rivalling the main home bases, extending its capacity to 50,400 tons, in a series of vast stores below the Corradino Heights beside French Creek (Fig 10.12).[54]

Fig 10.10
Port Royal's coaling jetty with sacks of coal in 1895. At the landward end of the jetty two huge brick-built coal stores were constructed late in the life of the base, but today only the stumps of the jetty and some of the outer walls of the stores remain.
(TNA ADM 195/49 fol 50)

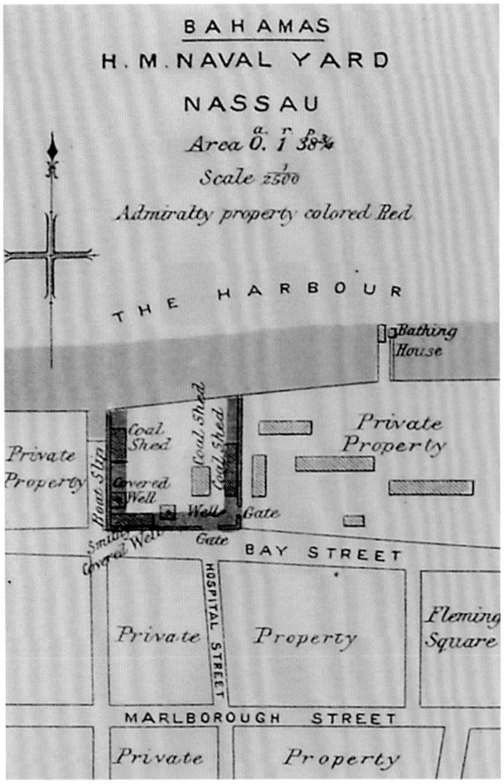

Fig 10.11
A plan of the tiny naval yard at Nassau in 1909, when its principal function was as a coaling and water point, with a small smithy for use by ships' engineers. (TNA ADM 140/1484 fol 73)

By 1876 Admiralty purchases of Welsh steam coal were considerable, its dominance along with North Country coal as boiler fuel reflecting their widespread availability (*see* Table 10.2).[55] Those coaling stations which formed part of a naval base had a degree of permanence; the fortunes of the remainder depended on changing strategic requirements and the availability of alternative commercial coal depots. The operation of these coaling stations relied very heavily on human muscle, usually a combination of local labour and ships' crews (Fig 10.13). Later, at a number of sites, manually operated tramways linked the stores with the wharf edge or jetty, where further assistance might be provided by a small steam crane (Fig 10.14). There was never the elaborate mechanical handling plant that was found at the principal home bases by the end of the 19th century.[56] The coal stores themselves were generally simple, large sheds, sometimes built of timber, as at Halifax (Fig 10.15), but more often constructed of masonry. Care was needed to ensure that coal was dry when put in store to avoid any problems of spontaneous combustion,

Fig 10.12
The huge coal depot alongside French Creek, Malta, reflecting the importance of the Mediterranean fleet. It was the largest such naval depot outside the British Isles. (TNA ADM 174/363)

Fig 10.13
Warships coaling alongside the new mole at Gibraltar in 1898. The entire ships' crew was roped in for this filthy, dusty work.
(Navy and Army Illustrated *10 Dec 1898)*

Fig 10.14 (below)
The large building with three pitched roofs was the coal shed in the lee of Fort Thornton at Georgetown, Ascension Island (see also *Fig 9.81). The jetty to the left with its small crane cannot have been the easiest transhipment point for coal (or anything else).*
(AdL Da 032)

Fig 10.15 (below bottom)
Timber coal stores in Halifax Dockyard in the 1890s.
(TNA ADM 195/49 fol 16b)

as happened in a coal store in Devonport in 1863.[57] The fuel was normally stored to a height of no more than 12ft to lessen handling problems. Such simple requirements meant that coaling stations could be set up and abandoned with comparative ease as circumstances changed, although rarely with the speed shown at Samoa where a coal shed was established on a 30ft-square plot fronting Apia Harbour in May 1889, but closed and sold only 2 years later.[58]

Following the 1882 report of the Carnarvon commission, extensive works were carried out at the port of Castries, St Lucia. This was already an important commercial coaling station, at the intersection of shipping between North and South America, and between Europe and the Gulf of Mexico. The harbour was extensively dredged, new wharves were constructed to plans by Sir John Coode, and the port was strongly fortified with heavy guns. Barracks for 1,500 troops were built, and existing garrisons at Trinidad, Demerara and Barbados were relocated here, along with a detachment of coastal artillery. In 1890 it was reported that 'the whole of the North American and West Indian Squadron has for the last two years, come right into the port, executed all necessary manoeuvres

with ease and safety, and taken in all the coal they required conveniently, and with a rapidity not surpassed at any coaling station in the world'.[59]

By 1887, Esquimalt, Aden, Mauritius, Colombo, St Helena and Table Bay had been added to the list of coaling stations, and Barbados removed.[60] In 1893 Fernando Po was closed, but 6 years later an acre of land for a coal depot was acquired at Fort Cromwell, Bonny, on the coast of Nigeria. A coal depot was also maintained at Apapa Wharf at Lagos, where a thousand tons of Welsh coal were still available in 1928.[61] In 1895 a substantial coaling depot holding 6,000 tons of coal was established at Stanley Harbour in the Falkland Islands, its management later transferred to the Falklands Islands Company (Fig 10.16).[62]

At the end of the 19th century British rivalry with European powers and the United States led to something of a drive to establish coaling stations across the Pacific, although not on the scale of the 175 acres purchased on Deception Island in the New Hebrides in 1874.[63] The small island of Vuo in Suva Harbour, Fiji, was likewise acquired in September 1893, when it was noted that the island was a sanctuary for blue and white herons. Neither of these islands was ever developed for naval purposes.[64] However, the year 1893 also saw land at Samarai Island, Papua New Guinea, set aside for a coaling station; a coal shed was built there 6 years later.[65] In 1900 three parcels of land were leased at Tonga from King George Tabou for the same purpose, but here the Admiralty apparently had more ambitious plans. The leases specified that they could 'erect wharves, jetties, storehouses and fortifications and place artillery' on one of the sites, while the other two were for coaling and repairing warships. Moreover, 'the Admiralty had the right ... to exclude ships of war of all other nations' from adjacent areas.[66]

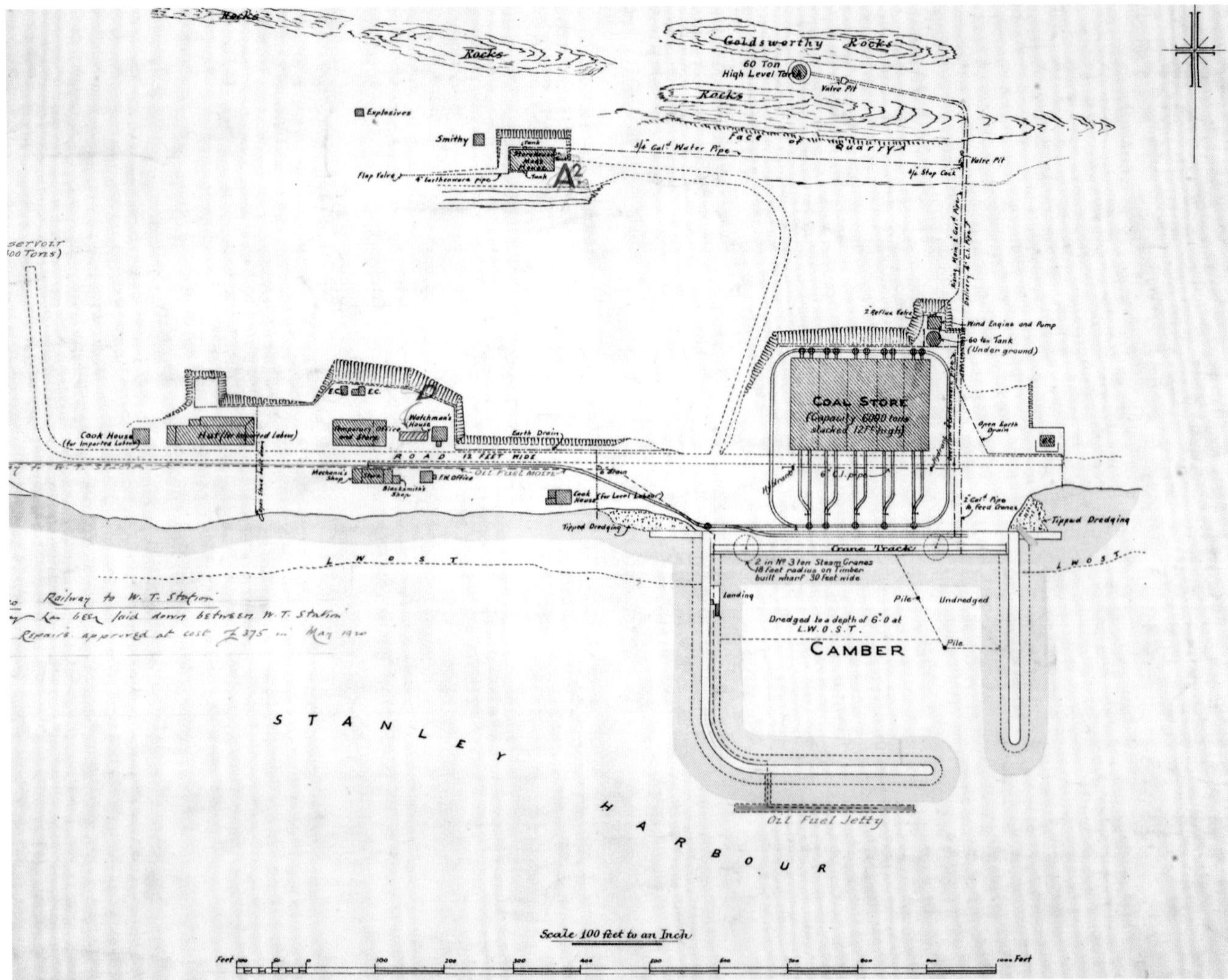

Fig 10.16
The strategically sited coaling depot at Port Stanley, Falkland Isles. Vice-Admiral Sir Doveton Sturdee's squadron was replenishing its bunkers here early on 8 Dec 1914 when Vice-Admiral Graf von Spee approached, believing the islands to be undefended. The destruction of the German squadron in the ensuing battle avenged the Royal Navy's defeat a month earlier at Coronel.
(AdL Vz 15/29)

In 1900 the Commander-in-Chief on the Australian station, clearly without visiting the site, favoured the acquisition of Trinity Island in Cairns Harbour on the eastern coast of Australia 'before the property becomes more valuable', became 'it might be desirable to establish a coaling station there in the future'. The Admiralty Hydrographer concurred, remarking that 'Cairns is a rising place'. The 1,600-acre island accordingly was vested in the Admiralty by the Governor of Queensland. However, in 1902 when HMS *Wallace* came to inspect it, Captain Noel reported that the island was 'an ordinary mangrove swamp very little above the wash of an ordinary tide ... if the mangroves were destroyed the mud banks supported by their roots would fall in. Docks could be built at great cost, but the situation is most insalubrious and infested with mosquitos ... it is not considered of any use for naval purposes'.[67]

In the Far East a further small coal depot was established in 1882 in Japan at Yokohama, making use of redundant Victualling Department storehouses, but was closed 6 years later in favour of a local contractor (Fig 10.17).[68] Coal supplied here supplemented far larger supplies available at Hong Kong and held at Kowloon, where the growing naval importance is reflected in the increasing size of the coal depot that by the first decade of the 20th century occupied 11 acres and contained around 19 coal stores.[69] At the southern end of the South China Sea, Singapore's key location on a major trade route had ensured that as early as 1869 its commercial coal stocks totalled nearly a million tons.[70] In 1863/4 the Admiralty acquired land at Pulo Brani in Singapore, part of which was leased to the Tanjong Pagar Dock Company and part developed as a coaling station. The War Office also maintained an ordnance depot here for the Admiralty land. In 1876 the coaling station held some 5,334 tons, a figure that rose to around 16,000 tons of coal and patent fuel by 1907, this comparatively low figure probably reflecting the

Fig 10.17
Japanese women coaling HMS Powerful *in 1899, possibly those employed by the contractor at Yokohama.* (Navy and Army Illustrated *4 Feb 1899)*

Fig 10.18
The coal store and loading jetty strategically located on Henjam Island overlooking the Straits of Hormuz in the Persian Gulf. This 1926 photograph gives a good impression of the bleak, arid and isolated terrain. The buttressed coal store is a standard pattern, also seen on Ascension Island. The purpose of the long white buildings left of the coal store is not known. (© National Maritime Museum, Greenwich, London, neg. P39726)

abundant availability of commercial supplies here.[71] It was only after the First World War that Singapore was developed into a major naval base.

The overseas coaling depots were never more than strictly utilitarian structures. They made little contribution to naval architecture and have left very few traces, though at Port Royal the former naval coal yard still retains its wharf and the ruins of two coal stores. The smaller coaling stations must have provided some of the loneliest postings, the lives of their solitary storekeepers enlivened only by occasional visits of a collier or warship. The coaling station of Basidu in the Persian Gulf, first established as a base in 1823 to protect the pearl fishers, was transferred to Henjam Island at the entrance to the Gulf in 1911 (Fig 10.18). On its closure in 1935 *The Times* noted in something of an understatement that 'even the provision of a recreation ground [for visiting ship's companies] did not make this malarious and torrid isle an ideal port of call'.[72]

11

The Mediterranean Bases: Buildings and Engineering Works, 1700–1914

When the Royal Navy relinquished Gibraltar in 1990, it ended an unbroken custom of using overseas bases that stretched back almost three centuries, the period encompassing the rise and zenith of Great Britain's maritime power. A substantial number of these former bases still retain buildings and civil engineering works of historic interest. As these are generally more thinly spread than in the home bases and as the operational dates of the yards vary considerably, this and the following two chapters have brief chronological histories covering the times when the yards were under Admiralty control. In most cases, these periods span the transition from sail to steam. There are descriptions only of the more notable surviving structures.[1] To make comparisons more meaningful, individual bases are grouped together, loosely according to the stations they served in the 19th century.

Gibraltar

The strategic and operational benefits of a secure base in the Mediterranean were apparent since the Royal Navy first starting operating there on a regular basis in the early 17th century. The capture of Gibraltar in 1704 gave Britain a great natural fortress overlooking the Straits, but its only berthing facility was a short quay, later known as the Old Mole, at the northern end of the town of Gibraltar, where it was vulnerable to any Spanish attack. This was in part remedied by a second mole built south of the town in the mid-1720s and which was to form the nucleus of the subsequent small naval base.[2]

In the 18th century Gibraltar was rapidly eclipsed in importance by the capture in 1708 of Minorca with its fine natural harbour at Port Mahon. In the 19th century, Malta and its Grand Harbour took their place, ensuring that Gibraltar remained largely undeveloped as a naval base, its importance chiefly lying in its role as a look-out post, victualling depot and site for a hospital. In 1751 an ambitious plan was produced to create a large harbour protected by a semicircular mole and with a range of dockyard buildings on reclaimed land, but the likely expense along with the potential civil engineering problems meant that it never went beyond the drawing stage.[3] By the mid-1750s the yard facilities were limited to a small careening quay and capstans, a smith's shop and pitch house and a timber mast house and boathouse.

This situation did not change significantly for over a century, sketch drawings of the yard in 1841 by William Scamp showing predominantly timber-framed buildings, including a handsome sail loft with a clocktower (Fig 11.1).[4] Scamp visited a number of times from Malta

Fig 11.1
William Scamp's 1841 sketch of the buildings at Gibraltar Dockyard. Alongside the old mole are two early paddle frigates. These frail craft were to prove invaluable for the anti-slavery work of the West Africa squadron. HMS Penelope, *possibly one of the warships in this sketch, was to become the squadron flagship in 1843, the first steamer to have this role. (AdL Portfolio B19 fol 30)*

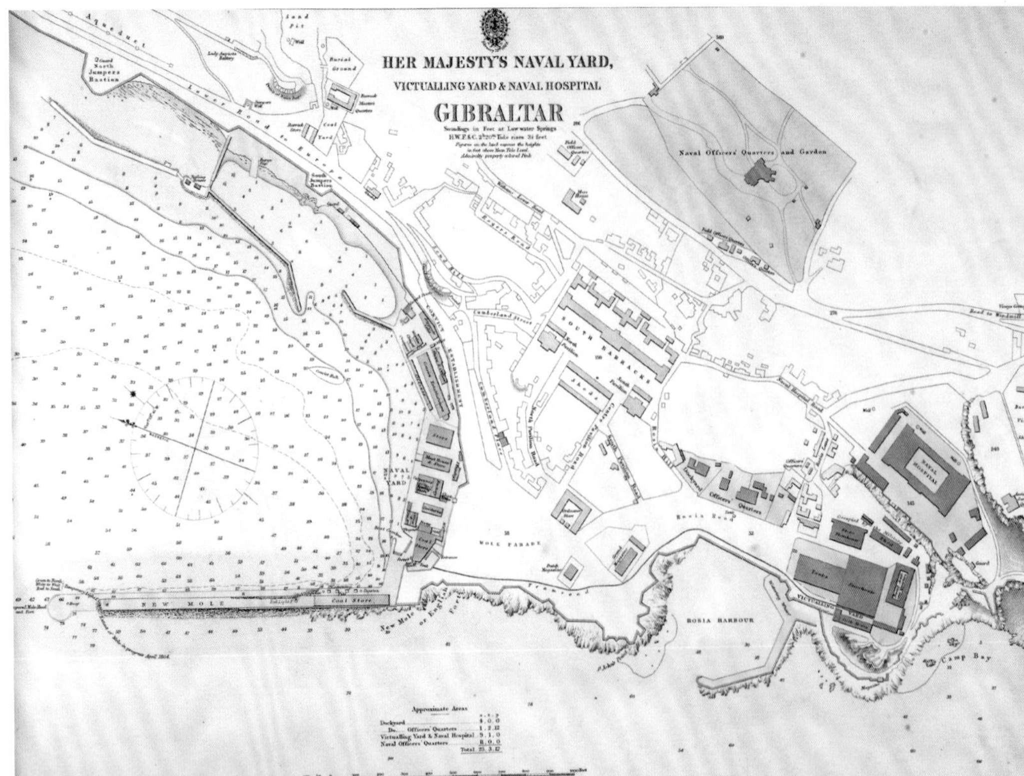

Fig 11.2
The naval estate at Gibraltar in 1863. The small dockyard in the curve of the bay was little different in size from a century earlier, but work was then under way extending the New Mole. (AdL Naval Establishments 1863 Da 02 fol 11)

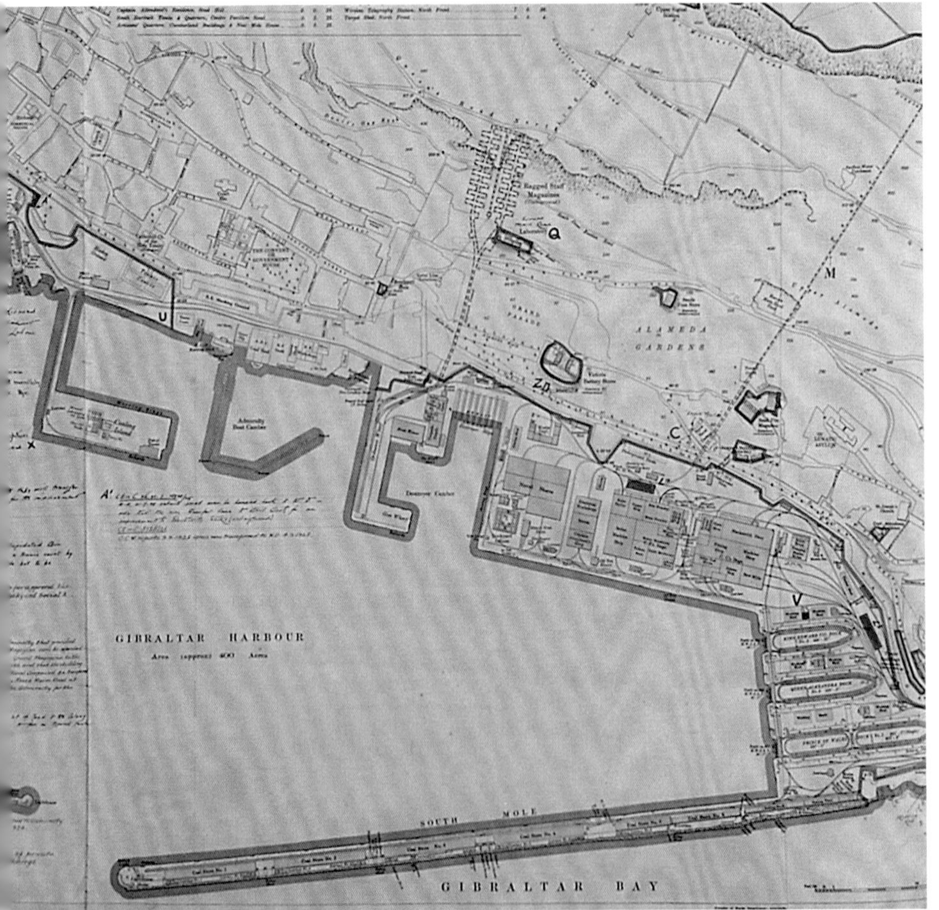

Fig 11.3 (below)
The modernisation plan that followed the 1895 Naval Works Act transformed the capabilities of Gibraltar Dockyard, and the original yard was now partly occupied by the three dry docks. (AdL Vz 15/39)

between 1841 and 1844, followed by a series of recommendations for improving the dockyard, including the construction of a breakwater. Some recommendations were carried out over the next few years, including construction of two coaling sheds for some 4,000 tons of coal, a smithery and various storehouses.[5] In 1851 the Admiralty proposed to construct a 'long projected' 1000ft extension to the existing mole (Fig 11.2), saying that 'the present [time] affords a favourable opportunity for the execution of the work at the least possible expense, by the extensive employment of convict labour, already available on the spot'. Work continued on the project well into the 1870s, by which time revised estimates suggest that costs had multiplied by a factor of at least four. The delays were in part blamed on a lack of convict labour, apparently a perennial problem at Gibraltar, sometimes caused by disputes by competing military and naval requirements.[6] This was the most ambitious engineering project hitherto at Gibraltar and was important in providing more adequate shelter and berthing. Even though it was not linked to any similar expansion of repair and maintenance facilities, by the late 1870s there was a boiler makers' shop and a steam hammer furnace, differing little in scale from those on Ascension Island.[7]

In 1893, following the Naval Defence Act of 1889, work began on extending the mole to 2,100ft, partly to provide more space for coaling ships alongside and partly to give increased protection against torpedo attack. However, it was to be the provisions of the 1895 Naval Works Act that would transform the base. When this modernisation was completed, Gibraltar for the first time could be considered as a major naval dockyard, with modern workshops and stores and a protected harbour of a size able to accommodate the Mediterranean fleet and the Channel squadron (Fig 11.3). The mole was to be extended northwards again to 3,700ft, and a commercial mole with extensive coaling facilities was to be grafted on to the Old Mole, effectively forming the northern boundary of the protected harbour.[8]

A detached mole formed part of the western boundary of the harbour, providing additional shelter and protecting the two harbour entrances. The initial proposals allowed for a much-needed graving dock; in the event three were constructed, in the process totally obliterating the site of the old yard. The associated workshops, stores and the dock pumping station were grouped alongside the harbour on reclaimed ground below the town defences, conveniently close to the new dry docks. These were all steel-framed buildings with handsome stone cladding, the metal and timber trades grouped in the two principal buildings, with a separate Electrical Workshop to the north, and beyond that a boat camber and a large coaling berth (Figs 11.4 and 11.5). The coaling berth was supplemented by a series of coal sheds along the New Mole. The principal buildings were later copied on a smaller scale by ones of a similar design constructed at Simon's Town. Following the tunnelling precedents established by the Royal Engineers during the Great Siege of 1779–83, a series of magazines were excavated deep inside the Rock at the back of Ragged Staff.

Fig 11.4
Work in progress at Gibraltar in August 1900. To the left a coffer-dam protects work on the dry docks; to the right the main dockyard workshops are under construction. (Author's collection)

Fig 11.5
By 1902 work was well advanced on the workshops at Gibraltar Dockyard. A century on, they remain substantially as completed. (Author's collection)

The comparative urgency of the work at Gibraltar is reflected in the time taken for this project, which was comparable in scale to the great steam yard extensions at home. The main contractors, Topham, Jones and Railton, had virtually completed the moles and breakwaters by 1903. On 9 April that year King Edward VII set the coping stone on the smallest of the three dry docks, which was named in his honour (Fig 11.6). The other two were named the Queen Alexandra and Prince of Wales docks. In their planning, the Admiralty Works Department was especially mindful of the growing size of capital ships and had sought to maximise the sizes of the dry docks within financial and physical constraints. All three had 95ft entrance widths; the King Edward VII dock (3 Dock) had a length of 450ft, the middle or Queen Alexandra Dock (2 Dock) was 552ft long, while No. 1 Dock or the Prince of Wales Dock had the astonishing length of 851ft 9in (Fig 11.7), a figure that would only just be eclipsed by the three slightly later docks begun in 1909 at Rosyth.[9] No. 1 Dock could operate as a double dock, a caisson part way along allowing the space to be subdivided into separate 380ft and 451ft docks.

Fig 11.6
Gibraltar Dockyard in 1904. Although the workshops have yet to be fitted out and the wharves completed, King Edward VII Dock is operational and the harbour works are sufficiently advanced for a fleet visit. In the distance is the commercial harbour that formed part of this vast scheme. (Author's collection)

Fig 11.7
The three dry docks at Gibraltar in January 1905. The two on the left are still under construction. (Author's collection)

By 1904 what was described as a large proportion of the main shops and store buildings were in use, the dock pumping station had been erected, King Edward VII Dock was practically complete apart from its caisson, and the remaining two docks 'were being rapidly advanced'. It was already found that the underground magazines were not large enough for revised requirements and were being extended.[10] By 1906 the dockyard was fully operational, its capacity such that there were to be few significant additions during the rest of the century.

Although this great reconstruction effectively obliterated the old dockyard, Gibraltar retains other important buildings that date from its use by the sailing navy. These notably include the Rosia Bay victualling yard, begun in 1799, and the naval hospital of 1741 (*see* Chapters 14 and 16).[11] The victualling yard, even lacking its recently destroyed underground reservoir, remains the most complete of the small overseas victualling establishments, with its bomb-proof storehouse and house for the Agent Victualler (Fig 11.8). The naval hospital, although long disused as such, is the earliest courtyard one to remain, predating the completion of Haslar by a decade (*see* Chapter 16).

The small size of the base in the 18th century meant that the few senior yard officials lodged with the garrison or in the town. This changed after the Great Siege, when the town was extensively damaged. A number of houses were subsequently built round Rosia Bay near the victualling yard. Documentary evidence is largely lacking, save for 5 and 6 Rosia Bay, known in 1800 as the 'Naval Officer's House' and originally home for the senior officer. It was later subdivided into a pair of dockyard residences. When a Navy Board commissioner was appointed at Gibraltar in 1793, he was accommodated at The Mount, in a commanding position on the Rock (*see* Chapter 7).

Fig 11.8
The victualling storehouse at Rosia Bay, Gibraltar. The vaulted reservoir beyond has since been destroyed. (Author)

Minorca: Port Mahon

In 1708 forces under General Stanhope captured the island of Minorca, with Port Mahon surrendering on 30 September. The attraction of the island to the Royal Navy lay in its sheltered deep-water anchorage at Port Mahon (Fig 11.9), some 250 miles south of the great French naval base of Toulon. Its drawback lay in the need for a strong garrison and a vigilant navy to protect the island from invasion. In 1756 it fell to French forces under the Duke de Richelieu after Admiral John Byng's failure and was not restored to the British until the Treaty of Paris in 1763, when Britain swapped the captured Belle Isle off the Brittany coast for Minorca. In 1782 the island again fell to the French, this time after a 5-month siege of Port Mahon by forces under the Duc de Crillon. The British occupied Minorca for a third time in 1798, but this occupation lasted only until 16 June 1802, when Thomas Merdon 'resigned the keys of the dockyard' to the Spaniards.[12] By then, the island's importance to the navy had declined following the capture of Malta in 1800.

Initially in 1708, the British rented accommodation and stores along with a convent for a naval hospital in the town of Mahon, but the obvious drawbacks of security and the temptations of the numerous taverns, especially for the sick, made other arrangements desirable. In 1711 Admiral Sir John Jennings arranged for the construction of the first naval hospital on an island in Mahon Harbour (*see* Chapters 3 and 16). In 1715 his successor, Vice-Admiral John Baker, established the nucleus of a naval base on the north side of the harbour, on uninhabited ground opposite the town.[13] Using his ships' crews to shift stones weighing between 2 and 6 tons, he rebuilt a derelict careening wharf there, but for reasons of economy and security he used empty rooms in the new hospital as stores, allocating its former home in Mahon to the Victualling Agent and constructing a cooperage adjacent.[14]

By the mid-1740s, facilities at the small dockyard had grown to include a mast house, sawpits, a smithery, a cordage store and a new sail store. James Montresor, engineer-in-ordinary on the island from 1743 to 1746, drew up ambitious proposals for officers' and artificers' houses, with a 12ft-high wall to surround the yard. None of these seem to have been implemented, but at the start of the second British occupation in 1763 a survey of existing structures also mentions a crane, a ropehouse and a boathouse.[15] Apart from the hospital, which had to be extensively repaired and enlarged, there are no surviving British naval facilities here earlier than the mid-1760s. The ambitious construction work then undertaken underlines the value of Port Mahon as a maintenance centre for the Royal Navy's Mediterranean operations at that time. Existing buildings were repaired and refubished, the hospital was largely rebuilt and its capacity dramatically increased.

Fig 11.9
The naval base with its cluster of storehouses and anchor rack at Mahon, Minorca, c 1750. Careening was carried out elsewhere in the harbour, but the rocky island on the right would later be developed as a careening base.
(TNA ADM 140/1316)

Fig 11.10
The naval base at Port Mahon, Minorca. Prominent are the former 1760s careening wharves and storehouses on the reformed and extended Saffron Island. (Author)

In October 1764 Marsh, the resident naval officer, obtained Navy Board agreement for a substantial reclamation project centred on Saffron Island, a small islet lying in the harbour just offshore from the existing base.[16] This was purchased in December 1765, and over the next 9 years was to be transformed into the largest careening facility then available at an overseas yard. The islet was levelled and reformed into an irregular octagon in plan and connected to the rest of the base by a small bridge. A report in 1774 noted that it was now 'formed into a wharf of eight sides; five of which are fitted with Pitts, Capstans etc for ships to careen at, one with sheers for taking out and putting in of ships' masts, and two for boats, stages and craft'. Each of the careening wharves was some 200ft in length, an adequate size for contemporary warships. In the centre were 'storehouses, sheds and other buildings ... for reception of small stores and lodging the officers and seamen of the ships whilst on the careen'.[17] These two large single-storey buildings constructed of the local stone remain much as built. Their completion, along with the setting up of an open-air ropewalk in a valley to the rear of the base, consolidated operations on this side of the harbour with facilities that were then superior to any other overseas base.

During the third British occupation beginning in 1798, there was no further construction work at the naval base, which was handed in 1802 to the Spanish navy who still make use of it. Save for the addition of a small covered slip, Saffron Island remains little altered (Fig 11.10), while elsewhere in the base a Georgian idiom is apparent in a number of the buildings constructed during the early years of Spanish use, notably the two handsome officers' houses with their sash windows and fanlights.[18]

Malta

The capture of Malta and its aptly named Grand Harbour from the French in September 1800 gained the Royal Navy its most important overseas base. It was well sited for the central and eastern Mediterranean, although less convenient for squadrons blockading Toulon, as Nelson noted in 1803, complaining that he could 'send nothing there [Malta] that I may want under six or seven weeks'.[19] In all other respects its geographical location was ideal for maintaining a naval presence in the heart of the Mediterranean, and at the Congress of Vienna in 1815 Britain retained hold of Malta and was also recognised as the protecting power for the Ionian Islands. These latter islands, especially Corfu with its harbour, were considered to have some strategic value, but their facilities in no way rivalled those of Malta. Although the British spent considerable sums fortifying Corfu, no naval base was established. At Malta, uniquely among foreign naval bases, Britain acquired from the Knights of Malta some of the strongest defences in Europe that protected an established

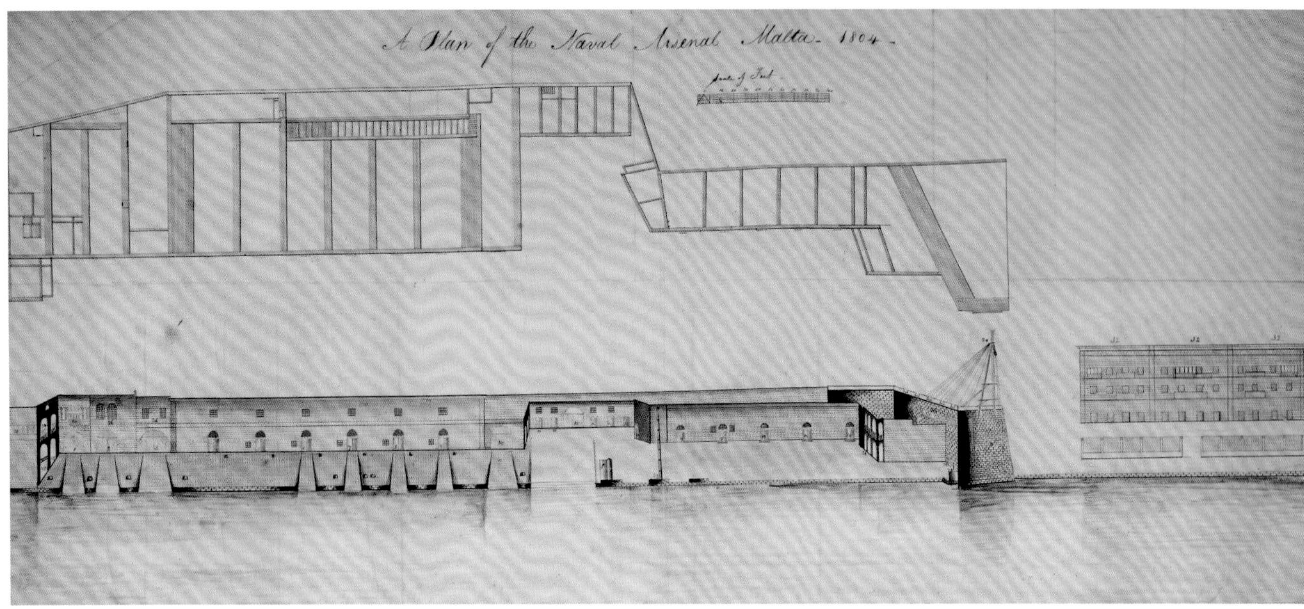

Fig 11.11
The earliest-known British survey of the naval premises inherited from the Knights at Malta. This 1804 drawing records a plan and elevation of the vaulted storehouses for the galleys along Dockyard Creek beside the Sheer Bastion. To the right is an elevation of three houses built nearby for the galley captains. All these buildings remain.
(TNA ADM 140/1281)

dockyard (Fig 11.11).[20] The dockyard, however, was principally designed to build and maintain the knights' galleys, and its facilities were split among the crowded cities of Valletta, Vittoriosa and Senglea, with an open-air ropewalk at Fort Ricasoli. Such dispersal did not make for efficient operations, while the dockyard buildings were generally inadequate for the larger scale of the Royal Navy's operations. The hazards of operating in such urban locations were also grimly demonstrated in July 1806, when a magazine explosion in the dockyard killed 149 people and caused damage estimated at £35,000 to buildings, including naval officers' houses, three offices, a spar store, sail loft, several storehouses and the anchor wharf.[21]

Before 1815, despite the uncertainty surrounding Britain's long-term relationship with Malta,[22] the Navy Board pressed ahead with two substantial construction projects. Both were for facilities hitherto not provided in foreign bases and reflect the importance attached to the island. In 1806 the Navy Board's first resident commissioner, William Brown, suggested constructing a ropery in a more convenient location on top of the range of vaulted galley storehouses built by the Knights along the west side of the head of Dockyard Creek (Fig 11.12). This would allow an 800ft ropewalk, shorter than those in the home yards, but long enough to be useful. It would replace the ropewalk at Fort Ricasoli that had been newly equipped in 1804 with a complete set of ropemaking machinery sent from Portsmouth. This was eventually agreed, and the building was constructed under the supervision of the master shipwright, William Bray. Initially 90 people were employed, including 8 ropemakers from Britain. In 1809, just over a year after completion, the ropery caught fire. Fibrous dust and the lines of yarn in roperies made them very vulnerable to the swift spread of fire, and in a vivid demonstration of the flammability of the process, 'in three minutes from its first appearance, the whole ropewalk was in a blaze'.[23] It was speedily rebuilt, and production resumed the following January, but ended in 1815 with its closure. There is no evidence to suggest any subsequent reopening.[24] Much of this arcaded, flat-roofed building still remains above the galley storehouses next to the Sheer Bastion, which was itself used as a hemp store (Figs 11.13 and 11.14).

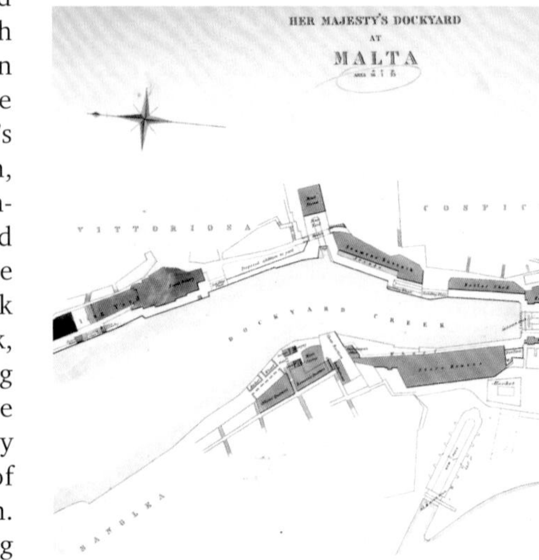

Fig 11.12
Naval premises along Dockyard Creek, Malta, in 1863.
(AdL Naval Establishments 1863 Da 02 fol 16)

Fig 11.13
Sheer Bastion in Dockyard Creek, Malta. To the left are the galley arches, with the ropery built for the Royal Navy forming its top storey. This photograph was possibly taken in the late 1840s.
(© National Maritime Museum, Greenwich, London, neg. C3592)

Fig 11.14
The galley arches, former ropery and Sheer Bastion, Malta, in 2007.
(Author)

The second and far more ambitious project was the attempted construction of a dry dock, the first at an overseas base.[25] This too was proposed in 1806 by Commissioner Brown and championed by William Bray, who in 1810 was in England where he persuaded the Admiralty and Bentham's department of the feasibility of providing one, using part of the landward moat defending Fort St Angelo.[26] In November Holl signed off a sum of £10,000 to be spent on the Malta dry dock, which was to be modelled on Bentham's South and South East Basin Docks (now 2 and 3 Docks) at Portsmouth.[27] Work began in 1811 after permission was obtained from Lord Liverpool, Secretary of State for War and the Colonies. Severe fissures and faults in the underlying rock soon caused insuperable problems and flooding of the works, despite the help of garrison troops in manning pumps. In September 1812 Bray was drowned in a boating accident, and with his death the project began to falter. In 1813 Lieutenant-Colonel Dickens[28] produced a report estimating that its completion would require an additional £70,000 on top of the £35,000 already spent, and in June 1816 the Admiralty ordered the abandonment of the works. The partly completed dock lay disused for most of the 19th century before its site was adapted as a boat camber.[29] It was to be 1841 before there was a fresh proposal for a dry dock.

Malta had a further enormous advantage for the navy in having a highly skilled local workforce available. One consequence was that housing needs were limited to comparatively few officials.[30] Early on, these were the

Fig 11.15
The handsome terrace at Malta, converted from former houses of galley captains. Few official quarters had such splendid views. Photograph in 1971, just after they had ceased to be used as quarters for senior dockyard officers, when the navy had vacated the base.
(Author)

commissioner, master shipwright, master attendant, storekeeper and clerk of the cheque, along with a small number of others associated with the victualling yard and naval hospital. These were accommodated in a variety of rented properties, of which the finest was a terrace of three houses overlooking Dockyard Creek in Strada San Giuseppe, Senglea, originally built in the 18th century as accommodation for the Knights' galley captains (Fig 11.15). In 1843 the navy acquired these and subdivided them between 1843 and 1846 to provide housing for the senior dockyard officers, who were now six in number, as they included a superintending engineer. The only external alteration was the addition of a shallow roof carried on cast-iron columns to shade the first-floor terrace. These remain among the most attractive of all former naval residences.

The arrival of more senior naval officers posted to the island led to further and rather grander properties being used. In the 1820s, the flag officer was accommodated in a rented property in Strada Mezzodi in Valletta; in 1832 with the abolition of the Navy Board, the last commissioner became an Admiral Superintendent and lived in Admiralty House in Vittoriosa.[31] Towards the end of the British period his successors lived in Calcara in the handsome 18th-century Villa Portelli set in its own spacious grounds (Fig 11.16).[32] The Commander-in-Chief of the Mediterranean fleet for much of the time was accommodated in considerable splendour in a handsome town house in South Street, Valletta.

In the quarter of a century following the end of the Napoleonic Wars, construction of new facilities at Malta was largely limited to the

Fig 11.16
The Villa Portelli, Malta, in 1971, shortly before it ceased to be the flag officer's official residence.
(Author)

ropeyard, the abortive dry dock and construction of a new naval hospital at Bighi overlooking Grand Harbour (*see* Chapter 16). The importance of the base was recognised when a powerful squadron was stationed here during the Syrian crisis of 1839–41. It is no coincidence that early in 1841 William Scamp was posted to the Mediterranean to see what repairs were needed at Gibraltar and, more importantly, to consider updating and increasing the output of the existing naval bakeries at Malta. The first of two naval bakeries had been established in 1801 in the Fondazione Manoel in Floriana outside the city of Valletta and was supplemented by a second in Strada Ponte in Valletta itself. The Floriana bakery operated with mule-powered grain mills, and the original intention had been to replace these with a spare set of engines and boilers, originally manufactured for the mills-bakery at the Royal William Victualling Yard at Stonehouse, and to use surplus power for dough-mixing machines and rollers for the production of ships' biscuits.[33] However, on inspection both Brandreth and Scamp agreed that a new building was the only practical solution, and it was Scamp who apparently suggested a location alongside Dockyard Creek, adjacent to the existing victualling storehouses and close to the granaries.

As constructed, the bakery followed the general layouts of the earlier ones at Gosport and Stonehouse and like them employed internal iron framing supporting stone jack-arches, both for load capacity and for fireproofing purposes. One side of the building contained the steam-powered mill, to which grain was fed by gravity from bins on the upper floors; on the other and separated by a central space used for receiving and issuing purposes, lay the bakery proper, with its 12 circular brick bread ovens arranged in two groups of 6 facing each other across a central working space (Fig 11.17). By 1861 a rotary bread oven had been added.[34]

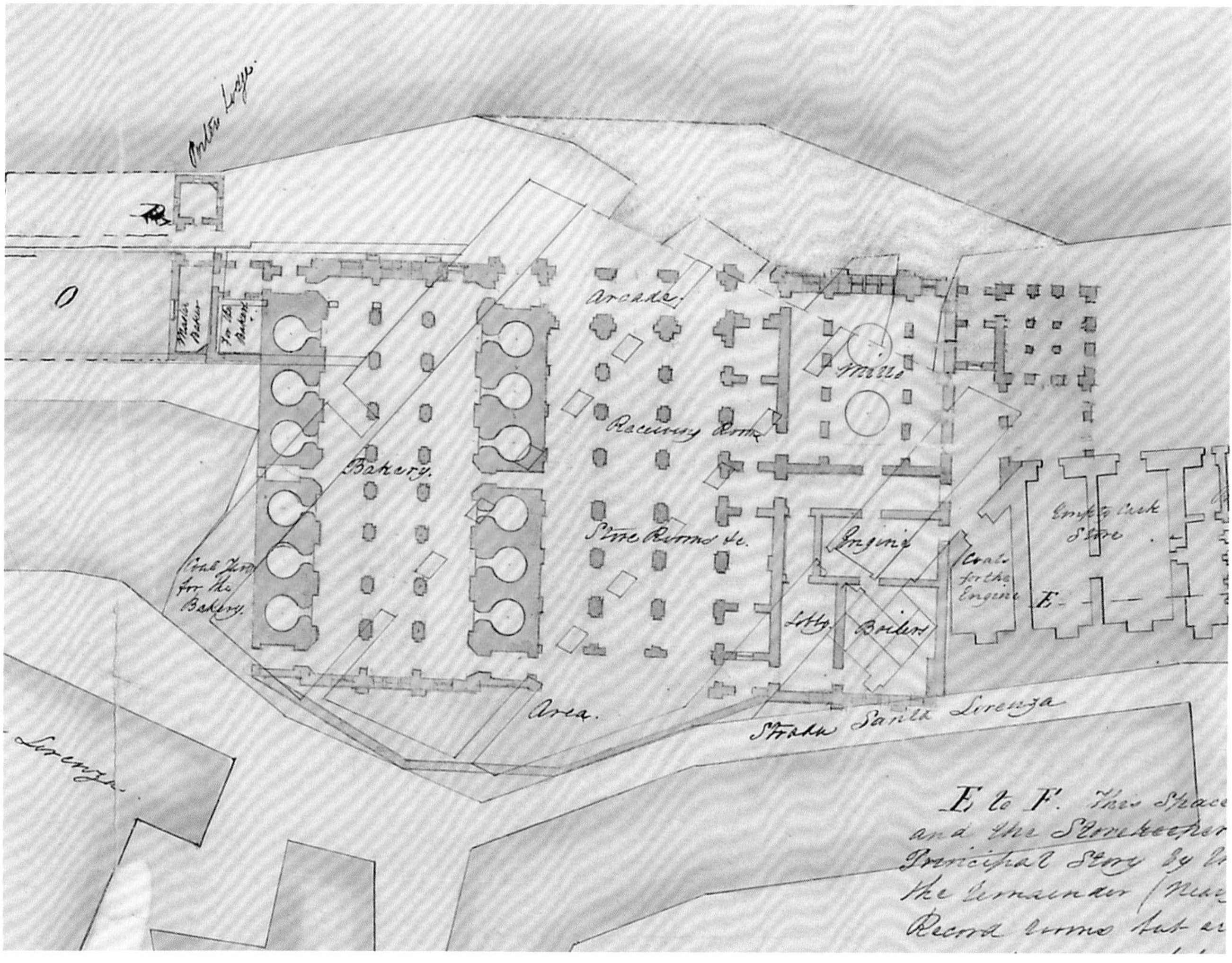

Fig 11.17
Scamp's plan of the naval bakery at Malta, showing the layout of mill, mixing room and ovens. The ovens still survive, and the building is now the Malta Maritime Museum.
(TNA ADM 140/1285-1)

The building, along with adjacent houses for the master miller and master baker, was constructed using local stone between 1842 and 1844 and remains a distinguished addition to the Vittorioso waterfront (Fig 11.18). Although Brandreth drew up the original plans, they were substantially modified by Scamp in the interests of more efficient working patterns. He also made use of local construction techniques, notably stone corbels to carry joists and roof members. Further Maltese influence is evident in the building's skyline, peppered with towers and turrets, while the stone balustrades on the main elevations owe much to similar features on the house of the General of the Galleys, which was used as an office by Scamp. Among the most conspicuous features are the blind arcades on the main elevations with their great recessed rows of windows that borrow heavily on his knowledge of Hugh May's earlier work on buildings around the upper ward of Windsor Castle.[35] The bakery, now the Malta Maritime Museum, is rightly known locally as Scamp's Palace, a reflection not just of his influence on its design, but also on his other contributions to Malta's architecture.[36]

The new bakery marked the start of much-needed Admiralty investment in infrastructure for the growing numbers of warships permanently based at Malta. In the early 1840s the dockyard lacked all but the most rudimentary repair facilities and none designed for steam warships. In 1840 a hauling-up or patent slip was seen as a solution to when works were required on a ship's hull, perhaps to avoid the earlier problems with the unfinished dry dock, and so £10,000 was put in the estimates. Patent slips were a comparatively new invention. The size of vessel able to be hauled up a slip was governed by the capacity of the cradle and the power of the steam winch, and at this stage it is doubtful if any had been constructed with the capacity to take a ship of the line. The plan was abandoned, possibly on recommendations from Brandreth, and was replaced by new proposals for a dry dock.[37] In itself, this was inadequate, and both Scamp and Brandreth would have been well aware that attendant engineering and metal-working facilities would also be required. Space for all these was not easy to find in the crowded urban waterfront environment of much of Grand Harbour, but acquisition of a number

Fig 11.18
The naval bakery alongside Dockyard Creek, Malta, in 1971. (Author)

of properties at the head of Dockyard Creek gave space for a dry dock and pump house flanked by two narrow ranges of store sheds, all conveniently located adjacent to the existing dockyard area (Fig 11.19).[38]

By the time work started on the dry dock (2 Dock) in 1844, purchase of further properties on the Cospicua waterfront had allowed Scamp to site a small steam factory here, its rear elevation forming the boundary wall of the yard.[39] The centre of the range was occupied by a metal workshop 90ft by 62ft, designed to contain punching, shearing, turning and boring machines. Flanking this were two smitheries, one for shipwrights and one for engineers. The shipwrights would have been responsible for the hulls and the engineers for the machinery. Adjacent to the engineers' smithery at the south end was a small foundry, while an engine and boiler house occupied the corresponding position at the other end of the building.[40] On the western side of the dry dock the original proposal of a long shed for spars and timbers was superseded by a two-storey, stone-built range, by 1863 described as a factory. Its heart was a sawmill, to which coppersmiths' and other workshops and stores were to be added.[41]

Although Scamp should be credited with the development of the entire original scheme, it is clear that Brandreth made a number of contributions, including recommending the purchase of 'four small houses' to improve access to the new dock.[42] The estimate for the dry dock was £45,000 and that of the steam factory and its machinery a further £30,000.[43] The dry dock came into operation in 1847, and its original

Fig 11.19
Part of the original dry dock at Malta, the first at an overseas base. This came into use in 1847 and was known as No. 1 Dock. The vessel is sitting in 2 Dock, which was added in 1857. On either side are the machine shops and stores, which have mostly been demolished since this 1971 photograph. (Author)

dimensions were 253ft long and 90ft wide, with a depth over the sill of 25ft.[44] The factory buildings were largely finished by 1850, but both were to be enlarged at intervals in the next half century. The extended dockyard was completed with a boundary wall and modest main gateway (Fig 11.20).[45] The foundry was demolished in 1971 and the dockyard wall more recently. The factory buildings on the western side of the docks remain standing, though altered.

Fig 11.20
The modest main gateway to the early Victorian dockyard at Malta in 1971. It has since been demolished. (Author)

Scamp and Brandreth had provided the necessary minimum with these works for maintaining and repairing steam warships at an overseas base, but their adequacy was to be shortlived. Already by the mid-1850s the dry dock was too small, and in 1855 it had to be extended further into Dockyard Creek, forming a double dock 'to receive two first-class ships, or one of extraordinary length' (*see* Fig 11.19). The new outer dock was 281ft long, but curiously only 82ft wide, compared to the 90ft of its predecessor that now formed the inner dock.[46] This double dock remains today substantially intact. Double docks in the home yards had gone out of favour half a century earlier, and their use here simply reflects the lack of available waterfront land; for the same reason the design was to be repeated later with 5 and 6 Docks.[47] Effectively, by the mid-1850s, the victualling yard and expanded dockyard occupied all available space in Dockyard Creek.

Malta's strategic importance meant that alone among overseas bases in the second half of the 19th century, it was home to a powerful squadron that included some of the navy's most modern capital ships.[48] This resulted in a series of dockyard expansions from the mid-1850s to the eve of the First World War, which were largely centred on the provision of more dry docks, larger in size, and attendant engineering and metal-working facilities. By the 1900s the facilities in Malta rivalled in size those in the main home yards. With no room remaining in Dockyard Creek, the new docks had to be located elsewhere round Grand Harbour. The initial proposal had been to incorporate a dry dock as part of the development of a commercial basin at Marsa at the western end of Grand Harbour, which would be deepened by extensive dredging. The Admiralty was prepared to share the dry dock with commercial shipping, in return for which the Maltese government would contribute £10,830 towards the cost. Although the commercial basin was constructed, rising costs and doubts about sharing the dry dock caused this part of the project to be abandoned.[49] Instead, in 1862 Scamp drew up with Sir Andrew Clarke proposals for a 'Deep Dock' on French Creek,[50] immediately west of Dockyard Creek and separated by the narrow promontory occupied by the fortified city of Senglea. This site

Fig 11.21
Part of French Creek with its naval installations in c 1910. From the 1860s the greater space here made it the focus for the expansion of Malta Dockyard. (TNA ADM 140/1484 pt 62)

was favoured by the Commander-in-Chief and by the Director of Works, and the principal components of the late Victorian dockyard gradually occupied the waterfront all round this creek (Fig 11.21). In 1861 £60,000 was allocated to relocate the merchant wharves elsewhere and to buy up existing properties, mainly on the Senglea side, where the dry dock was set below the St Michael Bastion at an oblique angle to the creek. The dry dock, begun in 1865, was named after the 12th Duke of Somerset, First Lord of the Admiralty from 1859 to 1866 and a firm supporter of the project. When completed it was 448ft long overall, with a width of 80ft at the caisson and a depth of 33ft 6in at the sill.[51] Early in the 20th century the dock was to be lengthened to 477ft 6in, but otherwise remains little altered.[52]

The warship-building programme following the 1889 Naval Defence Act had its impact on the overseas yards. At Malta a further dry dock was begun the previous year below the ramparts of Senglea adjacent to the Somerset Dock. This was named Hamilton Dock, after Lord George Hamilton, First Lord of the Admiralty from 1885 to 1892. Its site was chosen by the Director of Works, Major-General Smith, to be adjacent to Somerset Dock to allow for a common pumping system. It had a length of 520ft, a 94ft entrance width and a depth at the caisson sill of 33ft 8in, reflecting the growth in warship sizes since construction of the Somerset Dock a quarter of a century earlier.[53] Within a few years of its completion, as the European arms race gathered momentum, work began in 1899 at the head of French Creek on a further three dry docks. For reasons of space, Docks 5 and 6 were constructed as a double dock, with entrance widths of 95ft and a massive 776ft length when used as a single dock, one that outclassed anything then available in the home yards. It was exceeded overseas only by its near-contemporary 1 Dock at Gibraltar. When used as individual docks, 5 Dock had a length of 440ft, and 6 Dock had a length of 336ft 6in. The adjacent 7 Dock was some 30ft longer and 1ft wider at its entrance compared to the slightly earlier Hamilton Dock, again reflecting the increase in capital ship sizes at this period (Fig 11.22).[54]

Fig 11.22
French Creek, Malta, in 2007, with part of Hamilton Dock in the foreground. Docks 5–7 are in the distance. (Author)

Fig 11.23
The New Factory at the head of French Creek, Malta, photographed when nearing completion in August 1887. It was later named the Iron Ship Repairing Shop and is still in use. (Author's collection)

Fig 11.24
The Gun-Mounting Store and Factory at Malta, nearing completion in 1890 alongside French Creek. The building no longer exists. (Author's collection)

The seven dry docks constructed at Malta Dockyard between 1844 and 1909, a number unrivalled by any other overseas yard, remain a vivid testament to the singular strategic importance of this base for the Royal Navy at this period. All remain in use today. In 1897 there were 10 first-class battleships stationed here, a number that was briefly to rise to 14.[55] Investment in dry docks was paralleled with the development of a variety of associated workshops and stores. By the end of the 19th century these extended along the waterfront on both sides of French Creek and round the northern end of the Corradino Heights to the Marsa, where the coaling facilities and the naval ordnance were concentrated; here, as at Gibraltar, ammunition stores were quarried deep into the hillside below the Corradino Heights.

Since then much has been swept away by more recent developments, principally by a massive commercial dry dock occupying most of the western side of French Creek. However, two notable buildings, both used by the metal-working trades, remain from this epoch. Set alongside Somerset Dock and facing down French Creek stands the handsome Iron Ship Repairing Shop, originally known rather more prosaically as the New Factory (Fig 11.23). This was built to serve Somerset Dock and, when completed, Hamilton Dock as well, and to augment a series of now-vanished earlier and smaller metal-working shops ranged against the nearby dockyard boundary. Construction started in 1884, and the building was completed around the end of 1887.[56] Three ranges of stone-built machine shops surround a central smithery, its louvred roofs carried on metal columns. The main western range incorporates offices overlooking French Creek, while to the rear of the complex a boiler house provided power for the steam hammers. The main elevations are distinguished by their use of bold stringcourses, banded rustication and prominent architraves to windows and doorways. A massive hydraulic crane with a capacity of 160 tons once stood in front, on the adjacent Somerset Wharf. This was linked to the dockyard railway system and was used for lifting heavy machinery and gun turrets, the latter principally destined for the now-vanished Gun Mounting Store that lay beyond Hamilton Dock (Fig 11.24).[57]

Contemporary with the construction of 5–7 Docks is another large factory building known as the Machine and Fitting Shop. This lies adjacent to the southern side of 7 Dock, where its handsome stone elevations are a prominent landmark (Fig 11.25). Its classical detailing is very much in the Maltese tradition, setting it apart from its near contemporaries at Gibraltar and Simon's Town. This was the last of the great machine shops built at Malta for the Royal Navy and a century on remains very much in use.

Fig 11.25
The Machine and Fitting Shop built alongside 7 Dock, Malta. This was the largest dockyard building of its type at an overseas base. (Author)

By the turn of the 20th century the concentration of British naval power at Malta made the dockyard and the anchorage at Grand Harbour an attractive and vulnerable target for a lightning raid by fast attack craft armed with torpedoes and quick-firing guns and from the growing threat from submarines.[58] To counter these and to give better protection to the anchorage from northerly gales, the Admiralty constructed two moles at the harbour mouth. The shorter Ricasoli breakwater projected into the harbour mouth from Fort Ricasoli, while the longer detached St Elmo breakwater (Fig 11.26) ran approximately east from the northern tip of Fort St Elmo, to which it was linked by a short, two-span iron bridge. As with the contemporary breakwaters protecting the Admiralty Harbour at Dover, both were provided with gun emplacements and searchlight positions at their ends. The effect of these massive stone structures was to prevent torpedoes being fired into Grand Harbour from outside and to force ships into a dog-legged approach to its entrance, increasing their vulnerability to coastal artillery. King Edward VII laid the foundation stone in April 1903, while reviewing the Mediterranean fleet, and the breakwaters were completed in 1910.[59] They remain superb examples of engineering skills combined with Maltese craftsmanship and were to prove their worth in the Second World War, thwarting an Italian raid in 1941.[60]

Fig 11.26
The St Elmo breakwater, Malta. The masonry structure on the left originally supported a bridge linked to Fort St Elmo. The superb quality of the local masonry is apparent. (Author)

12

The West Indies and North American Bases: Buildings and Engineering Works, 1700–1914

For much of the 18th century, the Caribbean was a cockpit of competing European powers and a hunting ground for privateers and smugglers. The crescent-shaped necklace of islands of the Lesser Antilles that formed the boundary between the Atlantic and Caribbean was mostly colonised by mutually hostile British and French settlers. A thousand miles to the west lay Jamaica, Britain's only possession in the largely Spanish Greater Antilles.[1] By the start of the 18th century, the Royal Navy sought to protect Britain's trading interests in the region by retaining a powerful squadron at Port Royal in Jamaica to protect convoys bound to Britain and North America, while individual warships cruised the Caribbean islands. In the summer season of sickness and hurricanes, the navy tended to concentrate its activities in North American waters, returning south when ice and winter gales made operations there impossible.[2] Such patchy protection was increasingly unsatisfactory to the British settlers, especially on islands in the Lesser Antilles. Many of these were in sight of neighbouring French colonies, leading to fears that in wartime the arrival of an enemy fleet from Europe would do immense damage before any help could arrive from Jamaica, which was situated downwind in the prevailing trades.

The first and largest British naval base in the Caribbean was established at Port Royal late in the 17th century, conveniently next to the commercial centre and within reasonable reach of Spanish Town, the administrative capital. This was to be followed by others at Port Antonio, on the north coast of Jamaica, and English Harbour, Antigua. Two other small bases, more in the nature of supply depots, were at Barbados and at Nassau on New Providence Island in the Bahamas, just north of the Caribbean. During the Revolutionary and Napoleonic Wars, these were supplemented by additional stores depots on Martinique and briefly on Haiti in 1787–8.[3] At Barbados, the first port of call for vessels following the normal route from England via the Madeiras, lack of a good harbour precluded establishment of a naval base. However, the navy used the island as a watering point, for purchasing food and restocking ordnance supplies. In 1704, following his return to Jamaica in 1701 as chief engineer on the island, Colonel Christian Lilly was appointed chief engineer for the West Indies, with orders from the Board of Ordnance to fortify Barbados. Part of his work may have included constructing a naval ordnance depot there, because in 1709 the Board appointed him keeper of the depot.[4] Little is known about the depot, and it may have been subsumed into what was later described as the Old Naval Yard, transferred to the army in May 1816, but apparently used again by the navy, since monies were allocated in 1840 for constructing a water tank, in 1865 for 'an additional coal store' and in 1881 for a 'tramway between the coal yard and engineer's wharf .[5] A similar naval depot existed at Nassau, which by 1863 was a small walled yard with a jetty, smithy, well and two coal stores with a capacity of 390 tons adjacent to the military store yard.[6] Nothing remains of either of these two minor establishments.

Port Royal

The Venn and Pennables expedition that captured Jamaica in 1655 realised the strategic importance of Port Royal and rapidly fortified the site on the end of the Palisadoes, the sandy spit which sheltered Kingston Harbour. The extraordinary growth of the town with its flourishing entrepôt trade meant that space was at a premium, and although naval ships were based here, they generally seem to have made use of commercial storehouses and careening wharves. These and much else were destroyed in the devastating earthquake of 1692, which largely submerged 33 of the 51 acres of Port Royal, cut the Palisadoes and left it marooned as an island. Most of the population fled to the mainland, where the new town of Kingston was laid out in 1694 to plans by Christian Lilly, newly appointed commander of the siege train in the West Indies.[7]

Port Royal was rebuilt, but destroyed by fire in 1703 and severely damaged by hurricanes in 1712 and 1722, effectively ending its commercial future. It remained an island until the gap in the Palisadoes was repaired in the early 1730s.[8] During this time, naval use of the harbour had grown very considerably, but the disasters befalling Port Royal made the Admiralty understandably hesitant to invest in shore facilities, preferring to rely on the increasingly inadequate commercial facilities and storehouses in Kingston.[9] It remains unclear how early the navy had its own permanent facilities at Port Royal. Early in 1728 Captain John Gascoigne, back at Port Royal which he had surveyed a few years earlier, was unenthusiastic about either of the locations that were proposed by Sir Jacob Acworth for a careening wharf – he reported that the ground had sunk 2ft since 1726. Nevertheless, he felt that the number of warships using Port Royal did justify a wharf, 'that would serve to careen ships for twenty or thirty years, without any considerable charge for repairing (hurricanes excepted)'.[10]

Isaac Pearson's plan, perhaps dating from around 1730 and probably the earliest detailed one to survive, is the best evidence for the existence then of a small base (Fig 12.1). This shows an irregularly shaped walled yard centred on a 122ft-long careening wharf, with its capstan house, a small boathouse and mast house, a smith's forge, a pitch house and a range of 'Negroes Hutts or shedds' against the boundary wall. Pearson may have been successor to the 'Clerk of the Navy Office', a post known to have been in existence here since at least 1675.[11] Clearly, Pearson recognised the inadequacies of existing arrangements, and his plan proposed significant extensions, including a further 150ft careening wharf, with a new capstan house and new forge. His plans were not implemented, perhaps because Port Antonio was already under consideration, but they clearly formed the basis for the almost identical set of proposals put forward in 1734 by Sir Chaloner Ogle, Commander-in-Chief at Jamaica since 1732. These were estimated at £3,792 10s 0d, excluding a new hospital, which was the centrepiece of Ogle's scheme.[12]

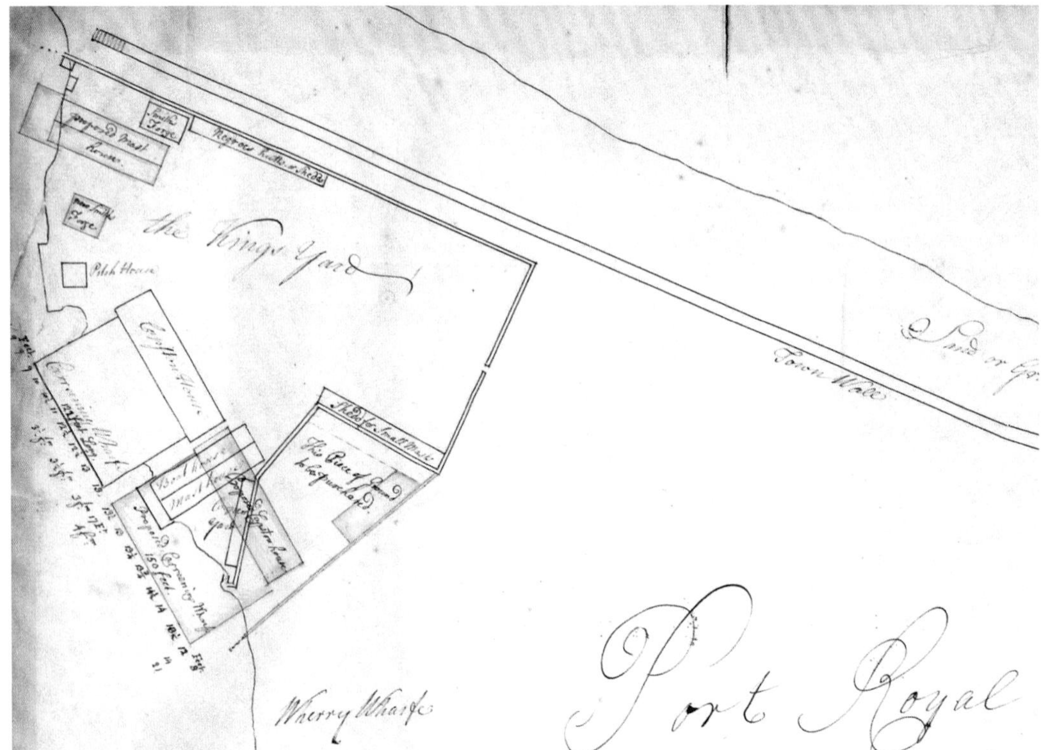

Fig 12.1
Isaac Pearson's c. *1730 plan of the yard at Port Royal, Jamaica, shows the existing limited facilities, with the proposed expansion and new buildings in pink. (AdL Vz 10/ 71)*

By now, the disadvantages of the new base under construction at Port Antonio were becoming apparent, and the Admiralty agreed in December 1734 that 'it appeared advisable to have careening wharves, receptacles for stores, and some stores lodged and officers, both at Port Royal and Port Antonio'.[13] It seems that Ogle's proposals were largely implemented at Port Royal in time for Admiral Vernon to praise the work of the base in refitting his squadron over the winter of 1739–40. A 1765 plan of the yard shows it much as proposed by Pearson and then Ogle, but with additional buildings including 'new cookrooms' for the crews of ships on careen, 'new sheds for seamen when on careen', 'apartments for the admiral ... captains ... lieutenants and other gentlemen while on careen', a blockmaker's shop, new cooperages, three sawpits by the careening wharf and additional 'negro houses'.[14] But even with these additions, naval facilities remained inconveniently dispersed, as Charles Knowles noted in 1748: 'The ships careen at Port Royal; send for their stores (7 miles) to Kingston; for their provisions (5 miles) to New Greenwich; for their water (12 miles) to Rock Fort; and for their Ordnance stores (5 miles) to Mosquito Point'.[15]

It was to be more than half century or so before facilities became more centralised at Port Royal. By 1799 additional land had been acquired to the east beyond the Polygon Battery for a separate victualling yard constructed that year, its buildings probably of timber (Fig 12.2).[16] The dockyard itself was to be extensively rebuilt, pride of place given to a handsome storehouse with a tall central clocktower constructed along its southern boundary and linked to the main wharf by a covered way (Fig 12.3). A house for the senior naval officer was incorporated at its northern end.[17] Along the south-eastern boundary was a further range of houses for the senior yard officers; these had what were described as yards and grass to their rear. The careening wharves were improved, and other buildings were constructed. With the exception of the main storehouse and the officers' houses that were built of brick, the majority of the buildings were timber framed, with weatherboarding and shingled roofs (Figs 12.4, 12.5 and 12.6). The date of this extensive reconstruction is uncertain and may have been towards the end of the Napoleonic Wars, with further works following the major town fire of 1815 that is known to have affected the southern end of the yard.[18] It seems to have been completed before the construction of Holl's naval hospital between 1818 and 1824.

Fig 12.2
The naval base at Port Royal in 1863, its three distinct parts separated by the town and defences. The narrow, low-lying spit meant that Port Royal has always been vulnerable to hurricanes and earthquakes. The victualling facilities were soon to be transferred to the main dockyard and replaced by a coaling station. (AdL Naval Establishments 1863 Da 02 fol 14)

Fig 12.3 (right)
The main storehouse at Port Royal, photographed in the 1890s. The covered way linking it to the wharf was probably as much for protection from sun as well as rainstorms. The tower to the left formed part of the commodore's house at the end of the range.
(TNA ADM 195/49 fol 41)

Fig 12.4 (below left)
The modest main gate at Port Royal in the early 1890s, with muster bell and police sergeant's quarters.
(TNA ADM 195/49 fol 36)

Fig 12.5 (far right)
Looking from the main storehouse c 1900 towards Port Royal harbour and the Urgent, *an iron screw troopship used as depot ship here since 1876. Below the flagstaff is the shipwrights' shed. To its left is the rigging house and sail loft, with a multitude of dormer windows, beyond which are two storehouses for victuals. Overlooking the centre of the yard is the terrace of houses for the officers, behind which are the huddled roofs of Port Royal town.*
(Author)

Fig 12.6 (right)
The waterfront of Port Royal dockyard, photographed in 1868, one of the earliest images of this yard. Prominent in the centre is the capstan house, with accommodation on the first floor for the crew of a ship on careen. The generally somnolent air was probably characteristic of many of these smaller overseas bases in their Victorian heyday.
(BB90/07334 ©Commander R A B Phillimore)

After the Napoleonic Wars the Caribbean became something of a naval backwater as its economic and strategic importance gradually declined. Such alterations and additions as were made to the base in the remainder of its life were in response to changing technology. By the late 1830s the victualling yard had closed, and the former 74-gun *Magnificent* after service as a hospital ship was in use as a victualling store. In 1840 it was realised that the cost of converting her to a coal hulk was greater than the £3,200 cost of purchasing the former victualling yard for a coal depot.[19] A jetty and coal shed were constructed here by the early 1860s (Fig 12.7; *see also* Fig 10.10). By 1904 the jetty had been rebuilt and extended and the original coal shed replaced by two huge coal stores.[20] In the yard itself, space for a victualling store and a dedicated wharf was found at the western end. In the early 1860s a new smithery was built, but had hardly been completed before it had to be enlarged to cater for the increasing numbers of steam vessels needing repair (Fig 12.8).[21]

Fig 12.7
Looking north-east over the commodore's house at Port Royal towards the roofs of the coal stores and coaling jetty with a warship alongside. On the right are two newly constructed brick buildings with louvred roofs. The nearest one was built in 1892 as a store for the chief engineer, the further one in 1890 as an engine house. Both were associated with the torpedo boat slip, apparently not yet completed, and all three survive. The town of Kingston is in the distance across the harbour. (Author)

Fig 12.8
The smithery and fitting shop built in the early 1860s at Port Royal to service steam warships on station. This building was subsequently extended and renamed the chief engineer's workshops. In general scale it was similar to the one at Ascension Island. A photograph taken in the 1890s. (TNA ADM 195/49 fol 38)

In the latter part of the 19th century Port Royal was seen as having a potential importance if the Panama Canal was excavated, leading to a revision of trade routes. It was this thinking that probably prompted the Gladstone Government in 1884 to include Port Royal among the first-class coaling stations which were to receive modern fortifications.[22] At the very end of the 19th century the base was provided with a double patent slip for torpedo boats for additional defence. This still remains in place; near its head are two surviving pairs of officers' houses built in 1904, possibly for the commanders of these craft.[23] These were the last additions to the yard. By then, a combination of the growing naval power of the United States and the need for the Royal Navy to concentrate its strength in home waters had led the Admiralty to the conclusion that it would not be possible in the face of any American hostility to defend the naval bases of Halifax, Bermuda and Jamaica and the coaling station at St Lucia. In 1905 Port Royal was closed.[24]

Port Antonio

The precise sequence of events leading to the founding of a naval base at Port Antonio on the north-eastern coast of Jamaica remain unclear, but one driving factor was an understandable anxiety on the part of the Admiralty over Port Royal's vulnerability to natural disasters, something highlighted by Captain Gascoigne in 1728. Whatever the reasons, Port Antonio remains the Royal Navy's only overseas dockyard to have been designed and constructed to a set of agreed plans in one short building campaign, rather than developed piecemeal. The documentary records demonstrate initial optimism, lack of knowledge of the effects of climate and remarkable feats of organisation. Perhaps above all else, the records highlight the difficulties facing a far-distant Admiralty in making judgements when lacking reliable information. Port Antonio had an active life of less than 20 years, and its site on Navy Island, the former Lynches Island, is now overgrown and mainly of archaeological interest.

In many ways the most tangible evidence of the navy's presence is the neighbouring small township of Titchfield, a settlement founded to support the naval base and preserving its original grid pattern of streets (Fig 12.9). It was almost certainly laid out by Christian Lilly.[25] In April 1729 Lilly had arrived back in Jamaica as chief engineer after an absence of 18 years. His brief was to superintend the fortifications and new settlement at Port Antonio, where he was to spend nearly a year.[26] In November 1731 Commander Charles Knowles, with his considerable building skills, arrived on the *Southampton*, which was to serve as the headquarters' hulk for the construction of the naval base itself. He was to remain here until 1735.[27] A number of largely undated and unsigned maps and plans survive,

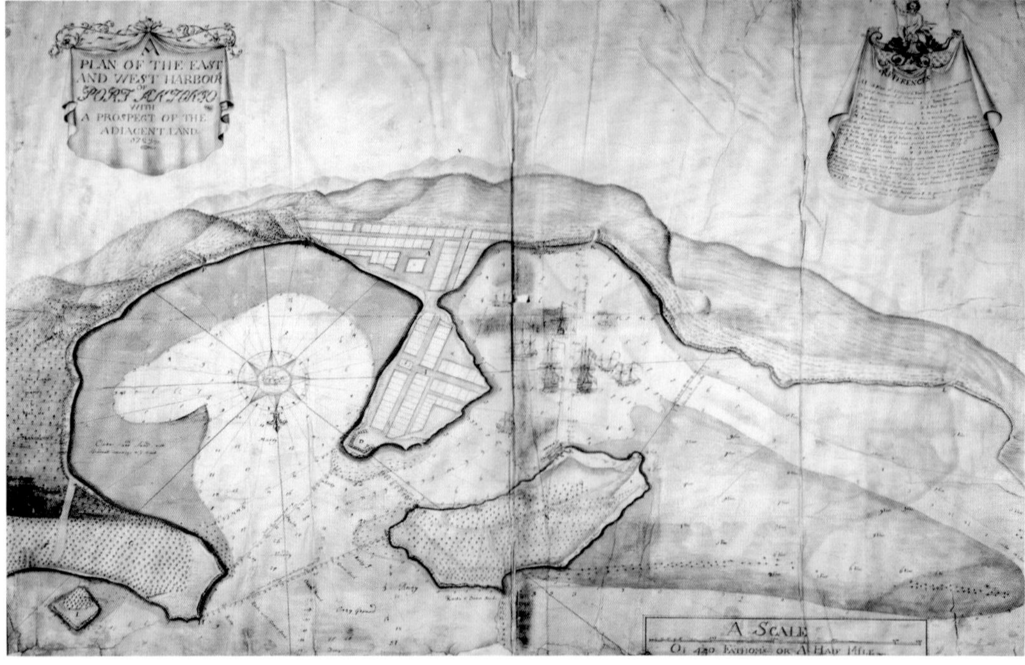

Fig 12.9
The town of Titchfield, Jamaica, as proposed in 1729–30. The grid pattern of streets and house plots, no doubt designed to tempt settlers to the location, can still be traced. Lynches Island is in the foreground. (AdL Vz 10/ 68)

and together with the reports from Knowles and Admiral Charles Stewart, they give us a good idea of the scale and complexity of the project.[28]

Port Antonio is a deep, north-facing bay divided into eastern and western harbours by a rocky peninsula projecting into the centre. This peninsula was to become the site of the township of Titchfield. The eastern harbour is protected on the north-east by Portland Point, while the 64-acre Lynches Island, which lies to the north-west of the Titchfield peninsula, protects the western harbour that is approached by a deep-water channel between the peninsula and the island (Fig 12.10). In 1729 the Navy Board purchased Lynches Island as the site for the new base. Much of the initial work was done by slaves, with Stewart suggesting that 30 be purchased to be apprenticed to 'the Master Caulker, carpenters of builder, or whoever are the Naval Officers, in order to be brought up to their several trades'. They were to live on the island, 'the ground allotted to them will produce them their bread and other necessaries usual for them', while the sea had 'abundant fish'. In addition, Stewart recommended that 'to make a distinction of his Majesty's Negroes I think it will be proper to allow a piece of beef or pork to each man a week to season their Negroes' pots, and also a bottle of rum'.[29]

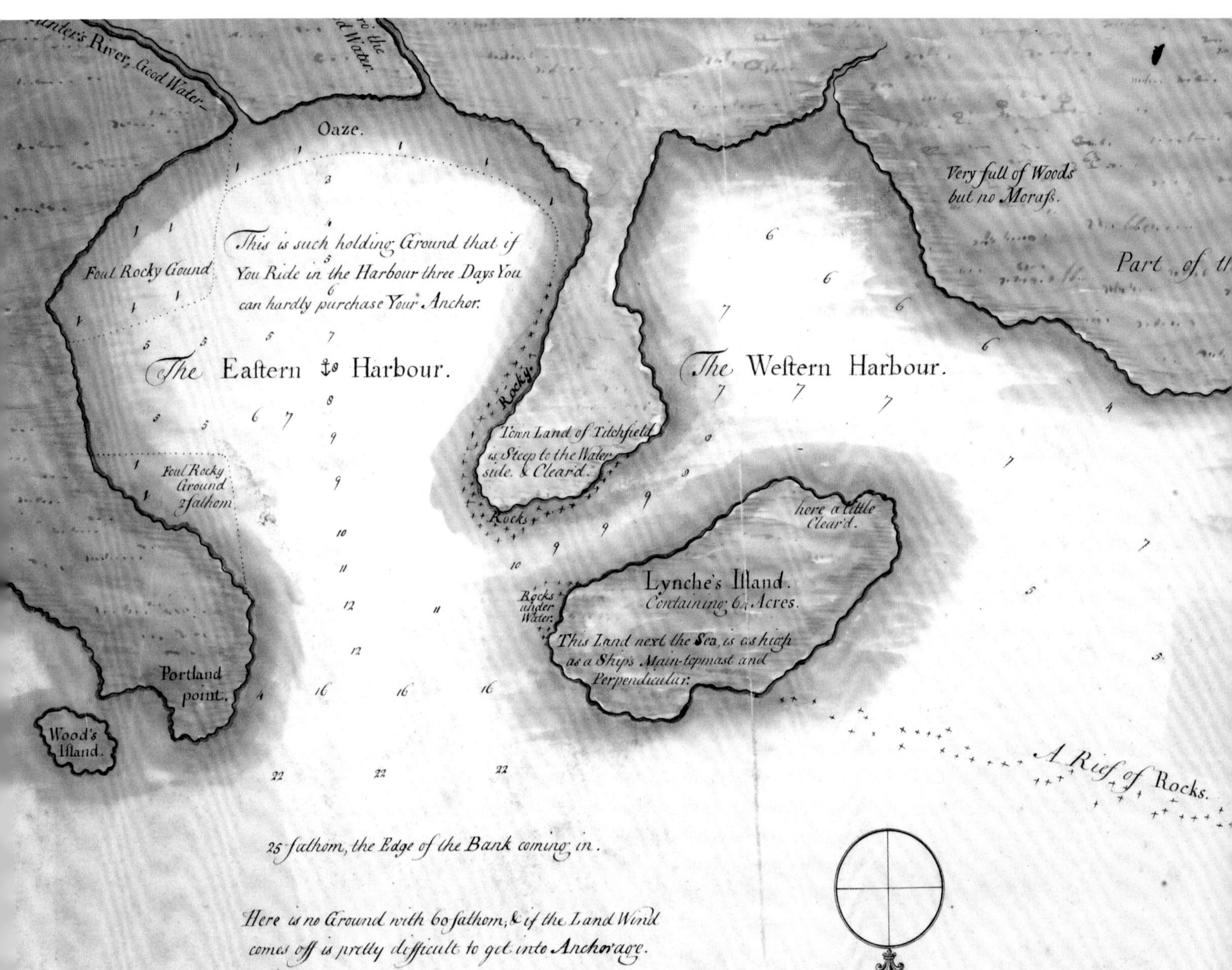

Fig 12.10
Christian Lilly's survey of c 1730 of the proposed site of Port Antonio on the north coast of Jamaica. Lynches Island is marked as the site for the naval base, with the township of Titchfield planned for the peninsula between the eastern and western harbours. (AdL Vz 10/69)

The following January Stewart sent home an optimistic report: 'I think there cannot be a better harbour for the bigness. It's true the entrance is narrow, but no ways difficult'. He noted the prevalence of winds off the land and how the *Lion* 'lay as in a mill pond', despite the 'considerable sea on the shoals and in the harbour's mouth'. Stewart had begun work clearing trees from the island and levelling parts for buildings, employing 70 men: 'I believe the island may afford brick; if not, stone may be had with no great trouble.' He was also investigating the possibilities of lime burning and enthused about the climate: 'it's my opinion a man may live as long here as in any part of the world … I have not had one man fallen sick by working, but on the contrary are better and in a good heart as ever I saw ship's company in my life.'[30]

The nucleus of the new base was at the southern end of Lynches Island, adjacent to the western harbour (Fig 12.11). Along the foreshore was a careening wharf, capstan house, storehouses, a small house for lodging naval officers and a mast house. Overlooking these from the higher ground to the rear, its commanding position reminiscent of Dummer's officers' terrace of 40 years earlier at Plymouth, Knowles planned a range of houses for the yard officers. Along the eastern flank of the island were the 'Negroes Hutts'. Towards the northern end of the island and to the rear of Lilly's proposed 26-gun fort guarding the seaward approach, Knowles sited a very substantial quadrangular hospital, in part surrounded by the garden plots of the slaves.[31]

Most of these naval buildings were prefabricated in timber, some possibly in North America, but the majority probably in one of the home yards. In March 1731/2 the Navy Board reported to the Admiralty that

> there was sent to Jamaica in 1730 a framed shed 150 feet long, 19 feet broad and 9 feet high … for a storehouse; one of a hundred feet long for a mast house, one of 35 feet long for a boathouse; and one for a smith's shop 21 feet 6 inches long that was sent in 1728; which shop with the boat-house and 118 feet of the said storehouse are already put up … with a house of about 30 feet by 35 feet bought by Mr Stewart. And in addition to these building[s] there are lately framed and sent two lengths of buildings, one of 153 feet long, the other 85 feet, of 22 feet broad and 10 feet 6 inches high to the raising, designed to be put up at Port Antonio to serve as an hospital, lodgings or for stores as the necessity of the service requires.[32]

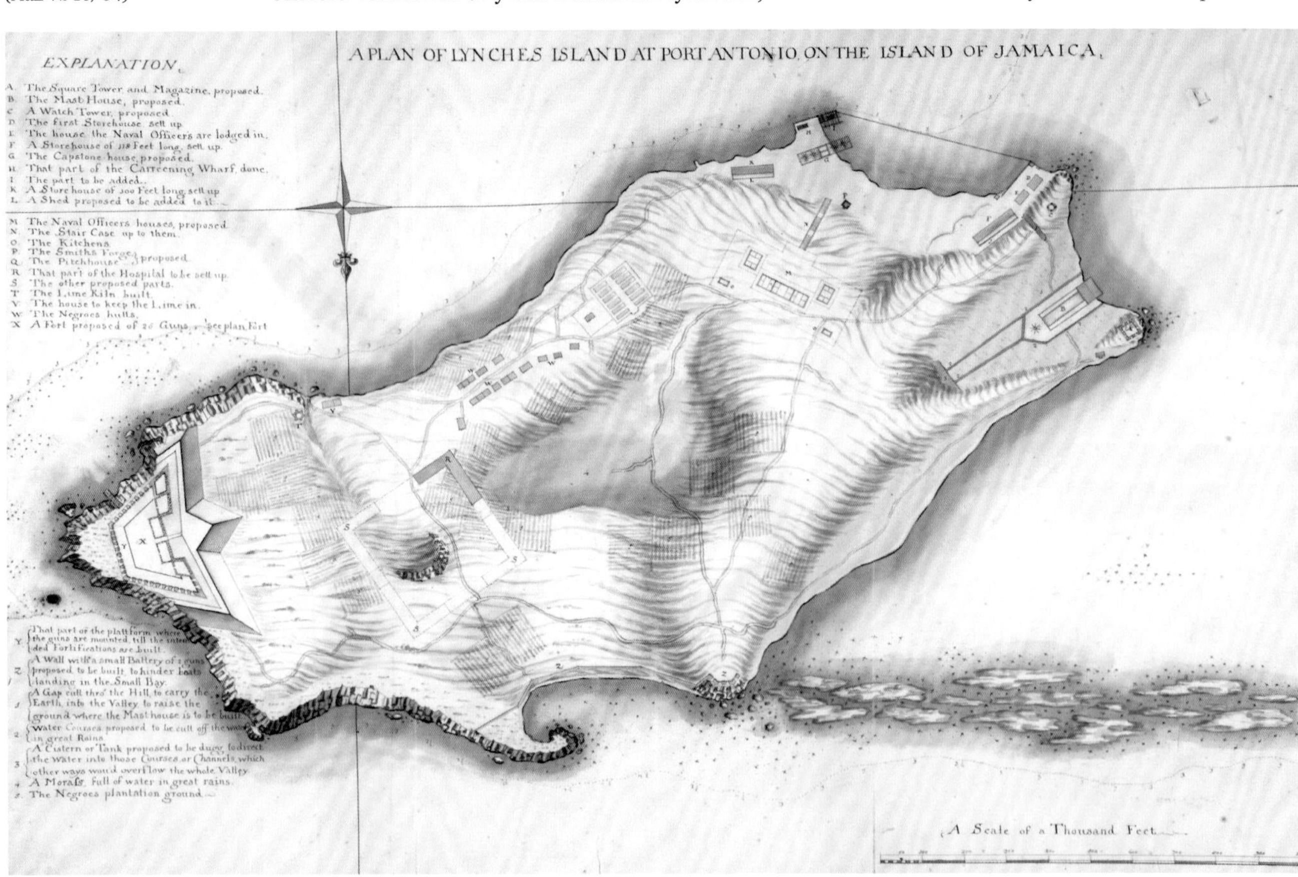

Fig 12.11
A plan of late 1731 showing the progress of construction of the naval base on Lynches Island at Port Antonio. Following convention, buildings and installations proposed but not yet built are coloured red.
(AdL Vz 10/64)

In July 1732 the naval surgeon at Port Royal was transferred to Port Antonio, suggesting that the hospital was coming into operation.[33]

Despite this progress, there were ominous signs. Port Antonio needed to attract settlers with skills and trades to generate commercial activity, provide manpower and help make the whole enterprise viable. But the mountainous and sparsely populated hinterland was the refuge of escaped and rebellious slaves. The previous December, 16 local slaves had absconded to join them, taking arms and ammunition from their owners and causing such great unease among the inhabitants that 'several about Port Antonio has talked already of leaving their settlements'.[34] A far more intractable problem was the local climate with its very high winter rainfall. Continuous downpours seriously affected maintenance and careening work, causing endless delays and harm to the ships; they also had a devastating effect on health. In December 1732 Knowles reported to the Admiralty that

> the rainy and sickly season ... has been severer than ever was known. I have sent home several of the workmen invalids, and buried most of the rest. The chief settlers are leaving the place, and I greatly fear its malignancy will soon make us. The few workmen now left if not closely looked after would run away, they are so terrified at the place. The misfortune is that not one in ten recovers, though sent round to Port Royal Hospital.

In spite of all these difficulties, construction work proceeded so that by March 1733/4 Knowles advised that 'there remains only to be done the officers' houses, lengthening the careening wharf, and setting up the other half of the capstan house to complete their Lordships' directions'.[35] But faced with something of an endemic labour shortage at Port Antonio, a climate that played havoc with ships, buildings and men and, perhaps above all, the isolation from the mercantile and administrative heart of Jamaica at Kingston and Spanish Town, the case for Port Antonio became steadily less compelling. This was tacitly acknowledged at the end of 1734, when it was agreed to develop in parallel similar facilities at Port Royal.[36] In November 1740 delays to the refitting of Vernon's ships at Port Antonio were caused by poor weather, when continuous rain over 9 days prevented the repair of the careening pits.[37] On 26 December 1749 the Admiralty bowed to the inevitable and declared that Port Antonio 'should be forthwith broken up', the stores sent to Kingston and the 'storehouses and other buildings let at an easy rent'.[38]

English Harbour, Antigua

English Harbour, the most picturesque and best preserved of all the Royal Navy's 18th-century overseas bases, owes its origins to the initiative of the island legislature and merchants. After two naval captains had done a survey in 1725, the legislature in 1728 successfully petitioned the Admiralty to establish a base here, promising to donate the land and pay for a careening wharf and a gun battery (Fort Berkeley) to guard the harbour entrance.[39] The navy had already made use of the harbour on occasions as an anchorage and for careening. A permanent naval base here, with its attendant fortifications, would increase the island's security and thus was highly attractive to the settlers (Fig 12.12). Apart from a storehouse at Barbados, the navy then had no other shore facilities in the Lesser Antilles. Antigua had a number of advantages as a base for the Leeward Islands station. English Harbour overlooked the Guadeloupe Passage and was reputed to be hurricane-proof. There was space on both sides of the harbour for wharves and storehouses, while gun batteries could easily command the dog-legged entrance to the harbour, and the surrounding hills, once suitably fortified, would make the base virtually impregnable.[40]

Fig 12.12
English Harbour, Antigua, from the defences at Shirley Heights. The main dockyard lies on the west side of the harbour, to the right, with the slightly earlier careening wharf and harbour entrance to the left.
(Author)

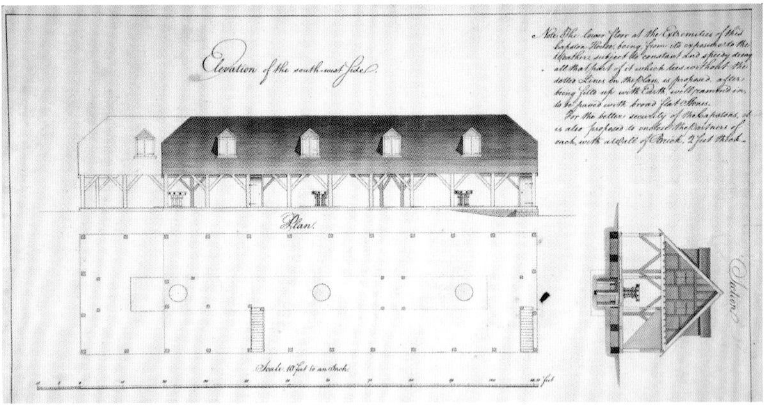

Fig 12.13
An undated late 18th-century drawing of the capstan house at English Harbour, Antigua. Capstans were the most expensive pieces of careening equipment, needing protection from the elements. The design shown was a standard pattern for such structures. (TNA ADM 140/1200)

There were also a number of disadvantages. The harbour entrance required skilled seamanship, and its shallowness meant that the largest warships had to be lightened before entering. If this was done at St John's, the capital of Antigua, it was impossible for them to turn up to windward to reach English Harbour. When crowded with shipping, the comparatively tideless harbour gained a reputation as 'a festering unhealthy hole', where yellow fever could be rampant among the crews.[41] Nevertheless, after a number of enquiries both the Admiralty and the Navy Board were in favour of establishing a base here. On 21 July 1729 the Navy Board proposed a careening wharf and capstan and a couple of storehouses, one of which was also to accommodate the crew of a ship on careen. In order 'to pursue the most frugal method for perfecting these buildings', the Board proposed to use local stone, lime and shingles, and 'all other materials of wood and iron necessary for completing those works should be prepared and framed in England and sent over on freight'.[42]

This first base initially was established on the eastern side of the harbour at St Helena, but in the 1740s it was considerably extended when the legislature gave a further 10 acres on the western side for mast and storehouses and lent '130 Negroes' to help. Commodore Knowles, who was in charge of these works, had instructions to create 'a proper careening place for any of His Majesty's ships of 70 or 80 guns'. The work was further aided when Commodore Peter Warren sent 100 Spanish prisoners, 'who with the encouragement he has given them of a *real* a day, work cheerfully'. The mast house was shifted across from the eastern side, and new wharves and storehouses constructed; at least one 'large building' was shipped from New England.[43] None of these early structures survive, but framed buildings by then were all prefabricated to broadly similar designs that altered little during the 18th century (Fig 12.13; *see also* Chapter 9).

English Harbour's heyday, when naval activities in the Caribbean were at a peak, was in the half century leading to the defeat of Napoleon in 1815. Apart from the dockyard, the base had ordnance facilities and a naval hospital; the latter has left no trace. The majority of surviving dockyard buildings date from this period, and the base assumed much of its final layout, with the boundary walls for the western base reaching their present extent in the 1770s (Fig 12.14).[44] The more important buildings were all constructed using bricks shipped from England, while many of the rest continued to be made of timber. In 1796 an ambitious plan was put forward for a double-ended double dock cutting across the full width of the western yard. As with the earlier proposal for a dry dock at Halifax, nothing came of the scheme, and it does not seem to have progressed beyond a preliminary plan.[45]

Dominating the centre of the western yard is a handsome brick storehouse, plans for which were drawn up in 1785; its construction was apparently completed 2 years later (Figs 12.15 and 12.16).[46] The storehouse had a set of water cisterns built against its main walls and were fed from the roof, each holding 50 tons of water. It was used as a general warehouse and was later known as the Copper and Lumber Storehouse. By the mid-19th century the first floor was used to accommodate crews of ships being careened. Such crews would have been fed from the small

Fig 12.14
English Harbour, Antigua, in 1858. By then the yard was little used and the nearby hospital had been demolished. The plan essentially shows the naval facilities as they had developed by c 1800. (TNA MF 1/6 fol 1)

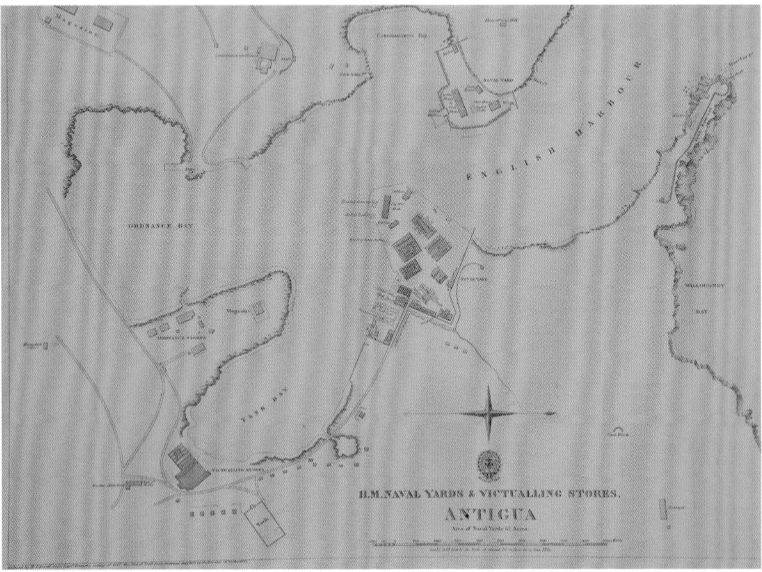

galley near the careening wharf (Fig 12.17). Near the main gate and contemporary with this main storehouse is a smaller storehouse, which was later used as a pitch, tar and paint store and joiners' shop, before becoming the engineer officers' building.[47] Nearby are the Porter's Lodge, part of the Canvas and Clothing Store, the mast house, sawpits and the smithery. The smithery was originally constructed to accommodate six forges, as shown on an early drawing (Fig 12.18).[48]

From 1784 to 1787 Nelson, as captain of the 28-gun frigate HMS *Boreas*, was based here. In 1786 he was joined by Prince William, who commanded HMS *Pegasus*. When ashore the prince occupied Clarence House, a handsome colonial building shaded by a deep veranda with fine views over the harbour, that was completed for him in 1787.[49] The records are unclear as to who paid for it, but the house was later used to

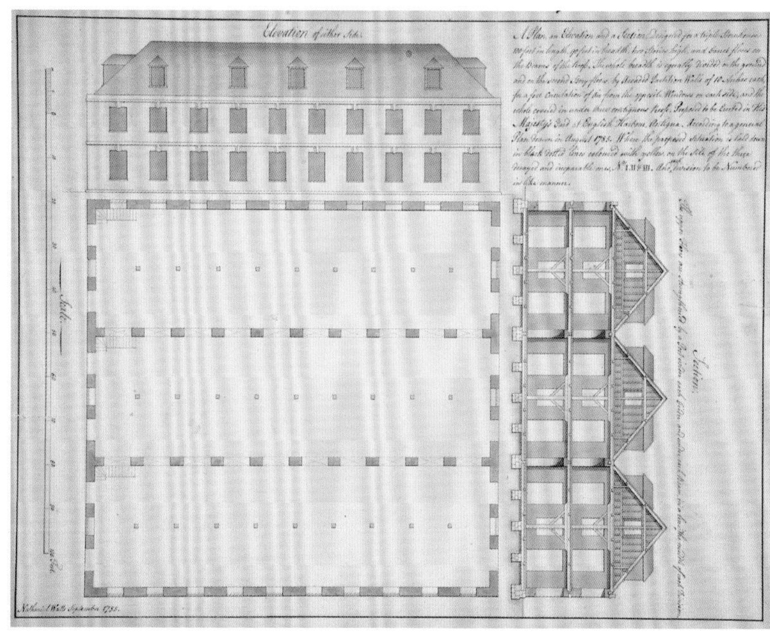

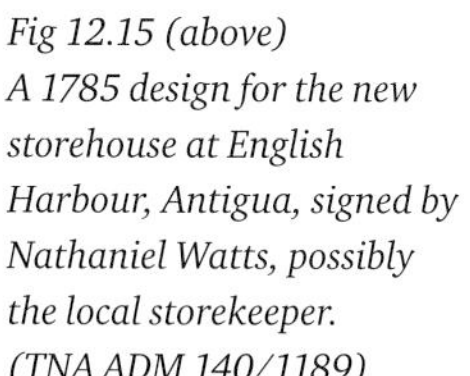

Fig 12.15 (above)
A 1785 design for the new storehouse at English Harbour, Antigua, signed by Nathaniel Watts, possibly the local storekeeper. (TNA ADM 140/1189)

Fig 12.16 (left)
The main storehouse with its brick water cisterns completed in 1787 at English Harbour, Antigua. To its right, constructed c 1807 above massive water tanks, is accommodation for the officers of warships being careened. (Author)

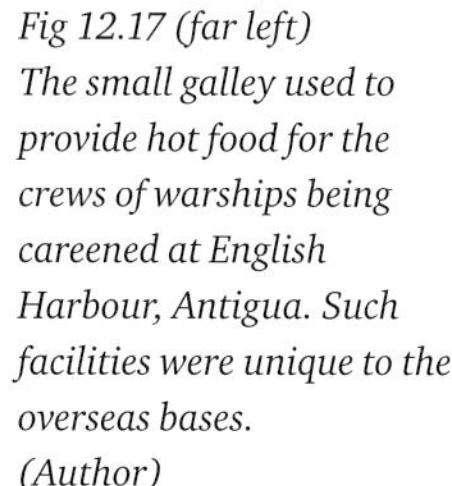

Fig 12.17 (far left)
The small galley used to provide hot food for the crews of warships being careened at English Harbour, Antigua. Such facilities were unique to the overseas bases. (Author)

Fig 12.18 (left)
An undated plan for the proposed smithery with six forges at English Harbour, Antigua. At smaller yards as here, these would generally have been worked by the warship crews. (TNA ADM 140/1203)

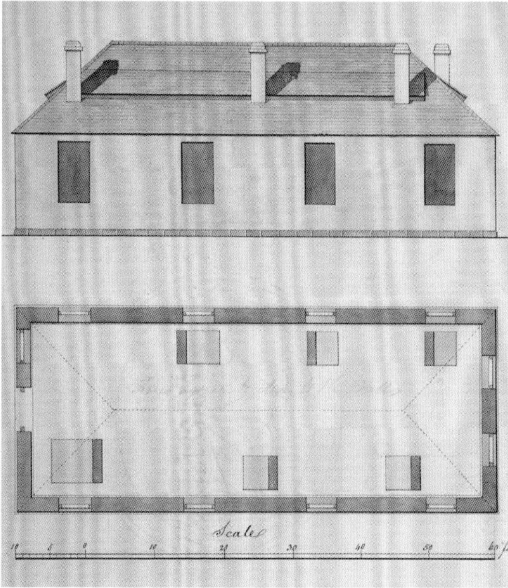

accommodate the senior yard official. It was renamed the Commissioner's House when the dockyard had a commissioner during part of the Napoleonic Wars.[50] Naval officers less exalted than Prince William and whose ships were on careen were accommodated from the early 19th century in a range of apartments next to the main storehouse. These apartments were built over a series of huge water cisterns, and the drawings for this building date to 1807. It seems to have been the last significant addition to the yard.[51]

After 1815 English Harbour continued in use, but never recovered its former importance. A stockpile of coal was kept on the eastern side of the harbour, but unlike Port Royal the base was never modernised with workshops to cope with the steam navy. In 1852 John Anderson, clerk of works at Bermuda, was asked to visit Port Royal and English Harbour to assess their condition. By then, many of the buildings in English Harbour were in a poor structural condition, the roof of the mast house and sail loft in an especially parlous state, which Anderson advised replacing with a new iron roof. The St Helena wharf was beyond repair and useless as a coaling point, and it was recommended that one possibility was the creation of a 2,000-ton coal store on the western side, adjacent to the officers' quarters.[52] Nothing apparently came of this report, and the coal store remained on the St Helena side. In 1860 it was first suggested that the base be closed, but inertia prevailed, and as Governor Berkeley minuted the Colonial Office in 1879 when the threat was repeated, 'it must not be lost sight of that the abandonment of the dockyard at English Harbour must be looked on as the severance of the last visible link existing between the colony of the Leeward Islands and the mother country'.[53]

At best, Berkeley's opinion may have secured a stay of execution, but development of coaling facilities at Castries, St Lucia, where there was a deep-water berth, effectively removed the only justification for retaining English Harbour. Ten years later the yard was closed, with HMS *Canada* reporting on 28 June 1889 that 'The Booms of the Naval Yard at English Harbour [were] formally closed yesterday'.[54] For just over half a century the yard lay decaying and abandoned until its historic importance was appreciated in the late 1940s, and it became the first naval base to have a remarkable conservation campaign to restore the buildings and to give it a new life and purpose as a yachting centre and historic monument.[55]

North American bases

The common factor linking the disparate and scattered naval bases of Esquimalt, the Great Lakes, Halifax and Bermuda lies in their location on, within or near the vast North American land mass. A journey of nearly 2,800 miles separates Esquimalt on the Pacific coast from Halifax on the eastern seaboard, only slightly less than the distance from Halifax to Portsmouth. Until the opening of the Canadian Pacific Railway's transcontinental line in 1886, most of Esquimalt's naval supplies came round Cape Horn. Halifax and the early naval facilities on the Great Lakes originated in Anglo-French rivalry at the time of the Seven Years' War, which led to the creation of the Royal Navy's only freshwater fleet. These bases were augmented first by Bermuda in the early 19th century and later by Esquimalt, at a time when the British and Canadian governments were both suspicious of America's expansionist intentions.

The Great Lakes

By the time of the Seven Years' War, the 94,360 square miles of the five Great Lakes of North America were important trade routes, increasingly well known to the French and British. The four upper lakes are interconnected, but remained separated from Lake Ontario until the completion of the first Welland Canal in 1829 allowed shipping to bypass Niagara Falls. Shoals and rapids on the upper waters of the St Lawrence river similarly prevented ships travelling between Lake Ontario and the North Atlantic. A lesser-known but strategic waterway system connected the St Lawrence and Hudson rivers. This involved porterage for part of the route, but relied for much of its length on Lake George and Lake Champlain, whose narrow waters linked together, stretching roughly north–south for some 155 miles.

It was inevitable that hostilities on land would spread to these trading arteries, leading to the establishment of separate naval forces on each water system. Little is known about the ships and their bases during the Seven Years' War. Adapted merchant vessels were pressed into use, but in 1755 Commodore Augustus Keppel was ordered to arrange for warships to be constructed at Oswego on the southern side of Lake Ontario to support land operations. Further warships were constructed at yards at Fort Niagara and Point Baril after their capture from the French. A small shipyard was also operated on the Niagara river on Navy Island, just above Niagara Falls. Further east on Lake George there was a British naval base at Fort William Henry and two further centres on Lake Champlain at Ticonderoga and St Jean.[56] The great majority of warships built at these sites were small vessels, described as schooners, sloops or snows; much of their equipment for fitting out, including ordnance, was transported with considerable difficulty from Halifax, more than 630 miles to the east; later, a store depot was established at Montreal for transhipment of supplies coming up the St Lawrence.[57] Shipbuilding on this small scale called for little more than a simple timber slip, a few sawpits and a forge, perhaps with a storehouse for supplies and equipment. Most structures, excepting the forge, were built of wood and were comparatively ephemeral; it is more accurate to describe these sites as shipyards rather than naval bases. A number were burned down in the course of hostilities, and their active use largely ceased with the end of the war, when the remaining vessels effectively became a transport service.[58]

The War of American Independence saw a resumption of this small-scale naval warfare and warship construction at a number of sites, this time to counter attacks from the American colonies to the south. It also marked an important change in the status of the new lake flotillas. In the previous war they had acted as loosely attached limbs of the Royal Navy, but in 1778 Governor Guy Carleton of Quebec obtained the secondment of one of the most able naval lieutenants on station, John Schank, as 'Commissioner of all His Majesty's Naval Yards or Docks upon the Lakes' and persuaded the Admiralty that to foster better local cooperation, the freshwater navy should come under the Governor's authority. This move marked the start of the Provincial Marine, which remained independent of the Royal Navy for nearly 35 years, until the War of 1812.[59] Like the earlier force it was never large, and at the end of the war in 1783 it had a total of 468 officers and men and 47 men in the yards, a number of which were by now in American territory.[60] The ensuing peace, punctuated with periods of tension with the new United States, again saw the ships of the Provincial Marine largely used as a transport service for both public and private goods.

The loss of former yards that were now in American territory was compounded by neglect of the surviving ones. In 1813 a new base had to be created at the Isle aux Noix on the Richelieu river north of Lake Champlain to replace the decayed former base at St Jean, and on Lake Huron Penetanguishene at the southern end of Georgian Bay was developed as the principal base for the upper lakes at the end of hostilities.[61] What was to become the Royal Navy's largest establishment on the Great Lakes was sited on a peninsula directly east of Kingston Harbour and its new and burgeoning loyalist town, immediately south-east of the estuary of the Cataraqui river on the northern shore of Lake Ontario. This was on land 'set apart from the Crown Reserve for Defensive purposes in 1783–85'.[62] The site of the dockyard was later selected with the aid of a young Royal Engineer, Lieutenant Alexander Bryce; it lay on the west side of Haldimand Cove, later Navy Bay, its entrance sheltered by Point Frederick and Point Henry. By 1800 Kingston Dockyard had store buildings, workshops, a sail loft and slips, on which a number of gunboats had been built.[63]

The growing tensions with the United States caused by Great Britain's imposition of trading restrictions with Continental Europe, which led ultimately to the War of 1812, furthered development of the base. Additional impetus followed the American decision in 1808 to construct at Oswego the 16-gun *Oneida*, the first United States warship on the Great Lakes and at some 262 tons also the most powerful. Two years later the Americans started to develop a new naval base at Sackets Harbor, only some 35 miles south of Kingston. In 1809 the British response was to launch the 330-ton, 20-gun *Royal George* at Kingston. Spurred by the outbreak of war and the successes of Commodore Isaac Chauncey's American squadron, the British followed this with a number of warships, culminating in the construction of HMS *St Lawrence*, a 102-gun first-rate, launched at the yard in September 1814 (Fig 12.19), outclassing anything else on the lake, but completed too late for the war.

By 1814 Kingston had developed into a fully fledged base of some 26½ acres rather than just a shipbuilding yard. One of the earliest views of it in the early 1820s by John Roebuck shows its three building slips, two with the frames of unfinished first-rates (Fig 12.20). Dominating the waterfront is the surviving four-storey stone storehouse constructed just after the war as a lay-apart store for the equipment of warships being placed in ordinary. Nearby is a variety of what appear to be mostly timber structures,

Fig 12.19 (above)
The 102-gun HMS St Lawrence *awaiting launch at Kingston, Ontario, in 1814. The ability to construct a warship of this size is indicative of the sophistication of the shore establishment. (Royal Ontario Museum ROM74 CAN258.967.106.1)*

Fig 12.20 (above right)
The naval base at Kingston, Ontario, c 1821–4, by John Roebuck, with a number of incomplete warships on the slips. To the right is the surviving storehouse. (National Archives of Canada C121249)

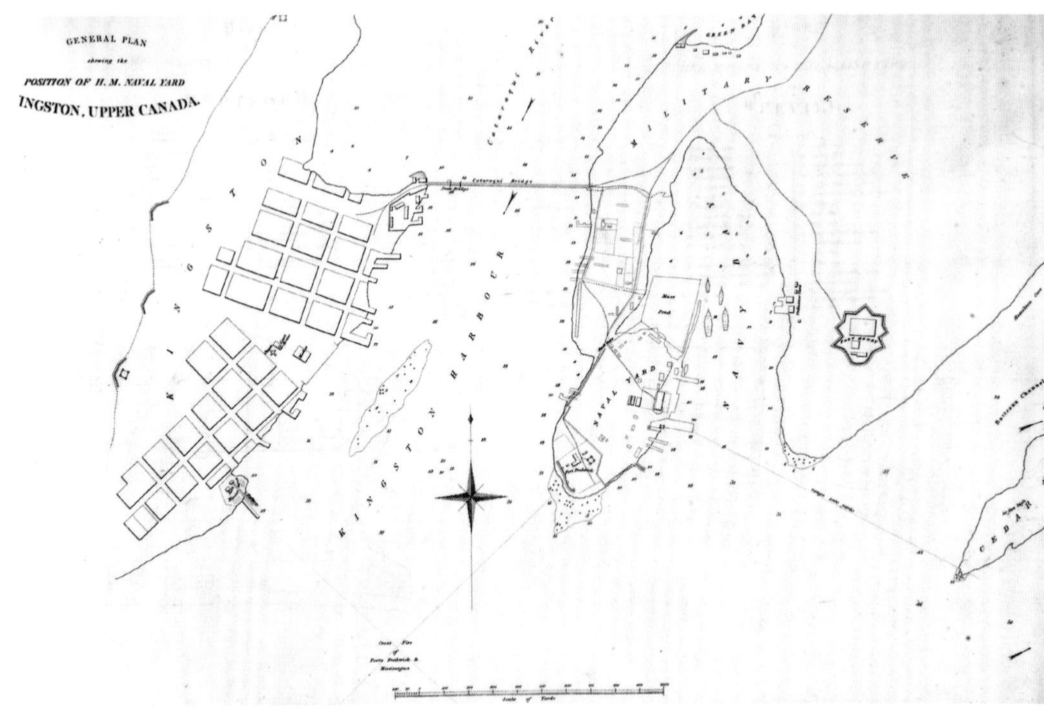

Fig 12.21 (right)
The town and dockyard of Kingston, Ontario, in 1840. By then the dockyard existed on a limited 'care and maintenance' basis. (AdL Plans of Naval Establishments c 1840 Da 01 fol 18)

many of which are probably those buildings listed on a yard plan of around 1840 (Fig 12.21). These included smiths' and joiners' shops, a tar house, offices, stables, three houses, two described as 'in temporary repair', a porter's lodge and a guardhouse. The three slips are also shown on this plan, although by then long disused.[64]

A little outside the yard, still standing in its own grounds, is a handsome two-storey stone building constructed soon after the war as a small naval hospital. Its designed use seems to have lasted only a few years, before it simply became the naval surgeon's quarters, and as such it is identified on an 1863 plan of the yard long after the navy had departed.[65] The stone storehouse became seamen's barracks in the last years of the dockyard, foreshadowing its later use as accommodation for the cadets at the military college (Fig 12.22); later it was given an additional wing. The hospital, storehouse, porter's lodge, guardhouse and a length of the dockyard wall remain the sole survivors of the many yard buildings constructed over an 80-year period for the various flotillas of the freshwater navy.

In 1817 the British minister in Washington, Sir Charles Bagot, and the Acting Secretary of State, Richard Rush, reached a formal agreement, named after them, to reduce naval forces on the lakes. Each country could maintain on the upper lakes two warships not exceeding 100 tons and armed with a single 18pdr gun, and a single warship of the same size on Lake Ontario and one on Lake Champlain.[66] Although this effectively marked the end of the freshwater navies, a number of proposals were put forward in the following years to improve the yards. Commodore Robert Barrie, commissioner at Kingston, remained concerned how to maintain his small fleet in ordinary there. Life expectancy of such ships in fresh water was only some 7 or 8 years,[67] and lack of a dry dock and a suitable place to excavate one made hull repairs difficult. In October 1819 he sent to the Admiralty a novel proposal by Robert Moore, the master shipwright, 'a very zealous and ingenious officer', to construct on the ice over the winter a timber dry dock that could be sunk into position on the creek bed in the spring thaw. Its hollow sides were to be ballasted with stones and secured on top of a stout timber raft. Its internal dimensions were to be some 230ft in length with an entrance width of 50ft, and the entrance would be closed by a caisson. Pumping out the dock would require a powerful steam engine 'and proper persons to erect and attend it', but this could also be used to power a sawmill 'and various other uses'. Barrie reckoned that as 'a very large engine would be difficult for us to get repaired in this country, I would propose two engines of about 40 horse power each, being sent out'.[68] Perhaps not surprisingly, in an era of post-war retrenchment, nothing more was heard

Fig 12.22
The former naval storehouse at Kingston, Ontario, now used as accommodation by the Royal Military College. (Author)

of the proposal. In 1829, a scheme was put forward for a new 'Naval Arsenal' at Penetanguishene to replace the existing timber buildings, and 2 years later a building was inspected for possible use as a naval barracks at the Isle aux Noix.[69] Nothing more was heard.

In March 1834 the Admiralty ordered Barrie to close all the Royal Navy yards on the lakes, and the Kingston yard was left in charge of a watchman. As it turned out, this did not mark the end of the Royal Navy's involvement with Kingston or the Great Lakes. The Upper Canada Rebellion of 1837 saw the yard reactivated by Captain William Sandom, who assembled a small fleet that included six steamers and five schooners. By 1839 operations had been heavily scaled back, but money for maintenance of the base appeared at intervals in the annual estimates up to 1849/50.[70] In 1866, threatened by armed raids into Canada from the States by the Fenian Brotherhood and by now lacking an operational yard, the Royal Navy despatched from Britain three of the smallest gunboats of the Britomart class to patrol the Great Lakes and supplement the local paddle steamers that had been hastily commandeered and armed.[71] These gunboats were withdrawn as the crisis subsided.

In 1868 the Admiralty ordered that any remaining stores and vessels should be disposed of and Kingston transferred to the Ordnance Department, 'to be held by that department and kept in repair so long as that may not be required for the Naval Service'. In 1870 what were described as 'The Naval Reserves at Point Frederick' were handed over to the Dominion Government with the stipulation that 'the properties were to be put to no other use than for naval purposes and for the Defence of Canada'.[72] In 1874 the Royal Military College of Canada was established here, which still fulfils the latter part of the Admiralty's 1870 stipulation.

Kingston itself was very much a 'frontier town' on the Canadian/United States border and in the first half of the 19th century was provided with a number of forts and redoubts and, at the time of the Oregon crisis, with a chain of Martello towers (Fig 12.23). Most of these fortifications still remain.[73] At the beginning of the 20th century, as part of a wider review of Canadian land defences, the Admiralty looked at the possibility of reviving the naval base, especially as there was now a government dry dock on the town waterfront, but concluded that the dockyard's position so near the border made it too vulnerable.[74] In January 1908 the Imperial General Staff noted that 'Naval Command of the Great Lakes, more especially of Lakes Erie and Ontario, would be of grave importance to Canada in the event of war with the United States, and recent increases in the number and power of United States' war vessels in the waters have inspired some anxiety in the Dominion'. The Rush-Bagot Agreement was cited, the General Staff noting that 'gradual modifications of the Agreement are more likely to engender ill-feeling than its total abrogation. If, however, abrogation is to come, the responsibility for it should be thrown upon the United States'.[75] There was no suggestion on this occasion that the navy should recolonise the Lakes, and like other such alarms, this one subsided.

Fig 12.23
One of the chain of Martello Towers constructed in the 1840s at the time of the Oregon Crisis to protect Kingston, Ontario, and its harbour.
(Author)

Halifax

Before the founding of the naval base at Halifax, warships on the North American station needing repairs, careening or supplies had to use commercial yards on the east coast, notably at Boston, Manhattan Island, Norfolk, Charleston and Philadelphia. Lack of a naval base was a concern of successive commanders, and a number of possible sites were proposed over the years. The fine natural harbour at Chebucto on the east coast of Nova Scotia was unsuccessfully recommended to the Admiralty by Captain Thomas Durell in 1732, 17 years before Halifax was founded here as the new capital of the province.[76] In 1745 the capture of the great French fortress of Louisbourg on Cape Breton Island led Commodore Warren to suggest that a careening wharf should be established there. In 1746 the Navy Board sent out the necessary equipment, but use of the facilities ended with the return of the fortress to France in 1749.

Over the next few years growing rivalry with France saw a substantial increase in the number of Royal Navy ships on station, and in the autumn of 1755–6 for the first time a squadron of seven ships under Commodore Sir Richard Spry overwintered at Halifax, his ships' crews overhauling the vessels.[77] The outbreak of the Seven Years' War, with its concentration on Anglo-French rivalries in North America, provided a further spur to the creation of a proper careening base. The catalyst may have been the hurricane in September 1757 that nearly destroyed Vice-Admiral Francis Holburne's squadron blockading Louisbourg. Damaged ships struggled back to Halifax, severely straining its limited facilities and supplies, and the following year the Admiralty authorised the Navy Board to create a base there (Fig 12.24). Edward Boscawen, preoccupied with the siege of Louisbourg, delegated the choice of site to Commodore Philip Durell.

A slightly earlier attempt to found a careening yard on Cornwallis Island (now McNab's Island) in the harbour was deemed impracticable.[78] Instead, Durell selected the site of an abandoned farm that included a watering wharf constructed by Spry in 1755 about a mile to the north of the new town. Here there was deep water close inshore, subsoil that would take foundation piles and a natural pond that could be adapted as a mast pond. At least one of the two surviving barns was adapted as a storehouse.[79] Contracts for the construction of the yard fell to the

Fig 12.24
The naval estate at Halifax in 1863, shortly before the railway was built parallel to Water Street, severing the grounds of Admiralty House. The dockyard itself had altered little since the 1770s.
(AdL Naval Establishments 1863 Da 02 fol 12)

storekeeper, Joseph Gerrish, as Durell was by then absent with Major-General James Wolfe on the expedition to Quebec. By 1760, when Captain James Cook was starting his 3-year survey of the harbour and its approaches, local contractors had completed the nucleus of the small yard, centred on a careening wharf and enclosed by a 10ft-high wooden fence.[80] The original extent of this yard was about 7 acres, but over the next quarter of a century further land was acquired, most notably in 1763 at its north end, in 1764 as the site for a naval hospital and in 1783, when 20 acres were added for a burial ground and a location for Admiralty House.[81]

The new base occupied a strip of land along the harbour's edge, the terrain sloping up to high ground to the west. The yard's layout, along with a number of its early buildings, remained largely intact from the early 1770s into the 20th century. At its centre was the first careening wharf with the capstan house at its head. Nearby were a boathouse and slip, mast house (Fig 12.25), smithery, pitch house, sawpits, guardhouse and porter's lodge by the yard entrance. Around 1770 a detached storehouse was constructed immediately to the south of the rear wings of the capstan house, effectively creating a courtyard (Fig 12.26). This courtyard was later laid out as a formal garden when part of the complex was used as barracks for the crews of ships being careened or repaired, a use first suggested in 1772 (Fig 12.27). Nearby stood the Commissioner's House of 1785, replacing an earlier and smaller residence originally built for the storekeeper (Fig 12.28). This was supplemented in 1793 by a handsome terrace of three weatherboarded houses, originally for the

Fig 12.25 (below top) The 18th-century mast house at Halifax, a timber-framed building of considerable size known as 7 Store at the time of this photograph in the 1890s. (TNA ADM 195/49 fol 15a)

Fig 12.26 (below bottom) The dockyard at Halifax in 1771 viewed from the harbour. A warship is shown being careened, while nearby is a stock of spare anchors. (© National Maritime Museum, Greenwich, London, Lad11 fol 51)

Fig 12.27
Part of the quadrangle of buildings completed at Halifax by 1770. By the time of this photograph in the 1890s, the buildings had been largely reconstructed in stone, and this range was in use as seamen's barracks. (TNA ADM 195/49 fol 7b)

naval officer, master shipwright and master attendant (*see* Fig 7.13 and Chapter 7).[82]

In 1771 Rear-Admiral James Gambier appears to have advocated construction of a dry dock here, the earliest to be proposed at an overseas yard. Nothing came of this suggestion, which would have revolutionised the ability of the yard to undertake major repairs, but in 1800 its importance as a careening base was emphasised by the adaptation of the existing anchor wharf to form a second careening wharf capable of accommodating a 50-gun warship. That year also saw construction of a second mast pond at the northern end of the yard.[83] At the very end of the Napoleonic Wars a new house standing in substantial grounds was built for the Port Admiral and was completed in 1819 (*see* Fig 7.12). Not surprisingly, the house saw little of its intended use, as the admiral had also been allocated a second house in the balmier climes of Bermuda. Admiralty House at Bermuda was burnt down in 1974; Admiralty House at Halifax is now the dockyard museum.[84]

Halifax was the only British naval base sited where winters were invariably harsh, sometimes with ice floes in the harbour and the waterfront rimmed with ice. Such extremes of weather had an impact on the dockyard, where severe frost could lead to 'ground heave', destroying roads and causing major settlement in buildings. Weight of snow also damaged roofs and gutters. Until proper storm drains were installed and maintained, the disadvantage of being at the foot of a steep slope was all too apparent during wet weather, Sir Samuel Hood noting 'the great impetuosity' of the rainwater rushing down and through the yard. Not surprisingly, the effect of the climate is evident in the amount of repairs and maintenance found to be necessary. The timber capstan house of 1760 was rebuilt in stone in 1768 and along with the storehouse of 1770 was again extensively rebuilt in 1783.[85] But in a land where timber was cheap and abundant, framed buildings remained very much part of the yard scene, with stone tending to be used only for the more important buildings, such as Admiralty House.

Fig 12.28
The Commissioner's House of 1785 at Halifax with its distinctive roof-top balcony. By the time of this late 19th-century photograph, the building was described as 'officers' barracks'. (TNA ADM 195/49 fol 4b)

After 1815 the base remained at the periphery of Royal Navy operations, supporting a station occupied with patrolling fishing grounds, showing the flag and keeping a distant eye on American activities. In general the North American squadron visited Halifax only in the summer. In 1819 the base was reduced to a minor stores depot; when the hospital burnt down that year a succession of hulks was used as unsatisfactory stopgaps, and a new building was not provided until 1863.[86] In practical terms of importance to the Royal Navy, Halifax Yard was on a par with English Harbour, but its closure would have been unthinkable so soon after the War of 1812 and amid recurrent suspicions of American intentions which caused occasional brief flurries of activities here. The term 'imperial fortress' had yet to be coined, but the withdrawal of the Royal Navy and the shutting of the naval base within the fortified harbour and beneath the guns of Halifax Citadel would have reverberated across the North American continent. In 1832 the Admiralty approved Halifax as the principal refitting yard for the North American and West Indies station, but the practical import of this may have been muted, as warships needing major repairs were still sent to Britain.[87]

This diminished role in the 19th century is reflected in the paucity of new buildings and the generally neglected state of the yard, the result of inadequate and irregular maintenance funds. Only the most essential new building work was authorised, as in 1832 when £250 was allocated to replace the pitch house destroyed in an accidental fire.[88] In June 1839 permission was requested by Vice-Admiral Sir Thomas Harvey to construct a coal shed for 400 chaldrons of coal 'for the use of steam vessels calling here'. Further coal stores were to be added over the next 60 years. A month later the Admiralty was 'pleased to allow Mr S. Cunard to occupy the vacant ground outside the dockyard at Halifax for the purpose of erecting a patent slip and an establishment for making and repairing steam machinery', with the proviso that Royal Navy ships should have priority use of the slip 'at the rate of five guineas for the first day and two guineas for each day after for a ship of 500 tons'.[89]

The 1860s saw a minor flurry of building activity and construction of a new smithery, coal store and jetty at the yard in 1868, but the general impression remains of a neglected establishment. An 1867 report referred to the rum store as 'damp and walls dirty', the guardhouse 'filthy from old age and rotten materials', the mast pond 'very offensive', as the drains from the officers' houses discharged into it, and the bread store full of 'old blankets used by fever patients'.[90] In February 1864 the Director of Works, Godfrey Greene, had signed off the year's estimates that included money for a new naval hospital and victualling buildings here. The new hospital was a long, narrow building of four floors built of brick with a stone basement, much of which survives, although obscured by more modern development.[91] The modest victualling yard at the foot of Observatory Hill (levelled in 1881–2) made use of an existing cooperage building at the north of the naval base. The space between this and the adjacent terrace of three timber-framed houses, built in 1815 for the medical staff of the nearby hospital, was filled by a large weatherboarded victualling store (Fig 12.29), the first tangible evidence in the yard of the Admiralty decision in 1832 to create a depot here, no doubt the result of the move to make the yard a refitting base.[92]

Fig 12.29
The victualling storehouse at Halifax in the 1890s. (TNA ADM 195/49 fol 17b)

Apart from further coal stores, the most conspicuous additions to the yard in the last decades of the 19th century were a pair of slips with a boat shed for two torpedo boats for local defence and a small brick-built gun-mounting workshop. In 1864 a Select Committee had recommended that Bermuda should have priority for a dry dock ahead of Jamaica or Halifax, but in 1886 the Admiralty made its largest investment at its Nova Scotia base when it agreed to part-fund the Dominion Government's construction of a commercial dry dock just outside the yard boundary, contributing $200,000 in 20 annual instalments. In the opening years of the 20th century, an ambitious plan was drawn up to reorganise and modernise the whole yard at a cost of some £330,000, but this was shelved in December 1902, the Admiralty preferring to concentrate on Bermuda. Geological problems at Bermuda prevented construction of a dry dock, and a floating one had to be sent from Britain (*see* Chapter 10).[93]

On 22 December 1904 the Commander-in-Chief North America was informed by the Admiralty that Halifax and Port Royal were to close, 'that is to say, they will be reduced to "cadres" on which no money will be spent in time of peace, but which can be developed in war according to necessity'.[94] In the global scheme both were modest yards. At the time, Port Royal had more facilities, but Halifax had the advantage of easy access to the adjacent commercial dry dock. After a few years of 'care and maintenance', Halifax was transferred in 1910 to the new Royal Canadian Navy.[95] Much of the yard still retained its 18th-century form, as well as many of the buildings. Subsequent redevelopment and especially the explosion of the ammunition ship *Mont Blanc* in the harbour in December 1917, when most of Halifax and the dockyard were destroyed, have meant that only Admiralty House, the hospital and some of the victualling yard residences predate 1900. Around 2,000 people lost their lives and 10,000 were injured in the explosion. Admiralty House is now a naval museum. The former hospital became a naval college and then offices. The residences remain in use.

Esquimalt

By the late 1860s the Royal Navy's Pacific Squadron numbered some 10 ships and around 2,000 men, with its headquarters at Valparaiso in Chile. A move north to Vancouver Island, suggested in 1859, became a reality in 1870 (*see* Chapter 10).[96] The new naval base at Esquimalt Harbour overlooked Juan de Fuca Strait at the southern end of Vancouver Island (Fig 12.30). Its location was more central to Canadian and British interests and shortened the time taken to reach China from 3½ to 2 months. The navy had been a regular visitor

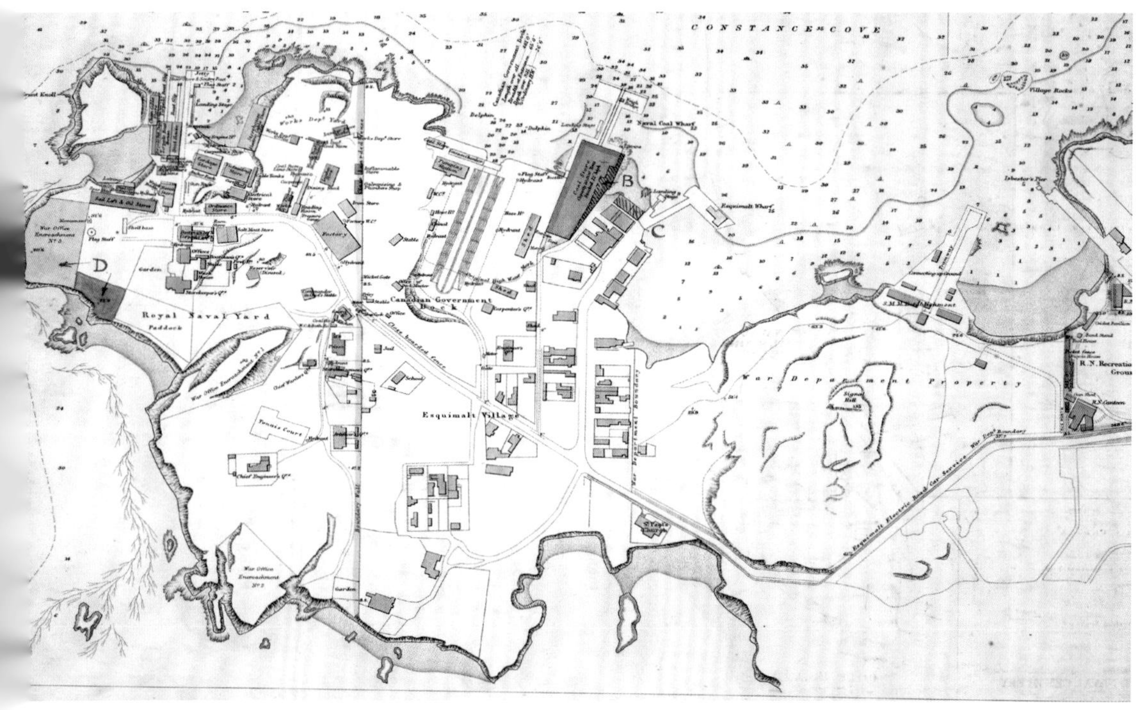

Fig 12.30
The naval base at Esquimalt in 1900, with the dockyard and the naval coal yard on either side of the government dry dock.
(AdL Vz 15/27)

to the coast of British Columbia since the 1840s, and following the Oregon Boundary dispute of 1846 had charted the waters at the southern end of Vancouver Island. At this time Victoria was first established, and the Hudson's Bay Company, already active in the area, set up a trading post. Following the 1850s gold rushes Victoria grew rapidly, in 1866 becoming capital of British Columbia.

The first modest naval installations were temporary sawpits and small stores buildings constructed on Thetis Island in the early 1850s, followed by three substantial timber huts erected in 1855 on Duntze Head by the harbour entrance as a hospital for 100 patients, in case of further naval casualties from Crimean War operations off the Kamchatka peninsula.[97] Stores were also kept here, and after the war the navy used one of the buildings as a hydrographic office for HMS *Plumper*, engaged in surveying the coast of British Columbia from 1857 to 1861. In August 1858 the War Department purchased land on the eastern side of the harbour adjacent to Pilgrim Cove for a hutted camp (Fig 12.31) for the Royal Engineers, who were sent out that year to work with their American counterparts on the Boundary Commission, establishing the frontier between the United States and British Columbia west of the Rocky Mountains. This work had added urgency in the wake of the 1846 Oregon Boundary Treaty and the huge influx of American and other gold prospectors, arousing suspicions of America's expansionist tendencies.[98] In 1859 when the Admiralty first seriously considered relocating the Pacific Squadron to Esquimalt to counter any American or Russian threats, it promised in a memorandum that 'If these powers have dockyards and resources in the North Pacific, and we have not, for every shilling spent by either of them … we shall spend a guinea.'[99] A naval base close to the American frontier was a very tangible part of the process of establishing British Columbia's territorial rights.

In the early 1860s a small naval armaments depot was established on Cole Island at the remote northern end of the harbour.[100] In 1862 the Admiralty took over the engineers' camp at Esquimalt as the naval hospital, acquiring nearby land for a cemetery (Fig 12.32) and freeing up space for a dockyard on the lee of the rocky promontory, ending at Duntze Head at the southern end of the harbour. Three years later the base was formally established, to be protected subsequently by coastal batteries here and across the harbour entrance at Rodd Hill.[101] Nearby in the harbour, a coaling depot was laid out on Thetis Island, physically joined to the dockyard by ensuing land reclamation (Fig 12.33). The base was the first to be built overseas for the steam navy and consequently never had a careening wharf. Its prime purpose was as a stores depot with workshops sufficient to maintain the squadron; its small size meant that victualling storehouses were also located within the yard rather than in a separate establishment, as at the larger bases. There was a flurry of building activity in the early years, but the sums allocated were small and were largely spent on further timber buildings, most probably storehouses (Fig 12.34).

Fig 12.31
The timber buildings constructed at Esquimalt for the Royal Engineers and adapted in 1862 as a naval hospital, replacing facilities at Duntze Head.
(© National Maritime Museum, Greenwich, London, Album 151, f.95)

Fig 12.32
A small naval cemetery and chapel were among the first facilities established at the new base of Esquimalt on Canada's Pacific coast. (Author)

Fig 12.33
The timber coal shed and coaling jetty on Thetis Island, Esquimalt. The island was joined to the mainland by the time of this photograph in the 1890s. (TNA ADM 195/4 fol 16)

Fig 12.34
The 'first generation' of buildings at Esquimalt, such as this storehouse, were nearly all timber framed. (TNA ADM 195/4 fol 10)

Fig 12.35 (below right) A naval working party ashore at Esquimalt c 1870 in the early days of this Pacific base. Anchored in the harbour beyond are ships of the Pacific Squadron. (© National Maritime Museum, Greenwich, London, L5703)

By 1869 the annual estimates for the yard had been reduced to £100 for maintenance, and in 1870 the yard staff amounted to fewer than a dozen people, comprising a paymaster, a clerk, two temporary writers and two labourers. With the exception of a single labourer, they all worked for the victualling department.[102] Until 1879 when a resident chief engineer was appointed, it would seem that the few yard workshops were manned as necessary by the engineering staff of visiting warships (Fig 12.35). The new house provided for the chief engineer is the only one dating from the Admiralty period and one of the few timber-framed buildings remaining in the yard.[103]

The change in importance of Esquimalt followed the decision by the Provincial Government to construct with the aid of an Admiralty subsidy a dry dock adjacent to the base. Although the first tenders were sought in April 1872, a series of problems delayed construction, and it was not completed until 1887 (Fig 12.36).[104] This was a spur to the modernisation and rebuilding of the yard, which were undertaken in the 20 years preceding the Royal Navy's withdrawal from Esquimalt in 1905. In 1901, echoing similar sentiments on the rebuilding of Portsmouth and Plymouth nearly a century and a half earlier, the Superintending Engineer, Mr T Sims, reported:

> The policy of gradually replacing the old wooden buildings by others of more permanent construction is being steadily followed … The new Storehouse and Shipwrights' Shop … reflect great credit on the Assistant Engineer and his staff. These buildings were both carried out by departmental labour in a very satisfactory manner, and appear to be excellently adapted to their respective purposes … in a few years time when the remainder of the wooden buildings are replaced by permanent structures the cost of maintenance should be less than at present.[105]

Fig 12.36 (below) HMS Phaeton, *a 2nd-class cruiser built at Napier's Clyde yard, in the government dry dock at Esquimalt. Such wintry conditions were more typical of Halifax than Esquimalt. (*Navy and Army Illustrated *16 July 1898, 388)*

In 1885 the naval storeskeeper was provided with a handsome and substantial house, now Admiral's House, in a commanding position overlooking the harbour entrance. This is a rare instance of a building here designed and very probably built by an outside architect and contractor, John Teague, who had an extensive practice in Victoria (*see* Chapter 4). He would also be responsible for the new buildings of the naval hospital, and it is possible he designed some of the more utilitarian dockyard buildings.[106] The majority of the dockyard buildings from this later period are comparatively small in scale, of red brick with simple functional design and minimal ornamentation. Notable buildings include the factory, which was originally constructed as a timber-framed building in 1866 and rebuilt in brick and extended in 1889, 1891 and 1903 (Fig 12.37). Also of note are the Rum and Salt Meat Stores of 1895–6, the Shipwrights' Shop of 1901 and the Ordnance Stores of 1902.

Perhaps the most remarkable building is the storehouse constructed in 1898, its concrete basement built into the slope of the rock and partly extending into the harbour, with entrances allowing small boats to enter the building to load stores, an arrangement matched by the two surviving Filled Shell Stores on Cole Island, but unparalleled in any other Royal Navy storehouses.[107] The two floors above are built of brick, their loading doors distinguished by rusticated quoins. The storehouse was designed by an engineer on the base, Thomas Woodgate, who may have trained as a Royal Engineer and was responsible for a number of other buildings here during this period.[108] The last substantial building to be constructed was the Sailors' Barracks for 74 men, 8 petty officers and a warrant officer. Built of random rubble with brick detailing, this two-storey building was designed to accommodate the crew of a warship in for a refit or repairs, but within a year of its completion the Royal Navy was being withdrawn, and in 1910 the base was formally transferred to the new Royal Canadian Navy. Today the surviving buildings, including those of the former naval hospital (*see* Chapter 16), are the most complete collection of late 19th-century naval buildings to remain from one of the Royal Navy's smaller overseas bases.

Fig 12.37.
The heart of the yard at Esquimalt, with the factory on the left and the Rum and Salt Meat Stores on the right. These brick buildings are typical of the final phase of redevelopment by the Royal Navy.
(Author)

Bermuda

Bermuda, an archipelago of small islands some 580 miles off the coast of North Carolina, was first settled in 1612 and became a Crown Colony in 1684. Its importance to the Royal Navy followed the loss of the American colonies and the use of their ports on the eastern seaboard of the United States. By 1795 a small contingent of dockyard workers were established at Bermuda's capital, St George, but shoals and the narrow approach channel precluded development of an adequate naval base. By then, Captain Hurd's meticulous survey, begun in 1783 of the waters and reefs surrounding the islands, was nearing completion, resulting in the crucial discovery of the 'Narrows Passage', a navigable channel for large ships into Great Sound, a vast stretch of water sheltered by the curving chain of islands terminating at its northern end in Watford, Boas and Ireland Islands.[109] Following the advice of Sir John Borlase Warren, the Vice-Admiral on station in 1808, the Admiralty started to acquire land on these islands in 1809.[110]

The site selected for the new dockyard was Grassy Bay on the southern side of Ireland Island overlooking Great Sound (Fig 12.38). Fortuitously for the Navy Board, this was largely composed of some of the hardest limestone in Bermuda, ideal construction material for naval buildings, the great breakwater and the massive defences that were to transform the island over the next half century. Its drawback lay in unexpected fissures and substantial hidden voids, which occasionally caused problems with foundations and would prevent the construction of any dry docks.

Between 1810 and 1816 over £145,000 was spent on levelling the site and constructing a piecemeal group of storehouse, residences and other buildings to enable the base to start functioning.[111] By 1814 the nascent yard had a workforce of 51 people. Although Edward Holl had been involved in London in the design process, local initiatives were clearly exercised, for as he subsequently complained, 'on examining the plans, elevations, and sections brought home by Mr Fulton, of the buildings already erected, I am sorry to observe that, on comparing them with the originals in my office ... there are very few instances in which they have been conformed to'.[112] By then Holl and John Rennie senior were completing estimates for a fully fledged dockyard containing a ropeyard and a dry dock centred on a large basin protected by a breakwater. Adjacent was to be a separate victualling yard. These were on an altogether grander scale than anything at Halifax, the nearest British yard.

The remote location on the island explains why outside the yard the proposals included 18 cottages, an inn or store and a covered market, the last also a feature of the contemporary development at the equally rural Pembroke Dockyard in Wales. Allowing for contingencies, the grand total was estimated at £648,548, of which the dry dock accounted for £156,174 and the breakwater £306,434. In an innovative move, Rennie proposed that the dry dock should be lined with iron plates to overcome problems with the porous and fissured rock.[113] The Navy Board then commissioned Josias Jessop to visit Bermuda to examine all possible options for the location of 'a principal naval station'. If the

Fig 12.38
An 1823 plan of Ireland Island, Bermuda. The early naval buildings are marked, while the proposed basin (part shown) was very similar in scale and plan to the one eventually constructed.
(TNA MPH 1/611)

Board had been motivated by the hope that there might be a cheaper alternative, Jessop's report in October 1819[114] was probably a disappointment, as he supported a base on Ireland Island and recommended that local stone rather than wood be used whenever possible for buildings. Significantly for the future, he also advised the demolition of the existing Commissioner's House, which was in the way of developments and was 'of little value and being of timber in a state of decay'. He suggested locating its successor on the northern tip of Ireland Island, where it would be out of the way of future dockyard works, 'and it would stand more conveniently to communicate by signal with the other parts of the islands and anchorages'.[115] In the event, the only elements of these proposals that were implemented were construction of the Commissioner's House and, over a rather longer period, the civil engineering works for the naval base. In a separate development in 1818, a naval hospital was also built at the southern end of Ireland Island. This was demolished in 1972 with the exception of the former zymotic or isolation block, constructed in 1899 and now known as Lefroy House.[116]

Progress on the new base was slow. In part, the immediately post-war years were a time for financial retrenchment on the part of the Admiralty, already preoccupied with rebuilding Sheerness and completing Pembroke, but a more fundamental reason was the need to coordinate work with the Royal Engineers who were constructing the defences. In July 1811 Captain Thomas Cunningham had arrived with instructions to secure the naval base and improve the islands' defences as relations with America drifted towards war. Cunningham departed in August 1816, and by the time his successor, Major Thomas Blanshard, arrived in 1822, only a defensive ditch protecting the western approach to the dockyard was completed. Blanshard had rather more ambitious plans for fortifications, noting the growth in the proposed yard and the addition of a breakwater. Levelling a larger area for the yard he felt would not only reduce the costs of forming escarps on the proposed fortifications, but would provide ashlar for these and the yard buildings, as well as rubble for the breakwater enclosing the basin. Work began in 1822, using a combination of local labour and the first of over 9,000 convicts held on prison hulks. The extensive quarrying and blasting involved in winning the stone and levelling the site led to damage to buildings in the vicinity and were major impediments to any progress with the naval base.[117] A number of modifications to the proposed fortifications were made after a visit in 1826 by Colonel Edward Fanshawe, and the work was finally finished in 1843, with the exception of the incomplete breakwater.[118] The fortifications included an irregular bastioned fort at the northern end of Ireland Island, linked to a bastioned defence work enclosing the western seaward side and landward end of the dockyard.

Between 1822 and 1845 the most significant investment in the naval base, apart from the gradual levelling of its site, was the construction of wharf walls, a slip and the careening wharf and capstan pits at the northern end of the basin. Holl's clerk of works, Smith, was in charge of the site work. All this and work on the breakwater, where diving bells were employed, cost £91,641 between 1823 and the end of December 1831.[119] By 1828 the broad outline of the base and the location of buildings were being planned,[120] but the only building to be constructed before 1845 was the commissioner's new house within the bastioned keep, where it overlooked the dockyard from a distance and was relatively safe from blasting operations (Figs 12.39 and 12.40). The house was designed by Holl in 1822, and construction started in May 1823 under the supervision of Smith. On Holl's death in November that year, his successor George Ledwell Taylor took on the responsibility for the detailed drawings and saw the building through to completion in 1831.

Commissioner's House is a remarkable essay in the use of local stone for the walls and cast and wrought iron for roof members and for veranda and floor supports (*see* Fig 7.4), following Holl's slightly earlier use of this combination of materials for the naval hospital at Port Royal. The ironwork was employed not just on account of its durability and strength, but because it could be prefabricated in Britain along with some of the architectural stonework and most of the fittings, including fireplaces, doors and frames, impost mouldings, skirtings, plinths, fanlights and shutters. Most of the joinery was apparently produced by Jeffrey Wyatt's workshop conveniently adjacent to the Navy Board's headquarters at Somerset House, allowing Holl, as he noted, to 'have an opportunity of attending personally' to check on the quality of materials and workmanship, before the items were shipped downriver to

Fig 12.39
Looking across to the Commissioner's House at Bermuda, from the southern rampart of Keep Yard, showing the sheltered location of the ordnance buildings (see also *Fig 7.4*). *In the centre is the small basin, with the boat tunnel through the fortifications to Great Sound on the right. (Author)*

Fig 12.40 (right)
An 1847 watercolour by Michael Seymour of the view from the Commissioner's House at Bermuda across the levelled area for the proposed dockyard to the fortifications at the southern end.
(Fay and Geoffrey Elliott Collection, Bermuda Archives, DAP 4.2.00047)

transports at Woolwich.[121] Holl hoped that using prefabricated parts would also lessen the ability of local officials to alter approved designs, but in this instance he met his match with the commissioner, who insisted on the expensive addition of a basement and the removal of domestic offices further from the main building. Ironically, the year after completion of the building, the post of commissioner was abolished, and for most of its life the house was used as marine barracks and its service area as a naval prison.[122] After decades of dereliction following the dockyard's closure in 1951, Commissioner's House was meticulously restored by the Bermuda Maritime Museum.

Following completion of Commissioner's House, work began on the ordnance yard, on an immediately adjacent site to the south, within the ramparts. This had its own dock for small craft formed from a natural void in the rock and defended by a portcullis where a short tunnel passed through the ramparts (*see* Fig 15.35). Known as Keep Yard, this still has its set of stone and brick-vaulted ordnance stores, magazines and shifting houses built between 1837 and 1852, their contents designed for use by both the navy and the land defences (*see also* Chapter 15). These are now part of the National Museum of Bermuda and used as exhibition halls.

Although quarrying and levelling operations on the site of the dockyard were finished by 1843, construction work did not start before 1845, when a sum of £5,000 in the estimates for New Works and Buildings is probably to be identified with the two handsome victualling yard storehouses facing each other across a courtyard to the south-west of Keep Yard. These were constructed using convict labour and are shown as 'now in progress of construction' on an 1847 yard plan.[123] The navy meantime was still relying on a few timber buildings completed a quarter of a century earlier. In 1849 the new Commander-in-Chief, Lord Dundonald, was moved to complain to the Admiralty that 'the space enclosed by ramparts is an entire void, except the half-finished victualling store, and two small wooden buildings to be pulled down'.[124] It is probably Dundonald's influence as much as anything that galvanised the Admiralty into further activity.

After a gap of some years when little was apparently done, the 1849/50 estimates included £66,000 for the naval yard and £30,000 for the Victualling Yard. A paragraph attached to the 1851/2 estimates noted that these sums were 'for continuing buildings at the victualling yard, for completing the buildings for factory purposes, and for proceeding with one of the large storehouses, the sum taken being no more than sufficient to give full employment to the convicts'.[125] Work was largely complete by 1860, when the annual estimate had dropped to £6,670 and it was noted that £1,330 would complete the buildings. The only outstanding item was the 'hauling up slip', where it was noted that there was 'slow progress'. This is the small patent slip that appears on one side of the main boat slip in later yard plans.[126]

The final addition that transformed the capabilities of the yard was the arrival in July 1869 of the ironclads HMS *Warrior* and HMS *Black Prince* towing the Royal Navy's first floating dock, constructed at the Thames yard of Campbell, Johnson and Co. Designed to lift 10,000 tons, the dock measured 380ft by 124ft wide and 72ft high and was then the largest in the world (*see* Fig 10.6).[127] Its estimated cost of £250,000 made it by far the most expensive component of the naval facilities here, its construction reflecting the requirement of the new ironclads coming into service and a tacit admission that a conventional dry dock at Bermuda was impossible because of the geological problems. Four years later money was provided for a 'machine shop for repairing iron ships', which was built to the south of the main storehouses. In 1875, heavy-lifting capacity for removing and installing machinery and gun turrets from warships was provided by a massive sheer-legs with a 90ft clearance at 30ft outward lean, which was erected on the main wharf.[128] As completed by the mid-1860s, the size and type of equipment in the yard reflected the role expected of Bermuda naval base.[129] It was not in such a strategically or politically sensitive location as to warrant the scale of facilities provided at Malta, but Bermuda was the principal base on a station that extended over a vast area of ocean. It therefore needed to have the requisite skills and equipment to maintain the ships and sailors of the squadron, and some spare capacity was needed in order to deal with any unexpected increase in the size of the squadron.

The new yard had been laid out on relatively spacious and formal lines (Fig 12.41). The principal buildings of the Victualling Yard were the two substantial storehouses (Fig 12.42), together with a cask store and cooperage; unlike Malta the numbers of sailors here were not considered sufficient to justify a bakery. To the south and flanking its main entrance, two pairs of semi-detached houses for the senior staff were constructed facing south over the main dockyard (Fig 12.43). In 1863, in the twilight years of the sailing navy, these housed the boatswain, foreman of shipwrights, Victualling Agent and storekeeper; by 1891 the first three had been replaced by the master attendant, the inspector of machinery and the engineer constructor.[130]

Immediately in front of the houses an inlet and boat slip led to a range of stone boathouses and mast and spar stores. At the time these buildings were constructed, it was still hoped to provide a conventional dry dock, and space was left for one running parallel to the inlet and extending to the rear of the curtain wall

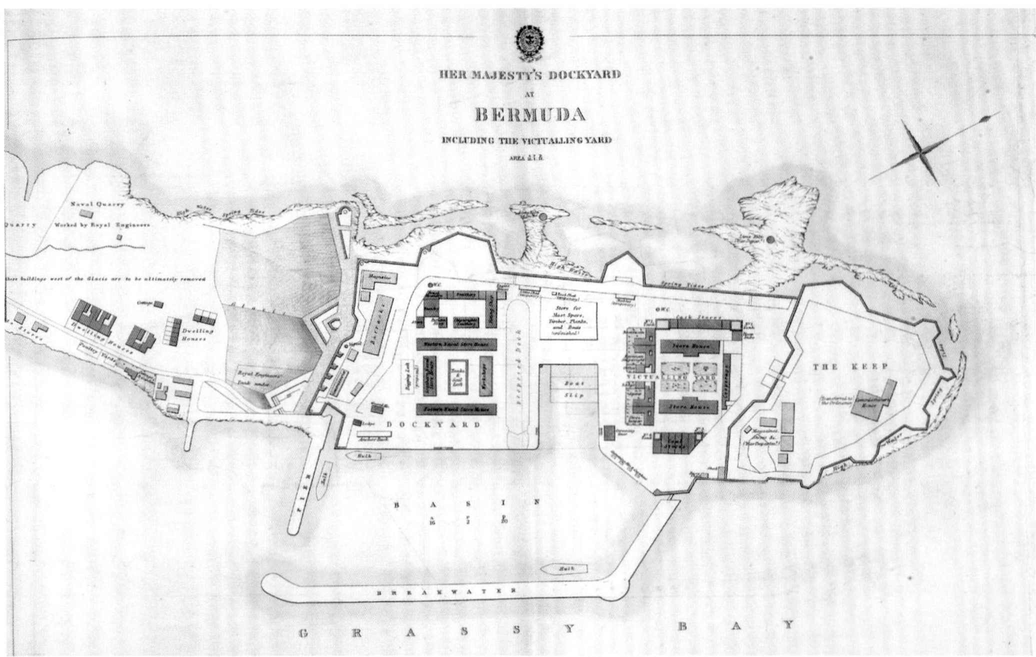

Fig 12.41
An 1858 plan of the dockyard at Bermuda. Although this allocated space for a dry dock, geological difficulties forced the Admiralty to provide a floating dock. The only major addition before 1914 was the second or South Basin, adding a further 22 acres of sheltered water. (AdL Da 022 fol X1)

Fig 12.42
One of the pair of victualling yard storehouses at Bermuda. (Author)

Fig 12.43
Houses for the senior officers at Bermuda, next to the entrance to the victualling yard. (Author)

protecting the seaward side of the yard.[131] South of the inlet, occupying most of the remaining space within the corset of the bastioned defences, lay the heart of the dockyard. Overlooking the basin and providing a distinguished focal point for the base was the Eastern Storehouse, one side of a quadrangle of detached storehouses and a workshop arranged round a central reservoir with a sail loft above. To their rear and largely hidden was a further irregular quadrangle of small iron and brass foundries, smitheries, pattern shops and fitting shops.

All these buildings are of the local stone and make extensive use of cast and wrought iron for their internal supports and roof structure.[132] Their composition, notably the handsome clocktower and bell tower on the Eastern Storehouse (Fig 12.44), along with their architectural detail, in particular the use of blind arcading on some of the main external elevations, the rusticated stone detailing to doorways, windows and quoins and the unusual employment of stone balustrades set within window spaces, give a sense of unity and order to this mid-Victorian naval base. The records are incomplete, but there is very little doubt that its plan and the design of the buildings are principally the work of William Scamp (Fig 12.45). Many of the architectural details are to be found in his slightly earlier work at Malta. Colonel Greene, the Director of Works, was to write of Scamp in 1860 that, ‘The present Admiralty establishments at Malta, Gibraltar and Bermuda, are almost entirely projected by him’.[133]

Fig 12.44 (below)
The Eastern Storehouse at Bermuda, now carefully adapted as a retail centre. (Author)

Fig 12.45 (accross both pages below)
Dominating the scene of Bermuda Dockyard in an 1856 panorama is Scamp's new Eastern Storehouse with its twin towers.
A number of accommodation and convict hulks are in the basin.
(National Museum of Bermuda, 75:145.001)

There have been few significant buildings added since Scamp's work, save for a number of coal stores later in the 19th century. The most notable addition to the base was the construction of the huge South Basin and wharf at the turn of the 20th century, which added a further 22 acres of protected moorings to the existing 16½ acres of the original basin, which was itself renamed the North Basin.[134] Much of the base remains as completed in the 1860s (Fig 12.46), its buildings now used for a variety of purposes. Along with the surrounding defences, they are a vivid reminder of the infrastructure supporting the Royal Navy's global reach throughout the 19th century and beyond.[135]

Fig 12.46
An aerial view in 2000 of the former naval base at Bermuda within its tight corset of bastioned defences. In the foreground is Commissioner's House and beyond it the ordnance yard; outside the Keep Yard defences is the victualling yard and beyond that the buildings of the dockyard overlooking the two great basins.
(National Museum of Bermuda)

13

South Atlantic and Australian Bases: Buildings and Engineering Works, 1700–1914

Ascension Island

In 1815 Ascension Island, an uninhabited and largely barren volcanic island towards the middle of the South Atlantic and nearly a thousand miles from the nearest coast of mainland Africa, was annexed to prevent it being used as a base to rescue Napoleon from St Helena. It was largely devoid of vegetation, its lower slopes covered in volcanic ash and its shores lacking a landing place safe from South Atlantic swells and occasional giant rollers. Some 1,800 miles to the north-east of Ascension, a subsidiary forward base off central West Africa was established in 1827 on the island of Fernando Po (now Bioko) just off the African mainland at the northern end of the Bight of Biafra, and a small framed hospital was constructed at Port Clarence on the north coast of Fernando Po. The unhealthy climate here leading to high mortality rates made this a deeply unpopular posting. It subsequently became a naval coaling station until closure in 1893.[1] Late in the 19th century a victualling store, agent victualler and an ordnance store were also established at Freetown in Sierra Leone.[2]

Ascension Island speedily found a use as a supply base, with medical facilities and limited equipment for repairing the ships of the West Africa Squadron, which were based here, on their arduous and disease-prone anti-slavery patrols. Christopher Lloyd has noted that 'again and again it was found that a sickly crew from the Bights [of Benin and Bonny] could be restored to health by a visit to this island'.[3] The facilities gradually provided at Ascension with its benign climate reflect the roles of supply, succour and repair. Lieutenant Brandreth's 1829 building proposals seem to have been the only occasion when any sort of coordinated development was pursued; the later somewhat piecemeal additions are witness to the reality of the island's remote location. All the buildings had to be constructed by the resident garrison helped by such seamen, and later by any available Kroomen, as might be available. Progress could be slow, as was noted in 1850 when it was recorded that as the construction of the main naval storehouse was being done by a working party of marines, so that 'a small progress only can be made'.[4] The principal naval buildings were sited at the largely military settlement of Georgetown (Fig 13.1), close to the pier head where they were protected by Fort Cockburn and later by Fort Hayes. Fort Cockburn was later replaced by Fort Thornton.[5]

Apart from the fortifications, a small victualling yard was the first to be established at

Fig 13.1
Georgetown, Ascension Island, in 1900 with the assortment of buildings of the naval base clustered near to Fort Thornton and the pier head.
(AdL Vz 15/7)

Georgetown, and a two-storey victualling store was completed by the end of 1827, when its facilities were shared with the Royal Marine garrison.[6] This was extended in the same style, probably in 1832 following Rear-Admiral Warren's visit, and a pay office was added at one end (Fig 13.2).[7] Later, in 1848, construction of a substantial naval storehouse, incorporating cast-iron beams, was begun nearby and completed in 1852.[8] Soon after the first steam warships joined the station, the Brigantine *Independencia*, a captured former slaver, was fitted up as a coal hulk. It is not until 1858 that records mention money for construction of a proper coal store (Fig 13.3). Two years later this was linked by a tramway to the crane at the pier head.[9] For further information on Ascension, *see also* Chapter 9.

Fig 13.2
The paymaster's quarters and the victualling store on Ascension Island in the 1890s. The crenellated blockhouse of Fort Thornton can be seen far left.
(AdL Da 032)

Fig 13.3
The coal stores, distinguished by their substantial buttresses, photographed in the 1890s alongside Fort Thornton, Ascension Island. To the right is the surviving main naval storehouse.
(AdL Da 032)

The early 1860s saw a considerable investment in metal-working facilities, with a new smithery and workshops, later known as the steam factory. This was a substantial single-storey building with partly louvred walls and metal furnace chimneys (Fig 13.4). It housed a moulding floor, a pattern-making workshop, a tinsmith and plumbers' workshop, a machine shop and furnaces for smelting iron and brass.[10] An 1862 report to the Director of Works noted that 'this most important department has been strengthened and is in the course of great improvement ... when the new workshops now in progress are completed and a cupola for casting erected, there will be scarcely any defect in the machinery of our cruisers'.[11] What was described as 'six huts for married artificers' were allowed for at the time of construction, and the following year money was allocated for a house for the senior engineer (*see* Fig 7.19) and residences for his small staff, as well as a new roof to the spar trench, a dormitory over the marines' barracks, extending the bread store, a further tank for water from roofs of buildings and a stable on Green Mountain, presumably for hospital use (Figs 13.5 and 13.6).[12] The roofed spar trench was used to keep spare masts and spars sheltered from the heat of the sun. By the end of the decade the base was equipped with all the facilities for simple maintenance and repair of steam-assisted warships on station, and its buildings were linked by the tramway that now extended from the pier head to the Turtle Ponds at Clarence Bay at the northern end and the carpenters' shop and sawpits to the south.[13]

The very high sickness and mortality rates suffered by the crews of the anti-slavery patrols made a naval hospital a priority on Ascension, a point emphasised in 1829 when over a quarter of the sailors in the West Africa Squadron died from yellow fever.[14] In 1830, following his return from the island, Brandreth put forward proposals for a single-storey hospital with a basement to be built at Georgetown. Following the earlier example of Holl's much larger hospital at Port Royal, he proposed to make extensive use of iron in its construction, offering the option of an iron 'gallery' round the outside,

Fig 13.4
The steam factory on Ascension Island in the 1890s. This was a substantial building, perhaps reflecting the island's remote location, and comparable to the one at Port Royal. (AdL Da 032)

Fig 13.5
The barracks for the Kroomen, recruited from West Africa to serve on the squadron's anti-slavery patrols. Overlooking these from the higher ground, to the left of the flagstaff, are the naval offices, with St Mary's garrison church in the distance. To the right of the flagstaff are the colonnaded barracks occupied by the Royal Marine garrison and on occasion by naval crews. A photograph taken in the 1890s. (AdL Da 032)

Fig 13.6
The new naval bakery on Ascension Island in the 1890s, its modest size reflecting the small naval and marine staff there, as well as the occasional needs of ships of the squadron. By this date there was no separate bread store. (AdL Da 032)

'which could be attached to the Building at any future period with facility'. The Admiralty approved the proposal minus the gallery and substituted timber for iron joists to reduce costs further. Work on the building was under way in 1832.[15]

Six years later, Brandreth suggested supplementing this with a temporary hospital 'in case of contagious diseases' – a very real fear of the anti-slavery patrols. Although he drew up plans and estimates for the amount of material to be sent out for the marines to construct, the proposal seems to have been abandoned. The hospital would have held 20 patients and 5 officers and included surgeons' quarters, a dispensary, kitchen and dead house.[16] A second naval hospital for convalescents, its single-storey ranges grouped round a courtyard, was constructed later near the top of Green Mountain. Here patients could benefit from produce from the adjacent farm and enjoy a more temperate climate, along with the delights of a croquet lawn and garden set with shrubs and olive trees.[17] The horrors of the West African coast with their unimaginable scenes, fevers, diseases and deaths must have seemed a world away from this misty mountain. Both these hospital buildings survive.

Perhaps less immediately apparent was the increasingly elaborate freshwater system needed for Georgetown. As at Bermuda, the navy had to conserve the limited supplies and construct large holding tanks. Brandreth's 1830 piped system from Green Mountain gradually had to be extended to cope with increased demands both from the garrison and visiting ships, and by 1896 a combination of the original spring, further catchments and water from roofs of buildings was estimated to yield some 3,065 tons a year, stored in a series of tanks constructed at Georgetown.[18]

In 1896 the Admiralty instructed a Royal Engineer, Lieutenant-Colonel James Lewis, to inspect the state of the facilities on Ascension and to suggest possible improvements. His very thorough report covered all aspects of the island, including its defences, buildings, roads, agriculture and water supply.[19] He made a number of recommendations for improving them all, before advising on ways to speed up the system of coaling warships. By replacing the existing crane on the pier head by three massive Temperly transporters similar to those at Portland naval base, he reckoned on increasing the hourly rate of coaling from the existing 20 tons to 90 tons.[20] To protect the warships and lighters from the notorious South Atlantic rollers and from the threat of torpedo attack, Lewis advocated a short breakwater arm running out from the shore by Fort Thornton and an 800yd breakwater parallel to the shore to protect the pier head and create a sheltered anchorage of some 16 acres, more than twice the size of the 1840s Steam Basin at Portsmouth Dockyard.[21] The justification for this immensely elaborate and costly scheme is not immediately apparent, for by then the anti-slavery patrols had been discontinued and Ascension's naval importance had diminished as a consequence.[22] Perhaps unsurprisingly, nothing more was heard of the proposal. Ascension Island's importance as a cable station did not begin until the end of 1899 when the Cape Town–St Helena–Ascension–Cape Verde line was laid to give London a direct and alternative link with South Africa. Apart from some minor works of modernisation, little more was done to the base.[23] In 1922 the Admiralty handed over the island to the Colonial Office, and the day-to-day administration devolved to the Superintendent of the Eastern Telegraph Company stationed on the island.[24]

Simon's Town

The occupation of the Cape of Good Hope in 1795 and its subsequent retention by Britain enabled the Royal Navy to take over the two bases used by the Dutch East India Company. The older of these at Cape Town had been developed since the 17th century as a victualling station for Company ships,[25] but Table Bay was an unsafe anchorage during north-westerly gales. After mounting ship losses, the Dutch East India Company in 1743 began development of facilities at Simon's Bay, a sheltered inlet off False Bay to the east of the Cape of Good Hope.[26] The Admiralty, not unreasonably, had no wish to maintain two bases less than 20 miles apart and opted to develop Simon's Bay with the 'safe anchorage at any season to at least eight sail of the line'.[27] In December 1812 the Admiralty ordered the transfer of the naval establishment at Cape Town to Simon's Town (Fig 13.7).[28]

For the British, a naval base at the Cape was strategically well placed to protect the sea route to India and the Far East. Possession would also help thwart any French ambitions to re-establish themselves as a naval power in the Indian Ocean and perhaps recapture their island bases at Réunion and Mauritius. In practice, after 1815 there was no serious threat for the rest of the 19th century, and for much of that time warships based at Simon's Town contributed to the anti-slavery patrols. From 1864, in addition to their work on the west side of Africa, they took over responsibility from the East Indies squadron for the eastern side of the continent, patrolling

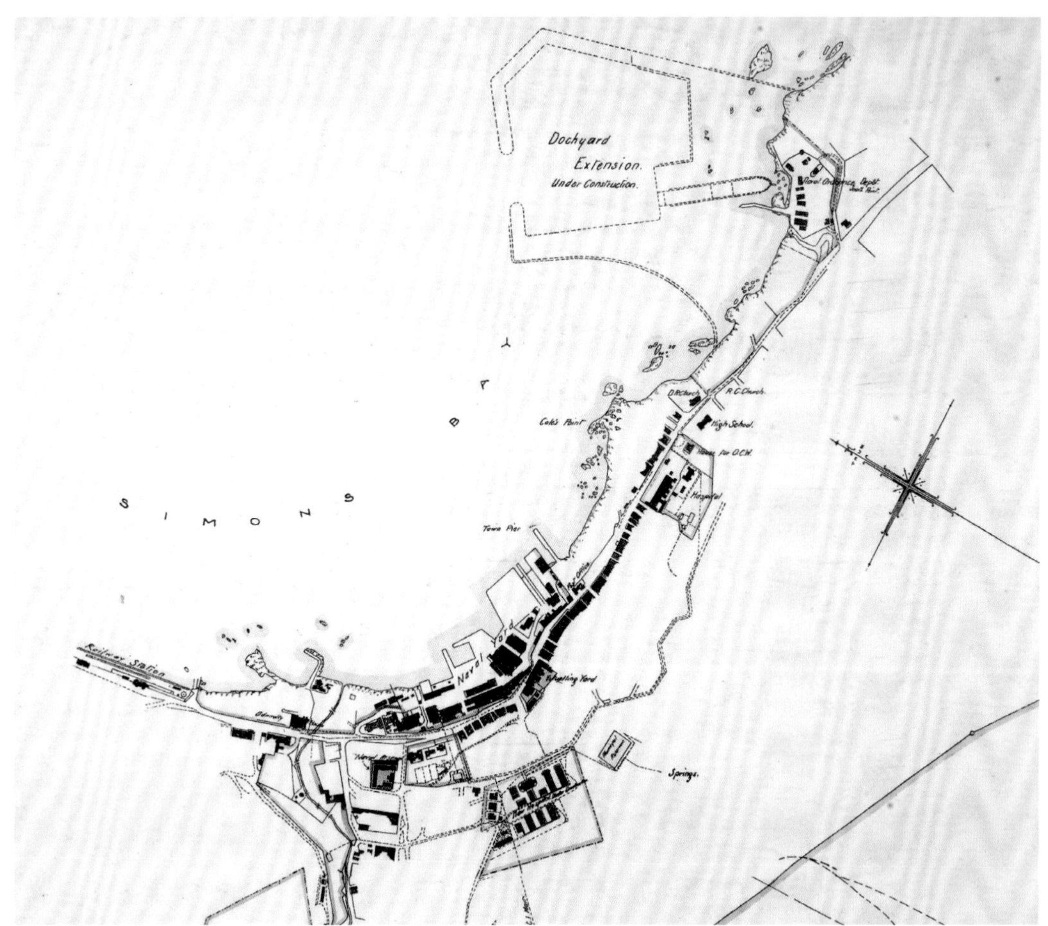

Fig 13.7
A plan of 1900 showing the various naval facilities at Simon's Town, with the original dockyard spread along the foreshore. The proposed steam yard is shown in outline. (AdL Vz 15/24)

Fig 13.8
The 1815 mast house and sail loft with its clocktower at Simon's Town. Beyond are the two storehouses built by the Dutch East India Company in 1743, with an extra floor added in the 19th century.
(Author)

as far north as the southern Arab states, following Livingstone's campaign against Arab slave traders. In 1869, although the opening of the Suez Canal considerably reduced traffic on the Cape sea route, one-seventh of Britain's trade still went round southern Africa, ensuring the continuing strategic importance of the base. In 1870–1 the yard employed some 42 people, putting it in the middle band of overseas establishments in terms of numbers and on a par with Halifax, Gibraltar and Trincomalee.[29] Radical transformation of the facilities only began in the late 1890s, with the need to provide for the larger and more powerful warships now considered necessary for the protection of trade and imperial communications. The changing strategic importance of Simon's Town is well reflected in the pre-1914 buildings and engineering works that remain.

Simon's Town shares the distinction with Malta of being one of only two locations where the Royal Navy inherited an existing base. The Dutch East India Company's small yard was on the foreshore at the head of the bay, sheltered by the mountains behind. Its principal buildings were two substantial storehouses authorised in 1743 by Baron von Imhoff, the Governor-General of the Dutch East Indies, when he visited the Cape.[30] These remain in what is now the West Yard, although later altered and each with an additional storey. For the Royal Navy consolidating its Cape operations here, the most urgent requirement was for adequate storage for masts and boats, along with a sail loft.[31] The handsome pedimented building, its gable surmounted by a small clocktower, which was completed around 1815 immediately to the west of the two storehouses, was built to serve these needs (Fig 13.8). The ground floor was for masts and ships' boats, with large double doors on its north side allowing direct access to the bay. Above was the sail loft, later used as the dockyard church. This was the first major building constructed by the British in the base. It remains the most distinguished building in the old yard, suggesting that the new arrivals wished to mark their presence with something of an architectural statement. Its designer is unknown, but possibly a Royal Engineer serving with the army.

In the early part of the 1820s Admiralty funding was concentrated on the construction of the Royal Observatory at the Cape, designed by John Rennie senior shortly before his death.[32] In the aftermath of the Napoleonic Wars, little funding was available for the naval base, and its subsequent development mirrors that of other similar-sized establishments. For most of the 19th century the only additions stemmed from changing technology rather than different operational requirements. A coal store first appears in the estimates for 1852/3, while the 1860s saw the addition of a boiler shop to the rear of the eastern 1743 storehouse and a machine shop and small foundry adjacent to its eastern end, providing a matching elevation to its older neighbour. Further coal stores were constructed, and in the 1870s pressure on storage space led to the addition of an extra floor to both the early storehouses.[33]

Although the Admiralty acquired the town's patent slip in 1885 (Fig 13.9), its capacity was limited and did not compensate for the lack of a dry dock here, although a commercial one had been available at Cape Town since 1870. In 1896, as part of the drive to improve facilities at key overseas stations, the Admiralty ordered proposals to be drawn up for a dry dock 'as near to the existing dockyard as possible'.[34] Space restrictions (*see* Figs 13.10 and 13.11) and the expense and scale of the necessary breakwaters led the committee chaired by the Civil Lord, Austen Chamberlain, to recommend an alternative separate site at the eastern end of Simon's Bay.[35] Here it would not encroach on the existing anchorage, which would benefit from additional protection by the new works. If necessary, the outer breakwater could

Fig 13.9 (above)
The paddle survey vessel HMS Pioneer *under repair on the patent slip at Simon's Town in 1864. The arcaded shed in the foreground is a coal store. (© National Maritime Museum, Greenwich, London, L5705)*

Fig 13.10 (left)
Simon's Town in the 1890s showing the increasingly cramped nature of the old yard with its tiny basin. (AdL Da 038)

Fig 13.11
*Part of the dockyard and Simon's Bay in the late 1880s. Prominent is the 1815 sail loft, mast house and boathouse with its clocktower. The open roadstead beyond provided the only anchorage until the completion c 1910 of the breakwater enclosing the west yard (*see *Fig 13.14). The principal ships at anchor (from left to right) are HMS* Landrail, *a torpedo gun vessel launched in 1886 at Devonport, HMS* Raleigh, *an iron steam frigate launched at Chatham in 1873 and the last Royal Navy ship to round Cape Horn under canvas, HMS* Flora, *a fifth-rate launched at Devonport in 1844 and relegated to harbour service from 1851, and HMS* Imperieuse, *an armoured cruiser undocked at Portsmouth in 1883, spending much of her life as flagship for the Pacific Squadron. Smaller vessels include several probably for coaling and three flat-iron gunboats. The assorted warships are typical of the varied types to be found on the quieter overseas stations. (© National Maritime Museum, Greenwich, London, L5694)*

be extended at a later date to further enclose the harbour.

Chamberlain's committee recommended a 750ft double dock with an entrance width of 95ft and a depth over the sill of 30ft.[36] For maximum flexibility, the caisson stops were to be so arranged that the double dock could either have an outer dock of 470ft, with an inner one of 250ft, or an outer dock of 320ft, with an inner one of 400ft. The eastern breakwater, provided with coaling facilities, and the western pier, in practice built as a mole, were to enclose a basin 'of about 25 acres', while alongside the double dock were to be the essential engineering workshops and associated facilities.

The Civil Engineer-in-Chief was unable 'at the present time to estimate with any approach to accuracy the cost of the plans', which the committee realised would 'very considerably exceed what was at first suggested as the sum necessary to provide a first class dock at the Cape'. Nevertheless, they felt that 'if ... a dock is to be constructed at all', their proposals could not be 'reduced with due regard to safety and efficiency'. A crumb of comfort was thrown to the Treasury by the suggestion that the new facilities would free existing ones in the dockyard, which could be used for much-needed storage, but the Treasury by then was no doubt wise to such optimistic cost-saving assumptions.[37]

The Chamberlain Committee's proposals were largely accepted, and in the spring of 1900 five engineering firms were invited to tender for the works.[38] In August the contract was awarded to Sir John Jackson, then busy with Admiralty contracts for part of the new harbour at Dover and with the Keyham extension at Devonport. The firm undertook to complete the work at Simon's Town within 7 years.[39] Most of 1901 was spent setting up a working base before the extensive land reclamation could start, along with construction of the breakwater, west pier and the coffer-dam to protect the double dock. The 1904 estimates noted that these had been commenced, but it was to be November 1906 before the double dock was advanced sufficiently for its foundation stone to be laid with suitable ceremony by the High Commissioner for South Africa, the Earl of Selborne, after whom the dock was named.[40] This was not operational before 1910, by which time the associated buildings were also largely complete (Fig 13.12).

Immediately adjacent, along the west side of the double dock, was the Main Factory, 575ft long and 80ft wide, recommended by the Chamberlain Committee 'to include engineer's shop, constructor's shop, boiler shop and engine house etc' (Fig 13.13). Near its northern end was the pumping station; beyond this on the west pier was the site for the sheer-legs. To the rear of the Main Factory was a separate Furnace House. Along the eastern side of the double dock were a number of other small workshops and two 100ft working sheds. A railway system linked the principal buildings and extended along the breakwater to three substantial coal sheds. The engineering works and principal buildings were all built of stone; the double dock especially is notable for the extremely high

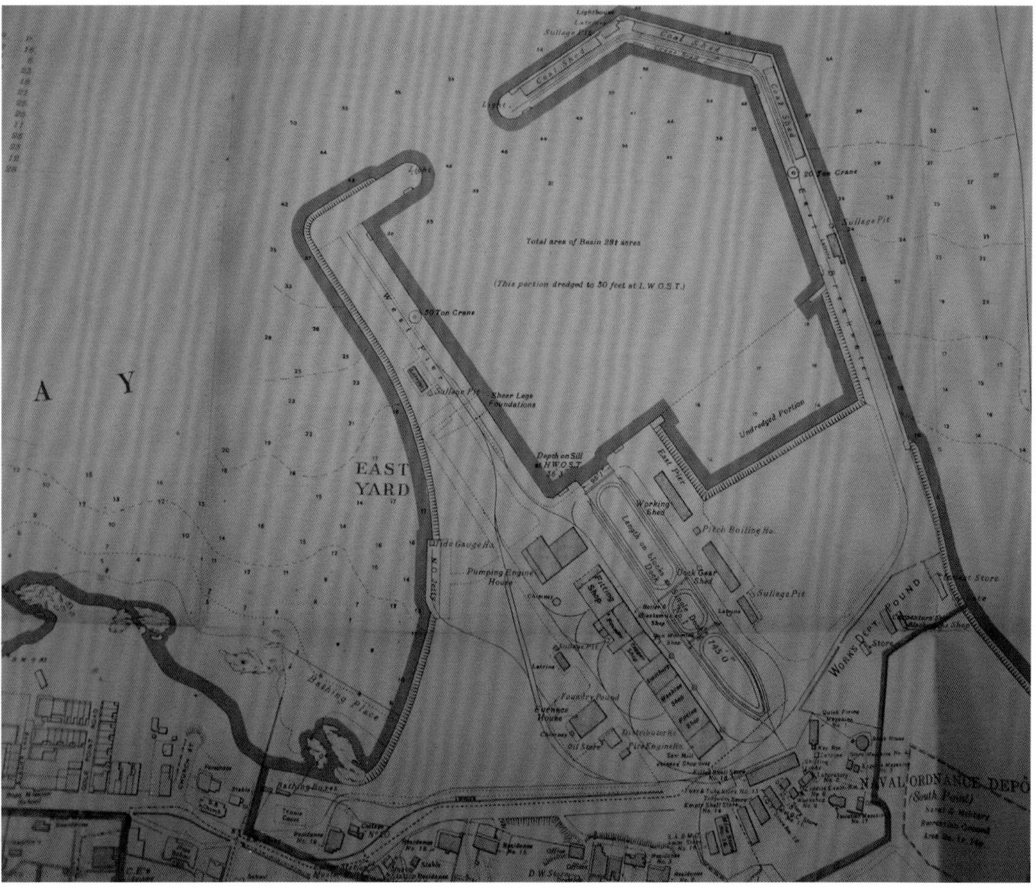

Fig 13.12 (left and below)
A 1909 plan of the base at Simon's Town.
The extension, then nearing completion, is shown enlarged below.
(TNA ADM 140/1484 fol 77)

Fig 13.13
A photograph taken at the end of December 1908 showing progress on the factory buildings and the double dock at Simon's Town. As at Gibraltar, the factory buildings are steel framed.
(TNA ADM 195/98 fol 42)

Fig 13.14
The new West Yard at Simon's Town nearing completion, photographed at the end of March 1910. In the distance is Cape Agulhas and the Indian Ocean.
(TNA ADM 195/98 fol 66)

quality of its masonry. The design of all these structures stems from the Admiralty Works Department; unsurprisingly, they have a family likeness to the slightly larger but contemporary works at Gibraltar.[41] In 1912 the new yard was formally named the West Yard (Fig 13.14), and the original was renamed the East Yard. A new naval hospital and ordnance stores were also constructed at this time (*see* Chapters 15 and 16). The West Yard remains much as completed, and the East Yard retains many of its early buildings.

Australia: Sydney

Distance from the mother country and sheer length of the Australian and New Zealand coastlines presented the Admiralty with formidable problems if it was to provide an adequate naval presence in these waters. Perhaps not surprisingly, it showed some reluctance, and although the first four governors of New South Wales were naval officers, the early decades were characterised by 'worn out and crazy ships, inadequate stores and indifferent authorities'.[42] This was gradually to change as further settlements were established on the continent, while whaling fleets and merchants increasingly demanded protection. In New Zealand the Maori uprisings of 1845–8 were significant influences in the Admiralty decision in 1848 to create a western division of the East Indies station.[43]

In the mid-1850s local concern about the inadequacies of naval protection led the states of New South Wales and Victoria each to acquire a small warship for local defence, moves later regularised by the 1865 Colonial Naval Defence Act that allowed the use of such vessels purely for harbour and coastal protection.[44] These initiatives were further encouraged by the Carnarvon Commission in 1882, but the proviso remained that 'any *sea-going* vessel that may be provided, equipped and maintained, at the cost of the colonies, should be manned by the Admiralty, and be placed in every respect in the same status as are her Majesty's vessels at present belonging to this station'.[45] Local defence was to be encouraged, but imperial defence was to remain very much in British Government and Admiralty hands.

In parallel with these moves, and partly stimulated by them, the Admiralty formed the separate Australia Station in 1859. The five vessels, a frigate, a sloop and three corvettes, in theory were responsible for an area north to the Torres Straits, south to the Antarctic Circle, east to Samoa and west to the tiny island of St Paul in the southern Indian Ocean.[46] The squadron was based at Sydney, used by the Royal Navy ever since the arrival of the First Fleet in January 1788. The magnificent natural harbour was an obvious draw, but the founding and growth of the city and the development of substantial commercial ship-repairing facilities added to its attractions for the Royal Navy (Fig 13.15).[47] These were substantially improved by the construction of the Fitzroy Dock on Cockatoo Island, begun in 1845 and the first overseas dry dock to be constructed with the aid of Admiralty funds.[48] In 1890 the much larger Sutherland Dock was also completed on the island. These and their attendant facilities were never Admiralty property, but were owned and operated by the Government of New South Wales.[49] Admiralty presence on shore until the latter part of the 19th century was limited to a commissariat storehouse and naval office on Circular Quay on the city's waterfront (Fig 13.16),[50] a site adjacent to Fort Macquarie

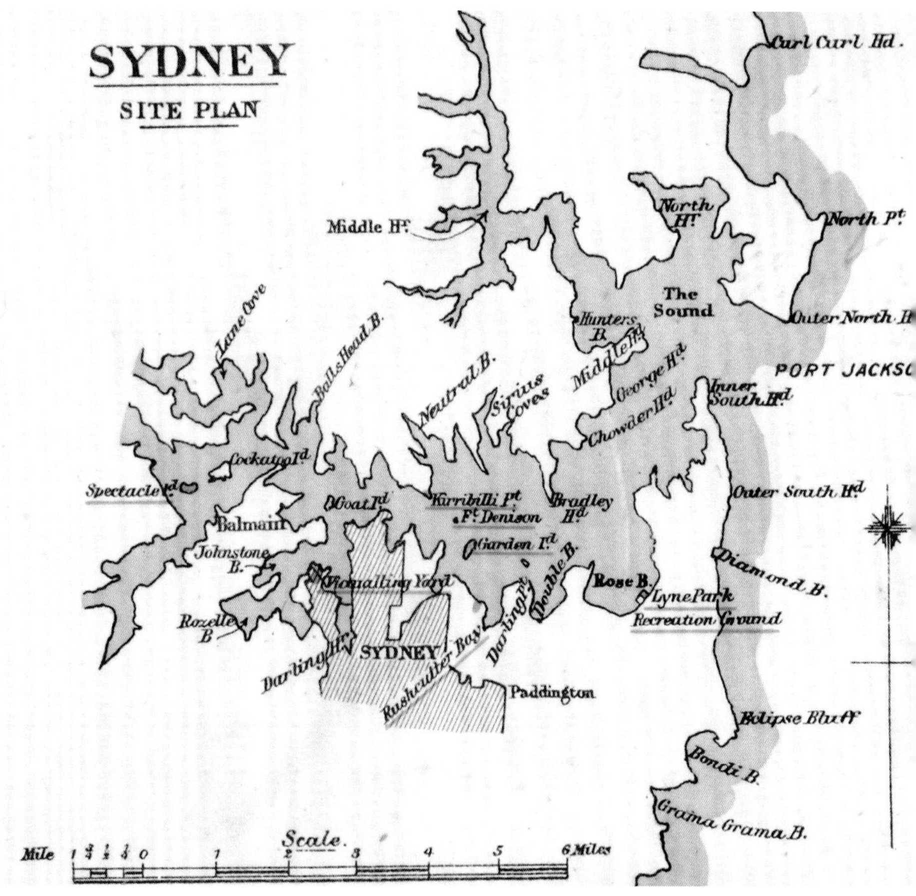

Fig 13.15 (above top)
An Admiralty location map of the Royal Navy's installations at Sydney Harbour c 1900.
(AdL Vz 15/80)

Fig 13.16 (above bottom)
The original Royal Navy offices and storehouse at Circular Quay, Sydney. They no longer exist.
(AdL Da 039)

that was briefly used in the middle of the century for minor repairs and is now the site of the Opera House. There was also land on the largely undeveloped Garden Island just off shore, as well as a small ordnance depot on Goat Island.[51]

In the second half of the 19th century, with financial assistance from the colonial governments, the Admiralty gradually acquired improved facilities at Sydney.[52] Spectacle Island, in the remote inner part of the harbour, was acquired by the Admiralty in the 1880s as an ordnance depot, replacing Goat Island which by then was too close to the expanding city. This was to be followed by the construction of the Royal Navy's main operational base on Garden Island. Finally, in the early 20th century,

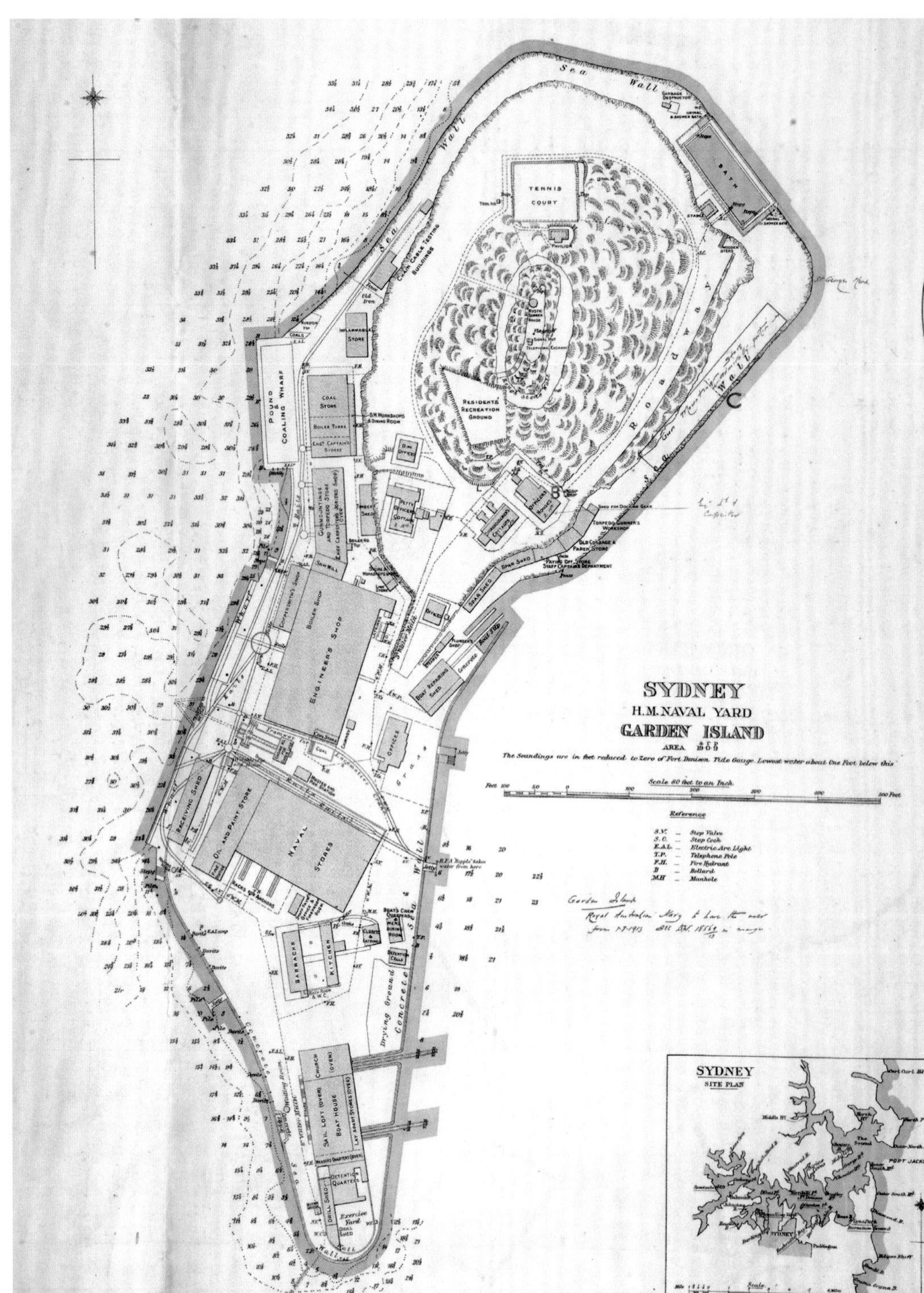

Fig 13.17
A 1900 plan of the Royal Navy's base at Garden Island, Sydney, soon after its completion.
(AdL Vz 15/ 80)

the now-vanished Royal Edward Victualling Yard was built by the New South Wales government on Darling Island, close to the city's main food markets. Its site is now subsumed in the Sydney suburb of Pyrmont.[53]

Garden Island was so named after being selected as the site for a garden for the ship's company of HMS *Sirius* just 16 days after the landing in 1788 of the First Fleet. In 1858 the Admiralty accepted an offer of land here from the Government of New South Wales for use as a base, acquiring the whole 10-acre island in 1866. It was unwilling to make a major investment, and for a number of years little more than a small residence, a boat shed and a blacksmith's shop seem to have been constructed.[54] In 1871 Commodore Stirling recommended that all naval facilities should be concentrated here, but the catalyst for development on both Garden Island and Spectacle Island did not come until 1883, when the Government of New South Wales offered £50,000 to construct a base (Fig 13.17), concerned that the Royal Navy would receive a more tempting offer to relocate to New Zealand.[55]

Two years were spent levelling much of Garden Island, constructing wharves and preparing plans for the buildings. Although the Admiralty sent out the engineer Mr Fishenden to assist with the planning of the buildings, responsibility for their design, at any rate before 1890, seems to have rested with the Colonial Architect James Barnet (*see* Chapters 4 and 15).[56] The base was constructed by local contractors between 1885 and 1896, when Garden Island was formally handed over to Rear-Admiral Cyprian Bridge. Proximity to Cockatoo Island meant that dry docks were unnecessary, but the yard was equipped with a substantial engineering workshop, along with a gun-mounting and torpedo store, a sawmill, a repair shed for ships' boats, a large central storehouse, coal stores, a central office and housing for a small number of staff (Fig 13.18). In common with some of the other more distant bases, a barracks building was also provided as living accommodation for crews in harbour for any length of time or whose ships were in dockyard hands. The continuing employment of sailing warships in the quieter and more remote

Fig 13.18
The Garden Island base at Sydney in 1898. To the left are the engineering workshops, with the main storehouse in the centre and the naval barracks and boathouse and sail loft on the right. Alongside the quay in front of the sheer-legs is the armoured cruiser HMS Orlando, *flagship on the Australia Station 1888–98. Moored in the foreground is HMS* Boomerang, *one of two Gossamer Class torpedo-gunboats then on station. (*Navy and Army Illustrated *29 Oct 1898, 131)*

Fig 13.19
The main storehouse on Garden Island, Sydney, photographed in the 1890s shortly after its completion, its size reflecting the need to keep adequate supplies at this station far from the home yards.
(TNA ADM 195/4 fol 62)

reaches of empire is reflected in the construction of a boathouse with a sail loft above. In July 1887 Captain Francis Clayton, commanding the Sheerness-built wooden screw corvette HMS *Diamond*,[57] visited the yard and noted that 'an immense sail loft is all but finished', adding, 'What it is to be used for, I can't think; it is big enough for Portsmouth Dockyard. It will make a fine ballroom'.[58] Belated enthusiasm of the New South Wales government and local officials ensured that the Admiralty had gained use of a much larger facility than the 'small Dockyard reserve dealing with minor defects', which it had viewed as adequate for the Australia squadron.[59]

The majority of the buildings then constructed are still in use, with the influence of James Barnet apparent in the Italianate style of many of the more important ones.[60] The centrepiece of the base remains the naval storehouse (Fig 13.19), a substantial building of four storeys constructed of polychromatic brick with sandstone detailing and granite door thresholds, generously provided with loading bays, each with a wall crane, originally hydraulically powered.[61] Internally, and similar to Taylor's and John Rennie junior's earlier victualling stores at Gosport and Stonehouse, the timber floors are carried on substantial cast-iron columns, and the building is divided by fireproof cross-walls. The storehouse was originally designed to accommodate victuals as well as a general naval store, but the former use ceased on completion of the Royal Edward Yard some years later. The nearby two-storey main offices, constructed in brick in 1894–5 and surmounted by a clocktower and cupola, rival the storehouse in the richness of the Italianate decoration. Later extensions have partly masked the elevations, but enough remains for the original design to be appreciated.[62] A little

Fig 13.20
In the forground overlooking the harbour are the main offices. To the rear is part of the engineer's shop with its tall boiler chimney. Beyond the offices, the boat repairing shed stands at the head of a small slip. In the distance are the superintendent's cottages and the officers' houses. (AdL Da 039)

further on stands the sail loft, the last to be built for the Royal Navy. It is a handsome, two-storey, rendered building, generously provided with loading doors and wall cranes. The gun-mounting and torpedo store was very similar in design. The sail loft had very few years of active use, and like the one at Simon's Town, part of it was converted into the dockyard chapel by 1902 (Fig 13.20).

As with all the navy's dockyards from the middle of the 19th century, the mechanical heart of the yard was the Steam Factory, a two-storey building constructed between 1889 and 1891. This was built of brick, using cast-iron columns, riveted girders and metal roof trusses to support the upper floor and roofs. The double-height main workshop incorporated a travelling crane. A foundry, pattern shop and engineering workshops were sited adjacent to this within the steam factory. In 1892 an eastern extension was built for an additional iron and brass foundry, engine and boiler house and associated workshops, pattern shops and tool shops. A dynamo room reflected the gradual introduction of electricity on board the navy's warships.[63] Since then, there have been further extensions and modifications, and the building remains in active use.

The one building from this period that is least influenced by local architectural fashion is

Fig 13.21
The former naval barracks on Garden Island, Sydney. (Author)

the naval barracks constructed in 1887–8 (Fig 13.21). The plain, three-storey, rendered brick building was designed for 239 officers and men; the officers and a small hospital occupied the top floor.[64] Timber floors were carried on metal girders supported by two rows of cast-iron Corinthian columns, but the roof trusses were entirely of timber. The main western elevation is distinguished by a three-storey verandah employing Tuscan columns with simple iron balustrades; this was later extended along the north and south ends of the barracks. Inside remain a number of hooks used to support the seamen's hammocks. To the rear is a single-storey range, originally the cookhouse and mess. The design is clearly derived from the barracks developed originally by the Royal Engineers for use in the West Indies and other hot climates, but modified to suit the healthier conditions of New South Wales.[65]

Completion of Garden Island, together with the modernisation of the ordnance depot on Spectacle Island, the availability of dry docks and further engineering workshops on Cockatoo Island and the construction of the victualling yard, gave the Royal Navy facilities that were to be unrivalled in the southern hemisphere until the completion of the West Yard at Simon's Town. The construction between 1940 and 1945 of the Captain Cook Graving Dock resulted in Garden Island being linked to the mainland. Despite this change in the topography and the modernisation of the base since the 1980s, the historic buildings here remain an appreciated and important element of the two country's closely linked naval histories.[66]

14

Feeding the Fleet: The Royal Victualling Yards

From 1683 to 1832 responsibility for obtaining and supplying victuals for the navy rested with the Victualling Board, replacing an earlier unsatisfactory system that had relied on contractors.[1] In 1832, as part of the wider administrative reforms, victualling became a department of the Admiralty. Through its centralised purchasing and manufacture, the Victualling Board became the country's first mass caterer, an onerous responsibility where any failure could have led to tragic consequences, but one that was on the whole discharged with considerable credit. Aware that the health, happiness and morale of crews depended in large part on their diet, the Admiralty early on insisted that the best-quality provisions should be supplied, and the Victualling Board constantly strove to improve the manufacturing processes and experiment with new foods and methods of preservation. On the whole, in terms of quality of food, diet and regularity of meals, it meant that a sailor in the Georgian navy was better fed than most of his peers ashore.[2] The same remained broadly true of his 19th-century successors, with the introduction of canned foods later that century allowing for a greater variety. Canned meat was first supplied to the army and navy in 1813, but until the costs of canning were reduced much later in the 19th century, its use was restricted to the sick.[3] In Daniel Baugh's opinion, 'the rise of the victualling department [in the first half of the 18th century] may have had more impact on the success of British arms than any other administrative development since the time of Pepys'.[4]

To control quality and costs and minimise fraud, the Victualling Board preferred to provision warships directly from its own yards or depots. But away from the home bases, contractors remained crucial. In 1685 the Board had agents at Chatham, Dover, Portsmouth, Plymouth, Kinsale, Livorno and Tangier, where there were two agents. The building used at Dover as the Victualling Office still exists.[5] Where the volume of provisions warranted, these were supervised by Agent Victuallers, notably on foreign stations, while ships' captains also had the powers to make local purchases, especially fresh foods. By 1700 the variety of provisions had become largely standardised, reflecting the fairly rudimentary food preservation technology. Beef, pork, fish, biscuits, butter, cheese, peas and beer formed a staple fare whose monotony was compounded by the very limited galley space on board warships, which reduced most hot meals to the ubiquitous stew. In the course of the 18th century oatmeal, sugar, sauerkraut and cocoa were added. A notable and popular introduction from 1756 was Mrs Dubois's Portable Soup, a slab of concentrate made largely of offal from naval slaughterhouses.[6]

Between 1774 and 1783 the number of men in sea pay rose from just over 17,000 to 105,000 and was to grow still further in the Napoleonic Wars, an indication of the hugely increased demands made on the Victualling Board.[7] Some indication of the quantity and variety of provisions required by the crew of a warship of around 500 men is given in Table 14.1 The navy's first victualling operations had been set up in the 16th century on Tower Hill using part of the dissolved Cistercian Abbey of St Mary Graces. This remained the Victualling Board's headquarters and centre of operations (*see* Fig 1.8) until a move to more spacious premises at Deptford in the mid-1740s.[8] In 1743 the Victualling Board drew up plans estimated at just under £70,000 for these new premises, which was the first of the major food-processing yards, as distinct from storage and distribution depots, since the establishment of the Victualling Board (Fig 14.1). It was proposed on a scale to match an expanding fleet, its facilities to be a model for the later but smaller manufacturing yards at Gosport and Stonehouse.[9] Close to the London food markets and barrel makers and a convenient supply depot for the Thames and Medway yards and the ships at the Nore, this was later renamed the Royal Victoria Victualling Yard, remaining in operation into the 1950s.

The buildings at Deptford fell into four distinct groups, centred on food production and purchase, the brewing of beer, packing and distribution. The principal foods processed in the yard were salt beef, salt pork, beer, bread and biscuits, while other food purchased from London markets and wholesalers included butter, cheese, peas, flour and fish; all had to be carefully packed in barrels. Only bread and ships' biscuits were issued in stout bags. As casks were the principal containers for food and drink, their purchase, production and repair were hugely important elements in the three main victualling yards, all of which had substantial cooperages and large areas for barrel storage. By the 18th century the Royal Navy was the largest user of casks in the country, buying the

Table 14.1 Provisions for the crew of around 500 of the 74-gun warship HMS Marlborough, being prepared for Channel service on 31 Aug 1779 (from Hattendorf et al 1993, 458).

	tons	*hundredweight*	*quarters*	*pounds*
beef	12	1	2	24
pork	11	14	0	18
beer	100	5	2	12
water	113	8	2	8
bread	30	10	2	24
butter	1	5	2	0
cheese	2	6	3	14
oatmeal	5	2	3	12
peas	7	14	1	4
flour	6	6	3	24
suet	0	9	3	1
raisins	1	9	2	8
spirits	7	9	0	16
vinegar	2	0	2	0
coals	50	0	0	0
wood	63	0	0	0

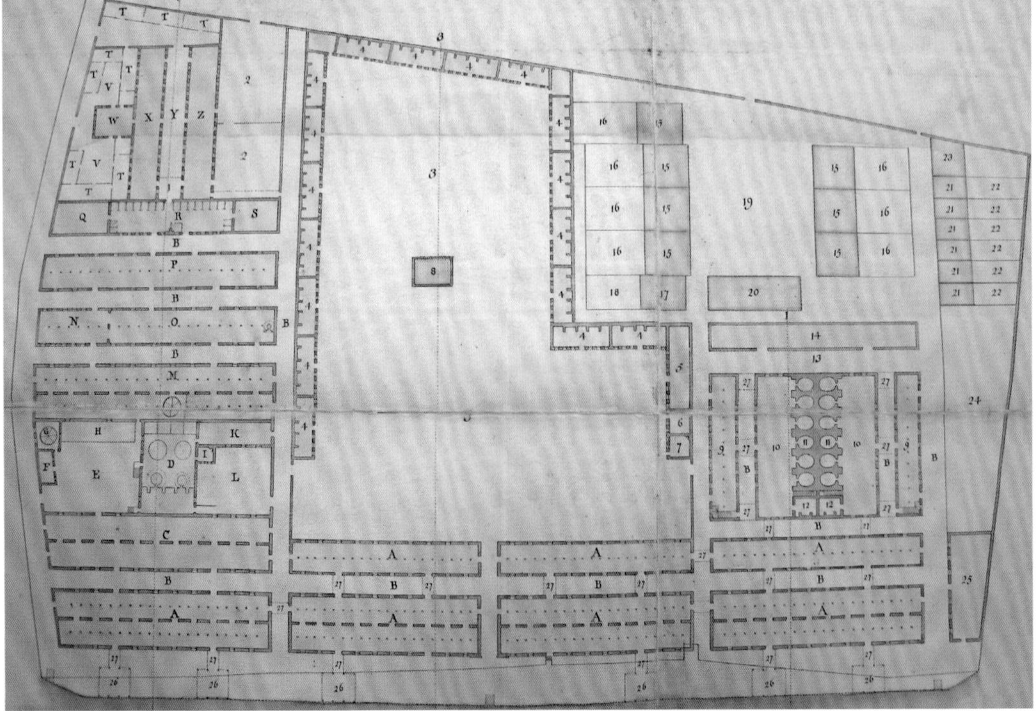

Fig 14.1
The 1743 proposals for the new Victualling Yard at Deptford. Perhaps nothing better conveys the growing scale of 18th-century naval operations than this plan. Although the yard differed in detail when constructed, it was the largest food-processing operation in Britain, if not in Europe. (AdL Portfolio B19/30 fol 27)

majority from London coopers and from the late 1740s distributing them from its new premises at Deptford. The cooperage here, in common with those at the other yards, devoted most of its time to repairing barrels. It also reassembled those taken apart after use to save space on ships and manufactured new ones from purchased staves. A cask used between 17 and 26 staves, depending on its size. Between 1803 and 1805 the Victualling Board's annual average consumption of staves was 99,800 for tight casks (used for liquids) and 25,200 for dry casks (for foodstuffs). The scale of operations at Deptford is apparent in the 1805 figures, when the yard issued 144,326 casks at a time when the average issue at Portsmouth was 10,000 and at Plymouth 21,700.[10]

The greatest space at Deptford was devoted to meat processing. Animals arrived on the hoof or by boat, the beef cattle and pigs held in lairage before going to separate slaughterhouses, the pigs then going to a hog hanging house. There were also separate cutting houses and salt houses where the carcasses were butchered and packed in salt in barrels. Associated with these were a suet loft and a pickle house. Nearby was the brewery with hop and malt lofts. The bakehouse was planned with 12 ovens for bread and ships' biscuits; adjacent was a bavin house for storing the bundles of brushwood for heating the ovens. Absence of a flour mill indicates that flour was bought from London millers.[11] However, the Board did propose 'a mill and other conveniences for making oatmeal, inasmuch as that is a species in which we have been particularly liable to be imposed upon ... [as the dealers] have always been sensible of our not having conveniences for making it ourselves, which we never had room for before'. They added that the oatmeal kiln could also be used for drying peas, 'which we find sometimes absolutely necessary for their keeping', especially in a wet summer.

Seven storehouses were proposed in 1743, along with a beer store and a pork store, and there was to be a terrace of six houses for the yard officers. As this was to be the headquarters of the Victualling Board, two terraces of seven rather grander houses were to be provided for the commissioners, together with a house for the secretary and an office with a boardroom and accommodation for the clerks.[12] How many of these proposals were implemented is not certain, as the yard was later redeveloped, and none of the 1743 buildings survive. What does survive at Deptford today are much later buildings – a grand late 18th-century terrace of seven houses built for the commissioners, along with the main gateway with its ox-head carvings, the Superintendent's House and two adjacent storehouses overlooking the Thames, once used for storing implements, raisins, biscuits and chocolate.[13] The scale of the original proposals and the quality of the surviving buildings are important in reflecting the determination of the Victualling Board to provide the best possible facilities on their new site.

As greater variety was introduced into the navy's diet during the 19th century, new foodstuffs that were required only in smaller quantities were stored and sometimes processed solely at this Deptford yard, before being distributed, reflecting its pre-eminence as well as its proximity to commercial suppliers. Cocoa beans were roasted here before being milled into chocolate; other specialised mills in the yard processed mustard and pepper. Sugar, tea, rice, raisins and wine were purchased in sufficient quantities to justify separate storehouses, and a significant section of the yard was given over to the storage of tobacco, purchased in bulk and repacked for onward distribution.

The fleet bases of Portsmouth and Plymouth were the only other locations that justified manufacturing victualling facilities on the scale of Deptford, but by the mid-18th century these had developed in a piecemeal and inefficient fashion, occupying scattered sites. Among other premises at Portsmouth were a bakery and storehouse in King Street, a slaughterhouse near the Sally Port and a grain mill by the Ordnance Yard. After the Square Tower ceased to be used as a powder magazine in 1779, it became a meat store for the Victualling Board, and hooks from this use still survive. Across on the Gosport side of the harbour the Board developed a substantial brewery and associated cooperage; the mid-18th-century cooperage buildings there are the oldest surviving victualling yard buildings.[14] At Plymouth there was a similar scattered piecemeal development, beginning with rented storehouses round the commercial harbour, followed in 1707 by a Victualling Office at Enty Comb and later by a brewery at Southdown on the opposite side of the Hamoaze from the dockyard.[15]

As Chatham declined as a fleet base in the 18th century, partly as a consequence of the shoaling of the Medway that also prevented warships at Chatham taking on stores there, the once-thriving victualling yard was also reduced in scale. By 1749 it was simply a store depot, 'calculated chiefly for petty warrant provisions for the Ordinary and Guardships, the ships fitting for the sea not being able to take in their provisions until they arrive at Blackstakes, where they are supplied from the stores in London'.[16] The approaching completion of a new victualling storehouse at Sheerness in 1821 led to further reductions at Chatham and a decision to supply all 'ships, craft and ordinaries at the Nore and in the Medway' from Deptford. However, 4 months of provisions were to be kept on guard ships at Chatham and 6 months on those at Sheerness 'for the use of any cruisers who may arrive in immediate want'.[17] Contractors still played a part in the arrangements at Chatham, supplying fresh meat to ships in commission there, as well to the depot ship where the beef was cut up for weekly distribution to the watchmen on ships in ordinary.[18] No trace of the naval victualling buildings survives at Chatham.

Elsewhere in the 18th century victualling stores at outstations such as Leith, Kinsale and Cork were generally hired. Rented accommodation was also used where the scale of activity warranted appointing a Victualling Agent to liaise with local contractors and merchants and to supervise the issue of stores. Such arrangements made for flexibility, allowing depots to be set up and closed according to need. If necessary, the Victualling Board was prepared to build premises. In the 1790s the inadequacy of existing arrangements at Kinsale and Cork was a key factor in the collaboration of the Victualling and Navy Boards to combine facilities in the proposed new yard at Haulbowline (*see* Chapter 1).[19] At Dover in 1665 the resident Agent Victualler had been provided with a house next to the Maison Dieu that was used as a store. When this ceased in 1831, the house was taken over by the Board of Ordnance for the Commanding Royal Engineer, but sold into private ownership in 1834 and is now the public library.[20] In 1836 the former victualling premises at Dover were limited to a wharf with two storehouses at the harbour. A little further away in Limekiln Street, there was what G L Taylor described as 'a well of water with some buildings over it of very inferior description – mere sheds'. These were let to 'Messrs Hayward and Walker' following closure of the victualling yard in 1831.[21]

At overseas bases, notably Gibraltar, Minorca and Jamaica, the 18th-century naval victualling system had to have a degree of spare capacity, as on occasion it was called upon to supply the military garrisons or expeditions sent from Britain.[22] Extensive use was made of contractors, especially in the West Indies where the substantial firm of Mason and Simpson held the victualling contract for a number of years from 1730, bringing in supplies from the British Isles, New York and the east coast of America, Barbados and Antigua.[23] Such agents worked to strict Victualling Board contracts. Naval operations in the Indian Ocean presented some of the most difficult victualling problems, if only because of the vast distances involved; Madras was at least 4 months sailing from Britain. In 1781 an Act of Parliament obliged the East India Company to transport the King's provisions from England and to provide all other victualling stores required by the navy.[24] Despite the varied complexities presented by the different theatres of operation, the 18th century saw the standards of British naval victualling steadily rising at the same time as costs were falling, leading N A M Rodger to state that 'Soldiers and passengers remarked with pleasure on the goodness of naval food'.[25]

The Victualling Board had the same approach to storage premises at foreign stations such as Port Royal or at ports such as Lisbon or Livorno, using commercial buildings where available. [26] Where they did not exist or were in short supply, the Victualling Board was prepared to construct buildings, relying on the greater experience of Navy Board staff for assistance. In 1743 a substantial two-storey bomb-proof victualling storehouse, vaulted on both floors, was proposed for Dutch Cove on the south side of Port Mahon Harbour, together with a cooperage and house for the Agent Victualler.[27] These do not seem to have been constructed, and it seems probable that the Board continued to rent the former convent in Mahon town.[28]

At Gibraltar a former White Convent was similarly used, along with a storehouse near the mole. In 1799 the storehouse stood in the way of new defence works and had to be vacated. Both buildings were replaced by a new and larger victualling yard at Rosia Bay, where it was also better protected from bombardment. The two key elements in the new establishment were a substantial victualling storehouse and an adjacent vast, vaulted, brick-lined underground reservoir that collected most of its water from the roofs of the storehouse. The plans for both resulted from discussions between the local contractor, John Maria Boschetti, and naval and military officials on the Rock. Although the Navy Board seems to have been kept informed, the Victualling Board apparently was not, commenting somewhat peevishly to a request from the Navy Board for their views on the proposals that 'Not ... having had a sight of any plan ... it is not in our power to offer any suggestion thereupon'.[29]

Although work began on the reservoir in 1799, it was not apparently until 1807 that the storehouse was started, to be completed too late to play a significant role in the Napoleonic Wars. This massive rectangular brick and stone building, some 190ft by 160ft, is vaulted on both floors (Fig 14.2; *see also* Fig 11.8). It faces a tiny courtyard entered through a handsome archway flanked by a small house and office for the Agent Victualler (Fig 14.3). This remained in use into the 1980s and, until recently, was the best and least altered example of a victualling depot at a foreign station. In its 19th-century heyday, the Gibraltar victualling yard would have obtained much of its stock from the manufacturing yards at Deptford, Gosport and Stonehouse, supplementing these with purchases from contractors.[30] Only two overseas victualling yards had any manufacturing capacity, and this was largely limited to bread. At Malta, the size of the Mediterranean fleet by the early 1840s justified construction of a bakery, rivalling in capacity those at the principal home victualling yards. At the other end of the scale, the tiny bakery on Ascension reflected the island's extreme remoteness (*see* Fig 13.6). The comparatively small numbers of those employed in these overseas victualling yards (Table 14.2) is an indication of their primary role as storage facilities.

Table 14.2 Numbers employed in overseas victualling establishments in 1865/6 (TNA ADM 181/77).

Place	*numbers*
Gibraltar	7
Malta	107
Halifax	1
Bermuda	14
Jamaica	9
Ascension	11
Sierra Leone	6
Cape of Good Hope	5
Trincomalee	2
Hong Kong	24
Esquimalt	3
total	**189**

Fig 14.2
The interior of the bomb-proof victualling store at Rosia Bay, Gibraltar. This 1971 photograph shows the building still in naval use. (Author)

For economy and security, the Victualling Board was happy to locate its stores within existing bases overseas if there was space. This happened at English Harbour and Trincomalee and eventually at Port Royal.[31] Here, after initially using commercial premises, the Board had its own establishment adjacent to the dockyard, but this was closed in the 1830s as its use declined, and after temporarily relocating supplies to a hulk, a storehouse was found in the main dockyard. The best example of integrated planning is the Victualling Yard at Bermuda, neatly sited between the ordnance yard and the main dockyard, its spacious layout one of the most attractive architectural spaces

Fig 14.3
The entrance to the Rosia Bay victualling yard at Gibraltar in 1971. The victualling store is to the left and the house for the Agent Victualler to the right. (Author)

on the islands. At Garden Island, Sydney, the main naval storehouse held victuals as well, until completion of the separate Royal Edward Victualling Yard (*see* Chapter 13). At Yokohama a victualling yard consisting of a small general storehouse and a tobacco store was located in the former naval sick quarters, in turn making way in 1882 for a coal yard.[32]

Freshwater supplies at established home bases were not generally a problem, except at Sheerness where fresh water was obtained from Chatham until deep wells were sunk in the 19th century.[33] At overseas bases adequate local supplies were not always readily available. At Jamaica ships had to obtain water from a watering pier linked by an aqueduct to a small reservoir constructed at Rock Fort some 12 miles from Port Royal. On barren Ascension Island in the early 1830s, the Georgetown catchments were supplemented when Brandreth engineered a piped supply from a spring some miles away on Green Mountain. At English Harbour, Bermuda, Gibraltar and Malta elaborate arrangements had to be made using catchments and water tanks, and their capacity at Malta indicated the growing size of the Mediterranean fleet. In 1844 a rock-cut tank on the Corradino Hills was excavated with a capacity of 7,568 tons; in 1849 and 1852 this was supplemented by two further 28ft-deep tanks holding over 19,000 tons of water, and in 1861 by a single tank of 40,000 tons.[34] Probably the smallest naval watering point was a solitary well at Dungeness on the Kent coast, and in the Napoleonic Wars this was 'a useful anchorage for the cruisers that watch the enemy ports on the opposite coast'. The site was still maintained as an Admiralty Watering Point in 1859, although the water here must have been somewhat brackish.[35]

Developments after the Napoleonic Wars

By the time war broke out in 1793, the Victualling Board's extensive investments at Deptford were not matched at its other establishments.[36] Although its supply system coped with demands of the greatly expanded navy during the Napoleonic Wars, by 1815 it was clear that the Victualling Board needed to centralise, modernise and expand manufacturing and storage facilities at the principal fleet bases of Plymouth and Portsmouth. The Victualling Board also had increasing responsibility for supplying the army, and a victualling depot for this purpose was established at St Katherine's Dock, next to the Tower of London. This was closed in 1816 and operations were transferred to Deptford.[37] Plymouth also supplied the important victualling station at Gibraltar and after 1815 the garrison on Ascension Island and the ships of the anti-slavery squadron; probably for these reasons the Plymouth facilities were the first to be modernised. By the time works began, responsibility for Victualling Board construction projects had been devolved to the Navy Board with its architect's department and far greater experience.[38]

The Royal William Victualling Yard, Stonehouse

In 1824 work started on a site for a new manufacturing victualling yard just west of Plymouth on the end of the Stonehouse peninsula, overlooking the entrance to the Hamoaze from the Sound and a little downstream from the dockyard (Fig 14.4).[39] The young John Rennie was appointed as architect. On his father's death in 1821 he had succeeded him as engineer for the Plymouth Breakwater, as well as carrying on his works at Sheerness, Deptford and Woolwich dockyards. In 1822 the Board had decided that its new victualling yard should be 'capable of embracing every requisite object', and it seems to have been left largely to the fortunate Rennie to realise this rather imprecise but grandiose goal.[40] Nearly three years were spent preparing a level 14-acre site for the new yard. This was won by cutting away the northern side of the rocky hill and using some of the material to extend its waterfront into the adjacent Stonehouse Pool. All this and the subsequent construction work were undertaken by the contractor, Hugh McIntosh, then busy with construction of Pembroke Dockyard and the completion of the Gloucester and Berkeley Canal (*see* Chapter 3).

Rennie's grand formal layout has at its centre a tidal basin for victualling craft; flanking this on the west was the brewery and on the east a flour mill and bakery. The bakery had two groups of six ovens arranged back to back. The northern part of the building was partly carried forward on columns to the edge of the quay so that grain boats could be unloaded directly into the building (Fig 14.5). On the south side of the basin the massive quadrangle storehouse dominates the centre of the yard (Fig 14.6). West of the storehouse Rennie placed a smaller irregular quadrangle for the coopers. To its east is an open space, now extensive lawns, overlooked by the houses for the senior

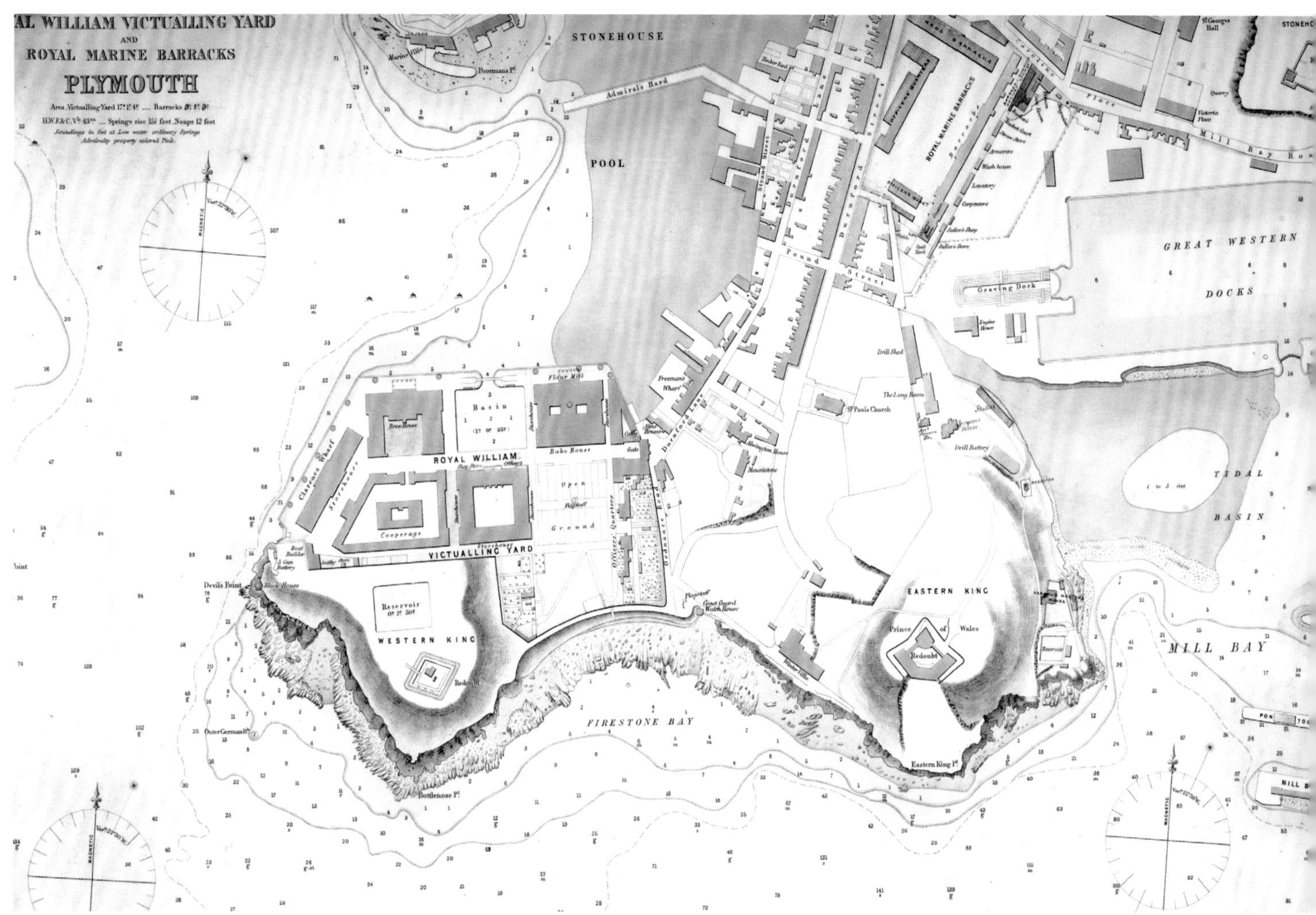

Fig 14.4
An 1863 plan of the Royal William Victualling Yard at Stonehouse. There have been few additions since then.
(AdL 1863 Naval Establishments Da 02)

victualling yard officers (Fig 14.7), but on an 1840 plan marked as a yard.[41] This suggests it was originally a pound for newly arrived cattle before they were taken to the slaughterhouse, which was adjacent to the monumental main gateway surmounted by its 13ft-high statue of King William IV (Fig 14.8).

Rennie terminated the vista from the gateway along the main road at its western end by Clarence Store, which fronted the wharf on to the Hamoaze. The contract for the Clarence Storehouse, the first building to be constructed on the levelled site, was let in November 1827. The next year saw contracts for the boundary

Fig 14.5
Looking across the frontage of the Royal William Yard, Stonehouse, the mills-bakery in the foreground and the brewery beyond. (Author)

Fig 14.6
The basin and Melville Square quadrangle storehouse at Stonehouse in naval use in 1974. On the left is the mills-bakery. (DoE)

Fig 14.7
The houses for the senior victualling officers at Stonehouse. (Author)

Fig 14.8
The grand entrance to Royal William Victualling Yard at Stonehouse, the gateway surmounted by a statue of William IV. (Author)

walls and the basin. At that time Rennie was completing his designs for the brewery and urging the Victualling Board to ask for reports from their brewers at Deptford, Portsmouth and Plymouth 'in order that any defects complained of in the existing establishments may be remedied, and the new one at Cremill be made as perfect as possible'.[42] In 1829 work began on the quadrangle storehouse, later named Melville Square after Lord Melville, First Lord of the Admiralty 1812–27. In 1830 it was the turn of the Main Entrance and Colonnade, Porter's Lodge, Warden's House, Guard House, Slaughter House, Cattle Yard, and Beef and Vegetable Store, 'the whole to be completed by October 1831'.[43] In September 1830 Rennie was still working on drawings for the flour mill-bakery and the officers' houses, but construction of the brewery seems to have been well under way, and this was completed by January 1832.[44] The previous November 'Mr Watt' was still building steam engines, presumably at this stage for the flour mill, and it appears that the mills-bakery was completed in 1834.[45] Rennie's estimate in 1825 had been £291,512 for the buildings, but the eventual total must have been considerably in excess of this figure, which did not include all the preliminary site work or the large reservoir cut into the top of the rock immediately above the yard.

As with all Rennie's projects, the detailing is superb and the masonry work of the highest quality. All the buildings were constructed of the local Devonian limestone, most of it won from the site, with detailing in granite. Rennie made extensive use of iron trusses for roofs, and iron columns were employed for their load-bearing properties inside the main manufactories and stores (Fig 14.9). Most of the buildings had shallow mansard roofs, their lower slopes clad in Delabole slates and their bonnets in copper sheeting. The wharves and basin are notable for their use of finely worked granite (Fig 14.10). Built in a single campaign on a new site, this was always the grandest of the royal victualling yards, and in its externally largely unaltered state it remains today one of the most magnificent industrial monuments in the country.

Fig 14.9
An upper floor of the mills-bakery at Stonehouse showing the flanges on the iron columns for boards that were inserted between columns to form grain bins. A 1974 photograph when the building was a naval store. (DoE)

Fig 14.10
Part of the central basin at Stonehouse showing the superb quality of the masonry. The cast-iron swing-bridge spanning the entrance is an original feature, made by the Horseley Iron Company at their foundry near Birmingham. (Author)

It is unlikely that the Royal William Victualling Yard was ever used to its designed capacity for victuals; indeed, there is some doubt as to whether the brewery ever brewed beer, and an author writing in 1832 noted that 'it is in contemplation to convert into a means of general accommodation'.[46] The Royal William yard and its sister manufacturing yard at Gosport were designed in the aftermath of one of Britain's most arduous and lengthy wars and understandably were laid out to cope with a future war on a similar scale. By the time they were operational, the Royal Navy needed only a fraction of the capacity and could probably purchase beer more economically from local breweries. At least by the middle of the 19th century, victualling staff here and in the other victualling yards were responsible for a variety of non-food stores, including seamen's clothing and 'books from the Seamen's Library and Religious Books'.[47]

Well before the end of the 19th century, the brewery had been given over to a variety of purposes. The former engine house had been adapted as a hydraulic engine house to power the yard cranes, and the west range had been divided into cattle lairs, a slaughterhouse and meat and vegetable stores. Only a rum store in the east range preserved a link with the building's alcoholic origins. By 1900 the coopers were rehoused in a new cooperage on part of the former cattle yard, because the naval Ordnance Department had taken over the cooperage as a gun-mounting store and armaments workshop. For much of the 20th century until the yard closed, the brewery was used as a torpedo workshop.[48] An elaborate narrow-gauge railway system connected most of the buildings with each other and with the basin and wharves. The bakery remained in production, but on a much reduced scale because larger warships from the 1900s were equipped with baking ovens, and ships' biscuits fell out of favour.[49]

The Royal Clarence Victualling Yard, Gosport

At Gosport a good source of fresh water used for supplying the fleet had encouraged the Victualling Board by 1716 to establish a brewery and cooperage on the waterfront, where it was known as Weevil Yard. Unusually, a windmill was used to pump the liquor in the brewery.[50] In the course of the century, the establishment gradually expanded, and in the mid-1760s the Board decided to concentrate all its local cooperage work here, constructing new buildings for the coopers. In 1771 the Earl of Sandwich commented favourably that 'the new cooperage lately finished is large and commodious'.[51] Its buildings are the oldest to survive in any victualling yard, forming a large, irregular, single-storey quadrangle around an open space used to store barrels (Fig 14.11). The original buildings, divided into a series of small workshops, each centred on a hearth, were built partly of brick, with timber-framed and timber-clad upper halves and tiled roofs. Remarkably, a few remained in use until the abolition of the naval rum ration in 1970.

In 1824 the Victualling Board, spurred by the

Fig 14.11
The little well house with barrels awaiting repair in the centre of the cooperage yard at Gosport, photographed in 1968. The cooperage remained in use until the end of the rum issue in 1970. (Author)

works starting at Plymouth, suggested that all the disparate operations on the cramped Portsmouth side of the harbour should be relocated in new facilities at Weevil Yard, where there was room within the fortifications if extra land was acquired from the Board of Ordnance.[52] Perhaps surprisingly, the Admiralty was unenthusiastic, citing the vulnerability in wartime of all supplies being in one place and objecting to the victualling officer being stationed on the opposite side of the harbour. The scheme would probably have foundered had it not been for the support of the Duke of Clarence, recently elevated to the honorary post of Lord High Admiral. In December 1827 the Duke enthusiastically endorsed the proposals and was 'pleased to direct that the whole of the Victualling Establishment at the Port of Portsmouth should be concentrated at Weevil'.[53] Until he was removed from his post the following September, he took a close interest in the project, urging it on and commenting on the plans.[54]

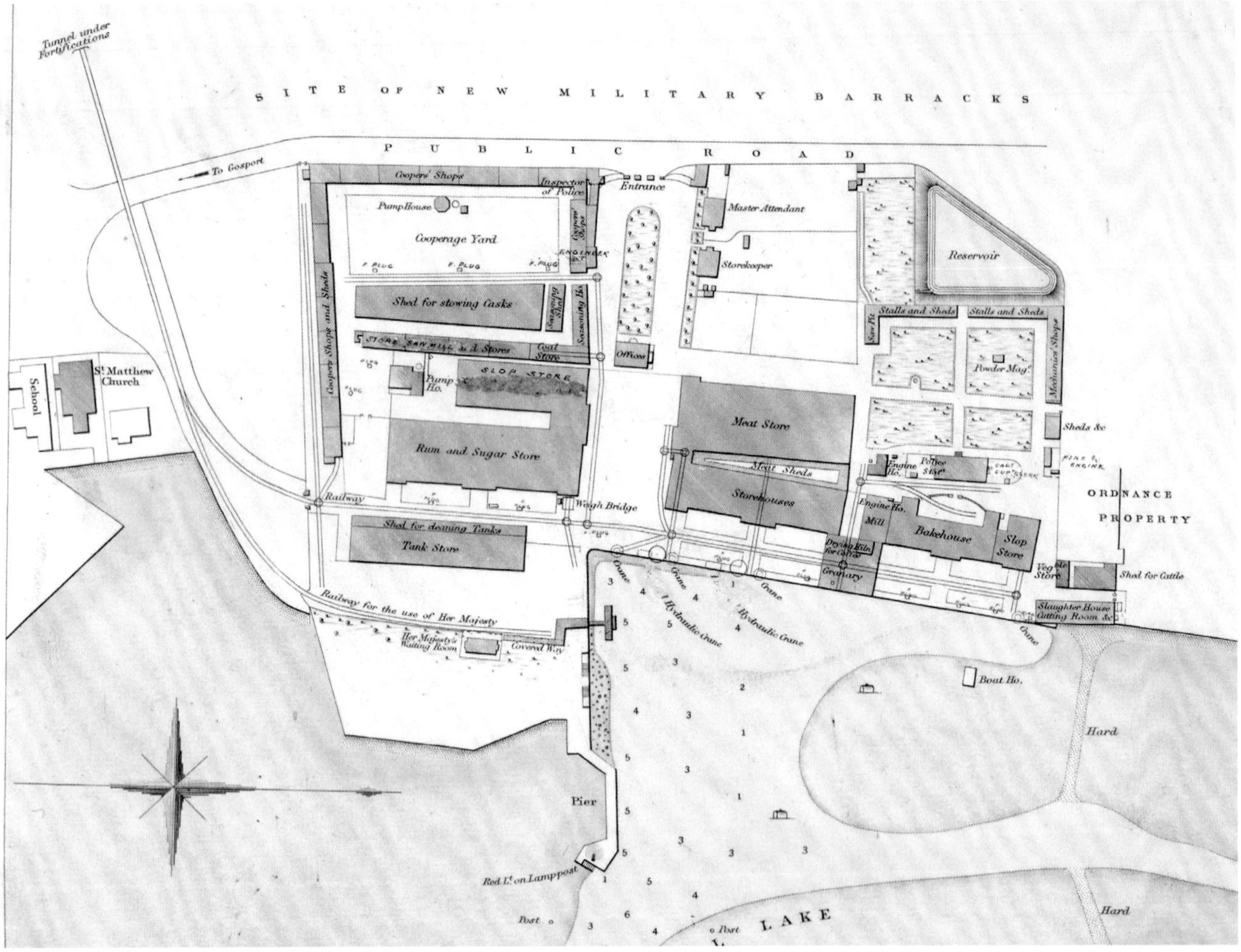

Fig 14.12
An 1863 plan of the Royal Clarence Victualling Yard at Gosport. Although substantially modernised and expanded in the 1830s, it incorporates earlier victualling buildings that largely account for its less formal layout compared to the Royal William Yard. (AdL Naval Establishments 1863 Da 02)

Fig 14.13
The Royal Clarence Yard at Gosport photographed from the Portsmouth side of the harbour c 1900. The mills-bakery dominates the centre and to the right is the slaughterhouse. The brewery to the left was largely destroyed in the Second World War. (Author's collection)

As the Weevil Yard already had an adequate cooperage and a brewery, which G L Taylor was then modernising and extending using the contractor Hugh McIntosh, the principal new facilities required were a flour mill-bakery, dry stores, slaughterhouse, reservoir, houses for the victualling officers and an entrance gateway and lodges. Rennie provided the 40hp engine and machinery for the flour mill.[55] The new buildings were mostly sited on land acquired from the Board of Ordnance along the waterfront, immediately north of Weevil Yard (Figs 14.12 and 14.13). An existing storehouse in Weevil Yard, probably the Long Storehouse, had an extra storey added and was said to contain 5,000 tons of provisions.[56] The extended yard was largely complete by the end of 1832; fittingly, on 1 July 1831, it had been renamed the Royal Clarence Victualling Yard. In 1830 questions had been asked in Parliament about the cost of the project, and in September 1831 it was noted in a House of Commons report that the final bill would probably be under £200,000, still a substantial sum for a project on a smaller scale and involving little expensive site preparation compared to the Royal William Yard.[57]

In appearance Taylor's new buildings were more conservative than those of Rennie, probably a result of the architect wishing to achieve an architectural cohesion with existing buildings. They were constructed of local brick with detailing in Portland stone (Fig 14.14), but Taylor's assured use of iron columns and roof trusses in the surviving mill-bakery matches that of Rennie. This building still retains its battery of brick bread ovens. Nearby, the main gateway, its colonnaded wings, porter's lodge and the pair of semi-detached houses for the senior victualling officers (Fig 14.15) remain much as Taylor completed them, their rendered elevations giving a pleasant Regency feel to this part of the yard. To the rear of the bakery, an area once known as North Meadow was used as cattle lairage and retains a number of former stables. The associated slaughterhouse remains largely intact on the wharf.

Fig 14.14 (below top) The mills-bakery building at Gosport in 2009. The bakery still retains its bread ovens. (Author)

Fig 14.15 (below bottom) The houses for the senior victualling officers just inside the main entrance to the Royal Clarence Yard at Gosport. The scale of accommodation was very similar to Stonehouse. (Author)

Completion of the extended yard in 1832 presented the same problems of over-capacity that faced the Royal William Yard, and by the 1850s the brewery had ceased to function and had become a slop store for clothing.[58] The bakery appears to have remained in use, with extra ovens being recommended in 1861 to enable it to keep pace with demand, but was probably closed soon after the First World War and used as a storehouse.[59] By the 1960s the only buildings still used for their original purpose were the cooperages. Royal Clarence Yard as a whole suffered considerable bomb damage in the Second Word War, leading to the destruction of the storehouse attached to the flour mill, the main offices and most of the brewery and its associated storehouses. The yard closed in 1991, since when most of its surviving buildings have been carefully conserved and found new uses.

Mechanisation

The Malta bakery of 1842–4 was the last of the great traditional bakeries to be constructed for the navy, as well as the only one of this scale at an overseas base. By then, food processing by mechanical power had appeared in the victualling yards, with the introduction of steam-powered flour mills at Deptford, Stonehouse and Gosport in the 1820s.[60] In 1834 the Victualling Department installed biscuit-making machines in the bakery at the Royal Clarence Yard invented by a Mr Grant. Tests of his machinery compared to making biscuits by hand at Deptford showed that there were considerable savings in labour costs; of equal importance, machinery allowed production to be rapidly increased when necessary. Similar machines had been ordered for Stonehouse but not yet installed, and it was calculated that if a third set was provided for Deptford, even with the current reduced demand, there would be an annual saving of £5,970.[61] Grant's machinery seems to have been limited to mixing the ingredients, for as late as 1901 the biscuit bakery at Deptford still manually handled the dough on rolling tables where it was pressed into shape, stamped and carried in trays to be baked in batches in the circular ovens (Fig 14.16). At that date, to satisfy demand and top up naval stores, Deptford baked biscuits for only 3 months every year, producing some 600,000lb, and Stonehouse baked once every 6 months.[62] The numbers employed in the three main victualling yards in the late 1860s (Table 14.3) probably remained reasonably steady for much of the 19th century after the introduction of bread and biscuit making machinery in the 1830s. The relative importance of the coopers in the three principal victualling yards reflects the importance of barrels for storage.

Although there was increasing emphasis on feeding sailors fresh provisions whenever possible, the basic range of foods processed and

Fig 14.16. Biscuit machinery in use in 1901at the Royal Victoria Yard at Deptford. The two cats on the biscuit trays suggest a relaxed approach to food hygiene. (Navy and Army Illustrated *14 Sept 1901*)

Table 14.3 Numbers employed in the three principal victualling yards of Deptford, Plymouth and Gosport in 1868 (TNA ADM 181/79).

Description of workmen	*Royal Victoria Yard*	*Royal Clarence Yard*	*Royal William Yard*
coopers and apprentices	50	19	19
sawyers	4	2	1
blacksmiths	6	5	4
millers and millers' boys	7	5	3
bakers and bakers' boys	21	13	13
other trades	47	16	13
leading men of stores, 1st class	3	3	3
leading men of stores, 2nd class	7	4	3
storemen, 1st class	2	–	–
storemen, 2nd class	10	6	6
leading men of labourers	7	2	2
labourers	60	17	16
total numbers	**224**	**92**	**83**

Fig 14.17
The Royal Victoria Victualling Yard at Deptford. This 1928 plan shows the yard in its final phase with its wide variety of specialised buildings alongside the Thames.
(TNA ADM 174/414)

Fig 14.18 (right)
Cocoa bean roasters in operation at Deptford in 1901.
(Navy and Army Illustrated *14 Sept 1901)*

Fig 14.19 (far right)
The salt meat store at Deptford in 1901, a scene little changed since the establishment of the Victualling Board.
(Navy and Army Illustrated *14 Sept 1901)*

Fig 14.20
An atmospheric evening scene at the main Thames-side wharf of the Royal Victoria Yard at Deptford, with a lighter being loaded.
(Navy and Army Illustrated *14 Sept 1901)*

stored at the victualling yards changed very little in the course of the 19th century. Additional machinery was installed for processing new foodstuffs (Fig 14.18)[63] and tinned food was used in increasing quantities, but most preserved food was still packed in barrels or timber boxes. In 1901 the Deptford yard alone was supplied with 30,000 barrels by its cooperage, the majority probably used for salt meat storage (Fig 14.19).[64] That year the *Navy and Army Illustrated* speculated that 'The time may yet come when some kind of cold chamber will be provided in ships of war to enable fresh meat to be served out regularly'.[65] This development was still some way in the future, and the Royal Navy entered the First World War using a range of preserved foods prepared and packed using methods that had not altered significantly since the end of the Napoleonic Wars a century earlier.

15

Naval Ordnance Yards

Detailed and authoritative accounts of the development of ordnance, explosives and their manufacture and naval ordnance depots are in Cocroft 2000 and Evans 2006. This chapter relies extensively on their researches, but attempts only a simplified overview sufficient to outline the technical developments that affected the ordnance yards and to set the surviving naval ordnance facilities in the wider context of their relationship to other naval shore establishments.

The smooth-bore era to 1855

The Royal Navy relied from the outset for its munitions on the ordnance office, an organisation headed since 1414 by the Master of Ordnance. In 1683 a royal warrant redefined the role of the Board of Ordnance, which continued with little modification until its abolition in 1855. The Board supplied weapons and ammunition to both the navy and the army; in the case of the army this included both fixed defences and field artillery. Such an arrangement made sense when the requirements of both services were very similar. Smooth-bore ordnance that fired solid shot propelled by the explosive force of black powder remained unchanged in their essentials from the late 15th century to the mid-19th century, the gun barrels interchangeable between army and navy use. The wooden truck carriages used on land fortifications, although differing in detail from sea-service carriages, were sufficiently similar for there to be no problems using a common manufacturer.

But developments from the 1830s were soon to challenge the supremacy of smooth-bore weapons. Explosive shells fired from rifled barrels with more powerful propellants by the 1850s were enormously increasing the range, accuracy and power of heavy guns, making existing ordnance very largely redundant. For the navy in particular, the middle years of the 19th century saw the end of the supremacy of the 'wooden walls', with their tiers of broadside armament, and the gradual replacement of the fleet by metal-hulled warships. Initially, these retained broadside armament with a single tier of the new weapons mounted on metal traversing carriages, but within a decade the range and accuracy of the new guns made the concept of such close engagement obsolete. The main armament was increasingly carried on the centre-line of warships on traversing mounts, initially sometimes protected behind barbettes, but soon in armoured turrets of increasing complexity. The divergence between sea and land service ordnance was becoming ever wider.

In 1855 the Board of Ordnance was abolished, partly because of shortcomings in the Crimean War, and its responsibilities were transferred to the War Office. This produced a number of efficiency gains and led to an initial upsurge in the modernisation and expansion of ordnance depots. It did not, however, overcome increasing naval resentment at not being in charge of the design and procurement of its own weapons. Under arrangements with the War Office, 'the Admiralty could not give direct orders to the gunwharves as to particular fitments for particular ships', but had to put their requests to the Ordnance Department.[1] In June 1888 a half-way house was reached, with the Admiralty gaining control by paying for its own weapons and the War Office agreeing to provide storage and staff. Finally, in 1891, a complete separation was achieved with the setting up of the Naval Ordnance Store Department and the formal dividing up of the ordnance depots between the army and navy.

By 1700 the Board of Ordnance had established a supply system dependent on a combination of outside suppliers and its own manufacturing capacity, which was to survive in part until the late 20th century. In the 17th and 18th centuries most iron ordnance came from gun-founders in the Weald of Kent and Sussex (Fig 15.1). By 1800 they had been supplanted by firms with better access to raw materials, such as Samuel Walker and Co of Rotherham and most famously by the Carron Ironworks, established near Falkirk in 1759. These were supplemented by wartime suppliers such as Brodie's Calcutts works near Ironbridge that flourished during the Napoleonic Wars (Fig 15.2). At the very end of the smooth-bore era in the 1850s the Low Moor Company, from near Bradford, and Walker of Gospel Oak were the principal gun-founders.[2] The new rifled guns introduced then became largely the preserve of the Royal Gun Factory at Woolwich and of great armaments firms, notably Armstrong at the Elswick works and a little later Vickers at Sheffield.

In parallel with these private suppliers, the Board of Ordnance developed its own manufacturing capacity, for long specialising in casting the far more expensive bronze pieces at its works at Moorfields. After a disastrous explosion in 1716, production was shifted to new facilities at Woolwich, marking the start of Woolwich Arsenal. For a period in the 1860s Woolwich had a virtual duopoly with Armstrong's Elswick works in the far more complex manufacturing process for large rifled breech-loading and muzzle-loading guns. This involved forging each barrel from coiled iron over which were shrunk a series of wrought-iron jackets to give added strength. The cost of manufacture was significantly reduced in 1867 when the Deputy Assistant Superintendent at the Royal Gun Factory at Woolwich, Mr Fraser, substituted a steel barrel for the forged iron.

Fig 15.1
Excavating a gun-casting pit and blast-furnace at Pippingford in the Sussex Weald in 1974. The gun-casting pit, a rare survival, still retains its timber lining. The small scale of this early 18th-century ironworks is probably typical of most Wealden sites.
(Author)

Until the Seven Years' War, gunpowder had remained the preserve of private manufacturers and suppliers, notably the East India Company. But serious supply and quality problems led the Government in 1759 to purchase an existing set of gunpowder mills at Faversham in Kent, followed in 1787 by mills at Waltham Abbey, north of London. In both cases, these royal gunpowder mills were to be extensively rebuilt and expanded and their manufacturing process vastly improved from 1783 under the superintendence of Major William Congreve. They set the standard for quality and safety for commercial manufacturers and, as Congreve was able to claim with some justification before he retired, 'so great a quantity of powder is manufactured by the Ordnance themselves, that they are enabled to keep the contractors in order, both as to price, and to the quality of the powder'.[3] From the mid-19th century Waltham Abbey was to be the centre for government development of the new chemical explosives, such as guncotton, which were largely to supplant gunpowder.

The Board of Ordnance for long kept its main supplies of gunpowder and guns at the Tower of London. After the humiliating Dutch raid on the Medway, Upnor Castle was converted in 1668 into a powder magazine, and by 1691 it stored 5,206 barrels of powder, compared to the 3,692 then at the Tower. By the early 1770s the need for extra powder storage led to the construction of a group of five huge powder magazines at Purfleet on the Thames, well positioned to receive powder from the works at Faversham. Each of the magazines, of which one still survives, could hold 10,400 barrels, making this by far the largest powder store in the country. Its completion in 1773 enabled the Board to close its magazine at Greenwich, constructed in the 1690s, to the relief of the local citizens.[4]

Just over 30 years later, as war was renewed with France, the Board began construction of a vast arsenal at Weedon in Northamptonshire, next to the Grand Junction Canal, under the superintendence of the Royal Engineer Captain Robert Pilkington. Its central location between London and many of the Board's suppliers in the industrialising Midlands enabled the distribution of ordnance supplies using the

inland waterway system, reducing dependence on coastal shipping that was vulnerable to attack. As well as storehouses for saltpetre destined for Waltham Abbey, four large magazines were completed at Weedon by 1810, each capable of holding 4,140 barrels of powder.[5] Munitions from these principal depots were distributed to ordnance yards located at the main fleet bases, and these yards in turn supplied the associated land defences.

Ordnance installations alongside the dockyards had two distinct functions. The ordnance yards, more commonly referred to as gunwharves, stored ships' guns, truck carriages and operating equipment of rammers, mops and sponges, as well as the small arms, boarding pikes, cutlasses and other weapons. From the 18th century most items would be supplied new from Woolwich or one of the principal depots, but private gun-founders might deliver direct from their works. Gun barrels could be kept in the open, but everything else needed to be kept under cover (Fig 15.3). Apart from the receipt and issue of equipment, most of the routine work on a gunwharf centred on maintenance and repair of weapons removed from warships ending a commission and being placed in ordinary, or undergoing a major repair or refit in the dockyard. Pressure on storage could be acute when fleets were reduced in size at the end of wars. The great majority of buildings to be found in these yards were storehouses, but there were a number of workshops, notably at Portsmouth gunwharf, for armourers, smiths, furbishers and joiners (*see* Fig 15.28).

Gunpowder required rather more careful handling and storage, as well as considerable space. By the end of the 18th century a first-rate warship might have to unload 479 barrels of powder when decommissioning. For safety reasons the powder magazines gradually came to be sited away from the ordnance wharves and urban areas. But gunpowder also had to be regularly checked, sifted to remove any lumps and mixed to ensure that the saltpetre, sulphur and charcoal did not separate. Initial inspection was done in a shifting room (after 1875 renamed the Examining Room), where the barrel tops were removed. This was normally close to the magazine. Gunpowder that had become damp

Fig 15.2
Brodie's Calcutts ironworks near Ironbridge in Shropshire. This 1788 engraving by Wilson Lowry after George Robertson shows what was to become briefly one of the largest producers of guns for the Board of Ordnance. Some cannon can be seen on the far bank of the river above the two figures in the foreground. Goodrich was to visit this works in December 1799 (Ironbridge Gorge Trust, AE185.760)

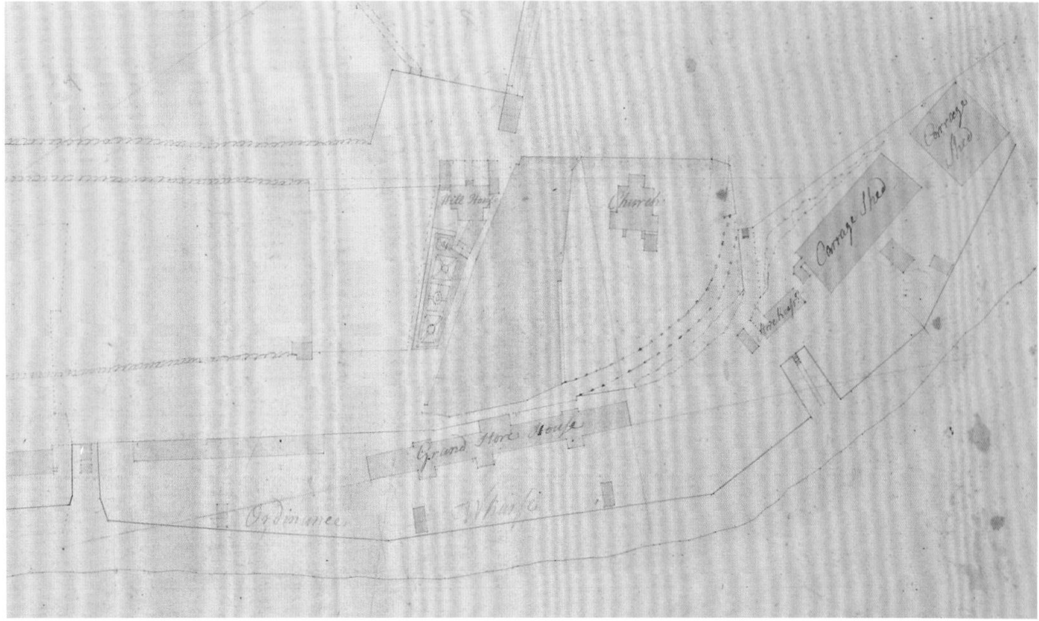

Fig 15.3
The Ordnance Yard adjacent to the dockyard at Chatham in 1704. The principal buildings were storehouses for the ordnance equipment and gun carriages.
(TNA ADM 140/4)

had to be returned to the manufacturing sites for drying, sorting and repacking. Part of Sir William Congreve's improvements included the installation in 1791 at Waltham Abbey of restoving machinery for the drying process, but early in the 19th century the Board of Ordnance decentralised some of its operations, including restoving, to the local yards. This was a dangerous process and tended to be carried out on isolated sites such as Horsea Island in Portsmouth Harbour.[6]

From the time of the Napoleonic Wars ordnance facilities included laboratories that were principally used for small arms and shell filling and were normally part of a magazine site, although they could be entirely separate installations. Associated with these laboratories were workshops used for a variety of other operations, including casting lead bullets and repairing damaged ammunition. At the north end of Portsea, to the rear of Frederick's Battery, the laboratory serving Portsmouth employed 353 people at its height in December 1813.[7] By contrast the laboratory at Upnor was accommodated in the cramped quarters of the south tower of the Tudor castle.

A dry atmosphere was essential within the main powder magazines and was usually achieved through the use of double-skinned walls with controllable ventilators. The magazines had to be constructed without any ferrous materials to avoid the risk of sparks, and doors and door and window frames were clad in copper sheet as a further precaution. Most purpose-built 18th-century powder magazines serving naval bases also had brick-vaulted roofs, copying those in fortresses which had to withstand bombardment. Although bombardment may have been a concern, it seems more likely that the engineers responsible for the magazines serving naval bases were simply following tradition. Vaults added considerably to the expense, and their efficacy in a heavy bombardment was suspect. When the new powder depot was constructed at Marchwood on Southampton Water towards the end of the Napoleonic Wars, the magazines had simple framed roofs.

It was clearly desirable to keep explosives separate from gunwharves, but in a century less concerned with safety than our own, this took time and the standards were very variable. Initially, separation was achieved at Chatham gunwharf, as all the powder could be stored at Upnor Castle, but in 1763 so much was returned that a further storehouse for 10,000 barrels had to be hired.[8] When a gunwharf was established at Portsmouth in the early 18th century, the Board of Ordnance used the 15th-century Square Tower at the end of Portsmouth High Street as a magazine. After the serious fire in the dockyard in 1760, there was mounting local concern, culminating in a petition to George III in December 1767 as citizens speculated on the unpleasant consequences of a similar blaze in the town centre.[9] The Square Tower was superseded in 1777 by a new magazine at Priddy's Hard on the Gosport side of the harbour.

At Morice Yard, Plymouth, Colonel Lilly with his considerable experience might have been expected when planning the yard to have located the magazine in a quieter area of the 1720s yard rather than on the main wharf close to the merchant ships' anchorage. Here, as a later engineer Horneck commented in 1743, 'when the ship company are saluting, rejoicing and firing their guns, the very flashes come ashore to the magazine without any regard being paid to its being open or shut'. By then, the inadequate size of the magazine meant that powder also had to be stored in the only other magazine available in Plymouth, at the Citadel. Sharing such facilities was probably common practice elsewhere and may well have presented the same hazards. At Plymouth it meant the 90lb barrels had to be carried on the backs of sailors through narrow, crowded streets close to shops with numerous small fires, adding to the potential risk of disaster.[10] One quick solution to gunpowder storage in times of crisis was the use of decommissioned warships as floating magazines, and they were extensively used during and after the Napoleonic Wars. These wars saw existing ordnance yards fully stretched and a number of new ones created to serve the fleet and the army. Space also had to be found in them for Congreve's rockets, which were first deployed in an attack on Boulogne in 1805 and remained in service into the 1850s.[11]

In 1790 further moves to expand powder storage at Portsmouth led to the acquisition of land on the comparatively little-developed north-west part of Portsea Island at Tipner. A single magazine for some 7,776 barrels was largely constructed by 1798, but the facility did not come into operation until the completion of the shifting house in 1800. A second and larger magazine with a capacity of 10,000 barrels was added in 1856, its external appearance very similar to its original building. In 1891 Tipner became an army explosives depot.[12] Great Yarmouth, an important rendezvous point for the North Sea fleet, already with a navy yard and soon to have a substantial naval hospital, acquired a major ordnance establishment in 1806. [13] James Wyatt laid this out centred on a magazine, six storehouses, an armoury, workshops, officers' quarters and a barracks for the guard. The establishment was abandoned in 1815, but the handsome pedimented armoury still stands (Fig 15.4).[14] The Marchwood depot on Southampton Water, constructed between 1813 and 1815, originally had three magazines, each holding 6,800 barrels. Four additional magazines to the same pattern were added in the flurry of activity following the problems revealed by the Crimean War. These brought the capacity of the site to an unrivalled 76,000 barrels.[15]

The decades after the Napoleonic Wars were a period of retrenchment for the Board of Ordnance, with little in the way of new works. This was to change dramatically in the mid-century following the strains of the Crimean War and the revolution in ordnance and its propellants.

Fig 15.4
The former Armoury of the naval ordnance yard at Great Yarmouth, begun in 1806 to designs by James Wyatt.
(BB 97/05968)

The rifled gun era 1855 onwards

The introduction and rapid development from the 1850s of rifled muzzle-loading and breech-loading guns for the navy affected the associated ordnance establishments in a variety of ways. The most obvious difference for the gunwharves was the growing size and weight of the largest weapons compared to their smooth-bore predecessors. In the mid-1880s this culminated in the 16.25in guns forming the main armament of the *Benbow, Sans Pareil* and *Victoria* where each barrel weighed 110 tons (Fig 15.5). Manoeuvring such monsters on the wharves required sheer-legs and bogies of commensurate strength; at Portsmouth gunwharf a pair of sheer-legs was obtained from Woolwich Dockyard on its closure and re-erected.[16] Fortunately, like their predecessors, the new rifled barrels could be stored in the open.

The demise of the smooth-bore guns also ended the era of the wooden truck carriages provided and maintained by the ordnance yards. For a time, the new weapons were mounted on traversing metal carriages, but the introduction of barbette mountings and then turrets for the main armament, as well as their growing weight and complexity, meant that increasingly they formed part of a warship's structure to be maintained in the dockyards. Lighter weapons, such as the later Quick-Firing (QF) guns and their mountings could be removed as units for storage and maintenance, but increasingly it was the dockyards that were provided with the gun-mounting workshops and stores, although the ordnance yards continued to be involved. At Devonport in the 1890s cooperage buildings in the Royal William Yard were allocated to storing and servicing these lighter guns and their mountings.[17]

The ordnance yards also became home from the 1870s for two new weapons, the torpedo and the electro-contact mine (Fig 15.6). The mines were designed to be laid to guard the approaches to ports and harbours, and they were fired electrically by an observer on shore. Although deployed extensively around Britain and at overseas bases such as Esquimalt, Simon's Town, Sydney and Trincomalee, they were cumbersome to maintain and lay and were superseded by the simpler contact mines by 1914.

More fundamental changes affected the powder depots. The distinctive bulbous nature of the new rifled guns resulted from the need to increase the strength of their breech ends to resist the enormous pressures generated by the substantial charges of gunpowder now required for such large-calibre weapons. This was ameliorated by the development of slower-burning prismatic powder in the 1870s, which put less strain on a barrel. The barrels could now be slimmed and lengthened to take advantage of the full force developed by this powder, increasing the range and accuracy of the shell. In 1882 Waltham Abbey began to manufacture prismatic powder, following this at the end of the decade by patenting cordite. Named after its

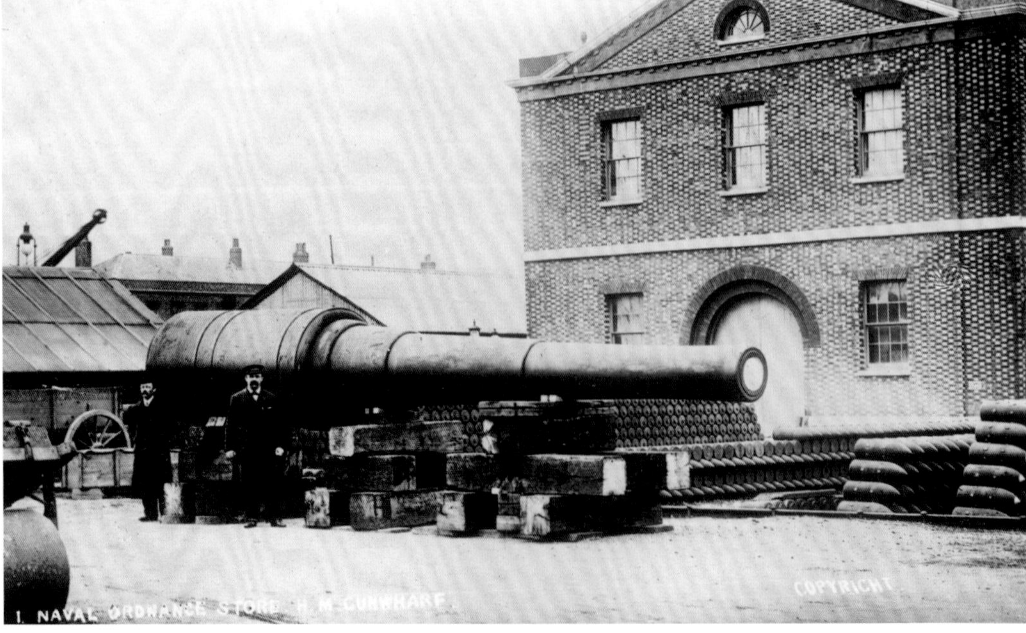

Fig 15.5
Portsmouth Gun Wharf in 1900, with an obsolete 16.25in gun barrel. (1981/193/14, Reproduced by kind permission of Portsmouth Museums and Records Service, Portsmouth City Council, All rights reserved)

resemblance when manufactured to bundles of cord, this marked a significant advance as the first smokeless propellant. Cordite was issued to the fleet in 1893, rapidly taking over from gunpowder. In a further development in 1895, lyddite started to be used as the explosive filling for shells, before being replaced at the start of the First World War by the far more stable trotyl (TNT). Guncotton, first invented in the late 1830s and notoriously unstable except when stored wet, was first manufactured at Waltham Abbey in 1872. It was to have a significant military use as the explosive for naval mines where damp conditions helped its stability but did not harm its explosive power.[18]

Gunpowder had been comparatively simple to store, mainly requiring dry conditions. Provided safety precautions were observed, it was a fairly straightforward operation to fill shells and cartridge bags and to empty them when coming out of service. Cordite was relatively stable, but had to be stored at a temperature no lower than 40°F to prevent it deteriorating, so magazines had to have hot water heating systems installed. Lyddite was the most complicated to handle, because it had to be carefully heated and poured as a hot liquid into shell casings, where it solidified. It was also found that in certain circumstances if it came into contact with bare metal, the resultant chemical reaction could cause a spontaneous explosion. As a consequence, all shell casings had to be carefully lacquered inside and out. Shells also had to be checked at intervals to ensure their fillings and fuses remained in good condition; in 1894 it was stipulated that shells on reserve ships had to be examined every 3 years, all of which made increased work for the ordnance yards.[19]

From the 1860s shell-filling rooms became important elements of ordnance depots, as did the concomitant spaces used for emptying those coming out of service. The QF guns introduced in the 1880s increasingly used shells that had

Fig 15.6
The gun carriage, torpedo store and foundry building at Simon's Town nearing completion c 1895.
At the smaller overseas bases, weapons and their support systems frequently shared storage and workshop facilities.
(AdL Da 038)

Fig 15.7
The mid-1880s shell-filling range of buildings at Priddy's Hard, separated by blast walls, photographed in 1991. This is the finest such set to remain.
(Author)

their cartridges already attached in brass cases. The cases were ejected from the guns after firing, to be returned for refurbishing and reuse. Along with the multiplicity of gun calibres, this added to the work, which was further augmented by the late 19th-century growth in the fleet. There was a need for additional magazines, stores and workshops and the modifying of some existing plant.

The attractions of these new explosives lay in their much greater power compared to gunpowder. However, this meant that careful thought had to be given to the layout of the armaments depots to minimise and contain the effects of accidental explosions. Shell filling was done individually, initially in substantial brick buildings separated by blast walls (Fig 15.7), and later in small, lightly constructed timber buildings, isolated either by space or by earth banks; magazines were similarly spaced well apart and surrounded by blast banks. Inevitably, a combination of lack of finance and lack of space led to compromises at existing naval depots. The only one to meet all criteria was Lodge Hill, a new site laid out at the start of the 20th century to the north of the Upnor depot to serve Chatham and the fleet at the Nore.

Ordnance facilities at Chatham

The first of the ordnance yards, or gunwharves, was established in the 17th century at Chatham, then the most important of the fleet bases. It was constructed just upstream from the dockyard on the site of the Tudor yard and by 1704 had one long storehouse, two carriage sheds, a further lean-to store against the boundary wall and a house for the storekeeper (Fig 15.8). Small treadwheel cranes on the wharf edge were used for transhipping guns and carriages.[20] Until well into the 18th century ordnance and small arms were also stored at Upnor; only later was the castle used almost exclusively as a powder depot.

In 1717, reflecting the importance of this Medway yard, the Board of Ordnance began construction of a huge three-storey brick storehouse on the gunwharf (Fig 15.9). Its Vanbrugian appearance with turrets and false machicolations indicates that its designer was almost certainly the same person responsible for the main gateway, the officers' terrace and other buildings then under construction in the adjacent dockyard. This remained the grandest of the gunwharf storehouses until its demolition after the Second World War. Nearby, the former ordnance storekeeper's residence is now a public house, but apart from a later carriage store of *c* 1805 at the southern end and the former clerk of the cheque's house of 1816, little remains of the former gunwharf that was closed in 1958.[21]

By contrast, much survives at Upnor and its associated magazines that supplied the Royal Navy from 1667 to 1983, a longer record of continuous service than any other comparable ordnance facility. After the humiliating Dutch raid in 1667, the decommissioned castle had the two floors in its main building converted into a powder magazine (Fig 15.10). These were the former living quarters for the garrison that initially seem to have been reused without any alterations.[22] Only later in the 18th century were the internal partitions removed to create the existing open floors. The present wood-block ground floor post-dates this work, as does the unique, manually operated windlass on the first floor, used to raise and lower barrels to the water bastion 30ft below, where shifting rooms were constructed and the powder was transhipped from hoys. The windlass was installed soon after a 1750 report by the Surveyor-General had commented unfavourably on the method then in use, where barrels were drawn up on a pulley,

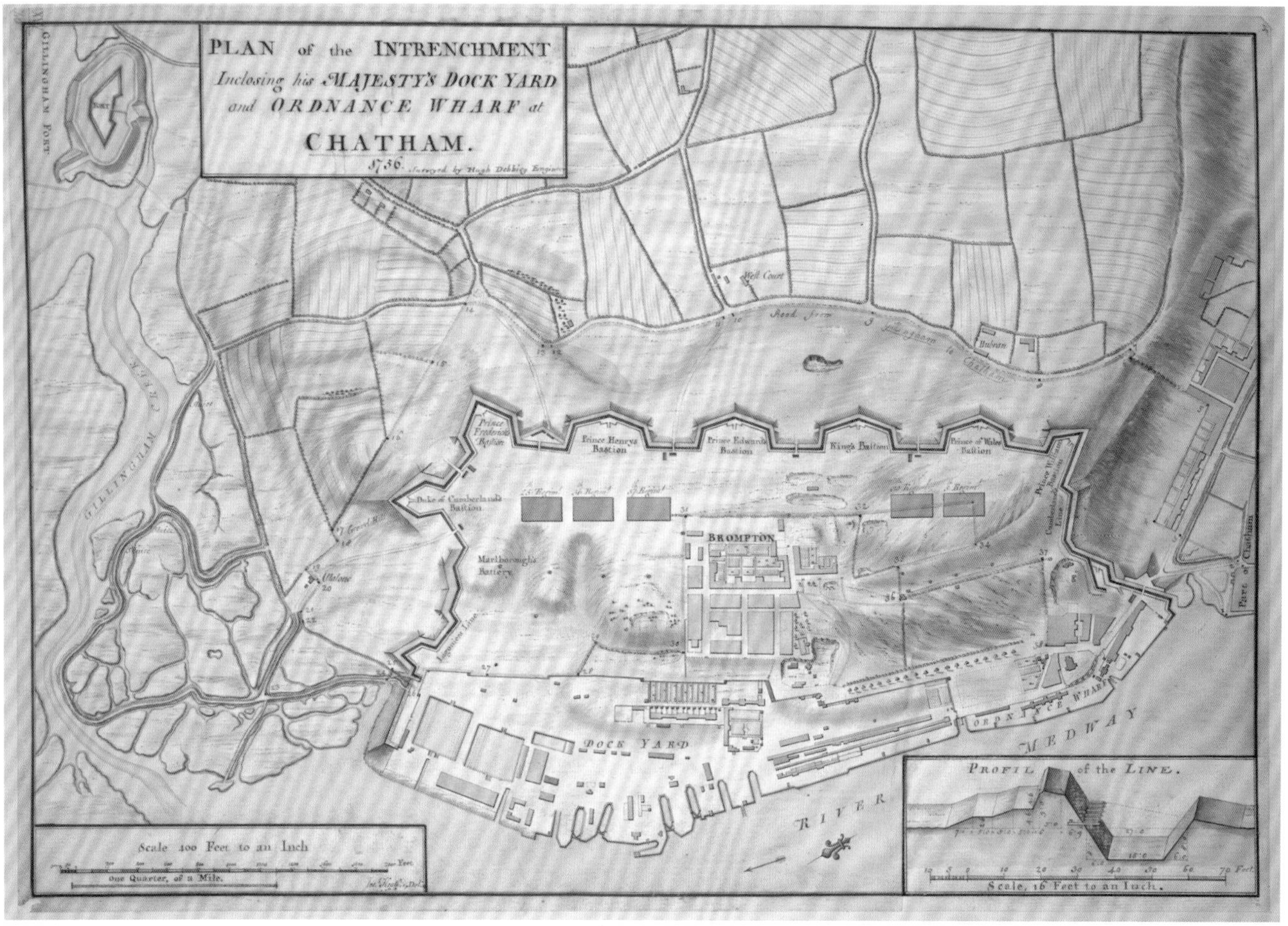

Fig 15.8
Hugh Debbieg's 1756 plan of Chatham. The ordnance wharf on the riverfront just upstream from the dockyard was well placed to serve both the dockyard and its new landward defences.
(© The British Library Board. Kings Top. 16:40)

Fig 15.9
The 1717 Ordnance Storehouse on the gunwharf at Chatham, its size reflecting the then importance of the naval base here.
(AA44/01481)

Fig 15.10
Upnor Castle a little downstream from Chatham, on the opposite bank of the Medway, was begun in 1559 to protect the new dockyard. From 1667, the main accommodation was used as a powder magazine, with powder boats berthing alongside the water bastion below. (Author)

the counterweight at the other end of the rope being provided by a man who 'jumps out of a window, and his weight draws up the barrel … which is a dangerous and uncertain method, for if he is too light the barrel will not ascend, and if he is too heavy, he is sure to bruise himself against the pavement'.[23]

A 1691 survey records that the castle then held 5,206 barrels of powder, along with 164 iron guns, 62 standing carriages, 100 ships' carriages, 7,125 round shot, 4 matchlock muskets, 200 snaphaunce muskets and 77 pikes.[24] Such a considerable inventory must have tested the castle's capacity, as a later plan of 1812 marks the main building as being able to hold 3,500 barrels. This may mean that one or other of the castle towers was pressed into service, although these would have been more suitable for the small arms and pikes. The gun barrels were most likely laid in the courtyard; it is not clear where the gun carriages were kept.[25] This substantial arsenal clearly supplied both the navy and land fortifications down the Medway to Sheerness. Its security was improved by the construction of barracks in 1718 for 2 officers and 64 soldiers, one of the oldest surviving barracks in Britain and one of the least altered (Fig 15.11).[26] A slightly later house once occupied by the ordnance storekeeper stands a little to the west of the castle.

After the construction of the barracks there were few additions to Upnor until the Napoleonic Wars, which saw the depot at full stretch. In the three years from 1801 to 1803, 164 named ships, including *Victory,* had their

Fig 15.11
The barracks constructed in 1718 at Upnor to accommodate soldiers guarding the castle magazine. (Author)

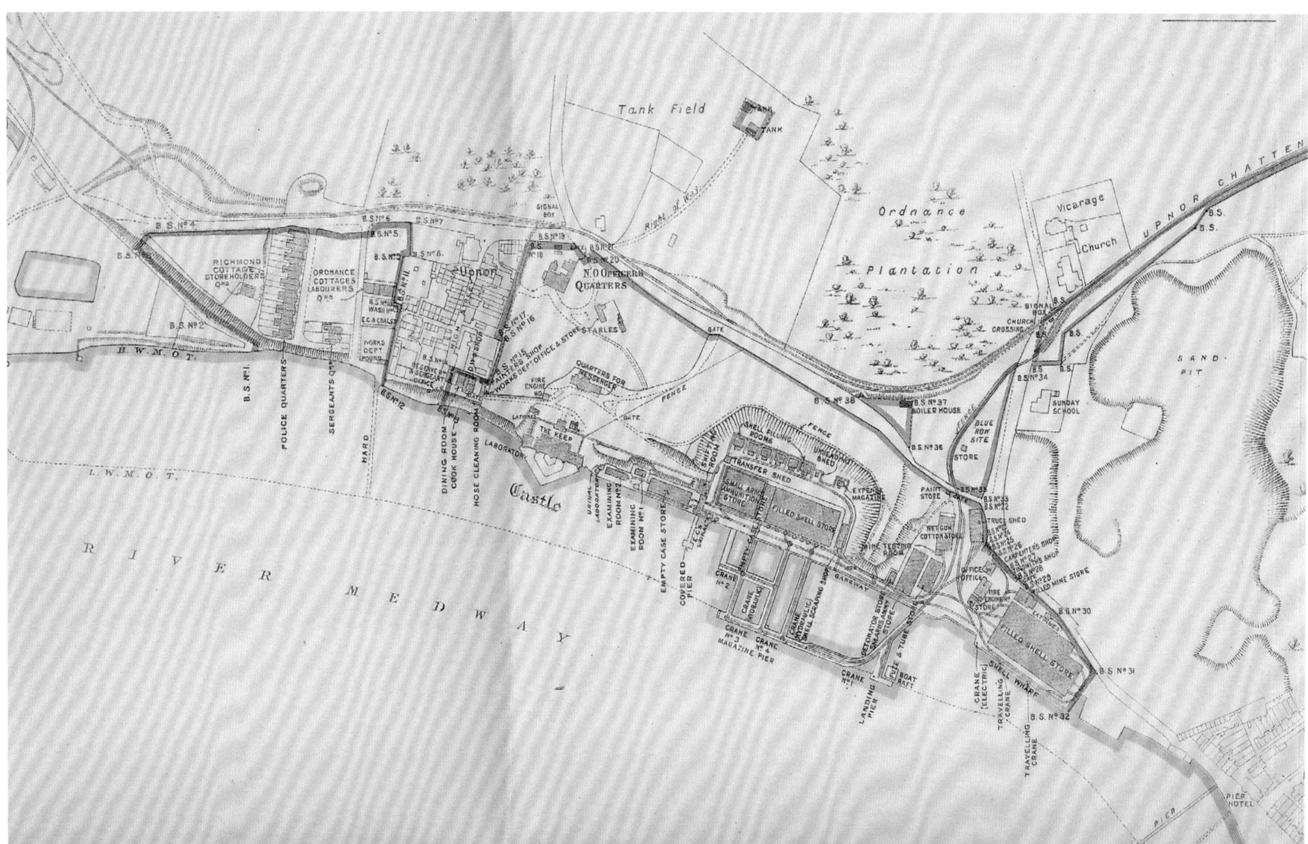

powder landed at the castle or received fresh supplies from it.[27] In 1808 a further magazine for 10,000 barrels was built, along with a shifting house on the banks of the Medway to the north of the castle.[28] The Crimean War and its aftermath saw the War Office authorise two further magazines and two shell stores, which were built between 1856 and 1862 (Fig 15.12). Along with other contemporary facilities, these increased Upnor's capacity to handle the new munitions to not far short of the new Bull Point ordnance establishment then under development to serve Devonport.[29]

Adequate powder storage at Upnor was impossible following official recommendations in 1865 that for safety reasons magazines should be limited to 2,000 barrels; it was not to be resolved until a new site a little way inland at Chattenden was purchased. Here a further five powder magazines were completed in 1875, set into the hillside where the slope formed a natural traverse (Fig 15.13). Each held 4,000 barrels, recognition that the 2,000-barrel limit was impracticable, because of the expense of constructing and operating large numbers of smaller magazines.[30] Chattenden was simply a storage depot, linked to Upnor by a tramway.

Fig 15.12
Upnor Ordnance Depot just before the First World War. The expansion of ordnance facilities during the first half of the 19th century along the riverside north of the castle is apparent, while to the south the village of Upnor is hemmed in by housing for the depot staff. (TNA ADM 140/1484 fol 10)

Fig 15.13
The five powder magazines completed at Chattenden in 1875. This 2009 aerial view shows clearly how the buildings are set into the hillside. (NMR 26475/029)

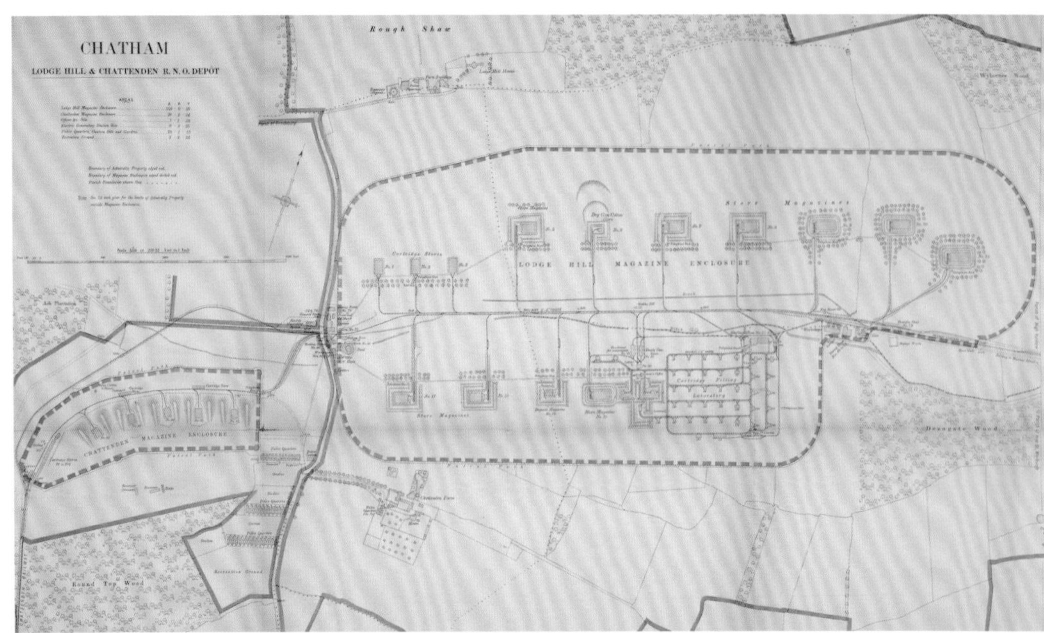

Fig 15.14
The plan of the magazines at Chattenden and Lodge Hill as they had developed by 1909.
(TNA ADM 140/1484 fol 11)

Fig 15.15
Lodge Hill from the air in 2009, showing the widely dispersed buildings. Belts of trees surround the cordite magazines to the right. The two large buildings in the left foreground are Filled Shell Stores built between 1918 and 1939.
(NMR 26475/012)

The 1891 division of ordnance premises between the army and the navy led to the loss of naval storage facilities at Woolwich, Purfleet and Chattenden. Although Chattenden ultimately was retained by the navy, the loss of the Thames magazines proved a serious problem. This was solved by the acquisition in 1898 of an extensive area of undeveloped land at Lodge Hill just north-east of Chattenden. Over the next few years a series of nine magazines for cordite with a further magazine for dry guncotton and one for returned ammunition were laid out, spaced 500ft apart and protected by low traverses (Figs 15.14 and 15.15). A further three magazines held QF ammunition in brass cases; nearby was a laboratory. The depot was serviced by a railway laid through the centre of the site and linked to the South Eastern and Chatham Railway, while a narrow-gauge railway connected Chattenden and Upnor.[31] The magazines were simple brick buildings with low-pitched, copper-covered roofs more reminiscent of a factory estate than the distinctive vaulted magazines on earlier sites. The laboratory buildings, a group of corrugated-iron huts, were even more utilitarian. Nevertheless, completion of Lodge Hill provided Chatham and Sheerness with the most up to date of the three main naval ordnance depots in the years before the First World War.[32]

Ordnance facilities at Portsmouth

Early ordnance stores at Portsmouth were located at the Domus Dei, the former pilgrim hospital on God's House Green that became the Governor's residence in the 16th century. It lay just inside the town's defences, but was less conveniently located for the dockyard at Portsea.[33] By 1717, when similar facilities were being built at Chatham and alongside the new yard at Plymouth Dock, a gunwharf was laid out near the Portsmouth yard. What were described as a 'storekeeper's house and several other works' were also constructed in the course of the 18th century (Fig 15.16).[34]

By 1800 the gunwharf size had more than doubled by the acquisition of adjacent land fronting the harbour across the millpond channel that separated Portsmouth from Portsea. A bridge linked the two yards, known as the Old Gunwharf and New Gunwharf. In the centre of the New Gunwharf, construction of the Grand Storehouse was started in 1811.[35] Built to a design almost certainly by Major-General John Evelegh, a Royal Engineer who had served at Gibraltar during the Great Siege, the Grand Storehouse was the focal point of the yard (Fig 15.17). Its pedimented main range

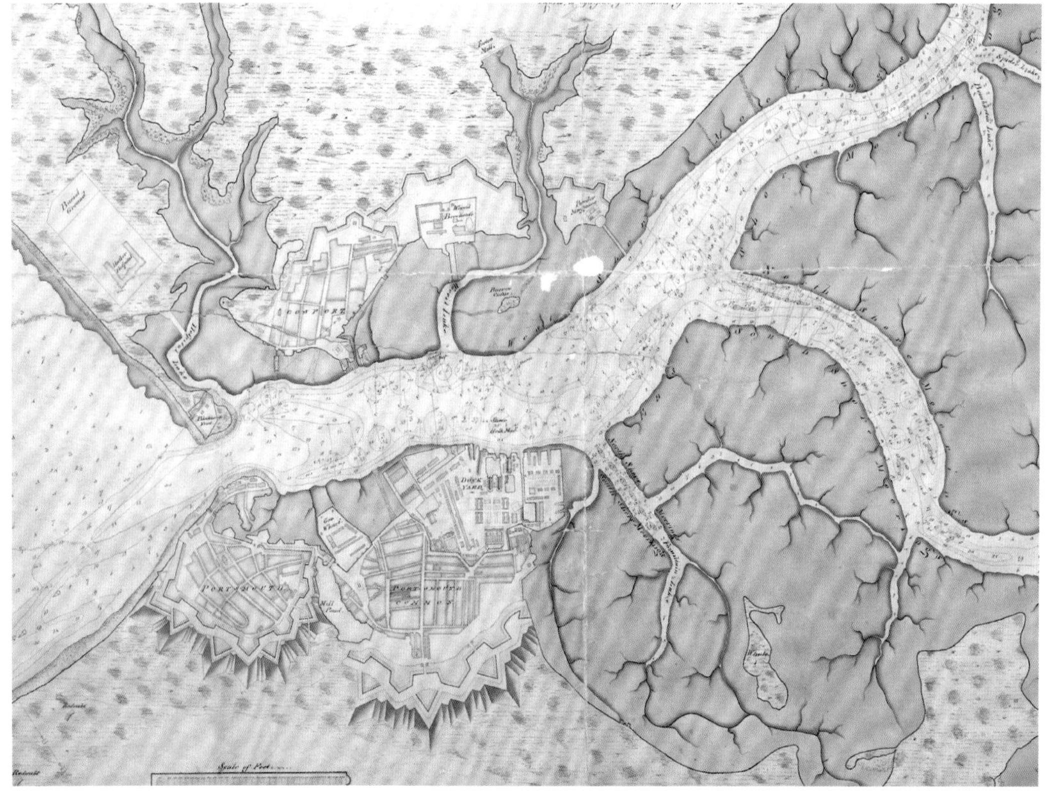

Fig 15.16
Portsmouth Harbour in 1785 looking west. This plan clearly shows the two settlements of Portsmouth and Portsea (here named Portsmouth Common), with the dockyard on the east side of the harbour. The gunwharf fronts the harbour between Portsmouth and Portsea. On the Gosport (west) side of the harbour are shown Haslar Hospital, Weevil Brewery – nucleus of the later Royal Clarence Victualling Yard – and the new powder magazine at Priddy's Hard.
(TNA ADM 140/555 fol 10)

Fig 15.17
Portsmouth Gunwharf c 1900. In the centre is the Grand Storehouse, partly rebuilt in the 1990s after war damage and now the centre of a new housing development.
(1132A/1/2/6, Reproduced by kind permission of Portsmouth Museums and Records Service, Portsmouth City Council, All rights reserved)

and two wings were generously provided with substantial arched entrances for the easy movement of stores. Inside, to support the required heavy floor loadings, Evelegh used a composite construction of iron columns carrying massive timber beams, probably the first time this was used by the Board of Ordnance and predating by several years Holl's use of this method at Sheerness and Pembroke. The main pediment bears the inscribed legend 'Major General Fisher, Commanding Royal Engineers' and the date '1814', in honour of Major-General Benjamin Fisher, who died at Portsmouth on 29 September 1814.[36]

By the end of the Napoleonic Wars the Portsmouth gunwharves had a wider range of building types than any other similar ordnance establishment. They included a gun carriage workshop, carpenters' shop, two substantial armouries, one specifically for sea-service weapons, and a Battering Train Storehouse, the last reflecting the dual nature of contemporary ordnance establishments.[37] In 1891, the division of ordnance facilities saw the Old Gunwharf being left in army control and the New Gunwharf passed over to the Admiralty.[38] Both gunwharves were partly redeveloped in the first half of the 20th century and then suffered considerable bomb damage in World War II. For most of the 20th century, the New Gunwharf was HMS *Vernon*, the navy's mine and torpedo establishment. The gunwharves were closed in 1986. In the subsequent commercial development, only a former Ordnance Office and the Grand Storehouse remain from the time of the Board of Ordnance. The Grand Storehouse had one wing destroyed by bombing, and this has been restored.

Fig 15.18 (opposite)
An aerial view of Priddy's Hard on the Gosport shore of Portsmouth Harbour. This 1996 photograph clearly shows the original powder magazine, its associated buildings and the small camber at the bottom of the picture, protected by the bastioned defences. Later ordnance buildings occupy much of the site.
(NMR 15543/05 22 Aug 1996)

The Board of Ordnance had the advantage that much of the land further up Portsmouth Harbour remained largely undeveloped until the 20th century, making it easier to find sites here for explosive storage and processing. Priddy's Hard was to be joined by Tipner by 1800 and a century later by a new depot at Bedenham.[39] Priddy's Hard, the earliest powder magazine to be specially built at Portsmouth for naval use, lies on the Gosport side of the harbour and was laid out following concern about the dangers of storing gunpowder in the centre of Portsmouth (Fig 15.18). Priddy's Hard was then an isolated location within the northern end of the Gosport Lines. The Board of Ordnance first considered the site in 1766, but construction was delayed until 1769, partly because of Admiralty fears about an explosion there damaging 'the centre of our line of capital ships laying in the harbour', as well as the adjacent Weevil victualling yard.[40]

To secure the agreement of the First Lord, Sir Edward Hawke, the proposals for three magazines were reduced to one, and the plans were mainly drawn up by Captain John Archer.[41] The site was approved in July 1769 when the chief engineer, Major-General William Skinner, visited. He is perhaps best known as the designer of Fort George near Inverness. The first phase of works was completed by 1777 when the brick-vaulted powder magazine came into use; it was

designed to hold 3,904 barrels (Fig 15.19). Riskily close within the walled enclosure were the shifting house and cooperage, the latter apparently pressed into service as a second examining room. The original proposal for a 600ft rolling way across the mudflats to link the depot with deep water was modified, and a much shorter rolling way substituted leading to a small octagonal basin approached by a short channel from the harbour (Fig 15.20). The buildings gained much of their present appearance in 1827, when the two shifting houses were linked by a store for empty barrels.[42] Immediately to the south and overlooking the magazine is a handsome two-storey pedimented building constructed towards the end of the Napoleonic Wars as the storekeeper's office and extended in similar style around 1920 (Fig 15.21).[43]

Facilities at Priddy's Hard were to be enlarged and modernised into the 1960s, reflecting the changing types of explosives, their storage and maintenance and the requirements of the fleet. Among the most important of the pre-1914 additions to remain are a very rare set of laboratory buildings. These date from the late 1840s when the Board of Ordnance, in a move to improve efficiency and safety, authorised their provision as part of a drive to ensure that every establishment had separate facilities for all the functions for which it was responsible.[44] Ordnance buildings of the latter half of the 19th century are well represented by E Magazine, built in 1878–9. This was among the last of the traditional vaulted magazines to be constructed, reflecting concerns about the vulnerability of the Portsmouth area to bombardment. Although designed for gunpowder, it was later used for cordite. At the southern end of the site, overlooking Forton Lake, is a remarkable row of brick Shell-Filling and Fuzing Rooms constructed in the mid-1880s; these are the most complete set to survive in any ordnance yard (*see* Fig 15.7). The small buildings were heated by a hot-water system and were separated by brick-revetted traverses. They were surrounded on the land sides by earth banks, precautions given added emphasis by the fatal explosion in a shell-filling room on the site in 1883.

Fig 15.19
The original brick-vaulted powder magazine at Priddy's Hard, completed in 1777 and now a museum of ordnance.
(Author)

Fig 15.20
The small tidal basin or camber adjacent to the main powder magazine complex at Priddy's Hard from where boats transported powder barrels to warships lying in the harbour and brought back powder needing to be checked or stored.
(Author)

Fig 15.21
The storekeeper's office at Priddy's Hard. (Author)

The introduction of QF weapons in the 1880s led to a need for further storage for their shells and the construction of a brick warehouse in 1896–7 to hold 6pdr and 3pdr ammunition. Later in the First World War it became a carpenters' shop, its survival today a useful reminder that the ordnance yards employed numbers of carpenters making and repairing ammunition boxes.[45] Priddy's Hard was closed in 1985 and its functions transferred further up harbour to Bedenham, which had developed as a naval ordnance depot between 1903 and 1920. Its linear layout followed that adopted at Lodge Hill, and the design of its magazines was based on the Cordite Cartridge Stores built at that depot from 1899.[46]

Ordnance facilities at Devonport

The establishment of Plymouth Dockyard in the 1690s and its growing use by the Western Squadron was soon followed by a small ordnance yard. A wharf and storehouses were constructed near Mount Wise, but the site was cramped, and when in 1717 the Board of Ordnance looked to expand the yard, the Navy Board asked that it be relocated closer to the dockyard. The new site lay immediately adjacent to Plymouth Dockyard on land owned by Sir Nicholas Morice, after whom the new ordnance yard was named.

In 1715 Colonel Lilly had been appointed as Engineer-in-Charge of the Plymouth division, and much of the preliminary work, including the selection of the site and negotiations with the owner, was delegated to him by the Board of Ordnance, which reasonably noted that it 'must be left to his judgement, being upon the spot'.[47] In March 1719 the 'buttings and boundings' were staked out, and in the early summer a Mr Gumb and Partners won a contract to furnish moorstone for the works. That year, Lilly was recalled to London,[48] and it was not until 1720 that Andrews Jelfe was sent to Plymouth to supervise the works. In January 1719 he had been appointed 'Architect and Clerk of Works of all buildings erected or to be erected in the several garrisons, forts, castles, fortifications etc, belonging to the Office of Ordnance', but for a number of years before that he had been employed by the Board as a clerk of works and from 1716 had been supplying 'draughts of buildings and fortifications'.[49] Lilly would have been perfectly capable of designing the buildings, which he must have discussed with Jelfe after his recall to London. However, his direct input may have been limited to the overall plan, together with the preliminary engineering works that quarried away the hillside to a depth of some 40ft to create the wharf and space for the main storehouses.[50] It was not until October 1720, when Jelfe was on site, that William Cowley, a London stonemason, was awarded a contract for the bulk of the buildings. These owe much to Hawksmoor's influence, something

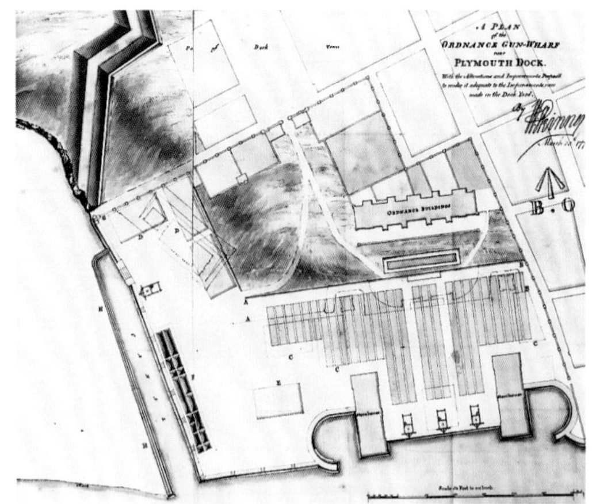

Fig 15.22 (right)
A plan of Morice Yard, Devonport, in 1774, little altered since completion. The two storehouses with their basins flank the open central storage area that is overlooked by the officers' terrace on high ground to the rear.
(TNA MPHH 1/703 fol 35)

to which Jelfe would have been much more exposed than Lilly, who had spent much of his career abroad.

The centre of Morice Yard was originally largely an open space for storing gun barrels. This was flanked on the north and south sides by two storehouses, set at right angles to the wharf and each provided with a small semi-circular basin that allowed loads to be transferred between the centre of each building and small craft alongside (Figs 15.22, 15.23 and 15.24). When first constructed, the storehouses were equipped with wooden railways to help move the heavier ordnance equipment kept here.[51] Three treadwheel cranes stood in a row along the wharf edge in front of a small powder magazine. Overlooking the yard from the rock above, Jelfe placed the officers' terrace, its varied skyline showing clear Hawksmoor influence (Fig 15.25). Originally, this provided houses for four senior officers, with the central part used as barracks for soldiers guarding the yard, though this use as barracks was soon discontinued. The terrace was linked to the yard below by a divided flight of steps constructed by Cowley, who was paid £853 14s 2d for cutting back the rock 'and making the great flight of steps leading up to the Officer's Pile on the hill' (Fig 15.26).[52] Morice Yard was surrounded by a wall with its gateway a little to the east of the

Fig 15.23 (above)
The least altered of the pair of original storehouses at Morice Yard.
(Author)

Fig 15.24
The interior of the same storehouse at Morice Yard, still retaining its early board-lined walls.
(Author)

terrace. The two lodge houses were originally occupied by workmen, a reminder that when this was built accommodation had to be provided, as the yard was in open countryside.

In 1743 the existing powder magazine was authorised, replacing the original one.[53] This is one of the earliest surviving vaulted magazines with double-skinned walls and copper-sheathed doors and shutters. Its exterior is distinguished by a quirky set of brick pilasters and pediment, below which are the arms of the Duke of Montagu, Master-General of the Ordnance from 1739 to 1749 (Fig 15.27). Much of its powder would have come from the Royal Powder Mills, which were established at St Budeaux, a little way up the River Tamar, and also had an important later role in restoving powder.[54]

Fig 15.25.
The officers' terrace overlooking the heart of Morice Yard and the Hamoaze beyond. (Author)

Fig 15.26
The great double set of steps leading up to the officers' terrace at Morice Yard, with vehicles now occupying the space where gun barrels were once stored. (Author)

Fig 15.27
The 1743 powder magazine at Morice Yard, one of the oldest such buildings to survive. (Author)

In the 1770s two small buildings were constructed as a furbishers' shop and a smiths' shop (Fig 15.28). Furbishers were responsible for repairing and maintaining small arms. In 1776 a two-storey gun-carriage store was added, and these buildings survive much as completed. The Morice Yard building is a very rare surviving example of a furbishers' workshop.[55] During the Napoleonic Wars a substantial number of temporary buildings, including a hospital for the Royal Artillery, were constructed in the yard, but have left no trace.[56] In the centre three handsome ashlar warehouses were added in the mid-19th century, the large arched entrances on two of them denoting their original use as carriage stores. Most of the buildings in Morice Yard remain substantially unaltered, making it the outstanding example of a naval ordnance yard, spanning from 1718 to the demise of the Board of Ordnance.

By the 1770s, when additional gunpowder storage was needed here, safety concerns favoured separation of powder magazines from the gunwharves. A new site was chosen a little way up the Hamoaze at Keyham for two 10,000-barrel magazines and associated facilities, which came into use in 1783.[57] Sixty years later, the site was needed for the new Keyham Steam Yard, and so their operations were relocated further up the Hamoaze at Bull Point, where the new powder depot subsumed the site of the St Budeaux powder works (Fig 15.29), making use of a number of its laboratory buildings.

Fig 15.28
The late 18th-century furbishers' shop at Morice Yard, Devonport. (Author)

Although the Admiralty had started work on the Keyham Steam Yard in 1844, it was to be 1849 before the Board of Ordnance produced an estimate of £97,627 for Bull Point; this included magazines for 40,000 barrels, 'or double the quantity of the present magazines ... by which means all occasions for ever employing floating magazines will be avoided' and 'houses for the workmen, barracks for the guard etc'.[58] The cost of purchasing the site was £27,000, and a further sum of £49,721 was later added to construct a Boat Basin 'in lieu of the Camber surrendered at Keyham'.[59]

On completion of the main building works in 1857, Bull Point became the best planned of all these magazine complexes, the first to be designed around the supply of filled shells, which were then rapidly displacing solid shot.[60] The crescent-shaped site curved along the shore south from Bull Point, round Kinterbury Point and towards Weston Mill Lake. Following the system adopted at Priddy's Hard, great care was taken to ensure that there were separate production and supply lines for powder and shells, with individual buildings linked by a tramway system. The four main powder magazines in the northern part of the site were supplied from their own powder pier. Powder from these magazines was taken to an expense magazine adjacent to the laboratory, with its ancillary buildings and shell-filling and cartridge-filling rooms at the southern end. The filled shells and cartridges were then sent to the issue magazine by the basin to await shipment (Figs 15.30 and 15.31). As ammunition could also be returned here, this magazine was divided for safety into two separate halves. Returned ammunition could also be landed at a jetty towards the southern end of the site, where it was processed in the adjacent laboratory buildings.

The five great magazines and the traverses are notable for their monumental stone architecture with rusticated quoins, bold stringcourses and substantial porches (Fig 15.32). The majority of the buildings from this first phase still remain. Between 1893 and 1906 the facilities were extended to accommodate cordage and guncotton storage and new magazines for QF ammunition, forming what Evans describes as 'the best surviving group representative of the development of these new

Fig 15.29
Bull Point powder depot. The receipt and issue magazine and its basin lie at the northern end at the top. Immediately south are the four principal magazines, then set back and heavily protected by blast banks is the later cordite magazine. The large flat-roofed building in the centre of the picture is the main shell store. In the division of ordnance facilities in 1891, the basin and two adjacent magazines became a Royal Army Ordnance Depot. (DAP UY14 © Frances Griffith, Devon County Council, 07/11/2012. Not to be reproduced in any way without the prior written consent of Devon County Council Historic Environment Service. Most archaeological sites in Devon are on private land. Depiction of a site on an aerial photograph, or its inclusion in the Historic Environment Record, does not imply any right of public access)

Fig 15.30
The receipt and issue magazine at Bull Point seen across the basin in 1981.
(DoE)

Fig 15.31
Interior of the receipt and issue magazine at Bull Point in 1981.
(DoE)

Fig 15.32
One of the main magazines at Bull Point.
(Author)

explosives at the end of the nineteenth century'.[61] On the hilltop to their rear stands a very rare set of defensible barracks, built in 1855–8 to guard the new powder depot. Inside its curtain walls, with their two small angle bastions at opposite corners, there remains a complete set of military buildings including a small powder magazine for the garrison.[62]

Overseas ordnance facilities

The role of overseas ordnance depots was essentially one of storage of ammunition sent out from Britain first by the Board of Ordnance and from 1855 by the War Department, until the Admiralty gained complete control in 1891. Limited supplies of expendable equipment, including rammers, mops and sponges, were kept at some of the larger establishments such as Bermuda, but maintenance and repair of gun carriages of warships on station normally remained the responsibility of the ships' carpenters. Magazines in general followed the pattern of their contemporaries in Britain, their scale depending on the importance of the base and whether they were also supplying powder for defence works. Associated facilities were generally limited to receiving and shifting rooms, as well as a cooperage for repairing powder barrels. Powder that was substandard or damp from the effects of climate or long periods at sea was dealt with when a warship returned home. Restoving equipment does not seem to have been supplied to overseas bases, although an earlier undated proposal at Port Royal for a magazine, shifting house and cooperage did indicate adjacent 'dry sandy land for starting of powder upon hides to dry in the sun which will give strength to the same'.[63]

As with overseas naval bases, distance from supervision by London allowed something of a proliferation of local standards, especially at the smaller bases where money was always tight and space could be at a premium. The great majority of overseas bases were protected by fortifications. On grounds of economy and security, it made sense for the local garrisons and the navy, at least in the early years of a naval base, to make joint use of magazines located within the defences, as was proposed at Port Antonio in the 1730s and as happened at Malta 70 years later.[64] Admittedly, when Admiral Byng was establishing the base at Mahon in 1709, he proposed a bomb-proof magazine, the implication being this was for the navy, but it does not seem to have been built, and throughout the British occupation the navy seems to have made use of powder stores in the fortifications.[65]

Unusually, the navy in Jamaica used magazines located some miles across harbour at Fort Clarence or at the army depot at Kingston, probably for fear of further earthquakes at Port Royal.[66] But sharing magazines could bring its own problems over the apportioning of the contents, especially if supplies were inadequate, and the gradual trend was for the navy and the local garrison to develop their own separate establishments.[67] Lieutenant Edward Henry Columbine's 1789 plan of English Harbour shows separate army and navy powder magazines at the head of the harbour adjacent to what was later named Ordnance Bay.[68] By the mid-19th century the naval magazine had been relocated to the small peninsula between Ordnance Bay and Tank Bay, where a number of ordnance storehouses had also been built.[69] At least one of these powder magazines remains.

On the Great Lakes, Kingston Navy Yard had a small powder magazine at one side of the yard, described in 1840 as 'in temporary repair'.[70] At Halifax warships coming into the dockyard at the end of the 18th century unloaded their powder at George's Island in the harbour, where there was what was described as a flimsy wooden magazine holding up to 1,200 powder barrels. As this was only some 80 yards from the ramparts of the island's fort, safety left something to be desired, and the hulk *Inflexible* was used as a floating magazine until she was broken up at Halifax in 1820. Not until some years later were a magazine, ammunition store and small wharf provided close to the dockyard beyond the seamen's hospital.[71] At Esquimalt a naval ordnance depot was established in the early 1860s on Cole Island at the remote northern end of the harbour.[72] By 1895 there were four powder magazines, a shell-filling house, a mine and shell stores and a caretaker's quarters. A number of these were described in 1901 as being very temporary and in poor repair, while the crowded nature of the ordnance depot due to lack of space meant that it did not meet magazine safety regulations. A new site was recommended, but the Royal Navy withdrew from the base before this could be implemented.[73] On Ascension during the smooth-bore era, the navy had what was described as a small ordnance shed opposite its main storehouse, but must have relied on the garrison magazines for powder. The changeover to shell guns was not matched here by any new storage facilities. An 1896 report, by the Royal Engineer Lieutenant-Colonel James Lewis, noted that ammunition was stored 'in an unused old house in the victualling yard' with 'all shells stored in two long sheds' nearby, and the guncotton kept in a 'disused cement store in Georgetown'.[74]

At Simon's Town a small ordnance yard with two magazines was established on the foreshore at South Point, and this was joined in 1888 by a Submarine Mining Establishment (Fig 15.33).[75] A number of the ordnance buildings dating from the first half of the 19th century remain within the present dockyard boundary, but the main ordnance depot was to be laid out in the 1890s in Kloof valley, inland from the dockyard.[76] A rather similar development took place at Trincomalee, where it seems likely that powder initially was stored in the former Dutch Fort Ostenberg just above the base. By 1863 a shed 'occupied by guns' lay to the rear of Pugett's Wharf with its coal store, then beyond the dockyard boundary.[77] By 1909 this area had developed into the main naval ordnance yard, with a shell store, naval reserve magazine, wet guncotton store, QF ammunition store and small laboratory. There were also plans to create a naval mining establishment immediately adjacent.[78]

The most complete overseas example of a pre-1850 ordnance yard is at Bermuda Dockyard (Fig 15.34), where it was located to serve both the navy and the Ireland Island fortifications. It was begun in the late 1830s within the newly completed bastioned defences of Keep Yard, just below the former

Fig 15.33
New magazines and mine stores at South Point, Simon's Town, photographed in the mid-1890s. The construction a few years later of the adjacent steam yard led to the partial relocation of the magazines.
(TNA ADM 195/2 fol 23)

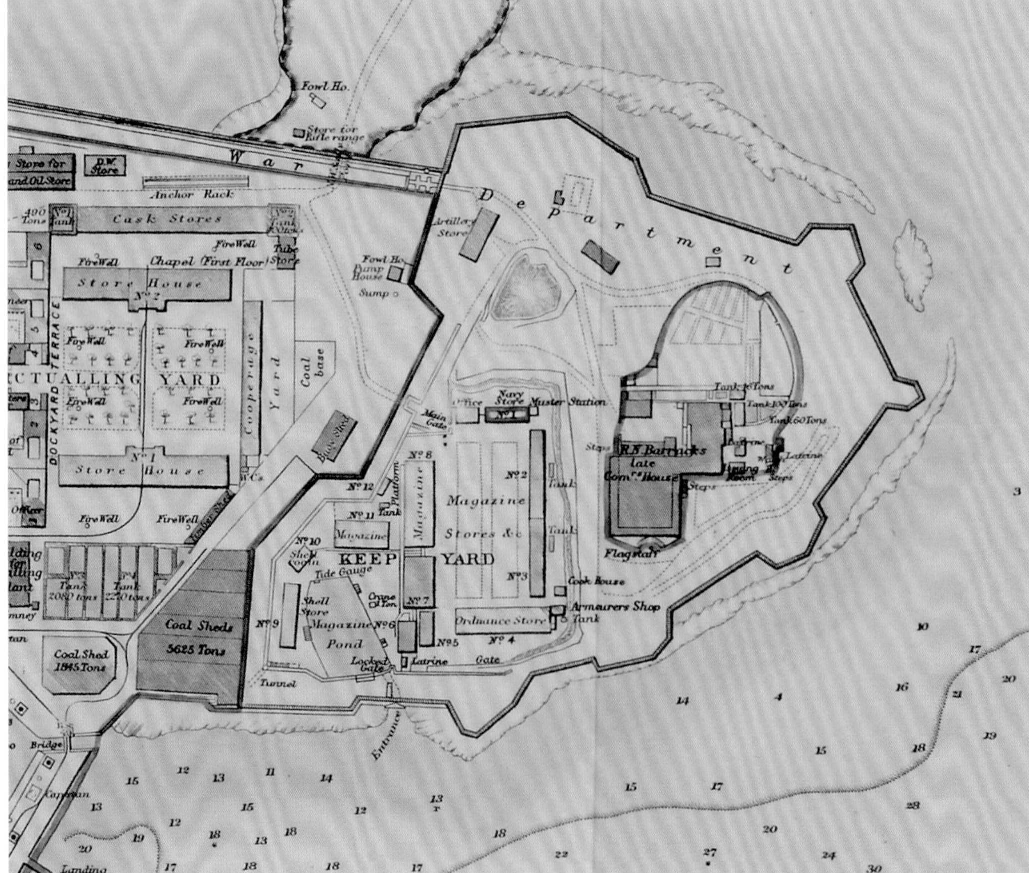

Fig 15.34
Part of a 1909 plan of the dockyard at Bermuda showing the location of the ordnance yard within Keep Yard inside the defences.
(TNA ADM 140/1484 fol 68)

Fig 15.35
The ordnance yard at Bermuda with the boat tunnel through the ramparts. The magazines on the left are those designed by Francis Fowke.
(Author)

Commissioner's House (*see* Fig 12.39). The heart of the yard is a small boat dock enlarged from a natural fissure in the rock. Ammunition boats were able to reach this dock along a short tunnel from Great Sound, protected by a portcullis where it passed through the ramparts (*see* Fig 15.35).

Around the dock are three disparate magazines constructed of the local stone with brick vaults. The earliest, a three-bay vaulted building constructed in 1837, stands just beyond the head of the dock. A second but smaller magazine later used for shells was added in 1849, its single brick barrel vault carried to the external faces of the gable ends. This magazine was designed by the young Lieutenant Francis Fowke, who was also responsible a year or so later for two adjoining buildings, very substantial and distinguished by their classical elevations with decorative external pilasters and heavy cornices (Fig 15.35). The southern of the two buildings was divided internally into three separate units forming a cooperage, a receiving room and a shifting room; the northern one was a great tunnel-vaulted magazine capable of holding 4,968 barrels, divided internally into bays by transverse brick vaults which, like the smaller magazine, are carried through to the external elevations of the building.[79] The reasoning behind Fowke's choice of a classical style is unknown, but the two buildings remain among the most striking of all magazine structures. East of this range of buildings were later ordnance storehouses of considerably more utilitarian design.[80]

In Sydney Harbour, Spectacle Island remains the finest surviving example of a small overseas ordnance depot developed at the end of the 19th century (Fig 15.36), to complement the dockyard facilities then being constructed on Garden Island. In 1865 the New South Wales Government selected Spectacle Island as the site for its official gunpowder store, and the newly appointed Colonial Architect, James Barnet (*see* Chapter 4), was responsible for its initial development. On the south side of the island (Fig 15.37), he constructed a three-bay vaulted magazine approached by a covered way from a short jetty for the powder boats (Fig 15.38). The associated shifting rooms, cooperage store and barrel store were housed in three ranges of single-storey buildings centred on the magazine. To the east of these buildings and overlooking the harbour, Barnet designed a pair of residences for the civilian staff (Figs 15.39 and 15.40), while to the west was a house for the labourers,

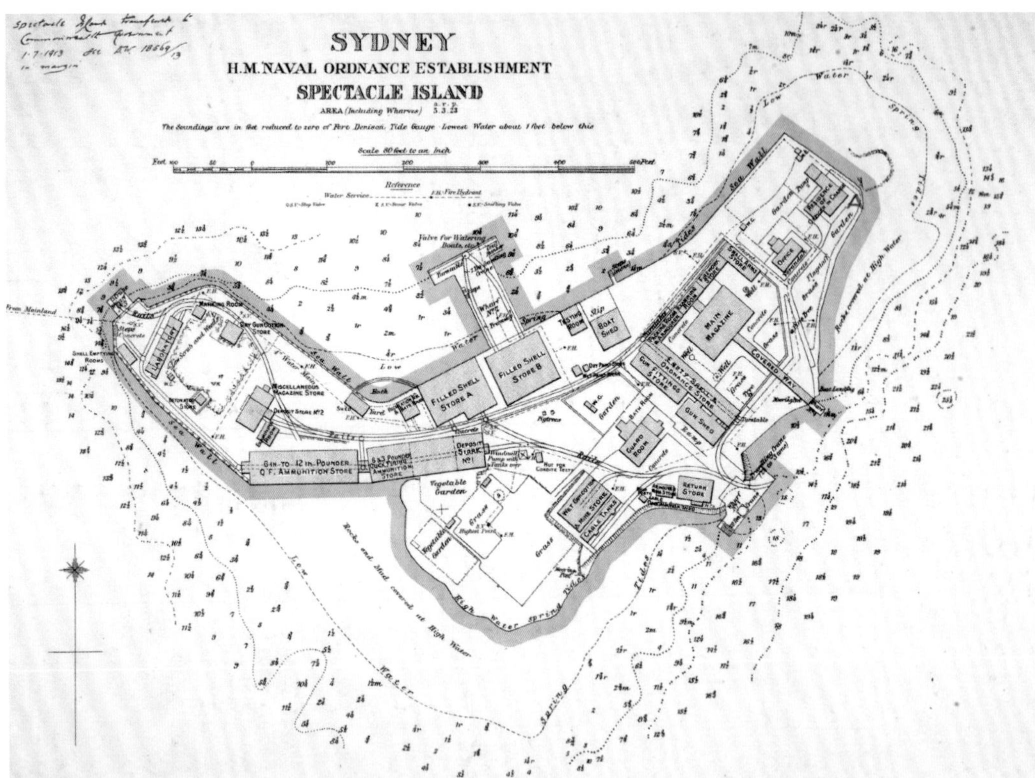

Fig 15.36 (right)
A plan of the ordnance depot on Spectacle Island, Sydney, soon after completion in 1900. (AdL Vz 15/80)

Fig 15.37
Spectacle Island, Sydney, from the south c 1900. (AdL Da 039)

Fig 15.38
The main magazine at Spectacle Island, Sydney, approached by a covered way. (Author)

Fig 15.39
The pair of residences constructed for senior civilian staff at Spectacle Island, Sydney. One was used as petty officers' quarters in the 1890s.
(AdL Da 039)

later the guard room.[81] All these were constructed in local sandstone with hipped slate roofs. In the 1870s a new laboratory, later a filled shell store was added, and in 1884 the island became an armament depot for the Royal Navy.

Over the next 20 years a series of buildings was added to Spectacle Island, which included Filled Shell Stores, QF Ammunition Stores, Examining Room, Return Store, a Dry Guncotton Store and a combined Wet Guncotton and Mine Store with its associated cable tanks. There were in addition a Test Room, an Armourers' Workshop, a Gun Shed and Gun Fitting Store. In 1894 a further laboratory was built in an isolated position at the western end of the island. The buildings are a mix of stone, rendered brick and corrugated iron. Filled Shell Store A unusually was built of polychrome brick with stone dressings; this and a number of other buildings from the 1890s reflect the Federation Free Style design, products of the Government Architect's office.[82] Although a number of buildings was added after 1905, the ordnance depot remains the most complete overseas example of its date, reflecting the rapid evolution of naval ordnance in the half century before the First World War.[83]

Security from bombardment was a factor when Spectacle Island was selected for an ordnance depot, but it was never a serious threat. By the 1880s the positions at Gibraltar and Malta were very different. At both places naval facilities were increasingly vulnerable to long-range bombardment, while existing ordnance storage was inadequate, inefficiently located and out of date. The Channel fleet's

Fig 15.40
The senior staff quarters at Spectacle Island, Sydney, today. The far bungalow had an extra floor added in 1915.
(Author)

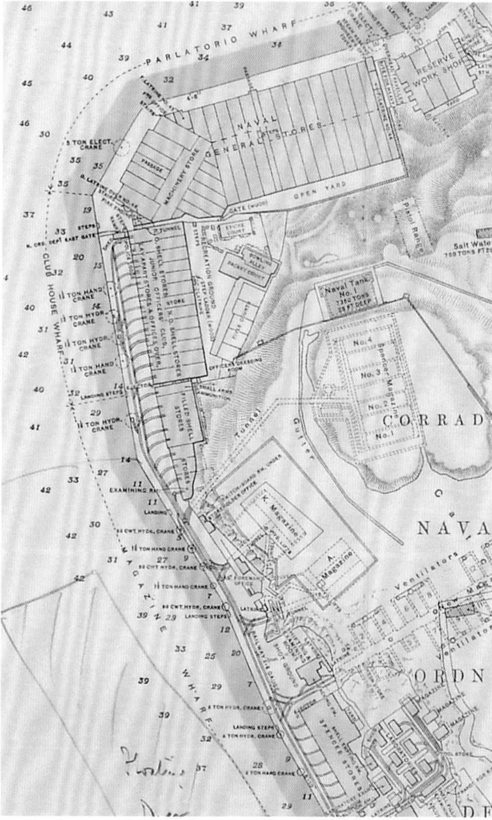

Fig 15.41
Part of a 1909 plan showing the underground magazines at Malta below the Corradino Heights and the new shell stores along the waterfront.
(TNA ADM 140/1484 fol 62)

entire reserves of ammunition were held at Gibraltar, along with one-third of the Mediterranean fleet's reserves, with Malta holding the balance. New warships coming into service following the 1889 Naval Defence Act would only exacerbate the problems. Both naval bases also had densely populated urban surroundings, while Gibraltar had little spare land. The solution in both cases was to create vast underground magazines. Those at Malta were located beneath the Corradino Heights (Fig 15.41) and were connected by tunnels to the ordnance yard overlooking Grand Harbour near the entrance of French Creek. In 1893 the Admiralty authorised excavation of space to store 24,000 barrels; in all, six magazines were excavated. At the same time, the capacity of the adjacent naval coal stores was reduced by some 10,400 tons and the waterfront space devoted to a series of Filled Shell Stores, with new and extensive laboratory buildings a little further along Grand Harbour, all linked by a railway system.[84]

At Gibraltar, considerable time and a great deal of money were spent trying to adapt and enlarge the existing land service magazine in North Gorge to the rear of the naval hospital. Only after the expenditure of nearly £34,000 was the project abandoned on grounds of cost and inconvenient location. Instead, 16 magazines with a designed capacity of 118,000 cubic feet and linked by parallel spine tunnels were excavated below Ragged Staff, with a communication tunnel emerging directly into the dockyard by the Torpedo Boat Destroyer Camber (Fig 15.42).[85] All these new facilities were completed in time for the First World War.

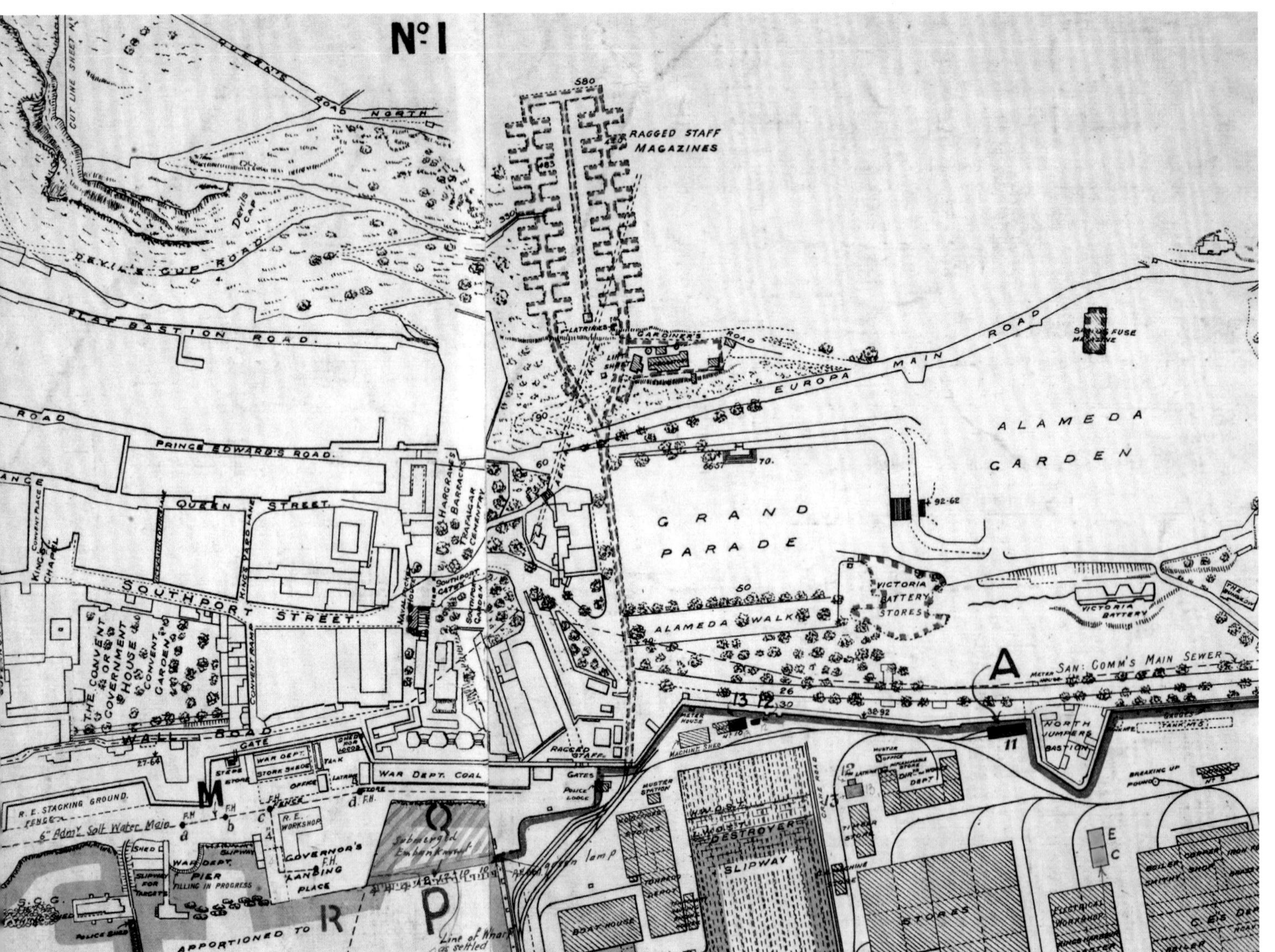

Fig 15.42
The underground magazines at Ragged Staff, Gibraltar, linked by a tunnel directly to the dockyard.
(AdL Vz 15/39)

16

Care of the Sick and Wounded: Naval Hospitals

The oldest surviving hospital built for the Royal Navy's sick and wounded has stood on an island in the harbour of Port Mahon since 1711 (*see* Fig 16.1). Its construction represented a significant but transitional stage in improvements in the care of British sailors, which had begun in the mid-17th century and was to come to fruition some forty years later at the great naval hospital at Haslar. Completion of Haslar and its slightly younger sister at Stonehouse marked the full recognition by the state that it had a duty of proper care for those injured in its service. The facilities at these hospitals were far in advance of those provided by other maritime powers and were to set the standard for all subsequent British naval hospitals.[1]

As long as the Royal Navy was restricted to comparatively short periods at sea in northern European waters, sickness on board its ships was not seen as a major problem by the authorities. During peacetime, the Surgeon-General hired surgeons for ships in commission; from the mid-17th century during wartime he was aided by commissions for sick and wounded and prisoners-of-war. The commissions saw to the appointment of additional surgeons and the hiring of sick quarters, frequently in alehouses and inns at the ports. Battle injuries were treated by the ships' surgeons, and on return to port injured survivors were transferred to the care of surgeons based in hired accommodation or, if near to London, to one of the great hospitals in the capital.[2] Such arrangements became steadily less sustainable in the 17th century as the navy ventured further afield. Longer voyages made scurvy a problem and in cold climates increased the risk of fevers (typhus). In warmer waters crews could be devastated by malaria, yellow fever and other tropical diseases. Admiral Francis Hosier's 1726 expedition to blockade Porto Bello and capture the Spanish treasure ships was to cost his own life and that of more than 4,000 sailors.

The conquest of diseases had to await 19th-century and later medical advances, but from the second half of the 17th century there were a series of *ad hoc* practical improvements in the care of the navy's sailors. At home, temporary hospitals were established during the three Dutch Wars (1652–74), with hospitals at Ipswich, Harwich, Rochester and Plymouth. In 1689 the Royal Navy's first permanent hospital in England for sick and injured seamen was established at Plymouth, just as construction of the new dockyard was getting under way. The purchase of a house to form the hospital, along with furnishings, marked a significant but not complete break with the existing contract system, as the contract surgeons here were still paid on a commission basis of 6s 8d a cure.[3]

In 1664 James Pearse, soon to be Surgeon-General, first advocated the use of hospital ships on major distant-water expeditions, an idea strongly supported by Charles II.[4] Hospital ships were a considerable improvement, but the sick and wounded in most cases benefited even more by being nursed ashore in more spacious surroundings, with access to fresh foods. Hiring civilian accommodation was not always practical overseas, where there might be a hostile population or no settlement with available rooms. In any event, by the end of the 17th century, with Royal Navy ships operating in the Mediterranean and Caribbean on a regular basis, practical as well as humanitarian reasons demanded permanent facilities to help the recovery of sick or injured seamen who were hard to replace overseas. By 1681 a hospital was in operation at Tangier, used by both the army and the navy and by civilians who were injured working on the mole. Although the hospital was shortlived, as Tangier was given up in 1685, it had set something of a precedent.[5]

In 1701 when fitting out his second expedition to the West Indies, Admiral Benbow requested from the Navy Board commissioners not just a hospital ship, but also a 'boarded house' – probably a timber building prefabricated in England to be shipped out with the expedition and quickly assembled – where the sick could be looked after by their ships' surgeons.[6] Significantly, the commissioners proposed that the hospital should be staffed by a salaried surgeon, an assistant and two mates, rather than having patients rely on contract surgeons or ships' surgeons who might be elsewhere. Contractors were to be engaged to provide food for the hospital, under the supervision of an agent sent from England, but medicine was to be supplied by the Surgeon-General. Although the Admiralty subsequently insisted that the patients should be cared for by their ships' surgeons, the agreement reached for the Jamaica hospital marked something of a sea change in improving naval medical care.[7]

In 1702 renewal of war saw the establishment of the Fifth Commission for Sick, Wounded and Prisoners. Its members condemned the existing system, which was based largely on renting inns and lodging houses, and they advocated construction of purpose-designed naval hospitals for the better and more effective care of the sick.[8] Hospitals were established at Rochester, Gosport and Deal, joining the existing one at Plymouth, together with a later one at Jamaica that replaced Benbow's 'boarded house'.[9] In 1705, Sir John Leake obtained agreement for a naval hospital at Lisbon operated on similar terms to the Jamaica hospital, although in this case it appears that initially rented accommodation was used.[10] In 1708, with the capture of Minorca imminent, the Fifth Commission members wasted no time, appointing an agent with the task of 'immediately upon arrival ... setting up a hospital'.[11] Although designs had been drawn up in 1709, nothing had been done by the time Admiral Sir John Jennings arrived on station in 1711 to find the sick still accommodated in cramped, rented properties in the town of Mahon. Using the Sick and Hurt Board's warrant as his authority, Jennings pressed ahead with the construction of a hospital on an isolated island in Mahon harbour. Although later substantially rebuilt, this remains the oldest extant purpose-designed Royal Navy hospital (Fig 16.1; *see also* pp356–7).[12]

Construction of hospitals owned and paid for by the Admiralty marked a significant advance over the previous arrangements using rented accommodation. However, despite the proposals for running them with salaried staff, put forward for Benbow's Jamaica hospital, they were still generally operated on the contract system, which could offer very varying degrees of care. In 1705 a scathing report on conditions in the new hospital at Plymouth noted men lying in their own excrement and the lack of clean linen and nursing care.[13] Action was taken in this instance, but similar problems persisted. In the 1720s at Jamaica 'the rapacious local physicians, the Doctors Tredway and Skeen' had a negative impact on the care of the sick, while in 1734 conditions in the hospital at Gosport were generally bad, with the sick being poorly housed, badly looked after and fed virtually a starvation diet.[14] In 1742 a report on the arrangements then in force in the Minorca and Gibraltar hospitals pointed out to the Admiralty that 'Beds are not furnished either by the Publick or the Contractors ... which cannot but be attended with great inconveniences to the people who are sent to them, and in all likelihood with the loss of many who have no beds of their own.' Although the Crown agreed the following January to supply beds (the thin mattresses placed in the bottom of sailors' hammocks) to both hospitals, the incident again emphasised the weaknesses of a contract system.[15]

The outbreak of war in 1739 proved to be the catalyst leading to the establishment of state-run hospitals for the Royal Navy. The inadequacies of the existing arrangements were pitilessly exposed as the navy increased to its wartime strength. Between July 1739 and August 1740, some 15,868 sick were sent ashore to the largest home ports, with Gosport and Plymouth taking 12,063 of this total, Rochester 1,830 and Woolwich, Sheerness and Bristol significant numbers.[16] At none of these places were the existing arrangements able to cope; similar situations prevailed at Gibraltar, Port Mahon and Jamaica. In February 1740 virulent typhus on board HMS *Canterbury* and HMS *Panther* at Plymouth led to an epidemic that spread to London, eventually killing more people than in any year since the Great Plague.[17]

In May 1740, in response to this deteriorating situation, the Admiralty took a decisive step, ordering the Navy Board

> to take into consideration the present method of treating the sick seamen in the hospitals and quarters ... and whether the same can be put on a better footing with regard to the men and cheaper with regard to the Crown, and to transmit to their Lordships an estimate of the expense of

Fig 16.1
The 1711 naval hospital at Minorca.
(BL Kings Top. LXXIV fol 39)

establishing the necessary number of hospitals and of the saving (if any) that may accrue to the Crown by a change of method in the treatment and care of sick seamen.[18]

In the meantime, consideration was once again given to the possibilities of adapting the ruined Portchester Castle as a hospital.[19] It was then used to hold prisoners-of-war, but it was easily accessible by water and was considered to have 'good wholesome air'. More importantly, the intact Roman walls meant that 'the seamen could not have it in their powers to straggle about', official language for saying that escape would be difficult, which was one of the principal weaknesses of most contract hospitals.[20] Leasing difficulties prevented any progress.

By the end of March 1741 the Admiralty had figures suggesting a powerful economic argument for a change from the existing system. From Michaelmas 1739 to Michaelmas 1740, the charge for sick quarters had amounted to £43,315 19s 5d; the optimistic estimated that the cost of building three royal hospitals was £17,354 11s 9d. During this period £3,907 7s 2d had been paid to the contract surgeons, based on the 6s 8d per head allowance for cured patients. This sum would have provided salaries for 26 surgeons, more than sufficient for the three projected hospitals. The annual cost of caring for 1,000 sick men in a contract hospital was put at £21,526 12s 8d, compared to £13,879 6s 8d for the same number in a royal hospital.[21] Admittedly, the cost of running such hospitals in peacetime was an unknown factor, but it was felt that a reduction in the number of staff would sufficiently answer the question.[22] Proposals were drawn up for a 1,500-bed hospital at Portsmouth and for two hospitals with 750 beds at Plymouth and Queenborough, with the men being looked after 'at His Majesty's expense'.[23] In October, when these were put to the King in Council, Chatham had been substituted for Queenborough. Because the course of the war gave priority to new hospitals at Gibraltar and Jamaica, these proposals were turned down.

The contract system remained in place, giving rise to further problems with quality of care, while the lack of security in the contract hospitals and even more so in the use of hired lodgings led to a substantial problem with the numbers of deserters. But by 1744, hostilities had come much closer to home, with France's declaration of war in March and the subsequent necessary increase of the Royal Navy's strength in the Channel. Casualties from any battle in home waters would overwhelm existing medical arrangements. The Admiralty went back with their 1741 proposals to the King in Council. Significantly, the faults of the contract system were emphasised: 'The want of Royal Hospitals is the cause of the lodging, diet and nursing of sick men performed by Contract: a method liable to such abuses as are often fatal to the health of seamen, notwithstanding all the care taken to prevent it'.[24] This time, the proposals were accepted for one hospital at Haslar on the Gosport peninsula close to Portsmouth Harbour for 1,500 sick, even though by November the cost had risen to £42,977 12s 8d (Fig 16.2).[25] This decision marked the decisive step in the establishment of navy-built and navy-run hospitals that were to be a valued and reassuring part of naval life for the next 250 years.[26]

Fig 16.2
Haslar Hospital drawn by the Rev J Hall, hospital chaplain 1798–1812. The prominent building with corner turrets in front of the main wall was the guardhouse. (© National Maritime Museum, Greenwich, London, 7095)

Although the decision to establish Haslar and further hospitals marked a turning point, it did not in itself guarantee an automatic improvement in the health and recovery rates of naval patients. Their medical care could only reflect current knowledge, but one important factor in the new arrangements lay in the recruitment of medical staff. Doctors were normally appointed by warrant to particular ships for the duration of the commission, but the new directly run hospitals with more extensive facilities could offer them permanent appointments, a career structure, better facilities and the opportunity for the growth of specialist knowledge on the treatment of diseases and injuries encountered in naval service. The navy was fortunate in the 18th century in the number of talented doctors such as James Lind, Sir Gilbert Blane and Thomas Trotter, who 'exerted a profound influence on the health and medical practice of the navy, which led to significant reform'.[27] It was also fortunate that by the early 18th century the Royal Navy was becoming noted for the emphasis placed by its officers on the cleanliness of their ships and the clothes and bedding of their men, even though the link between poor hygiene and sickness and disease had yet to be fully understood and scientifically proven. The Admiralty and Victualling Boards' desire to provide the best-possible victuals, supplying fresh food wherever opportune, also made a major contribution to keeping crews healthy.

An indication of improving standards at the end of the 18th century is provided in Blane's paper published in 1815, which showed that between 1779 and 1813 the proportion of sick to the number of men voted dropped from 1 in 2.45 to 1 in 10.75.[28] The death rate over the

Fig 16.3
In spatial terms, the ward seen here at Haslar Hospital in 1897 was little altered since construction. The effect of more generous funding and changing attitudes to the proper care of the navy's sick and injured are evident. (Navy and Army Illustrated *19 Feb 1897)*

same period reduced from 1 in 42 to 1 in 143. This was no mean achievement at a time when it was not understood that typhus (often known as ship, camp, hospital or jail fever, references to its prevalence in crowded conditions) was a disease spread by body lice, and that infectious diseases were caused by parasites including bacteria and fungi. The deadly danger in warmer climates of mosquito-borne diseases was totally unsuspected. Until these causes were understood in the 19th century, the long-established 'miasma' theory held sway. This blamed air polluted by vaporous exhalations from a variety of sources, including stagnant water, infected and putrefying animal and human bodies and general urban filth. A bad smell denoted corrupted air.[29] The corollary to this lay in ensuring that hospitals preferably should be located where there were fresh breezes, but even then there could be mistakes. Admiral Vernon's championing of a new hospital at Jamaica in 1740 led to its construction on what seemed a perfect site at New Greenwich; the dangers of the nearby morass and its mosquitoes were not appreciated. The soaring rate of fevers and deaths remained a mystery, forcing the abandonment of the hospital in 1755 and a return to Port Royal.[30]

This did not invalidate the general premise that patients benefited from wholesome surroundings. In the Admiralty letter of June 1745, which authorised Haslar, the architects were directed that they should 'consider attentively to the dispositions of the wards for sick men, the convenience of light and air; to avoid narrowness as also crowding the beds too close together'.[31] The spacious wards at Haslar (Fig 16.3) were in marked contrast to the claustrophobic ones in the earlier hospital on Minorca (Fig 16.4). This trend for better light and air was to continue, and a 1785 report by the Commission for Sick and Hurt recommended that hospital wards should have opposing

Fig 16.4
A ground-floor ward in the former naval hospital at Minorca. Barred windows added to what must have been a claustrophobic atmosphere.
(Author)

windows to encourage air circulation.[32] This was to culminate in the pavilion plan, with the hospital wards set at right angles to a linking corridor and thus able to be ventilated and lit on both sides. William Scamp was to pioneer this design in his hospital built for the Royal Marine barracks at Woolwich in 1858 (Fig 16.5).[33]

The royal hospital at Haslar was followed in 1758 by Stonehouse hospital at Plymouth (Fig 16.6). These remained the two most important naval hospitals, with Haslar accommodating some 2,100 patients by 1778 and Stonehouse built with a capacity for 1,200. By then it was realised that Chatham's role as a fleet base had effectively ended and that little purpose would be served by constructing a large naval hospital this far up the Medway. The Napoleonic Wars highlighted the continued needs for hospitals on coasts close to naval anchorages, where sick seamen and battle casualties might be expected. In the 1790s, a building for a naval hospital for 300 patients was constructed at Deal in Kent, just south of the castle and Navy Yard, where it was well placed to serve the Downs anchorage within the Goodwin Sands. The hospital was largely replaced in 1811 by the surviving range, constructed to a design by Edward Holl (Fig 16.7). Both these Deal buildings had wards with opposing windows, but in other respects were not as advanced as Alexander Rovehead's design for Stonehouse.[34]

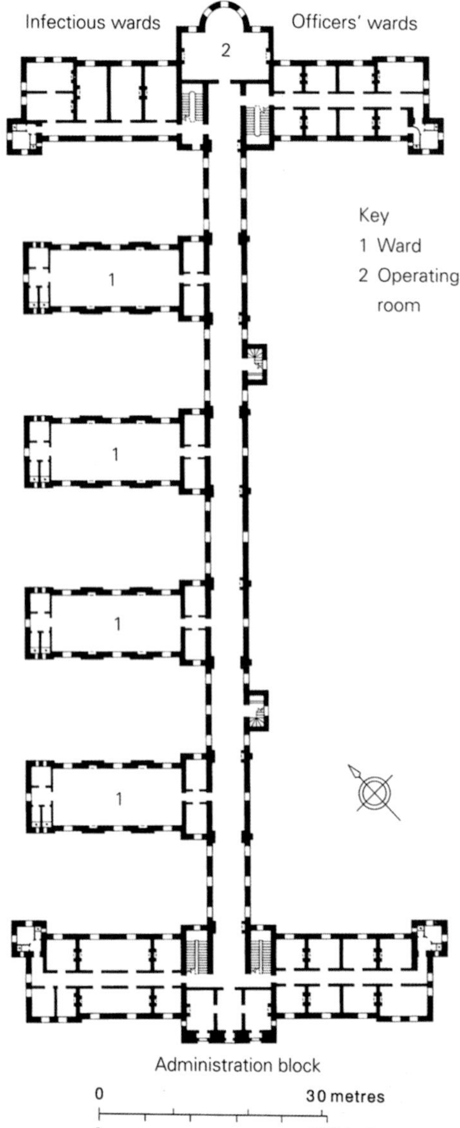

Fig 16.5
Scamp's 1858 pavilion plan hospital for the Royal Marine barracks at Woolwich.
(Richardson 1998, Fig 83)

At Great Yarmouth the needs of the Eastern Squadron during the Revolutionary War from 1793 to 1802 continued to be served by a contract hospital, probably the 80-bed hospital considered in 1807 to be 'by no means adequate to the exigency of the service'.[35] That year the Admiralty decided to replace the contract arrangements here with a purpose-built hospital under full naval control, and although Bentham and Holl produced designs, one of which was based on the Deal building, when work started in 1809 it was to plans by William Pilkington (Fig 16.8).[36] He designed the hospital as four ranges round a courtyard, with the majority of the wards occupying the full width of the ranges (Fig 16.9). A continuous colonnade linked these at ground-floor level, as at Stonehouse, allowing wards to be isolated. An operating theatre was included from the start.[37]

Some years after the Napoleonic Wars, Chatham was provided with the much smaller 228-bed Melville Hospital, including 84 beds for Royal Marines, tailored more closely to the immediate needs of the navy here. Designed by G L Taylor and estimated to cost £35,027 5s 9d, work on site began on 1 June 1826.[38] The layout and plans of the three hospital blocks, each with nine wards linked by a colonnade (Fig 16.10), was also very similar to Stonehouse hospital. By the 1890s it was proving too small and were replaced in 1905 by the present buildings that now form the heart of Medway Maritime Hospital (Fig 16.11).[39]

Where existing buildings were converted, as at Haulbowline where the southern victualling store later became a hospital, such layouts were not usually possible, and low ceilings might make it more difficult to achieve the minimum of 600 cubic feet of air deemed necessary in 1785 for each patient.[40] Haulbowline hospital remained in use until the closure of the base,

Fig 16.6 (above)
An 18th-century engraving of Stonehouse hospital looking east along the main axis. The two blocks of wards nearest the entrance are depicted as ground plans to avoid obscuring the view. Externally the buildings and layout have changed little since completion.
(© The British Library Board. Kings Top. XI fol 84)

Fig 16.7 (left)
The former naval hospital at Deal in Kent, as rebuilt by Holl in 1811.
(Author)

Fig 16.8 (above)
Pilkington's elevation of the north range of the quadrangle of the hospital at Great Yarmouth, begun in 1809.
(TNA ADM 140/405)

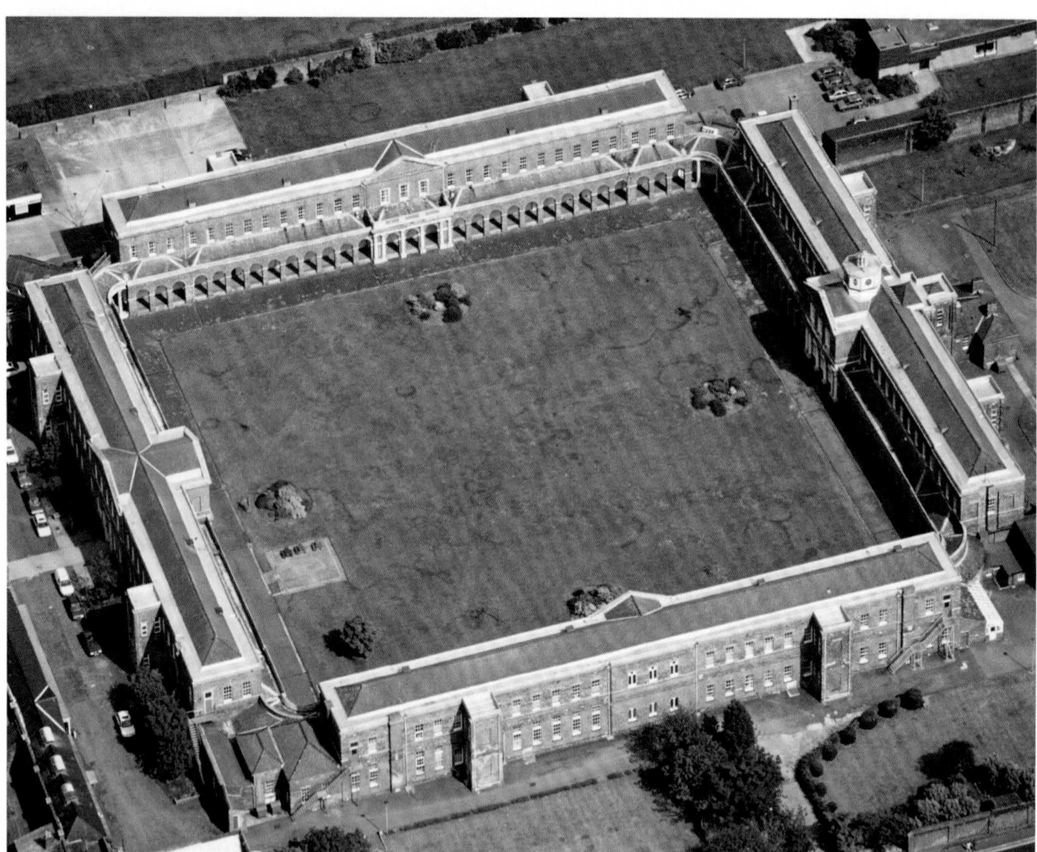

Fig 16.9 (right)
A 1993 photograph of William Pilkington's naval hospital at Great Yarmouth. Although the country was at war, this was conceived and executed on a magnificent scale. It is now in residential use.
(NMR 4864/29 7 Jun 1993)

Fig 16.10 (below)
Ground plan of the Melville naval hospital at Chatham designed by G L Taylor in 1826.
(Richardson 1998, Fig 82)

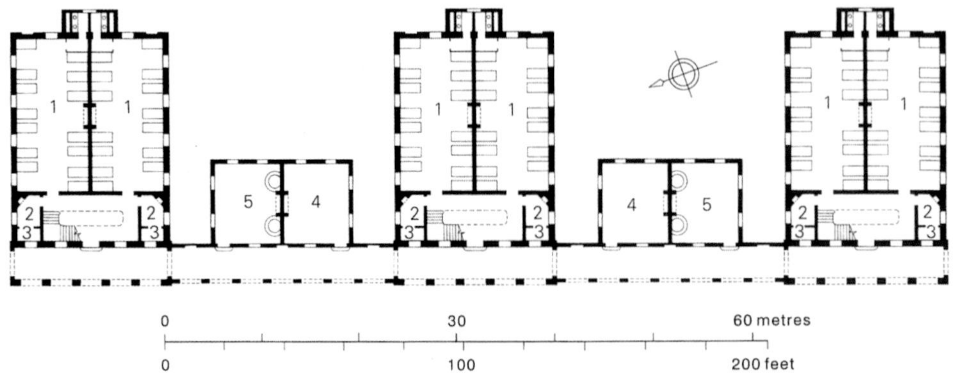

Fig 16.11
The former naval hospital at Chatham that replaced Taylor's building in 1905. (Peter Kendall)

and by 1909 three small zymotic or isolation blocks had been added to the south, replacing a terrace of labourers' cottages.[41] Such zymotic blocks were provided at most of the larger naval hospitals at this time, following the Isolation Hospitals Act of 1893.[42] The last naval hospitals to be built in Britain before the First World War were at Portland, begun in 1901, and at South Queensferry, started a few years later on the opposite side of the Forth from the new dockyard under construction at Rosyth. Both hospitals were comparatively small establishments, the one at Rosyth significantly referred to as 'sick quarters', but still with an operating theatre and surgeon's accommodation. The Portland hospital was laid out on the pavilion plan, while that at Queensferry was arranged as an informal group of separate buildings (Fig 16.12).[43]

Overseas, hospitals of varying sizes, designs and materials were to be found at virtually every base before the end of the 18th century. Occasionally, these were supplemented by the use of hospital ships, with further facilities intermittently used at Lisbon, Baia[44] and later Madras.[45] Minorca, Gibraltar and Jamaica had purpose-built hospitals operational by 1720, superseding rented accommodation.[46] Port Antonio in its brief existence had a hospital in the early 1730s, almost certainly one of the prefabricated timber buildings sent there. Antigua had a more ambitious, two-storey, colonnaded hospital at the head of Tank Bay; a construction contract drawing for this is dated May 1763. Nine years later a severe hurricane struck English Harbour, driving ashore four ships of Rear-Admiral William Parry's squadron,

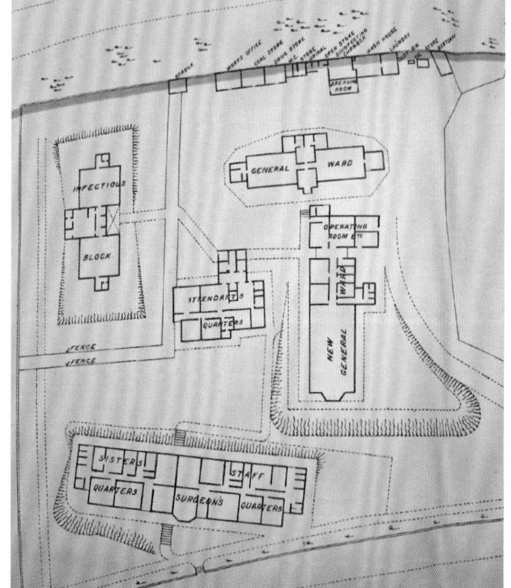

Fig 16.12
The small naval hospital built at South Queensferry to serve the needs of the new dockyard at Rosyth. (TNA ADM 140/1484 fol 49)

including his flagship HMS *Chatham*. It also destroyed the hospital, which was 'levelled to the ground crushing in its fall the unfortunate patients and attendants'.[47] In January 1778 the Admiralty ordered that 'three hospital buildings with apartments for officers and all necessary offices' should be erected here at a cost not to exceed £10,909 6s.[48] A more ambitious 1779 plan for a new hospital on the old site had five detached two-storey blocks (Fig 16.13), each with four wards containing 12 cradles, reminiscent of the detached blocks at Stonehouse.[49] In the event only two blocks appear to have been built following representations by Admiral Sir Richard Hughes in 1783, and nothing now remains of the buildings.[50]

By 1783 there was a naval hospital on St Lucia at Pigeon Island,[51] while further north, the American War of Independence saw one set up on Long Island.[52] At Halifax a series of makeshift and unsatisfactory premises served in the years immediately after the founding of the base. However, in 1782 the Admiralty approved construction of a proper hospital on the waterfront just north of the dockyard. Like many of the local buildings this was of timber; it held up to 127 seamen and 20 officers. The new

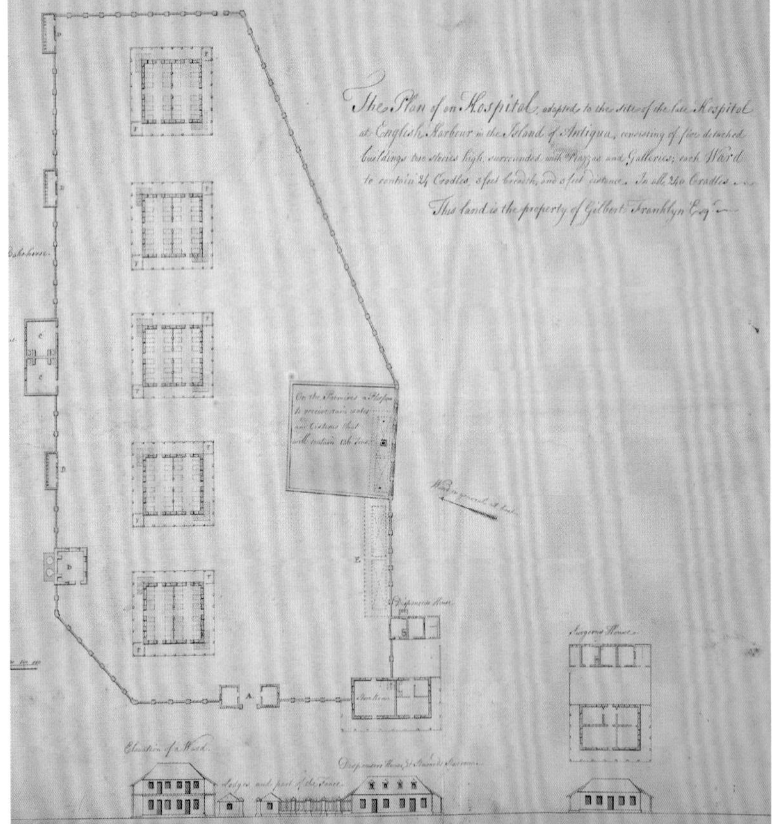

Fig 16.13
The 1779 plan of the naval hospital at Antigua. Only two of the ward blocks seem to have been built.
(TNA ADM 140/1220 pt 2)

Halifax hospital may have replaced one in Newfoundland that in 1785 was reported by Admiral John Campbell, the Governor and Commander-in-Chief Newfoundland, as needing repair.[53] Little is known about the hospital, which was presumably in St Johns. At Barbados during the Napoleonic Wars, Admiral Sir Alexander Cochrane, in a move reminiscent of that of Jennings at Minorca, had a hospital for around 100 patients constructed with 'timber lathed and plastered' at the considerable cost of £35,290 12s 0d.[54]

After the capture of Malta in 1800, sick and injured were accommodated in the former armoury at Vittoriosa and in a building in Valletta once used as a prison for Turkish slaves; such arrangements held until the completion of the naval hospital at Bighi in 1832 (*see* pp370–72). A further building in Strada Forni was also used.[55] At Bermuda a succession of hulks was used as hospital ships prior to the completion of a hospital on Ireland Island. In 1813 the Admiralty had ordered Holl to draw up plans for a 250-bed hospital, capable of being doubled in size if later required. Holl's drawings for this do not appear to survive, and it is not known if the building completed in 1818 was to his design.[56] The hospital had new facilities added and remained in use until 1951. The only building still standing is the former isolation or zymotic ward of 1899.[57]

By 1825 post-war retrenchments had led the navy to close a number of its hospitals, transferring those at Barbados, Gibraltar and Great Yarmouth to the army.[58] Ones that remained in use, with their estimated annual running costs, were as follows: Haslar (£8,146), Stonehouse (£6,047), Port Royal (£2,409), Malta (£2,005), Bermuda (£1,995), Cape of Good Hope (£556) and Halifax (£80). A further sum of £35,000 was allocated in 1825 for equipment, bedding and medicines.[59]

The size of overseas medical establishments in the 19th century after the Napoleonic Wars largely correlated with the distribution of warships on these foreign stations, with the largest hospitals at Malta and Gibraltar. However, climate also played a part. Holl's comparatively large hospital at Port Royal reflected the incidence of disease and sickness in the Caribbean. Similarly, the two hospitals built on Ascension Island and the one on Fernando Po were a consequence of the high mortality concomitant with the work of the anti-slavery patrols. Hospitals at Esquimalt and

Fig 16.14
The naval hospital at Trincomalee in 1895. (TNA ADM 195/2 fol 82b)

Halifax serving the more benign stations were comparatively modest in scale. At Simon's Town a small naval hospital outside the base sufficed until the dockyard was extended early in the 20th century, at which point a new and larger hospital and sanatorium were built on the mountainside behind the base, to which they were linked by an aerial cableway.[60]

Further east the navy had a hospital at Madras for a time during the wars with France. Trincomalee generally had a healthy climate, and in 1821 a Madras architect, Mr Stringer, who had already built a local hospital, submitted plans for one for the new naval base. This was probably not the most propitious time, and nothing more was heard of the proposal.[61] Later, a hospital was started but only the footings were completed before it was abandoned. By 1871 one was in operation at the base and is probably to be identified with the two-storey buildings with verandas in an 1895 photograph, labelled perhaps more accurately as 'sick quarters' (Fig 16.14).[62]

Hulks as hospital ships still had their champions. At Hong Kong the navy relied for many years on a succession of these, the last of which, HMS *Melville*, served at the base from 1857 until she was sold in 1873. In 1860 Admiral Sir James Hope had first proposed a naval hospital at Kowloon, but in 1867 the Director of Works, Colonel Sir Andrew Clarke, minuted the Admiralty that

> the difficulty of obtaining a site for such a building, the sufficiency of the *Melville* to meet the want of hospital accommodation for the fleet, and the opinion expressed of the superior salubrity of a floating hospital over one on shore, combine to induce me to recommend to My Lords the abandonment of the idea of erecting at Hong Kong or Kowloon a permanent naval hospital, leaving the question of building such an establishment at Yokohama for future decision.[63]

In the event, the Admiralty purchased the Seamen's Hospital in 1873 that had been opened in 1843 at Wanchai and which with later additions was to remain the navy's hospital until 1941 (Fig 16.15).[64] It was extensively bombed in 1941 and was demolished after the war.

Concerns about the effects of the climate on the sick at Hong Kong seem to have been one factor that led the Government in 1869 to acquire sites from the Japanese government for a naval convalescent hospital and a house for the flag officer at Yokohama, joining a small victualling yard and coal depot already established there. In 1875 an alternative site for the hospital was agreed and leased from the Japanese government. The Admiralty paid for the new hospital, which was handed over to the Medical Department in March 1876. Described by a correspondent in 1902 as 'one of the most pleasant stations at which Naval Officers and men who are unfortunate enough to be taken ill in this part of the world may recuperate',

Fig 16.15
The naval hospital at Hong Kong c 1900. (AdL Da 039)

the hospital was laid out as a series of detached, single-storey buildings that included four wards each with between 70 and 80 beds. There was also a separate isolation block and staff accommodation (Fig 16.16). The milder climate at Yokohama meant that sick were sent here from Hong Kong during the hot summer months.[65] The hospital remained in operation, save for part of the First World War, but was destroyed along with the depot in the great earthquake of 1923.[66] On the Chinese mainland the port of Wei Hai Wei, leased to Britain between 1898 and 1930, was home to a small naval base on the island of Leu-Kung-Tao at the entrance to Wei Hai Wei bay. This included a hospital, cemetery and recreation ground.[67] The irregular layout of the hospital suggests it may have been formed from rented buildings or, more likely, was a simple hutted establishment.

On the other side of the Pacific, modernisation of the small base at Esquimalt following construction of the government dry dock in the 1880s included the rebuilding of the naval hospital at Naden, on the eastern side of Esquimalt Harbour. This had been housed since 1862 in the former Royal Engineers' timber huts. Apart from a detached, two-storey house for the Medical Officer, the principal buildings of the new hospital were all single storey. They included an administrative building, which was linked by a timber veranda flanked to a men's wards on each side. There was also a separate ward for officers. These were constructed between 1887 and 1891, with a number of stores and outbuildings completed between 1890 and 1894. The majority of these former hospital buildings remain in use. All the principal buildings are of brick with rendered detailing, and they were designed by John Teague in a similar style to his contemporary buildings in the dockyard (Fig 16.17).[68]

Remarkably, a number of the more significant naval hospitals survive, their designs reflecting advances in medical knowledge, the needs of the

Fig 16.16 (above)
The convalescent hospital at Yokohama c 1900, with a number of street vendors outside the main gate.
(AdL Da 039)

Fig 16.17 (left)
The officers' ward and administrative building of the former naval hospital at Esquimalt, designed by John Teague.
(Author)

bases they served and the changing official attitudes to their inmates. With the exception of the former naval hospital of 1905 at Chatham, now part of the National Health Service, none of these remain in medical use. The two oldest extant hospitals at Mahon and Gibraltar were both navy provided, but initially contractor run; the remainder, including the pioneer hospital at Haslar, were completed after 1745, the date when the navy began to take over the running of its hospitals, as well as their construction. The building histories of the most significant of the surviving hospitals are briefly described in chronological order.

The Naval Hospital, Port Mahon

The disasters of Admiral Sir Cloudesley Shovell's 5-month deployment to the Mediterranean in 1703, when 'upwards of 1500 men had died on the voyage, and three-quarters of the rest were so ill and weak that there was scarce sufficient to man the ships', must have weighed in the minds of the Sick and Hurt Board when Byng's expedition sailed in 1708 to capture Minorca.[69] The Board's agent, Peirce Griffyth, had firm instructions 'immediately upon ... arrival' to consult both with senior naval officers and with the 'Governor of the Garrison ... where and in what manner, the said hospital may be erected ... and to get a draft of the same drawn up by some able and skilful workmen'.[70] In 1709 a scheme for a hospital costing £9,000 was put forward, but not adopted; in the meantime, Griffyth hired accommodation in the town of Mahon.

When Admiral Sir John Jennings arrived early in 1711, he found the hospital premises 'extraordinarily prejudicious to Her Majesty's Service' and forthwith ordered the construction on an island in Port Mahon harbour of a new hospital, 'which according to the estimates will amount to but Three Thousand Pounds'.[71] The designer was almost certainly the military engineer attached to the garrison, Captain Robert Latham (*see* Fig 16.1), and to speed construction Jennings borrowed most of the money from his fellow officers on station.[72] The harbour island location fulfilled two aims that for long exercised the Admiralty and its subordinate boards when considering hospitals: it made escape difficult and it put patients beyond reach of the twin evils of liquor and women of easy virtue. Captain Latham's design was for a single-storey, stone building some 310ft in length, with wings at each end (Fig 16.18). In the centre of the main range was a chapel and bell tower flanked on either side by five barrel-vaulted wards, which were linked by a colonnaded veranda leading to a kitchen at the north end. The wings each contained a further three wards, as well as accommodation for the surgeon, the naval officer and staff. Rainwater from the flat roof was probably collected in underground cisterns. The hospital apparently held 336 patients and was completed in a year.[73]

This speed of construction was to have unfortunate consequences. Three years later the building was leaking badly, and 'all the arches and pillars which make the piazza of the north wing' had collapsed. Among the remedial works was a new screed on the roof and the addition of 42 buttresses.[74] As such, the building appears to have survived little altered until 1770, when neglect of the fabric during the French occupation from 1756 to 1763 and subsequently by the contractor led to a partial collapse. Commodore Charles Proby reported to the Admiralty that 'the same is utterly irreparable by any means whatever, unless directions are given for rebuilding it, there will not be a place for the surgeon or a single seaman to inhabit'.[75] By the early 1740s the hospital had been housing up to 500 patients, but 30 years later, faced with a major rebuild, the Admiralty favoured increasing the number to 1,200.[76] In 1770 Commodore Proby ordered the resident surveyor, Milbourn Warren, who he charged with producing plans and estimates for the new

Fig 16.18
A late 18th-century view of the harbour at Minorca, with the naval hospital on its island.
(© National Maritime Museum, Greenwich, London, PX9694)

hospital, 'to rebuild it upon its present plan', and the dimensions of the ground plan of the rebuilt hospital do essentially match the earlier building.

Over the next year or so various proposals were put forward, and as late as October 1771 Proby's successor, Rear-Admiral Sir Peter Denis, was sending home alternative plans.[77] Reconstruction or, at the very least, repairs to the original building must have been under way by then, for in August 1772 Warren was to take the blame for the second storey, with the Sick and Hurt Board noting that 'there seems to have been a great want of judgement in Mr Warren's making such a plan for a second storey as failed to secure the walls from bulging out'.[78] This tight timescale suggests that much of the earlier building must have been incorporated in the new structure. By the autumn of 1774 Admiral Robert Man 'found everything in the department of the Navy at Port Mahon in good order'.[79]

In the rebuilt hospital, the chapel was replaced by a central staircase leading to the first-floor wards. A ground-floor passage by the staircase led to the rear of the building where there was a storeroom or dispensary, a separate kitchen and a well. Two houses, presumably for medical staff, were added to the ends of the wings of the hospital. A number of the surviving detached single-storey buildings were probably used for further staff quarters, operating theatre and morgue in a similar fashion to later ones that survive at the hospital at Port Royal. In 1774 the completed hospital had 40 wards, 12 on each floor of the main range and a further 4 on each floor of the wings. The wards in the main range were slightly larger than those in the wings, internally measuring some 22ft by 32ft. Those on the ground floor originally all had stone barrel vaults and each contained a fireplace; these wards were lit by heavily barred windows at each end (*see* Fig 16.4), with stout doors opening on to the verandas.

There are few references to conditions in this hospital. In 1742 it was recorded that clean linen was issued every 14 days 'or oftener if needed' and that each man was allowed 1¾ lb of meat daily, together with a pint of wine and a pound of soft bread. It was also reported that

> For breakfast they have water gruel, and those who are in flux milk morning and evening. When any of the sick are by surgeon's orders prohibited meat, they are served rice, with milk cinnamon and sugar one day, and flour boiled in like manner the next till they are again allowed to eat meat; greens, such as are in season, and proper for the sick, are constantly provided.[80]

In 1711 Jennings had reckoned his new hospital had a capacity of 356 patients, averaging 21 to 24 to a ward.[81] By 1770 the hospital held 550, raising the average to 34 to each ward. The rebuilt hospital, at its full capacity of 1,200 sick, reduced this to 30 to a ward, but even so conditions must have been crowded, the barred windows more reminiscent of a prison than a place of healing (*see* Fig 16.4). After the British withdrawal from Minorca, the Spanish navy took over the dockyard, and the hospital remained in use until about 1960.[82] Even allowing for its rebuilding and an extra storey, this remains not only the earliest but also one of the least altered of the 18th-century naval hospitals (Fig 16.19). Comparing what must have been claustrophobic and crowded wards here with the more spacious ones of only 30 years later at Haslar (*see* Fig 16.3) is to appreciate the strides made in Georgian Britain in the care of the navy's sick and injured.

Fig 16.19
Part of the main range of the former naval hospital at Minorca photographed in 1971. An extensive conservation programme is now under way here. (Author)

Gibraltar's 1741 naval hospital

Little is known about the first naval medical facilities established on Gibraltar soon after its capture in 1704. During the siege of 1727–8, these facilities were acquired by the army for use as barracks, and the navy was reduced to caring for its sick in what amounted to little more than huts that were bitterly cold in winter and insufferably hot in summer.[83] In the 1730s there was mounting pressure to provide a purpose-built naval hospital on a site a little inland from Rosia Bay, where the buildings were protected by a shoulder of rock from Spanish land batteries and the patients were a little removed from the temptations of the town. In 1734 three different sets of plans for hospitals capable of holding between 140 and 170 men were drawn up, but nothing was done.[84] In 1740, when Admiral Nicholas Haddock arrived and found that the hospital comprised two sheds for 30 men, he had to hire quarters for around 200 sick men from his squadron.[85] Haddock's request for a proper hospital was echoed by Sir Chaloner Ogle, who had joined him on station and been appalled by conditions in the huts and tents during the rainy season. These complaints stirred the Admiralty into making enquiries, and in 1741 they approved construction of a proper hospital. This seems to have been based on a 1739 design for 1,000 patients.[86] A number of craftsmen from Portsmouth were recruited to help with the construction work, and it seems likely that apart from stone, most of the original building materials were shipped out from Britain. The building was completed in 1746.

The new hospital was a plain, two-storey, quadrangular design, some 350ft by 150ft, with projecting three-storey corner towers. Covered verandas served as corridors and 'airing spaces' for patients; the wards appear to have occupied the full width of the ranges and to have been more spacious than those at Mahon. In the centre of the main west range, a three-storey block originally accommodated offices, dispensary and senior staff quarters, while to the rear of the hospital a number of outbuildings provided a kitchen and store rooms. This was the only naval hospital to be completed to a quadrangular plan until the later construction of Great Yarmouth hospital, and it was to remain in use until after the Napoleonic Wars, when it passed temporarily into army hands.[87] Later, after completion of a new naval hospital on the Rock, it was converted into naval married quarters. The external elevations remain much as completed (Fig 16.20), but the interiors have been extensively altered, masking the original arrangements.

The Royal Naval Hospital at Haslar

On 18 June 1745 the Admiralty authorised construction of the Royal Hospital at Haslar on the Gosport Peninsula close to Portsmouth Harbour, the largest and most famous of the Royal Navy's hospitals in Britain.[88] The timing meant that the long-serving Surveyor of the Navy, Sir Jacob Acworth, probably had to be asked for a design, but by then he was nearing

Fig 16.20
Part of the courtyard of the former naval hospital at Gibraltar.
(Author)

the end of his career and had lost the confidence of many of his official colleagues and Board members.[89] His proposals were shown to the Sick and Hurt Board, but they had called in Theodore Jacobson, architect of the Foundling Hospital then under construction in London. When the Board showed him Acworth's plan, the minutes record that 'Mr Jacobson not entirely approving of it, has promised to make one of his own, which he believes may be better for the purpose'.[90] Jacobson then took over responsibility for the design, helped, as with the Foundling Hospital, by James Horne, who was responsible for much of the on-site supervision.[91]

The foundations were laid in 1746 and the whole building completed in 1761 after a number of modifications.[92] The original design seems to have been for a great quadrangle of double ranges of wards separated by narrow courtyards, an arrangement possibly derived from the Queen Anne Block at Greenwich. In the event, the south-west ranges were never built (Fig 16.21). Constructed by a contractor, John Spenser, of local red brick with Portland stone dressings, the three-storey hospital with its part-vaulted brick cellars and attic accommodation fulfilled the Admiralty's instruction that it should be 'a strong, durable, plain building' (Fig 16.22).[93] Ornament was largely restricted to Thomas Pearce's carving within the pediment of the main range of the Royal Arms of George II and personifications of 'Navigation' and 'Commerce' (Fig 16.23). This 567ft range with its 553ft wings made the hospital the largest brick building in Britain.[94]

It had originally been intended that the hospital should hold 1,500 patients, a figure raised to 1,800 after modifications in 1754–5, a year after pressure on facilities had forced the incomplete hospital to admit its first patients. By 1778 there was provision for over 2,000.[95] When first opened, the hospital had 114 wards, most containing 19 or 20 beds. A number of the original wards were in pairs, which were linked end-on by communicating doors, and later these became single large wards. Each ward had a water closet, and there was a bath house for

Fig 16.21
Looking north over Haslar Hospital, a photograph taken in the 1950s. The grand formal scale of the original buildings is apparent. St Luke's Church is hidden in the trees (left). In the right foreground is Canada Block, opened as quarters for nursing staff in 1917. The water tower completed in 1885 is prominent on the left beyond the north wing of the hospital. Fronting Haslar Creek in the distance and distinguished by roofs of its boat sheds is Haslar Gunboat Yard. Top right are the buildings of HMS Hornet, *the Coastal Forces Base established in the Second World War. (Haslar Heritage Group)*

Fig 16.22
The front elevation of the former naval hospital at Haslar. Semi-detached houses at each end provided quarters for senior medical staff. (Author)

Fig 16.23
The main pediment at Haslar with the arms of George II and personifications of Navigation and Commerce. (Author)

Fig 16.24
Haslar Hospital from the Gosport foreshore photographed in the 1880s. (Haslar Heritage Group)

newly admitted patients.[96] In the 1780s Robert Dodds, the hospital surgeon, oversaw the setting up of the first operating theatre, years before one was available in Stonehouse Hospital. A significant drawback to Jacobson's design lay in the wards generally being the full width of the ranges, their double duty as corridors making isolation of patients difficult. In this respect they were less satisfactory than Latham's earlier hospital on Minorca.

In 1756 the hospital chapel of St Luke was completed. Placed south-west of the hospital and aligned on its main axis, this simple rectangular brick building has an internal gallery and a pedimented west front surmounted by a clock turret, making it similar, but on a smaller scale, to Georgian dockyard churches such as St Ann's across the harbour. As in those churches, seating was strictly according to rank.[97] More or less contemporary with the chapel are two pairs of residences facing each other across the front of the main hospital range. These plain, three-storey brick houses for the senior staff are distinguished by their enclosed timber porches, characteristic features of nearly every Georgian naval residence. In 1794 management of the hospital was removed from the medical officers and made the responsibility of serving naval captains.[98]

Inevitably, further accommodation was required for the new Governor and other officers. They were housed in a terrace of nine substantial three-storey residences built to the south-west of the hospital on the same axis as the chapel (Fig 16.25). To emphasise its importance, the Governor's House in the centre, as well as being by far the largest building, was partly set back from the four houses on either side. The contract was let to a Mr Jno Shean in May 1796, and the houses were completed by November 1799.[99] To their rear are the traditional walled gardens, with that of the Governor occupying the lion's share of the area. The architect of the whole terrace in all probability was Samuel Bunce, newly appointed to Bentham's staff.[100]

Fig 16.25
The terrace of nine houses completed at Haslar in 1799 for the hospital governors. (Author)

Fig 16.26
Patients enjoying the airing grounds at Haslar in 1897. (Navy and Army Illustrated *19 Feb 1897)*

Haslar Hospital is unique in the extent of its walled grounds, traditionally used for exercise by both patients and staff (Figs 16.26 and 16.27). An 1897 writer noted that 'the Airing ground, as it is called in old documents, is nearly a mile in circumference';[101] today this still remains largely intact. Within it, a number of additional buildings were constructed in the 19th and 20th centuries without undue loss of this sense of space. Among the more notable of these and dominating the skyline is the ornate 120ft brick and stone water tower, completed in 1885 and holding 100,000 gallons. In the following decade a series of four ward blocks with a central administrative building was laid out overlooking the Solent. This was the zymotic or infectious diseases establishment, its surrounding wall with its hatch, through which supplies could be passed, making it almost a hospital within a hospital. In the early years of the 20th century further accommodation was provided, with a new block for officer patients south of the west wing of the main hospital. In both cases the Admiralty Works Department was involved in the designs.

Fig 16.27 (right)
The same view at Haslar in 2011. (Author)

The Royal Naval Hospital Stonehouse

Although the 1744 Order in Council had specified a naval hospital at Plymouth for the Western Squadron, construction on a site adjacent to Stonehouse Creek did not start until 1858, and the hospital was completed in 1862 (Fig 16.28).[102] The architect was an Alexander Rovehead or Rouchead, of whom little is known except that he was a mason and active as a builder in London by the mid-1720s.[103] As far as is known, he undertook no other work for the navy, but in selecting him the Sick and Hurt Board – probably unwittingly – was to achieve a very significant advance in hospital planning.

The earliest specification was for a hospital for 600 patients, which soon increased to 900 and then to 1,200.[104] Rather than Jacobson's solution of a single monumental building, Rovehead chose to design 10 three-storey blocks of wards arranged round a substantial rectangular courtyard some 720ft by 128ft. The three-storey blocks had two wards on each floor, separated by a spine wall containing two fireplaces and with stairs at one end of the building.[105] Each ward held 20 patients, a number similar to those in the original wards

Fig 16.28
An 1863 plan of Stonehouse Hospital showing its detached wards. To the right are the officers' houses. Naval patients were normally rowed up Stonehouse Creek to the hospital's landing stage. Facing the naval hospital across the creek is the garrison hospital.
(AdL 1863 Naval Establishments Da 02 fol 24)

Fig 16.29
A view along the main axis of Stonehouse Hospital towards the original chapel. The view is today little different from this 1898 photograph.
(Navy and Army Illustrated *18 March 1898)*

in Haslar. In the centre of the eastern range and facing along the main axis to the twin entrance lodges, Rovehead placed the pedimented administrative block, which also contained the chapel and was surmounted by a clocktower and cupola (Fig 16.29).

In between the three ward blocks on the northern and southern sides, Rovehead designed four single-storey buildings, which by 1796 were used as stores, a kitchen, a smallpox ward and a lunatic ward.[106] All these were linked by a Tuscan colonnaded walk and were built of the local limestone with Portland stone detailing. The original layout was completed with a jetty on Stonehouse Creek, at the landward end of which were clothing and bedding stores and small receiving wards (Figs 16.30 and 16.31). Sick and injured were rowed here by their shipmates, verminous or missing clothing and bedding were replaced by fresh, and after assessment in the receiving wards they were allocated to beds in the main hospital.[107] Surprisingly, there were no operating theatres here before the mid-1790s. Until then, operations still took place in the wards, and Thomas Trotter noted that 'It is not decent to operate in a full ward, where the cries of the patients offend others'.[108]

In July 1787 Jacques Tenon and Charles-Augustin Coulomb, two members of a French Commission investigating foreign hospitals, visited Stonehouse. Afterwards, they enthusiastically reported that 'in not one of the hospitals of France or England, we would say in the whole of Europe, except the Plymouth hospital are the individual buildings destined to receive patients as well ventilated and as completely isolated'.[109] Mortality rates here, compared to Haslar, further underlined the success of this layout. The design was not, however, copied in the subsequent hospitals at Deal and Great Yarmouth, but it reappeared in the early 1820s in a modified form at Holl's Port Royal hospital and at Taylor's slightly later Melville Hospital at Chatham. As long as the miasma theory held – that fevers stemmed from foul air and putrefaction – the emphasis tended to be on eliminating these perceived causes and encouraging fresh air. It was only later that the importance of properly isolating sick patients was fully appreciated.

In 1763 a short brick terrace with a mansard roof and oversized central pediment was constructed south of Stonehouse Hospital, looking along its main axis to the administrative block. These provided accommodation for the physician, steward, surgeon and agent. The appointment of governors in 1795 led to the construction of two further houses on either side of the earlier terrace, creating something of a formal square opposite the inner entrance gates of the hospital. The earlier designs for these houses were signed by Bentham, but Holl took over the project in 1804 soon after his appointment.[110] Notable subsequent additions were an octagonal stone water tower and, in 1883, a Gothic chapel to the north of the hospital that replaced the original.[111]

Fig 16.30
A patient arriving in a canvas cot at the landing stage of Stonehouse Hospital in 1898. The buildings to the rear were storerooms and a bath house for new patients.
(Navy and Army Illustrated *18 March 1898, 342)*

In 1837 a young Dr Edward Cree began his career here as Assistant Surgeon, leaving an account of his routine that had its lighter moments:

> Our duties were not arduous: at 8.30 a.m. to attend the Physician (Sir David Dickson) round his wards, afterwards to the Dispensary to assist in making up medicines with the Apothecary. Generally nothing more till the evening visit, at 8 p.m., which lasted about half an hour. Old Sir David had then evidently dined, and was sometimes a little thick in his speech and very crabbed, and I have seen him feel for the pulse of the leg of an empty bed which had been put up against the wall, much to the suppressed mirth of the nurse and Assistant Surgeon, but he was a clever old Scotchman.[112]

Fig 16.31
The former storerooms at Stonehouse Hospital looking through the entrance archway to the infilled Stonehouse Creek.
(Author)

By then, physicians at both Stonehouse and Haslar had to be concerned with more than just the sick and injured. Naval hospitals were specifically constructed to heal and care for these men and to return as many as possible to the fleet. At Haslar and Stonehouse in particular, the huge number of patients inevitably meant that there were many whose injuries, age or mental state made a return to duty impossible. In the 18th century regular Boards of Survey reviewed such cases. Most of those deemed unfit for further service could simply be discharged, with luck to be cared for by their families, while those deemed insane were generally sent to Bethlem Hospital in London. For anyone too old for further service or permanently incapacitated by injury and with no means of support, the Royal Hospital for Seamen at Greenwich since 1705 had provided a home.

Such arrangements were far from perfect, and it was not long before both Haslar and Stonehouse apparently held numbers of permanent inmates. By 1838 Haslar accommodated 118 patients 'labouring under mania in different forms', and by 1863 the east wing of the hospital had wards 'for lunatics'. The same seems to have been the case at Stonehouse.[113] In 1869 the Royal Hospital for Seamen at Greenwich was closed, and 'out-pensioner' payments were substituted. This may have put further pressure on the two main naval hospitals to care long term for elderly and infirm seamen who had no family or relatives to look after them. Late 19th-century photographs show numbers of such pensioners at both Haslar and Stonehouse hospitals (Fig 16.32).[114] None of the other naval hospitals, either at home or overseas, appear to have had similar provision.

The Naval Hospital, Port Royal

At Jamaica after the disastrous experience of the hospital at New Greenwich (p 347), medical facilities were returned to Port Royal in 1755. Subsequently, the hospital at Port Royal was badly damaged by the earthquake of 1771, further damaged by a hurricane in 1787 and finally destroyed by another hurricane and fire in 1815.[115] In the immediate aftermath of these disasters, arrangements were made for a temporary hospital, and Edward Holl was asked to design a new one.[116] There can have been few more challenging briefs for an architect, given the history of Port Royal, the fate of the earlier hospital and an absence of any guidance on constructing substantial buildings in such a vulnerable part of the world.[117]

At the time, Holl may well have been smarting from his dispute with Admiral Sir Alexander Cochrane over the design of a hospital for Bermuda, and this may have influenced his decision to make use of prefabricated ironwork to prevent local alterations at Jamaica. Holl's complete drawings do not appear to survive, but in June 1818 the yard officers sought tenders for the new buildings, and the following month

Fig 16.32
Invalids at Stonehouse Hospital. This 1898 photograph, entitled 'Sheer Hulks', a play on the naval term for a decommissioned ship equipped with sheer-legs for stepping and unstepping masts, would not pass muster in a more politically correct age.
(Navy and Army Illustrated *18 March 1898, 344)*

Fig 16.33
The naval hospital at Port Royal in the 1890s with jalousies shading the upper veranda. The detached ward blocks are visible at ground-floor level.
(TNA ADM 195/49 fol 54)

a contract was awarded to a local firm of builders, Messrs Campbell, Logie and Anderson. The outline site plan accompanying these documents shows two parallel ranges of wards separated by a courtyard and with ancillary buildings nearby.[118] The records are very incomplete, but it is clear that objections to the design came from Admiral Douglas and Dr Macnamara, the senior medical officer on station. Macnamara wished for extra land to be purchased for the hospital and for the verandas surrounding the wards to be widened. It was calculated that these proposals would add some £88,000 to the cost, much of which was attributed to the need for piling the foundations because of the unstable ground on the preferred site at the western end of Port Royal, overlooking the harbour entrance.[119] Some two years were to be spent resolving this dispute and acquiring the necessary land.

Holl's eventual solution for the actual buildings, which he estimated would cost just over £26,000, was a single line of two-storey blocks of wards linked by 15ft-wide verandas under an oversailing common roof (Fig 16.33). The blocks were built of brick, and the surrounding verandas and stairs between each block were of cast iron (Fig 16.34). The roof structure was a mixture of cast and wrought iron, all the ironwork supplied by the Bowling Ironworks at Bradford. The roof was to be boarded and covered with copper sheets.[120] This design went through a series of drafts before construction started on three blocks, with a further block added at the north end and two at the south end as more land was acquired.

Fig 16.34
Details of the cast-iron structure of the first floor and staircase of the hospital at Port Royal.
(Author)

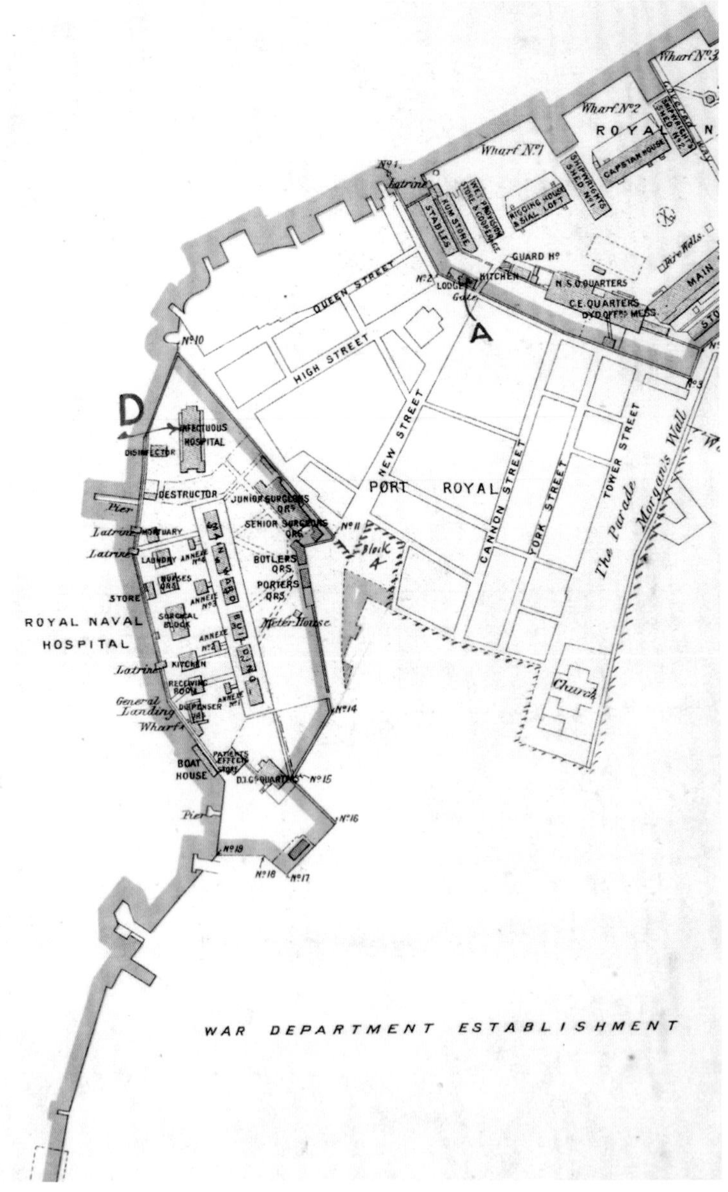

Fig 16.35
A 1904 plan of the naval hospital at Port Royal with the town and part of the dockyard beyond. (AdL Vz 15/55)

The blocks provided a single ward on each floor, with four sash windows on opposite sides; each ward probably held 16 beds, suggesting a total of 192 patients (Fig 16.35).[121]

There were problems with the quality of some of the ironwork and complaints that some dimensions did not accord with the plans, and it was to be 1820 before work finally got under way.[122] Conscious of the unstable nature of the ground, Holl used extensive piling. The cast-iron veranda columns sit on stepped brick foundations built on a continuous planking base, with five timber piles under each column and two or three between the columns, giving a total of over 800 piles for these alone. Although drawings do not survive, it is highly likely that the blocks of wards, whose walls are 2½ bricks thick, were built on similar massive foundations. Holl and the Rennies were collaborating on the reconstruction of Sheerness Dockyard at this time, and it would be surprising if Holl had not sought the latter's advice on his Port Royal project.

The ground-floor veranda columns support a first-floor ring beam. Cast-iron beams bolted to this have their opposite ends resting on cast-iron pads built into the walls of the blocks. The central beams on opposite sides of each block are linked to each other with metal straps, helping to bind the iron framework. U-shaped housings on the webs of the beams provide seats for cast-iron joists. The joists were designed to carry stone slabs, but these may never have been installed, and the existing lime concrete slabs may be original.[123] Indicative of Holl's attention to detail are the pairs of vertical ribs cast on opposite sides of the first-floor columns which once housed full-height wooden jalousies that could be lowered to shade the upper veranda.

The mansard roof is carried on metal roof trusses spanning the full 52ft width of the building. The principal members of the trusses are bolted together, with the compression members within the trusses located in slots top and bottom and held in place by three vertical, evenly spaced, bolted wrought-iron rods. Metal purlins were secured in place by wrought-iron clamps tightened by pairs of metal wedges (Fig 16.36). Holl was employing roof trusses with similar profiles to those in the now-demolished Quadrangle and Victualling Stores at Sheerness, and his successor Taylor was to use a similar truss at the dockyard offices at Sheerness in 1825. None of these, however, approached the span of the Port Royal hospital.[124]

The main roof was hardly completed before it developed serious leaks and had to be covered

Fig 16.36 (right)
The hospital roof at Port Royal showing Holl's use of cast-iron and wrought-iron trusses and purlins. (Author)

Fig 16.37
The naval hospital at Port Royal in the 1890s viewed from the harbour. To the right is the landing stage and behind this a number of ancilliary buildings with Holl's main hospital wards to the rear.
(TNA ADM 195/49 fol 51)

with tarred canvas 'to render it habitable during the rainy season'. The cause was 'the intense heat of the sun' that twisted the roof boarding and split the covering of copper sheets. The contractor blamed the thinness of the 16oz sheets and recommended replacing them with 28oz to 30oz copper sheets, of a similar weight to those used for hull sheathing. An 1849 drawing suggests that by then the roof was covered in slates or shingles; 14 dormer vents set in the roof have long gone.[125]

The first patients were admitted in April 1821, and the hospital was finally completed in 1828. As with many such projects, its eventual cost is largely unknown. By the time the first patients arrived, the commissioner reckoned the costs had reached £54,309 10s 5d.[126] The naval hospital was to remain in use until the Royal Navy withdrew in 1905. It was then passed over to the army. Holl's main building was to prove remarkably durable, withstanding at least a dozen hurricanes and earthquakes and a long period of neglect.[127] It is rightly famous as one of the earliest buildings in the West Indies to employ prefabricated structural ironwork on this scale.

It is not so widely appreciated that a number of its ancillary buildings also survive.

West of the hospital a row of eight small, single-storey brick and slate buildings was constructed overlooking the harbour (Figs 16.37 and 16.38). Next to the landing stage at the southern end stood a store for 'patients' effects', the dispenser's quarters and the receiving room where incoming patients were assessed. Only the footings of these buildings survive. Adjacent to them in varying degrees of repair still stand the kitchen with louvred roof, the surgical block with its small operating theatre, the nurses' quarters and the former laundry. The row was

Fig 16.38
The hospital at Port Royal from the north in 2008. The structural importance of Holl's main hospital wards has tended to overshadow the significance of the associated and now derelict service buildings on the right.
(Author)

completed by a small mortuary, now demolished. On the north-eastern part of the site the footings remain of the Infectious Hospital, certainly in existence in 1887 when money was allocated for improvements to the fever ward. Nearby, footings mark the site of the Junior and Senior Surgeons' Quarters, probably built in 1864.[128]

Between the eight ancillary buildings and the hospital are small brick latrines, the northernmost one being two storey, probably built shortly before the hospital closed.[129] Although traditionally built of brick and architecturally less important, the hospital could not have functioned without these buildings, and the survivors are now rare examples of their type. Further away along the Palisadoes, the narrow isthmus linking Port Royal to the mainland, lies the overgrown naval cemetery. Its headstones record young lives lost through the ubiquitous fevers that frequently defied the best endeavours of naval doctors before their cause was identified.[130]

The Naval Hospital at Malta

The surrender of the French garrison on Malta in September 1800 and the subsequent use of Grand Harbour as a fleet base made the provision of medical facilities imperative. That December Admiral Keith directed his ship's surgeon to set up a hospital in Valletta; this was quickly established in an armoury in Vittoriosa and in the erstwhile Turkish slave prison in Strada Christofora. It is possible that the Vittoriosa one may have met the Sick and Hurt Board's minimum requirement of 600 cubic feet of space per patient; it is improbable that the former slave prison achieved either this standard or the concomitant 'open, elevated and airy situation with windows in every ward in opposite directions', set as the Board's desirable minimum in 1785. Nevertheless, after a hiatus in 1802–4, both were to serve the navy for nearly 30 years.[131]

By 1818 the inconvenience of running two separate hospitals led to discussions about using the former Inquisitor's Palace at Vittoriosa, a gaunt building of late 16th-century date set round a central courtyard. Although probably an improvement, it was by no means ideal as it was still in a crowded urban setting. Nothing came of the proposal. Instead, attention turned to the unfinished Bighi Palace that occupied a dramatic site high on the end of the Calcara peninsula overlooking the entrance of Grand Harbour. Its strategic importance was considered such that the palace and its surrounding grounds had been purchased for the British Government in 1801 by the Civil Commissioner, Sir Charles Cameron,[132] specifically for possible use as a naval hospital. In December 1803 Dr John Snipe, physician to the Mediterranean fleet, wrote to Nelson, its Commander-in-Chief since May:

> I beg leave to acquaint your Lordship that with Sir A Ball I examined the Palace of Bighy which is a most desirable situation for a Naval Hospital, in Summer it is cooled by the refreshing sea breeze and in winter perfectly dry. A convenient landing place close to the palace and sufficient ground belonging to it in a high state of cultivation to produce abundance of vegetables for the use of the sick and if lemon and orange trees were planted the fleet on this station might be amply supplied.[133]

Nelson himself was enthusiastic, if more cautious about likely costs, writing to Sir Thomas Troubridge: 'Bighi is certainly the only proper place as it stands insulated with grounds, and has every means of comfort. But to complete it for 150 men would cost beside the purchase of house and grounds, £1,000 to £2,000 to put it in order. Ball says £5,000 would do the whole, but I say for 5 read £10,000'.[134] This was hardly a propitious moment to advocate expenditure on such a project. The First Lord of the Admiralty, Earl St Vincent, was in the midst of an ill-considered attack on all the navy's shore establishments because of their suspected inefficiencies and corruption. As Roger Knight has put it, 'Contracts were cancelled. Dockyard officials were summarily dismissed'. As part of his drive for economy, St Vincent had ordered the closure of the naval hospital at Malta in May 1802, forcing the then Commander-in-Chief, Rear-Admiral Sir Richard Bickerton, to rely on the army hospital on the island. Dr Snipe's suggestion received a measure of support in London, but although nothing then came of his proposal, Bighi was not forgotten.[135]

In 1824 Captain Charles Ross, the commissioner of the dockyard, and Colonel George Whitmore of the Royal Engineers collaborated on drawing up plans for a hospital at Bighi for approval in London.[136] Official permission was still not forthcoming, although the inadequacies of existing medical arrangements were emphasised by Vice-Admiral Sir Edward Codrington in 1827 shortly before he sailed with the Mediterranean fleet to the Peloponnese and the Battle of Navarino. Two years later, plans were finally approved after Codrington's successor, Sir Edward Pulteney Malcolm, had demanded action. The foundation stone was laid on 24 March 1830, recording that the hospital was 'designed by Colonel George Whitmore, of the Royal Engineers, in concert with Vice-Admiral Pulteney Malcolm and Captain Charles B.H. Ross.' Incised at the base of the plaque were the names 'Gaetano Xerri, Architect, and Jos.B.Collings, Clerk of Works'.[137] However, the Navy Board correspondence shows that his brother Salvador Xerri was the original architect, and that Gaetano Xerri took over that role on his death. It would be reasonable to assume that it was Gaetano who was responsible for the final design, working in consultation with Colonel Whitmore.

The new hospital was constructed by local craftsmen and was completed in 1832 (Fig 16.39).[138] An 1840 handbook to Malta glowingly described it as a 'superb, elegant and extensive naval hospital which is an adornment to the Island and an immortal honour to its founder'.[139]

Fig 16.39
An 1863 plan of Malta Naval Hospital.
(AdL 1863 Plans of Naval Establishments Da 02 fol 25)

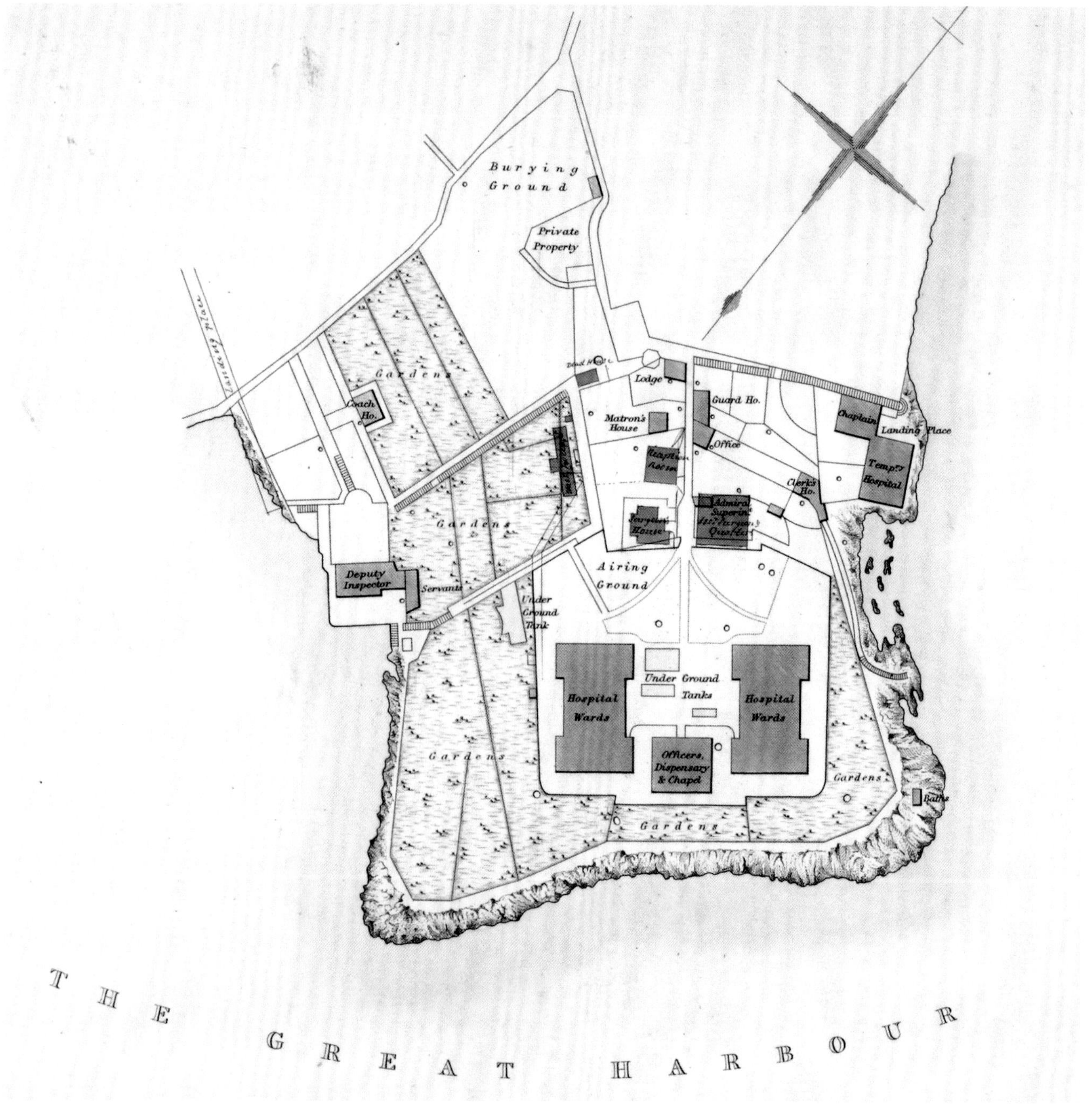

Fig 16.40
The former naval hospital at Malta from Grand Harbour. The building on the extreme right is the later zymotic block. (Author)

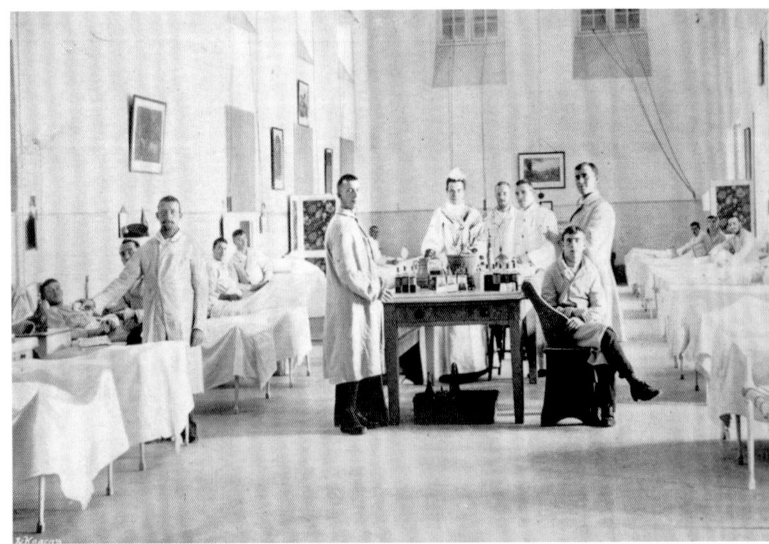

Fig 16.41
One of the wards in the hospital at Malta in 1898. The hospital was noted for its spacious and airy accommodation.
*(*Navy and Army Illustrated *10 Dec 1898, 274)*

At its heart was the unfinished Bighi Palace, which in 1804 Dr Snipe had considered could hold 160 patients, with a further 120 to be accommodated in two new wings and additional ancillary buildings constructed.[140] As completed in 1832, the former palace provided accommodation for administrative offices, quarters for senior medical staff, a dispensary and chapel. Its design was clearly rooted in the local island Baroque.

By contrast, the two substantial new colonnaded detached blocks that held 240 patients were constructed in an austere Greek Revival style and are unlike any other Royal Navy hospital (Fig 16.40). The records are silent on this choice of style, but the hospital was designed at a time when, further east in the Mediterranean, the Greeks were fighting their War of Independence, its successful outcome substantially boosted by the destruction of the Turkish and Egyptian fleets at Navarino. It may not be too fanciful to suggest that the prominent new naval hospital at Malta was built in a style that celebrated Greek emancipation, as well as providing a classical building worthy of its Grand Harbour setting.[141] The ward blocks, raised on substantial rusticated basements containing storerooms, kitchens and laundries, had double rows of wards, separated by a spacious central passage and opening on to the colonnaded verandas along both sides. The large wards are distinguished by their high ceilings and generous windows, fulfilling the 1785 criteria for patient space (Fig 16.41). The small pedimented blocks at the corners of the wings contained the officers' wards.

In the 1860s, pressure on space led to the construction of houses for senior medical staff, enabling the old palace to be adapted as further sick quarters for officers.[142] At the end of the century separate zymotic wards were added, and soon afterwards a tall, freestanding stone lift shaft was constructed to allow patients to be brought up from a landing stage on Calcara Creek. Although Bighi Hospital suffered some war damage, it was little altered and finally closed in 1970. It remains a prominent and distinguished group of buildings.

17

Barracks and Training Establishments

The economic impact of the royal dockyards on the evolution of their associated dockyard towns was very considerable. Similarly, naval and dockyard training establishments and later naval barracks made increasingly distinctive contributions to the architectural development of a number of bases and their civilian communities. These are considered in outline here, sufficient only to set them in their wider naval context.[1]

Apart from the watchmen, yard porters and senior civilian and naval officers responsible for the various shore establishments, everyone else lived in towns and villages closely linked to the fortunes of the naval bases.[2] The impact of the bases on their local communities increased as the dockyards expanded from the early 18th century. This was less noticeable in large, mature urban settlements, such as Deptford and Woolwich with a variety of alternative employment, or where the yards remained small, as at Harwich and Deal. But where major yards were constructed in rural areas, the effect was dramatic. In 1690 the establishment a few miles from the port of Plymouth of a new dockyard in open country on the banks of the Hamoaze led to the growth there of the new town of Plymouth Dock to house the yard workforce. In 1824 the town was renamed Devonport, the dockyard adopting the same name in 1843. Subsequent urban growth has led to Plymouth and Devonport becoming a single conurbation. In the 18th century Portsea, now a suburb of Portsmouth, grew up on open commons adjacent to the dockyard that lay outside the old settlement of Portsmouth and its defences.[3] Here, too, the dockyard town soon rivalled in size its far older neighbour.

At Chatham, the village of Brompton developed on the hillside above the dockyard in the 18th century, its grid pattern of streets in marked contrast to the older community of Chatham where most of the labour force continued to live.[4] On Jamaica in the 1730s the planned town of Titchfield was laid out to attract the workforce for the new base of Port Antonio; when the latter failed, the town lost its principal economic driver and was largely abandoned (*see* Chapter 12). All these communities seem to have developed without direct Admiralty input beyond the wages of its workforce. However, in less attractive, more expensive or remote locations, the Admiralty found it had to play a more active role to attract and keep workers. At Sheerness, lacking adequate housing and long considered unhealthy, the Navy Board early on provided hulks for accommodation and by the end of the 18th century had – uniquely for a home yard – constructed ranges of workers' lodgings. These were inside the garrison and supplemented Blue Town, which was gradually developing in the lee of the fortifications.[5]

Workers attracted to the new dockyard at Pembroke were faced with considerable problems because of the lack of an adjacent settlement, and the Admiralty had to facilitate the development of land outside the boundary, as well as petition for the establishment of a market in 1819. The resultant town of Pembroke Dock, which developed from rival developments of Pater Town and Melville Town, still retains it early grid pattern of streets (*see* Chapter 1).[6] A century later the creation of Rosyth Dockyard led to similar housing problems. During the construction phase, the Admiralty saw the solution lying in special workers' trains from Edinburgh and other population centres. By 1912 these trains had to be supplemented by prefabricated corrugated iron huts, which by 1914 housed some 2,650 people in two communities, Bungalow City East and Bungalow City West.[7] Permanent housing for the yard workers and their families was gradually provided in the years during and after the First World War with the creation of Rosyth Garden City, fruition of collaboration between the Admiralty, Dunfermline Town Council and the Scottish National Housing Association.[8]

The smaller overseas bases in the 18th century had less impact on local communities, particularly as ships' crews would provide the bulk of the labour force for careening and simple repairs. However, an undated drawing, probably of the 1770s, for a 'proposed artificer's cabbin' at English Harbour submitted by the dockyard officers suggests that at times accommodation had to be provided to tempt skilled trades from Britain.[9] On Ireland Island, Bermuda, in 1818 the Admiralty was urged to build a market and a number of workmen's houses to encourage settlement near the new base.[10] The cost of local accommodation here later forced the Admiralty to construct a series of 16 houses in the 1860s for 'artificers and watchmen' and a further 7 with verandas for 'clerks and foremen' at the considerable cost of £27,339.[11] Nearer to home, the island location of Haulbowline made the provision of cottages for workmen essential, and a number were provided from the mid-1820s (*see* Chapter 1).[12]

As long as the navy manned its ships by recruiting or pressing crews and dismissing them after a commission, there was little pressure for the Admiralty to provide barracks for its sailors. However, there were a number of exceptions where accommodation was provided well before the end of the 18th century. At overseas bases with careening facilities, a crew had to come ashore while their ship was heeled over on the careening wharf. The officers were generally lodged in houses built for this purpose. By 1771 Halifax Yard had 'sea officers' apartments while their ships careen', while a 1765 plan of Port Royal shows 'The Apartments for Lieutenants and other Gentlemen to mess in while careening'.[13] In the centre of the yard at English Harbour, Antigua, is a handsome row of lodgings built over the water cisterns for this purpose during the Napoleonic Wars. Small kitchen buildings were built at a number of bases to provide hot food for crews while their ships' galley fires were extinguished. By 1787 English Harbour had two 'kitchens for ships' people', as well as a small provisions storehouse 'for ships under careen'.[14]

Initially, sailors were not provided with accommodation and probably made shift constructing tents with sails and spars. However, on the careening wharves the batteries of capstans used to haul down the warships were almost invariably protected from the weather by timber-framed buildings, and their first floors or loft spaces were intended for stowing equipment. There is evidence that at Port Royal, English Harbour and doubtless at other yards, these spaces were also used by crews to sling their hammocks. Such arrangements were gradually regularised at a number of yards where there was vacant space. By the 1770s at English Harbour a single-storey building 62ft by 21ft was allocated for crews on careen, while by 1853 part of the first floor of the surviving main storehouse was used as quarters for ships' companies.[15] At Halifax, part of a quadrangular range of single-storey buildings by the careening wharf was used as a capstan house by 1771. Part of the same range is marked as 'seamen's barracks' in 1859,[16] by which time careening was no longer possible with steam-assisted warships. The wording perhaps suggests more permanent occupation by the seamen, and the building could well have been used while a warship was in for repairs, though an additional use may have been as quarters for crews on station during the bitter winter months.

No such extremes of climate affected Bermuda, but an 1858 plan of Ireland Island marks a small group of buildings east of Cockburn's Cut as 'naval barracks'.[17] At Malta a former storehouse near the dry dock had been adapted as seamen's barracks by the early 1860s.[18] Thirty years later the development of Garden Island at Sydney included a handsome, purpose-designed, three-storey naval barracks surrounded by cast-iron verandas and clearly modelled on contemporary military accommodation (*see* Fig 13.21).[19] One of the last buildings to be constructed for the Royal Navy at Esquimalt in 1904 was a small barracks for 74 seamen, 8 petty officers and a warrant officer. The building was largely self-contained, with 42 men in one room on the first floor and 32 on the ground floor. The ground floor also had a galley, reading room, lavatories, four baths for the men and two for the petty officers and the warrant officer.[20] In these four instances the main functions of the barracks seem to have been to house crews whose ships were temporarily in dockyard hands and to accommodate sailors awaiting onward passage.

In the home yards, Sheerness was unique by 1863 in having a barracks. By 1880 this was used, along with a number of depot ships, to house very young ordinary seamen under training and awaiting posting to training ships. This may have been the reason for the original creation of this barracks in part of the Victualling Store.[21] The eventual provision of proper naval barracks stemmed from the launching of Long Term Service in 1853. This was introduced to retain sailors in order to reduce the wastage of trained men, which was becoming more critical as the steam navy demanded much greater technical training and skills.[22] Such men had to be housed between postings to commissioned ships; however, with large numbers of accommodation hulks available, it was to be another 30 years before they would come ashore to purpose-built barracks.

Military barracks had been introduced only following the development of a small standing army in the latter half of the 17th century. The earliest recorded use of the word 'barracks' as opposed to 'soldiers' lodgings' in the English language is in 1670 and relates to the new 'Irish Barracks' at the Tower of London.[23] Although ones for the navy were not to be built until the last quarter of the 19th century, the Admiralty by the 1850s had considerable experience of barrack building and maintenance, having provided them for the marines after they had been formed into a permanent force of three divisions in 1755. Marine barracks were established at Portsmouth by 1768, at Chatham in 1780[24] and at Stonehouse in 1781 (Fig 17.1).[25] A further set of barracks was constructed at Woolwich in the 1840s, while between 1862 and 1867 a vast defensible barracks at Eastney was built as new accommodation for the marines at Portsmouth. Eastney was a collaborative design between Greene and Scamp, with advice from Lieutenant-Colonel William Jervois, who had been appointed to the army Barrack Construction Committee in 1855. Scamp was also credited by the Director of Works with additional works at the marine barracks at Stonehouse and Chatham.[26] The introduction in 1860 of the Metropolitan Police to provide security for all naval bases also led to the construction of police barracks on a small scale in the yards.[27] At Haslar Gunboat Yard, the recently completed North Guardhouse was adapted to provide extra accommodation.[28] At Chatham a substantial three-storey brick Police Station and Barracks crowned by a small cupola was constructed at the north end of the dockyard, overlooking the mast ponds. Police married quarters here were located outside the dockyard gate.[29]

In 1860 three possible locations within Devonport Dockyard were considered for sailors' barracks, but in every case the site was too small or was wanted for other development. Instead, it was recommended that extra land be purchased to the north of Keyham Yard.[30] In 1862 £80,000 was allocated for the construction of naval barracks at Keyham, to be followed a year later by a sum of £104,000

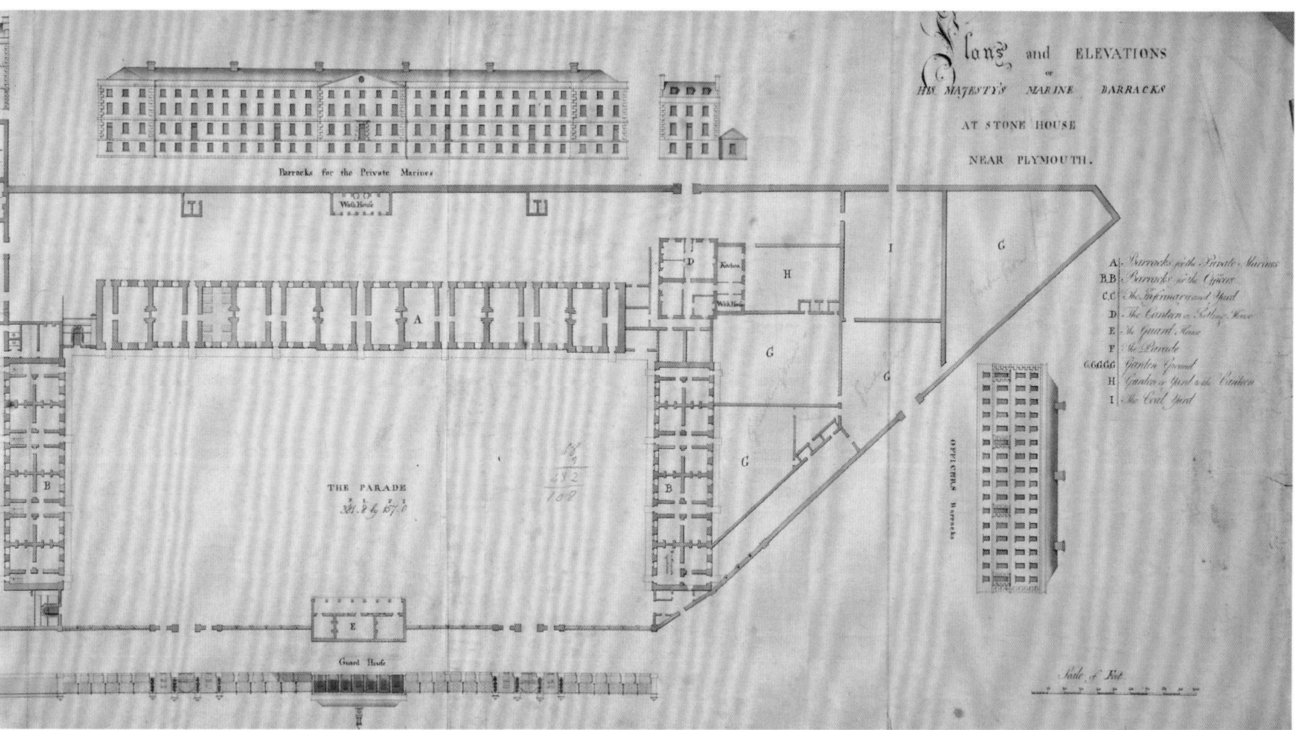

Fig 17.1
This 1788 plan shows Stonehouse Royal Marine barracks as first completed. There have been subsequent additions, but most of the original buildings survive, and the barracks remain in use by the marines. (TNA ADM 140/310)

for barracks at Portsmouth, to include the construction of a defensible wall, presumably following the precedent set at Eastney.[31] The origin of these sums is unclear, for in August 1864 G T Greene was writing to the Admiralty Board asking for clarification of their intentions as no sites had been agreed.[32] The matter then lapsed. However, the continued use of hulks as accommodation ships was becoming steadily less acceptable. They were used not just as living quarters, but also for storage and training. The Royal Navy's torpedo school took its name from HMS *Vernon*, a hulk that became its first home in 1876. Although an Act of 1866 had encouraged the setting up in hulks of 'Industrial School Ships', of which there were a number moored round the coasts of England and Scotland, the public mind associated hulks with housing prisoners-of-war during earlier wars and later as convict prisons and quarantine ships (Fig 17.2). The vessels were considered cramped, unhealthy and unhygienic, views reinforced by periodic outbreaks of fevers on board.[33] Moreover, their continued use reflected increasingly badly on the Admiralty at a time when the War Office was making considerable progress in getting rid of the worst of its barracks and replacing them with more spacious, healthy and hygienic quarters.[34]

In 1876 the Admiralty revived the barracks scheme, proposing ones for 4,000 seamen at Portsmouth and 3,500 at Keyham. In 1879 construction of the naval barracks began at Keyham, but 20 years were to pass before similar establishments were built at Portsmouth and Chatham.[35] These three great bases, the only ones to be provided with such barracks, were the 'manning ports' that, especially since the introduction of Long Term Service, were developing a tradition of supplying recruits from their hinterland to the navy. The career prospects created by the 1853 changes, with sailors and their ships being based at specific dockyards, also allowed sailors to establish their families in the vicinity of the bases, giving them a better opportunity of home life when their ships were under repair or maintenance.[36]

Changing requirements meant that although the first phase of Keyham barracks for 1,000 men was ready for occupation in 1886, further construction was to be spread over the next quarter of a century (Fig 17.3).[37] In 1884 the Admiralty Barrack Committee recommended that a further thousand should be accommodated 'and that space should be left in this arrangement so that it may be expanded to suit either 3,000 or 4,000 men'.[38] In 1891 the barracks was first occupied fully when it also housed the men of the Steam Reserve Depot. By 1907, when the third phase of works was complete, Keyham's capacity had risen to a total of 4,895 personnel.[39]

Naval ratings were accommodated in a series of pairs of parallel, three-storey barracks (Figs 17.4 and 17.5), each floor an open dormitory heated by stoves and with space for

Fig 17.2
Accommodation hulks moored alongside Chatham Dockyard. These continued to be used until the opening of the naval barracks in 1903. Such hulks remained common sights at naval bases well into the 20th century.
(Illus London News)

Fig 17.3
This 1909 plan shows the formal layout of the Devonport Royal Naval Barracks with its extensive parade and sports grounds. (TNA ADM 140/1484 pt 36)

125 hammocks. The men messed in their barrack rooms (Fig 17.6), collecting their food from a cookhouse in the central blocks between the barracks, which also housed washing facilities and latrines (Fig 17.7).[40] Plans prepared in 1878 show that the original intention had been to house officers in small buildings at the end of each of these barracks. Two were built before the idea was abandoned in 1885; instead, a large central wardroom crowned with a domed belvedere was constructed, linked by bridges to accommodation blocks on either side (Fig 17.8). The barracks at Keyham were completed with a gymnasium, drill hall, swimming baths, classrooms, canteen, church, commodore's house and parade ground.

Fig 17.4
The first seamen's barracks and drill shed newly completed at Devonport Royal Naval Barracks, a photograph probably taken in 1890. Until the Keyham extension was begun in 1896, the barracks looked across open ground to the Hamoaze. (TNA ADM 195/60 fol 68)

Fig 17.5
Looking towards the main gateway of Devonport Royal Naval Barracks with the seamen's barrack blocks on the left.
(Author)

Fig 17.6
The interior of one of the seamen's barracks in 1897 at Devonport Royal Naval Barracks. Hammock spaces and mess arrangements reflected the deck layouts in the old sailing warships.
*(*Navy and Army Illustrated *13 Apr 1897)*

Fig 17.7
One of the wash-houses at Devonport Royal Naval Barracks in 1897. Although to a modern eye conditions look primitive, the provision of a mangle, running fresh water and sinks in place of buckets was a vast improvement on earlier arrangements afloat.
*(*Navy and Army Illustrated *13 Apr 1897)*

Fig 17.8
The officers' mess at Devonport Royal Naval Barracks (HMS Drake*) and beyond it the former drill shed.*
(Author)

The Keyham barracks, renamed HMS *Drake* in 1934, were built on a grand scale using the local limestone, with details in Portland stone, their design a free Italianate style, forerunner of the slightly later Imperial Baroque. Dominating the barracks, as intended, is the tall clocktower, its six storeys enriched with pilasters, pediments and elaborate corbelled balconies with cast-iron balustrades. Its top originally housed a semaphore (Fig 17.9). Despite the protracted building period and changes of plan, the complex retains an architectural cohesion, but it remains unclear who was responsible for the design. Those most closely involved over the period were the four successive Directors of Works,[41] with considerable input by the local Superintending Engineers. In 1897 the author of an article on

Fig 17.9
The main gate, guard house and clock tower at Devonport Royal Naval Barracks soon after completion in 1897. Apart from the removal of the semaphore from the top of the tower, there have been few subsequent alterations.
*(*Navy and Army Illustrated *13 Apr 1897)*

Fig 17.10
The main buildings on this 1909 plan of Portsmouth Royal Naval Barracks (HMS Nelson*) are very similar in design to those at Devonport and Chatham, but the restricted nature of the Portsmouth site is reflected in the Officers' Mess being located across a busy road, still an inconvenience a century later.*
(TNA ADM 140/1484 fol 18)

Fig 17.11
This 1909 plan of Chatham Naval Barracks (later HMS Pembroke*) shows that the design of the barrack blocks and the overall layout followed the pattern established at Portsmouth and Plymouth. Since the closure of the naval base in 1984, the barrack buildings have been used as universities.*
(TNA ADM 140/1484 fol 5)

the barracks somewhat mysteriously wrote that 'Their construction and appearance are pleasing to the eye and creditable to the architect – whose name, unfortunately, cannot be given at the moment.'[42]

Unlike Keyham with its virgin site, Portsmouth naval barracks, now HMS *Nelson*, had to be fitted into a crowded urban area. Construction could not begin in earnest until late 1899 after the navy had obtained Anglesea Barracks from the War Office and demolished most of the buildings. Even so, the officers' mess had to be awkwardly situated on a separate site across a main road (Fig 17.10). At Chatham, the naval barracks were located on the site of the former convict prison, conveniently near the Steam Yard. Work began here in 1897, and the barracks here and at Portsmouth were first occupied in 1903 (Fig 17.11).[43] Both sets of barracks were modelled on the Keyham pattern of pairs of parallel ranges of accommodation blocks, with ablutions and cookhouses in between and with the other training and recreation facilities ranged round them. The Portsmouth and Chatham barracks were built of brick with stone detailing, but ornamentation was rather less elaborate than at the Keyham barracks. However, the officers' messes were notable for the richness of carved decoration and the great Wyllie murals of famous British naval victories.

Portsmouth barracks held 4,000 men, while Chatham could accommodate 4,742, rising to 7,720 during what were described as 'Total Emergency' periods. The cost of the Chatham barracks was said to be 'about £425,000 up to the date of occupation', and the anonymous author of a booklet on the barracks ascribes their design and the supervision of their construction to the Civil Engineer-in-Chief of the Naval Loan Works Department, Major Henry Pilkington. Given their similarity, it would be reasonable to credit Pilkington also with the design of those at Portsmouth.[44]

Training

From the early 18th century onwards the growing size and complexity of the fleet and its bases gradually forced the Admiralty to adopt more systematic methods of training those involved in their operation. Even so, for the majority of naval officers and dockyard craftsmen until well into the 19th century, training remained a somewhat haphazard affair, in which apprenticeship played a large part. Spurs to change came from three principal sources: concern that foreign rivals with superior training were stealing a march, the introduction of complex machinery ashore and afloat, and lastly the voracious demand for trained manpower in the final decades before the First World War. The teaching methods, curricula and success or otherwise of the various separate training schemes for the navy and its civilian dockyard staff are outside the scope of this brief survey, which focuses on the accommodation.[45] This was almost all first located within dockyard boundaries or in hulks moored close by. Later, as pressure on dockyard space grew and training needs increased, a number of establishments moved to separate sites.

Naval training establishments

By 1700 most naval officers were trained by a system of apprenticeship, starting their careers between the ages of 11 and 14 as volunteers-by-order, or as captains' servants. Their training, done entirely at sea, depended on the qualities of their captain, who might be assisted by the ship's chaplain and by a schoolmaster if the ship carried one. Depending on their aptitude, after 6 or 7 years, if these midshipmen passed a theoretical and practical examination, they were ranked as third lieutenants. The system generally produced officers with a sound knowledge of seamanship and navigation, but lacking a broader education, including foreign languages and the arts of war and diplomacy.

By the 1720s there was a growing feeling that a more broadly based and formal training would benefit the individual, the navy and the nation. This culminated in 1729 in an Order in Council to establish a Naval Academy at Portsmouth, forerunner of Greenwich and Dartmouth. The original instructions made clear that its aims were 'the reception and better educating and training up of 40 young gentlemen for His Majesty's service at sea, instead of the establishment now in force for volunteers on board His Majesty's ships'.[46] The 3-year course originally included mathematics taught by two masters, French, drawing, dancing and fencing lessons, as well as practical instruction that involved the yard's master attendant, master shipwright and boatswain.[47] Later on, physics, astronomy, gunnery, fortification and other subjects were added.[48]

The Naval Academy, estimated at £5,772 4s, was begun in 1729 and completed in 1733.[49] Construction of such an important institution here may be taken as early recognition by the Admiralty of the growing importance of this south coast yard and of the gradual eclipse of Chatham. It is a three-storey, H-plan building of brick with detailing in Purbeck stone (Fig 17.12). The two pedimented front wings originally housed the head mathematics master and the 'Commissioner of the Navy residing there as Governor of the Academy'.[50] Although the original draft of plans for the building does not appear to survive, the accompanying letter of 16 March 1729 from the Navy Board 'to direct and require' the Portsmouth officers 'to cause the said building to be gone in hand' is signed by five Navy Board officials, including the Surveyor Sir Jacob Acworth.[51] The importance of this project, requiring a type of building outside the normal remit of the yard officers, would strongly suggest that the Surveyor was responsible for the design.[52]

The rear wings, mostly used as dormitories, were gradually extended and a cross-wing added early in the 19th century, creating a courtyard to the rear.[53] The prominent cupola was added as an observatory in 1770 (Fig 17.13), but its floor space seems to have been used principally to teach fleet tactics using small armadas of ship models that could be overlooked by the pupils from a timber gallery above.[54] In 1806 the number of pupils was increased to 70 and the Naval Academy was renamed the Royal Naval College. In 1837 the college closed, but reopened the following year as a centre for scientific and professional training of officers; this course transferred to Greenwich in 1872 where it was able to expand. In 1906 the former Royal Naval College buildings became home to the Navigation School, a function it maintained until wartime bombing forced its relocation in 1941.[55]

In the 20 years following the closure of the Royal Naval College, cadets – or Volunteers as they were officially known – reverted to the old system of being trained exclusively at sea. In 1857 they were again brought together, first on the *Illustrious*, a hulk moored at Haslar Creek, and then in 1859 on the *Britannia*. In 1862 the *Britannia* was moved to Portland, before finding a permanent home the following year at Dartmouth. *Britannia* was joined in 1864 by the *Hindustan* and in 1869 was replaced by the *Prince of Wales*, which was renamed *Britannia*. In 1874 it was first suggested that the cadets should be brought ashore, and in 1875 the Wellesley Committee considered 52 possible sites, before opting for land at Dartmouth adjacent to the cadets' playing fields.[56] Financial restrictions put a stop to any progress for the next 20 years, and in the meantime a more pressing problem had to be solved.

In 1871 HMS *Devastation* had been launched at Portsmouth, the navy's first capital ship to

Fig 17.12
The former Naval Academy at Portsmouth in 2010, latterly used as a staff officers' mess. (Author)

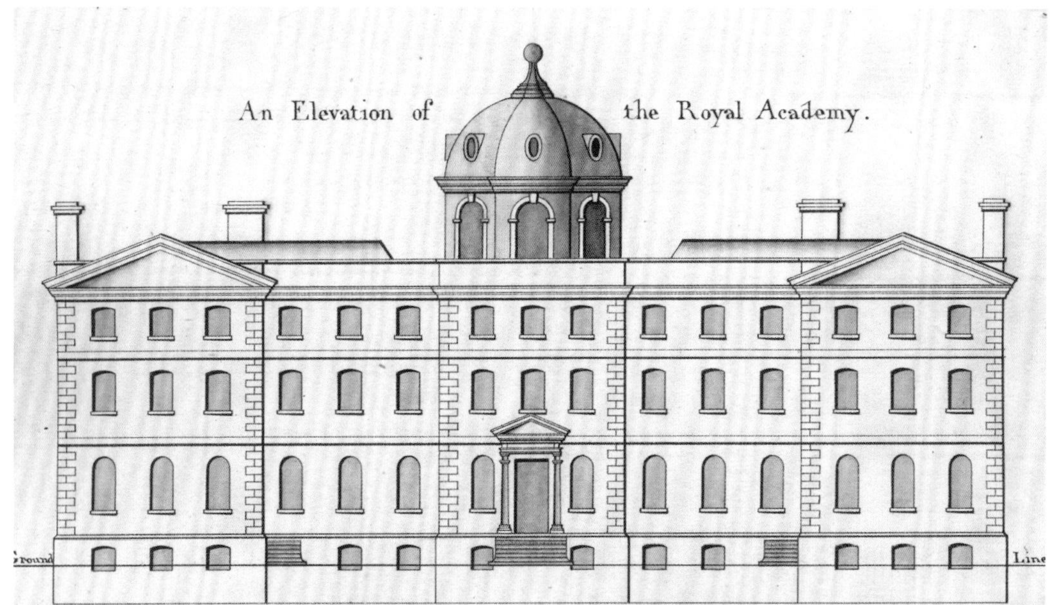

Fig 17.13
A late 18th-century drawing of the Naval Academy at Portsmouth, here labelled as the 'Royal Academy' in recognition of George II's role in its establishment. (NMRN Plans of HM Dockyard, Portsmouth, c 1786, MS 1993/443)

Fig 17.14
The Royal Naval Engineering College at Keyham, Devonport, in the late 1890s. This photograph shows its convenient location just outside the dockyard boundary and immediately adjacent to the great quadrangle engineering complex. (TNA ADM 195/60 fol 61)

dispense entirely with sails and be wholly reliant on steam propulsion. The future clearly lay with such vessels, and with them came a need for more and better-qualified engineers. To encourage recruitment, they needed to have enhanced status and be more fully integrated into the officer class, rather than being regarded by the officers as mere mechanics. In 1875 a committee chaired by Admiral Sir Astley Cooper Key made a number of recommendations, including establishing what became known as the Royal Naval Engineering College at Keyham. This was built just outside the dockyard wall from the Quadrangle to accommodate 120 students, who joined at the age of 15. The college opened in July 1880, and in 1897 a second accommodation block was added to the south for a further 50 students.[57] The design of the college, which was built of stone, was unlike any other naval building, with its Jacobean appearance and steep mansard roofs (Fig 17.14). It was a product of the Admiralty Works Department, the designer possibly influenced by Colonel Andrew Clarke, its Director from 1864 to 1873.[58]

The engineering course of five years, with a further one or two at Greenwich, was the longest training course in the navy. As all instruction

Fig 17.15 (below) Engineering College students gaining practical experience in the engineering workshops in the Quadrangle in the adjacent Keyham Yard. (Navy and Army Illustrated *6 Aug 1898, 459)*

Fig 17.16 (below bottom) The dining hall of the Royal Naval Engineering College at Devonport in 1898. (Navy and Army Illustrated *9 July 1898, 364)*

was done in the well-equipped engineering workshops in the adjacent Keyham Yard (Fig 17.15), the college initially provided only accommodation and meals, but some lectures were transferred to the college in 1886, and the new accommodation block incorporated classrooms.[59] Meals were taken in what a writer in the *Navy and Army Illustrated* described as a 'fine dining hall ... with its lofty open-timbered roof, and appropriate adornments, [it] is comparable to like halls at Oxford and Cambridge' (Fig 17.16). Rather than large open dormitories, the engineering students had individual cubicles with beds.[60]

The facilities at Keyham were something of a spur for the Admiralty to provide shore accommodation for its Dartmouth cadets, and in 1896 Viscount Goschen, the First Sea Lord, was able to authorise construction of what became Britannia Royal Naval College. This was financed by the Naval Works Loan Act of the previous year. The buildings were designed by Sir Aston Webb in a monumental Edwardian Palladian style and dominate this part of the Dart valley (Fig 17.17). They were constructed in brick and stone and formally opened in September 1905.[61] The college was designed to house 260 cadets between the ages of 13 and 17. As well as accommodation and messing for students and staff, classrooms and recreation facilities were also provided.

The construction of the college coincided with a major shake-up in naval training following a memorandum in February 1902 from Admiral Sir John Fisher, then Commander-in-Chief, Mediterranean fleet, to Lord Selborne, First Lord of the Admiralty. Fisher remained acutely concerned at the continuing divide between the engineers and the deck officers of the fleet, a division made almost inevitable by their separate training, which frequently led to mutual incomprehension. He felt passionately that 'it would be good for our officers ... to get much more than the present scanty attendance of the midshipmen when the ship is under steam and their entire absence when the maximum propelling power is being exerted which is the most impressive time for instruction'.[62] The First Lord agreed, and in a famous memorandum backed Fisher's proposals, which in essence aimed to create a unified and better-trained officer corps by providing a common and broader-based training, including engineering. This would be undertaken by every cadet between the ages of 12 to 19, after which those who had successfully passed the exam for Sub-Lieutenant could specialise as Executive (Seamen), Engineer or Royal Marine officers.[63]

The proposals, which were accepted by the Admiralty after much public debate, had immediate practical consequences. As the proposed new course was longer than the original training scheme for which Dartmouth was being built, until further accommodation was provided here, a new 'feeder' college would be necessary where the cadets could receive two years of preliminary training. Both colleges would have to be equipped with extensive engineering workshops. In late 1901 King

Fig 17.17
Britannia Royal Naval College at Dartmouth. Sir Aston Webb's monumental building was opened in 1905, replacing a series of accommodation hulks moored nearby in the Dart estuary. It remains the home of the Royal Navy's officer training. A 1959 photograph. (HAW 9394/42 22 Jul 1959 Harold Wingham Collection, EH)

Fig 17.18 (below top)
*The former stables of Osborne House after conversion to classrooms and a dining hall for Osborne Royal Naval College. (NMRN 1986/60 [9*22])*

Fig 17.19 (below bottom)
The officers' quarters and dormitories of Osborne Royal Naval College in 1917. (NMRN 1980/47)

Edward VII offered part of the Osborne Estate on the Isle of Wight as a site for the new college. To meet the training schedule, the first Osborne cadets would arrive in September 1903.[64]

Economy and speed were essential in setting up the Royal Naval College Osborne, and the task was given to the Office of Works and their architect Henry Hawkes.[65] The former royal stables were converted to a dining hall and classrooms, with additional classrooms attached to the east range (Fig 17.18). Twelve parallel ranges of dormitories, each with their own washrooms, were laid out on a north–south axis to the east of the stables, a connecting passage at their south end separating the dormitories from small reading rooms. Separate staff quarters, a small hospital, a rather larger gymnasium and extensive playing fields completed the college.[66] The dormitories or bungalows and most of the new buildings were all single storey of timber-frame construction, clad with a composite sheet material called uralite.[67] Their gable ends and half-hips to their roofs were given a more homely appearance with the liberal application of half-timbering (Fig 17.19).

After a visit to see progress in September 1903, Fisher was delighted to be able to record that the college had been 'built in one-twelfth of the time and one-eighth of the cost, of the

Fig 17.20 (above) The engineering workshops of Osborne Royal Naval College, situated at Kingston. (NMRN 1981/1061[8])

Fig 17.21 (below) Practical instruction for youthful cadets in the carpentry shop of Osborne Royal Naval College in 1903. (NMRN 1981/1061 [5])

palatial stone buildings at Dartmouth, but equally effective and to hold the same numbers'.[68] The engineering workshops, similar to ones at Dartmouth, were located separately in a series of brick workshops at Kingston in nearby East Cowes (Fig 17.20). These included lecture rooms, a drawing office, fitting and machine shop, carpentry and pattern-making shops, a foundry, smithery and boiler-making shop (Fig 17.21). Post-war retrenchments led to the closure of the Royal Naval College Osborne in 1921, with its courses transferred to Dartmouth.[69] A number of the college buildings, but not the dormitories, remain at Osborne. The Selborne-Fisher Accord also had a considerable impact on the Royal Naval Engineering College at Keyham, where the proposed common entry scheme meant the end of the existing courses here. In 1910 the college closed, only reopening in July 1913 in time to receive the first of the older intake of lieutenants arriving from Greenwich in September. Keyham then resumed the training of naval engineers until the college was relocated to new buildings at Manadon near Plymouth in 1958. The Keyham buildings became the Dockyard Technical College, but were demolished in 1985.[70]

In the19th century the increasing sophistication of naval weapons led to specialist training for those operating them. In 1832 HMS *Excellent*, a 74-gun third-rate launched at Harwich in 1787, was moored in Portsmouth Harbour as home for the navy's first gunnery school for training seamen gunners and gunnery instructors destined to form the nucleus of ships' companies. The first *Excellent* was replaced by a succession of vessels given her name, but by the 1880s such elderly warships were increasingly unable to mount the sophisticated weapons then being installed in the steam fleet, while their living accommodation left much to be desired. By 1851, the tiny Whale Island near the head of Portsmouth Harbour had been purchased to provide *Excellent* with a drill ground and a little later with rifle ranges. The start of the dockyard extension in 1867 led to the island being increased in size from around 10 to 80 acres as soil was added from the dockyard excavations. In 1886 a decision was taken gradually to move *Excellent*'s training facilities ashore.

The first structure to be constructed on the enlarged island was a covered gun drill battery, closely followed by the necessary magazines and associated stores.[71] In the late 1880s the officers' mess and accommodation were constructed overlooking the main parade ground, while laid out at right angles to its rear were 11 accommodation blocks for warrant officers and seamen. Two large latrine blocks, a cookhouse, canteen, sick bay, small bowling alley, large provisions store, classroom and guardhouses were all part of the original layout, together with a smaller winter parade ground and drill shed south of the main parade ground. For instruction purposes, the drill shed contained a range of guns then in use in the fleet (Fig 17.22). A second and larger covered drill battery for mounting heavier guns was added on the north side of the island at the start of the 20th century (Figs 17.23 and 17.24).[72] In all, accommodation was provided for nearly a thousand men.[73] The buildings were almost all single storey, built of brick with stone details, and with tiled roofs. The staff of the Director of Works was responsible for the design of the establishment.[74]

Fig 17.22
Rifled breech-loading guns used for instruction in the drill shed on the southern side of Whale Island, Portsmouth, in 1896. The nearest four guns are 6in breech-loaders on Vavasseur mountings, distinguished by their inclined planes up which the guns recoiled, to be further slowed by hydraulic buffers. (Navy and Army Illustrated *26 June 1896)*

Fig 17.23
Portsmouth. Whale Island. This 1909 plan of Whale Island at Portsmouth shows the spacious layout of HMS Excellent, *with the gun drill sheds at the perimeter. (TNA ADM 140/1484 fol 19)*

Dockyard training establishments

Until the early 19th century, apprenticeship remained the principal method of passing on skills in the royal dockyards. This system lacked both theoretical and formal training, and while it may have sufficed for the majority of skilled workers, its essentially conservative approach took little account of technical innovations and did not necessarily encourage the more able apprentices to develop their ambitions. Since the establishment in 1741 of a School of Naval Architecture in Paris, French dockyards had benefited from master shipwrights who had received a rigorous theoretical and scientific training.[75] Even if this did not necessarily translate into warships that were inherently superior to those of the Royal Navy, its mere existence provided ammunition for critics of the British approach.

In 1791 the establishment of the Society for the Improvement of Naval Architecture provided a more public platform for critics of the status quo, numbering among its members the Duke of Clarence and Charles Middleton, then Controller of the Navy, later Lord Barham and First Lord.[76] In 1795 one of Samuel Bentham's first acts on being appointed as Inspector General of Naval Works was to propose to the Admiralty a system of reforming the current apprenticeship arrangements and establishing apprentice schools specifically aimed at providing a theoretical as well as a practical education for shipwright apprentices and to identify possible future master shipwrights.[77] In 1802 St Vincent reformed the apprentice system along lines advocated by Bentham, but did not introduce the schools, a mistake that contributed to the failure of the reform.[78]

In 1806 renewed impetus came from the report of the Commissioners for Revising and Digesting the Civil Affairs of the Navy. This noted with concern that the nation's principal weapons of war were designed and built by men who had enjoyed no formal training in mathematics, mechanics or marine architecture. They further noted that the only qualifications required by aspiring shipwright apprentices were that they should be aged at least 14, in good health and over 4ft 10in tall. If these minimum requirements were met, there followed a 7-year apprenticeship. The weaknesses in this had already been acknowledged in some yards, where local arrangements sought to remedy educational deficiencies. At Plymouth a schoolmaster had been employed unofficially, and at Chatham the commissioners noted with approval that the officers had set up a small school to educate shipwright apprentices in the evenings. This was funded privately by the commissioner of the yard and his senior staff.[79]

The solution proposed by the Commissioners for Revising and Digesting the Civil Affairs of the Navy was the continuation of the apprenticeship scheme for the great majority of shipwright apprentices, supplemented by part-time schooling modelled on the arrangements at Chatham. However, a 'superior class' of apprentice was to be selected by competitive examination from the dockyard and from outside schools. These apprentices were to attend a 7-year course at a new School of Naval Architecture, continuing their classroom education in the mornings and receiving practical instruction in the afternoons.[80] From their ranks it was hoped to select future master shipwrights and Surveyors of the Navy.

In 1809 the main element of these recommendations was adopted, with George III issuing an Order in Council 'for introducing a better and more skilful description of shipwright officer into His Majesty's Royal Dockyards'.[81] Again, with the apparent exception of Chatham, dockyard schools for the ordinary apprentices were not provided, and they continued to receive a purely practical education around the yards. In 1811, 12 out of the 30 who had applied for the superior apprentice training were accepted, initially sharing classrooms and possibly accommodation with students attending the Royal Naval College at Portsmouth. Numbers gradually increased, and in 1815 money was put in the estimates to build the School of Naval Architecture at Portsmouth. This faces the Commissioner's House and the Royal Naval College across a green and was almost certainly designed by Edward Holl. Perhaps in deference to the Commissioner's House, it was constructed in yellow stock bricks with detailing in Portland stone (Fig 17.25). Completed in 1817, it is a simple rectangular building of two storeys with a pedimented centre and slight projections to its end pairs of bays. The output of the school was comparatively small,[82] but included a number who were to rise to positions of great responsibility in the Victorian navy. These included Isaac Watts, the Chief Constructor who designed HMS *Warrior*, and Thomas Lloyd who after leaving the School was responsible for

Fig 17.24 (opposite) Whale Island from the east, photographed in 1996. The original buildings are clearly visible, formally grouped overlooking the central parade ground. (NMR 15543/15 22 Aug 1996)

Fig 17.25
The former School of Naval Architecture at Portsmouth completed in 1817. (Author)

operating the Portsmouth Block Mills in 1831, before becoming inspector of steam machinery at Woolwich 2 years later and rising to be chief engineer of the navy in 1847.[83] Many others became master shipwrights. The school was closed during the reorganisations of 1832.[84]

After a 12-year gap, the most successful and longest running of the dockyard education schemes was started by the Admiralty in 1843. Schools in each of the larger dockyards had a board of governors that included the Admiral Superintendent, the master shipwright and the chaplain. Progress by the apprentices, who attended part time, was strictly on merit.[85] The less able spent 3 years at the schools, the more gifted a further year. Out of annual intakes that reached 1,500, one or two would be selected for higher education and sent to college to train as naval constructors; the rest staffed the royal yards with foremen, inspectors and dockyard officers.[86] In 1903 Sir Alfred Ewing was appointed Director of Naval Education, updating the syllabus and introducing a number of valuable reforms. With some justification he was able to say in 1911 that 'The Admiralty may fairly claim to be a model employer with regard to technical education'.[87] This system of dockyard training was finally abolished in 1972.

By a chance of fate the only dockyard school building to survive is the original School for Naval Architecture at Portsmouth. After its closure in 1832 it was used for a variety of purposes before reverting briefly to a different educational use as a War Course College in the approaches to the First World War.[88]

EPILOGUE

Sustained government finance and support provided the means and incentive for the extraordinary growth of the fleet after 1700, but it is no exaggeration to state that without the royal dockyards there could have been no Royal Navy. The crucial role of naval bases has not always been appreciated. Lacking the drama of great sea battles and the glamour associated with famous commanders, the royal dockyards until comparatively recently remained largely unknown, hidden behind their high walls and little studied by historians and industrial archaeologists. As a consequence, the scope and extent of the many skilled tasks undertaken in naval bases and the contribution of the bases to the nation's history have been little understood. This seclusion similarly has led to widespread ignorance of the sometimes remarkable buildings and civil engineering works that survive from the period covered by this book.

In 1700 few could have foreseen the phenomenal naval growth during the following two centuries as Britain's overseas interests expanded and the Royal Navy became the dominant force with a global reach. By the mid-18th century the Admiralty had become responsible for what in effect had become the greatest and most widespread industrial organisation in the western world. The dockyards were central to the navy, maintaining the fleet and building many of the navy's ships. They were also the focus of long and complex supply chains for a multitude of items, ranging from smaller warships that were mostly built in merchants' yards to the increasingly large, varied and complex assortment of raw and semi-processed materials. These were supplied by manufacturers, merchants and contractors to be stockpiled, converted, amalgamated, shaped, fitted and finished by the yard workforces. As the navy's bases expanded at home and overseas, such supply chains grew even longer and the logistics became increasingly daunting. Similar challenges had to be overcome to supply the fleet with ammunition, victuals and medical support.

From the middle of the 19th century, as the navy changed from wood and canvas to metal and steam and smooth-bore ordnance gave way to far more complex weapons, the naval bases virtually had to be reinvented. It was not just a question of providing the necessary infrastructure such as the new machine shops and docks; new materials, technologies and methods of production had to be understood and mastered, both by the dockyard staff and by the navy. Training became increasingly important, and allowances had to be made for the steam fleet's much greater dependence on dockyard skills. For a sailing navy the limitations to a warship's time at sea had been largely dictated by the amount of victuals a ship could carry and the skills of the ship's carpenter and crew to carry out running repairs. In contrast, warships of the steam navy required frequent refuelling, while permanent hull repairs were beyond the ability of their crews. Above all, the increasingly complex machinery on board was far from reliable, requiring constant vigilance by engine room staff and more regular time for maintenance and overhauling in dockyard workshops. In mid-October 1914, shortly after the outbreak of the First World War, Admiral Beatty in a memo to Winston Churchill, First Lord of the Admiralty, reported that 'We [the First Cruiser Squadron and the Light Cruiser Squadron] have been running now hard since the 28th July; small defects are creeping up ... the men can stand it, but the machines can't, and we must have a place where we can stop for four or five days every now and then to give the engineers a chance'.[1] In writing this, Beatty was only restating a concern that had been a problem for the navy ever since the first steam warships had joined the fleet more than 60 years earlier.

The long wars with Revolutionary and Napoleonic France at the end of the 18th century saw the Royal Navy sustained by the largest and best-equipped dockyards in Europe. The ability of the yards to support the fleet throughout two decades of near-global conflict with its convoy work, cruiser actions, relentless naval blockades and great naval victories was a vindication of the foresight of the politicians who had provided the political support and the men who had planned and carried out the dockyard modernisations from the 1760s. Similar planning and foresight were to prove equally crucial as the 19th century drew to a close. In the decade or so before 1914, the navy's influence in the life of the nation had never been more apparent. The Naval Works Act of 1895, the doubling of naval manpower and the naval arms race had seen almost 2.25 per cent of the male population in work in 1900 being employed directly or indirectly on naval orders. As the threat of war with Germany increased, the royal dockyards were reorganised, the less important were closed, and resources were concentrated on further expansion and modernisation of the principal home yards and the construction of Rosyth. As the Royal Navy prepared to face Germany's High Seas Fleet and the looming menace of submarine warfare, it once again had the reassurance of being backed by modern, well-equipped naval bases unrivalled in Europe.

The men who planned, built and maintained the royal dockyards are comparatively little known, and this book has been able to draw attention only to a few. Until the end of the 18th century the planning of the yards and the design of their buildings and engineering works had of necessity to be very largely done within the navy's own organisation, with occasional help from military engineers. At the start of the 18th century Dummer and Lilly stand out for their achievements, while their surviving plans and drawings enable us to further appreciate their skills. By the end of the 18th century the Industrial Revolution was starting to benefit the royal dockyards, not just with the new steam technology, but also with the widening of the country's skills base. Although the Navy Board and dockyard officers at the time may not have appreciated his methods, the navy had good reason to be grateful to Bentham. His support of Brunel's proposals for block-making machinery, and with it the establishment at Portsmouth Dockyard of the first factory in the world to use machine tools for mass production, may be his most famous achievement, but perhaps his more valuable legacy was to end the dockyards' comparative industrial isolation and bring them within the orbit of a wider industrial Britain. From Bentham's time onwards a small but constant stream of military, civil, structural and mechanical engineers, architects and surveyors, along with specialist industrial firms, contributed their skills and experience to projects in the naval bases; probably the best known of the outside consultants were the Rennies, but later Sir John Coode was to be closely involved with projects on similar epic scales. From 1837 the Admiralty Works Department was to be extensively staffed with military engineers, but this was never to the exclusion of other disciplines and backgrounds. Brandreth, Greene, Pasley and Pilkington were notable members of the former; Scamp probably the most versatile of the latter.

The construction of a naval base usually presented formidable civil engineering problems, while the sheer scale and variety of the buildings and engineering works added to the complexities of the task. This was especially the case when such operations depended almost exclusively on manual labour. In the 19th century harnessing of steam power marked a major step forward, but equally important were advances in geological knowledge, civil and structural engineering and the introduction of new construction materials. Even so, with projects that could take a decade or longer, few were completed without set-backs of one form or another and the need for additional funding.

Establishing overseas bases presented further challenges as, with a few exceptions such as Malta, the navy had to start from scratch. Before 19th-century improvements in communications allowed the Admiralty to exercise a much closer control, responsibility for the precise location and construction of these bases had to be left largely to the men on the spot, sometimes leading to problems stemming from over-ambitious or inexperienced naval officers. Scarce manpower and expensive materials added considerably to costs, and it was no surprise that the Admiralty complained from time to time about the expenses involved. Nevertheless, with the sole exception of Port Antonio, the bases were completed and generally fulfilled their intended role. The abiding impression from the records is of the exercise of local initiative, hard work and of the generally successful overcoming of sometimes daunting obstacles. This was most evident in places with unhealthy climates such as the Caribbean, or the more isolated locations such as the Great Lakes and Ascension Island.

A century on from the start of the Great War a surprising number of Georgian and Victorian

buildings and engineering works remain as witness to the rise and supremacy of the Royal Navy between 1700 and 1914. Overseas many of the former bases are still operational, the buildings constructed in them now used by other navies. Halifax and Esquimalt are homes to the Royal Canadian Navy, while the Royal Australian Navy has its principal base at Garden Island, Sydney. The Royal New Zealand Navy's dockyard at Devonport on North Island is centred on the Calliope Dock, and Simon's Town remains home of the South African Navy. The Spanish navy still uses a number of British buildings at Port Mahon. The former dockyard at Malta is now a commercial shipyard; nearby, Scamp's bakery has been carefully conserved and is now the Malta Maritime Museum. Closer to home the Irish navy occupies part of the former base at Haulbowline. Perhaps most remarkably, two of the abandoned overseas bases have been successfully saved almost entirely by voluntary efforts. In a pioneer move starting in the late 1940s the picturesque and long-derelict dockyard at English Harbour, Antigua, was gradually conserved, becoming a highly successful yacht harbour and tourist destination. Thirty years later a similar move has been instrumental in conserving the heart of the former naval base at Bermuda, making it one of the most popular attractions on these islands.

Although this book terminates in 1914, the Royal Navy broadly retained its supremacy and most of its home bases until its eclipse by the United States Navy in the Second World War. Since then a combination of economic stringency, changing strategic requirements and a shrinking fleet has meant that the only bases operational in 1914 and still used by the Royal Navy are Portsmouth and Devonport. Both were heavily bombed in the Second World War, Devonport especially losing many buildings. More succumbed to dereliction and redevelopment; some of the latter losses might have been avoided had there been a greater awareness

The former home for injured seamen established at Greenwich by Queen Mary following the battle of La Hogue in 1692. Following its closure in 1869, Wren's buildings became home until 1998 of Greenwich Royal Naval College, the navy's staff college specialising in scientific and professional training of naval officers. Appropriately, it remains in educational use, now home of the University of Greenwich and Trinity College of Music. The buildings form the heart of the Greenwich World Heritage Site. This view is terminated by the Queen's House and the buildings of the National Maritime Museum. (NMR 24452/025)

of their importance at the time.[2] This was gradually to change, and by the 1970s research was leading to a much better understanding of the historic and architectural worth of the naval estate, which was increasingly being protected by conservation legislation. Such legislation has never been an automatic passport guaranteeing a building's immortality; rather, its value lies in alerting owners and planners of its importance and that demolition, inappropriate alterations or additions are not acceptable. Most importantly, it encourages owners to find sympathetic new uses that will give such buildings economic and viable futures.

In the last 40 years much has been accomplished, with the Ministry of Defence working closely with English Heritage and local authorities to secure the future of buildings in the operational yards of Portsmouth and Devonport and to ensure that they are appropriately maintained. Many of the great Victorian workshops remain in use and have been sensitively modernised, a tribute to their versatile design and robust construction; former naval and ordnance storehouses have been carefully adapted as offices or handed over to trusts for museum and related functions. Inevitably, there are problem buildings for which no immediately appropriate uses can be found. However, there is an acceptance that such buildings should be kept intact as experience shows that new uses are almost invariably eventually discovered for them.

Fortunately, the drastic shrinking of the naval estate in the last two decades of the 20th century came at a time when its historic importance was understood. As a consequence, the demolitions and unsympathetic developments that earlier had done such harm at Pembroke and Sheerness after their closure have been largely avoided. Finding new uses for redundant naval buildings has generally been made easier by their durable construction and in many cases their sheer scale. The Royal Naval College at Greenwich continues in its educational role as a university, and the same use has been found for the former Royal Naval Barracks at Chatham. The two great victualling yards at Gosport and Stonehouse are gradually being adapted for a mix of residential and commercial use, while the buildings of the former naval hospital at Stonehouse have been partly converted to residential use and also house a school. At Portsmouth the three finest surviving 18th-century storehouses, together with three 19th-century boathouses, were given to the Portsmouth Naval Base Property Trust that was set up with an endowment to help their conservation. Appropriately, two of the storehouses are the home of the new National Museum of the Royal Navy.

The greatest conservation challenge came with the announcement in June 1981of the closure of Chatham naval base. The Georgian and early Victorian part of the dockyard contained buildings that had been little altered internally or externally. At the southern end the 18th-century ropery was still in production using machinery that is some cases had been operating in the building since 1811.This part of the dockyard had very largely escaped wartime damage, the buildings here spanning every decade from 1700 to 1860. In their totality they are unique, representing virtually every type of building and engineering installation used to build and maintain the warships of the Georgian and early Victorian navy. Further value lay in the survival of much early equipment. As well as the ropery machinery, this included hand tools, steam hammers and foundry machinery, dock-side cranes, locomotives and rolling stock, ship models, plans and drawings. Such was Chatham's importance that following pressure from conservation bodies and local authorities the Government endowed a Trust to conserve and run the yard. This it has done with great success, bringing buildings back to life, preserving skills and demonstrating to increasing numbers of visitors a little-known but fascinating side of naval and British history.

The importance of preserving HMS *Victory*, the *Mary Rose*, *Warrior* and other historic warships has long been appreciated. It is entirely appropriate that the historic buildings and installations that made the fleet possible should be similarly conserved to be appreciated and enjoyed by future generations. Together, the navy's ships and bases helped shape much of this country's modern history.

NOTES

1 The Royal Dockyards in Great Britain, 1700–1835

1 Friel 1995, 153.
2 Friel 1995, 156.
3 Moorehouse 2006, 9. Knighton and Loades (2011, xxvii) date the creation of a standing navy to the war of 1512–14. At the end of hostilities, Henry VIII retained a number of ships in active service and decommissioned rather than disposed of the rest.
4 Coad 1997, 164; Rodger 1997, 70.
5 Colvin 1982, 491. This convincingly challenges the more familiar date of 1495 proposed by Oppenheim (1896, 39–40) and repeated by Carr Laughton (1912, 371), or the date of 1498, more recently suggested by Dietz (2002, 144). Colvin argues that later references are to a rebuilding of the dock.
6 Duffy 2003, 104.
7 Oppenheim 1926, 338–40.
8 Coad 1997, 164. For Erith, *see* Rodger 1997, 222.
9 Capp 2008.
10 Oppenheim 1926, 353.
11 Morriss 1983, 4. TNA ADM 140/1251 is a plan of Deal Yard after the Napoleonic Wars. For Plymouth Dock, *see* BL Lansdowne 847, Dec 1694 and Coad 1983, 341–51. A detailed account of the new work at Plymouth, including costings, is given in full in Duffy 2003.
12 MacDougall 2001, 21.
13 Rodger 2004, 188. An undated late 18th-century plan is in AdL MS 259-13.
14 AdL MS 259/13, 2 Nov 1790, 28 Oct 1795, 6 Dec 1806. TNA ADM 106/198, 24 Apr 1820.
15 Rodger 2004, 481. *See* AdL uncatalogued plan of yard, 1880–1907.
16 Lavery 2007, 122–3; Morriss 1983, 4.
17 Lavery 2007, 180–3, 201. Merriman (1961, 103) mentions a survey of 1709 recommending construction of a wet dock and dry dock at Leith and the subsequent construction of the latter in 1720. If so, this appears to have been by local rather than Admiralty initiative.
18 Carr Laughton 1912, 374–6.
19 Rodger (2004, 368, 608) has the most up-to-date and authoritative figures. Nevertheless, the author wisely adds a number of caveats to be considered when assessing the size of the fleet at any one time.
20 The economic background that allowed the state to expand the armed forces and especially the navy is outside the scope of this work. A succinct account is given by Morriss 2011. Lambert (2008b, 154) has said of Anson, 'As a strategist, tactician, trainer of fleets, naval politician and administrator he had no peer… His navy gave Britain a world empire.'
21 Rodger 1993, 327. This biography of Sandwich is essential reading for an understanding of the operation of the dockyards at this time.
22 Rodger 1993, 197.
23 Rodger 2004, 368.
24 Lambert 2008b, 132. For supply operations in 1759, *see* Lambert 2008b, 150.
25 TNA ADM 7/659, 5 June 1771; *see* Coad (1989, 13) for more detail.
26 NMM ADM/B/167, 2 Nov 1761. This letter sets out in great detail the proposals for the replanning and expansion of Plymouth Dockyard and the reasons for the work. On the back of the letter is a scribbled note, '4th November. Approved of the enlargement and directed them to do what they propose. J'. The J is possibly John Cleveland, Secretary to the Board of Admiralty. TNA ADM 3/69, 11 Nov 1761, is a formal record in the Admiralty minutes of the Board's agreement to the proposals.
27 NMM ADM/B/175, 21 Nov 1764, is a letter from the Navy Board to the Admiralty confirming the Admiralty Board's general views on yard replanning and new buildings.
28 NMM ADM/B/167, 2 Nov 1761.
29 A plan of Portsmouth Dockyard dated 21 July 1760 shows the proposed north extension and the site for the new ropery (TNA ADM 140/555 pt 1). In Dec 1760 the Navy Board ordered the Portsmouth officers to reclaim this area measuring 1,283ft east–west by 600ft north–south from the mudflats (NMM POR/A/21, 12 Dec 1760). At Plymouth, the 6 acres required belonged to the St Aubyn family, who were possibly holding out for £5 an acre, 'a high price accounted for by the proximity of the yard' (TNA ADM 174/113, 18 Dec 1761).
30 Coad 1989, 203–6.
31 TNA ADM 7/660, 13 July 1773. For more details of the problems of the Medway and attempted remedies, *see* Coad 1989, 13–17. The smaller yards at Deptford and Woolwich suffered to a lesser extent from similar problems that would not be solved until the introduction of steam dredging in the 19th century.
32 TNA ADM 140/8, dated 1771, shows the outline of the new storehouse superimposed on the plan of the existing one, which itself is shown on another plan of 1771 (TNA Work 41/71), annotated with the date 1686. The 1771 Visitation noted that the old storehouse was partly propped up and 'said to be in a very bad condition' (TNA ADM 7/659).
33 The Fitted Rigging House appears in the 1791 estimates (NMM CHA/B1), and a plan of the final design is in TNA ADM 140/86 pt 1, signed as 'Approved 10th April 1793 JH'.
34 The yard officers were pressing for a new smithery in May 1805, and construction seems to have started the following year (NMM POR/B/220, 4 May 1805). The building is now partly home to the National Ship Model Collection.
35 Coad 1983, 361–4.
36 TNA ADM 7/662, 31 Oct 1775.
37 These numbers are culled from the following dockyard plans: Chatham TNA ADM 140/7 (1766), TNA ADM 140/21 (1814); Plymouth BL Kings 44 fol 13v (1774), TNA ADM 140/167 (1820); Portsmouth TNA ADM 140/555 pt 1 (1760), ADM 140/555 pt 18 (1814).
38 Morriss 1983, 54.
39 Oppenheim 1926, 375–6, 381.
40 Evans 2004, 18. For shoaling problems of the Thames and Medway yards, *see* Oppenheim 1926, 381.For early steam dredgers, *see* Skempton 1977, 99–103. MacDougall (2008) provides a good oversight of the problem and limitations of early steam dredgers.

41 Skempton 1980, 88–93.
42 Morriss 1983, 53.
43 TNA ADM 106/2677, 31 July 1812; MacDougall 2009, 77–8.
44 TNA ADM 140/675.
45 TNA ADM 106/2064, 9 Aug 1810. Rennie's plan does not appear to survive.
46 TNA ADM 140/1404.
47 NMM ADM/BP/316, 6 Dec 1811. Edmund Aiken was not an obvious choice, described by Colvin (1995, 67) as 'shy, nervous and physically delicate' and a 'fastidious and scholarly Greek Revival architect'. Apart from the porticoed entrance to the offices, Aiken clearly had had to suppress all his Greek Revival instincts.
48 TNA ADM 106/2677, 25 Feb 1812.
49 Hills 2006, 233.
50 TNA ADM 140/678 is signed by the committee and dated 17 July 1812. *See* ADM 106/2677, 21 Aug 1812, for the Admiralty approval.
51 NMM ADM/BP/30b, 1 Sept 1810.
52 The proposals are shown in outline in TNA ADM 140/679, dated 15 March 1813.
53 TNA ADM 181/34 annual estimates for 1824. (NMM ADM/BP/33b).
54 This location was suggested by the Admiralty in 1824, TNA ADM 106/2158 pt 1, 30 Apr 1824. In 1826 the basement of the Ordnance Armoury was ordered to be fitted up as a temporary chapel while the existing one was demolished and the new one built (TNA ADM 106/2162, 19 June 1826).
55 AdL plan Da 02 fol 4 shows that part of this warehouse was in use as a naval barracks by 1863. Later named HMS *Wildfire*, the building no longer exists.
56 Smiles 1862, 248–9.
57 TNA ADM 106/2160, 15 Apr 1825. *See also* Coad 2008.
58 TNA ADM 106/2679, 7 Sept 1813.
59 Smiles 1862, 249.
60 TNA ADM 106/2750, 20 March 1821; Cox and Cox (1999, 17) note that the Bowling Ironworks 'had the reputation for producing cold blast iron of the very highest quality', an important consideration when strength and durability of dock gates were of paramount importance.
61 TNA ADM 140/980–9 are the final drawings for this building, signed by W Miller, Holl's former draughtsman, and dated between 1829 and 1831. The 1832 annual estimates, TNA ADM 181/43, have a final payment of £15,000 'for completing the Ordnance Wall, the Admiral's, Commissioner's and Officers' houses'.
62 TNA ADM 106/2158 pt 1, 24 July 1824.
63 Morriss 1983, 54. The author notes that the Navy Board maintained its view that operations here should remain restricted. Rodger (2004, 481) makes the case that local manpower and timber supplies were available to be exploited.
64 TNA ADM 140/490 pt 1.
65 TNA ADM 140/492. This is a development of ADM 140/490 pt 2, which shows some of these buildings and others in outline. The designer may have been Rule, although Holl's involvement might have been expected. Given the Welsh climate, the open-air ropery was somewhat optimistic and can only have been an economy measure.
66 NMM ADM/BP/30b, 21 Dec 1810.
67 TNA ADM 106/1966, 13 May and 15 June 1814. The total valuation came to £42 11s 9d. The muster bell was valued at £3 15s 10d.
68 TNA ADM/BP/37a, 8 and 9 Apr 1817.
69 TNA ADM 106/1967. In an undated report of an inspection of the yard, but probably second half of 1816, Holl was instructed to put his proposed modifications to the yard layout to Rennie. What these were is not stated.
70 TNA ADM 106/1966, 29 March 1814.
71 TNA ADM 106/1966, 25 May 1814.
72 TNA ADM 106/1967, 5 Sept 1816.
73 TNA ADM 106/1967, 20 June 1818. The majority of these are unlikely to have been local.
74 TNA ADM 106/1967, undated inspection report, probably second half of 1816.
75 NMM ADM/BP/39a, 24 March 1819; NMM ADM/BP/39a fol 95, undated. *See* TNA ADM 106/1968, 17 Oct 1822, for a plan showing the extent of the town development at that date. Its grid of streets still includes a Melville Terrace and a Melville Street.
76 TNA ADM 106/1967, undated report, probably mid-1816. TNA ADM 106/1967, 26 June 1823.
77 TNA ADM 140/427 and 429. TNA ADM 106/1967, 19 Dec 1821, refers to a tremendous gale damaging these three roofs, as well as the temporary chapel and the mould loft. Replacing timber slips with stone seems to have been undertaken in the 1830s.
78 TNA ADM 106/1967; both ships were later converted to screw ships at Chatham and had comparatively long lives (Colledge and Warlow 2006, 297, 301).
79 TNA ADM 181/64. This sum almost certainly excludes the cost of roofing. Money for building slips and extending existing ones appears at frequent intervals from the early 1830s to the mid-1850s in the annual estimates for Pembroke (TNA ADM 181/45–71).
80 A plan of Pembroke in 1909 (TNA ADM 140/1484) and a plan between 1860 and 1904 (AdL Vz 14 fol 83) confusingly number slips from 1 to 13, omitting 3 Slip, which is probably to be identified with one of the three small and unserviceable slips replaced by two in the mid-1850s. All except Slips 1 and 2 and the adjacent graving dock have been infilled as the modern port has developed.
81 The acquisition of Hobbs Point lessened but did not remove the necessity for fitting out elsewhere. Hobbs Point was supplemented in the early 20th century by the surviving Carr Jetty at the western end of the dockyard.
82 These appear in the 1841/2 yard estimates, TNA ADM 181/52.
83 TNA ADM 181/36, 1826 estimates.
84 TNA ADM 140/447, dated 1817.
85 In June 1818 McIntosh had a further 350 masons and labourers at work in the yard, TNA ADM 106/1967, 20 June 1818. On 8 Sept 1819 the houses were said to be within 2 months of completion (TNA ADM 106/1967).
86 TNA ADM 140/444–54.
87 TNA ADM 106/1968, 16 Apr 1823. Also a plank boiling trough for the shipwrights.
88 TNA ADM 1/3413, 9 Aug 1834, records an Admiralty order for his appointment dated 7 June 1833.
89 TNA ADM 1/3501, 28 Nov 1833. The surgeon's house was completed by Sept 1834 (TNA ADM 1/3501, 30 Sept 1834). On 1 Aug 1835 the new Captain Superindent Bullen was asking for shutters for his new house (TNA ADM 1/3413). The stonework of the lodge houses clearly shows the additional storey.
90 TNA ADM 181/43 annual estimates for 1832/3 include £2,000 for 'final payment'. Dockyard plans show that at times the strip of parkland had formal garden features, probably dependent on the enthusiasms of the adjacent residents. *See* Chapter 7 for details of the dockyard church.
91 Admiralty Board Minutes, 5 Oct 1683; Hattendorf *et al* 1993, 245. The Admiralty Terrier for Kinsale records that the earliest reference to a yard there is dated 8 Feb 1660. Little is known about these facilities, which may have been only temporary.
92 In July 1752, for example, a blockmaker from Cork travelled to Kinsale to repair the ship's pump of the sloop HMS *Badger*, TNA ADM 106/1100, 3 July 1752.
93 AdL MS 259/13. This undated plan and description accompanied a letter by John Peake dated 7 Jan 1805. It would be reasonable to assume the plan is of the same date or slightly earlier.
94 TNA ADM 106/1982, 16 Oct 1813.

95 TNA ADM 106/1982. The existing premises were rented at an annual cost of 330 guineas between 1 Jan 1799 and 30 Sept 1803. The writer was possibly John William Dunsterville, the Victualling Agent there by March 1805.
96 AdL MSS 259/13, 2 Nov 1790, 28 Aug 1804, 6 March 1805; AdL Admiralty Terrier. On 6 March 1805 Bentham noted 'there is not at present any building on Haulbowline Island except those within the enclosure of a small fort erected a long time ago' (AdL MSS 259/13). *See also* Brunicardi (1982, 9–15) for details of the fort.
97 AdL MSS 259/13, 28 Oct 1795. John Schank (1740–1823) had just been appointed a commissioner to the transport board. He had a distinguished naval career, but is perhaps better known for his invention of a 'sliding keel' or centreboard and for designing in 1800 the first of the two paddle steamers, named *Charlotte Dundas*, for the Forth and Clyde Navigation Company (Cock 2004).
98 AdL MS 259/13, 28 Oct 1795.
99 AdL MS 259/13, 15 Aug1804. Cockerell pointed out that costs had risen significantly since his original estimate in 1795.
100 AdL MS 259/13, 8 Nov 1804 This was a joint report prepared with Admiral Gardner, commander on the Irish Station.
101 NMM ADM/Q/3322, 16 Nov 1804.
102 AdL MS 259/13, 16 Nov 1804. Peake was later to be appointed as extra assistant architect and civil engineer; his post was abolished in 1812 (Collinge 1978, 128). NMM ADM/Q/3322, 12 Dec 1804.
103 AdL MS 259/13, 6 March 1805.
104 Coad 1989, 32; NMM ADM/Q/3323, 20 and 30 July 1805.
105 AdL Admiralty Terrier.
106 AdL MS 259/13, 6 Dec 1806.
107 AdL Admiralty Terrier.
108 Photograph signed W Miller 5 Apr 1816 (information from D Brunicardi). AdL 1840 yard plan details the buildings on top, which are now mostly shells.
109 The Haulbowline cottages, some of which survive, were single-storey, two-room dwellings, originally with gardens and privies to the rear.
110 AdL MS 259/13, 6 and 31 Dec 1806, 8 and 27 Jan 1807.
111 AdL MS 259/13, 15 June 1810, 9 Feb 1811; TNA ADM 106/1982, 13 July 1815; AdL 1840 plan of Haulbowline.
112 Collinge 1978, 117; in Feb 1827 Kingdom signed a design for iron railings for the Port Admiral's new office (TNA ADM 106/1983).
113 TNA ADM 106/1982, 13 July 1815.
114 TNA ADM 106/1982, 6 and 27 Feb 1817. A note by Holl on the back of this document refers to the original contract, presumably for all outstanding buildings and engineering works here, to be completed by 1 Aug 1819.
115 TNA ADM 106/1982, 12 June and 15 Nov 1817. In 1820 Holl approved an estimate for removing mud from the canal 'abreast the naval storehouse', TNA ADM 106/1982, 22 Feb 1820.
116 TNA ADM 106/1982, 1 Nov 1815, 15 Nov 1817, 20 Jan and 27 March 1819, 5 Apr and 13 July 1821. In 1825, Thomas Deane was given the contract for building an office for the Port Admiral at Cove (TNA ADM 106/1983, 7 March 1825).
117 TNA ADM 106/1982, 27 March 1819. The Kinsale premises were given up 'about 1817–8' and those at Cork at about the same time according to a note in the terrier (AdL Ireland Terrier).
118 TNA ADM 106/1982, 29 Jan 1821.
119 TNA ADM 106/1983, 4 Apr and 20 Nov 1822; Colledge and Warlow 2006, 359.
120 TNA ADM 106/1983, 8 Dec 1823 and 30 March 1824. There is some ambiguity about this figure, which could relate to works undertaken since June 1820, although this would imply major works that are not entirely borne out in the records.
121 TNA ADM 106/1983, 26 Jan 1824.
122 TNA ADM 106/1982, 18 Feb 1820. A plan of the chapel conversion survives in these papers.
123 TNA ADM 106/1983, 20 Apr 1822. This follows the conversion of 'reporting rooms' into a temporary hospital 2 years earlier.
124 TNA ADM 174/398, an 1897 plan of the dockyard, shows this. Early in the 20th century a series of wards were built *en echelon* to the south.
125 TNA ADM 106/1983, 25 Apr 1831; ADM 106/1984, 10 Sept 1831.

2 The Royal Dockyards in Great Britain, 1835–1914

1 For early steamboats and their builders, *see* Armstrong and Williams 2011. For the *Kent*, brain-child of the 3rd Earl Stanhope, *see* Ditchfield 2004.
2 Hore 2000, 161–3.
3 Buchanan and Doughty 1978, 330. *See* Owen 2002 for the history of the Post Office fleet.
4 Owen 2002, 169. Before the creation of this department, responsibility for steam vessels had been vested in one of the Lords of the Admiralty and the Surveyor of the Navy, assisted by Peter Ewart.
5 Coad 1994, 169; Hattendorf *et al* 1993, 682.
6 TNA ADM 1/304, 15 June 1839. *Columbia* was a wooden paddle packet, an ex-Cherokee class brig-sloop, launched at Woolwich in 1829.
7 *See* Brown 2004 for a detailed technical explanation of Seppings's innovations. *See also* Lambert 1984, 31–6, Lambert 2006, 18, and Lambert 2008a, the best introduction to the development of the early steam navy.
8 TNA ADM 181/48 extra estimates; Evans 2004, 28–35. Evans gives the most detailed account of the creation of the Woolwich Steam Factory. From 1837 Lieutenant William Denison RE was in charge of the Woolwich project, later being posted to Portsmouth (*see* Arbuthnot 2004).
9 The basin first appears in the extra estimates for 1826, TNA ADM 181/36, and the final payment in the extra estimates for 1832/3, TNA ADM 181/43. Works on the dry docks appear for the first time in the following year's estimates, TNA ADM 181/45. The new inner basin appears for the last time in the 1842/3 extra estimates, TNA ADM 118/53.
10 Evans 2004, 61, 67.
11 Riley 1985, 15–16. The estimated construction figures come from the annual estimates, TNA ADM 181/55 to 73 (1844–63).
12 Evans 2004, 71–4. Money for modernising the slips appears in the annual estimates at intervals from 1851/2 (TNA ADM 181/62) to 1860/1 (TNA ADM 181/71).
13 The new powder magazines at Bull Point were a substantial investment, estimated in 1849 at some £97,627; this included magazines for 40,000 barrels and 'houses for the workmen, barracks for the guard etc' (TNA ADM 181/60, estimates 1849/50; Evans 2004, 104).
14 Evans 2004, 113–14; TNA ADM 181/65 estimates. Keyham remained in use as a name alongside North Yard into the 20th century.
15 Ballard 1980, 58; Lambert 1994, 181.
16 Brown 1983, 31–2; Hattendorf *et al* 1993, 688. *See* Quinn 2001 for an assessment of Airy and other pioneers who helped solve the problems of magnetic compasses.
17 Ballard 1980, 50.
18 Ballard 1980, 224–7; Brown 1983, 43. For a detailed account of HMS *Captain*, *see* Hawkey 1963.
19 Hamilton 1993, 201. Riley 1985, 22. *See* 'The Second Report of the Select Committee on Basin and Dock Accommodation, 15 July 1864', *in* Hattendorf *et al* 1993, 588–91.

20 Hattendorf *et al* 1993, 683; Oppenheim 1926, 386. For investment at Deptford, *see* ADM 181/55–6 annual estimates. The Admiralty records of numbers employed in dockyards show men employed at Deptford as late as 1901, when the ADM series ends. That year an average of 232 worked here, but these figures by then relate to the Royal Victoria Victualling Yard, which earlier had absorbed part of the former dockyard (TNA ADM 49/181). *See* Courtney 1974 and 1975 for reports on archaeological excavations on part of the former Woolwich Dockyard.
21 Figures in annual estimates TNA ADM 181/65 (1854/5) to ADM 181/70 (1859/60).
22 TNA ADM 1/5775, 4 May 1861.
23 TNA ADM 1/5838, 25 March 1863.
24 Coad 1982, 156–71, Coad 1989, 15–17. For Northfleet and the Isle of Grain, *see* Oppenheim 1926, 385–7, and Evans 2004, 183–5. In 1812 the idea of Northfleet was still alive (Hills 2006, 233).
25 TNA ADM 181/66 and 69, estimates 1855/6 and 1858/9; Brodie *et al* 2002, 126–30. For a detailed history of the development of the steam facilities at Chatham, *see* Evans 2004, 182–7.
26 TNA ADM 181/66, estimates 1855/6; Evans 2004, 90. For the Royal Commission Defences, *see* Saunders 1989, 171–89. *See also* Oppenheim 1926, 387.
27 Evans 2004, 187; Oppenheim 1926, 387. Evans (2004, 184) rightly suggests that along with his Keyham factory, this production line was Scamp's greatest achievement.
28 Brodie *et al* 2002, 130–1; Evans 2004, 184; Hattendorf *et al* 1993, 590; TNA ADM 181/81, estimates for 1870/1.
29 TNA ADM 181/86, estimates 1875/6. From 1885, the extension work no longer appears as a separate item in the annual estimates.
30 Scamp's proposal was based on his knowledge of the United States Navy experience of protecting warships from damage from ice during winter that can be traced back to 1802, when President Jefferson was advocating safe storage for new 44-gun frigates. Scamp's scheme in 1849 was considered too grand and impracticable, although a model of it was shown at the Great Exhibition of 1851. *See* Chapter 8 for Haslar Gunboat Yard. Plans for Scamp's Chatham proposals are in TNA ADM 1/5703 and 1/5838. A version of the 1863 plan is also in AdLVz 14 fol 134.
31 Sutherland 1985, A1–A3; Sutherland 1997, 136.
32 Colonel Raban's proposals dated 12 Aug 1904 and a plan are in TNA ADM 214/4.
33 Evans 2004, 189. Scamp may have been thinking of local defence; in this, he may not have been alone – Clarke's later dockyard wall to the extension has rifle loops and bartizans at intervals.
34 Riley 1985, 22–3.
35 TNA ADM 181/76–78, 81 and 86; Brodie *et al* 2002, 126; Riley 1985, 22–3.
36 Riley 1985, 22, 25; TNA ADM 181/99 fol 20.
37 Hattendorf *et al* 1993, 661. This was the repeat of a memo he had first submitted in June 1855.
38 Tracy 1997, 121–8. A memorandum of July 1910, 'Principles of Imperial Defence', gave the thinking on the various classes of dockyards, ports and harbours that were of use to the navy then. For Dover's Admiralty Harbour, *see* Hasenson 1980. For its defences, *see* Coad and Lewis 1982, 192–6.
39 TNA ADM 140/1484 fol 60 shows the extent of construction of the breakwaters by 1909.
40 TNA ADM 1/5730, reproduced in Evans 2004, pl 192. *See also* Chrimes *et al* 2008, 654.
41 These developments are well charted in Evans 2004, 173–80.
42 TNA ADM 1181/99, 1903/4 estimates, includes a summary of works in progress.
43 Coad 1994, 171.
44 TNA ADM 181/99 Statement of Work, 1903/4.
45 TNA ADM 116/464.
46 Hattendorf *et al* 1993, 676.
47 Brown 1983, 71; TNA ADM 181/99 Statement of Works, 1903/4.
48 TNA ADM 174/398, 1897 plan; AdL plan of Haulbowline Yard 1897–1905 with subsequent annotations.
49 Riley 1985, 26; TNA ADM 181/99, 1903/4 review.
50 Riley 1985, 27.
51 Coad 1994, 171, 173. *See* Chapter 17.
52 Evans 2004, 196–7. For Long Dock, *see* TNA ADM 181/71–4 estimates. The estimated cost was £70,000. For 3 Dock, *see* TNA ADM 181/87 estimates; the estimated cost was £135,000. By December 1880 £106,000 had been spent, and it last appears in TNA ADM 181/92. *See also* AdL Devonport Dockyard plan *c* 1900 (uncatalogued).
53 Sargent 2008, 109.
54 TNA ADM 214/39 contains the seven tenders. Jackson's tender was for £2,835,455 (Coad 1994, 172).
55 Coad 1994, 172; TNA ADM 181/99, 1903/4 Statement of Works fol 21. The 1895 contract documents had specified a finishing date of 31 March 1903, barring unforeseen alterations or exceptionally bad weather (TNA ADM 214/39).
56 Lavery 2007 is the indispensable reading for Scottish naval history.
57 Lavery 2007, 180–3. AdL map of site of Rosyth Dockyard *c* 1904 shows the five farms that needed to be purchased.
58 Lavery 2007, 189.
59 Information from AdL uncatalogued contemporary plans of Rosyth. The dimensions of the docks and basins come from these and differ slightly from those quoted by Lavery (2007, 192).
60 Lavery 2007, 201. The author quotes the final cost of Rosyth, including the extra work necessary to convert the tidal basin into a wartime submarine base, as £11,335,207. For Cromarty, *see* Lavery 2007, 196–8. For Scapa Flow, *see* Hewison 1985, 49–58.
61 Brunicardi 1982, 29; Davies 2008, 2. The Irish Navy has a commendable track record in gradually conserving and using its legacy of historic buildings.
62 Running down a naval base inevitably took several years following the announcement of closure.

3 Planning and Building the Royal Dockyards to 1795

1 Morriss 1983 (chapter 6) gives a detailed background to yard management.
2 Coad (1989, 333–9) traces the architectural evolution of the buildings. Harland (2003, 263–6) gives a detailed account of the founding and operation.
3 Coad 1989, 311.
4 NMM T/1/154, 1 Apr 1711; T/1/151, 12 Aug 1712.
5 Morriss 1983, 173–4.
6 Coad 1989, 55. Like the remuneration boards of many modern companies, there was probably an element of self-interest in the Navy Board's decisions in these cases.
7 Lavery 1983, 45.
8 NMM Lad/7, 29 May 1693.
9 Fox 2007, 2, 9, 20–2; 2009, 48–66. Fox (2007) is the best detailed account of Edmund Dummer's remarkable career, particularly his contribution to warship design and construction, which is outside the scope of this book. Dummer's Mediterranean drawings are in a bound volume in BL Kings MS 40.
10 Rodger 2004, 188.
11 BL Kings MS 43 'A Survey and Description of the Principal Harbours with their Accommodation and Conveniences for Erecting, Moaring Secureing and refitting the Navy Royall of England'.
12 Fox 2009, 49.
13 Fox 2009, 54–5.
14 Fiennes 1983, 281–2.
15 The building contractors Sir Thomas and John Fitch also worked for the Board of

Ordnance, notably constructing at the Tower of London the Great New Storehouse, begun in 1688 (Colvin 1976, 381).

16 Fox 2007, 2. The author gives a very detailed account of this tangled tale in which Dummer was almost certainly the injured party. *See also* Skempton *et al* 2002, 193–4.

17 TNA ADM 1/3633, 23 March 1719; TNA MPH 1/247, Lempriere's 1719 plan, shows the new boundary wall but no buildings proposed on the new land. TNA ADM 140/4, a 1704 plan of Chatham yard, has the additional land marked, together with the outline of the new officers' terrace and what appear to be a small storehouse and sawpits. These additions are undated, but probably *c* 1720.

18 NMM ADM/B/167, 2 Nov 1761.

19 TNA ADM 106/1101, 24 Dec 1752.

20 At the start of the 18th century the Crowley Ironworks had its business headquarters at Greenwich and manufacturing premises at Winlaton and Swalwell in Co Durham, with nailmaking at Stourbridge. It was one of the main contractors supplying iron to the royal dockyards, and with a workforce of several hundred was probably the only industrial enterprise then to rival the naval dockyards. *See* Flinn 1962. I am grateful to David Cranstone for drawing my attention to this firm.

21 NMM ADM/B/167, 2 Nov 1761.

22 Lavery 1983, 96–9. Slade's long-serving predecessor, Sir Jacob Acworth, has tended to be compared unfairly with Slade. For a reassessment of Acworth, *see* Hemingway 2010.

23 Lavery 2004.

24 Rodger 1993, 64–5.

25 Wilkinson (1998) gives a concise account of the complicated financial manoeuvres undertaken by Egmont to secure continued funding in the financial retrenchments following the end of the Seven Years' War.

26 These can be traced in the dockyard plans in the TNA ADM 140 series, notably ADM 150/149–158, 301, 555.

27 TNA ADM 6/659, 15 June 1771. This model most closely matched a 1769 plan of Plymouth in TNA ADM 140/151.

28 NMM CHA/E/27, 10 Dec 1771; CHA/E/28, 17 Jan 1772; CHA/E/29, 20 Aug and 24 Nov 1773; POR/A/25, 21 July 1772; POR/A/26, 20 Aug1773. The two house carpenters at Portsmouth who built the model of the Hampshire yard were Nicholas Junior and John Doughty, both commended by the Navy Board, NMM POR/A/26, 20 May 1774. A key to the Plymouth Dock model dated Jan 1774 is in NMM MS 76/128. The NMM also curates the models that are currently on display in Chatham Historic Dockyard. For the much larger and later model of Sheerness Dockyard, *see* Coad 2008.

29 TNA ADM 174/16, 30 Nov 1761.

30 NMM POR/A/22, 28 Oct and 23 Nov 1763; TNA ADM 140/522 pt 1. £6,000 was inserted in the 1764 estimates (NMM POR/A/22, 13 Feb 1764).

31 NMM POR/A/22, 2 Apr 1764.

32 Ibid.

33 NMM POR/A/22, 28 March and 4 Apr 1764.

34 TNA ADM 106/1969, 17 Jan 1826.

35 NMM POR/A/23, 28 Jan 1766.

36 TNA ADM 140/522 pt 2, 19 June 1776. For a brief synopsis of Hunt's early career, *see* Knight 1987, 149.

37 NMM POR/A/30, 8 July 1782; POR/A/32, 24 Apr 1784; POR/A/34, 3 May 1790.

38 NMM POR/A/26, 21 Jan 1775; POR/A/27, 28 May 1776, 21 Aug 1776, 28 Feb 1777; ADM/B/193, 28 May 1776. For completion of the building, *see* NMM POR/A/29, 10 Nov 1779, and for the South Storehouse, *see* NMM POR/A/30, 8 July 1782.

39 NMM CHA/E/36, 5 Apr 1787. It is not clear from the correspondence if this letter related to wholly new drawings or ones sent in by the yard and merely modified by the surveyor.

40 Coad 1989, 35–6. For a detailed history of the contractor Templar and Parlby, *see* Drabble 2010.

41 Knight 1987, xlix; TNA ADM 1/3525, 31 May 1798.

42 NMM ADM/B/183, 8 Aug 1770.

43 The Gourock Ropeworks at Port Glasgow, founded in 1797, had a ropewalk that eventually extended to 400m, while the Firth and Clyde Roperie at Kirkaldy had one of 374m. Both were single storey (Hay and Stell 1986, 93–6).

44 TNA ADM 7/661, 25 June 1774.

45 Coad, 1989, 103. The external committee comprised the architect Samuel Wyatt and two Royal Engineers, Colonel Mulcaster and Captain William Twiss.

46 Ritchie-Noakes 1980, 5–8.

47 Saint 2007, 71. Despite these, the theatre was destroyed by fire in 1809.

48 NMM POR/A28, 24 July 1777; POR/A30, 15 Feb 1782.

49 Riley, 2007, 51–3. This article makes clear the complexities of attributing inventions to any one person. What Cort can claim is that he was the first person successfully to introduce these processes on a commercial scale.

50 Ritchie-Noakes 1980, 27–42; Skempton *et al* 2002, xxviii. The wider background of the Industrial Revolution is discussed in Floud and Johnson 2004.

51 Skempton *et al* 2002, xvii. In 1818 the Institution of Civil Engineers was founded (Chrimes 2010).

52 Lane 2004.

53 Buchanan 2004b; Fox 2009, 98–9; Paxton 2004. Skempton *et al* (2002, 627) credits Josias as being the resident engineer for the Eddystone Lighthouse. As such, he must have been closely involved in Smeaton's pioneering experiments using cement mortar in its construction.

54 Chrimes (1994) gives the best account of his remarkable career.

55 TNA ADM 106/1967, 20 June 1818.

56 Burton 1972, 176.

57 Coad 2005, 52; Rolt 1986, 82–9. Maudslay's life is summarised by Evans 1995, 166–72.

58 Hudson 2004, 37; Tann 1981, 249; Wakelin 2011, 8. Consolidation of ironworks after the Napoleonic Wars led to a huge change in the industrial landscape, with the massive South Wales ironworks at Cyfarthfa and Dowlais both employing around 5,000 men by 1830. There is a survey drawing of the early 19th-century engineering shop at the Carron Works in Hay and Stell 1986, 116–17.

59 Hills 2006, 233.

60 The best account of the various reforms is in Morriss 1983, chapter 7. *See also* Pool 1966, 112–30.

61 *Fifth Report of the Commissioners on Fees (VII)* 1806.

62 Sainty 1975, 117. Cockerell was also Surveyor to the Victualling Office at this time, responsible for early plans for Haulbowline. His limited work for the Navy Board included designing buildings for Haulbowline in 1795 (*see* Chapter 2). *See also* Colvin 1995, 79, 262, 411, 418; Sainty 1975, 76.

4 Planning and Building the Royal Dockyards, 1795–1914

1 Fox 2009, 116–17.

2 For Jeremy Bentham's ideas and designs for a Panopticon prison, *see* Brodie *et al* 2002, 58–9.

3 In 1804, as Viscount Melville, Henry Dundas became First Lord of the Admiralty

4 Coad 1989, 29–30; 2005, 23.

5 Morriss 1983, 47; NMM ADM/Q/ 3320, 22 Apr 1795.

6 NMM ADM/Q/ 3320, 2 June 1795.

7 Details of Bentham's relationships with the Admiralty and Navy Boards are outside the scope of this chapter. *See* Coad 1989, 31–3, Coad 2002, 52–3, Morriss 1983, 211–15.

8 Structural engineering developed as a separate discipline much later. The Institute of Structural Engineers was originally founded in 1908 as The Concrete Institute, only assuming its present name in 1922.
9 These were not particularly notable and seem to have marked the end of Bentham's involvement in ship design, although he remained passionate about mechanising warship construction (Coad 2005, 29).
10 Colvin 1995, 179. Colvin notes that two of Bunce's buildings survive, at Hampstead and at Felpham in Sussex.
11 NMM ADM/Q/3321, 11 Apr 1801, 25 March 1802. NMM POR/A39, 14 March 1796, is a letter from the Navy Board to the Portsmouth officers asking for an estimate for the cost of these nine houses. It is possible they may have forwarded a design as well.
12 Torrens 2004.
13 Coad 2005, 31.
14 Coad 1989, 30.
15 Coad 2005, 61.
16 Goodrich failed to see inside the ironworks itself as William Reynolds was away.
17 Coad 2005, 34–6.
18 Trinder 2000, 75.
19 Bracegirdle and Miles 1974, 78–83; Fox 2009, 113; Hadfield 1966, 156–7. The inclines have been partly restored.
20 Fox 2009, 113.
21 This use of rollers was following in Cort's footsteps at Funtley. John Wilkinson had launched his first iron barge in July 1787; 70ft long and made of riveted plates 5/16in thick, it transported castings along the Birmingham Canal. For the Wilkinson brothers, *see* Skempton *et al* 2002, 783–5.
22 *See* Skempton *et al* (2002, 777–8) for Whitmore.
23 Tann (1981, 12) also notes the 'frequently poor quality' of Boulton and Watt's goods produced in the early years of the foundry.
24 The details of this tour are all in the Science Museum Arch: Good. E1.
25 Fox (2009, 118–30) gives the most detailed modern account of Goodrich's career with the navy.
26 Fox 2009, pl 57.
27 NMM ADM/Q/3323, 20 and 30 July 1805; Coad 2005, 64–6.
28 Coad 2005, 49–59, 75.
29 Early drawings indicate that the sawmill was to be sited either at Woolwich or Chatham (TNA ADM 140/98).
30 Fox 2009, 66.
31 Naish 1992, 43–4.
32 Coad 1989, 32–3; Morriss 1983, 214. Morris (2006) looks at technological innovations during Bentham's time as Inspector General. Pease-Watkin (2004) provides a useful summary of his career and an assessment of his work.
33 Holl was buried at Chelsea Old Church. His plaque beside the chancel east window reads, 'In memory of Edward Holl Esq of this parish surveyor and architect to the Navy Board who departed this life November 2nd 1823 in the 58th year of his age. He lived respected and died lamented'.
34 NMM ADM/Q/3322, 12 March 1804, is a letter from the Admiralty to the Navy Board recommending the appointment of a Mr Hobbs as Inspector of Works at Deptford, as this post had been vacant since Mr Holl had been appointed to succeed Mr Bunce. TNA ADM 1/3526, 3 Dec 1802, is a letter from Bentham, following Bunce's death, to Nepean, Secretary to the Admiralty Board, asking that Holl should supervise works in the London area and a Mr Adams to do the same for Plymouth.
35 Collinge 1978, 19, 143.
36 NMM ADM/Q/3323, 29 March 1806.
37 Collinge 1978, 123.
38 Colvin 1995, 501; TNA ADM 1/3501, 10 July 1832.
39 Sutherland 1997, 123. For the slip and dock canopies, *see* Chapter 5.
40 NMM ADM/BP/34b, 30 Aug 1814.
41 Colledge and Warlow 2006, 297. Gwyn (2004, 344) notes that in 1814–15, Samuel Sellon, a leading man of shipwrights, was at St Andrews, Newfoundland, inspecting wood purchased for three timber-framed buildings for a Bermuda naval hospital. It is not clear on whose authority he was operating.
42 This hospital was extended and remained in use until the closure of the base in 1951. It was deliberately burnt down in 1972 after becoming derelict (Stranack 1990, 69–70).
43 Coad 1983, 365. GC 394 30 July 1812 and GC 399 October 1812 detail discussions on the size of iron members. TNA ADM 140/260 shows a cross-section of the reconstructed building. At the time of the fire, the Theatre Royal at Plymouth, with its extensive use of ironwork for fireproofing, was under construction. It would be surprising if its architect, John Foulston, and Holl were unaware of each other's work, but it is not known if they met (Saint 2007, 73).
44 Coad 1989, 240–1; Tucker 2007, 32.
45 Cox and Cox 1999, 16–18. An 1848 plan and elevation is in TNA ADM 105/89.
46 Coad 1982, 165–73.
47 Colvin 1995, 812–13; Diestelkamp 1990, 15.
48 GC, Book 32, 2 March 1814; GC, A519, 21 June 1814.
49 GC, A519, 21 June 1814.
50 Hattendorf *et al* 1993, 646–50.
51 Colvin 1995, 960–1.
52 TNA ADM 1/3501, 13 May 1834. The work was completed on Christmas Eve 1834. The concrete was probably a mix developed by William Ranger. *See* Chrimes *et al* 2008, 543. Taylor would almost certainly have been aware of the earlier successful use of concrete in London by the architect Robert Smirke and Samuel Baker, his builder brother-in-law, to underpin the failing foundations of the Millbank Penitentiary, the Savoy Precinct in Lancaster Place and the Custom House. The success of concrete at Sheerness no doubt helped to give Taylor the confidence to use this material with great success to underpin one of the Anchor Wharf storehouses at Chatham (TNA ADM 1/3502, 13 May 1834). *See* Saint (2007, 207–9) for a succinct account of the early development of concrete.
53 Saint 2007, 212; Skempton *et al* 2002, 543; TNA ADM 1/3502, 14 Aug 1837. Clarke ceased to be Director of Works in 1867 when he became Governor of the Straits Settlement and left for Singapore, demonstrating yet again the varied careers open to Royal Engineers in the 19th century (Chrimes *et al* 2008, 180).
54 Taylor's financial control of works at the Royal Clarence Yard also appears to have been somewhat loose (Coad 1989, 276–7). *See also* Chapter 14. After the abolition of his post, Taylor returned to private practice, almost immediately becoming responsible for designing the 170ft-high Hadlow Tower near Tonbridge. This remarkable Gothic edifice with its similarities with Beckford's Fonthill may also have owed something to the Rennies' unbuilt dock pumping station for Chatham (*see* Fig 6.30). It is quite conceivable that Taylor may have been inspired by these 1815 drawings, which were almost certainly in his official office.
55 Taylor 1870, 179; Weiler 1987, 125. In his memoirs, Taylor sourly notes that Brandreth was to marry the niece of Lord Dalmeny, then a member of the Board of Admiralty. He also commented unfavourably on the putative savings from the new arrangements, noting that his office 'cost the government £2,000 a year, including myself and three assistants; I had a clerk of works at Portsmouth, but attended by myself alone at all the other dockyards ... Captain Brandreth found he must have an establishment at every dockyard, and the expense became enormous'.

56 Coad 1989, 249.
57 Vetch 2004a.
58 Coad 1989, 334–5.
59 The Corps of Engineers was renamed the Royal Engineers in 1787 (Evans 2006, 35–9).
60 Coad 1989, 368; Weiler 1987, 24.
61 Harris 2010. The powder magazine is now the Queen's Exhibit Hall, part of the Bermuda Maritime Museum (Chrimes *et al* 2008, 300).
62 Weiler 1987, 9.
63 Skempton *et al* 2002, 39.
64 Skempton *et al* 2002, 34
65 Port 2010, 66, 268–9; Skempton *et al* 2002, 35.
66 TNA MR1/1771.
67 Weiler 1987, 125–7.
68 However, the new organisational arrangements were not all plain sailing (MacDougall 2009, 323–4, 361–2).
69 Weiler 1987, 127.
70 TNA ADM 128/1, 4 Aug 1843.
71 Quoted in Colvin 1995, 853. TNA ADM 1/6015, 7 Aug 1867, also records Greene's regret at Scamp's wish to retire after 'his devoted service over half a century', and quotes an earlier memo by Greene dated 9 Dec 1858 that bears out much of the quote above. *See also* MacDougall 2007, 29. Scamp died on 13 Jan 1872.
72 TNA ADM 128/1, 3 March 1842.
73 Beare 2004; Evans 2004, 172–7.
74 Chrimes *et al* 2008, 191–5. These included notable new harbours at Cape Town and Colombo. In Australia and New Zealand 'he designed or at least advised on, most of the harbours built in the late nineteenth century' (Chrimes *et al* 2008, 193).
75 Nelson and Oliver 1982, 42.
76 Bach 1986, 203; Martin and Tanner 1988, 386–7. McDonald (1969) states that in 1889 defence work was removed from Barnet's control after problems with military contracts and that 1890 saw 'a regrettable end to a distinguished career'. Barnet died in 1904.
77 Richards (1958, 64–5) first drew attention to the importance of the Sheerness Boat Store. For 7 Slip and a more detailed appraisal of the boat store, *see* Evans 2004, 121–30. For Greene's career, *see* Chrimes *et al* 2008, 351.
78 *See* Chrimes *et al* 2008, 606.
79 Colson and Colson nd, 2. For Smith's career, *see* Chrimes *et al* 2008, 720.
80 Weiler 1987, 126–30.
81 Coad 1989, 236; NMM CHA/E/101, 15 Oct, 31 Oct and 10 Nov 1811. The pipe runs and site for a well and 20hp steam pump are shown on an 1811 yard plan, TNA ADM 140/16, signed by Bentham. This may have remained no more than a proposal.
82 Although sewerage systems were well established long before 1900, Portsmouth Dockyard uniquely had batteries of earth closets in the late Victorian extension, extant as late as 1909, although marked 'disused' (TNA ADM 140/1484 fol 16). By 1854 it was the turn of smaller yards, notably Sheerness, to have gas lighting. The annual estimates noted that 'the substitution of gas for oil is much required in this yard' (TNA ADM 181/65).
83 TNA ADM 1/5803, 22 Sept 1862. The proposal may have been intended for use on board harbour hulks rather than active warships, as Scamp did not favour linking ships to pipes, but favoured gas holders, forerunners of today's ubiquitous gas cylinders.
84 Evans 2004, 192–4; Smith 1992, 64–5. The Royal Victoria Victualling Yard had a hydraulic system for cranes and victualling machinery budgeted for in1855 (TNA ADM 181/66 estimates).
85 The Works Loan Act of 1903 devoted £715,000 to the provision of electricity 'for light and power' for Chatham, Sheerness, Portsmouth, Devonport, Pembroke, Malta and Simon's Town, to be spent over two financial years, 1904–6 (TNA ADM 181/99 estimates).
86 TNA ADM 181/51, 1840/1 estimates. In 1849 the Woolwich estimates included monies for 'tram roads' of cast iron capable of withstanding the weight of traction engines. This system, designed by Beatson, remained in use until the closure of the dockyard. It seems improbable that such an elaborate tram road would have been installed if the railway proposed in 1840 had been implemented (TNA ADM 181/60 estimates; Guillery forthcoming).
87 Rolt 1960, 15. The Railways Inspectorate was to remain the exclusive preserve of the Royal Engineers into the 1960s.
88 Imperial Service Calendar 1848. The Harbour and Railways Department's principal task was to discharge statutory powers given to the Admiralty to approve harbour works, railway bridges and other projects likely to affect navigable waterways. These responsibilities were passed to the Boards of Trade in 1862.
89 Evans 2004, 191.
90 TNA ADM 181/60, 1849/50 estimates.
91 TNA ADM 181/61, 1850/1 estimates; ADM 181/62, 1851/2 estimates. The type of tramway proposed to link the victualling yard with the dockyard at Gibraltar is not stated, but its sinuous curves on an 1863 plan of Gibraltar suggest it could have used rails (AdL Naval establishments 1863, Da 02). By 1859 tramways were to be found in Woolwich, Portsmouth, Chatham, Devonport, Deptford and Sheerness, when it was estimated they had cost about £25,000 (MacDougall 2009, 94).
92 MacDougall 2009, 94; White 1961, 117. The line into the Royal Clarence Yard had to pass through the ramparts of the Gosport defences, a breach that the Board of Ordnance would probably not have sanctioned merely for the convenience of the Admiralty.
93 TNA ADM 181/67, 1856 estimates.
94 Interestingly, the tunnel constructed between 1854 and 1857 to link Devonport Dockyard with the new Keyham Yard was designed for road traffic. Only in 1879 was a railway laid through it, as well as cutting through the corner of the North Smithery that blocked the direct approach to the southern end of the tunnel. *See* Chapter 2.
95 Evans 2004, 191.
96 Vetch 2004b.
97 Evans 2004, 191. Lengths of this plateway may still be seen *in situ*.
98 Dendy Marshall and Kidner 1963, 338. An 1887 dockyard plan held in the archives of the Chatham Historic Dockyard Trust shows the original extent of the full-size railway. Linking Chatham to the main line was not easy, hence the late date; in 1869 the Director of Works had advocated that Sheerness Dockyard be linked to the London, Brighton and South Coast Railway's Sheerness branch (TNA ADM 1/6117, 7 Dec 1869).TNA ADM 140/1484 shows both systems in 1912 at their full extent.
99 TNA ADM 181/82, estimates for 1871/2, allowed monies for a link at Pembroke with the Pembroke and Tenby Railway; ADM 181/84 estimates for 1873/4 allowed money for a link at Portland with the Castletown Railway. The original terminus of the branch line to Sheerness, opened in 1860, was by the dockyard, only being extended to its present terminus nearer the town in 1883 (Dendy Marshall and Kidner 1963, 529).
100 Evans 2006, 145–6.
101 Imperial Service Calendar 1914.
102 TNA ADM 181/96, fol 22.

5 Engineering Works of the Sailing Navy, 1700–1835

1 TNA ADM 1/376, 9 Aug 1715.
2 TNA ADM 106/1967, undated report, probably mid-1816. NMM ADM/BP33c, 5 Nov 1813.
3 NMM ADM/A/1765, 29 July 1692.
4 NMM POR/A44, 7 Jan 1802. Dummer's basin at Plymouth Dock relied on a single set of inward-opening gates, but at Portsmouth he fitted a double set.
5 Dietz 2002, 147.

6 Harris 1999, 397–8; Merino 1985, 36–7.
7 For the early history and evolution of these docks, *see* Dietz 2002 and Coad 1989, 90–9. At Chatham, the 'First New Dock', probably constructed *c* 1685 and valued at £4,404 8s in 1698, needed repairs estimated at nearly £7,000 in 1735 (Coad 1989, 92).
8 Morriss 1983, 44.
9 Coad 1989, 94–5. The dock was enlarged during construction, when the decision was taken in 1690 to make Plymouth a major dockyard capable of taking the largest ships of the line. Dummer claimed that his sets of twin gates required only 4 to 6 men to operate, compared with up to 70 men needed for triple gates (BL Lansdowne 847).
10 BL Lansdowne 847; TNA ADM 174/1, 24 Apr 1697, 8 March and 18 Sept 1699. For a detailed account of Dummer's works at Portsmouth and Plymouth, *see* Fox 2007, 26–30.
11 Coad 1989, 96. NMM ADM/A/1770, 15 Dec 1690, is the Admiralty order for the dry dock.
12 NMM POR/A2, 19 May 1699; POR/A10, 5 Aug 1737. Dummer's plan of the developed scheme in 1698 is in BL Harley MS 4318 fol 44.
13 Dummer's drawing and description of this whole ingenious installation are in BL Harley MS 4318 fol 42. The North Stone Dock does not appear to have been incorporated into this arrangement.
14 NMM POR/A2, 27 Apr 1702.
15 Fox 2007, 51–7. The author's detailed account sums up Dummer's fall from grace as largely due to technical over-ambition, bad man-management and political intrigue, 'thus ended the official Navy career of a visionary inventor, sophisticated in his awareness of the desirability of applying reason to industry, highly skilled at expressing his schemes for design and control on paper, yet perhaps on account of these same remarkable qualities fatally flawed when it came to executing his plans in practice' (Fox 2007, 56).
16 The final costs of the works at Portsmouth and Plymouth are by no means clear; the estimated costs of the dry dock and associated basin at Plymouth between 1691 and 1700 came to £21,887 14s 8¾d (Coad 1992, 194). At Chatham, No. 2 Dock was described in 1855 as being 'at present a wooden dilapidated dock, with a good stone entrance' (TNA ADM 181/66 annual estimates).
17 NMM POR/A6, 17 Sept 1716; POR/A22, 15 March and 17 Apr 1765; POR/A23, 6 March 1767, 1 Feb 1768. As late as 1895 a substantial section of the North Corner wall at Portsmouth, largely constructed in the 1840s, collapsed following alterations to the now-vanished 9 Dock (TNA ADM 195/79 fol 16).
18 Johnson 1976, 57.
19 Coad 1989, 101. NMRN Plans of HM Dockyard, Portsmouth *c* 1786, MS 1993/443.
20 Dietz 2002, 150.
21 Coad 2005, 27.
22 NMM POR/A43, 11 Oct 1799. Bentham's use of the inverted arch just predates its employment in a similar situation by John Rennie senior, who combined it with cellular walls and thus reduced the ground pressure, employing this system successfully from the summer of 1800 in his works at Grimsby harbour (Skempton *et al* 2002, 560–1).
23 TNA Por/A43, 21 Oct 1799; TNA ADM 1/3525, 10 Sept 1798. Inverted arches in earlier docks referred to the timber floors that could be curved by up to 6in depending on the size of the dock. These were considered to be important elements in the stability of the structure. *See* Dietz 2002, 150. Bentham's original proposal had been to replace the timber dock floor with a masonry one supported from the inverted arches.
24 Rennie also used piles at No. 3 Dock at Chatham in 1816 (MacDougall 1989, 186).
25 MacDougall 1989, 179, 190.
26 NMM ADM/BP/38b, 23 Sept 1818. Their report went on to record that 'we have however the satisfaction to find that the late correspondence between the Board and Mr Rennie has led to the correction of a similar expense which was proposed by Mr Rennie in the plans for the docks at Sheerness'. The contemporary model of Sheerness shows the dry docks supported on massive timber rafts secured to piles (Coad 2008, 53).
27 Merino 1985, 38.
28 NMM ADM/A/1906, 4 July and 27 Aug 1703.
29 Bentham first put these proposals for a caisson to Nepean, Secretary to the Board of Admiralty, in Aug 1798 (TNA ADM 1/13525, 4 Aug 1798).
30 MacDougall 1989, 180; TNA ADM 140/678. *See* Chapter 8 for his iron gates at Sheerness
31 *See* Gardberg and Palsila 1998, 49–50 for Sveaborg. Hällström (1986, 144) has an illustration of the galley dock and two windmills.
32 Merino 1985, 43–6.
33 *See* TNA ADM 140/496 pt 1 for Sadler's pump design.
34 TNA ADM 181/45 and 46, annual estimates 1834/5, 1835/6.
35 TNA ADM 106/2154. Boulton and Watt were paid £4,027 for the engine and pumps.
36 TNA ADM 106/2154, 2 June 1822.
37 TNA ADM 174/139, 15 Jan 1816. For Rennie's report on the Plymouth proposal, *see* NMM ADM/BP/36a, 22 May 1816. For Woolwich, *see* Evans 2004, 81.
38 TNA ADM 140/675.
39 The slip in the Great Basin at Portsmouth had been constructed *c* 1730 and was replaced by the present No. 4 Dock by 1767 (NMM POR/A8, 27 Feb 1729, 14 Apr 1731; TNA ADM 140/555 pt 2). At Sheerness the small slip opened into the Mud Dock (TNA ADM 140/665). Deptford had three slips opening into the basin in the latter part of the 18th century (TNA Work 41/595), reduced to two by the time of the yard's closure, their survival largely due to the absence of space to site slips that could launch directly into the Thames.
40 TNA ADM 140/223 is an 1815 plan for a slip at Plymouth with a 1:20 incline.
41 *See* Coad (1989, 108–10) for a detailed breakdown of the costs of building and repairing 18th-century slips.
42 NMM ADM/BP/6b, 14 June 1786.
43 Sutherland 1997, 126; TNA ADM 3/72, 21 June 1764.
44 TNA ADM 7/662, 31 Oct 1775.
45 Building accounts for individual slips have not always survived, and their evolution is most easily followed in the dockyard plans in the TNA ADM 140 series.
46 BL Kings MS 44 fol 13; TNA ADM 140/4; Coad 1989, 109.
47 TNA ADM 140/555 fol 18; ADM 140/159; ADM 140/16.
48 TNA ADM 140/670 fol 1.
49 TNA Work 41/595; Morriss 1983, 45. For Harwich, *see* AdL Da 01 fol 35. Banbury (1971) remains the only general account of commercial shipbuilding yards on the Thames and Medway and gives useful lists of warships built at Deptford and Woolwich.
50 Morriss 1983, 45.
51 In one example, the housing was to be constructed of 'the outside of fir timber' (NMM POR/A59, 8 Dec 1814). NMM ADM/BP/41b, 7 June 1821, has a cross-section 'of a roof as fixed over His Majesty's ship *Prince of Wales* in Portsmouth Yard in 1792'. This warship was not launched until 1794, after spending a remarkable 10 years on the stocks. The roof, bolted to her bulwarks, can only have been fixed late in her construction.
52 Sutherland 1997, 125.
53 NMM ADM/BP/41b, 7 June 1821.
54 Bentham 1862, 47.

55 NMM ADM/BP/32a, 23 Feb 1812; TNA ADM 140/1404. *See* Sutherland (1997, 126) for a description of Bentham's remarkable Sheerness buildings.
56 TNA ADM 181/21, 1814 estimates.
57 NMM ADM/BP/41b, 7 June 1821.
58 The Navy Board officials subsequently dismissed Pering's claim to have made a significant and reward-worthy contribution to the design of slip roofs, effectively accusing him of plagiarising the slightly earlier design of his fellow yard officers. He was probably the same Richard Pering recorded as Clerk to the Surveyor from Feb to Oct 1791, before being appointed as Clerk of the Survey at Sheerness (Collinge 1978, 130). His work with the Surveyor may account for his interest in designing slip housings.
59 NMM ADM/BP/41b, 7 June 1821.
60 Probably to be identified with Lionel Lukin, lifeboat designer and inventor with a number of important naval connections (Chichester 2004b). TNA ADM 49/105, Correspondence with the Admiralty 1810–11, details 'Mr Lukin's plans for ventilating ships'.
61 NMM ADM/BP/32c, 8 Dec 1812. The drawings that Mr Lukin appears to have sent with his suggestions seem not to survive in the official records. Holl's reference to discontinuing the use of timber in new buildings in the dockyards seems a little impracticable. More probably, he meant discontinuing the use of timber buildings, an aim within the dockyards since at least the 1760s.
62 Skempton *et al* 2002, 600.
63 TNA ADM 181/21, 1815 estimates.
64 For Plymouth, *see* MacDougall 2009, 62; Sutherland 1997, 127; and NMM POR/A61, 12 Dec 1815.
65 NMM ADM/BP/37b, 25 Oct 1817.
66 Crimmin 2008, 226.
67 TNA ADM 181/21, 1817 estimates.
68 Between 1815 and 1821, when they cease, considerable sums appear in the Plymouth estimates for covering slips and docks. TNA ADM 181/21 has the comparatively large sum of £6,000 for a slip roof at Plymouth in 1820 and the following year a smaller sum 'to complete the roof'.
69 TNA ADM 181/47–9, 1836/7–1838/9. The annual estimates allowed a total of £8,500 for construction, including the actual slip.
70 In 1843 No. 3 Slip at Pembroke was provided with a timber roof of 30m span, compared to the 28.5m span of 3 Slip at Chatham (Sutherland 1997, 132).
71 Naish 1992, 37. This is the best detailed account of the project.
72 TNA ADM 7/659, 5 June 1771.
73 The original survey drawing dated 22 Apr 1806 is in TNA ADM 140/369 pt 1. Rennie and Whidbey were assisted by James Hemmans, then master attendant at Chatham but formerly at Plymouth Dockyard, where he had surveyed the Sound. Hemmans is described by various authors as James or Samuel Hemmans, Hemans or Hermans.
74 This was to be augmented by a further four quarries (Coad 1994, 167).
75 Whidbey's house still stands at Bovisand, where he was also responsible for constructing a freshwater reservoir and jetty for the Victualling Board. G L Taylor (1870, 178) recorded that Whidbey planted the banks of the reservoir with strawberries, 'and when a ship came in at a time they were ripe, he allowed the crew to come ashore and feast on the strawberries, to the number of 500 or more at a time; a most excellent anti-scorbutic'.
76 Naish 1992, 46–50.
77 Ibid.
78 Smiles 1862, 263.

6 Buildings of the Sailing Navy

1 Colvin 1995, 818–19.
2 Colvin 1995, 262.
3 Grainger and Phillpotts 2010, 81.
4 Port 1995, 24.
5 The convoluted history of the Admiralty is well described in Port 1995, especially pp 269–71.
6 Mallinson 2005, 81–2; Sainty 1975, 77; Wilson 1976, 13, 26. Wilson provides the definitive and detailed account of the Admiralty telegraph systems, supplemented by Mallinson's later work, and he identifies a house at Saltram (p 32) as the only surviving example of a shutter telegraph structure.
7 Wilson 1976, 16. For details of the entirely separate chain of coast signal stations used to report enemy shipping movements to the nearest naval station, *see* Wilson (1976, 64–7) and Kitchen (1990), who includes a location map of the sites.
8 Wilson 1976, 34.
9 Wilson 1976, 60–1. The Chatley Heath tower is looked after by the Surrey Wildlife Trust and is occasionally open to visitors.
10 McGowan 1999, 12. This is probably a conservative figure as Crimmin (2008, 192) quotes 3,000 loads being required for a 74-gun ship, of between 1,600 and 1,900 tons.
11 NMM ADM/BP 32c, 26 Sept 1812; Crimmin 2008, 191; Morriss 1983, 78–84.
12 Crimmin 2008, 191–3.
13 NMM ADM/BP 32c, 26 Sept 1812; King 1995, 17. Broken-up ordnance had long been used as ballast. Redundant cast-iron ballast also found a ready use in yards to provide a hard surface. Much still survives in this form in Chatham, Portsmouth and doubtless elsewhere.
14 BL Kings MS 43.
15 Morriss 1983, 75.
16 McGowan 1971, 94–5; Merriman 1950, 145–6.
17 TNA ADM 3/30, 15 June 1716.
18 Baugh 1977, 252, 275.
19 McGowan 1999, 86.
20 Coad 1989, 161–2; Lavery 1989, 73–5.
21 Morriss 1983, 73; NMM ADM/BP 32c, 26 Sept 1812.
22 Coad 1969, 146.
23 NMM ADM/BP 32c, 26 Sept 1812; Coad 1969, 163.
24 NMM ADM/BP/346, 14 Feb 1814.
25 *See* Cock (2001, 456) and Bingeman *et al* (2000) for the introduction of copper sheathing.
26 Defoe 1962, 129. Timber from the Weald was generally taken by road to the River Medway at Maidstone, a distance probably 25 miles or less. According to Defoe, this was done in a series of short stages: ''tis carry'd so little a way, and then thrown down, and left for other tugs [heavy timber wagons] to take up and carry on.' At the Medway the timber was conveyed downriver to Chatham.
27 Coad 1989, 126. The Chatham building of 1718 was demolished to make way for the existing storehouses in the 1780s. The Board of Ordnance storehouse, considerably altered and now known as the New Armouries Building, constructed at the Tower of London 1663–4, had very similar features. Parnell (1993, 64–6) includes a 1717 survey drawing. I am grateful to Simon Thurley for drawing my attention to this building. One of the two Morice Yard storehouses remains little altered since completion. See Chapter 15.
28 Calvocoressi 1986, 32.
29 TNA ADM 140/1484. The building stood against the boundary wall at the north end of the dockyard.
30 TNA MPH/247.
31 NMM ADM/BP 32c, 26 Sept 1812. The figure of 4,214 is made up of 3,128 shipwrights, 781 servants, 197 quartermen, 61 submeasurers, 2 converters and 45 cabin keepers. As might be expected, Portsmouth had the most, with 980 shipwrights, followed by Plymouth with 824 and Chatham with 453.
32 Abell (1981, 72), quoting late 17th-century practice.

33 Documentary references to the use of this as a mould loft have not been found. The upper part of the building was extensively reconstructed by Samuel Bunce in 1802 (Coad 1982, 149–50).

34 'The scrieve gets its name from the practice of *scriving* the lines around a curved batten pinned in place with a special tool – a hook with a point, like a gouge chisel, called a 'scrieve-hook' (Abell 1981, 131).

35 TNA ADM 181/60, annual estimates. The date of the conversion of 5 Slip is not yet clear, but it was certainly used as a scrieve floor well before 1900. Remarkably, the building and its floor still survive.

36 Painted honours boards in the building record the names of the later warships.

37 Coad 1973, 133–4; McGowan 1999, 12.

38 NMM ADM/BP 32c, 26 Sept 1812; TNA ADM 140/692. The first floor housed a mould loft and carpenters' workshops. The building still stands.

39 TNA ADM 7/660, 13 July 1773.

40 TNA ADM 7/659, 13 May 1771.

41 NMM ADM/B/185, 24 July 1771, sets out where the 7,470ft of sheds were to be built; by Aug 1771, the total run was reduced to 2,490ft, with a further 500ft ordered in Oct 1773. The final totals for each yard were Deptford 530ft, Woolwich 400ft, Chatham 600ft, Sheerness 60ft, Portsmouth 600ft and Plymouth 700ft (NMM ADM/B/188, 26 Oct 1773).

42 Coad 1982, 156–7. TNA ADM 106/2508, 4 Apr 1771, Standing Order no. 567, sets out in considerable detail precisely how long timber was to be seasoned, how it was to be stacked and when it was to be used.

43 NMM ADM/BP 32c, 26 Sept 1812.

44 NMM CHA/E5, 6 Aug 1740; CHA/E/6, 11 May 1742. An original elevation drawing is in the NMM (reproduced in Coad 1982, pl 14).

45 NMM ADM/BP 32c, 26 Sept 1812.

46 Goodwin 1998, 29–33. The French navy had introduced use of iron knees in the 1740s. Their use would certainly have been known to the British Admiralty following the capture of a French '74 off Cape Finisterre in 1747. Renamed HMS *Invincible* and subsequently wrecked off St Helens in 1758, this warship has been the subject of a major archaeological excavation when over 200 iron knees were recovered. (Bingeman, 2010)

47 NMM POR/A/46, 17 Aug 1803; NMM ADM/BP 39b, 13 May 1819.

48 Coad 1989, 153.

49 NMM POR/A35, 8 March 1791; POR/A37, 7 Feb 1794.

50 NMM ADM/B/220, 4 May and 18 Sept 1805.

51 NMM C7520-D, signed by Holl on 28 Jan 1806; NMM ADM/B/221, 14 March 1806; NMM CHA/E/94, 29 July 1809.

52 NMM ADM/B/232, 8 June and 1 July 1808.

53 NMM ADM/BP 32c, 26 Sept 1812.

54 Coad 1989, 154–5. The equipment was salvaged by the Inspectorate of Ancient Monuments after the closure of the building and was handed over to the Chatham Historic Dockyard Trust on its inception in 1984.

55 Coad 2005, 20.

56 Their unmistakable outlines appear on a dockyard plan of 1761, TNA ADM 140/149, and are identified as such on a plan of 1782, TNA ADM 140/153.

57 TNA ADM 140/555 fol 16.

58 Coad 1989, 226.

59 At the naval base at Sveaborg, then part of Sweden's Baltic possessions, a windmill installed by 1749/51 to power a sawmill and grist mill also drove dock pumps (Gardberg and Palsila 1998, 49–50).

60 Coad 2005, 28–32. This book contains a far more detailed account than is possible here of the pioneer use of steam power in Portsmouth between 1799 and *c* 1810.

61 Despite air circulation being encouraged by drawing air for the boiler furnaces from this level.

62 The Boulton and Watt drawing of this engine house is in GC Good C17.

63 Coad 2005, 36, 42, 44–6. Brunel developed three types of sawing machinery for these wood mills, circular, reciprocating and pendulum saws, but no trace of these remains.

64 The block-making machines forced the introduction of new working practices that are outside the scope of this book. *See* Coats (2006) and Riley (2006) for detailed assessments of the impact of this technology on labour and working practices.

65 TNA ADM 106/3519, 19 Oct 1809. Materials came to £12,210 9s 8d; workmanship to £24,508 4s 5d.

66 Fearful that a fire in the Block Mill might cripple the navy's supply of blocks, the Navy Board had a duplicate set of frames for the block-making machinery constructed by Maudslay and stored in a fireproof space in Brunel's Chatham sawmills. These incorporated a number of modifications and improvements resulting from experience gained by the original sets of machines. Goodrich felt that the mechanisms themselves could be quickly manufactured if necessary. When some of the last frames were delivered to Chatham in Jan 1819, the dockyard officers noted that 'most of the articles are sent in a rough state and will require filing and fitting' (TNA ADM 106/3519, 7 Sept 1814, 14 Jan 1819). Maudslay's firm had a high reputation for the quality of its products and in this instance had deliberately left the frames 'to be finished hereafter when thought proper' (Coad 2005, 99).

67 Not always with the approval of Goodrich, who thought there was a danger of misuse of public funds (Coad 2005, 68–9). For Brunel's Battersea sawmill, boot manufactory and decorative tinfoil works, *see* Thom 2010.

68 Coad 1989, 236–9.

69 TNA ADM140/98 pt 3, 24 Jan 1812.

70 TNA ADM140/98 pt 2, 24 Jan 1812, is a drawing of a mill that could be built at either yard.

71 TNA ADM 140/2 clearly shows this.

72 MacDougall (2009, 139), quoting a description of the sawmill.

73 TNA ADM 140/98–101 has an extensive set of drawings of the sawmills.

74 TNA ADM 140/99.

75 Holl's signature appears against a number of these drawings in TNA ADM 140/100, along with a marginal note that 'ironwork to be provided by Mr Brunel', probably indicating that the latter was responsible for ordering all the metal components of the mill. It is always possible that the cast-iron shoes owe something to Bentham and his desire to simplify procedures to enable the use of unskilled labour.

76 TNA ADM 140/99.

77 Dempsey 1843.

78 As late as 1829 the older docks here were still being pumped out individually by manual labour. The proposal to link the docks by a culvert to a central pump (in this case the new steam one) was suggested by the shipwright officers to Commissioner Charles Cunningham, who passed the suggestion to the Navy Board in a letter of 23 Apr 1829 (MacDougall 2009, 87).

79 MacDougall 1989, 173–91; 2009, 63–4, 71.

80 TNA ADM 140/96, dated 1816.

81 TNA ADM 140/97 are signed Rennie drawings showing the building largely as completed.

82 MacDougall 2009, 116 (30 Jan 1816). No plans appear to survive showing the location and extent of the system. It was probably modelled on Bentham's earlier 1811 proposals, which centred on a well and steam pump to be located north of the bricklayers' pound, presumably intended for supplying fresh water that could also be used for firefighting (TNA ADM 140/16).

83 Coad 1989, 240. In 1815 Rennie estimated the cost of the engine, engine house, well and drain at £14,700; the dry dock figure was £143,000 (MacDougall 2009, 64).

84 A very full set of drawings is in TNA ADM 140/107. Hobbes, writing *c* 1849, mentions that lead pipes were also manufactured here; MacDougall 2009, 114, 124, 145.

85 Coad 1989, 240–2.

86 Oppenheim 1926, 343–4.

87 Coad 1983, 346–7 .

88 TNA ADM 140/670; ADM 106/2064, 9 Aug 1810.

89 TNA ADM 140/492.

90 *See* Chapter 9 for additional information. TNA ADM 140/1303 is a drawing of a proposed house for a ropemaker at Minorca in 1743. AdL Da 01 fol 4, a plan of Port Royal *c* 1840, marks the ropehouse, which was described in 1846 as a lean-to building, out of use and in poor repair when Captain J J Hope RE was seeking permission for its demolition (uncatalogued letter of 9 Nov1846 in Bermuda Maritime Museum). For Malta, *see* Coad 1989, 343–4.

91 For a detailed description of the ropemaking process and its buildings, with especial reference to Chatham, *see* Coad 1969, 143–65.

92 Coad 1969, 158. This description of the ropemaking process is based on a detailed record compiled by Goodrich during his visit to Chatham ropery in April 1808.

93 Coad 1989, 199, 204, 343. Malta was the only overseas yard to have a ropehouse as distinct from an open-air ropewalk. The double ropehouse at Chatham had its window openings glazed for the first time after the Second World War. It still retains some of its wooden shutters. At Plymouth, the spinning house has many of its cast-iron shutters that were installed after the fire of 1812. Here, Holl introduced limited glazing in the segmental heads of the window openings above these shutters.

94 NMM ADM/BP 32c, 26 Sept 1812.

95 Tann 1981, 317, 396.

96 TNA ADM 140/555 pt 17; MacDougall 2009, 129. The date of installation of this steam engine and its details have not so far been found.

97 Skempton *et al* 2002, 275; TNA ADM 1/3526, 27 Sept 1802, 1 Jan and 18 Feb 1803.

98 Goodrich papers 50/51. Significantly, Grimshaw lit his ropery with specially designed lanterns that Bentham purchased in 1805 to light the Portsmouth Block Mills (Coad 2005, 72–3).

99 Skempton *et al* 2002, 275; TNA ADM 1/3526, 18 Feb 1803; ADM 1/3527, 15 Jan 1804. TNA ADM 140/291 is a 'sketch of Mr Grimshaw's Spinning Frame' dated 6 Sept 1804 in the Inspector General's Office and signed by Simon Goodrich.

100 MacDougall 1986, 124. GC 50/51, undated but watermarked 1801, indicates that the ropery was to be fireproof.

101 TNA ADM 7/661, 25 June 1774.

102 Morriss 1983, 87.

103 NMM ADM/B/231, 4 and 9 April and 4 May 1808. The Navy Board's request to the Admiralty was in a letter of 25 Feb 1808. The Board itself felt strongly that the engine's use should be limited to the 'formation of strands' and to help with the tarring process.

104 GC Good A242, dated 27 Apr and May 1808. A near-identical set of forming machines, but without the maker's nameplate, is in the ropery in the Swedish naval base at Karlskrona. For Huddart and his rope making, *see* Skempton *et al* 2002, 344.

105 NMM CHA/J/1, 14 July 1836.

106 TNA ADM 181/47, 1836/7 estimates; TNA ADM 1/3502, 2 March 1836. G L Taylor visited Chatham in March 1836 'to arrange ... the best methods of placing the machinery'. The boiler was also intended to provide steam to heat a tar kettle located on the spinning floor, suggesting that yarns were to be tarred here rather than in the adjacent tarring house. Penn supplied siphons, steam pipes and cocks in connection with this (NMM CHA/J/1, 4 Nov 1836). The most detailed account of the installation of the steam engine and its equipment is in NMM CHA/J/1, especially 24 June and 10 July 1836 and 31 Aug 1837. The steam engine was replaced by an electric motor, which still drives the capstans. TNA ADM 181/84 estimates for 1873/4 have £600 for an engine house 'for a new engine and boilers for the ropery'. This is probably the extant former engine house to power spinning machinery on the first floor of the hemp store.

107 TNA ADM 1/5979, 11 Oct 1866.

108 A steam engine for Devonport appears in 1838/9 estimates (TNA ADM 181/50), with a note that it is to be diverted to Deptford. A 20hp engine reappears in the 1849/50 estimates, TNA ADM 181/60, but an 1863 plan of Devonport Dockyard (AdL 1863 Yard Plan Da 02) shows no engine or boiler house by the ropery. A high-pressure boiler house estimated at £204 was proposed for the Portsmouth ropery in the 1856/7 estimates (TNA ADM 181/67), but this may have been connected with the tarring process and was quite possibly not installed. The 76 ropemakers at Portsmouth all lost their jobs as there were no vacancies at either Chatham or Devonport (Hamilton 2005, 63).

109 The detailed evolution of these rebuildings is described in Coad 1989, 199–223.

110 NMM ADM/B167, 2 Nov 1761.

111 TNA ADM 140/555 pt 1, 21 July 1760. The proposals were reworked and are shown in more detail in ADM 140/555 pt 2.

112 NMM ADM/B/183, 8 Aug 1770.

113 For a lively description, *see* Warner 2005, 119–28 .

114 At the time, the buildings were not protected by historic building legislation. While one may quibble about some aspects of the modernisation, this did at least preserve the form and scale of the buildings, which the Admiralty could simply have demolished.

115 The Ministry of Defence continued to make cordage here for the fleet until the closure of the naval base in 1983. Since 1984, the ropery has been the responsibility of the Chatham Historic Dockyard Trust and its commercial subsidiary, Master Ropemakers Ltd. Except where indicated, much of the information on Chatham ropery here comes from Coad 1969, 143–65, and Coad 1989, 207–21.

116 The 'Dutch yacht' was probably the ketch-rigged *Fubbs*, built by Phineas Pett at Greenwich in 1682 and finally broken up in 1781 (NMM CHA/E/10, 4 May 1753).

117 NMM ADM/B/181, 12 Sept 1768.

118 NMM ADM/BP/6b, 16 Oct 1786. The new storehouse had been mooted for a number of year, first appearing as a proposal on a yard plan in 1771 (TNA ADM 140/8).

119 NMM CHA/E/31, 18 Apr 1787; NMM CHA/B1, 25 June 1792.

120 Ibid.

121 Plan of Chatham *c* 1840, AdL Da 01 fol 28, and *c* 1909, TNA ADM 140/1484. The building was later used as a stationery store.

122 References to these later alterations have not been identified in the records, and the approximate dates are based on G L Taylor's 1831 yard plan (NMM A5911), an 1840 yard plan (AdL Da 01) and a 1909 plan (TNA ADM 140/1484).

123 TNA ADM 1/3634, 18 Nov 1728; NMM CHA/E/103, 18 Apr 1812. A sum of £9,048 appears in the estimates for 1813 and again in those for 1814 'to build a new hemp house 123 feet long'. Although slightly ambiguous, these sums almost certainly refer to this additional storey. A later sum of £6,605 in 1818 'to raise the old North Single Hemp House one storey' would seem to refer to the smaller hemp house demolished to make way for the ropery steam engine house in 1836 (Navy estimates 1792–1854, Parliamentary Papers).

124 The most likely date for this last extension is around 1836 when the engine house for the ropery was built on the site of a second hemp house at the north end of the double ropery. The cellars of this 19th-century addition are fireproof.

125 Three drawings in the Chatham collection in the NMM (H61, H63 and one unnumbered), dated between 1858 and 1864, show the alterations required. This work involved removing the existing first-floor timber pillars supporting the roof trusses and strengthening the trusses, partly to support a glazed and louvred ridge light running the length of the building. The dates correspond with entries in the annual estimates for 'additional accommodation for spinning machinery' in 1861/2 (TNA ADM 181/72), 'lining the floor of the hemp store' in 1862/3 (TNA ADM 181/73) and 'additional accommodation for spinning machinery' in 1864/5 (TNA ADM 181/75).

126 The engine house does not appear on an 1863 yard plan (AdL Da 02 fol 29) and does not appear in the annual estimates, unless ii was subsumed under 'additional accommodation for spinning machinery'. The building has long been used to test ropes and cables.

127 *Chatham News and North Kent Spectator,* 10 Dec 1864, quoted in MacDougall 2009, 152.

128 May 1999, 63.

129 *See* Chapter 8 for the later 6 Boathouse at Portsmouth.

130 Coad 1981, 36; Coad 1983, 360–1; AdL 1863 plan of Devonport, Da 02. For Sheerness, *see* TNA ADM 140/692 and 1484.

131 BL Kings MS 43. This was probably used principally for repairing sails from ships in ordinary.

132 Coad 1982, 146–7.

133 NMM POR/A/4, 28 May 1709.

134 NMM CHA/E4, 13 Apr 1736.

135 TNA ADM 140/1030.

136 TNA ADM 1/3502, 2 March 1836.

137 TNA ADM 1/3503, 31 Aug 1839. None of the pitch houses or their equipment survive.

138 Coad 1989, 143–4.

139 The process of plank bending is treated in some detail in Coad 1989, 142. Drawings of the Sheerness installation are in TNA ADM 140/1035–9.

140 Dockyard plans of the time show steaming kilns concentrated by the working boathouses and the boiling troughs near the building slips. No boiling troughs or steaming kilns survive.

141 BL Kings MS 43.

7 Dockyard Housing, Offices and Chapels

1 For the lists of yard officers in 1697, *see* Merriman 1950, 344. The skills of the tenants reflected the technology of the age. One of the houses in the Chatham officers' terrace in the 1970s housed the nuclear manager.

2 The house at English Harbour was originally built for Prince William Henry when on station in the Caribbean. The yard only had a resident commissioner for part of the Napoleonic Wars. It is only marked as 'Commissioner's House' on later plans, such as TNA MF 1 fol 5, dated to 1855.

3 I am grateful to H Gordon Slade for drawing my attention to the similarities in the massing of the palace front of Les Invalides. Dummer is not known to have visited Paris, but could have seen Thomas Povey's manuscript on the building that was circulating in London among those concerned with founding a similar hospital for army veterans at Chelsea. For a fuller account, *see* Ritchie 1966 and Coad 1983, 348–50.

4 NMM unsorted MSS 1695–1832, 8 Feb 1695.

5 Quoted in Fox 2007, 25. In this, Dummer was probably too optimistic, because in the 1790s Commissioner Fanshawe bemoaned the 'repeated pilferings and embezzlements' (Morriss 1983, 171). At Chatham in 1743, Commissioner Brown had a small timber building erected in the upper part of his garden, 'the roof to project about three feet above the Wall to give a better opportunity to observe the Workmen coming in and going out of the Dock Gate' (quoted in Hall and Lear 1992, 143).

6 NMM unsorted MSS 1695–1832, 8 Feb 1695.

7 For Port Royal *see* TNA ADM 195/49, fols 34, 41.

8 NMM ADM/BP/38a, 20 July 1818; TNA ADM 106/1993, 8 May 1823.

9 TNA ADM 1/3596, 10 July 1703. This letter was sent by the Navy Board to the Admiralty to seek guidance from the Lord High Admiral, Prince George of Denmark. Accompanying it was an elevation drawing of the proposed house that is much as built, but lacking the balcony and cupola clearly shown in slightly later views of the yard. A letter of 14 July 1703 (NMM ADM/A/1906) signified the Admiralty's approval for the construction of the house. The earliest illustration of it with its balcony and cupola is in a view of the yard from across the Medway in 1708 in BL Kings Top. XVI 42a.

10 Coad 1989, 53–4.

11 TNA ADM 140/444–60. These detailed drawings of the houses are mostly signed by Edward Holl, but a number are signed by Miller, his assistant.

12 TNA ADM 140/812; ADM 106/2151 pt 1, 11 March 1824. The terrace was apparently completed in 1826 (TNA ADM 106/2162, 6 June 1826).

13 TNA ADM 106/2166, 7 Oct 1828; ADM 106/2168, 18 May 1829. With the exception of Woolwich and Deptford terraces, all these survive. However, 10 of the 12 houses at Plymouth were destroyed in an air raid in 1941.

14 A plan of Deal Yard *c* 1840 marks an 'Admiral's Office' just outside the dockyard, probably once used by the Port Admiral (AdL Da 01 fol 33).

15 Baugh 1977, 2.

16 NMM ADM/BP/32a, 17 Feb 1812.

17 TNA ADM 106/2064, 9 Aug 1810; ADM 181/43, estimates 1832/3. The entry is noted as 'final payment'. In 1800 the *Vindictive* is shown moored alongside in the mast pond (TNA ADM 140/670).

18 TNA ADM 106/2156 pt 1, 6 Aug 1821, noted that no progress could be made with plans until a site had been selected; *see also* TNA ADM 106/2164, 30 May 1827 and 16 Aug 1827.

19 Taylor 1870, 171. By 1835 Taylor had 10 children.

20 Gwyn 2004, 54–61; Stranack 1990, 62–3.

21 Gwyn 2004, 31.Other housing is shown on an 1845 plan of Halifax yard (TNA ADM 174/362), but its small scale suggests piecemeal construction rather than a designed terrace.

22 Coad 1989, 348.

23 TNA ADM 106/2168, 1 Apr and 2 June 1829. The estimates for 1881/2 for Devonport provided baths for the officers' residences (TNA ADM 181/92).

24 TNA MPH 1/247.

25 The wall at the end of the Chatham gardens was probably reduced in height soon after it ceased to be the dockyard boundary here, when the boundary was extended in connection with the construction of Brunel's sawmill. It now seems likely that the existing garden gates were inserted then rather than earlier, as I had surmised in Coad 1989, 84. The Portsmouth terrace completed in 1719 is known as The Parade, or Long Row, to distinguish it from the later terrace of four houses known as Short Row. *See* Chapters 14–16 for residences in the ordnance yards, victualling yards and hospitals.

26 TNA ADM 140/1743. Montresor spent much of his military career as an engineer in the Mediterranean and North America (Latcham 2008).

27 For Halifax, *see* TNA ADM 174/362, dated to 1859. At Trincomalee the grounds extended to over 25 acres, only an acre less than the dockyard itself (TNA ADM 140/1484).
28 Coad 1989, 325.
29 NMM POR/A/6, 21 Sept 1719.
30 Quoted in Hall 1989, 61.
31 Hall and Lear 1992, 136.
32 Hall and Lear (1992, 133) cite Rosemary Sutcliffe's autobiography *Blue Remembered Hills*, where she recalls living in one of the Chatham terrace houses with their walled gardens.
33 To this was added a trellised extension, probably in the 1860s (Hall and Lear 1992, 144).
34 Hall 1989, 64; Hall and Lear 1992, 144. Other evidence suggesting keen horticultural interest is the survival of a small, glass, lead-lined plant case in the best surviving garden room.
35 TNA ADM 195/4 has an illustration *c* 1903.
36 TNA ME 1 fol 1 indicates a 'clerk in charge' of the dockyard; for Prince William, *see* Pocock 1991, 90.
37 Both the Admiralty Library and The National Archives have bound volumes of photographs of the overseas yards at the end of the 19th century. For Halifax *see* TNA ADM 174/36.
38 TNA ADM 195/4.
39 TNA ADM 1/362.
40 TNA ADM 140/1484; ADM 195/4.
41 Coad 1989, 81–4. The contemporary wall turrets along the dockyard wall at Chatham provided occasional cramped accommodation for, among others, model makers responsible for the 1774 dockyard model now at the NMM.
42 TNA ADM 106/2168, 27 Dec 1827.
43 No building accounts have been found for the porter's residence at Antigua; a building in this location first appears on Columbine's 1789 survey (NMM Com-01 fol 63). The two buildings at Kingston were most probably constructed during the War of 1812 with the United States and first appear on a dockyard plan of *c* 1840 (AdL Da 01 fol 9; *see also* Osborne and Swainson 1988, 60.
44 BL Lansdowne 847 fol 46, dated 1694; Coad 1989, 46.
45 *See* the Kip engraving of *c* 1700 (BL Add MS 9329 fol 180).
46 Coad 1989, 46. TNA ADM 140/7 is a yard plan of 1766 showing the location of the various offices at Chatham. The tap-house provided a more convivial and possibly more productive meeting place than the usually soulless and generally airless conference rooms in its modern successors
47 Coad 1989, 46, 154. For the linking building, *see* TNA ADM 140/532 pt 2. The later use is shown on a plan of *c* 1840 (AdL Da 01 fol 30) and on an 1849 plan (TNA Work 31 fol 302). During the refurbishment work of the former smithery in the late 1980s, English Heritage archaeologists found substantial remains from its industrial phases *in situ* beneath the ground floors.
48 Coad 1983, 386–7; TNA ADM 140/1484.
49 NMM POR/A/13, 21 Apr 1744. For a seamen's pay, *see* Rodger 1986, 124–37. Those seamen discharged before a ship ended her commission were given a 'ticket', only redeemable at the end of the commission.
50 NMM ADM/Q/3323, 28 Oct 1808. Pitch houses and 'glew rooms' – the latter usually constructed inside joiners' shops – had long been given simple brick vaults as a fire precaution. In 1799 the Navy Board turned down a proposal for a new room on the roof of the previous pay office to store ships' books prior to their transmission to London (NMM POR/G/1, 26 Jan 1799).
51 TNA ADM 106/2168, 2 Jan and 23 March 1829.
52 TNA ADM 106/1970, 26 June 1827.
53 TNA ADM 140/74 fol 3. The Chatham Chest was a benevolent fund established in 1590 by Sir Francis Drake, Sir John Hawkins and Lord Howard of Effingham. Seamen paid 6d a month into this from their pay for the benefit of wounded sailors and the widows of those killed in action. Despite seven different locks requiring the presence of seven keyholders, the chest was not immune to peculation. The original chest is now in the NMM. There is an elevation drawing of the Pay Office in TNA ADM 140/74 fol 3.
54 AdL Da 01 fol 28, plan of the yard *c* 1840, shows this arrangement.
55 Rodger 1997, 306–10; the author notes that 13 were serving in 1588. *See also* Harland 2003, 456–77.
56 TNA ADM 140/1321. Latham died at Minorca in 1713 (Conolly 1898, 118).
57 It is not known whether or not John Evelyn included a chapel in his 1666 design for a quadrangular naval hospital for 500 men at Chatham (*see* Harland 2003, 442–3).
58 *See* Saunders (2004, 140–8, 155–6) for a description of these fortifications.
59 NMM POR/A/2, 23 Feb 1703. Money was raised locally and the workmen had 2d a month deducted from their wages to endow a priest. Portsea was not to have its own church until 1753, the existing St George's, when an Act of Parliament was passed to create Portsea as a parish and 'for building a Chapel on the Common, in the parish of Portsea' (Clarke 1963, 218). *See* NMM ADM/B/130, 3 Aug 1767, for Plymouth chapel.
60 NMM ADM/B/180, 3 Aug 1767. The proposed design may be found with this letter.
61 For the Act of Parliament, *see* Clarke 1963, 224.
62 NMM CHA/E4, 4 Oct 1738.
63 Coad 1989, 69–70. The chapel apparently needed further extensive repairs by 1782, suggesting that the monies allocated the previous year had not been spent (NMM POR/A/30, 27 March 1782).
64 Pew rents were certainly being charged at the chapel in Plymouth Dockyard when it was proposed to add an extra aisle in 1767 (NMM ADM/B/180, 3 Aug 1767). For pew rents and the problems caused, *see* Clarke 1963, 22–31.
65 TNA ADM 106/1967, 23 Feb 1819; ADM 106/1969, 4 Apr 1825.
66 Haslar Hospital had St Luke's Chapel by 1756. This lies in the centre of the grounds and like the dockyard chapels is a plain rectangular 'preaching box' with a gallery. At Stonehouse the chapel formed part of the main administrative block.
67 In 1786 at St Giles's, Camberwell, a new south aisle was proposed 'to prevent the rising generation from assembling with Dessenting congregations', quoted in Clarke 1963, 25.
68 Langford 1989, 264–73; Morriss 1983, 99. This whole subject requires further research. It should not be assumed that all in authority in the navy were opposed to the rise of nonconformity. Charles Middleton, appointed Comptroller of the Navy in 1778, proved over a long career to be one of the most outstanding naval administrators and reformers, but was also 'narrow-minded, intolerant, priggish, and devoted to the novel and alarming doctrines of the Evangelical movement' (Rodger 2004, 373).
69 NMM POR/A32, 1 Dec 1784. On 23 Dec 1784 Marquand was ordered by the Navy Board to survey the existing building and the proposed new site. His designs for the new chapel were sent to the yard for their comments later that month. An incomplete set of original drawings is in TNA Work 41/389–399.
70 NMM POR/A32, 31 Jan, 20 May, 21 June and 28 Dec 1785, and 7 March 1786. The 1786 estimates allowed £600 for completing the chapel and £140 for demolishing its predecessor.
71 Coad 1989, 72. On 30 Oct 1805 Simon Goodrich approved Holl's drawings on behalf of 'the Inspector General of Naval Works [Bentham] absent on service' (TNA ADM 140/68).

72 *See* Oppenheim (1926, 359–60) for early complaints about Sheerness.
73 MacDougall 1990b, 213–14.
74 A plan of 1813 (TNA ADM 140/679) marks the well as 'new'.
75 The chapel is marked on TNA ADM 140/678, the outline modernisation plan agreed in June 1812. This was broadly based on one drawn up 2 years earlier and agreed by Bentham, a point noted with asperity by the Admiralty when Bentham strongly objected to the chapel's location (TNA ADM 106/3188, 14 Feb 1812). For Holl's plan and order for construction, *see* TNA ADM 106/2064, 13 July 1812. In Feb 1815, the garrison chapel was ordered to be demolished on account of its dangerous condition (TNA ADM 103/3188, 10 Feb 1815).
76 TNA ADM 106/2158 pt 1, 30 Apr 1824.
77 A plan of G L Taylor's chapel dated Jan 1826, with the modifications requested by the Navy Board, is in TNA ADM 140/851. TNA ADM 106/2161, 1 July 1826, notes the Board's concern about the size. *See* TNA ADM 106/2161, 25 May 1826, for the order to demolish the existing building. This was to start only after an alternative temporary chapel had been created in the basement of an existing ordnance storehouse (TNA ADM 106/2161, 19 June 1826).
78 TNA ADM 140/851; ADM 106/2162, 19 June 1826; ADM 106/2166, 15 Sept 1828.
79 At the time of writing, there is hope that a Trust may restore the building.
80 TNA ADM 140/465–67 are Taylor's surviving drawings. *See also* TNA ADM 181/39, 1829/30 estimates; TNA ADM 181/43, 1832/3 estimates (which include £2,000 as a 'final payment' for the chapel).
81 TNA ADM 181/46, 1835/6 estimates; ADM 1/3413, 7 July 1835.
82 Summerson 1969, 315–17. The commissioners built some 214 churches in urban areas with expanding populations.
83 Nelson and Oliver 1982, 159–61; Stranack 1990, 71–2.
84 AdL Vz 10 fol 75. Crewe (1993, 231) describes Knowles as 'an obsessive dockyard builder'.
85 TNA ADM 106/1983, 14 June 1822; an attached plan shows the arrangements.
86 *See* TNA ADM 174/379 for Simon's Town; ADM 140/1484 for Garden Island, Sydney, and Trincomalee.
87 TNA ADM 140/1282–92.
88 Scamp had arrived on the island in 1841 to oversee construction of his naval bakery and had been called in to help with the cathedral when structural failures became apparent. He was responsible for making structurally sound and then completing the half-built Anglican cathedral of St Paul that remains a conspicuous landmark in Valletta (Hughes 1969, 247; MacDougall 2007, 38). Hughes credits Scamp with a more fundamental and extensive redesign. He also made additions to the Protestant College at St Julian's Bay (Colvin 1995, 853).

8 Buildings and Engineering Works of the Steam Navy, 1836–1914

1 The history of Rosyth is well covered in Lavery 2007, 180–3.
2 The figures for the English yards come from TNA ADM 140/1484; for Deptford from TNA Work 41/595 and Cres 34–66; for Haulbowline from TNA ADM 174/398; and for Rosyth from AdL Vz 14 fol 144, plan *c* 1918, and from Lavery 2007, 201. In addition, by 1914 Portsmouth and Devonport each had a single 10-acre tidal basin. For the growth of commercial basins and docks in London from the late 18th century, *see* Skempton 1980 and 1983.
3 Buchanan 2004a; Smiles 1863, 291. Significantly, Nasmyth's most famous invention, the steam hammer, appears at the same time in the annual yard estimates, TNA ADM 181/56, for 1845/6. Every home yard except Deptford was to be equipped with one at a cost of £2,000 for a hammer and boiler. For other pile drivers, *see* Sargent 2008, 104.
4 Sargent (2008, 111) gives a detailed account of this method, noting that some of the columns reached 90ft in length.
5 Hunter (2005, 40–2) goes into considerable detail.
6 Riley 1985, 22, 25; Sargent 2008, 104; TNA ADM 181/99 fol 20. Sargent (2008, 112–13) gives valuable details of the excavation and construction methods, including the later use of Lidgerwood and Brothers cableways employed at the Keyham Extension.
7 Evans (2004, 195–9) summarises these dilemmas in considerably more detail than is possible here.
8 Admiralty papers are full of references to the problems of providing adequate docks and basins. The following references to Devonport are fairly typical: TNA ADM 1/5838, 6 Jan 1863, on inadequate size of No. 1 Dock and possible solutions; TNA ADM 116/464 details similar conundrums regarding the Keyham extension.
9 Riley 1985, 25, 26.
10 NMM ADM/BP/38b, 23 Sept 1818. At Sheerness, Rennie continued with Bentham's inverted masonry archway to anchor the two sides of the docks, setting this on piles. *See* TNA ADM 140/777 for an 1824 drawing of the Frigate Dock, later 4 Dock. Docks 1–3 were buried in the 1970s by the harbour board.
11 Sargent 2008, 101, 105–7.
12 Ibid.
13 Heads and entrances of docks have tended to be modified over the years and the pumping equipment upgraded. At the time of writing, the 854ft No. 1 Dock at Rosyth is having its 114ft-wide entrance enlarged to accommodate the Royal Navy's two new 65,000-ton aircraft carriers.
14 MacDougall 2009, 331. The Navy Board on their visit to Chatham on 30 Sept 1819 proposed that gates for Chatham and Sheerness docks should be put out as a single contract 'to induce the masters of the first respectability to offer tenders'. Cox and Cox (1999, 17) note that the Bowling Ironworks, who won the contract, 'had the reputation for producing cold blast iron of the very highest quality', an important consideration when strength and durability of dock gates were of paramount importance. The surviving pair of gates at Sheerness has the maker's nameplate of Bowling Ironworks and the date.
15 These were hefty pieces, and Sargent (2008, 94) reports a weight of 70 tons for the larger gates of Docks 1–3. These were infilled by the port authority in the 1970s. Sargent also identifies the surviving gates of the former frigate dock as the oldest iron dock gates in the world.
16 Sargent 2008, 96–7. Before Mitchell modified the caisson, it apparently took 1½ hours and 50 men at the pumps to empty it. Mitchell's timber caisson was replaced by the surviving wrought-iron caisson made by Easton and Anderson in 1868. The entrance to the wet dock at the dockyard at Suomenlinna in Finland still retains an early iron caisson, its bulbous cross-section akin to the profile of a submarine's hull.
17 Riley 1985, 15. The caisson to the entrance of the steam basin at Portsmouth was buried *in situ* when a new entrance was constructed in the early 1870s. It was revealed during road repairs in 1984.
18 This exclusive use of caissons in preference to gates was not without its critics. *See* TNA ADM 1/5604, 30 March 1850, for a report to Lord John Hay.
19 Sargent 2008, 99. *See* Chrimes *et al* (2008, 178) for a brief summary of Clarke's contribution to caisson and penstock design.
20 The same sequence of motive power was applied to the capstans installed in significant numbers around dry docks to help with the docking and undocking of warships.

21 A pump house adjacent to the solitary dry dock at Pembroke is shown on an 1832 yard plan, TNA ADM 140/429. Its size suggests that it could have contained a horse gin. TNA ADM 140/1484, a plan of *c* 1909 of the yard, shows no separate pump house, but it is possible that pumping equipment for this dock could have been installed in the No. 3 Ship Fitters Shop immediately adjacent.
22 This building does not appear in the annual estimates, but its construction may have been subsumed in the dry dock costs. Possibly significant is the entry for 1880/1 of £6,000 for 'culverts for draining docks', TNA ADM 181/91 annual estimates.
23 Evans 2004, 194.
24 Evans (2004, 194) notes that the original machinery was designed by the Rennies.
25 Traces of the original machinery still remain in the Block Mills, but electricity replaced steam here in 1911 (Coad 2005, 109). Docks 1 and 6 were apparently linked to this system at a much later date.
26 Evans 2004, 194–5. The author notes a drawing of the chimney signed in July 1874 by Pasley who held the post of Director of Engineering Works and Architecture at the Admiralty from 1873 to 1882.
27 The building does not appear even as a proposal on an 1877 plan of the dockyard (TNA Work 21/200), but first appears as a separate figure in the 1883/4 estimates when its total cost was projected to be £20,000 and £2,510 noted as 'already expended' (TNA ADM 181/94).
28 For details of the system, which proved to be notably reliable, *see* Evans 2004, 194–5.
29 TNA ADM 140/56 pt 2. Slip dimensions are taken from AdL Naval Estates plan Da 02.
30 *Africa* gained her place in the history books when in January 1912 Lieutenant Samson became the first navy pilot to fly from a warship when he took off in a Short S27 from a ramp on the fore deck of the battleship.
31 The proposed new steam basin at Portsmouth meant that the north-facing pair of slips had to be relocated adjacent to the three existing ones on the western side of this part of the yard. Monies were first allocated in the 1839/40 estimates for two new roofed slips at a total cost of £15,000. The 1842/3 estimates refer to three slips with roofs. By 1846/7, the last year the three slips appear in the estimates, the total cost had risen to £171,000; TNA ADM 181/50–57, ADM 140/1484 and Work 41/302. No. 5 Slip here was again extended in 1912. None of the Portsmouth slips survive. Evans (2004, pl 108c) shows Slips 1–3 in 1902. *See* Riley (1985, 20) for uses of the slips by 1900.
32 Slip dimensions for 1850 come from TNA ADM 140/189. The 'graving slip' on the north side of the Camber Channel, first shown on a dockyard redevelopment plan of *c* 1764 (TNA ADM 140/150) is not included in these five. It was originally known as a 'graving place'. In 1850 it had a length of 169ft and a maximum width of 62ft. It was filled in some years later.
33 *See* TNA ADM 140/489 for 1850; AdL for Devonport plan of 1912. At the time of writing, this remains the last survivor of the slips adapted to construct the battleships of the Dreadnought era.
34 TNA ADM 140/189. In the 1859 estimates (TNA ADM 181/70), £74,000 was allocated for 'lengthening slips 3, 4 and 5 by the stern, reconstructing the floors and raising the roofs'. There is some doubt if this programme was fully completed. The later slip dimensions come from TNA ADM 140/1484 fol 16 (1909–12) and an uncatalogued AdL plan of Devonport in 1900.
35 Slip locations and dimensions taken from TNA ADM 140/149, 140/153, 140/167 and 140/1484 and AdL Vz 14 fol 43. Slips 3,4 and 5 had monies inserted in the 1859/60 estimates for lengthening (TNA ADM 181/68).
36 TNA ADM 140/51, pts 1 and 3.
37 TNA ADM 140/63. The design for these was possibly by Captain Thomas Mould RE. G L Taylor's 1836 design for the new 3 Slip to replace 5 Dock at the yard used the floor of the dock as a base for the slip floor built on a series of diminishing brick arches. This turned out to be a disaster, and the whole slip had to be rebuilt in 1849, 'the old floor, which was of faulty construction, having given way' (TNA ADM 181/60, estimates 1849/50).
38 TNA ADM 140/55 shows an 1838 proposal to roof Slips 3 and 4 at Chatham; only 3 was proceeded with at this point.
39 Mornement and Holloway 2007, 10–12. Henry Palmer had previously worked for Thomas Telford. Unable to develop his new material, he sold the patent to Richard Walker who began its manufacture.
40 Mornement and Holloway 2007, 14–15. In 1837 a Commander Craufurd RN filed a patent (No. 7355) for using a thin coating of zinc to cover the iron sheet, and in 1841 this process was improved by Edward Morewood's patent No. 9055 that used tin to give a shinier finish.
41 The distance from centre to centre of standards across the slips was to be 82ft 6in and alongside the slips 13ft 4in (Evans 2004, 44).
42 The outline of the slip roofs appears on a number of yard plans, notably James's 1849 plan (TNA Work 41/302).
43 Two of these Deptford roofs survive, although modified for subsequent use as a cattle market and then further degraded when used for a newsprint warehouse.
44 TNA ADM 181/55–57, annual estimates 1844/5–1846/7. *See* NMM CHA/H/67, 6 Sept 1847, for the contract for 4–6 Slips at Chatham. These may not have been complete before Baker also started work roofing 1 and 2 Slips at Pembroke, which appear in the estimates for that yard between 1848 and 1850 at a total cost of £30,000 (TNA ADM 181/59–60 annual estimates).
45 This is discussed in some detail in Sutherland 1997, 117–20. It is not known how far the surviving Chatham slip roofs differed in detail from the demolished ones at Pembroke and Portsmouth.
46 NMM CHA/J/2, 14 Jan 1843.
47 *See* Evans (2004, 47–9, 123) for a detailed account of foundation problems here. Evans also draws attention to the existence of roof drawings signed by Baker alone and Baker and Mould jointly.
48 Doubts about the stability of 6 Slip roof caused by the partial subsidence of the standards in 1852 gave urgency to the construction of 7 Slip roof so that it could act as a support and buttress (Evans 2004, 123).
49 Sutherland 1997, 137. Attributing the design of a building or engineering work to a single individual becomes less meaningful in an inverse ratio to the scale and complexity of the structure concerned. Many of the drawings for 7 Slip are signed by Greene, whose guidance and approval as Director would have been needed, but significant inputs would have come from the master shipwrights, who had to use the building, and probably also from Rivers, the clerk of works, who was to oversee its construction.
50 Evans (2004, 123) cites St Peter's Shipyard at Newcastle. I am grateful to Keith Falconer for drawing my attention to the use of overhead travelling cranes in the Swindon locomotive works.
51 TNA ADM 181/68, estimates for Woolwich, records 'Iron roof over Slip 5 with traveller, £12,719'.
52 In 1857–8 Grissell won contracts to supply all the ironwork for the Royal Opera House and the adjacent Floral Hall in London (Saint 2007, 96–9). The success of the travelling cranes above 7 Slip led to the installation of brackets and girders to carry travelling cranes in 4–6 Slips in 1863 (Saint 2007, 125).
53 *See* Chapter 2 for unrealised expansion plan of 1904.

54 5 and 6 Slips were floored over and used as workshops for 7 Slip *c* 1907.

55 Birse 2004. Cowper was a talented engineer at Fox Henderson, supervising the preparation of the contract drawings for the buildings of the Great Exhibition of 1851. After he set up his own consultancy business that year, he designed the 211ft-span metal roof for the original Birmingham New Street Station, completed in 1854.

56 Weiler 1987, 467.

57 Evans (2004, 66–8) gives a detailed description of the construction of this building.

58 It is still marked as a brass foundry on the 1909 plan of the dockyard; on its west side is the coppersmiths' shop (TNA ADM 140/1484).

59 Vetch 2004c. The Admiralty may well have been relieved to see him go as his experience in the Ordnance Survey had given him little experience in budget management, resulting in substantial additional costs for the steam factory (Evans 2004, 67). James ended his career as Director-General of the Ordnance Survey from 1854 to 1875.

60 Evans (2004, 115) favours Greene, but it is at least possible that James's temporary iron-framed and corrugated iron-clad smithery led him to explore the possibilities of a permanent and grander structure using these materials and that Greene developed this further; a number of drawings signed by Greene also survive.

61 Evans (2004, 134–6) gives a detailed description of this building and its equipment. *See also* Coad 1983, 361. A Hercules was a heavy iron weight attached to a stout rope threaded over a pulley hung on a beam. The weight was raised by a team of men on the opposite end of the rope. The iron weight then fell by gravity. It was used in metal-working shops and smitheries for helping to forge large pieces of ironwork, such as anchors, and was also used to drive in piling. It was very labour intensive and was largely superseded by Nasmyth's steam hammer in the 1840s.

62 This was estimated to cost £20,000, including equipment. It first appears in the 1855/6 estimates; by the 1857/8 estimates – the last year it features in these – £7,828 is recorded as already expended (TNA ADM 181/66–68).

63 Evans 2004, 134–7.

64 £30,000, the estimated total cost, was inserted in the 1856/7 estimates (TNA ADM 181/67). What the inhabitants of the officers' terrace thought of this smoky and noisy new neighbour is not recorded.

65 Evans 2004, 118–19. Tenders had also been sought from Baker and Son and Rigbys (NMM POR/P62, 29 Aug 1856). Riley (1985, 21) dates the extension to 1873. The foundry ceased to operate in the 1970s and has recently been carefully converted to office use.

66 Evans (2004, 71–5, 92–105) provides a very thorough and detailed account of the construction and equipping of the Quadrangle.

67 MacDougall (2009, 365–9) lists ships built at Chatham from 1815 to 1865; MacDougall (1982) lists Chatham ships since 1860.

68 TNA ADM 181/52–54, estimates 1841–4.

69 NMM CHA/C/2, 18 Oct 1855. The gable ends of Holl's building were reconstructed and heightened in the late 1880s.

70 Evans (2004, 56) suggests that the building may have been designed by Rigby's rather than by John Fincham, the master shipwright. Firm evidence is lacking.

71 NMM CHA/H/53, 10 Apr 1844; CHA/H/57, 20 March 1845. The original drawings for this building are in TNA ADM 140/109.

72 Evans 2004, 58.

73 *See* MacDougall (2009, 147) for a scathing criticism of the arrangements of 2 Smithery, written by William Scamp in 1857.

74 Clearly shown on an unreferenced 1879 plan of the yard held by the Chatham Historic Dockyard Trust.

75 MacDougall 2009, 98–9, 155–9. An indication of the urgency of the project is reflected in its absence from the annual estimates.

76 TNA ADM 140/1356.

77 TNA ADM 181/94. The foundry was estimated to cost £15,000. No figure was included for the coppersmiths' shop. Both buildings were demolished after the closure of the naval base.

78 Preston and Major 2007, 33.

79 *See* Hamilton (2005, 251) for a contemporary report on the difficulties of maintaining these gunboats in reserve.

80 TNA ADM 1/5674. The other three sites were at Chatham, the Royal William Victualling Yard, Stonehouse, and at Keyham Yard.

81 TNA ADM 181/68. Estimates for 1857/8 record that 'The sum of £30,000 was authorised by Treasury letter of 15th September 1856 to be expended in the year 1856–57 and charged against the general surplus of the Vote No 11 for the year'. Hamilton (2005, 63) indicates that eight gunboats had been hauled up by mid-Jan 1857.

82 This was later resited and has since been destroyed. The site of the original patent slip remains largely intact.

83 In July 1857 it was felt that the Captain of the Steam Reserve had so many responsibilities that the Commander-in-Chief suggested to the Admiralty that the gunboats at Haslar might be put in the charge of the Captain Superintendent of Haslar Hospital who, fortuitously, 'is, as their Lordships are aware, a very active and experienced Steam Officer' (Hamilton 2005, 251). The Captain Superintendent was Captain Sir Sidney Colpoys Dacres.

84 A plan of the establishment in 1861 is in TNA ADM 1/5764. TNA MFQ 1/58 is an 1860 plan of the northern guardhouse showing it as police barracks with the proposed dormitory subdivisions. Further drawings (a number signed by Greene) are in the NMR at Swindon, especially nos NMR 95-0694, 08505 and 06517.

85 TNA ADM 1/5764. The plan is dated 19 June 1861 and signed by John Murray.

86 It is not known whether the yard was rented out. Two of these sheds were located next to 8 and 9 Docks for use as ironworking sheds (Hamilton 2005, 63). The 1871/2 estimates (TNA ADM 181/82) allowed a further £1,550 for 're-erecting sheds from Haslar over timber' in the dockyard.

87 TNA ADM 181/94.

88 In the Second World War the yard was closely associated with the adjacent HMS *Hornet*, the RN base for small attack craft. After the Second World War it became part of the Admiralty Small Craft Experimental Establishment based at Haslar, formed out of three wartime directorates (Miscellaneous Weapons Development, Combined Operations Material and Coastal Forces Material), and was responsible for sea trials and development of coastal attack craft and their equipment. It survived the closure of HMS *Hornet* in 1957. Its records, which include extracts from the German Hydrofoil Committee reports 1941–5, are in TNA ADM 250/80 and 81.

89 Weiler 1987, 463.

90 Bentham was also responsible for the design and construction of the surviving chain cable store there (Evans 2004, 51–3).

91 TNA ADM 181/53. There was a further £3,000 for water pipes and the cost of their installation, suggesting either an extension of the existing main or its renewal.

92 TNA ADM 140/529, dated Nov 1840.

93 TNA ADM 140/530 and 543–549 are all early designs for a two-storey building.

94 Such girders were to gain notoriety in 1847 after the collapse of a railway bridge over the River Dee.

95 There is some uncertainty about precise construction dates. Riley (1985, 16) gives 1844 for its completion. Evans (2004, 53) notes 'the first surviving drawings ... date from the beginning of 1845'. This could imply that Beatson had left for Woolwich before completion of the boathouse.
96 MacDougall 2009, 90.
97 Evans 2004, 127; Richards 1958, 65. A very comprehensive set of original drawings is in TNA ADM 140/1328–47. It has been standing empty for many years, its future something of a cause for concern.
98 One immediate effect was to raise costs. In 1853 a proposed new sawmill at Pembroke to replace one built only some 10 years earlier at an estimated cost of £3,500 and described as 'quite unequal to the work of the yard' was estimated to cost £7,000. By 1856 this had been revised to £16,000 'by an additional storey for the workshop and by fire-proof construction' (TNA ADM 181/51, 65 and 67 estimates). *See* Evans (2004, 131–4) for a detailed account of the buildings and new machinery.
99 A workshop and store for treenails. It first appears on a dockyard plan of 1814, with a much smaller joiners' shop on its west side (TNA ADM 140/21).
100 The original Napoleonic Wars treenail workshop was much larger than the adjacent joiners' shop and is indicative of the importance of the treenail makers to a major warship-building yard. Detailed documentary references for this building have not so far been found. This account is largely based on a study of the building and on the annual estimates, TNA ADM 181/58, 65 and 73. It is possible that the £7,000 allocated for the joiners' shop in 1847/8 may have included a steam engine, but normally this would have been a separate item in the estimates.
101 Archibald (1971, 13–26) gives a succinct account of the early development of these warships.
102 Evans 2004, 199; TNA ADM 181/98, 1888/9 estimates, allows an unspecified sum of 'Stores, workshops etc for gun mounting'. The Portsmouth building suffered war damage. Chatham was to have a rather smaller gun-mounting workshop and store, now demolished, near 2 Basin (TNA ADM 140/1484).
103 TNA ADM 181/96, annual estimates 1886/7. The torpedo range still survives at the north end of Portsmouth Harbour. Ripley (1982) provides a short history.
104 Part of this funding came from the Works Loan Act of 1903.
105 Riley 1985, 27.
106 TNA ADM 181/158. Considerable sums were also earmarked for re-equipping naval factories with modern machinery.
107 TNA ADM 181/99. £713,000 was allocated 'to commence the large programme of installations of electric light and power in naval establishments on shore'. These included ordnance yards, victualling yards and naval hospitals.
108 Riley 1985, 27.

9 Growth of Empire: The Overseas Bases of the Sailing Navy, 1700–1835

1 After Parliament in 1652 had resolved to have a permanent naval presence in the Straits of Gibraltar, this suggestion surfaced again but was rejected by Cromwell on the grounds that the harbour was inadequate and the Rock would be difficult to defend (Donaldson 2002, 425–6).
2 Coad 1989, 306.
3 In 1620 Mansell had visited Port Mahon and seems to have been the first naval officer to have appreciated its magnificent natural harbour and convenient location for operations in the western Mediterranean (Donaldson 2002, 425–6).
4 Harland 2003, 86, 98, 136–42.
5 Coad 1989, 346; Wadia 1957, 39–40.
6 Mayes (1972, 7) reckons that 60% of the 'wickedest city on earth' slid into the sea.
7 Coad 1989, 355. The virtues of English Harbour had first been extolled by two naval captains in 1725.
8 Wadia 1957, 158.
9 Gwyn 1973, 50. Commodore Warren in a letter from English Harbour dated 7 Feb 1744/5 noted that 'There was formerly a dry dock there [Boston] fit to receive a ship of 50 guns. I am persuaded there might be one made for one of 60 or more.'
10 Gwyn 2004, 6; Malcomson 2001, 8.
11 Syrett (2004, 42–50) gives a good account of these sort of peacetime operations in the mid-century.
12 Hattendorf *et al* 1993, 381–4. In January 1757 there were 72 vessels and 22,381 sailors based at the home yards; the figures for the following July are 55 vessels and 17,981 sailors. The most significant rise in numbers, reflecting both the climate and the political situation, can be seen in the Plantation figures where 30 ships and 7,645 men were deployed in the winter, rising to 63 ships and 18,295 men the following summer.
13 In the 1814 Treaty of Ghent following the War of 1812, the Americans recognised the legitimacy of British North America and the establishment of the frontier along the 49th parallel west to the Rockies.
14 Malcomson 2001, 112.
15 NMM ADM/BP/34b, 28 Aug 1814. The Admiralty order to move to Simon's Town was dated 10 Dec 1812, but the move had still not been completed 6 years later (NMM ADM/BP/38b, 26 Sept and 12 Dec 1818).
16 Facilities were not necessarily very satisfactory. An 1814 report noted that the stores were kept in 'one very bad loft' in the 'centre of a Portuguese Oil Manufactory' 5 miles from the town on the opposite side of the river (TNA ADM 106/3214, 25 Apr 1814).
17 The variable quality of record keeping was compounded by the loss of material when the overseas bases were closed. 'Much [has been] ... torn up which would now be of great interest', wrote an officer of HMS *Canada*, recording the closure of Antigua dockyard in June 1889. Tropical climates, mould and insects proved to be even more effective weeders of records, so most overseas bases are much less fully documented compared to home yards.
18 NMM ADM BP/34b, 14 Dec 1814, contains a list of officers and numbers then employed in the overseas yards. *See* Chapter 12 for the Commissioner's House at Bermuda. Quebec was chosen as the headquarters for a commissioner, as earlier that year it had been decided to establish a depot there to supply the navy on the Great Lakes (NMM ADM/BP/34a, 27 Jan 1814).
19 TNA ADM 106/3216, 5 July 1814. The commissioner noted that if he had asked the engineers, who would have been East India Company rather than Royal Engineers, at the Presidency to do this work, the cost would have been double.
20 Crewe 1993, 228.
21 Gwyn (2004, 6–10) gives a detailed account of the initial establishment of the yard. For the impact on the town, *see* Raddall 1993, 54. This author gives a detailed account of the history of Halifax.
22 TNA ADM 106/839, 23 March 1733. TNA ADM 106/3029, 6 Dec 1806, records that the navy still owned the land and buildings, though long abandoned.
23 NMM ADM/BP/50a, 5 Sept 1829; Malcomson 2001, 138–40. Nothing came of the arsenal, a proposed that was late in the day, as the Americans had closed their naval base on the Lakes in 1825.
24 Coad 1989, 312; Crewe 1992, 228.
25 TNA ADM 1/3503, 11 July 1838. The hospital was to hold 20 patients and 4 officers and included a surgeon's quarters, sergeants' room and dispensary, a kitchen and dead house. An extra ward for 20 was to be added if needed. This is probably to be identified with the naval hospital on the outskirts of Georgetown.
26 Navy Board to Admiralty Secretary, 19 Sept 1730; Baugh 1977, 356.

27 29 Jan 1730, quoted in Baugh 1977, 357.
28 TNA ADM 106/3216, 14 June 1813.
29 TNA ADM 106/3216, 20 Sept and 2 Oct 1812, 14 June 1813. The Bombay stores as well as some from Madras are noted in the AdL Admiralty Terriers, Ceylon. Curiously there is no capstan house shown on an 1840 plan of the yard (AdL Plans of Naval Establishments 1840, Da 01).
30 AdL Admiralty Terriers, Ceylon. This dates the completion of the purchase by the Admiralty to 17 Jan 1814.
31 *Navy and Army Illustrated* 4 Feb 1899, p 482.
32 Perhaps unsurprisingly the house does not appear to feature in the sparse records. It seems more probable that it was purchased from some local nabob rather than being built, which would have attracted more notice in London. It must have remained the envy of every other naval storekeeper
33 Schurman 2000, 113. *See* Chapter 10. It remains a naval base but access is not easy.
34 NMM T/1/154, 1 Apr 1711; T/1/151, 12 Aug 1712.
35 Gwyn 2004, 8–9. A flood of immigrants from New England to Halifax and Nova Scotia had swiftly followed the French defeats at Louisbourg and Quebec, doubtless adding to the pool of skilled labour (Raddall 1993, 61–2).
36 TNA ADM 106/2021, 27 June 1800. The wily Boschetti, in his dual role as architect and builder, seems to have exploited a degree of ignorance and confusion between the Navy Board and Victualling Board and raised his original estimate from £22,053 5s 2d to £43,078 16s 10d, and possibly to £62,103 3s 4d (Coad 1989, 322–3).
37 NMM ADM/BP/38a, 20 July 1818; TNA ADM 110/1996, undated memorandum, probably July 1831.
38 Baugh 1977, 349, 361.
39 Baugh 1977, 372.
40 Weiler 1987, 416–17.
41 AdL Misc Foreign Property Letting Book 1 records the renting of three small properties on St Helena in 1816. Gosse (1938) is still the best general history of the island.
42 This is shown on Brandreth's 1829 survey (TNA MR1/1771).
43 TNA ADM 109/93. The letter from the 'Victualling Depot, Island of Ascension' is dated 14 Dec 1827 and includes a sketch of the new building.
44 TNA ADM 109/93. On 23 Oct 1822 they were requested to send out carrot, turnip, radish, lettuce, leek, parsley, beetroot, onion, cabbage, mustard, cucumber and broccoli seeds. Trees and shrubs were also imported; TNA ADM 1/5775, 9 March 1861, records the Comptroller of Victualling informing the Admiralty of the safe arrival of 50 orange trees from Lisbon.
45 TNA ADM 1/5775, 15 Feb and 16 Nov 1829. By then, a turtle pond had been constructed so as to have a ready supply for eating or bartering.
46 TNA ADM 109/93, 9 Dec 1828. Brandreth arrived back at Portsmouth on 7 Sept 1829. The plans and drawings accompanying his subsequent report of 10 Nov 1829 are in TNA MR 1/1771. A series of letters in TNA ADM 114/46, written by Brandreth in England and on his later return to Ascension, records the implementation of many of his recommendations. These were highly praised by the senior officer resident on the island in a letter of 26 June 1831 (TNA ADM 109/93).
47 These are illustrated in TNA MR 1/771. None survive. Brandreth's three proposed Martello Towers (TNA MR 1/771 fol 10) were each armed with two guns with carriages that traversed on cranked links to a central pivot, possibly a unique design for this type of tower.
48 TNA ADM 114/46. The cast-iron tanks, and possibly the pipes, were supplied by the Gospel Oak Ironworks near Birmingham. The specification drawn up by Brandreth included 8,000ft of ¾in pipe and 20,000ft of 5/8in pipe. These were also tendered for by the firm of Baily in High Holborn, London, on 15 Dec 1829. *See also* Clements 1999, 151.
49 Rees 2009, 308.
50 Hunter 2006, 284–6.

10 Heyday of Empire: The Overseas Bases, 1835–1914

1 Schurman 2000, 5. The colonies were generally considered of secondary importance, with a feeling in some political circles that colonial self-government logically should be responsible for colonial self-defence, a debate outside the scope of this book.
2 Preston and Major 2007, 14.
3 *Navy and Army Illustrated* 8 Dec 1900, quoted in Hughes 1981, 172.
4 In Apr 1812 the purchase of storehouses was authorised at Madras, but in 1816 it was ordered that 'the rope-walk and buildings of every description' should be disposed of to the highest bidder (TNA ADM 106/3216, 8 Jan 1816). Rear-Admiral William Drury, when flag officer on the East Indies station, had first suggested a move from Madras to Trincomalee. After visiting the island, Commissioner Peter Puget produced a report along with three alternative plans for a base at Trincomalee (TNA ADM 1/3441, 3 Oct 1811). *See also* TNA ADM 106/3216, 20 Sept and 2 Oct 1812, 10 June 1813, 8 Jan 1816.
5 Harland 1985, 6. This book gives a succinct history of the naval base here.
6 Martin and Tanner (1988) give the early background.
7 Jeremy 2005, 24–5.
8 AdL Terriers, Auckland. Land for the naval depot was originally acquired under the 1858 Waste Land Act.
9 The first two of four second-class torpedo boats for harbour protection had arrived from England in 1887, a spur to providing shore facilities.
10 TNA ADM 1/266, 27 Feb 1839, 17 June 1840, 27 July 1843. The engineer appointed in 1839 was serving as the First Engineer on HMS *Spitfire*, a wooden paddle vessel subsequently wrecked near Jamaica.
11 Bermuda Maritime Museum Misc Papers, letter dated 27 Oct 1852.
12 Hattendorf *et al* 1993, 596. Memorandum by Colonel Sir William Jervois on the defence of colonial bases, 1 Jan 1875.
13 Schurman 2000, 159. AdL Admiralty Terriers, Misc Foreign Property Letting Book 1 (Esquimalt).
14 TNA ADM 116/744, '1879 Report on the Defence of British Columbia' by Lt Col T Bland Strange RA, Dominion Inspector of Artillery. *See also* Schurman 2000, 103–15.
15 TNA ADM 181/91, Appendix 3, subhead C Coal, p 68.
16 TNA ADM 116/744, 12 May 1887.
17 Cardwell was Secretary of War 1868–74.
18 Hattendorf *et al* 1993, 595.
19 As late as 1905 the impact of the Panama Canal on the strategic importance of English Harbour and Port Royal was a factor in favour of retaining them (AdL Misc Foreign Property Letting Book 1).
20 Schurman 2000, 14. The Duke of Cambridge, Commander-in-Chief of the army 1856–95 and a fierce opponent of the Cardwell reforms, favoured the addition of Quebec, Kingston (Canada) and Mauritius to the list.
21 TNA ADM 116/744, 25 Nov 1889. The Admiralty had its own plans to counter these commerce raiders. In 1889 the Canadian Pacific Railway Company ordered three steamers for their Pacific service from Victoria, as the Governor-General noted: 'The steamers are built under an arrangement by Imperial authorities by which they may be used as cruisers in time of war'.
22 Hattendorf *et al* 1993, 692–3.
23 Hattendorf *et al* 1993,754. These were all

small gunboats of less than 1,000 tons, capable of no more than 13 knots. In the same memo dated 25 Feb 1902 to Lord Selborne, First Lord of the Admiralty, Fisher forecast the closure of Esquimalt, 'which cannot be held in case of war with the United States', and the abolition of the Pacific squadron, 'of what use then is a Pacific squadron? And even if reduced to say a single vessel – of what use is that vessel?'

24 For Hong Kong see Harland 1985, 14–15. These were the Lamont and Hope dry docks. TNA ADM 116/536 is a world-wide list compiled by the Admiralty of dry docks in use in 1899. This gives dimensions.

25 Stranack 1990, 56–7. Stranack credits the utility of this second dock, demonstrated by its lifting of the hull-damaged 17,500-ton HMS *Dominion,* in persuading Admiral Fisher not to close the base but to reduce it to care and maintenance.

26 Hattendorf *et al* 1993, 604.

27 Jeremy 2005, 7–12. The estimated cost was for using convict labour. It was calculated that the work would require 100 convicts for 470 days. As the work took the best part of 10 years, there is reason to believe that costs overran. Fitzroy Dock was to be extended twice.

28 TNA ADM 181/72 and 74 estimates.

29 TNA ADM 1/6015, 17 Apr 1867.

30 Nelson and Oliver (1982, 48–55) give the most detailed account of the construction of the Esquimalt dry dock.

31 Jeremy 2005, 13–15.

32 TNA ADM 116/993, 1905 Admiralty report on Canadian yards. TNA ADM 116/993, report on yards at Halifax and Esquimalt.

33 AdL Admiralty Terriers, Misc Foreign Property Letting Book 1; TNA ADM 140/1484 fol 83, uncatalogued site plan *c* 1900.

34 AdL Admiralty Terriers, Misc Foreign Property Letting Book 1; this terrier includes a paper detailing expenditure on the dry dock up to 1948, when Ceylon became independent.

35 AdL uncatalogued plan of Halifax with annotations.

36 AdL Admiralty Terriers, Misc Foreign Property Letting Book 1 (Jamaica) fol 6.

37 TNA ADM 116/993–4.

38 Cost was an ever-present concern to the Admiralty and a significant element in the annual expenditure. In 1878/9, as a fairly typical example, steam vessels on the home stations consumed coal to the value of £52,545, while those on the foreign stations burnt through coal costing £113,963 (TNA ADM 181/90).

39 In the 1870s replacement of low-pressure rectangular shell boilers by the cylindrical Scotch fire-tube boilers and then a decade later the introduction of water-tube boilers raised steam pressures from 20lb to 30lb per sq in eventually to around 250lb, which further improved economy.

40 Rabson and O'Donoghue 1988, 19–20. Harcourt (2006, 1) makes the point that the early steamship companies, notably P&O, were only able to develop with the aid of government mail and troop contracts.

41 TNA ADM 1/5521, 28 Feb 1841. Grant was only one of a number of entrepreneurs hoping to convince the Admiralty of the superiority of their fuels.

42 Admiral Napier was appointed to command the Baltic fleet in February 1854.

43 Lambert 1984, 61–3.

44 TNA ADM 181/92, annual estimates 1881/2, Appendix 3, p 69. This gives some details of the types of coal, but less is said on patent fuels. Quinn (2007) gives a good account of experiments to improve boiler combustion efficiency and to develop and produce patent fuel for the merchant service.

45 Schurman 2000, 29–30, 48.

46 TNA ADM 181/92, annual estimates 1881/2, Appendix 3, 69. Even so, 4 to 6 months' stock was considered prudent at both bases.

47 The Third Report of the 'Royal Commission to enquire into the defence of British possessions and commerce abroad' (extract in Hattendorf *et al* 1993, 602). *See also* Schurman 2000, 86. In 1884 the Government announced that £976,760 would be allocated to fortify the first-class coaling stations at Aden, Trincomalee, Colombo, Singapore, Hong Kong, Cape of Good Hope, Mauritius, Jamaica and St Lucia. A further £178,500 was allocated to protect second-class stations (Schurman 2000, 136).

48 Schurman 2000, 152, 157. Schurman gives a detailed account for the period 1868–87, which is beyond the scope of this book

49 Tracy 1997, 186. Such battle-cruisers were seen to have an imperial role.

50 TNA ADM 140/1198, report by John Anderson, clerk of works, Bermuda, dated 15 June 1853.

51 TNA ADM 1/3452, 21 Apr 1838; TNA MF 1/6. In the 1860s two other small buildings were similarly converted. In comparison, when coaling facilities were first proposed for Portsmouth in the early 1840s, a site capable of holding between 10,000 and 20,000 tons was considered necessary (Evans 2004, 170).

52 TNA ADM 174/379; AdL Misc Foreign Property Letting Book 1.

53 TNA ADM 174/361; ADM 140/1484 fol 72. By 1905 Esquimalt's storage capacity had been increased to 10,000 tons.

54 TNA ADM 174/363; ADM 140/1484 fol 62 shows that by 1909 the coaling facilities had been relocated and the former site was used for 'naval general stores, machinery and shell stores'.

55 The navy devoted a great deal of time to tracking down sources of coal and analysing the different types. TNA ADM 181/92, annual estimates 1881/2, Appendix 3, contains a long report on the various qualities of what were described as 'native coals', and it is clear that very considerable efforts were devoted to searching out local supplies wherever the navy was operating.

56 Evans 2004, 177–80.

57 TNA ADM 1/5838, 5 Feb 1863.

58 AdL Misc Foreign Property Letting Book 1.

59 Devaux 1975, 2–3. The works were completed in 1890 at a cost of £100,000.

60 TNA WO 78/5429. This set of plans details the protective shore batteries for these establishments. Aden had originally been acquired by the East India Company in 1838 to use as a base to quell pirate attacks. Its importance as a coaling and watering station was immeasurably increased by the opening of the Suez Canal 30 years later. Mauritius included a patent fuel depot; by 1914 the Admiralty was scaling back facilities here and returned them to the Mauritius authorities in 1923 (AdL Misc Foreign Property Letting Book 2).

61 AdL Misc Foreign Property Letting Book 1. The buildings were later handed to the government of Southern Nigeria. At Apapa Wharf, some of the coal was stored in the hulk *Diana.*

62 AdL Misc Foreign Property Letting Book 1.

63 Ibid. The purpose of this purchase is not known. It was described as covered in dense scrub in 1903 and was never developed.

64 Ibid. It is not known whether respect for the herons was a factor in not developing Vuo. The island is now a protected nature reserve.

65 Ibid. In 1929 the shed was described as 'long demolished'.

66 Ibid. The Admiralty held the land until 1959, although the original leases were apparently terminated in 1918.

67 Ibid, letter of 10 Sept 1902. The Board of Admiralty meeting on 4 Feb 1903 decided to keep the property on the curious reasoning that 'although it may not be of much use, it costs nothing to retain'. The property was returned in 1926. The island was also known as Admiralty Island.

68 AdL Misc Foreign Property Letting Book 1. The operational dates of these Japanese depots have yet to be established.
69 AdL uncatalogued plan of 1905. TNA ADM 140/1484 fol 81 *c* 1909 shows what appear to be 19 coal stores. At this time the actual dockyard at Kowloon extended to only 5 acres.
70 Schurman 2000, 29.
71 AdL Misc Foreign Property Letting Book 1 contains details of the complicated land transactions here from the 1860s onwards.
72 *The Times* 3 Apr 1935. Henjam (Hanjam, Hengam) Island had been the location of a cable station base for the Indo-European Telegraph since Dec 1868.

11 The Mediterranean Bases: Buildings and Engineering Works, 1700–1914

1 For this reason, Trincomalee, Singapore, Hong Kong and Devonport NZ are omitted but have passing mention elsewhere in this book.
2 Coad (1989, 315–27) gives a more detailed account of the early dockyard buildings.
3 TNA ADM 140/1262.
4 AdL Portfolio B19 fol 30 contains Scamp's 1842 sketch drawings of Gibraltar.
5 TNA ADM 1/5715, 11 Apr 1859, is a valuable report detailing improvements here. Many of the buildings constructed then seem to have been timber framed (MacDougall 2007, 35).
6 TNA ADM 181/62, 1851/2 estimates. The cost was put at £25,000; the following year £18,500 was allowed 'to complete the work'. However, the project reappears in the estimates into the late 1870s. *See* TNA ADM 1/5697 pt 1, 30 July 1858, for earlier problems with construction work on the mole.
7 TNA ADM 181/88, 1877/8 estimates, indicates that at least one steam hammer furnace already existed.
8 Hattendorf *et al* (1993, 675) gives an extract from the 'Statement of the First Lord of the Admiralty explanatory of the Navy Estimates for 1894–95'. These estimates increased the length of the mole to 3,700ft for better protection against torpedo attack and to provide space for additional coaling facilities. Black (2006) gives useful background information.
9 TNA ADM 140/1484 fol 61.
10 TNA ADM 181/99.
11 Coad (1989, 318–24) describes both in some detail.
12 TNA ADM 106/3213, 16 June 1802; ADM 106/2045, 5 Aug 1811.
13 Baker died at Port Mahon on 10 Nov 1716 aged 56. His monument at Westminster Abbey describes him as 'a brave, judicious and experienced officer, a sincere friend, and a true lover of his country'.
14 This included a bakehouse, described as 'in tolerable good condition' in 1763 (TNA ADM 1/84, 4 June 1763). An undated plan and elevation in AdL B20 appear to show this building.
15 TNA ADM 1/84, 6 June 1763. The 'rope house' probably refers to a cordage store. TNA ADM 140/1310 dated 1745 is a design for a Ropemaker's House, but the cordage was manufactured in an open-air ropewalk. This survey was undertaken to assess the neglect and damage to the buildings during the French occupation. In 1763 Montresor was to design and oversee the construction of the huge and partly surviving powder depot at Purfleet on the Thames (Latcham 2008).
16 NMM ADM/B/175, 1 Oct 1764; TNA ADM 1/385, 5 March 1767. I previously attributed authorship of this project entirely to Marsh (Coad 1989, 331). Although credited in 1767 by Commodore Spry with 'carrying out this work with great diligence, judgement and frugality', it is more likely that Marsh had help with the plans from the military engineer in charge of repairing the island's defences.
17 TNA ADM 1/385, 29 Nov 1763.
18 The influence of British carpenters and joiners is evident in the architecture of much of the town of Mahon, where sash windows are common.
19 Nicolas 1845, 244. The account of Malta before 1850 in this chapter is a modified, updated and shortened version of Coad 1989, 341–54.
20 *See* MacDougall (1990) for the early history of this base under British control. The elaborate defences of the island are well covered by Hughes (1969 and 1981) and Spiteri (1996). For the Ionian Islands under British protection, *see* Pratt 1978. For Corfu, *see* Hughes (1981, 104–18) for its fortifications.
21 TNA ADM 106/3210; Wood 2008, 209.
22 The 1802 Treaty of Amiens stipulated that Britain should hand the island back to the Order of St John
23 TNA ADM 106/2044, 11 July 1809. Wood (2008, 209) and MacDougall (1990, 209) give detailed accounts of the construction of the ropery.
24 TNA ADM 106/2046, 28 Aug 1815.
25 A double dock had been proposed in 1795 at English Harbour, but nothing had come of the suggestion (TNA ADM 140/1191).
26 Brown had favoured a different location (MacDougall 1990a, 210). There is some confusion in the records over the choice of site.
27 TNA ADM 106/2044, 4 Sept 1810; TNA ADM 106/2045, 1 Nov 1811; NMM ADM/BP/30b, 29 Nov 1810.
28 Almost certainly Samuel Trevor Dickens, later Lieutenant-General, KCH (Conolly 1898, 11).
29 *See* TNA ADM 106/3210, 6 March 1813; TNA ADM 106/2046, 30 June 1816; TNA ADM 140/1484 fol 63; AdL Da 01 Plans of Naval Establishments *c* 1840.
30 This was in contrast to Ireland Island, Bermuda, which suffered from a labour shortage (*see* Chapter 17).
31 Coad 1989, 347–8.
32 The Villa Portelli owed its bright pink exterior in its final years as official naval residence to the last flag officer, Rear-Admiral Templeton-Cotill. For obituaries *see The Times* 2 and 6 June 2011.
33 MacDougall (2007, 207) gives a detailed account of the evolution of the Malta bakery. TNA ADM 181/51, estimates for 1840/1, allows £10,000 for 'alterations to a building, machinery for grinding corn and making biscuit'. Two years later the sum of £8,000 was allowed 'for erecting a new bakery and machinery for grinding corn etc' (TNA ADM 181/53).
34 TNA ADM 1/5775, 24 June 1861.
35 Colvin 1995, 853.
36 In the midst of his works for the Admiralty, Scamp found time to rescue from collapse and complete the protestant church of St Paul at Valletta. Scamp's works on the island are well-documented in Thake (2010). The museum conversion of the former bakery has been skilfully carried out, making it possible to appreciate the original internal spaces. The bread ovens survive.
37 TNA ADM 181/51, 1840/1 estimates.
38 Scamp's investigations revealed sound bedrock here (MacDougall 2007, 40).
39 To improve security, a sum of £119 appears in the 1850/1 estimates for 'iron gratings for back windows of factory buildings' (TNA ADM 181/61).
40 TNA ADM 140/1289, dated 1843, shows the dry dock with the outline of a paddle steamer in it and the new workshops along its east side. A metal colonnade fronting the factory and providing shade on the wharf was allowed for in 1863 (TNA ADM 181/74, estimates 1863/4) and appears in later Victorian photographs.
41 An 1896 plan of the yard lists the uses (TNA ADM 174/363).
42 TNA ADM 140/1284. This is signed and dated by Scamp on 31 Dec 1841 and is very similar to the plan in MacDougall 2007, fig 5.
43 TNA ADM 181/57–58, annual estimates 1846/7 and 1847/8. The caisson was estimated to cost £4,500; this may not

have been included in the overall cost of the dry dock. The machinery element of the steam factory was estimated at £10,000.

44 Sargent 2008, 99. MacDougall (2007, 40) gives the dimensions for the Malta dry dock as 310ft long by 60ft wide. The dimensions quoted here come from an 1863 plan in AdL Da 02. The dock was extended at least once, and by 1895 was 269ft 7in long (TNA ADM 174/363).

45 Money for a porter's lodge, guard room and entrance gate appears in the 1849/50 estimates (TNA ADM 181/60).

46 TNA ADM 181/66, 1855/6 estimates, allowed £40,000 for the work. Money for completing the work last appears in TNA ADM 181/73, estimates for 1862/3. Dimensions are from the 1863 plan of the yard in AdL Naval Establishments 1863, Da 02.

47 The last double dock in a home yard was at Deptford, where there was similar pressure on waterfront space. The double dock at Deptford partly survives below ground.

48 In 1862 Britain handed over the Ionian Islands to Greece, and, as a Select Committee subsequently noted, thereby increased the value to Britain of Malta. *See* 'Second Report of the Select Committee on Basin and Dock Accommodation', 15 July 1864, cited in Hattendorf *et al* 1993, 589.

49 TNA ADM 1/5838, 20 Jan and 7 Feb 1863. By then, the Governor wished to cut costs and the Commander-in-Chief at Malta favoured French Creek as more central to other naval facilities. £118,758 was allocated 'for dredging and extending the Great Harbour'.

50 TNA ADM 1/5803, 8 Dec 1862.

51 Hattendorf *et al* 1993, 589. Dock dimensions come from an 1863 plan in AdL Naval Establishments 1863 Da 02; this agrees closely with the 1896 plan in TNA ADM 174/363. It appears that a proposal to enlarge the dock in 1869/70 (TNA ADM 181/80, estimates) was not implemented. A contemporary model of this dock is in Malta Maritime Museum.

52 TNA ADM 140/1484 fol 62.

53 TNA ADM 174/363; Chrimes *et al* 2008, 720.

54 TNA ADM 140/1484 fol 62.

55 Hughes 1981,172. An additional dry dock has been constructed by the Malta Docks Company to cater for supertankers.

56 Documentary references are scarce. TNA ADM 181/96, estimates for 1885/6, records that £23,752 had already been expended out of a total estimated cost of £45,000.

57 The Gun Mounting Store and Factory was a handsome stone building, its architectural details very similar to the Iron Ship Repairing Shop. For its location on the eastern side of French Creek, *see* TNA ADM 174/363. Much of the work of a gun-mounting shop involved relining or fitting fresh inner tubes to gun barrels that lost their accuracy due to corrosion from the powder gases after firing a limited number of rounds. To preserve gun barrels, the Royal Navy used reduced charges for peacetime firing practice (Hughes 1981,173).

58 Malta was well protected by coastal artillery, outside the scope of this book. For further information, *see* Hughes 1981, Maurice-Jones 1959 and Spiteri 1996.

59 Hughes 1969, 255. TNA ADM181/99, 1904/5 estimates, notes that 'much progress has been made under the contract for the construction of Ricasoli and St Elmo breakwaters'.

60 On 24 July 1941 Italian special naval forces made a spectacularly unsuccessful night-time attack and were thwarted by the combination of submarine nets and the breakwaters (Hughes 1969, 265).

12 The West Indies and North American Bases: Buildings and Engineering Works, 1700–1914

1 Hispaniola was half French.

2 This system was introduced by Commodore Warren in the early 1740s (Gwyn 1973, xviii).

3 Morriss 1983, 5.

4 Vetch 2004a.

5 AdL Admiralty Terriers, Misc Foreign Property Letting Book 1; TNA ADM 181/51, 1840/1 estimates; ADM 181/76, 1865/6 estimates; ADM 181/92, 1881/2 estimates. A letter from the Navy Board of 11 May 1810 (NMM ADM/BP/30a) grants permission to advertise for a contract for constructing a storehouse and 'to accept the most advantageous tender'. In 1867 Scamp was looking at the possibilities of extending the wharf alongside the 'old naval yard', presumably to make coaling easier (TNA ADM 1/6015, 29 Jan 1867).

6 AdL Plans of Naval Establishments 1863, Da 02.

7 Vetch 2004a.

8 Mayes 1972, 5–8. AdL Vz 10 fol 76 (plan of proposed Port Royal Dockyard 1734) notes that the gap in the Palisadoes 'has been made good by the industry of the inhabitants of Port Royal'. AdL Vz 10 fol 80 is a 1704 plan by Christian Lilly showing Kingston Harbour, the new town of Kingston, Port Royal and the severed Palisadoes. Lilly had time only to draft this as 'I was by an Order from the Office of Ordnance suddenly call'd away to go upon the fortifications of Barbados'. This order was issued by the Board on 4 May 1704 (Vetch 2004a).

9 Baugh 1977, 327; Pawson and Buisseret 1975, 129.

10 Baugh 1977, 345. This was based on the premise that the ships would suffer unduly if not careened and checked.

11 Pawson and Buisseret 1975, 46–7.

12 Pawson and Buisseret 1975, 130. The plan referred to by Ogle is almost certainly AdL Vz 10 fol 76. At the time there were functioning naval hospitals in a number of rented houses in Port Royal and Kingston; plans for a new one were under consideration, but not in the location proposed by Ogle (Harland 2003, 379–80).

13 Baugh 1977, 364.

14 Baugh 1977, 131; AdL Vz 10 fol 73, plan of Port Royal 1765. In 1748 Admiral Knowles proposed a hugely ambitious scheme for an entirely new fortified naval base at Port Royal that would have eclipsed even the later one at Bermuda (AdL Vz 10 fol 75; Laughton 2004). For Knowles's opinions of the base then, *see* Rodger 2004, 303.

15 Baugh 1977, 391.

16 Mayes 1972, 27.

17 In 1838 Port Royal ceased to be an independent command and became the headquarters of the Jamaica Division of the North American and West Indian Station, under a commodore (Pawson and Buisseret 1975, 140).

18 Pawson and Buisseret 1975, 139. AdL Da 01 fol 14 (plans of Naval Establishments *c* 1840) shows Port Royal yard after these alterations. Commissioner Ross in 1824 refers to the western capstan house built in 1786 and the eastern capstan house built a year later (TNA ADM 106/2039, 31 June 1824).

19 TNA ADM 181/51, estimates 1840/1, records that 'coals will be deposited there [the former Victualling Yard] for the steam vessels, which could not be put on board the *Magnificent*'. AdL Admiralty Terriers, Misc Foreign Property Letting Book 1, records that the 34½ acres of land were purchased from Alexander Grant for £3,200 on 9 June 1840.

20 Shown on an uncatalogued 1904 plan (AdL Port Royal 1904 plan). Part of the jetty and the brick walls of the coal sheds remain. Mayes (1972, 30) states that the coal sheds were constructed in 1861–2 by Commander Dunlop.

21 TNA ADM 181/74, estimates 1863/4, records that for 'Enlarging smithery, boundary wall at coal stores, machinery foundations, alterations and reconstructions etc', £2,462 was required

for this financial year. The following year, £4,208 was required to complete the works.

22 Schurman 2000, 51–4, 136.

23 AdL 1904 plan of Port Royal, uncatalogued.

24 Tracy 1997, 26–9. At the time, there were ambitious plans for improving the yard – *see* TNA ADM 116/993. Among the projects for 1905/6, it was proposed to spend £3,500 on the foundations for a 25-ton steam crane, £2,850 for the reconstruction of the torpedo boat slip, £4,700 for the extension of wharves 2 and 3, £1,330 for a high-level reservoir extension, £530 for a dry provision store, £430 for improving and extending tramways and £400 for the reconstruction of No. 1 boat slip.

25 AdL Vz 10 fol 68 is a 1729/30 plan, almost certainly by Lilly, showing an early grid plan of streets and tenements on the Titchfield peninsula and adjacent mainland. Locally, Navy Island is probably now more famous as the one-time home of Errol Flynn. Although closed and abandoned by the navy in 1749, it remained in naval ownership into the 19th century (TNA ADM 106/3029, 6 Dec 1806). Titchfield retains a number of early houses and Fort George at the end of the peninsula. The former barracks are now a school.

26 Vetch 2004a.

27 Laughton 2004.

28 The Admiralty Library has the most extensive collection of maps and plans of Port Antonio for this period.

29 Writing on 11 Nov 1729 (Baugh 1977, 351). An AdL plan of Lynches Island, undated but *c* 1730, shows the plots for potatoes, corn and yams, the careening wharf and the quadrangular hospital.

30 Writing on 29 Jan 1729/30 (Baugh 1977, 352).

31 AdL Vz 10 fol 64. This undated plan of Lynches Island shows the progress of construction and probably dates from 1731/2.

32 Report of 11 March 1731/2 (Baugh 1977, 361). For the buildings being prefabricated a little earlier in home yards, *see* Baugh 1977, 342.

33 Harland 2003, 381. The arrival of the surgeon at this early date suggests that already there were concerns about the health of the workforce here.

34 Reports of 9 Jan 1731/2, from Admiral Charles Stewart to the Admiralty Secretary, and March 1733/4, from Commander Charles Knowles to the Admiralty Secretary (Baugh 1977, 360, 363).

35 Reports from Commander Charles Knowles to the Secretary of the Admiralty, 17 Dec 1732 and March 1733/4 (Baugh 1977, 362–3).

36 On 20 Dec 1734 (Baugh 1977, 364).

37 The careening pits were sited on the careening wharf, and the ends of the ship's yard were lodged in them when the vessel was hauled over for careening.

38 Baugh 1977; Crewe 1993, 221. Letting Navy Island was not a success. By the early 19th century, the local garrison used the island as grazing for their stock, which was 'a very essential benefit to them', and as a result proposals then to lease the island were turned down. *See* TNA ADM 106/3209, 8 Nov 1811, 3 Feb 1812.

39 TNA ADM 116/307, 2 July 1889; AdL Misc Foreign Property Letting Book 1; Baugh 1977, 346–7. TNA ADM 140/1173 is a 1727 survey of English Harbour, probably by a naval officer, that shows a number of buildings and defence works already there.

40 The extensive system of fortifications protecting the naval base that were manned until the Crimean War are outside the scope of this book. Jane (1982) has a useful introduction.

41 Pares 1963, 274–5. The author notes that a number of commanders sent their largest ships to be refitted at Jamaica or Halifax, Nova Scotia.

42 Baugh 1977, 349.

43 Baugh 1977, 372. The work of establishing the base is detailed in a series of reports from Knowles, dated 17 March 1743/4, 22 June and 6 July 1744, 26 Feb and 2 March 1744/5 (Baugh 1977, 380–7). Although Knowles was censured by the Admiralty (23 Feb 1744/5, *see* Baugh 1977, 382) for exceeding his brief, the Admiralty eventually approved his work (Admiralty minute 2 May 1746, *see* Baugh 1977, 387). Knowles also found time to construct a gun battery, later Fort Charlotte, overlooking the eastern side of the harbour entrance and supplementing Fort Berkeley's coverage. He also constructed a temporary field work for 20 guns in Freeman's Bay, facing the harbour entrance (Baugh 1977, 380).

44 Documentary evidence for these works is slight. The 1789 Columbine plan is one of the earliest to show the base at English Harbour with much of its present plan (NMM Com-01 fol 62). AdL Admiralty Terriers, Misc Foreign Property Letting Book 1, notes that additional land was acquired in 1775 and 1785, which would fit well with these various improvements.

45 TNA ADM 140/1191. There are no indications of any pumping arrangements, which would have been essential here.

46 TNA ADM 140/1189 is a drawing of this building, signed by Nathaniel Watts in Sept 1785. He was possibly the storekeeper.

47 TNA ADM 140/1190 is an unsigned drawing of the smaller storehouse, dated 1785. *See also* TNA ADM 140/1198 for the mid-19th-century uses of these two buildings. The smaller storehouse became an inn in the 1960s.

48 Blackburne 1972, 13. TNA ADM 140/1203 is an undated drawing of what is probably the existing smithery.

49 Coad 1989, 360.

50 NMM ADM/BP/39b (14 Dec 1814) lists overseas bases with commissioners. English Harbour had one appointed by 1810.

51 TNA ADM 140/1196. Further documentary evidence for this building remains elusive; it has a rainwater hopper dated 1810, suggesting a likely completion date.

52 TNA ADM 140/1198, Antigua, Mr Anderson's report, March 1853, with an additional report of 15 June 1853. Pt 3 is the accompanying plan. TNA ADM 181/65, estimates 1854/5, has a sum of £500 for 'corrugated iron roof over the masthouse slip and boat camber'. A late 19th-century photograph of the yard in the author's possession suggests that this work may have been done.

53 TNA ADM 116/688, 25 July 1879.

54 TNA ADM 116/307, 28 June 1889. An uncatalogued 1905 AdL plan of the dockyard has marginal notes stating that the Admiralty nevertheless retained an interest in the yard and seems to have employed a caretaker to prevent squatters occupying the site. In 1899 the Admiralty 'decided that the yard shall be abandoned, but the site retained as Admiralty Property in view of possible future needs'. AdL Admiralty Terriers, Misc Foreign Property Letting Book 1, states that on 18 June 1906, the base was transferred to the colonial government, 'subject to, that if at any time the C.G. have it under consideration to lease the property for coaling purposes, the Ady are to be first consulted and their approval obtained'.

55 Blackburne (1972, 34–8) gives a succinct account of this remarkable conservation campaign that had its genesis in one family's enthusiasm in the late 1940s that led to the foundation of the Society of the Friends of English Harbour in 1951.

56 Malcomson 2001, 8–9, 17, 19. This author gives a detailed account of the warships and the maritime operations on these waters. Much of the information here comes from this source.

57 TNA ADM 1/3451, 28 July 1835, records the supply depot at Montreal comprising

one 60ft by 30ft brick storehouse, one 35ft by 34ft stone storehouse, one 36ft by 28ft guardhouse, one 77ft by 21ft timber shed for iron, a 35ft by 20ft stone dwelling house, a stable, wood shed and wooden privy. In the War of 1812 Quebec was an important additional supply base.

58 The rather larger-scale 18th-century warship-building yard at Buckler's Hard in Hampshire, where the former slips survive as shallow depressions on the river bank, still gives a flavour of the simplicity of such establishments, although here the brick housing of the workers reflects the far longer lifespan of this yard compared to most on the Great Lakes.

59 Malcomson 2001, 35–6. *See* Cock (2004) for a succinct biography of John Schank (1740–1823), who rose to become an Admiral of the Blue and whose expertise included building floating bridges for the army, the invention of the sliding keel for shallow-draft vessels and the construction in 1796 of a steam canal tug for the Duke of Bridgewater.

60 Malcomson 2001, 26, 39. During this war there were facilities on Lake Ontario at Oswego, Oswegatchie, Niagara and Carleton Island. On Lake Erie the yards were at Detroit and Navy Island and on Lake Champlain at St Jean, Ticonderoga, Skenesborough and Isle aux Noix.

61 Malcomson 2001, 120, 138. None of the original buildings survive, but the reconstructed 'Discovery Harbour' in its wooded setting at Penetanguishene gives a good idea of the small scale of the majority of these bases.

62 AdL Admiralty Terriers, Misc Foreign Property Letting Book 1; NMM ADM/BP/34a, 27 Jan 1814.

63 Chichester 2004a; Osborne and Swainson 1988, 48. Bryce also recommended a number of fortifications to protect the new yard. He was to have a distinguished career with the Royal Engineers, rising to be Colonel-Commandant and acquiring a knighthood for his services in Sicily, Egypt, France and the Netherlands in the Napoleonic Wars.

64 The Roebuck watercolour, reproduced by Malcomson (2001, 144), is in Library and Archives Canada, C121249. The yard plan of *c* 1840 is in AdL Plans of Naval Establishments Da 01 fol 17.

65 AdL Naval Establishments 1863, Da 02 fols 17, 18.

66 TNA FO 93/8/9c, 29 Apr 1817, sets out the terms agreed by the Prince Regent. *See* NMM ADM/BP/39b for a report of 15 Aug 1814 by Rich. O'Conor, acting commissioner at Kingston, setting out rather more ambitious proposals for the future of naval bases for the freshwater navy. He advocated a major supply depot at Montreal and the maintenance of a commissioner at Kingston. A subsequent document dated 14 Dec 1814 indicates that the commissioner was then based at Quebec.

67 Malcomson 2001, 50.

68 NMM ADM/BP/39b, 18 Oct 1819. This report also has the detailed drawings. The stated dimensions are curious. HMS *St Lawrence* had a gun deck length of 191ft 2in, but her extreme breadth was 52ft 6in (Malcomson 2001, 112). Further proposals for a sawmill here were sent to the Navy Board in June 1820 (NMM ADM/BP/40a, 14 June 1820). NMM ADM/BP/40b, 22 Dec 1820, contains a report on the area, along with the names of the homesteaders. Although nothing came of this proposal at Kingston for a floating timber dock, such docks were in use at the Port of Quebec from 1827 into the 1930s (*see* Marcil 1995).

69 NMM ADM/BP/50a, 31 Aug and 5 Sept 1829. At Penetanguishene, Sir James Kempt, Governor-in-Chief, pointed out his preferred site for the new dockyard to Captain Phillpots of the Royal Engineers. In 1819 new fortifications at the Isle aux Noix necessitated the removal of some of the naval buildings including sheds accommodating shipwrights (NMM ADM/BP/50a, 30 Nov and 18 Dec 1819).

70 TNA ADM 181/60, estimates 1849/50, has a sum of £260 for 'ordinary maintenance'.

71 Preston and Major 2007, 64–5. The new Britomart class, armed with a hefty 68pdr gun, were the only ones whose dimensions and shallow draft allowed them to use the Canadian canals, including the Welland Canal. *Britomart* patrolled Lake Erie, *Cherub* guarded Lake Huron, and *Heron* protected Lake Ontario.

72 AdL Admiralty Terriers, Misc Foreign Property Letting Book 1.

73 Osborne and Swainson 1988, 60. For a detailed account of the fortifications, *see* Allcorn 2011.

74 Tracy 1997, 21. This Admiralty report, 'The Naval Position on the Lakes', was marked as 'secret' and dated 'c March 1903'.

75 Tracy 1997, 80–3. The Treaty was modified in 1946 to allow vessels used for training purposes to be armed, but it still forms the basis of the frontier agreement between the two countries. The naval defence of Canada, if faced with American aggression, had already caused concern in 1905 (Tracy 1997,42).

76 Gwyn 1973, xxvii, note 3.

77 Gwyn 2004, 5–7. Professor Gwyn's very detailed account of the development of the Halifax base is the definitive work on the subject.

78 Smith 1985, 6.

79 TNA ADM 106/1179, 16 Jan 1770, describes 'the old south storehouse being a patchwork piece of building, added to an Old Barn run up in haste to receive the Stores for the Squadron going against Quebec in the years 1758 and 9'. NMM ADM/B/163, 14 Nov 1759, allocates £8,000 for a careening wharf. *See also* Gwyn 2004, 8–9.

80 Gwyn 2004, 10.

81 AdL Admiralty Terriers, Halifax. This records that the original yard was granted 'for ever' from the Crown on 7 Feb 1759. Land for Admiralty House and the burial ground was held on similar terms, dated 23 June 1783. By 1890 the yard was just over 12 acres in extent, the hospital site just over 5 acres, and the burial ground just over 3. Admiralty House and its grounds occupied just over 17 acres (TNA ADM 174/362). The extension of the railway into central Halifax in the early 1870s reduced the extent of Admiralty land and severed the hospital grounds and Admiralty House and grounds from the rest of the base.

82 Gwyn 2004, 30; Smith 1985, 20.

83 Gwyn 2004, 16–31.

84 Gwyn (2004, 53–9) gives a detailed account of the saga of the construction of Admiralty House, Halifax. *See also* Colvin (1995, 761–2) for John Plaw. For Bermuda, *see* Stranack 1990, 61–3. *See* Chapter 6 for a fuller description of Port Admirals' houses.

85 Stranack 1990, 13, 32.

86 Smith, 1985, 35; Stranack 1990, 60–1, 146–7.

87 TNA ADM 128/1, 27 Sept 1832.

88 TNA ADM 1/3446, 30 Oct 1832.

89 TNA ADM 1/304, 19 June and 4 July 1839. Halifax, as the nearest port to northern Europe on the North American mainland, stood to benefit from the new steamships. The Cunard family were wealthy local shipowners and timber merchants before Samuel branched out into steam passenger ships. Cunard's request stemmed from his successful tender following the British Government's request for bids for steamships to carry mail between Britain and New York via Halifax (Raddall 1993, 180).

90 TNA ADM 1/6015, 11 Apr 1867; TNA ADM 1/6064, 9 May and 20 Oct 1868. In 1885 further money was allocated to convert this into a fully fledged machine shop (TNA ADM 181/96, estimates 1885/6).

91 TNA ADM 181/75, estimates 1864/5. TNA ADM 195/49 fol 23b has a photograph of the building *c* 1895. I am grateful to Ian Doull for information on the survival of this building.

92 Smith 1985, 13.The observatory is shown on an 1863 plan of the yard (AdL Naval Establishments Da 02 fol 12).

93 *See* Hattendorf *et al* (1993, 588–91) for Second Report of the Select Committee on Basin and Dock Accommodation, dated 15 July 1864. TNA ADM 116/993 records the proposal, abandoned in Dec 1902, to modernise Halifax.

94 AdL uncatalogued memo DW19239/04, marked confidential and clearly written in happy ignorance of the effects of the local climate on unmaintained buildings and other installations.

95 AdL Admiralty Terrier, Halifax. Order in Council dated 13 Oct 1910.

96 Preston and Major 2007, 64. The Childers reforms of 1869 surprisingly suggested maintaining Valparaiso as the headquarters. It remained a supply base for some years (Hattendorf *et al* 1993, 594). For correspondence between 1851 and 1857 relating to the possible establishment of a base at Esquimalt, *see* WKL 1942.

97 The previous year, the navy had been unable to land casualties here owing to lack of facilities, and the wounded had to be taken to San Fransisco (Nelson and Oliver 1982, 9). AdL Admiralty Terrier, Esquimalt, records that the £952 5s cost of the buildings was paid to the Hudson's Bay Company, which remained the landlord until the base was properly established. I am grateful to Ian Doull for the information on Thetis Island.

98 AdL Terrier records that the land was purchased from the Puget Sound Company for £9, with a further £484 15s 3d paid for the buildings. The Puget Sound Agricultural Company was a subsidiary of the Hudson's Bay Company who presumably constructed the hutted camp for the War Office (Nelson and Oliver 1982, 107). The 1818 agreement establishing the national boundary along the 49th parallel had been settled only as far as the Rocky Mountains. The 1858 Boundary Commission had the task of agreeing the line of the 'missing' frontier and marking it out on the ground. In their time in British Columbia, the Royal Engineers also laid out towns, constructed roads, designed public buildings, established the Government Printing Office, set up the first building society and inaugurated the first observatory (Hill 1987, 90–1).

99 TNA ADM 1/5969 (memo Y.81/1866), quoted in Preston and Major 2007, 64.

100 Nelson and Oliver 1982, 163–5; AdL Terrier, Esquimalt. Cole Island was abandoned in 1938. Of the 17 buildings existing then, only 5 have survived. Cole Island is now looked after by the Province of British Columbia.

101 Preston and Major (2007, 65) note that even after the 1871 *Alabama* Claims Settlement, which reduced tensions between Britain and the United States and led to the withdrawal of most imperial troops, Halifax and Esquimalt uniquely retained garrisons of British regular troops. TNA ADM 116/744 contains a detailed 1879 report on the defences by the Dominion Inspector of Artillery, Lt Colonel T Bland Strange RA. There were six coastal-defence batteries (and one submarine mining establishment) built during the British period, of which those at Duntze Head (Dockyard) and Fort Rodd Hill were only two. The largest was a twin, 9.2in counterbombardment battery on Signal Hill, on Army Ordnance Corps property near the dockyard, which was not actually armed until *c* 1917. Information from Ian Doull.

102 TNA ADM 181/76–81, estimates 1865 to 1871.

103 Nelson and Oliver 1982, 19. £500 for a residence for an engineer first appears in the 1873/4 estimates (TNA ADM 181/84). Unless otherwise indicated, the dates of the buildings are taken from Nelson and Oliver 1982, 177–83.

104 TNA ADM 116/744 contains a detailed account of the vicissitudes surrounding the construction. Not until 19 Sept 1876 was the first pile for the new dock driven in at a ceremony attended by the Governor-General, Lord Dufferin (Dufferin and Ava 1891, 284). Earlier in Victoria, the Marchioness had noted in her journal that 'the feeling here is British, but anti-Canadian on account of the railroad' (*ibid*, 252). Dry dock and railroad were key factors leading to British Columbia joining the Dominion of Canada in 1871 following the passing in 1867 of the British North America Act. In a letter of 25 Nov 1889 Lord Stanley, Governor-General of Canada, reported to Lord Knutsford the Colonial Secretary that the dry dock was well used and that 'shipping was increasing rapidly'. He also advocated that the dock be extended to cater for the larger steamers then being constructed for the Canadian Pacific Railway Company, noting that 'The steamers are built under an arrangement by Imperial authorities by which they may be used as cruisers in time of war'.

105 TNA ADM 116/675, 9 Sept 1901. Other parts of the report refer to local contractors as being expensive and unsatisfactory.

106 Segger 2000.

107 Nelson and Oliver 1982, 86–7. The building's use in 1903 was to store electric cables, probably for use in the yard. I am grateful to Ian Doull for the information on Cole Island.

108 Doull (2007, 107–11) gives detailed histories and illustrations of these buildings.

109 Coad 1989, 365–6. The Narrows Passage could be tricky in certain weather conditions, leading Commissioner Ayscough in 1830 to ask for a steam tug for 'towing any man of war in or out of this intricate navigation' (TNA ADM 106/1996, 1 Nov 1830).

110 Stranack 1990, 4–6. A number of small islands in the Sound were also acquired, together with some 5,500 cedar trees growing on them. AdL Admiralty Terriers, Misc Foreign Property Letting Book 1 (Bermuda), details the owners of land at Ireland Island whose properties were acquired in 1809 and 1810.

111 On 15 May 1810, Warren reported that a contract for the large storehouse on Ireland Island had been signed (NMM ADM/BP/30b).

112 NMM ADM/BP/38a, 20 July 1818.

113 NMM ADM/BP/38a, 30 Apr 1818. The 1823 estimates in TNA ADM 181/33 allowed for £264,910 'towards forming a naval establishment', but do not specify what was included. Until then a notional £20,000 had appeared in the estimates. As an alternative to an iron-lined dry dock, Mr Smith, the foreman of works, on site later suggested that stone be sent from England, 'the island not producing stone of a quality for that purpose' (TNA ADM 106/1994, 18 Oct 1826). Nothing came of his proposal.

114 Josias Jessop's report is dated 'Adelphi. Oct.1819' (NMM ADM/BP 39B).

115 NMM ADM/BP/39b, Oct 1819.

116 Stranack 1990, 70–1.

117 For instance, TNA ADM 106/1996, 9 Aug 1831.

118 Harris (1997, 182–6) gives a succinct account of the construction of the defences. Fanshawe visited on the express instructions of the Duke of Wellington. His plan showing the initial defences and the embryonic dockyard is in TNA MPH 1/622, dated 1 Sept 1823. Fanshawe's 1826 proposal is in TNA MPH 1/604 fol 4. Hope's 1847 plan (TNA MR 1/1059) clearly shows the incomplete breakwater.

119 TNA ADM 1/3446, 15 Sept 1832. Later, the naval diving bells were to be used helping the Royal Engineers construct the curtain on the west side of the yard (TNA ADM 106/1995, 30 Sept 1829).

120 TNA MPH 1/604 contains 1826 and 1828 plans of the yard that show preliminary thinking on the disposition of buildings. These were drawn by S B Howlett, then Assistant Military Surveyor and Draughtsman to the Board of Ordnance (Baigent 2004).

121 TNA ADM 106/1996, 24 June 1831 and an undated memo; Coad 1983.
122 *See* White (1999, 110–12) for the later history of the house. The use as a prison is shown on a number of plans of the dockyard, including TNA ADM 174/397 (dated 1891).
123 TNA MR 1/1059.
124 Quoted in Stranack 1990, 14. Dundonald is better known to history as Sir Thomas Cochrane, among other achievements founding father of the Chilean navy in that country's successful struggle to break free from Spanish rule.
125 TNA ADM 181/60 and 62.
126 TNA ADM 181/71, estimates 1860/1. The patent slip appears on TNA ADM 174/397, dated 1891. One of the last construction projects was to repair one of the victualling stores damaged by a fire, when £8,000 was allowed in the 1862/3 estimates (TNA ADM 181/63). TNA ADM 181/76, estimates 1865/6, is the last year when money appears for the buildings of the naval and victualling yard.
127 Stranack 1990, 54
128 Stranack 1990, 59; TNA ADM 181/83, 1872/3 estimates. A succession of dry docks served at Bermuda until the closure of the base. The sheer-legs were removed in 1930.
129 Detailed documentation, as so often with the overseas bases, is lacking for much of this phase.
130 AdL Vz 15 fol 13; TNA ADM 174/397, 1891.
131 AdL Vz 15 fol 13, 1863, has the outline of the proposed dry dock.
132 The victualling storehouses have cast-iron beams from Robinson and Son, Pimlico, London.
133 Colvin 1995, 853.
134 TNA ADM 181/99, 1904/5; ADM 140/1484 fol 68. This was financed by the Naval Works Loan Act; concrete blocks were used extensively for the construction of the breakwater protecting the new basin.
135 The surrounding defences, developed in the 19th and 20th centuries on a scale commensurate with those protecting the main naval bases in Britain, are outside the scope of this book. For the definitive work, *see* Harris 1997.

13 South Atlantic and Australian Bases: Buildings and Engineering Works, 1700–1914

1 Rees 2009, 137; AdL Misc Foreign Property Letting Book 1. A memo of 10 June 1893 records the closure 'as soon as the stock of coal is exhausted'.
2 For details of the health of seamen on these patrols, *see* Watt 2002. Lloyd (1949, 134) quotes Bryson's 1819 *History of the British West Indies*, which refers somewhat discouragingly to the location of the Fernando Po hospital: 'there is not perhaps any known spot in the whole known world more detrimental to health'. A small coaling depot was maintained here until 1893, long after the rest of the facilities had been abandoned. AdL Admiralty Terrier, West Africa, indicates that facilities at Freetown were maintained at least until 1914.
3 Lloyd 1949, 133.
4 Kroomen were generally West African fishermen living along the coast of what is now Liberia and the Ivory Coast and who were recruited to serve ashore and afloat, principally with the West Africa squadron ships. TNA ADM 181/61, 1850/1 estimates.
5 *See* Clements (2010) for a detailed account of the defences of Ascension Island.
6 TNA ADM 109/93, 14 Dec 1827. A letter of 9 July 1830 lists the garrison as numbering 160 European men, 34 women and 45 children, plus 46 African men, 14 boys, 12 women, 13 children and 22 'supernumeraries', possibly freed slaves.
7 TNA ADM 109/93, 11 Apr 1832. Warren ordered works to begin immediately on the 'new victualling store' and to complete the hospital and Fort Cockburn
8 This building appears in the annual estimates from TNA ADM 181/58 (1847/8) to ADM 181/62 (1851/2). In the absence of much other documentation, this incomplete series is the main guide for the approximate dates of construction of many of the Ascension Island buildings.
9 Hart-Davis 1976, 84; TNA ADM 181/69–71, estimates 1858 to 1861. In 1862 it was reported that 'great benefit has resulted from the tramway … from the pierhead to the victualling yard, with this and the steam hoist that is kept constantly in work' (TNA ADM 1/5803, 6 Sept 1862). Additional coal stores appear in later estimates. Hart-Davis (1976, 130) records that by the 1880s the island held some 4,000 tons of coal for the West Africa Squadron. Most of these buildings appear in TNA ADM 195/4, an invaluable photographic record of the naval buildings on Ascension Island in 1904.
10 Hart-Davis (1976, 87) mentions an engine fitter on the island in 1851.
11 TNA ADM 1/5803, 6 Sept 1862.
12 TNA ADM 1/5803, 7 Jan 1862, is a report on the buildings, mentioning that work was 'in progress' on the new workshops. *See* TNA ADM 181/73–4 for the 1862 to 1864 estimates.
13 AdL uncatalogued plans of Georgetown and Ascension 1900–8 (annotated up to 1922).
14 *See* Watt (2002, 70, 72), who gives a sickness rate for the West Africa Squadron for the years 1837–43 of over 1,500 men per 1,000 and a mortality rate of 70 per 1,000. The author notes that between 1837 and 1843 alone, these squadrons employed an annual average of 4,645 men and suffered 62,541 cases of disease and injury and 1,353 deaths. Rees (2009, 308) credits the Royal Navy with freeing around 160,000 slaves during the 60 or so years of the anti-slavery patrols, but at a cost of the lives of 17,000 British seamen from disease, battle and accident.
15 TNA ADM 114/46, 12 Feb 1830; ADM 109/93, 11 Apr 1832. An early drawing by Brandreth shows two wards (TNA MR 1/1771). TNA ADM 195/4 shows the hospital in 1904, with a rendered arcade shading the verandas. *See also* TNA ADM 181/77, estimates for 1866, which included £50 for 'removing privies to leeward side of hospital', no doubt welcomed by patients and staff.
16 TNA ADM 1/3502, 11 July 1838. The hospital was criticised as being inadequate by Admiral Sir Patrick Campbell, Commander-in-Chief at the Cape of Good Hope, who suggested the size should be doubled.
17 TNA ADM 105/91 is an 1882 plan of the Green Mountain hospital and grounds.
18 TNA ADM 116/680.
19 For more on the defences, *see* Clements 2007 and 2010.
20 Evans 2004, 179; TNA ADM 116/680. Lewis based these figures on his understanding that 'the Flagship on the Station can take 50 tons and hour', and he reckoned it should be possible to coal two cruisers simultaneously. He would have been well aware of the new arrangements at Portland completed a year or so earlier (Hattendorf *et al* 1993, 675). TNA MT 23/258 describes a coaling trial here in 1911 when HMS *Glasgow* was able to load 50 tons an hour of bagged coal using more traditional but labour-intensive methods.
21 TNA ADM 116/680, Report on Jetty and Coaling Facilities.
22 *See* Schurman (2000, 110) for details of the Carnarvon Commission appointed in 1879 to consider the 'Defence of British Possessions and Commerce Abroad'.
23 The base probably mostly came to the attention of the Lords of the Admiralty when they enjoyed the annual gift of turtles for turtle soup This custom apparently had started in 1816. TNA ADM 1/8634/187 records correspondence between 1922 and 1935 by the Admiralty Board, anxious not to lose their agreeable culinary treat. It was not something that the Colonial Office felt could be part of any formal contract with the Eastern

Telegraph Company, but was more in the nature of a 'gentlemen's agreement'. The Admiralty feared that the telegraph company might lack sufficient gentlemen in its ranks to maintain the agreement and ensure the continued arrival of their soup.

24 AdL Misc Foreign Property Letting Book 1.

25 Gaastra 2003, 80. Cape Town was a compulsory victualling stop for Dutch East India Company ships.

26 Fawcett 1984, 441.

27 TNA ADM 123/57, 'A History of the Acquisition of Naval Property at Simonstown'.

28 NMM ADM/BP/34b, 28 Aug 1814.

29 TNA ADM 181/71, estimates 1870/1. Malta was the most populous base, then employing 381 people.

30 Fawcett 1984, 441. These were used for a number of storage purposes, including victuals, and under the Dutch initially were part occupied by hospital patients. The precise number and condition of the buildings inherited by the Royal Navy are not entirely clear, as the army claimed a number for its own purposes. *See* Rodger 1985, 467–9. Myers (1997) contains detailed histories of surviving buildings.

31 Proposed by Rear-Admiral Robert Stopford in a letter to the Admiralty of 31 March 1811 (quoted in Rodger 1985, 469).

32 The observatory, operated by the Admiralty, lies outside the scope of this book. Warner (1995) is the definitive account of the establishment and early operation of the Simon's Town observatory, first suggested to the Board of Longitude at a meeting on 3 Feb 1820. Rennie's preliminary drawings are in TNA ADM 140/1251, dated 1 March 1821.

33 TNA ADM 195/2 fol 9 is a late 19th-century photograph showing this last group of buildings. The annual estimates for the yard in the 1870s have frequent sums for storehouse repairs and restoration. The year 1879 seems the most likely date for the addition of these upper floors.

34 TNA ADM 123/57, Admiralty letters of 10 and 15 July 1896.

35 TNA ADM 123/57, committee report. AdL uncatalogued plan of Simon's Bay *c* 1900 shows this separate site in outline. A similar plan dated 1909 has an annotated margin giving the date of approval for the name changes of East and West Yards.

36 Sill depth calculated for Low Water Ordinary Spring Tide.

37 TNA ADM 123/56. The committee's report is dated 12 May 1898.

38 TNA ADM 123/56, 31 Jan 1899, 9 Apr 1900. The year 1899 was taken up with preparation of the specifications and with securing the passage of 'The Simon's Town Naval Defence Act 1898' through the Cape Legislature. The five firms invited to tender in 1900 were Messrs Pauling & Co, Sir John Jackson Ltd, Messrs S Pearson & Son Ltd, Mr John Price and Messrs Punchard Lowther & Co. For Jackson, *see* Spencer-Silver 2004.

39 TNA ADM 123/56, 13 Aug 1900.

40 TNA ADM 123/56, 10 Nov 1906.

41 TNA ADM 181/99, 1904/5, 1 Feb1904. An uncatalogued plan of Simon's Town dated 1909–12 in AdL is annotated with notes on the later progress of the contractors; they were finally asked to vacate the site of their operations no later than 1 Feb1912. TNA ADM 140/1484 fol 77 shows the dockyard as completed in 1910.

42 Bach 1986, 12.

43 Bach 1986, 18. New Zealand was formally established as a British colony in 1841.

44 Jones (1995) gives useful background detail. These state navies survived in Australia until the Federation of the Australian States in 1901 gave the Commonwealth Government responsibility for defence (Martin and Tanner 1988, 366, 387).

45 Author's italics. The Commission noted, 'The Australian Colonies – growing rapidly in wealth and population – are year by year, by their own efforts, becoming more able to resist hostile attack, and to assist in the common defence of the Empire' (Hattendorf *et al* 1993, 604). Rear-Admiral Sir George Tryon, C-in-C Australia, in a letter to the several Governors of the Australasian Colonies dated 24 Dec 1885 (Hattendorf *et al*, 1993, 610). The proviso that such vessels should be kept in Australasian waters did not entirely reassure the colonies.

46 Frame 2004, 47. The author points out that this was 1/6th of the earth's surface, admittedly with Australia in the middle. Ten years later, in 1869, the reorganisation of overseas squadrons by Hugh Childers reduced this squadron by one warship (Hattendorf *et al* 1993, 594). For a vivid description of the duties of a Royal Navy warship on this station in the mid-1880s, *see* Jones 2003.

47 A small government yard was laid out by Governor Hunter between 1796 and 1800 on the western side of Sydney Cove to build and maintain small craft for the government of the new colony. This was not an Admiralty yard (Proudfoot 1996, 17–18).

48 Jeremy 2005, 7–12. The author notes that the Fitzroy Dock was the first such dock in the Pacific. Its location on the island was determined by the existence there of the convict prison whose inmates provided most of the labour for its construction. From 1838 the navy had been able to use a patent slip in Sydney. *See also* Chapter 10.

49 Cockatoo Island became the responsibility of the Commonwealth Government from 1913 and was developed as a major naval shipbuilding and repair base in the 20th century. Jeremy (2005) provides an authoritative history of its naval facilities, which were closed in 1991, though a great deal of historic and architectural interest remains on the island.

50 This was still in naval use in 1895 when it was photographed for Admiralty records. It may have been the 'depot on the mainland' that the Admiralty in 1894 noted was to be exchanged for Garden Island once new buildings there were completed (Hattendorf *et al* 1993, 675).

51 Bach 1986, 200.

52 In 1887 the Australia Naval Defence Act allowed for Australia and New Zealand to contribute a sum not exceeding £126,000 towards the establishment and maintenance of Royal Navy forces in Australasian waters; in 1903 the Naval Agreement Act raised this to a maximum of £240,000; and in 1908 the Naval Subsidy Act allowed for New Zealand to contribute £100,000 annually. These sums were principally for the costs of warships and their crews, but an indirect result was the need for adequate shore facilities (Tracy 1997, 344).

53 The victualling yard had a comparatively short life and was apparently just a purchasing and storage operation. TNA ADM 181/99, estimates for 1904/5, notes a victualling store as being 'under way'. No precise location or sums of money are given. A plan of Garden Island *c* 1896 (AdL uncatalogued) marks the new storehouse here as 'naval and victualling stores'. By 1909, TNA ADM 140/1484 fol 82 marks the building simply as 'naval stores', suggesting that the Royal Edward Yard was then functioning (Bach 1986, 214).

54 Bach (1986, 200) mentions that by 1863 there was a naval workshop here in the charge of a chief petty officer. *See also* Martin and Tanner 1988, 366–8; much of this account of the buildings on Garden Island is based on the work of these authors. Frame (2004, 55) states that it was 1871 when the NSW Government formally dedicated Garden Island 'as a depot for the use of Her Majesty's ships'.

55 Martin and Tanner 1988, 370; Frame 2004, 59. Among very few references in the Admiralty estimates for works here are £10,000 for a storehouse in 1873/4 (TNA ADM 181/84) and in 1881/2 £50 for maintenance of buildings on the island (TNA ADM 181/92). The storehouse was to replace rented ones on Circular Quay.

Although , the Colonial Architect was asked to design the building (Martin and Tanner 1988, 370), it never went ahead.
56 Bach 1986, 203; Martin and Tanner 1988, 371, 387.
57 *Diamond* was a slightly larger sister ship of *Gannet*, launched at Sheerness 4 years later and now preserved at Chatham Historic Dockyard. Both were the classic 'up-funnel down screw' steam-assisted sailing warships specifically designed for use in the more remote parts of the British Empire.
58 Jones 2003, 360.
59 Bach 1986, 213, quoting TNA ADM 1/7112, 5 July 1892. Local ship-repairing firms were to deal with major problems.
60 McDonald 1969. The sawmill, torpedo and gun-mounting store and coal sheds are the principal buildings that have been demolished.
61 Martin and Tanner 1988, 381–3.
62 Martin and Tanner 1988, 384–6; AdL uncatalogued plan of Garden Island *c* 1896.
63 Martin and Tanner 1988, 380–1.
64 Martin and Tanner 1988, 377–9.
65 Weiler 1987, 426–30. The use of verandas, raised ground floors and large windows protected by jalousies was derived from plantation houses in the West Indies. On Garden Island a raised ground floor and jalousies were unnecessary. Earlier barracks with all these features remain on Morne Fortune, St Lucia, where they were constructed for the Royal Garrison Artillery.
66 Concluding his book, Bach (1986, 221) noted that 'when the last Imperial ships sailed from Sydney for New Zealand in 1913 they left to the new Royal Australian Navy a modern, efficient and self-supporting naval establishment which, despite the legal conflicts with New South Wales, allowed the new dominion organisation to begin its career with confidence. It was not the least of the Royal Navy's many legacies to Australia'.

14 Feeding the Fleet: The Royal Victualling Yards

1 Baugh (1977, 401–6) gives a succinct account of the administrative background of the 18th-century Victualling Board.
2 Rodger 1986, 82–7.
3 Coad 1989, 273. Hattendorf *et al* (1993, 655–7) show how little the basic diet had changed by 1850.
4 Baugh 1977, 406. A century later the Victualling Department's knowledge of food preservation may have been why David Livingstone used it to supply his 1854–64 Zambezi expedition, leading to an expense claim of £198 5s 3d from the Comptroller (TNA ADM 1/5725, 1 June 1859).
5 Hattendorf *et al* 1993, 245.
6 For the very similar victuals of the Tudor navy, *see* Knighton and Loades 2011, 236–9. NMM ADM/E/24 is a letter of 26 Dec 1763 from the Sick and Hurt Board to the Admiralty saying they are proposing trials of the 'portable broth' to combat scurvy.
7 The figures come from Lloyd and Coulter (1961, 123) and Rodger (2004, 395).
8 The site of the Victualling Yard was later occupied by the Royal Mint. After the mint closed in 1976 the most extensive archaeological excavations on any former naval site were undertaken (Grainger and Phillpotts 2010).
9 The Redhouse site at Deptford included a number of buildings that were retained and adapted for reuse. This probably accounts for the brewhouse costing £596, whereas its attendant storehouse was estimated at £2,037.
10 Morriss 2007, 45–7.
11 In 1826 £32,000 was put in the estimates for a corn mill for Deptford (TNA ADM 181/26).
12 Baugh 1977, 442–4, letter from the Victualling Board to the Admiralty Secretaty 8 Sept 1743. AdL Portfolio B19-30 fol 27 is a 1743 plan of the proposed Deptford victualling yard that may well have accompanied the report quoted by Baugh.
13 TNA ADM 174/414.
14 Coad (1989, 274–6) goes into more detail of these individual buildings.
15 Coad 1989, 282–3.
16 TNA ADM 7/658. NMM ADM/BP/38a, 19 May 1818, shows the victualling yard sited a little upstream from the gunwharf by the Sun Hard. TNA ADM 111/255, 10 Nov 1821, also mentions a scatter of rented premises.
17 TNA ADM 111/255, 10 Nov 1821; ADM 111/257, 5 Aug 1822. TNA ADM 140/692 is a plan of Sheerness in 1825, showing the victualling storehouse to be comparatively small.
18 TNA ADM 111/257, 25 Sept1822; ADM 111/257, 19 Nov 1822, records a decision by the Victualling Board to lease off much of their Chatham premises, including the cattle shed, pound, yard and jetty.
19 Knight and Wilcox (2010, 218) list the following depots operated by contractors and active around the British coasts during the Napoleonic Wars: Falmouth, Penzance, Dover, Chatham, Yarmouth, Newcastle, Leith, Greenock, Liverpool, Milford Haven, Swansea, Bristol, Appledore, Dublin, Waterford, Cork, Kinsale, Limerick, Lough Swilly and Londonderry.
20 Information from Jon Iveson, Dover Museum.
21 TNA ADM 1/3502, 9 Dec 1836. Presumably the naval facilities at Deal were adequate during peacetime.
22 Bannerman 2008, 21. In the early 18th century there were comparatively few army garrisons overseas, and local military commanders arranged contracts locally or obtained supplies from the navy's victualling depots.
23 Crewe 1993, 150.
24 Wilcox (2011) gives a detailed account of the East Indies victualling operations between 1780 and 1815.
25 Rodger 2004, 306.
26 Alsop (1995, 468–9) sheds light on the workings of the Agent Victuallers at Lisbon during part of the 18th century.
27 AdL B19 fol 30, plan dated 28 Dec 1743.
28 Coad 1989, 330.
29 TNA ADM 106/2021, 23 March 1799.
30 Coad (1989, 321–4) gives a more detailed building account.
31 TNA ADM 1/5740, 20 Aug 1862, records that a victualling store at Trincomalee was sold to the Ceylon Government.
32 *See* TNA ADM 140/1185 pt 2, 1785, for Antigua; ADM140/1484 *c* 1909 for Trincomalee and Port Royal; AdL Miscellaneous Foreign Property Letting Book 1 and TNA ADM 140/1484 for Yokohama.
33 Sheerness had long suffered from a shortage of fresh water, as most wells sunk there tended to be brackish. Using a steam pump, the new well was intended to raise fresh water from a much greater depth.
34 TNA ADM 174/363.
35 TNA WO 44/52, 4 Apr 1813, Lt Colonel Ford to Lieutenant General Mann; TNA ADM 181/53 records that £165 was put in the 1842/3 estimates for 'watering place repairs'. *See also* AdL 1859 plan, Da 022 fol 12.
36 For detailed accounts of the administrative history of the Victualling Board during the Napoleonic Wars, *see* Knight and Wilcox 2010 and MacDonald 2010.
37 Coad 1989, 283.
38 TNA ADM 111/258, 12 July 1823.
39 The site had been selected in 1822, but individual property owners had to be bought out (TNA ADM 111/258, 12 July 1823).
40 TNA ADM 111/257, 14 Nov 1822. Significantly, when Taylor drew up his proposals for the Gosport establishment, this was headed 'Estimate for a War and Peace Establishment at Weevil'. The Victualling Board was perhaps more conscious than most that it had to build spare capacity into its manufacturing yards. The Duke of Clarence was highly

enthusiastic about Rennie's work at Stonehouse. After visiting the yard in July 1828, when he was briefly Lord High Admiral, his report noted, 'The new victualling establishment at Cremill Point promises everything to satisfy my utmost expectation of advantage from a plan so well considered in its origin' (TNA ADM 7/665, 22 July 1828). For a more detailed building account of Stonehouse, *see* Coad 1989, 282–90.

41 AdL Da 01, Plans of Naval Establishments *c* 1840. An 1863 plan in the same series shows the open space divided into what looks like a series of rectangular holding pens.

42 TNA ADM 111/262, 1 Feb 1828.

43 TNA ADM 111/262, 17 Nov 1827; ADM 111/263, 20 and 30 Aug 1828; ADM 111/265, 27 Jan and 30 Aug 1830.

44 TNA ADM 111/265, 17 Sept 1830; ADM 111/267, 19 Jan 1832.

45 TNA ADM 111/266, 23 Nov 1831.

46 Britton and Brayley 1832, 88.

47 TNA ADM 174/376, 'General Instruction to be Strictly Complied with by All Officers and Others in Her Majesty's Victualling Yards, Home', 1855, London, p 111. Separate but very similar instructions were issued for Abroad Yards.

48 TNA ADM 174/415, 1891 yard plan.

49 Akiyama 2008, 427. The bakery was badly damaged by a fire after the First World War; it was probably then that the bread ovens were removed, and it became largely stores and workshops.

50 BL Gough MS Antiq 2 fol 20. For a more detailed building account of this yard, *see* Coad 1989, 274–82.

51 NMM POR/A/23, 11 Nov 1766; TNA ADM 7/659.

52 In 1813 Bentham had suggested such a move, but the proposal had lapsed with his dismissal (NMM ADM/BP/33b, 14 Apr 1813). *See* Coad (1989, 276) for details of the land transactions.

53 TNA ADM 111/262, 31 Dec 1827. *See* Rodger (1979, 95) for an assessment of the Duke's well-meaning desire to improve the navy and the conditions of the sailors.

54 Coad 1989, 276. This contains a more detailed account of the building of the yard and its tangled financial history.

55 TNA ADM 111/263, 5 June 1828.

56 Taylor regarded McIntosh's tender for this as adequate and told the Victualling Board that 'a contract was not necessary'. Financial control of projects does not seem to have been his strongpoint (TNA ADM 111/263, 24 Jan 1828).

57 TNA ADM 114/42, 28 Sept 1831.

58 TNA ADM 174/399, plan dated *c* 1858. In 1861 it was recommended as suitable for a new clothing store (TNA ADM 1/5775, 26 Apr 1861).

59 TNA ADM 1/5775 (26 Apr 1861) recommended a rotary oven 'similar to one recently fitted at Malta'.

60 TNA ADM 181/36, estimates for 1826, has an entry of £8,000 required that year towards the total cost of £32,000 for building a corn mill at Deptford. Although the motive power is not stated, a steam engine can be assumed in the absence of any other practical alternative.

61 TNA ADM 181/44.

62 *Navy and Army Illustrated* 7 Sept 1901, 616; 14 Sept 1901, 639; 29 Sept 1901, 47. Clarence Yard appears to have had a similar output of biscuits to Stonehouse.

63 TNA ADM 174/360 shows the location of these on the 1888 yard plan. *See* Hattendorf *et al* (1993, 655–7) for victualling improvements proposed in 1850.

64 *Navy and Army Illustrated* 21 Sept 1901, 24.

65 *Navy and Army Illustrated* 14 Sept 1901, 639. 'Cold Chambers in ships of war' were then still some decades away, but the victualling authorities were alive to the chilled meat then starting to arrive from South America and New Zealand. A few years later at Gibraltar, the abortive North Gorge Magazine found a remarkable new use as a cold meat store supplying both the garrison and the navy (Evans 2006, 112).

15 Naval Ordnance Yards

1 Evans 2006, 107.

2 Lavery 1987, 83; Rogers 1971, 77. Wealden gun-founding was always on a small scale; *see* Crossley 1975 for one such site. The most complete 18th-century ironworks to survive with its furnace is at Bonawe, Argyll (Hay and Stell 1986, 108–14).

3 Cocroft 2000, 33. The author gives a succinct account of the early years at both these sites.

4 Coad 1989, 247; Evans 2006, 17; Saunders 1967, 15.

5 Evans 2006, 35–40.

6 At a cramped site such as Upnor, restoving was impossible, and powder requiring the process was sent to the Faversham powder works (Evans 2006, 247).

7 Between 30 Aug 1807 and 7 Apr 1814, 52,953,970 rounds of small-arms ammunition were produced at the Portsmouth laboratory (Evans 2006, 50). *See* TNA WO 44/643 for a plan.

8 Evans 2006, 43. At the time, the Admiralty would not permit floating magazines at Chatham because of lack of river space to moor them with safety. This was not a problem at Sheerness where the estuary allowed more room, and floating magazines were occasionally anchored there.

9 Coad 1989, 260.

10 TNA ADM 1/4008, 3 May 1743.

11 These were perhaps most famously used against Fort McHenry in the War of 1812, inspiring the fifth line of the first verse of the The Star-Spangled Banner: 'And the rockets' red glare, the bombs bursting in air'.

12 Evans (2000b, 141–50) gives a detailed history of the Tipner site. The surviving buildings, including both magazines that have had their vaults removed, are now in the centre of a scrap yard.

13 *See* TNA ADM 140/388 for a 1799 plan of the navy yard, which was principally a stores base. The hospital was designed by William Pilkington.

14 Evans 2006, 49. The storekeeper's house, clerk of the cheque's house, two barracks and a building used as a smiths' shop and carpenters' shop also remain (Anon 2002, 43–4).

15 Anon 2002, 45–7, 66. Marchwood was badly bombed in 1940 and closed in 1961. A number of the buildings, including original magazines, remain.

16 Evans 2006, 94.

17 TNA ADM 140/1484 fol 39.

18 In 1868 it was discovered that wet guncotton could be detonated using fulminate of mercury surrounded by dry guncotton as an initiatory explosive (Cocroft 2000, 122).

19 This very simplified account ignores the complexities of the associated fuses. *See also* Evans 2006, 129.

20 TNA ADM140/4; MPH 1/247.

21 The clerk of the cheque's house was designed by Colonel Robert D'Arcy RE. I am grateful to Peter Kendall for this information.

22 BL Kings Top. Coll XVIII certainly shows the ground floor as late as 1725 with internal partitions that have long gone, with no alterations or additions to the castle, such as storehouses.

23 TNA WO 47/35, 22 June 1750. Curiously, safety does not seem to have been the paramount consideration leading to the installation of the windlass; rather, as the report notes, it was 'very difficult to get men who will run such a risk upon labourer's pay'. The shifting rooms on the water bastion no longer exist, but the marks of their roofs remain visible on the castle walls. The hoist system was modified after the Napoleonic Wars (Evans 2000, 3–4).

24 Saunders 1967, 15.

25 TNA WO 44/140. The castle courtyard later became a proof ground, remarkably retaining this use in 1931 when the

adjacent building housed an ordnance museum (Evans 2000a, 4).

26 TNA WO 51/102, 30 Sept 1718.

27 Saunders 2005, 161. This article gives a very good account of the scope of work undertaken by an ordnance establishment serving the navy during a period of hostilities.

28 Evans 2006, 44. These no longer exist.

29 Evans 2000a, 11. Both magazines (one with a capacity of 20,000 barrels) and one of the shell stores remain.

30 Evans 2000a, 20. In 1875 the Magazine Committee raised the limit to 8,000 barrels.

31 Evans 2000a, 171–7. Evans gives a detailed account of the complications of establishing this new site. The layout is clearly shown on a 1910 plan (AdL Da 0 36 fol 54).

32 Sheerness had a small gunwharf in the centre of the dockyard from the 18th century; its configuration prior to the rebuilding of the yard in the 1820s is best shown on TNA ADM 140/665. After the rebuilding it was relocated alongside the Garrison, but never consisted of more than a single, large, L-shaped storehouse, clearly shown on an 1863 plan of the yard (AdL Naval Establishments 1863, Da 02). Probably for reasons of space and vulnerability to bombardment from the sea, there were no magazines apart from those in the fortifications.

33 TNA WO 47/30, 16 Aug 1717, records the construction of a new storehouse for planks and standing carriages at God's House Green.

34 TNA WO 47/30, 14 Apr 1717. The substantial sum of £801 7s was paid to Messrs Lidgbirds, master bricklayers (Coad 1989, 257–9).

35 Coad 1989, 258.

36 Conolly 1898, 9.

37 TNA WO 55/2657; MR 1/827. The full list is in Coad 1989, 259. Interestingly, this does not mention a magazine recorded in 1835 as being there since 1814 (Evans 2006, 53).

38 A plan of 1907 (AdL Da 036 fol 20) shows the new gunwharf as it had evolved by the time of the First World War.

39 In 1918 a mine depot was established at Frater, replacing the former frigate HMS *Vernon* that from 1872 had been used to repair and test mines. She was originally moored in Fountain Lake and from 1895 in Portchester Creek. In 1923 the mines went to Frater, and the mine school transferred to the former gunwharf, renamed HMS *Vernon*. Further magazines were constructed near Fort Elson in 1925 (Semark 1997, 250, 440–5).

40 NMM POR/F/13, 4 Apr 1766; Coad 1989, 260–2.

41 TNA WO 47/72, 18 Nov 1768, reports that 'the proposal for erecting the other two magazines may be postponed until a convenient situation is agreed upon'. It never was. The plans were modified by Skinner and probably others on the Board as well (TNA WO 47/73, 5 June 1769).

42 Evans 2006, 21, 50. Evans records that Archer reckoned to lift the total of barrels to 5,742 by using a different stacking configuration.

43 Evans 2000b, 4–5. The storekeeper's house was demolished in 1952; Evans (2006, 25) has an illustration.

44 At Portsmouth the move was also prompted by the existing laboratory at Frederick's Battery standing in the way of a dockyard extension.

45 Evans 2000b, 66–7; Evans 2006, 54–5, 96, 101–4.

46 The Bedenham magazines were given pitched rather than flat roofs. Evans (2000b 133–40) gives a comprehensive account of the development of Bedenham. This remains in use; the old centre of Priddy's Hard is in the care of the Portsmouth Naval Base Property Trust and is open to visitors as an ordnance museum.

47 TNA WO 47/30, 15 Oct 1717.

48 TNA WO 47/32, 26 March, 7 Apr and 26 June 1719; Vetch 2004a.

49 Colvin 1995, 542. *See* Hewlings (2004) for a detailed biography. Jelfe was to hold the position of Architect until 1727 and early on was responsible for a number of barracks in Scotland, including the surviving one at Ruthven. He was a master mason with a considerable business.

50 This quarrying was still under way in 1722 (TNA WO 49/229, 29 Sept 1722).

51 TNA WO 49/230, 20 Nov 1724. The records mention '551 feet running of fir quarter 3 ½ inches by 2 ½ inches planed and spiked to the floors for truckways'. This is the earliest instance I have found for the use of guided railways within buildings for stores' handling, but the casual mention in the records suggests this may have already been practised by the Board of Ordnance. Wooden railways were well established in Britain in the 17th century, mainly in the coal-mining districts (Lewis 1970).

52 Lewis 1970.

53 TNA ADM 1/4008, 10 May 1743.

54 The St Budeaux mills declined in importance after the Napoleonic Wars. In 1828 an explosion caused some damage to the site (TNA WO 44/307, 26 Nov 1828). Subsequent correspondence considered various options including sale and conversion of some of the buildings into barracks. Part of the site was later incorporated into Bull Point.

55 TNA WO 47/87, 22 May 1776; TNA MR 1/572 is a 1791 plan of the yard. TNA WO 55/2485 contains the first known reference fto mention one of the buildings being used as a blacksmiths' shop in 1821. *See* Parnell (1993, 64) for a description of the duties of furbishers at the Tower of London in the 1660s.

56 Coad 1989, 256.

57 Evans 2006, 22–3.

58 TNA ADM 181/60, estimates 1849/50.

59 TNA ADM 181/66, 1855/6 estimates. In Sept 1854 a tender of £46,572 had been accepted from the contractors Clifford and Drew to construct the basin (Evans 2006, 67).

60 *See* Evans (2006, 67–72) for a detailed description of the operation of Bull Point.

61 Evans 2006, 232.

62 A similar set of defensible barracks of the same period exists outside Pembroke Dockyard.

63 AdL Portfolio B25. The style of drawing is suggestive of a mid-18th-century date. The magazine does not appear to have been constructed.

64 At Port Antonio the principal magazine was proposed for Fort George at Titchfield Town; no ordnance facilities were planned for Lynches Island (AdL Vz 10 fol 67, undated plan).

65 TNA ADM 1/376, 24 May 1709.

66 The drunken angles of the late 19th-century gun emplacements at Port Royal show that the navy had every reason to be concerned about earthquakes. Knowles's 1748 proposals for a grand fortified base at Port Royal had magazines only within the fortifications (AdL Vz 10 fol 75).

67 Evans (2006, 114) highlights the problem at St Lucia in the late 19th century.

68 NMM Com-01 fol 62. Lt Columbine became a distinguished naval hydrographer and was later appointed the first Governor of Sierra Leone.

69 TNA MF 1/6 fol 1, 1858. Tank Bay referred to the adjacent naval water tank.

70 AdL Plans of Naval Establishments *c* 1840, Da 01 fol 17.

71 Raddall 1993, 145–6. TNA ADM 174/362 is an 1859 plan of naval facilities at Halifax that shows the naval powder magazine.

72 Nelson and Oliver 1982, 163–5.

73 TNA ADM 174/361; Evans 2006, 114.

74 TNA ADM 116/680, 7 Sept 1896.

75 Rice 2010, 8, 215

76 TNA ADM 140/1484 fol 77 is a 1909 plan showing the Kloof depot. A photograph in Rice (2010, 75) of the earlier ordnance depot shows at least one metal-framed building with windows set high in the walls, characteristic of Admiralty design for ordnance buildings in the 1890s.
77 AdL Naval Establishments Da 02 fol 15.
78 TNA ADM 140/1484 fol 77. It is not known if any of these buildings survive.
79 Harris 2010. Documentation for all these buildings is sparse; fortunately a number of date stones survive.
80 White (1999, 113–14) suggests that the withdrawal of nominally free convict labour in the 1850s led to a more utilitarian architecture.
81 AdL Album Da 039. In 1915 the western house had a first floor added when it became the senior officer's residence.
82 AdL Vz 15 fol 81 is a 1900 plan of Spectacle Island that identifies all these buildings. A slightly later plan of 1909 is in TNA ADM 140/1484 fol 82.
83 Spectacle Island is still used by the Royal Australian Navy, and its historic importance is appreciated.
84 TNA ADM 140/1484 fol 64; Evans 2006, 112–13. The Shell Stores no longer exist.
85 AdL Vz 15 fol 37; Evans 2006, 112.

16 Care of the Sick and Wounded: Naval Hospitals

1 For the administrative and other developments in the century after 1650, *see* Harland (2003), the most detailed and authoritative account.
2 Merriman 1961, 216–23. In effect, until the 18th century this meant St Thomas's and St Bartholomew's Hospitals, the best available ones with the requisite experience and medical skills.
3 Harland 2003, 114–15.
4 Harland 2003, 86–7. Stevenson (2000, 173) makes the point that hospital ships largely prevented desertion and kept patients away from drinking and gambling.
5 Harland 2003, 99. This was not a navy hospital as such.
6 Merriman 1950, 217 n 1. Since July 1699 the Navy Board had taken on peacetime responsibility for sick and wounded from the Commissioners of the Register.
7 Harland 2003, 136–42, 239.
8 Merriman 1961, 218. This Fifth Commission was to remain in existence throughout the 18th century, although responsibility for prisoners was transferred to the Transport Board in 1796.
9 Harland 2003, 146. None of these survive.
10 The naval hospital at Lisbon was still in existence into the latter half of the 19th century. AdL Misc Foreign Property Letting Book records that in 1859 the establishment was formed of three houses, one occupied as a hospital, one for the medical officers' quarters and one as a coach-house.
11 NMM T1/110, 30 Dec 1708.
12 *See* Coad (1989, 333–9) for a more detailed architectural history. *See* Harland (2008) for the crucial role played by Sir John Jennings in securing construction of the hospital.
13 Harland 2003, 219.
14 Harland 2003, 355, 388.
15 NMM ADM/F/3, 30 Nov 1742, Sick and Hurt Board to the Admiralty. Harland (2003, 276) says, 'there was no absolutely typical contract hospital of Queen Anne's War. Within certain parameters there was diversification. This was because the hospitals were established in different regions, at different dates and in different circumstances.'
16 Harland 2003, 408.
17 Lloyd and Coulter 1961, 109. Harland (2003, 397–407) gives a detailed narrative of this typhus outbreak and its effects.
18 TNA ADM 99/12, 5 May 1740, quoted in Harland 2003, 404.
19 A similar proposal, made for the same reasons, had been put forward in 1653 (Harland 2003, 90).
20 TNA ADM 1/3529, 31 March 1741; NMM ADM/E/8a, 22 Oct 1740; NMM ADM/E/8b, 22 Jan 1740. A plan is in TNA ADM 1/3528. Conversion costs for providing a 1,100-bed hospital were estimated at £1,800.
21 Harland 2003, 410–11. TNA ADM 1/3529, 31 March 1741. On past experience the Admiralty may well have had doubts about estimated costs for new buildings. Similar savings in running costs were put forward for the Minorca hospital in 1742 (Coad 1989, 294).
22 Harland 2003. The author goes into considerable detail, not least in comparing the staffing levels and supervision with the great London hospitals, notably St Bartholomew's.
23 NMM ADM/E/8b, 4 Apr 1741.
24 Quoted in Lloyd and Coulter 1961, 194. The authors credit Sandwich with approaching the Crown, but he was not appointed to the Admiralty Board until Dec 1744, although they quote a date for the submission of 28 Feb 1744. Harland(2003, 430) quotes a date of 15 Sept 1744 from a published source, but was unable to find any reference in the Privy Council Registers.
25 Harland 2003, 431.
26 With the closure of the navy's last directly run hospital at Haslar in 2007, the Royal Navy has effectively reverted to the old contract system, only this time with the National Health Service.
27 Watt 2011, 148–9. The author notes the establishment in 1746 of the Association of Naval Surgeons that met to hear original papers based on their own work and whose rules 'seem to have provided the basis of the rules of the Medical Society of London, founded in 1773 and the oldest continuing medical society in this country'. Thomas Trotter (1760–1832) was one of the most influential and distinguished naval physicians.
28 'Statements of the comparative Health of the British Navy', published in 1815 in *Medico-Chirurgical Transactions* and quoted in Lloyd and Coulter (1961, 183). Blane's work, successively as naval surgeon from 1779, physician at St Thomas's Hospital from 1783 and Commissioner of Sick and Wounded from 1795 to 1802, gave him opportunity to follow his professional interest and zeal in seeking to emphasise that prevention was better than cure. Building on the earlier work of Trotter and Lind, Blane in 1795 authorised the regular issue of lemon juice throughout the fleet to combat scurvy.
29 Stevenson 2000, 159, 162. The author notes that at Haslar those patients considered the most contagious were placed on the top floor, as nobody could safely be accommodated above them.
30 Crewe (1993, 30–51) gives an excellent account of this disastrous move. A report of 1806 noted that 'of the hospital there is scarcely a vestige to show where it stood', but associated storehouses had been lent to the Ordnance Board for stores and barracks and in part as a cooperage (TNA ADM 106/3209, 23 Apr 1806).
31 Quoted in Richardson 1998, 79.
32 Richardson 1998, 82.
33 Richardson 1998, 85. TNA ADM 1/5775, 26 Nov 1861, records the final cost of this as £72,294, an excess of £7,994 over the original estimate.
34 TNA ADM 1/5775, 2 Apr 1861, mentions the 'imminent transfer of Deal Hospital to the Royal Marines'. Three years later the small naval base here was closed and its site sold.
35 TNA ADM 1/3526, 9 June 1803; ADM 1/3527, 6 June 1807.
36 Richardson 1998, 84; TNA ADM 140/393–409. In TNA ADM 1/3527, 6 June 1807, Bentham proposed a 116-bed hospital to cost £8,534; he and Holl revised this to hold 238 beds and to cost £19,689. On 24 Dec 1807 the Admiralty asked for a 300-bed hospital; Bentham put forward proposals in April 1808 estimated at £32,242.
37 TNA ADM 140/1484 fol 58 indicates that by 1909 the hospital's capacity had been

reduced to 50 officers, 177 seamen and marines and 28 attendants.

38 TNA ADM 114/40, 6 Jan, 23 May and 1 June 1826. In Jan 1826 a Mr Barker of Rochester had tendered to construct the hospital; in May the contractor Hugh McIntosh submitted a tender for £22,222.

39 *Navy and Army Illustrated* (12 Nov 1898, 170–1) states the cost of Taylor's hospital as £70,000, but gives no source. The 1905 hospital was designed by J C T Murray (Richardson 1998, 86).

40 TNA ADM 98/14 fol 463.

41 A precise date for this work has not been found. Perhaps because it was a comparatively simple conversion, it does not appear in the annual estimates. It was certainly operational by 1861 when various improvements were requested, including a dead house, a drying house and other amenities (TNA ADM 1/5775, 25 Oct 1861). A 'cottage for the hospital laundry maid' appears in TNA ADM 181/92, estimates for 1881/2. TNA ADM 140/1484 fol 47 shows the later zymotic blocks in existence by 1909; they no longer survive.

42 Richardson 1998, 140. From the early 1890s to 1914 over 300 local-authority isolation hospitals were also built in Britain.

43 A plan of the South Queensferry Hospital is in TNA ADM 140/1484 fol 19.

44 Harland 2003, 360. Baia near Naples was in use between 1718 and 1720.

45 NMM ADM/BP/34b, 30 July 1814. At Madras a hospital was in use during the Napoleonic Wars. In 1814 the agent in charge was a Mr W Taylor, who was also being required to act as storekeeper at the proposed yard at Trincomalee.

46 The hospital at Jamaica was located near Kingston, not Port Royal.

47 Letter from the Governor, Sir Ralph Payne, quoted in Blackburne (1972, 13). Following this disaster, houses were hired (TNA ADM 98/14, 10 Dec 1781).

48 TNA ADM 98/14, 5 Nov 1783.

49 TNA ADM 140/1220 is a 1779 plan of the proposed hospital 'adapted to the site of the late Hospital at English Harbour'. TNA MPH 1/890 is a plan dated 25 Apr 1831 'to accompany an estimate for repairs'. This shows only two blocks and the necessary ancillary buildings such as lodges, bog houses and kitchen. In some ways this hospital with its detached blocks could be said to anticipate the pavilion plan, save for the absence of a linking corridor or colonnade. The 1779 plan (TNA ADM 140/1220 pt 2) shows the floor plan divided by a central partition, but with windows on three sides. In the 1831 plan of the two blocks (TNA MPH 1/890), the central partition has gone, allowing the large single wards to have windows on all four sides. In 1730 Admiral Stewart had proposed a series of small block wards for a proposed hospital at Jamaica (Harland 2003, 381).

50 Part of the reason for the delay lay in changing operational patterns, the Sick and Hurt Board noting in 1781 that Antigua 'was less resorted to by the King's ships than the other islands' (TNA ADM 98/14, 10 Dec 1781).

51 TNA ADM 98/14, 29 Aug 1783. Pigeon Island was equipped with gun batteries, two barracks for troops and a naval hospital. The hospital may be the building shown as a plan in TNA MPH 1/890 fol 10, dated 1831. Fort Rodney remains, along with a number of footings of buildings below; these may relate to army buildings proposed here in the 1820s.

52 TNA ADM 98/14, 2 Oct 1783. This was in existence by Sept 1779 and is also referred to as 'New York Hospital'.

53 Gwyn 2004, 44; TNA ADM 98/14, 4 Feb 1785.

54 NMM ADM/BP/34b, 30 Aug 1814. Cochrane was made Commander-in-Chief of the Leeward Islands in 1805, remaining in the West Indies until 1814. The hospital numbers are based on Holl's estimate that each bed there cost £367 10s 2½d

55 Coad 1989, 350–1.

56 NMM ADM/BP/34b, 30 Aug 1814. The Admiralty order to Holl to design a hospital was dated 23 March 1813. *See* Chapter 4 for the problems Holl had over this hospital with Admiral Cochrane.

57 Stranack 1990, 70–1. The Isolation or Zymotic Block is now a retirement home known as Lefroy House.

58 At Barbados the buildings of 'old Naval Yard' were handed to the army on condition the navy could have them back if required. This arrangement was approved by Lord Bathurst on 24 May 1816 and seems to have been a general requirement (AdL Admiralty Terriers, Misc Foreign Property Letting Book 1). The hospitals at Gibraltar and Great Yarmouth both reverted to use by the navy.

59 TNA ADM 181/35, 1825 estimates.

60 Location of the earlier hospital is clearly shown on an 1890 plan of the yard (TNA ADM 174/379). Construction of the later hospital began in 1899. The aerial cableway was discontinued after the First World War. Pers comm Sandy Myers.

61 TNA ADM 106/3216. The plans were sent to Holl in England. If Mr Stringer won the contract, he stated he would prefabricate much of the timberwork at Madras or Cochin.

62 TNA ADM 181/82, estimates 1871/2. TNA ADM 1/3454, 30 Aug 1862, mentions the 'foundations of an abandoned hospital building'. AdL Admiralty Terriers, Misc Foreign Property Letting Book 1, mentions the hospital and grounds in 1889.

63 TNA ADM 1/6015, 22 March 1867. Yokohama was seen as a suitable location for 'the projected erection of an invalid establishment'.

64 Harland 1985, 75–9 (with a good photograph of the hospital on p 75).

65 *Navy and Army Illustrated* 6 Dec 1902, 281.

66 AdL Admiralty Terriers, Misc Foreign Property Letting Book 1. The coal depot was closed and a contract given to a local supplier in 1888. The flag officer never got his house. The site of the hospital was returned to the Japanese government in 1929.

67 The original hospital was a traditional local building that was demolished (*Navy and Army Illustrated* 26 Nov 1898, 227–8; TNA ADM 140/1484 fol 84). The plan also shows that the flag officer did get a house here. Wei Hai Wei was to be developed later as a naval air base before being returned to China in 1930.

68 Nelson and Oliver 1982, 116–19. The hospital became the naval training establishment HMCS *Naden* in 1922. The original timber hospital of 1855 at Duntze Head held 100 patients; probably a similar number could be accommodated at Naden. *See* Appleton (2008) for a good account of the sort of life led by young naval medical officers at these more remote naval stations in the latter part of the 19th century.

69 Callender 1920, quoted in Keevil 1958, 213.

70 TNA T1/110, 30 Dec 1708. Coad (1989, 333–40) gives a more detailed account of the building. *See also* Harland 2003.

71 Journal of Sir John Jennings, 11 April 1711, quoted in Kepler 1973, 27.

72 TNA T1/151, 12 Aug 1712. Jennings needed to engage the Catalan and Majorcan workmen, who were then finishing work on the fortifications. For the problems resulting from Jennings's initiative, *see* Coad 1989, 334–5.

73 TNA ADM 140/1321 is a plan of this building. Jennings mentions the hospital as having 14 wards, but the plan indicates 16, unless 2 were used for other purposes.

74 NMM ADM/E/5, 3 Sept 1715.

75 TNA ADM 1/386, 3 Apr and 20 Aug 1770.

76 The Sick and Hurt Board favoured rebuilding the hospital as a single-storey building for 550 patients.

77 TNA ADM 1/386, 26 Oct 1771.

78 TNA ADM 1/386, 26 Oct 1771; ADM 98/10, 22 May 1772. Little is known about Warren. It is possible he designed the

rebuilt hospital, but it is more likely that he sought advice from local contractors and from the army garrison, which almost certainly included an engineer. TNA ADM 98/10 records that on 1 Jan 1771, the Sick and Hurt Board forwarded to the Admiralty drawings for a new hospital for 1,200 patients; the former considered the cost and numbers excessive. Unfortunately, the plan does not appear to survive; however, it is clear that the Sick and Hurt Board was overruled by the Admiralty, who wanted a larger hospital. TNA ADM 98/10, 22 May 1772, notes the bulging walls. The existing buttresses, not part of the original reconstruction, were probably strengthened to cure the problem.

79 TNA ADM 98/10, 20 Oct 1774.

80 NMM ADM/F/3, 23 Nov 1742, 25 May 1743. These were part of a very detailed set of instructions drafted by the Sick and Hurt Board for the care of the sick at Mahon, but doubtless represent the standards the Board then expected in all its contract hospitals. TNA ADM 1/3529, 9 Sept 1742, suggests that the reality at Mahon may have been different. An anonymous letter to the Board complaining of mismanagement by the contractor at the hospital moved the Sick and Hurt Board to set out a detailed letter to the Admiralty recommending that the contract system here be replaced with one where the Crown appointed staff and ran the hospital. Apart from improving patient care, the Board reckoned that the new arrangements would cost annually £9,016 4s 7d compared to £13,154 5s of the existing contract. NMM ADM/F/3, 20 Jan 1743, notes that as a half-way mark, the Sick and Hurt Board agreed to supply beds to both the Mahon and Gibraltar hospitals.

81 The different numbers reflect Jennings's statement that there were 14 wards, whereas TNA ADM 140/1321 suggests there were 16.

82 At the time of writing a local group is starting to conserve the buildings.

83 Harland 2003, 370–3.

84 Coad 1989, 319. Harland (2003, 373–4) makes the point that the station was considered healthy and at the time the number of sick there was low.

85 TNA ADM 1/3528, 12 Nov 1739, records that there were then 'upwards of 600 sick people at the hospital' and that extra accommodation had to be hired. This may be a reference to the army hospital being used in a crisis.

86 NMM ADM/E/8a, 5 Apr 1740; NMM ADM/Y/G/52.

87 NMM ADM/BP 41b, 31 July 1821.

88 TNA ADM 98/2, 27 June 1745. NMM POR/H/5, 22 Feb 1745, is a report by Portsmouth officers who recommended the purchase of Haslar Farm as the ideal place for a hospital 'both with regard to the easiness of its access for the sick seamen, the wholesomeness of its air, and the goodness of its soil being all gravel'.

89 Acworth was a carpenter by trade and had been Surveyor since 1715. In 1744 Admiral Vernon described him as 'a half-experienced and half-judicious surveyor' who had 'half ruined the navy' (Lavery 2008). NMM ADM/Y/G/55 has a number of undated and unsigned plans that may be early proposals for the hospital.

90 TNA ADM 98/2, 27 June 1745.

91 Colvin 1995, 516. Colvin (1995, 997) noted also that John Turner, who had supervised construction of the new Town Hall at Portsmouth, 'is said to have assisted in the construction of the Naval Hospital at Haslar in 1745'.

92 Birbeck, Ryder and Ward (2009) provide the best modern illustrated history of the hospital.

93 NMM POR/A15, 25 July 1747. The Navy Board turned down Spenser's request to be allowed to remove a 2ft layer of brickearth from 6 acres of the site, so he must have obtained his supplies from elsewhere. *See also* Richardson 1998, 79. The cellars were used in the 1790s to prepare lemon concentrate as an anti-scorbutic before its production became the responsibility of the Victualling Board; in the 1940s they were used as operating theatres and air-raid shelters.

94 In 1776 it was described by the chaplain of the Brunswick Dragoons as 'a large copper roofed building' (Lloyd and Coulter 1961, 213).

95 NMM ADM/F/12, 17 March 1755, for 1755 figures. Lloyd and Coulter (1961, 212–13) give a later capacity of 2,100; Birkbeck, Ryder and Ward (2009, 13) suggest 'probably nearer 2,500'.

96 Lloyd and Coulter 1961, 213.

97 The building was extensively restored in 1963.

98 Birbeck, Ryder and Ward 2009, 33. This revised system of governance lasted some 75 years.

99 NMM POR/A39, 14 March 1796; POR/A43, 13 Nov 1799. The new occupants were already complaining about shoddy workmanship.

100 NMM ADM/Q/3321, 11 Apr 1801. In his letter to Bentham, Bunce stated that the 'Governor's House was built under my direction'; it would be reasonable to assume that he was also responsible for the rest of the terrace.

101 *Navy and Army Illustrated* 19 Feb 1897, 115.'Airing Grounds' were specified in a 1785 report by the Commission for Sick and Hurt on the future design of naval hospitals (Richardson 1998, 82).

102 Lloyd and Coulter (1961, 216, 261) attribute this delay to lack of finance and a desire to see if Haslar was a success. As at Gosport, some time was spent considering whether a local prison could be converted more cheaply. Pugh (1974) gives a useful short history of Stonehouse Hospital.

103 Colvin 1995, 835.

104 NMM ADM/F18, 14 Nov 1758. By 1909 the number had been reduced to 819 men and 34 officers (TNA ADM 140/1484 fol 42).

105 Internal modifications would later remove lengths of the spine walls. *See* TNA ADM 140/1484 fol 42, dated 1909.

106 TNA ADM 140/321 pts 1 and 2. Pt 2 is dated 22 June 1796.

107 In 1795 Captain Richard Creyke arrived as Governor and left a detailed description of the layout and use of the hospital buildings (Coad 1989, 300–1).

108 Quoted in Lloyd and Coulter 1961, 238.

109 Quoted in Richardson 1998, 81.

110 TNA ADM 140/323 and 325. Holl was to use a version of his design here in 1813 for the proposed houses at Deal Hospital (TNA ADM 140/139).

111 Aptly described in Pevsner's *Devon* as 'engineer's Gothic'. More recent hospital buildings, mostly unobtrusive, have been in yellow stock brick. The hospital is now divided between private housing and a school.

112 Levien 1981, 18. Cree remained in the navy until 1869.

113 Revell 1978, 42. AdL Naval Establishments 1863 Da 02 fol 17 has an 1863 plan showing part of Haslar's east wing reserved 'for lunatics'. TNA ADM 140/1484 fol 25 shows this was still being used in 1909. Revell (1978, 19) notes that a separate, purpose-built mental department was built near the sea wall in 1910 and remained in use until 1960. Stonehouse Hospital appears to have had broadly similar arrangements, with dedicated 'lunatic wards' shown on a 1909 plan (TNA ADM140/1484 fol 42).

114 None of the other naval hospitals seem to have had long-term patients, although this subject has been little explored. For the best account of the early work of the Boards of Survey, *see* Lloyd and Coulter 1961, 278–90.

115 TNA ADM 106/2151, 27 July and 4 Nov 1815.

116 Early drawings, some signed by Holl, are in the National Archives, Jamaica. These relate to the surviving building and are listed in Cox and Cox (1999, 41–2). Otherwise, detailed surviving documentation is largely lacking.

117 This account relies heavily for its analysis of the building on Cox and Cox (1999), who undertook a great deal of research in the Jamaica Archives, as well as on the fabric of the building itself. Holl was not the first designer to use cast and wrought iron in Jamaica. In 1801 a substantial iron bridge (which still survives) was constructed at Spanish Town from parts shipped from England (Brown and Francis 2005). The designer was the Sunderland schoolmaster and engineer Thomas Wilson (Chrimes *et al* 2008, 788–9).
118 TNA ADM 106/2035, 20 June and 9 July 1818.
119 TNA ADM 106/2035, 18 Oct and 11 Dec 1818. The contract awarded in July for the hospital amounted to £6,968 for the buildings, with a further sum of £1,554 for various additions. It seems unlikely this could have been the whole cost for the original scheme. TNA ADM 106/2036 has numerous letters referring to the hospital and how it would encroach on private land.
120 TNA ADM 106/2154, 26 Apr 1822.
121 Cox and Cox (1999, 21) suggest 15 to a ward, allowing a table for a nurse, giving a total of 180 patients. TNA ADM 181/33, 1823 Estimates, notes that the hospital then had a staff of one surgeon, an agent, dispenser, chaplain, agent's clerk, steward, matron, porter and one other. Nursing staff are not mentioned, but if space was at a premium it seems unlikely that a bed space would have been lost in favour of a table. Holl's estimate is in TNA ADM 106/2036, 24 Apr 1819.
122 TNA ADM 106/2151, 8 Jan and 13 March 1820.
123 As late as Sept 1828 the contractor was still awaiting 130yd of flagging from England, but this may have been for the ground floor (TNA ADM 106/2040, 15 Sept 1828). Unreinforced lime concrete slabs were certainly in place by 1860 (Cox and Cox 1999, 23).
124 TNA ADM 140/996 and 1007 are cross-sections of the Sheerness buildings; TNA ADM 140/473 is that of the Pembroke offices.
125 TNA ADM 106/2038, 9 Feb 1824; ADM 106/2040, 21 June 1826 noted that the new copper for the roof would be supplied by 'the government' (the Admiralty), to whom the contractor would return the old copper. TNA ADM 105/89 is a drawing of the building in 1849, but is not entirely accurate in depicting the roof profile.
126 TNA ADM 106/2037, 24 Feb 1821. Holl appears to have accepted these figures in his accompanying note.
127 In 1828 a visiting captain considered the new hospital to be in no immediate danger, but 'in a very insecure state from the defective casting of the iron work and from the site not having been selected with due care to support the piling, which has been badly performed and the heavy weight of building resting on it' (TNA ADM 106/2166 fol 2, 30 June 1828). This pessimistic view was not borne out by events, and the buildings are now in the care of the Jamaica National Trust.
128 The row of buildings appears on a plan of 1849 (TNA ADM 105/89) and is identified on TNA ADM 140/1484 fol 73. The improvements to the fever ward are noted in TNA ADM 181/98, estimates for 1887/8, and the two houses appear in TNA ADM 181/74, estimates for 1863/4.
129 Perhaps 'the important alterations to the hospital to be completed 1904/05', noted in TNA ADM 181/99, in an Admiralty report dated 1 Feb 1904.
130 AdL Admiralty Terrier for Jamaica records that when the cemetery was closed in 1903, there were 260 naval and 75 military interments there.
131 TNA ADM 98/14 fol 463; Coad 1989, 350–2.
132 Borg 2001, 27.
133 Despatches, quoted in Borg 2001, 148. Captain Alexander Ball had commanded the British squadron besieging the French garrison before becoming the well-respected first Governor of Malta 1799–1801.
134 Borg 2001, 148. Nelson was unaware that the British Government already owned the site, but he showed a healthy mistrust of building estimates. Two years earlier, he had purchased Merton Place as his home, and by 1803 may well have had practical experience of the frequent differences between builders' estimates and final bills. *See* Knight 2005, 421–6.
135 Borg 2001, 149; Knight 2005, 438, 443.
136 TNA ADM 106/2049, 19 Apr 1824, 10 Jan 1826. This correspondence mentions that owing to a misunderstanding with the local Land Revenue Office, the commissioner had to ask Guiseppe Bonavia to prepare a plan that would be acceptable to the Office. It cost £25 16s 8d.
137 TNA ADM 106/2051, 26 Jan 1829. Sir Pulteney Malcolm had succeeded Sir Edward Codington as Commander-in-Chief Mediterranean. The inscription is reproduced in Borg 2001, 152. For the involvement of Gaetano Xerri, *see* TNA ADM 106/2051, 12 March and 14 Nov 1829, and ADM 1/3446, 24 May 1832.
138 TNA ADM 1/3446, 28 May 1832, has a detailed contract and progress report attached, recording that repairs to Bighi Palace were begun in Dec 1829, work to the North Pavilion on 23 March 1830 and work to the South Pavilion on 22 July 1830. The approved cost was £20,107 16s 8d. TNA ADM 106/2051, 28 July 1830, is one of a series of letters that expressed hope that stone quarried earlier for the abortive dry dock and left at the quarries on Gozo could be used, but much of this had vanished or been used by other contractors. However, the architect reckoned that the hard stone on the end of Gozo would be suitable for the columns.
139 MacGill 1839, quoted by Borg 2001, 151. MacGill credits William IV with ordering construction of the hospital. This is just the sort of project that would have appealed to the future king. He may well have encouraged it, but he had resigned as Lord High Admiral in Aug 1828, just over a year before the Navy Board gave authority for the project to go ahead.
140 Borg 2001, 28.
141 Vice-Admiral Codrington was strongly philhellene.
142 TNA ADM 1/5775, 28 and 31 Dec 1861; ADM 1/5838, 23 May and 19 June 1863.

17 Barracks and Training Establishments

1 For further information on these subjects, *see* Douet 1998 and Partridge 1999. The architectural and historical development of the buildings of the former Royal Naval College, Greenwich, has been covered by many authors.
2 A policy of providing official housing for civilian employees lasted into the second half of the 20th century; it is now almost exclusively confined to senior naval officers serving short-term postings and to those in naval barracks.
3 Clearly shown on TNA ADM 140/555 pt 11, dated 1785, by which time the dockyard community of Portsea was protected by its own bastioned defences.
4 The growth of Brompton is clearly shown between TNA MPH 1/247, dated 1719, and Hugh Debbieg's 1756 survey in BL Kings Top. 16-40.
5 TNA ADM 140/666; ADM 140/670 fol 1 has a good plan of Blue Town in 1800.
6 NMM ADM/BP/39a, 24 March 1819; TNA ADM 106/1969, 19 May 1826; ADM 106/1968, 17 Oct 1832.
7 AdL uncatalogued plan of Rosyth *c* 1918; Lavery 2007, 194. The corrugated iron huts had previously been used during the building of Immingham Docks.
8 Lavery 2007, 193–5. The idea of a Garden City at Rosyth had been raised in Parliament in 1903, the year when the first such development was being laid out at Letchworth.
9 TNA ADM 140/1202.

10 Ibid, 30 Apr 1818. Bermuda was especially expensive, and a series of terraces and semi-detached houses grew up in the 19th century outside the dockyard to house foremen and other skilled workers seconded to the dockyard from the home bases. These are clearly seen on TNA ADM 140/1484 fols 67–8.
11 TNA ADM 1/57, 20 June 1859. Plans for these buildings were drawn up 'by the later Civil Engineer, Mr Anderson, but were modified by Mr Remington'. TNA ADM 1/5939, 19 Aug 1865, records that the foundations were begun in May 1856. The buildings, which include Prince Albert's Terrace, still survive.
12 These are clearly shown on an 1840 plan (AdL Da 01 fol 34), when two additional terraces were proposed.
13 NMM LAD 11/52; AdL Jamaica Vz 10 fol 73.
14 TNA ADM 140/1185 pt 4.
15 TNA ADM 140/1208, undated but *c* 1770; ADM 140/1198 pt 3.
16 NMM LAD 11/51, 1771; TNA ADM 174/362, 1859.
17 AdL Da 022 fol 13. Wooden barracks shown on an 1823 plan of the island (TNA MPH 1/611) almost certainly belong to the garrison.
18 TNA ADM 140/1284 shows this as a storehouse in 1843; AdL Da 02 fol 8 *c* 1863 marks the building as 'Seamen's Barracks'.
19 TNA ADM 174/365, 1896. The barracks building still exists, and a contemporary photograph is in ADM 195/4 fol 59b.
20 Nelson and Oliver 1982, 26.
21 On the 1863 plan, AdL Da 02 fol 4, the barracks are shown in the west range of the victualling store; they had gone by 1900. A proposal dated 19 Sept 1859 in TNA ADM 1/5715 includes the allocation of funds for alterations and improvements and increasing the barrack accommodation from 954 to 2,000 men. It is not known if these proposals were carried out, but 2,000 men would have put a strain on the space unless more of the victualling store was made available.
22 *See* Hattendorf *et al* (1993, 708–15) for details of the new scheme.
23 Douet 1998, 7, 8.
24 NMM CHA/E/32, 26 Apr 1776. A letter from the Navy Board to the Chatham officers tells them to prepare plans for a barracks for 200 marine privates and officers, capable of expansion to hold 600 privates and officers. The design should be similar to recently approved Ordnance barracks. NMM ADM/BP/6b, 22 Feb 1786, records that John Marquand, the Navy Board's Surveyor of Buildings, supervised the construction of the extension of the barracks. These had been authorised in June 1780 (NMM ADM/BP/1, 2 June 1780).
25 Douet 1998, 48–9. The author credits the provision of barracks for the marines as reflecting 'in part the special difficulties … keeping in good order a force billeted for long periods in the same town – less of a problem for the army, which could move its units regularly.' The barracks at Chatham and Stonehouse were purpose built; those at Portsmouth were converted from the former Victualling Board brewery and cooperage; they were later enlarged and named Clarence Barracks. The Chatham barracks have been demolished; those at Stonehouse are the best preserved and retain their original use.
26 TNA ADM 1/5939, 23 Sept 1865. The Director's memo noted that Scamp deserved special notice 'in consideration of his plans for the RM Barracks at Eastney', suggesting that he played the key role in their design. TNA ADM 1/5888, 29 Sept 1864, records that Scamp sent plans for the extension of the Chatham barracks.
27 The Metropolitan Police had provided security for the Thames yards and Woolwich Arsenal since the 1840s.
28 This had been constructed in 1857, providing limited accommodation. NMR plan 95/06506 shows this before conversion. The building survives.
29 A series of plans are in TNA ADM 1/5803, 2 July 1862. The buildings survive.
30 TNA ADM 1/5752, 10 Oct 1860; ADM 1/5775, 4 Nov 1861, details purchase of land.
31 TNA ADM 181/73, 1862/3 estimates; ADM 181/74, 1863/4 estimates.
32 TNA ADM 1/588, 9 Aug 1864.
33 In 1862 *Britannia* had a severe outbreak of fever at Portland, resulting in 43 cases including 4 deaths among her cadets (Dickinson 1998, 439–40). The use of hulks as training ships is explored in some detail in Carradice (2009) and provides useful background information for this chapter.
34 Douet 1998, 128–41. The Barrack Accommodation Report of 1855 was followed in 1857 by the damning Sanitary Commission Report of 1857, which exposed the full squalor of army barracks and ushered in major reforms and improvements.
35 TNA ADM 116/727, 14 and 18 Jan 1876 – the letter of 14 Jan refers to plans for barracks at Portsmouth and Keyham 'prepared about 14 years ago'; ADM 116/727, 14 and 18 Jan 1880; ADM 181/90, estimates for 1880/1, allowed £130,000 for Keyham Barracks for 1,000 officers and men. Convicts were at work excavating foundations for barracks at Portsmouth in 1880, but this work did not apparently progress far, partly because of site difficulties and partly to see how Keyham turned out.
36 Lavery 2007, 192–3. The author points out that at the time these barracks were under construction, the navy, unlike the army, did not provide married quarters and did not pay the men's travel expenses between home and ship or station. A number of proposals to make Rosyth a manning station and develop links with Scotland came to nothing.
37 *Navy and Army Illustrated* (6 Aug 1897, 166) gives 1889 as the date the barracks were first occupied.
38 TNA ADM 116/727, 16 Apr 1884.
39 Douet 1998, 192. These were divided between the captain, 118 officers, 84 warrant officers, 388 chief petty officers, 520 1st- and 2nd-class petty officers and 3,360 seamen and stokers, with 52 NCO marines, 336 marines and 36 domestics.
40 Separate dining rooms in military barracks were an innovation of the 1890s, although one or two had appeared in the 1870s. The first of these barracks precedes, by a few years, broadly similar arrangements of military barracks at Tidworth (Douet 1998, 173, 185).
41 Pasley, Smith, Pilkington and Raban (Douet 1998, 190).
42 'The Royal Naval Barracks, Devonport', *Navy and Army Illustrated* 6 Aug 1897, 169.
43 Douet 1998, 193. *Navy and Army Illustrated* (31 Jan 1903, 499) noted that the Chatham Barracks were 'rapidly approaching a stage when it will be ready for occupation'. TNA ADM 181/99, 1 Feb 1904, notes that Chatham barracks were opened on 30 Apr 1903 and those at Portsmouth in Sept 1903.
44 Anon nd *Chatham Royal Naval Barracks.* Portsmouth barracks suffered from a degree of war damage, but the Officers' Mess remains much as completed. Chatham Naval Barracks closed in 1984 and has been successfully adapted as a university campus.
45 More detailed accounts of training are in Brown 1983, Lavery 1989 and 2007, Morriss 1983 and Partridge 1999.
46 NMM POR/A/8, 16 March 1729.
47 NMM POR/A/9, 2 Nov 1733. A rival private Naval Academy at Gosport also trained up to 80 young gentlemen, but even with this input, formal training remained restricted to a small minority of officers (Lavery 1989, 88).
48 Lavery 1989, 90. There is a useful account of the Naval Academy and its drawing masters in Surry 2008, 21–32.

49 NMM POR/A/8, 12 March 1729. For a more detailed description, *see* Coad 1989, 75–8.
50 NMM POR/A/9, 2 Nov 1733.
51 NMM POR/A/8, 16 March 1729.
52 Apart from an abortive early design for the Royal Hospital at Haslar, no other naval buildings can be ascribed with any probability to Acworth, despite his long period in office.
53 TNA ADM 140/555 pt 18 is a plan dated 1810, but signed by Holl in Dec 1814, suggesting that he may have been responsible for one of the phases of later extensions.
54 NMM POR/A/24, 6 Aug 1770.
55 More recently, the building was used as the Staff Officers' Mess. The former commissioner's accommodation retains much of its early panelling. The Navigation School was relocated as HMS *Dryad* to Southwick Park; since 2004 it has been part of HMS *Collingwood* at Fareham.
56 Payton (1994, 192–3) gives a succinct account of the training regime on the River Dart.
57 TNA ADM 181/90, estimates for 1879/80, allowed £30,000 for the building, an increase of £10,000 on the previous year's estimate.
58 Clarke's model for the proposed New Public Offices at Whitehall in 1867 employs a number of common features (Port 1995, 121).
59 Penn 1984, 36, 52. Lecture rooms were also provided in the Foundry Store, and a small gym was built nearby in the dockyard.
60 *Navy and Army Illustrated* 9 July 1898, 364; 23 July 1898, 418. An indication of the importance attached in official circles to the Royal Naval Engineering College is reflected in the *Navy and Army Illustrated* running in July and August 1898 a four-part series on the college and its work, more than the magazine devoted to many of the dockyards.
61 Aston Webb, knighted in 1904, was well known for his work completing the Victoria and Albert Museum (1899–1909), designing Admiralty Arch (1905–11) and refacing the front of Buckingham Palace (1913). Parallel with Dartmouth was his work designing and supervising the new buildings of Christ's Hospital School near Horsham.
62 Hattendorf *et al* 1993, 972–4.
63 Payton 1994, 193.
64 Partridge 1999, 19–20. The author also deals in some detail with the debates arising from the Selborne Memorandum.
65 Turner 2007, 50. Hawkes also carried out the conversion of Osborne House into a convalescent home. Among other buildings, he was responsible in London for the western extension of the National Gallery (1907–11) and the offices of the Board of Agriculture in Whitehall Place, the latter completed after his death by his colleague H D Collins (Port 1995, 250, 272).
66 AdL Da 0 36 fol 54 is a 1910 plan of the college.
67 At the time, the Office of Works was in the forefront of using new materials and techniques enabling the construction of sizeable buildings at moderate cost, one reason for using its skills at Osborne Naval College (Port 1995, 271).
68 Quoted in Partridge 1999, 26. Much the same economical approach to the provision of accommodation was adopted when the Admiralty established its huge training establishment in 1905 at Shotley for boy seamen. This was closed in 1976 and the course transferred to HMS *Raleigh* at Torpoint, Cornwall. The famous 143ft ship's mast on the former parade ground is the principal surviving memento of the Shotley establishment, renamed HMS *Ganges* in 1927 in commemoration of the warship used for training there from 1899 until the opening of the 'stone frigate' in 1905.
69 Already in 1914 Dartmouth was being expanded to take extra numbers.
70 For a detailed account of the fortunes of the college at Keyham and Manadon, *see* Penn 1984.
71 TNA ADM 181/96 estimates include a sum of £6,000 for the gun battery. Drawings are in the NMR – PMT/1926–36.
72 This are shown on NMR PMT/1941–1947. TNA ADM 140/1484 pt 19 shows the layout of Whale Island in 1909.
73 Carr Laughton 1912, 405.
74 Many of the original buildings remain in use. Close by, Horsea Island was developed at the same time with a torpedo range for the torpedo school attached to HMS *Vernon*. Its original name was the Whitehead Torpedo Adjusting and Experimental Range. Apart from the 800yd enclosed stretch of water used for testing, little else remains. Ripley (1982) gives a good account of the history of Horsea Island and its naval connections. HMS *Vernon* was not transferred ashore until after the First World War.
75 Haas 1990, 326.
76 Brown 1983, 24. The society only lasted for 8 years.
77 This interest in labour management stemmed from his time in Russia.
78 Morriss 1983, 111–13. The Commissioners of Revision in 1806 criticised their 'want of foresight and due consideration'.
79 'First Report of the Commissioners for Revising and Digesting the Civil Affairs of the Navy' 1806, 194–5. It was not published until 1833.
80 'First Report of the Commissioners for Revising and Digesting the Civil Affairs of the Navy' 1806, 194–5; Haas 1990, 326; Morriss 1983, 113. The minimum age of the superior apprentices was to be 16, and the qualifications for entry included an ability to understand the first six books of Euclid's *Elements*, along with a sound knowledge of French 'so as to receive instructions from the publications in that language on subjects connected with the construction of ships' (Coad 1989, 78).
81 NMM POR/G/4, 10 May 1816.
82 Morriss (1983, 114) gives a figure of 41; Brown (1983, 26) states that only 32 completed the course.
83 Brown 1983, 26; Coad 2005, 105–6.
84 For assessments of the effectiveness of education and training in these establishments, *see* Brown (1983, 27) and Morriss (1983, 114). A second School of Naval Architecture opened in Portsmouth Dockyard in 1848, but was closed after 5 years; a third school was opened in cramped accommodation in 1864 in Kensington, London, and amalgamated with the new Royal Naval College at Greenwich in 1873 (Brown 1983, 34, 39–40).
85 Brown (1983, 33) has noted: 'Fierce competition, a blend of theory and practice, a gradual selection process by examination and a total absence of social distinction and nepotism were the principles adopted.'
86 By 1945 the Civil Service regarded the fourth year as equivalent to a degree (Brown 1983, 34).
87 Haas 1990, 325, 330.
88 TNA ADM 140/1484 pt 16 marks it as such *c* 1909.

Epilogue

1 Ranft 1989, 141. At the time Rosyth was incomplete and did not have a protected anchorage. Scapa Flow was still being prepared for the latter role.
2 For a more detailed history of the conservation and reuse of the Royal Navy's bases *see* Coad 2011.

REFERENCES

Abell, W 1981 *The Shipwright's Trade.* London: Conway Maritime Press

Akiyama, Y 2008 'Trained Cooks and Healthy Boys: Reforming the Mess in the Royal Navy before the First World War'. *Mariner's Mirror* **94**, 420–31

Allcorn, W 2011 'Forts of Eastern and Northern Lake Ontario'. *Fort* **39**, 94–140

Alsop, J D 1995 'Royal Navy Victualling for the Eighteenth Century Lisbon Station'. *Mariner's Mirror* **81**, 468–9

Anon nd (*c* 1904) *Chatham Royal Naval Barracks.* Old Brompton: Charlesworth and Morehen, Photographers

Anon 2002 'Thematic Survey of the Ordnance Yards and Magazine Depots. Summary Report. Thematic Listing Programme'. Unpublished final draft, English Heritage

Appleton, P C 2008 *Resurrecting Dr Moss. The Life and Letters of a Royal Navy Surgeon, Edward Lawton Moss MD, RN, 1843–1880.* Calgary: University of Calgary Press

Arbuthnot, A J 2004 'Denison, Sir William Thomas (1804–1871)', revised by A G L Shaw, *in Oxford Dictionary of National Biography* (online edn 2008). Oxford: Oxford University Press

Archibald, E H H 1968 *The Wooden Fighting Ship in the Royal Navy 897–1860* London: Blandford Press

Archibald, E H H 1971 *The Metal Fighting Ship in the Royal Navy 1860–1970.* London: Blandford Press

Armstrong, J and Williams, D M 2011 'The Beginning of a New Technology: The Construction of Early Steamboats 1812–1822'. *International Journal of the History of Engineering* **81**, 1–21

Bach, J 1986 *The Australia Station. A History of the Royal Navy in the South West Pacific 1821–1913.* Kensington NSW Australia 2033: New South Wales University Press

Baigent, E 2004 'Howlett, Samuel Burt (1794–1874)', *in Oxford Dictionary of National Biography* (online edn 2008). Oxford: Oxford University Press

Ballard, G A 1980 *The Black Battlefleet.* Lymington: Nautical Publishing Company and Society for Nautical Research

Banbury, P 1971 *Shipbuilders of the Thames and Medway* Newton Abbot: David and Charles

Bannerman, G E 2008 *Merchants and the Military in Eighteenth Century Britain: British Army Contracts and Domestic Supply.* London: Pickering and Chatto.

Baugh, D A 1977 *Naval Administration 1715–1750.* London: Navy Records Society **120**

Beare, T H 2004 'Coode, Sir John (1816–1892)', revised by A M Wood, *in Oxford Dictionary of National Biography* (online edn 2008). Oxford: Oxford University Press

Bentham, M S 1862 *The life of Brigadier-General Sir Samuel Bentham, KSG.* London: Longmans

Bingeman, J M, Bethell, J P, Goodwin, P and Mack, A T 2000 'Copper and other Sheathing in the Royal Navy'. *International Journal of Nautical Archaeology* **29**, 218–29

Bingeman, J M, 2010 *The First HMS Invincible (1747-58): Her excavations (1989-1991).* Oxford: Oxbow Books

Birbeck, E, Ryder, A and Ward, P 2009 *The Royal Hospital Haslar. A Pictorial History.* Chichester: Phillimore

Birse, R M 2004 'Cowper, Edward Alfred (1819–1893)', *in Oxford Dictionary of National Biography* (online edn 2008). Oxford: Oxford University Press

Black, J 2006 'The Background to the Establishment of a Naval Dockyard at Gibraltar following the Naval Defence Act of 1889'. *Transactions of the Naval Dockyards Society* **2**, 65–71

Blackburne, K 1972 (5 edn) *The Romance of English Harbour*. Antigua: Friends of English Harbour

Borg, M 2001 *British Colonial Architecture, Malta 1800–1900.* San Gwann, Malta: Publishing Enterprises Group

Bracegirdle, B and Miles, P H 1974 *The Darbys and the Ironbridge Gorge*. Newton Abbot: David and Charles

Britton, J and Brayley, E W 1832 *Devonshire & Cornwall illustrated from original drawings byThomas Allom, W.H. Bartlett, &c.* London: H Fisher, R Fisher & P Jackson

Brodie, A, Croom, J and Davies, J O 2002 *English Prisons. An Architectural History.* Swindon: English Heritage

Brown, D K 1983 *A Century of Naval Construction. The History of the Royal Corps of Naval Constructors.* London: Conway Maritime

Brown, D K 2004 'Seppings, Sir Robert (1767–1840)', *in Oxford Dictionary of National Biography* (online edn 2008). Oxford: Oxford University Press

Brown, F B and Francis, P 2005 *The Old Iron Bridge, Spanish Town, Jamaica.* Jamaica: Faculty of the Built Environment, University of Technology

Brunicardi, N 1982 *Haulbowline Spike and Rocky Islands in Cork Harbour.* Fermoy: Éigse Books

Buchanan, R A 2004a 'Nasmyth, James Hall (1808–1890)', *in Oxford Dictionary of National Biography* (online edn 2008). Oxford: Oxford University Press

Buchanan, R A 2004b 'Jessop, William (1746–1814)', *in Oxford Dictionary of National Biography* (online edn 2008). Oxford: Oxford University Press

Buchanan, R A and Doughty, M W 1978 'The Choice of Steam Engine Manufacturers by the British Admiralty, 1822–1852'. *Mariner's Mirror* **64**, 327–47

Burns, K V 1984 *The Devonport Dockyard Story.* Liskeard: Maritime Books

Burton, A 1972 *The Canal Builders.* London: Eyre Methuen

Callender, G A R (ed) 1920 *The Life of Admiral Sir John Leake, vol 1*. London: Navy Records Society **52**

Calvocoressi, P 1986 'Lost Buildings in Dockland' *in* Carr, R J M (ed) *Dockland. An illustrated Historical Survey of life and work in east London.* London: North East London Polytechnic and the Greater London Council, 31–46

Capp, B 2008 'Bourne, Nehemiah (1611–1691)', *in Oxford Dictionary of National Biography* (online edn 2008). Oxford: Oxford University Press

Carr Laughton, L G 1912 'Maritime History' *in* Page, W (ed) *The Victoria County History of Hampshire and the Isle of Wight, vol 5*. London: University of London, 359–408

Carradice, P 2009 *Nautical Training Ships. An Illustrated History*. Stroud: Amberley Publishing

Chichester, H M 2004a 'Bryce, Sir Alexander (1766–1832)', revised by D Gates, *in Oxford Dictionary of National Biography* (online edn 2007). Oxford: Oxford University Press

Chichester, H M 2004b 'Lukin, Lionel (1742–1834)', revised by R C Cox, *in Oxford Dictionary of National Biography* (online edn 2007). Oxford: Oxford University Press

Chrimes, M M 1994 'Hugh McIntosh (1768–1840), national contractor'. *The Newcomen Society* **66**, 175–92

Chrimes, M M 2010 'Society of Civil Engineers (*act.* 1771–2001)', *in Oxford Dictionary of National Biography* (online edn). Oxford: Oxford University Press

Chrimes, M M, Cox, R C, Cross-Rudkin, P S M, Hurst, B L, McWilliam, R C, Rennison, R W, Ruddock, E C, Sutherland, R J M and Swailes, T (eds) 2008 *Biographical Dictionary of Civil Engineers in Great Britain and Ireland. Volume 2: 1830–1890.* London: Thomas Telford Publishing

Clarke, B F L 1963 *The building of the eighteenth-century church.* London: SPCK

Clements, W H 1999 *Towers of Strength. The Story of the Martello Towers.* Barnsley: Leo Cooper

Clements, W 2007 'The Fortifications of Ascension Island'. *Casemate* **80** (Fortress Study Group), 32–4

Clements, W 2010 'Barren Rocks – Aden and Ascension Island: Two Volcanic Fortresses 1815–1945'. *Fort* **38**, 14–55

Coad, J G 1969 'Chatham Ropeyard'. *Post-Medieval Archaeology* **3**, 143–65

Coad, J G 1973 'The Chatham Mast Houses and mould Loft'. *Mariner's Mirror* **59**, 127–34

Coad, J G 1981 'Medway House, Chatham Dockyard', *in* Detsicas, A (ed) *Collectanea Historica. Essays in Memory of Stuart Rigold.* Kent Archaeological Society, 273–7

Coad, J G 1982 'Historic Architecture of Chatham Dockyard, 1700–1850'. *Mariner's Mirror* **68**, 133–88

Coad, J G 1983 'Historic Architecture in H.M.Naval Base, Devonport 1689–1850'. *Mariner's Mirror* **69**, 341–94

Coad, J G 1989 *The Royal Dockyards 1690–1850.* Aldershot: Scolar Press

Coad, J G 1992 'The Development and Organisation of Plymouth Dockyard 1689–1815', *in* Duffy, M, Fisher, S, Greenhill, B, Starkey, D J and Youings, J *The New Maritime History of Devon vol 1.* London: Conway Maritime Press and University of Exeter, 192–200

Coad, J G 1994 'Architecture and Development of Devonport Naval Base, 1815–1982', *in* Duffy, M, Fisher, S, Greenhill, B, Starkey, D J and Youings, J *The New Maritime History of Devon vol 2.* London: Conway Maritime Press and University of Exeter, 167–76

Coad, J G 1997 'Defending the Realm: the changing technology of Warfare', *in* Gaimster, D and Stamper P (eds) *The Age of Transition. The Archaeology of English Culture 1400–1600.* Oxford: Oxbow, 157–69

Coad, J G 2002 'Bentham, Sir Samuel' *in* Skempton, A W, Chrimes, M M, Cox, R C, Cross-Rudkin, P S M, Rennison, R W and Ruddock, E C (eds) 2002 *A Biographical Dictionary of Civil Engineers in Great Britain and Ireland. Vol 1: 1500–1830.* London: Thomas Telford, 52–3

Coad, J G 2005 *The Portsmouth Block Mills.* Swindon: English Heritage

Coad, J G 2008 'The Sheerness Dockyard Model', *Country Life* **202** (32), 6 August 2008, 52–5

Coad, J G 2011 'Indifference, Destruction, Appreciation, Conservation: A Century of changing attitudes to historic buildings in British Naval Bases'. *Mariner's Mirror* **97**, 313–43

Coad, J G and Lewis, P N 1982 'The Later Fortifications of Dover'. *Post-Medieval Archaeology* **16**, 141–200

Coats, A 2006 'The Block Mills: new labour practices for new machines?' *Transactions of the Naval Dockyards Society* **1**, 59–84

Cock, R 2001 '"The Finest Invention in the World": The Royal Navy's Early Trials of Copper Sheathing'. *Mariner's Mirror* **87**, 446–59

Cock, R 2004 'Schank , John (1740–1823)', *in Oxford Dictionary of National Biography* (online edn 2008). Oxford: Oxford University Press

Cocroft, W D 2000 *Dangerous Energy. The archaeology of gunpowder and military explosives manufacture.* Swindon: English Heritage.

Colledge, J J and Warlow, B 2006 *Ships of the Royal Navy.* London: Chatham Publishing

Collinge, J M 1978 *Navy Board Officials 1660–1832.* London: London University, Institute of Historical Research

Colson, C and Colson C H nd 'Malta Dockyard Extension and Removal of Rock in Entrance Channel of Hamilton Dock'. Unpublished bound typescript lodged with the Institute of Civil Engineers 1892

Colvin, H M (ed) 1976 *The History of the King's Works, Vol 5.* London: HMSO

Colvin, H M (ed) 1982 *The History of the King's Works, Vol 4, pt II.* London: HMSO

Colvin, H M 1995 *A Biographical Dictionary of British Architects 1600–1840.* New Haven and London: Yale University Press

Conolly, T W J 1898 *Roll of Officers of the Corps of Royal Engineers from 1660–1898.* Chatham: Royal Engineers Institute

Courtney, T W 1974 'Excavations in the Royal Dockyard, Woolwich, 1972–1973, Part 1'. *Post-Medieval Archaeology* **8**, 1–28

Courtney, T W 1975 'Excavations in the Royal Dockyard, Woolwich, 1972-1973, Part 2'. *Post-Medieval Archaeology* **9**, 42–102

Cox, J and Cox, R 1999 *Naval Hospitals of Port Royal, Jamaica.* Kingston, Jamaica: University of Technology, Faculty of the Built Environment

Crewe, D 1993 *Yellow Jack and the Worm. British Naval Administration in the West Indies.* Liverpool: Liverpool University Press

Crimmin, P K 2008 'The Supply of Timber for the Royal Navy c1803–c.1830', *in* Rose, S (ed) *The Naval Miscellany, Volume VII.* Aldershot: Navy Records Society **153**, 191–234

Crossley, D 1975 'Cannon-Manufacture at Pippingford, Sussex: The Excavation of Two Iron Furnaces of c. 1717'. *Post-Medieval Archaeology* **9**, 1–41

Davies, D 2008 'The Future of Pembroke Dock'. *Dockyards. The Naval Dockyards Society Newsletter* **13** (1), 2–4

Defoe, D 1962 *A Tour Through the Whole Island of Great Britain, Vol 1.* London: Everyman's Library

Dempsey, W D 1843 'Description of the Saw Mills and Machinery for Raising Timber in Chatham Dockyard'. *Professional Papers of the Corps of Royal Engineers* **6**, 148–60

Dendy Marshall, C F and Kidner, R W 1963 *History of the Southern Railway.* London: Ian Allan

Denison, W T 1842 'Description of a Dock lately constructed in Woolwich Yard'. *Professional Papers of the Corps of Royal Engineers* **5**, 224–6

Devaux, R J 1975 *A Century of Coaling in St Lucia, including a Description of the Coaling Tokens*. London: Spink and Son (reprinted from *Numismatic Circular*)

Dickinson, H W 1998 '*Britannia* at Portsmouth and Portland'. *Mariner's Mirror* **84**, 434–43

Diestelkamp, E 1990 'Architects and the Use of Iron', *in* Thorne, R (ed) *The Iron Revolution. Architects, Engineers and Structural Innovation 1780–1880.* London: RIBA, 15–23

Dietz, B 2002 'Dikes, Dockheads and Gates: English Docks and Sea Power in the Sixteenth and Seventeenth Centuries'. *Mariner's Mirror* 88, 144–54

Ditchfield, G M 2004 'Stanhope, Charles, third Earl Stanhope (1753–1816)', *in Oxford Dictionary of National Biography* (online edn 2008). Oxford: Oxford University Press

Donaldson, D W 2002 'Port Mahon, Minorca: the Preferred Naval Base for the English Fleet in the Mediterranean in the Seventeenth Century'. *Mariner's Mirror* **88**, 423–36

Douet, J 1998 *British Barracks 1600–1914*. London: The Stationery Office

Doull, I 2007 'Problems in the Conservation of Historic Resources, HMC Dockyard, Canadian Forces Base Esquimalt, British Columbia'. *Transactions of the Naval Dockyards Society* **3**, 103–13

Drabble, S 2010 'Templer and Parlby: Eighteenth Century Dockard Contractors'. *Trans Naval Dockyards Society* **6**, 93–102

Dufferin and Ava, Marchioness of 1891 *My Canadian Journal*. London: John Murray

Duffy, M 2003 'Edmund Dummer's 'Account of the General Progress and Advancement of His Majesty's New Dock and Yard at Plymouth', December 1694', *in* Duffy, M (ed) *The Naval Miscellany vol 146*. Aldershot: Ashgate for The Navy Records Society, 93–148

Evans, D 2000a 'A historical account and Gazetteer of the Medway Magazine Systems'. Unpublished report, English Heritage, London

Evans D 2000b 'A historical account and Gazetteer of the Priddy's Hard Magazine system'. Unpublished report, English Heritage, London

Evans, D 2004 *Building the Steam Navy. Dockyards, Technology and the Creation of the Victorian Battle Fleet*. London: Conway Maritime Press

Evans, D 2006 *Arming the Fleet. The Development of the Royal Ordnance Yards 1770–1945*. Gosport: Explosion! Museum, in association with English Heritage

Evans, F T 1995 'The Maudslay Touch: Henry Maudslay, Product of the Past and Maker of the Future'. *Transactions of the Newcomen Society* **66** (1994–95), 153–75

Fawcett, N 1984 'Storehouses at Simon's Town'. *Mariner's Mirror,* **70**, 441–3

Fiennes, C 1983 *The Journeys of Celia Fiennes*. London: Macdonald & Co

Flinn, M W 1962 *Men of Iron. The Crowleys in the Early Iron Industry*. Edinburgh: The University Press

Floud, R and Johnson, P (eds) 2004 *The Cambridge Economic History of Modern Britain. Volume 1, Industrialisation,1700–1860*. Cambridge: Cambridge University Press

Fox, C 2007 'The Ingenious Mr Dummer: rationalising the Royal Navy in late seventeenth-century England. *The Electronic British Library Journal* **10**, 1–54

Fox, C 2009 *The Arts of Industry in the Age of Enlightenment*. New Haven and London: Yale University Press

Frame, T 2004 *No Pleasure Cruise: The Story of the Royal Australian Navy*. Crows Nest, New South Wales: Allen and Unwin

Friel, I 1995 *The Good Ship. Ships, Shipbuilding and Technology in England 1200–1520*. London: British Museum Press

Gardberg, C J and Palsila, K 1998 *Sveaborg, Suomenlinna*. Helsinki: Otava Publishing Company

Gaastra, F S 2003 *The Dutch East India Company. Expansion and Decline*. Zutphen: Walburg Pers

Goodwin, P 1998 'The Influence of Iron in Ship Construction: 1660–1830'. *Mariner's Mirror* **84**, 26–40

Gosse, P 1938 *St Helena 1502–1938*. London: Cassell

Grainger, I and Phillpotts, C 2010 *The Royal Navy Victualling Yard, East Smithfield, London*. London: Museum of London

Guillery, P (ed) forthcoming 2012 Survey of London*, vol 48: Woolwich*. London and New Haven: Yale University Press in association with English Heritage and the Paul Mellon Centre

Gwyn, J 1973 *The Royal Navy and North America. The Warren Papers, 1736–1752*. London: Navy Records Society **118**

Gwyn, J 2004 *Ashore and Afloat. The British Navy and the Halifax Naval Yard before 1820*. Ottawa: University of Ottawa Press

Haas, J M 1990 'The Best Investment Ever Made: The Royal Dockyard Schools, Technical Education and the British Shipbuilding Industry, 1800–1914'. *Mariner's Mirror* **76**, 325–36

Hadfield, C 1966 *British Canals. An Illustrated History*. Newton Abbot: David and Charles

Hall, E 1989 'The Georgian Gardens of the Royal Naval Dockyard at Chatham'. *The Georgian Group, Report and Journal 1988,* 61–6

Hall, E and Lear, J (eds) 1992 'Chatham Dockyard Gardens'. *Garden History* **20**, 132–52

Hällström, O af 1986 *Sveaborg Viapori Suomenlinna. The Island Fortress off Helsinki*. Rungsted Kyst, Denmark: Anders Nyborg

Hamilton, C I 1993 *Anglo-French Naval Rivalry 1840–1870*. Oxford: Oxford University Press

Hamilton C I 2005 *Portsmouth Dockyard papers 1852–1869. From Wood to Iron*. Winchester: Hampshire County Council

Harcourt, F 2006 *Flagships of Imperialism. The P&O Company and the Politics of Empire from its Origins to 1867*. Manchester: Manchester University Press

Harland, K 1985 *The Royal Navy in Hong Kong since 1841*. Liskeard: Maritime Books

Harland, K 2003 'The Establishment and Administration of the First Hospitals in the Royal Navy 1650-1745'. Unpublished PhD thesis, Univ Exeter

Harland, K 2008 'The Royal Naval Hospital at Minorca, 1711: An Example of an Admiral's Involvement in the Expansion of Naval Medical Care'. *Mariner's Mirror* **94**, 36–47

Harris, D G 1999 'Charles Sheldon and the Baltic's First Dry Dock'. *Mariner's Mirror* **85**, 396–404

Harris, E C 1997 *Bermuda Forts 1612–1957*. Bermuda: Bermuda Maritime Museum Press

Harris, E C 2010 'Discovering Bermuda's Royal Albert Hall' (*in* Heritage Matters). *The Royal Gazette* (Bermuda), 21 August 2010, 13

Hart-Davis, D 1976 *Ascension. The Story of an Atlantic Island*. London: Constable

Hasenson, A 1980 *The History of Dover Harbour*. London: Aurum Special Editions

Hattendorf, J B, Knight, R J B, Pearsall, A W H, Rodger, N A M and Hill, G 1993 *British Naval Documents 1204–1960* (Navy Records Society **131**). Aldershot: Scolar Press

Hawkey, A 1963 *HMS Captain*. London: G Bell and Sons

Hay, G D and Stell, G P 1986 *Monuments of Industry*. Edinburgh: Royal Commission on the Ancient and Historical Monuments of Scotland and HMSO

Hemingway, P 2010 'Sir Jacob Acworth and Experimental Ship Design during the Period of the Establishments'. *Mariner's Mirror* **96**, 149–60

Hewison, W S 1985 *This Great Harbour Scapa Flow*. Kirkwall: The Orkney Press

Hewlings, R 2004 'Jelfe, Andrews (*c.*1690–1759)', *in Oxford Dictionary of National Biography* (online edn 2008). Oxford: Oxford University Press

Hill, B 1987 *Sappers. The Royal Engineers in British Columbia*. Ganges, B.C: Horsdal and Schubart

Hills, R L 2006 *James Watt Volume III: Triumph through Adversity*. Ashbourne: Landmark Publishing

Hore, P 2000 'Lord Melville, the Admiralty and the coming of Steam Navigation'. *Mariner's Mirror* **86**, 157–72

Hudson, P 2004 'Industrial Organisation and Structure', *in* Floud, R and Johnson, P (eds) *The Cambridge Economic History of Modern Britain. Volume 1, Industrialisation, 1700–1860*. Cambridge: Cambridge University Press, 28–56

Hughes, Q 1969 *Fortress. Architecture and Military History in Malta*. London: Lund Humphries

Hughes, Q 1981 *Britain in the Mediterranean and the defence of her naval stations.* Liverpool: Penpaled Books

Hunter, M C 2006 'The Hero Packs a Punch: Sir Charles Hotham, Liberalism and West Africa, 1846–1850'. *Mariner's Mirror* **92**, 282–99

Hunter, R B 2005 *Rosyth. The Building of a Royal Naval Dockyard 1903–1922.* Banbury: 4Bears Publications

Jackson, M H and de Beer, C 1973 *Eighteenth Century Gunfounding.* Newton Abbot: David and Charles

Jane, C W E 1982 *Shirley Heights. The Defence of Nelson's Dockyard.* Antigua: Nelson's Dockyard National Park Foundation

Jeremy, J 2005 *Cockatoo Island. Sydney's Historic Dockyard.* Sydney: University of New South Wales Press

Johnson, S 1976 *The Roman Forts of the Saxon Shore.* London: Paul Elek

Jones, C 1995 'The Purchase of the Australian Colonial Gunboats'. *Mariner's Mirror* **81**, 182–94

Jones, M 2003 'The Letters of Captain Francis Starkie Clayton on the Australia Station, 1885–8', *in* Duffy, M (ed.) *The Naval Miscellany vol 6.* Aldershot: Ashgate for The Navy Records Society, 312–77

Keevil, J J 1958 *Medicine and the Navy 1200–1900, Volume 2, 1649–1714.* Edinburgh and London: E & S Livingstone

Kepler, J S 1973 'Sir John Jennings and the Preparations for the Naval Expedition to the Mediterranean of 1711–1713'. *Mariner's Mirror* **59**, 13–33

King, P W 1995 'Iron Ballast for the Georgian Navy and its Producers'. *Mariner's Mirror* **81**, 15–20

Kitchen, F 1990 'The Napoleonic War Coast Signal Stations'. *Mariner's Mirror* **76**, 337–44

Knight, R J B 1987 *Portsmouth Record Series. Portsmouth Dockyard Papers 1774–1783. The American War.* Portsmouth: City of Portsmouth

Knight, R J B 2005 *The Pursuit of Victory. The Life and Achievement of Horatio Nelson.* London: Allen Lane

Knight, R and Wilcox, M 2010 *Sustaining the Fleet 1793–1815. War, the British Navy and the Contractor State.* Woodbridge: Boydell Press

Knighton, C S and Loades, D (eds) 2011 *The Navy of Edward VI and Mary I.* Farnham: Ashgate Publishing for the Navy Record Society

Lambert, A 1984 *Battleships in Transition. The Creation of the Steam Battlefleet 1815–1860.* London: Conway Maritime

Lambert, A 1987 *Warrior. Restoring the World's First Ironclad.* London: Conway Maritime Press

Lambert, A 1994 'The Impact of Naval Technology on Warship Construction and Repair at Devonport, 1815–1986', *in* Duffy, M, Fisher, S, Greenhill, B, Starkey, D and Youings, J (eds) *The New Maritime History of Devon* Vol 2. London: Conway Maritime Press and University of Exeter, 177–87

Lambert, A 2006 'Science and Seapower: The Navy Board, the Royal Society and the Structural Reforms of Sir Robert Seppings'. *Transactions of the Naval Dockyards Society* **1**, 9–19

Lambert, A 2008a 'Symonds, Sir William (1782–1856)', *in Oxford Dictionary of National Biography* (online edn 2008). Oxford: Oxford University Press

Lambert, A 2008b *Admirals.* London: Faber and Faber

Lane, M R 2004 'Rendel, James Meadows (1799–1856)', *in Oxford Dictionary of National Biography* (online edn 2008). Oxford: Oxford University Press

Langford, P 1989 *A Polite and Commercial People. England 1727–1783.* Oxford: Oxford University Press

Latcham, P 2008 'Montresor, James Gabriel (1702–1776)', *in Oxford Dictionary of National Biography* (online edn). Oxford: Oxford University Press

Laughton, J K 2004 'Knowles, Sir Charles, first baronet (*d.* 1777)', revised by R Harding, *in Oxford Dictionary of National Biography* (online edn 2008). Oxford: Oxford University Press

Lavery, B 1983 *The Ship of the Line. Volume 1. The Development of the Battlefleet 1650–1850.* London: Conway Maritime Press

Lavery, B 1987 *The Arming and Fitting of British Ships of War 1600–1815.* London: Conway Maritime Press

Lavery, B 1989 *Nelson's Navy. The Ships, Men and Organisation 1793–1815.* London: Conway Maritime Press

Lavery, B 2004 'Slade, Sir Thomas (1703/4–1771)', *in Oxford Dictionary of National Biography* (online edn 2007). Oxford: Oxford University Press

Lavery, B. 2007 *Shield of Empire: The Royal Navy and Scotland.* Edinburgh: Birlinn

Lavery, B 2008 'Acworth, Sir Jacob (*c.*1668–1749)', *in Oxford Dictionary of National Biography* (online edn 2008). Oxford: Oxford University Press

Levien, M (ed) 1981 *The Cree Journals*. Exeter: Webb and Bower

Lewis, M J T 1970 *Early Wooden Railway.* London: Routledge & Kegan Paul

Lloyd, C 1949 *The Navy and the Slave Trade.* London: Longmans, Green and Co

Lloyd, C and Coulter, J L S 1961 *Medicine and the Navy 1200–1900, Volume III, 1714–1815.* Edinburgh: E & S Livingstone

McDonald, D I 1969 'Barnet, James Johnstone (1827–1904)', *in Australian Dictionary of Biography, Vol 3*. Carlton: Melbourne University Press, 100–2

MacDonald, J 2010 *British Navy's Victualling Board, 1793–1815.* Woodbridge: Boydell Press

MacDougall, P 1982 *Chatham Built Warships Since 1860.* Liskeard: Maritime Books

MacDougall, P 1986 'The Royal Dockyards of Woolwich and Deptford' *in* Carr, R J M (ed) *Dockland. An illustrated Historical Survey of life and work in east London.* London: North East London Polytechnic and the Greater London Council, 111–26

MacDougall, P 1989 'Granite and Lime: The Building of Chatham Dockyard's First Stone Dry Dock. *Archaeologia Cantiana* **107**, 173–91

MacDougall, P 1990a 'The Formative Years of Malta Dockyard 1800–1815'. *Mariner's Mirror* **76**, 205–14

MacDougall, P 1990b 'Countering Pernicious Tenets… The Building of the Sheerness Dockyard Chapel'. *Bygone Kent* **11**, 212–14

MacDougall, P 2001 'Hazardous Waters: Naval Dockyard Harbours during the Age of Fighting Sail'. *Mariner's Mirror* **87**, 15–29

MacDougall, P 2007 'William Scamp and his Early Naval Works in the Mediterranean'. *Mariner's Mirror* **93**, 28–42

MacDougall, P 2008 'Harbour Navigation and Moorings of Naval Dockyards in the Atlantic Region'. *Transactions of the Naval Dockyards Society* **4**, 69–90

MacDougall, P 2009 *Chatham Dockyard 1815–1865* London: Navy Records Society **154**

MacGill, T 1839 *A Handbook or Guide for Strangers Visiting Malta*. Malta: Luigi Tonna

McGowan, A P 1971 *The Jacobean Commissions of Enquiry 1608 and 1618.* London: Navy Records Society **116**

McGowan, A P 1999 *HMS Victory. Her Construction, Career and Restoration.* London: Chatham Publishing

Malcomson, R 2001 *Warships of the Great Lakes 1754–1834.* London: Chatham Publishing

Mallinson, H 2005 *Send it by Semaphore. The Old Telegraphs During the Wars with France.* Marlborough: Crowood Press

Marcil, E R 1995 'Wooden Floating Docks in the Port of Quebec from 1827 until the 1930s'. *Mariner's Mirror* **81**, 448–56

Martin, E J and Tanner, H 1988 'Historic Architecture of H.M.A. Naval Dockyard, Garden Island N.S.W. Australia'. *Mariner's Mirror* **74**, 363–90

Maurice-Jones, K W 1959 *The History of Coast Artillery in the British Army*. London: Royal Artillery Institution

May, W E 1999 *The Boats of Men-of-War*. London: National Maritime Museum

Mayes, P 1972 *Port Royal, Jamaica. Excavations 1969–70*. Kingston: Jamaica National Trust Commission

Merino, J P 1985 'Graving Docks in France and Spain before 1800'. *Mariner's Mirror* **71**, 35–58

Merriman, R D 1950 *The Sergison Papers*. Navy Records Society **89**

Merriman, R D 1961 *Queen Anne's Navy*. Navy Records Society **103**

Moorehouse, G 2006 *Great Harry's Navy*. London: Phoenix

Mornement, A and Holloway, S 2007 *Corrugated Iron. Building on the Frontier*. London: Frances Lincoln

Morriss, R 1983 *The Royal Dockyards during the Revolutionary and Napoleonic Wars*. Leicester: Leicester University Press

Morriss, R 2006 'The Office of the Inspector General of Naval Works and Technological innovation in the royal dockyards'. *Transactions of the Naval Dockyards Society* **1**, 21–30

Morriss, R 2007 'The Supply of Casks and Staves to the Royal Navy, 1770–1815'. *Mariner's Mirror* **93**, 43–50

Morriss, R 2011 'Promise of Power. The British Maritime Economy and the State in the Eighteenth Century'. *Transactions of the Naval Dockyards Society* **7**, 49–56

Myers, S A 1997 'The Changing Shore. A History of the West Dockyard 1743–1996'. Unpublished MS, Simon's Town

Naish, J 1992 'Joseph Whidbey and the Building of the Plymouth Breakwater'. *Mariner's Mirror* **78**, 37–56

Nelson, F D H and Oliver, N E 1982 'C.F.B. Esquimalt Military Heritage'. Unpublished MS, C.F.B. Esquimalt Library, accession #720

Nicolas, N H 1845 *The Despatches and Letters of Vice-Admiral Lord Viscount Nelson. Vol 5*. London: Henry Colburn

Oppenheim, M 1896 *The Administration of the Royal Navy 1509–1660*. London: Bodley Head

Oppenheim, M 1926 'The Royal Dockyards', *in* Page, W (ed) *The Victoria History of the County of Kent, Vol 2*. London: University of London, 336–88

Osborne, B S and Swainson, D 1988 *Kingston, Building on the Past*. Westport, Ontario: Butternut Press

Owen, J R 2002 'The Post Office Packet Service, 1821–37: Development of a Steam-Powered Fleet'. *Mariner's Mirror* **88**, 155–75

Pares, R 1963 *War and Trade in the West Indies 1739–1763*. London: Frank Cass

Parnell, G 1993 *The Tower of London*. London: Batsford

Partridge, M 1999 *The Royal Naval College, Osborne. A History 1903–21*. Stroud: Sutton Publishing

Pawson, M and Buisseret, D 1975 *Port Royal, Jamaica*. Oxford: Clarendon Press

Paxton, R 2004 'Telford, Thomas (1757–1834)', *in Oxford Dictionary of National Biography* (online edn 2008). Oxford: Oxford University Press

Payton, P 1994 'Naval Education and Training in Devon', *in* Duffy, M, Fisher, S, Greenhill, B, Starkey, D and Youings, J (eds) *The New Maritime History of Devon, Vol 2*. London: Conway Maritime Press and University of Exeter, 191–203

Pease-Watkin, C 2004 'Bentham, Samuel (1757–1831)', *in Oxford Dictionary of National Biography* (online edn 2007). Oxford: Oxford University Press

Penn, G 1984 *HMS Thunderer. The Story of the Royal Naval Engineering College Keyham and Manadon*. Emsworth: Kenneth Mason

Pocock, T 1991 *Sailor King. The Life of King William IV*. London: Sinclair-Stevenson

Pool, B 1966 *Navy Board Contracts 1660–1832*. London: Longmans

Port, M H 1995 *Imperial London. Civil Government Buildings in London 1850–1915*. New Haven and London: Yale University Press

Port, M H 2010 'Founders of the Royal Institute of British Architects (*act*. 1834–1835)', *in Oxford Dictionary of National Biography* (online edn). Oxford: Oxford University Press

Pratt, M. 1978 *Britain's Greek Empire*. London: Rex Collings

Preston, A and Major, J 2007 *Send a Gunboat. The Victorian Navy and Supremacy at Sea, 1854–1904*. London: Conway Maritime Press

Proudfoot, P 1996 *Seaport Sydney. The making of the city landscape*. Kensington NSW: University of New South Wales Press

Pugh, P D G 1974 *The History of the Royal Naval Hospital, Plymouth* (reprinted from *J Royal Naval Medical Service* **58**, 78–94, 207-226)

Quinn, P 2001 'The Early Development of Magnetic Compass Correction'. *Mariner's Mirror* **87**, 303–15

Quinn, P 2007 'Charles Wye Williams, Boilers and Fuel'. *Mariner's Mirror* **93**, 450–68

Rabson, S and O'Donoghue, K 1988 *P&O. A Fleet History*. Kendal: World Ship Society

Raddall, T H 1993 *Halifax, Warden of the North*. Halifax: Nimbus Publishing

Ranft, B McL 1989 *The Beatty Papers*. Aldershot: Scolar Press for Navy Records Society

Rees, S 2009 *Sweet Water and Bitter. The Ships that Stopped the Slave Trade*. London: Chatto and Windus

Revell, A L 1978 *Haslar. The Royal Hospital*. Gosport: The Gosport Society

Rice, B 2010 *Simon's Town Dockyard – the first hundred years*. Simon's Town: Simon's Town Historical Society, South African Naval Heritage Trust

Richards, J M 1958 *The Functional Tradition in Early Industrial Buildings*. London: The Architectural Press

Richardson, H (ed) 1998 *English Hospitals 1660–1948. A Survey of their Architecture and Design*. Swindon: Royal Commission on the Historical Monuments of England

Riley, R C 1985 *The Evolution of the Docks and Industrial Buildings in Portsmouth Royal Dockyard 1698–1914* (Portsmouth Papers **44**). Portsmouth: Portsmouth City Council

Riley, R 2006 'Marc Brunel's pulley block-making machinery: operation and assessment'. *Transactions of the Naval Dockyards Society* **1**, 85–92

Riley, R 2007 'Henry Cort and the Development of Wrought Iron Manufacture in the 1780s: The Naval Connection'. *Transactions of the Naval Dockyards Society* **3**, 51–5

Ripley, B 1982 *Horsea Island and the Royal Navy*. Portsmouth: Portsmouth City Council

Ritchie, C I 1966 'The Hostel of the Invalides by Thomas Povey, 1682 (Lambeth Palace Library MS.745)'. *Medical History* **10**, 1–22, 177–97

Ritchie-Noakes, N 1980 *Jesse Hartley. Dock Engineer to the Port of Liverpool 1824–60*. Liverpool: National Museums and Galleries on Merseyside

Rodger, N A M 1979 *The Admiralty*. Lavenham: Terence Dalton

Rodger, N A M 1985 'The Buildings of Simonstown Dockyard'. *Mariner's Mirror* **71**, 467–73

Rodger, N A M 1986 *The Wooden World. An Anatomy of the Georgian Navy*. London: Collins

Rodger, N A M 1993 *The Insatiable Earl. A Life of John Montagu, 4th Earl of Sandwich*. London: HarperCollins

Rodger, N A M 1997 *The Safeguard of the Sea. A Naval History of Britain, Volume 1, 1660–1649*. London: HarperCollins.

Rodger, N A M 2004 *The Command of the Ocean. A Naval History of Britain. Volume 2, 1649–1815*. London: Allen Lane

Rogers, H C B 1971 *Artillery Through the Ages*. London: Seeley, Service & Co

Roland, H 1899 'The Revolution in Machine Shop Practice'. *Engineering Magazine* (New York) **18**, 41–58

Rolt, L T C 1960 *Red for Danger*. London: Pan Books

Rolt, L T C 1986 *Tools for the Job. A History of Machine Tools to 1950.* London: HMSO

Saint, A. 2007 *Architect and Engineer. A Study in Sibling Rivalry.* New Haven and London: Yale University Press

Sainty, J C 1975 *Admiralty Officials 1660–1870.* London: Athlone Press

Sargent, E. 2008 'The development of dock construction at the royal dockyards in the nineteenth century'. *Transactions of the Naval Dockyards Society* **4**, 91–114

Saunders, A D 1967 *Upnor Castle.* London: HMSO

Saunders, A D 1989 *Fortress Britain.* Liphook: Beaufort Publishing

Saunders, A D 2004 *Fortress Builder. Bernard de Gomme, Charles II's Military Engineer.* Exeter: Exeter University Press

Saunders, A D 2005 'Upnor Castle and Gunpowder Supply to the Navy 1801–1804'. *Mariner's Mirror* **91**, 160–74

Schurman, D M 2000 *Imperial Defence 1868–1887.* London: Frank Cass

Segger, M 2000 'Teague, John', *in Dictionary of Canadian Biography* (online version)

Semark, H W 1997 *The Royal Naval Armaments Depots of Priddy's Hard, Elson, Frater and Bedenham 1768 to 1977.* Winchester: Hampshire County Council

Skempton, A W 1977 'A History of the Steam Dredger, 1797–1830'. *Transactions of the Newcomen Society* **47** (1974–5 and 1975–6), 97–116

Skempton, A W 1980 'Engineering in the Port of London, 1789–1828'. *Transactions of the Newcomen Society* **50** (1978–9), 87–108

Skempton, A W 1983 'Engineering in the Port of London, 1808–1833'. *Transactions of the Newcomen Society* **53** (1981–2), 73–96

Skempton, A W, Chrimes, M M, Cox, R C, Cross-Rudkin, P S M, Rennison, R W and Ruddock, E C (eds) 2002 *A Biographical Dictionary of Civil Engineers in Great Britain and Ireland. Vol 1: 1500–1830.* London: Thomas Telford

Smiles, S 1862 *Lives of the Engineers, Vol II.* London: John Murray

Smiles, S 1863 *Industrial Biography* (reprinted 1967). Newton Abbot: David and Charles

Smith, M G 1985 *The King's Yard. An Illustrated History of the Halifax Dockyard.* Halifax: Nimbus Publishing

Smith, T 1992 'Hydraulic Power in the Port of London'. *Industrial Archaeology Review* **14** (1991–2), 64–88

Spencer-Silver, P 2004 'Jackson, Sir John (1851–1919)', *in Oxford Dictionary of National Biography* (online edn 2008). Oxford: Oxford University Press

Spiteri, S C 1996 *British Military Architecture in Malta.* Malta: Stephen C Spiteri

Stevenson, C 2000 *Medicine and Magnificence. British Hospital and Asylum Architecture 1660–1815.* London and New Haven: Yale University Press

Stranack, I 1990 *The Andrew and The Onions. The Story of the Royal Navy in Bermuda.* Bermuda: Bermuda Maritime Museum Press

Summerson, J 1969 *Architecture in Britain.* Harmondsworth: Penguin Books

Surry, N 2008 *A Portsmouth Canvas. The Art of the City and the Sea 1770–1970.* Sudbury: The Fortune Press

Sutherland, R J M 1985 'Interim Statements for the Victorian Society on the Iron-Framed Buildings in Chatham Dockyard outside the Historic Area'. Unpublished report for the Victorian Society

Sutherland, R J M (ed) 1997 *Structural Iron 1750–1850. Studies in the History of Civil Engineering, Vol 9.* Aldershot: Ashgate

Syrett, D 2004 'A Study of Peacetime Operations: The Royal Navy in the Mediterranean, 1752–5'. *Mariner's Mirror* **90**, 42–50

Tann, J (ed) 1981 *The Select Papers of Boulton and Watt, Volume 1, The Engine Partnership 1775–1825.* Cambridge, Massachusetts: MIT Press

Taylor, G L 1870 *The Autobiography of an Octogenarian Architect.* London: Longmans

Thake, C 2010 *William Scamp (1801-1872). An Architect of the British Admiralty in Malta.* Malta: Midsea Books

Thom, C 2010 'Fine veneers, army boots and tinfoil: New light on Marc Isambard Brunel's activities in Battersea'. *Construction History* **25**, 53–67

Torrens, H S 2004 'Sadler, James (*bap.* 1753, *d.* 1828)', *in Oxford Dictionary of National Biography* (online edn 2010). Oxford: Oxford University Press

Tracy, N 1997 *The Collective Naval Defence of the Empire, 1900–1940.* London: Navy Records Society **136**

Trinder, B 2000 *The Industrial Revolution in Shropshire.* Chichester: Phillimore

Tucker, M 2007 'Structural Ironwork at Pembroke Dock. A Microcosm of Naval Practice'. *Transactions of the Naval Dockyards Society* **3**, 31–5

Turner, M 2007 *Osborne.* London: English Heritage

Vetch, R H 2004a 'Lilly, Christian (*d.* 1738)', revised by R T Stearn, *in Oxford Dictionary of National Biography* (online edn 2008). Oxford: Oxford University Press

Vetch, R H 2004b 'Pasley, Charles (1824–1890)' revised by E Baigent, *in Oxford Dictionary of National Biography* (online edn 2008). Oxford: Oxford University Press

Vetch, R H 2004c 'James, Sir Henry (1803–1877)', revised by E Baigent, *in Oxford Dictionary of National Biography* (online edn 2008). Oxford: Oxford University Press

Wadia, R A 1957 *The Bombay Dockyard and the Wadia Master Builders.* Bombay: priv printed

Wakelin, P 2011 *Blaenavon Ironworks and World Heritage Landscape.* Cardiff: Cadw, Welsh Government

Warner, B 1995 *Royal Observatory, Cape of Good Hope 1820–1831. The Founding of a Colonial Observatory.* Dordrecht: Kluwer Academic Publishers

Warner, J 2005 *John the Painter.* London: Profile

Watt, J 2002 'The Health of Seamen in Anti-Slavery Squadrons'. *Mariner's Mirror* **88**, 69–78

Watt, J 2011 'Naval and Civilian Influences on Eighteenth- and Nineteenth-century Medical Practice'. *Mariner's Mirror* **97**, 148–66

Weiler, J M 1987 'Army Architects. The Royal Engineers and the Development of Building Technology in the Nineteenth Century'. Unpublished PhD thesis, Univ York, Institute of Advanced Architectural Studies

White, D L (ed) 1999 *Bermuda's Architectural Heritage: Sandys.* Hamilton: Bermuda National Trust

White, H P 1961 *A Regional History of the Railways of Great Britain. Volume II, Southern England.* Newton Abbot: David and Charles

Wilcox, M 2011 '"This Great Complex": Victualling the Royal Navy on the East Indies Station'. *Mariner's Mirror* **97**, 32–48

Wilkinson, C 1998 'The Earl of Egmont and the Navy, 1763–6'. *Mariner's Mirror* **84**, 418–33

Wilson, G 1976 *The Old Telegraphs.* Chichester: Phillimore

W K L 1942 'Correspondence relating to the Establishment of a Naval Base at Esquimalt, 1851–57'. *British Columbia Historical Quarterly* **6**, October 1942, 277–97

Wood, J 2008 'James Bray, Master Shipwright, Malta 1806–12'. *Mariner's Mirror* **94**, 209–12

INDEX

Page numbers in **bold** refer to illustrations, page numbers in *italic* refer to tables.

A

Abbot, Charles 72
accommodation. *see also* barracks; housing, senior officers
  Chatham **56**
  labour force **50**, 374–5
  officers 17, 19–20, **19**, 20, **56**
  Pembroke 17, 19–20, **19**, **20**
accommodation hulks **376**, 377
Achilles, HMS 199, **199**
Act of Union 3, 50
Acworth, Jacob 252, 358–9, 382
Adams, Robert 107
Aden 230
Admiral Superintendents 79
Admiralty, the
  authorises Plymouth Sound breakwater 105
  Barrack Committee 377
  and Bentham 77
  boardroom **109**
  and Chatham steam yard 35
  conservatism 31
  and Esquimalt 272
  Harbours and Railway Department 84
  London headquarters 107, **107**
  and mechanisation 72
  and naval hospitals 344–5
  and Pembroke 17
  Plymouth modernisation and enlargement proposals, 1761 6–7
  resistance to establishing Scottish dockyards 3–4
  responsibilities 4, 391
  and sail production 112
  and slip roofs 101
  Steam Department created 25
  victualling department 299
Admiralty, the, Whitehall 107, **107**
Admiralty and War Office building, London 109–10, **110**
Admiralty House, Bermuda 269
Admiralty House Halifax, Nova Scotia 154, **154**, 156, 269, 271
Admiralty House, Trincomalee 214, **214**
Admiralty Order, 23 March 1796 72
Admiralty Works Department xvii, 79, 79–86, 109
  Chamberlain recommendations 86, 289–90
  Director of Works 82–3
  naval barracks programme 86
  planning system 82–3
  staff 86, *86*, 392
  workload 86
Africa, HMS 185, 192
Agamemnon, HMS 26, 32
Agent Victuallers 299
Aiken, Edmund 12
Airy, George 31
Aitchison, G 218
Aitken, Thomas 137
Alderney 43
Alderney Breakwater **41**, 42–3, 106
Alecto, HMS 25
All Hallow's Cog 1
Allin, Thomas 209
American Civil War 221
ammunition 315
anchor smiths 119, **119**
Anchor Wharf, Chatham 7, 65, **65**, 79, 114, **114**, 138, **138**
anchorages 4
Anderson, John 262
Anson, Admiral Lord 5, 59–60
Antigua xvii, *212*, 213, 215. *see also* English Harbour, Antigua
Anti-slave Trade Act, 1807 217
armour plate 31–2
Armstrong 316
Armstrong, William 83
Arrow, James 70
Ascension Island
  annexation 283
  bakery 285, **286**
  Brandreth's map **216**
  breakwater 286–7
  cable station 287
  coal store 284, **284**
  coaling station **229**
  construction 213, 215–16, 283–4
  defences 283, **284**, 286–7
  Fort Cockburn 216
  Georgetown 283, **283**, 286
  housing, senior officers 159, **160**, 285
  metal-working facilities 285, **285**
  naval hospital 285–6, 352
  officers' gardens 159, **160**
  ordnance yard 337
  paymaster's quarters 284, **284**
  strategic importance 286–7
  victualling store 284, **284**
  victualling yard 283–4, 303
  water supplies 286, 304
atmospheric engines 95
Auckland, New Zealand *176*, 218, 223–4, **224**, 393
Auckland Harbour Board 223–4
Australia xvii, 218, 223, 231, 293. *see also* Sydney

B

Bagot, Charles 265
Baker, John 238
Baker and Son, George 188–9, 189
bakeries 203, 243–4, **243**, **244**, 285, **286**, 301, 303, 305, 312
Ballard, Admiral 32
Banks, Sir Joseph 69
Bantry Bay, Battle of 20
Barbados 77, 212, *212*
  coaling station 230
  naval hospital 352
  supply depot 251
Barlow, Peter, *An Essay on the Strength and Stress of Timber* 80
Barnet, James 295, 339
barracks xvii, 4, 86
  accommodation 377–8, **379**
  accommodation hulks 377, **377**
  capacity 377, 382
  Chatham 381, 382
  Devonport 46, 376–7, **377**, **378**, 379, **379**, **381**
  early 375
  facilities 378, 382
  military 376
  overseas bases 375
  Portsmouth 381, 382, **xiv**
  Royal Marine xvii, 376
  Sheerness 375–6
  Sydney 298, **298**, 375
  wash-houses **379**
barrel storage 300–1, 314
Barrie, Robert 213, 265–6
Barrow, John 81
Barry, Charles 30, 195–6
basins 11, 28, 39, 88, 90, 95
  benefits of 11
  Bermuda 282, **282**
  caissons 181–3, **182**, **183**
  Chatham 36–7, 171, **172**, **173**
  construction materials 180, **180**
  design 172
  Devonport 171, **172**, **175**
  dimensions 171, 175
  expansion, 19th century 171, 171–5, **172**, **174**, **175**, 179–84, **179**, **180**
  foundations 173–4, **175**
  gates 182–3
  Haulbowline **45**, 171
  Keyham Extension 47, **47**

labour force expansion, 19th century 172, **172**
Portsmouth 39–40, 41, 46, 171, 174–5, **175**, 180, 182
Rosyth **50**, 51, **52**
Sheerness 14, 172–3, 182
Simon's Town **289**
spoil **175**
Bately, William 61–2
Baugh, Daniel 299
Beachy Head, battle of 55
Beatson, Roger 203–5
Beatty, Admiral 391
Beddoes, Thomas 73
Bellerophon, HMS **93**
Bellona, HMS **60**
Belper 74
Benbow, John 210, 343–4
Bengal Engineers 80
Bentham, Jeremy 12, 71, 72
Bentham, Samuel 7, 11, 21, 71–3, **71**, 74, 76–9, 187, 364, 392
appointment as Inspector General of Naval Works 53
apprenticeships 389–90
covered slips 98–9
dry dock foundations 92–3
dry dock innovations 92–5, **94**
introduction of steam power 121–3, **121**, 133
pay offices 164
redevelopment of Sheerness 11–13, **13**
smitheries 120
structural ironwork 202
woodworking machinery 71–2, 123
Beresford, John 153
Bermuda xvii, 52, 79–80
Admiralty House 269
aerial view, 2000 **282**
barracks 375
basins 282, **282**
boat tunnel **278**, 279, 339, **339**
boathouses 279
breakwater 277
careening wharves 277
chapels 170
Commissioner's House 149, **149**, 156, 203, 215, 277, 277–8, **278**, **282**, 339
conservation 393
construction 276–7
convict labour 35
cottages 276
defences 277, **278**, 281, **282**, 337, **338**
dry dock *176*, 222, **222**, 225, 271, 276, 279
Eastern Storehouse 281, **281**
expansion, 19th century 279–82
foundation 10
housing, senior officers 277, 277–8, **278**, 279, **280**, **282**, 339
Keep Yard 80, **278**, 279, **282**, 337, **338**
labour force *212*
local community 375
machine shop 279
magazines **338**, 339, **339**
Narrows Passage 276
naval hospital 77–8, 212, 277, 352
ordnance yard 278–9, **278**, **282**, 336, 337, **338**, 339, **339**
panorama, 1856 **281–2**
plan, 1823 **276**
plan, 1858 **280**
plan, 1909 **338**
site 276
storehouses 279, **280**, 281, **281**
strategic importance 211, 262, 276
Victualling Yard 279, **280**, **282**, 303–4
water supplies 304
Bermuda Maritime Museum 278
Bernays, E A 37, 82
Bethlehem Hospital, London 148
Bickerton, Richard 370
Birkenhead, HMS 31
biscuit production 312, **312**
Black Battlefleet, the 32
Black Prince, HMS 30, 279
Blackwall, Brunswick Dock 11
Blaenavon Ironworks 68
Blane, Gilbert 346
Blanshard, Thomas 277
Blenheim, HMS 210
Bligh, Richard 3–4
Block Mills 76, 121, 123, **124–5**, 126
block-making yards **180**
Board of Ordnance 14, 21, 315, 319, 328, 330
boat building 142
boathouses 142
Bermuda 279
overseas bases **220**, 221, **221**
Portsmouth 203–5, **204**, 394
Sheerness **204**, 205
Simon's Town **290**
boiling troughs 144–6, **145**
Bombay Dockyard 210, *212*
boring mills 74–5
Boscawen, Edward 267
Boschetti, John Maria 303
Boulton and Watt 14, 27, 68, 74, 75, 122–3, 128, 133
Bourne, Nehemiah 2
Bowling Ironworks 15
Brandreth, Henry 79, 80–1, 86, 188, 215, 216, 243, 244, 245–6, 283, 285–6
brass 113
brass foundries 194
Bray, William 240, 241
breakwaters
Ascension Island 286–7
Bermuda 277
Malta 250, **250**
Plymouth Sound **xvi**, 41, 77, 103–6, **104**, **105**
Portland 67
protected harbours 41–4, **42**, **43**
Brest 29
Brett, Timothy 6, 65
breweries 301, 307, 309, 311
brickyards **180**
Bridgewater canal 67, 74
Britannia, HMS 34, 103, 382
Britannia Royal Naval College 384, **385**
British Columbia 272
British naval bases
Britain **xi**
world **xii–xiii**
Brodie, Alexander 74–5
Brompton 374
Brown, David 31
Brown, William 240, 241
Brunel, Marc 11, 76, **76**, 112, 123, 126, **126**, 127–8, 392
Brunswick Dock, Blackwall 11
Bryce, Alexander 263
building contractors, appointment 58
building contracts 62–3
building design, the Great Rebuilding 61–3
Bull Point powder depot, Devonport **xvi**, 334, **335**, 336, **446**
Bunce, Samuel 72–3, 77
Burgmann, George 195–6

C

Cadiz 95
caissons 88, 94–5, **94**, 181–3, **181**, **182**, **183**
Calcutts ironworks 316, **317**
Camber Wharf Rigging House, Portsmouth **59**
Cameron, Charles 370
Campbell, Johnson and Co 279
Canada, HMS 262
Canadian Pacific Railway 219, 262
canal building programme 67, 113
canned foods 299, 314
canvas supplies 112–13
Cape of Good Hope 212, *212*, 213, 222, 287, 288
Captain, HMS, loss of 32
Captain Cook Graving Dock, Sydney 298
Captain Superintendents 81
careening 33
careening wharves 210, **210**, 239, **239**, 252, 253, **259**, 260, 267, 269, 277
Caribbean, the 251, 255
Carleton, Guy 263
Carnarvon Commission, the 223, 226, 229, 293
carpenters 118
Carron Ironworks 316
Cartagena 95
carvers 118
casks 300–1
cast iron 78, 82, 112, 297, **367**, 368, **368**
Castries, St Lucia 229–30, 262
Catherine II, Empress 71
cement 180, **180**
centralisation 81–3
chain pumps 90, **90**, 95
Chamberlain, Austen 86, 289–90
Chambers, William 109
chapels and churches 165
Chatham 166, 168, **168**, 170
Esquimalt **273**
first 165
Haslar naval hospital 361
layout 169–70
Minorca 165
overseas bases 170
Pembroke 166, 169, 170, **170**
Plymouth 165, 166
Portsmouth 165, 166, 167, **167**, 170
Sheerness 151, **151**, 168–9, **169**, 170

- Simon's Town 288
- Stonehouse naval hospital **364**

Chappe, Claude 110
Charybdis, HMS **219**
Chatham Dockyard **2**
- 1814 **9**
- access problems 7, 35
- accommodation hulks **376**
- Anchor Wharf 7, 65, **65**, 79, 114, **114**, 138, **138**
- apprentices 389
- barracks 376, 381, 382, **xv**
- basin expansion, 19th century **172**, **173**
- basins 11, 36–7, 39, 171
- brickyard **180**
- caissons 94
- canal tunnel 126, **126**, **127**
- canal tunnel shaft 126–7, **127**
- chapels 168, **168**, 170
- the Chatham Chest 165
- Chattenden Magazines **xv**, 325, **325**, **326**, 327
- church 166
- Clocktower Storehouse 73
- closure 52
- Commissioner's House **138**, **150**, 155, 157, **157**
- conservation xvii, 394
- convict labour 35, 37
- decline 35
- Dockyard, 17th–18th Century xvii, **xv**
- dry dock expansion, 19th century 179
- dry docks 1, 45, 88, 89, 93, **93**, *176*, 181
- expansion and modernisation 1860s 35–6, **36**
- Factory Basin 36–7
- Farington's painting **9**
- Fitted Rigging House 7
- Fitting Out Basin 36–7
- foundation 2
- foundry 198, 199
- gateway towers 160, **160**
- the Great Rebuilding 7, 61
- and growth in warship sizes 34
- hatchelling house 141
- hemp house 137, 141–2, **141**
- hoop house 144
- housing, senior officers 149–50, 150, **150**, **151**, 152, **152**, 155
- iron shipbuilding shop 199, **199**
- joiners' shops 206
- lack of planning 58
- land purchases 35
- last quarter of the 18th century 10–11
- Lead and Paint Mills 128, 130, **130**
- Lempriere plan **4**
- local community 374
- Lodge Hill magazines **326**, 327
- mast houses 116, **116**
- mast pond 114, **114**
- metal mills 198, **198**
- model, 1770s 61, **61**
- mould loft 115, 116
- naval hospital 345, 349, **350**, **351**, 364
- naval installations **xv**
- Naval Works Act extension 45
- No. 1 Smithery 198, 199
- No. 2 Smithery 198, 199
- numbers employed 6
- obsolescence 8
- officers' gardens 157–8, **157**, **158**
- officers' terrace **56**, 150, **151**, 152, **152**, 157–8, **158**
- offices 162, 162–3, **162**
- Ordnance Storehouse 322, **323**
- ordnance storekeeper's residence 322
- Ordnance Yard **318**, 322–7, **323**, **324**, **325**, **326**, **xv**
- pay office 165
- pitch house 144
- plan, 1756 **323**
- pre-eminence 4
- pump house 128, **129**, 183, 183–4
- pumping engines 37, 95
- railway **xv**, 84, **85**, 127
- Repairing Basin 36–7
- role 15
- ropery **2**, 7, 35, 65, 74, 113, 130–1, **132**, 133, 133–5, **134**, **135**, 137–41, **138**, **139**, **140**, **141**, 394
- ropery forming machines 134–5, **134**
- ropery labour force 132
- ropery laying floor 138–9, **139**, **140**
- ropery winches 132, 135, **135**
- Royal Marines Barracks 77
- sail loft **138**, 142–3, **142**, **143**
- St. Mary's Island 35, **36**, 39
- sawmill **9**, 112, 126–8, **126**, **127**, **128**, 206
- sawmill roof trusses 128, **128**
- Scamp's warship storage proposals 39
- School of Military Engineering 80
- and the Seven Years' War 5
- slips 8, 35, 82, **96**, 98, 99, 101, **102**, 103, **103**
- slips expansion, 19th century 185, **185**, 187–8, **187**, **188**, 189–90, **189**, **190**, **191**, 192–3
- small buildings 146
- smithery 120, **120**, 193, 198, 206
- spinning house 138
- steam factory 198–9, **198**, **199**
- steam saw mill 76, 117
- Steam yard **xv**, 29, 35–9, **36**, **37–8**, **173**
- storehouses 65, **65**, 73, 114, **114**
- strategic value 7
- structural ironwork 205–6, **206**
- suppling boilers 145–6
- surviving buildings 7
- timber processing modernisation 205–6, **206**
- timber seasoning sheds 117, **117**
- Upnor Castle barracks **324**
- Upnor Castle powder magazine **xv**, 316, 318, 322, 324–5
- Upnor Ordnance Depot **325**
- victualling yard 301–2
- wagon ways 84, **85**
- warship production line 36–7
- wharves 88
- workshops 39, 118
- yarn houses **132**, 138, 141

Chatham Historic Dockyard 7, 83, 84
Chatham Lines **9**
Chatham Prison 35
Chatley Heath semaphore tower 111, **111**
Chattenden Magazines, Chatham **xv**, 325, **325**, **326**, 327
Cherbourg 29, 43, 77
Chief Constructor of the Navy 83
Childers, Hugh 220
chocolate 301
churches. *see* chapels and churches
Churchill, Winston 391
Civil Architect 72, 77
civil engineers, emergence of 67–9
Clarence, Duke of 153, 310, 389
Clarence House, English Harbour, Antigua 158, 261–2
Clarke, Andrew **36**, 39, 41, 45–6, 79, 174, 182, **184**, 246, 353, 384
Clayton, Francis 296
coal
- consumption 26
- logistics 31
- quality 225–6
- sources 225, *226*, 228
- strategic importance 225

coaling stations
- Ascension Island 284, **284**
- Australia 231
- classes 226
- coal stores 227–9, **228**, **229**, **231**
- contribution 231
- defences 226
- English Harbour, Antigua 262
- Esquimalt 272, **273**
- facilities 227–8, **227**
- Far East 231
- Gibraltar 229, 235, **235**
- Halifax, Nova Scotia 270
- operation 228–9, **229**
- Pacific 230
- Persian Gulf 231, **231**
- Port Royal, Jamaica 255, **255**
- Portsmouth 40, **40**, 256
- stockpiles 226, *226*, 227
- strategic importance 218–19, 225

Cochrane, Alexander 77–8, 212, 352, 366
Cockatoo Island, Sydney 293, 298
Codrington, Edward 370–1
coffer-dams 88, 91, 172, **172**, **235**
Colonial Dock Loan Act, 1865 223
Colonial Naval Defence Act, 1865 293
Colombo 230
Columbia, HMS 25
Commission for Sick and Hurt 347–8
Commission on Fees, 1785 70
Commission on Fees, 1806 71
commissioners 54–5
- overseas bases 212–13

Commissioners for Revising and Digesting the Civil Affairs of the Navy 11, 389

Committee of Imperial Defence 226
communications 83
Congo, HMS 25
Congreve, William 316, 318
conservation 392–4
consulting engineers 82
convict labour 11, 14, 23, 34–5, 35, 37, 40–1, 172, **172**
Coode, John 37, 47, 82, 229, 392
Cook, James 268
Cooper Key, Astley 384
cooperages 300–1, 309, **309**, 311, 314
Copenhagen 88, 95
copper 113
cordage manufacture. *see* roperies
cordage requirements 66, 112, 113
cordite 321
Corfu 239
Cork 20–1, 302
Cornish, Samuel 210
Corps of Engineers 79
Corps of Military Engineers 80
corrugated iron 188, 194, 205
corruption 69–70
costs
  chapels and churches 167, 169
  dry docks 1, 90, 223–5, 241, 245
  floating docks 279
  Haulbowline 21, 22, 23
  Keyham Extension 47
  labour 11
  naval hospitals 345, 352, 356, 367, 370
  Pembroke 17, 18
  Plymouth modernisation and enlargement proposals, 1761 7
  Plymouth Sound breakwater 106
  Portsmouth Great Extension 40–1
  Portsmouth modernisation and enlargement proposals, 1761 7
  powder magazines 336
  roperies 133
  Rosyth 51
  Sheerness modernisation 12, 13
  sick quarters 345
  slip roofs 99, 101, 103, 189
  smitheries 120
  steam factories 198
  steam yards 29
Cott, Henry 67
Coulomb, Charles- Augustin 364
Courageux (French warship) 59
Cowley, William 331
cranes 118–19, **127**, 189, 249
Cree, Dr Edward 365
Crewe Railway Works 84
Crimean War (1854–5) 31, 35, 197, 315, 319, 325
Cromarty Firth 4, 52
Cunningham, Thomas 277

D

Deal 2–3, 153
  naval hospital 348, **349**, 364
Deane, Thomas 22–3
defences
  Ascension Island 283, **284**, 286–7
  Bermuda 277, **278**, 281, **282**, 337, **338**
  Chatham Lines **9**
  coaling stations 226
  Esquimalt **220**, 221
  Gibraltar 221, 233, 235
  Halifax, Nova Scotia 271
  Malta 221, 239–40, 250
  overseas bases 210, 221, **221**
  Port Royal, Jamaica **220**, 221, 256
  Portsmouth 39
  Sheerness 13
  Simon's Town 221
Defoe, Daniel 113
Denis, Peter 357
Deptford 4
  access problems 11
  caissons 182
  closure 34
  cooperage 300–1
  dry dock 88
  dry docks *176*
  numbers employed *6*
  Royal Victoria Victualling Yard 52, 109, 299–301, **300**, 312, **312**, **313**, *313*, 314
  sawmill 35
  slips 96, 98, 100, **100**
  slips expansion, 19th century 189
  storehouses 301
  wet dock 95
  wharves 88
Derby 74
Devastation, HMS 32–3, **33**, 34, 207, 382–3
Devonport 4
  basin expansion, 19th century **172**
  basins 171, **175**
  Bull Point powder depot 334, **335**, 336, **446**
  church 166, **166**
  dry docks 45, 46–7, *176*
  foundry **196**, 197
  furbishers' shop 334, **334**
  gun-mounting workshop 207
  housing, senior officers 332–3, **333**
  Keyham extension 47–9, **47**, **48**, **49**, **175**, 179, **179**, 183
  Keyham Steam Yard (North Yard) 29–30, 30, **30**, 31, **47**, 84, 171, *176*, 182, 195–6
  Keyham Steam Yard tunnel link 30
  local community 374
  Morice Ordnance Yard 29, 79, **319**, 331–6, **332**, **333**, **334**, **335**, **336**
  mould loft 115–16
  Naval Works Act extension 46–7
  ordnance yard 29, 79, 320, 331–6, **332**, **333**, **334**, **335**, **336**
  Port Admiral's House **152**
  powder magazine 333, **333**, 334, **335**, 336, **336**
  pump house 183, **183**
  pumping station 49
  the Quadrangle 196–7, **196**, **197**
  railway 84, 332
  ropery 136, **136**
  sailmakers 142
  sawmill 206, **206**
  slips 30, **97**, 101
  slips expansion, 19th century 186–7, **186**
  smithery 119, 194, **194**
  South Yard 30, 34, 101, 115–16, *176*, 195
  steam factory labour force *197*
  storehouses 332, **332**
  structural ironwork 206
  survival 393–4
  torpedo workshop 207
  workshop **118**
Devonport Royal Naval Barracks 46, 376–7, **377**, **378**, 379, **379**, **381**
Diamond, HMS 296
diet 299, 301
Director of Works 82–3
disease 260, 344, 347
dockyard buildings
  metal trades 118–20, **119**, **120**, 198, **198**, 245
  the sailing navy 112–13
  storehouses 113–14, **114**
  timber trades 115–18, **115**, **116**, **117**, **118**
dockyard officers, senior resident 55
  housing. *see* housing, senior officers
dockyard offices 162–5, **162**, **163**, **164**
dockyard superintendent engineers 81
dockyards xvii, 1–2
Dover 43
  Victualling Office 299, 302
Dover, HMS 31
drainage systems 83
Drake, HMS 380
Dreadnought, HMS 34, 192, 208
Dreadnought building programme 51
dredgers 11
Drinkwater, C R 84
dry docks 276
  Auckland *176*, 223–4, **224**
  Bentham's innovations 92–5, **94**
  Bermuda *176*, 222, **222**, 225, 271, 276, 279
  caissons 88, 94–5, 181–3, **181**, **182**, **183**
  chain pumps 90, **90**, 95
  Chatham 1, 45, 88, 89, 93, **93**, *176*, 179, 181
  commercial 222
  construction 88–95, **89**, **90**, **91**, **92**, **93**, **94**
  construction materials 180, **180**
  costs 1, 90, 223–5, 241, 245
  Deptford 88, *176*
  design 172
  Devonport 45, 46–7, *176*
  dimensions 47, 89–90, 91, 171, *176–8*, 179, 223, 236, 246, 247, 290
  drainage systems 89, **90**, 95, 121
  Dummer's innovations 56, **57**, 89–91, **89**, **90**, 95
  Esquimalt *176*, 219, 220, 223, 274, **274**
  European 88

expansion, 19th century 171, 171–5, *176–8*, 179–84, **181**, **182**, **183**, **184**
facings 180
floors 179
foundations 91–3, **91**, **92**
gates 88, 89, 90, 92, 94, 181, **181**, 182–3
Gibraltar *176*, 179, 236–7, **236**
and growth in warship sizes 33–4
Halifax, Nova Scotia *176*, 223, 271
Haulbowline 45, **45**, *176*
Hong Kong *176*, 222, **222**
inverted arch 92, **92**
Keyham Extension 47, **48**
Keyham Steam Yard 30
later developments 95
location *176–8*
Malta 88, *176*, 210, 217, **217**, 223, 241, 244–6, **245**, 247, **247**, 249
origins 88
overseas bases 210, 222–5, **222**, **223**, **224**
Pembroke 17, *176*
Plymouth 56, **57**, 88, 89, 90
Portsmouth 7, 8, 29, 39, 45–6, 72, 88, 89, 89–93, **90**, **91**, **92**, 121, *176–7*, 179
Portsmouth, 1492 1
pumping systems 183–4, **183**, **184**
Rennie's innovations 93
Rosyth 51, *176–7*, 179, 236
Sheerness **92**, *177*, 179, 181, **181**
shipbuilding 96
Simon's Town *177*, 179, 289–90
stepped 89, **89**
Sydney *177*, 223, **223**, 295
Trincomalee *177*, 225
walls 91–2
Woolwich 88, *177*
Dummer, Edmund 1, 3, 55–8, **56**, **57**, 76, 88, 89, 95, 121, 162, 392
Dundas, Henry 71–2
Dundonald, Lord 279
Dungeness 304
Durell, Philip 213, 267–8
Durell, Thomas 267
Dutch East India Company 287, 288
Dutch Wars 4, 343

E

East India Company 80, 210, 212, 215, 302, 316
Easton Gibb and Sons 51
Edward VII, King 236, 250
Edye, John 26
Egmont, Lord 5, 59–60
electrification 83, 208, 297
electro-contact mines 320
Empress of India, HMS **192**
English Harbour, Antigua 210, 259–62, **259**
advantages 259
barracks 375
capstan house **260**
careening wharves 210, **259**, 260
chapels 170
Clarence House 261–2
closure 262
coal stock 227
coaling station 262
conservation 225, 393
construction 260
Copper and Lumber Storehouse 260
disadvantages 260
facilities 260–1, **260**
foundation 251, 259
galley 261, **261**
gateway 161, **161**
housing, senior officers 261–2
local community 375
naval hospital 351–2, **352**
officers' gardens 158
plan, 1750 **211**
sawpits 117
site choice 213
smithery 261, **261**
storehouses 260, **261**
victualling yard 303
water supplies 304
wharf walls 87
wharves 88
English Heritage 394
Erith 1
Esquimalt 82, 170, **219**, 271–5, 393
armaments depot 272
barracks 275
cemetery **273**
chapel **273**
closure 225
coaling jetty **273**
coaling station 230, 272, **273**
defences **220**, 221
dry dock *176*, 219, 220, 223, 274, **274**
Duntze Head 272
the factory 275, **275**
first naval installations 272, **272**, **273**, **274**
foundation 219–20, 271
housing, senior officers 275
land reclamation 272
location 271
naval hospital 272, **272**, 352–3, 354, **355**
ordnance yard 337
plan, 1900 **271**
redevelopment 274–5
Royal Navy withdrawal from 274, 275
storehouse 275
strategic importance 219, 262, 272
weather **274**
yard staff 274
Evans, David 30
Evelegh, John 327–8
Evelyn, John 55, 157
Ewart, Peter 27
Ewing, Alfred 390
Excellent, HMS, Whale Island, Portsmouth 386–7, **387**, **388**
explosives storage 321–2

F

Factory, the, Portsmouth 46
Fairy HMY 31
Falmouth 3
Falmouth Dock Company 223
Fanshawe, Edward 277
Faslane submarine base 52
Fenian Brotherhood, the 266
Fernando Po *220*, 226, *226*, 230, 283, 352
Ferrol 95
Fiennes, Celia 56
Fifth Commission for Sick, Wounded and Prisoners 344
finance xvii
fire, risk of 8
fireproofing **66**, **67**, 78, 130, 165, 195, 206, 243
First World War 52, 312, 314, 321, 331
Fishenden, Mr 82
Fisher, John 51, 221, 225, 384–6
Fitch, John 57
Fitted Rigging House, Chatham 7
flag makers 142
Flaxman, John 72
floating docks 222, **222**, 225, 271, 279
Flora, HMS **290**
food 299, 300, 314, 346
food preservation technology 299, 314
Fort Cockburn, Ascension Island 216
foundations 58, **59**, 87
basins 173–4, **175**
Sheerness 14, **15**, 88, **92**, 93
foundries 28, **28**, 193, **196**, 197, 198, 199, 245, 246
Fowke, Francis 80, **80**, 339, **339**
Fox, Celina 56
Fox Henderson 188
France
dry docks 88
naval bases 29
semaphore telegraph system 110
threat of 43
French Creek, Malta **228**, 246–7, **246**, **247**, **248**, 249, 342
French Navy 26, 31–2, 221
Funtley 67

G

Gambier, James 269
Gannet, HMS 187
Garden Island, Sydney 82, 294–5, **294**, **295**, 296, 298, **298**, 304, 339, 375, 393
Gardner, Admiral 21
Gascoigne, John 252, 256
gateways 160–1, **161**, **246**, 306, **307**, 311
George III, King 389
Georgetown, Ascension Island 283, **283**, 286
German Navy 50, 52, 221
Germany
naval arms race 208
Navy Law 50
threat of 43, 50, 392
Gibraltar 52, 84, 233, **342**
base established 209
block-making yards **180**
breakwater 106
capture of 210, 233
chapels 170
coaling station **229**, 234, 235
coffer-dam **235**
construction 214–15
defences 221, 233, 235

Dockyard, 1841 233–4, **233**
dry docks *176*, 179, 236–7, **236**
Electrical Workshop 235
harbour 235, **235**
housing, senior officers 156, **156**, 237
improvements, 19th century 234
labour force *212*, 234
magazines 235, 237, 342, **342**
modernisation 225, **234**, 235–7, **235**, **236**
naval hospital 237, 358, **358**
ordnance yard 341–2
plan, 1863 **234**
pumping station 184, 235, 237
reservoir 237, **237**
Rosia Bay victualling storehouse 302–3, **303**
Rosia Bay victualling yard 237, **237**
siege of, 1727–8 358
strategic importance 233
Torpedo Boat Destroyer Camber 342
victualling yard 237, **237**, 302–3, **303**, **304**
water supplies 304
workshops 235, **235**
Gillingham 2
Glanville, Benjamin 70
Gloire, the (French warship) 31–2
Gloucester and Berkeley canal 68
Goat Island, Sydney 294
Goodrich, Simon 11, 21, 68, 73, 74–6, 120, 133
Goschen, Viscount 384
Gosport **200**. *see also* Royal Clarence Victualling Yard
naval hospital 344
Gourock Ropeworks Company 133
Grand Storehouse, Portsmouth 78, 327–8, **328**
Great Basin caisson, Portsmouth 88, 94–5, **94**
Great Lakes 211, 213, 262, 262–6, **264**, **265**, **266**, 337
Great Rebuilding, the 4–10, **6**, **8**, **9**, **10**, 392
accounts, Portsmouth 62
building design 61–3
Chatham 7, 61
contracts 62–3
labour force 64–5
master plans 60
materials **63**
planning system 59–65
Plymouth 5–6, **6**, 7, 8, 59, 60
Portsmouth 5–8, 7, **8**, 59, 60, 62–4
scale 59
Great Yarmouth 3
naval hospital 349, 364
ordnance yard 319
Greek War of Independence 372
Green, William 156
Greene, Godfrey Thomas 30, 35, 39, 81, 82–3, 189, **190**, 194–5, **194**, **195**, 196, 199, 205–6, **205**, **270**, 377
Greenwich 1–2
Greenwich World Heritage Site **393**
Gregory, Edward 157
Griffyth, Pierce 356
Grimsby Docks 14
Grimshaw, John 133
Grissell, Henry 190, 199, 205
ground anchors 58
Gumb and Partners 331
gun barrels
rifled 315, 316, 320, **320**
smooth-bore 315, 316
storage 317
gun turrets 32
gunboats 200, **200**
guncotton 316, 321
gun-founders 316, **316**
gun-mounting workshops 207, 320
gunpowder
production and storage 316–17, 317–18, 321, 322, 324–5, **324**, 328, **329**, **330**, 333, **333**, 334, **335**, 336, **336**
technological developments 320–1
guns, early 1
gunwharves. *see* ordnance yards

H

Haddock, Nicholas 358
Haiti 251
Halifax, Nova Scotia **211**, 267–71, 393
additions, 19th century 270–1
Admiralty House 154, **154**, 156, 269, 271
barracks 375
capstan house 268, 269
careening wharves 269
chapels 170
closure 225, 271
coal stores 228, **229**, 270
Commissioner's House 268, **269**
defences 271
dockyard 268, **268**
dry dock *176*, 223, 271
foundation 210, 267–8
garden 159, **159**, 268
housing, senior officers 268–9, **269**
labour force *212*
mast house **268**
Mont Blanc explosion 271
naval hospital 270, 352, 353
officers' terrace 154–5, **154**
ordnance yard 337
plan, 1863 **267**
site choice 213, 267
strategic importance 262, 270
victualling storehouse 270, **270**
weather 269
Hamilton Dock, Malta 82, **183**
harbours of refuge 42, **42**, 44
Hartley, David 67
Hartley fireproofing system 66, 67
Harvey, Sir Thomas 270
Harwich 2, 6
Haslar Gunboat Yard **xiv**, 31, 39, 52, 199–202, **200**, **201**, **202**
barracks 376
boat sheds 200, 201–2, **201**, **202**
closure 202
housing, senior officer 201, **201**
plan, 1909 **200**
slips 200–1
traverser 200–1, **201**
workshops 201
Haulbowline xvii, 3, 5, 77, 393
1863 **22**
basin **45**, 171
breakwater 23
canal 22
chapels 170
closure order, 1831 24
construction 21–3
convict labour 23
costs 21, 22, 23
dry docks 45, **45**, *176*
foundation 10, 20–1
ironwork 24, **24**
local community 375
mast houses 22
naval hospital 24, 349
Naval Works Act extension **45**
reservoir 23
slips 21
storehouses 21, 23–4, **23**, **24**
transfer to Irish Navy 52
Hawarden Iron Works 198
Hawke, Edward 328
heavy engineering 193
hemp 113
hemp houses 131, 137, 141–2, **141**
Henjam Island 231, **231**
Henry Grace de Dieu 1, **2**
Henry V, King 1
Henry VII, King 1, 88
Henry VIII, King 1–2
Highflyer, HMS 218
Hindustan, HMS 382
Hobbs, Samuel 77
Holl, Edward xvii, 7, 12, 17, 19, 22, 23, 23–4, 77–9, 100–1, 120, **120**, 127–8, 130, **149**, 151, 163, **163**, 166, **166**, 168, **168**, 170, 188, 202–3, 206, 241, 253, 276, 277–8, 348, **349**, 364, 366–8, 389
Holland, Henry 67
Holloway, Charles 21
Holyhead harbour of refuge 42
Hong Kong
coaling station 231
dry docks *176*, 222, **222**
foundation 218
naval hospital 353, **354**
Hood, Samuel 269
Hooke, Robert 148
hoop houses 144
Hope, James 353
Horne, James 359
horse gins 121
hospital ships 209–10, 343–4, 352, 353
Hots, Susan 82
housing, senior officers
Admiralty House, Bermuda 269
Admiralty House Halifax, Nova Scotia 154, **154**, 156, 269, 271
Admiralty House, Trincomalee 214, **214**
Ascension Island 159, **160**, 285
Bermuda 269, 277, 277–8, **278**, 279, **280**, **282**, 339
Chatham 149–50, **150**

Commissioner's House, Bermuda 149, **149**, 203, 215, 277, 277–8, **278**, **282**, 339
Commissioner's House, Chatham 150, **150**, 155, 157
Commissioner's House, Halifax 268, **269**
Commissioner's House, Plymouth 148, 155
Commissioner's House, Portsmouth 147, **147**, 155
commodore's house, Port Royal 148, **149**
decoration **150**
Devonport 332–3, **333**
Dummer's innovations 148
early 147
embellishments 148, 152, **152**
English Harbour, Antigua 261–2
Esquimalt 275
gardens 155, **155**, 156, 156–9, **157**, **158**, 268
Gibraltar 156, **156**, 237
Halifax, Nova Scotia 268–9
interiors 155
Malta 241–2, **242**
officers' terrace, Chatham 150, **151**, 152, **152**, 157–8, **158**
officers' terrace, Pembroke 151
officers' terrace, Plymouth 148, **148**, 149
officers' terrace, Portsmouth 150
officers' terrace, Sheerness 151, **151**
ordnance yards 332–3, **333**
overseas bases 154–5, **154**, 155–6, 214, **214**, 215
Port Admirals accommodation 152–4, **152**, **153**, **154**
Port Antonio, Jamaica 258
Port Mahon 239
Port Royal, Jamaica 253, **254**
Royal Clarence Victualling Yard 311, **311**
Royal Hospital, Haslar 361, **361**
Royal William Victualling Yard 305–6, **307**
and status 149
tenancies 156
tree plantings 156–7
victualling yards 305–6, **306**, **307**, 311, **311**

Huddart, Joseph 12
Hudson's Bay Company 272
Hughes, Richard 58, 352
Hughes, Robert 165
hulls
- armoured 31–2
- iron 31, 32, **32**
- structural developments 26, 31
- vulnerability of iron 31

Hunt, Edward **63**, 64
Hurd, Thomas 211
hydraulic power 83

I

Illustrious, HMS 382
imperial fortresses 220–1, 226, 270
Imperieuse, HMS **290**
Inchiquin, Earl of 21
Industrial Revolution xvii, 65–70, 71–9, 392
Industrial School Ships 377
Inspector General of Naval Works 72
Inspector of Repairs 70
invalids 366, **366**
Ireland **xi**, 20–1
Irish Navy 52, 393
Iron Bridge, Severn Gorge 74, 78
iron shipbuilding shop, Chatham 199, **199**
iron supplies 112
ironmasters 68
ironworks 67, 68–9, 74–5
Isaacs, James 17
Isla del Ray naval hospital 53, **54**
Isle aux Noix 263
Isle of Grain 11
Isolation Hospitals Act, 1893 351

J

Jackson, John 47, 290
Jacobson, Theodore 359
Jamaica 251. *see also* Port Antonio, Jamaica; Port Royal, Jamaica
- capture of 209, 251
- labour force *212*
- local communities 374
- naval hospital 344, 347, 366
- water supplies 304

James, Henry 29, 193–4, **193**
Jelfe, Andrews 331–2
Jennings, John 53, 79, 212, 238, 344, 356, 357
Jervois, William 218–19, 376
Jessop, Josias 12, 68, 276–7
Jessop, William 68
joiners 118, 206

K

Karlskrona, Sweden 12, 88, 95, 98, **98**
Keep Yard, Bermuda 80, **278**, 279, **282**, 337, **338**
Kent, HMS 25
Keppel, Augustus 262
Keyham barracks, Devonport 377, 380
Keyham extension, Devonport 47–9, **47**, **48**, **49**
Keyham Steam Yard (North Yard), Devonport 29–30, 30, **30**, 31, **47**, 84, 171, *176*, 182, 195–6
Kingdom, George William 22, 23
Kingston, Ontario 161, 263, **264**, 265–6, 337
Kinsale 3, *6*, 20–1, 302
Knight, Roger 370
Knights of Malta 239
Knowles, Charles 213, 253, 256–7, 258, 259, 260

L

labour force 87, 391
- accommodation **50**, 374–5
- basin expansion, 19th century 172, **172**
- Gibraltar 234
- the Great Rebuilding 64–5
- home yards, 1865/6 *34*
- ironworks 68–9
- Malta 241
- overseas bases *34*, 212, *212*, 213–14
- Plymouth Sound breakwater 105
- roperies 132
- steam factories 197, *197*

Lake Champlain 263, 265
Lake George 263
Lake Ontario 262–3, 263, 265
Landrail, HMS **290**
Latham, Robert 53, 79, 165, 356
lead 113
Lead and Paint Mills, Chatham 128, 130, **130**
Leake, John 344
Leeming Brothers 109
Leith 3, 302
Lewis, James 286, 337
Lewis, John **149**
lift-pumps 95
lighting 83
Lilly, Christian 79, 251, 252, 256, **257**, 258, 319, 331, 392
Lind, James 346
Lisbon 209, 344
Liverpool, Lord 241
Lloyd, Christopher 283
Lloyd, Thomas 389–90
local communities 373–4
local initiatives 53
locks
- Keyham Extension **48**
- Portsmouth 46, **46**
- Rosyth **52**

lodge houses 160, **160**
Lôme, Dupuy de 32
London
- Admiralty and War Office building 109–10, **110**
- Bethlehem Hospital 148
- East and West India Docks 11
- Seething Lane 53, **53**
- Somerset House 53, 107, **108**, 109
- Tower Hill **108**, 109
- West India Docks 114

London, Chatham and Dover Railway **xv**, 84
Long Term Service 376, 377
long-span building structures 77
Lord Warden, HMS 187
Louisbourg, siege of 267
Low Moor Company 316
Lyddite 321

M

machine tools, steam powered 76
McIntosh, Hugh 17, 19, 68, 305, 311
Madras 212, *212*
magazines
- Bermuda **338**, 339, **339**
- Chattenden **xv**, 325, **325**, **326**, 327
- costs 336
- Devonport 333, **333**, 334, **335**, 336, **336**
- Gibraltar 235, 237, 342, **342**

Lodge Hill **326**, 327
Malta 342
Priddy's Hard **xiv**, **327**, 328, **329**, 330–1, **330**
Upnor Castle **xv**, 316, 318, 322, 324–5
Magnet, HMS **200**
Magnificent. HMS 7, 255
Majestic, HMS 34, 44
Malta xvii, 233, 288, 392, 393
bakery 243–4, **243**, **244**
barracks 375
caissons **183**
capture of, 1800 10, 212, 217, 238, 239, 370
chapels 170
closure 52
coaling station **228**
defences 221, 239–40, 250
dry docks 88, *176*, 210, 217, **217**, 223, 241, 244–6, **245**, 247, **247**, 249
expansion, 19th century 244–9, **245**, **246**, **247**, **248**
facilities inherited 240, **240**
foundry 245, 246
French Creek **228**, 246–7, **246**, **247**, **248**, 249, 342
the galley arches **240**, **241**
gateway **246**
Grand Harbour **26**
Gun-Mounting Store **248**, 249
Hamilton Dock 82, 183
housing, senior officers 241–2, **242**
labour force *212*, 241
Machine and Fitting Shop 249, **249**
magazines 342
metal workshop 245
naval hospital 243, 352, 370–2, **371**, **372**
naval premises, 1863 **240**
the New Factory **248**, 249
ordnance yard 337, 341–2, **341**
plan, 1909 **341**
power station 208
recent developments 249–50
ropery 132, 240
ropewalk 240
St. Elmo breakwater 250, **250**
the Sheer Bastion 240, **240**, **241**
site choice 213
smithery 245
strategic importance 217–18, 239–40, 246, 249
torpedo test range 207
victualling yard 303, 312
Vittoriosa 370
water supplies 304
Malta Maritime Museum 393
Man, Robert 357
Mansell, Robert 209
Marchwood depot, Southampton Water 319
maritime focus, westward shift 3
Marlborough, HMS *300*
Marquand, John 54–5, 64–5, 167, 170
Marshall, Thomas and George 128
Martello towers, Kingston, Ontario 266, **266**
Martin, Henry 54–5
Martin, Thomas Byam 25, 101
Martinique 251
Mary Rose 183, 394
mast houses 116, **116**
Halifax, Nova Scotia **268**
Haulbowline 22
Simon's Town **288**, **290**
mast ponds 14, 19, **114**
master house carpenter 58
master shipwright 55, 58
masts 112
Maudslay, Henry 68, **69**, 111, 123
Mauritius 230
Meadows Rendel, James 67
meat processing 301
mechanisation 71–9
victualling yards 312, **312**, **313**, 314, **314**
Mediterranean, the 209, 210
Medway, River 2, 10
Medway Maritime Hospital 349
Melville, HMS 353
Melville, Viscount 25, 101
Melville Town 17, 374
Merdon, Thomas 238
metal trades
dockyard buildings 118–20, **119**, **120**, 198, **198**, 245
dockyard buildings, Ascension Island 285, **285**
steam factories 193–9, **193**, **194**, **195**, **196**, **197**, *197*, *198*, **199**
Metropolitan Police 376
Middleton, Charles (later Lord Barham) 72, 389
midshipmen 381
Milford Haven 3, 10, 16, **16**, 131. *see also* Pembroke Dockyard
military engineers 79
Miller, William 19, 23, 77, 145–6, **145**
Ministry of Defence 394
Minorca 87, 233. *see also* Port Mahon, Minorca
base established 209
capture of 344
chapel 165
construction 213
housing, senior officers 155–6
naval hospital 212, 238
strategic importance 210, 213
Mitchell, James 182
models 60–1, **61**
Montreal 263
Montresor, James 155–6, 238
Moore, Robert 265
Morice, Nicholas 331
Morice Ordnance Yard, Devonport **xvi**, 29, 79, 319, 331–6, **332**, **333**, **334**, **335**, **336**
Morrison and Mason 46
Mould, Thomas 189
mould lofts 115–16, **115**, **116**
Murray, Matthew 68

N

Napier, Charles 225
Napoleon, Emperor 215
Napoleonic Wars 3–4, 10, 21, 22, 26, 54, 75, 112, 117, 131, 133, 141, 211–12, 251, 269, 299, 304, 319, 324–5, 334, 349, 352, 391
Nassau 227, **228**, 251
National Museum of the Royal Navy 62
Naval Academy, Portsmouth 381–2, **382**, **383**
naval arms race 208, 221, 392
Naval Defence Act, 1889 44, 221, 235, 342
Naval Defence Act, 1913 218
naval hospitals xvii
ancillary buildings 369–70, **369**
Ascension Island 285–6, 352
Barbados 77, 352
Bermuda 77–8, 212, 277, 352
Boards of Survey 366
capacity 357, 359, 363, 372
chapels 165, 361, **364**
Chatham 345, 349, **350**, **351**, 364
closure 52
contract system 344, 345
costs 345, 352, 356, 367, 369, 370
Deal 348, **349**, 364
development 343–55
early 343–5
English Harbour 351–2, **352**
Esquimalt 272, **272**, 352–3, 354
first permanent 343
food 346, 357
Gibraltar 237, 358, **358**
Gosport 344
Great Yarmouth 349, **350**, 364
grounds 362, **362**
Halifax, Nova Scotia 270, 352, 353
Haulbowline 24, 349
Hong Kong 353, **354**
hygiene 344, 346
Isla del Ray 53, **54**
Jamaica 344, 347, 366
Kingston, Ontario 265
Lisbon 344
Malta 243, 352, 370–2, **371**, **372**
Minorca 212, 238
mortality rates 346–7, 364
Newfoundland 352
operating theatres 364
ornamentation 359, **360**
Plymouth 343, 344, 345
Port Clarence 283
Port Mahon 343, 344, **345**, 347, **347**, 356–7, **356**, **357**
Port Royal, Jamaica 15, 78, 203, 253, 258–9, 352, 364, 366–70, **367**, **368**
Portland 351
Portsmouth 345
receiving wards 364
Royal Hospital for Seamen (Greenwich), [later, Royal Naval College, Greenwich] 55, 165, 366, 382, 394
Royal Hospital, Haslar **xiv**, 55, 58, 73, 165, **327**, 343, 345–6, **346**, 347, **347**, 358–62, **359**, **360**, **361**, **362**, 366
Simon's Town 353
South Queensferry 351
staff 344
staff quarters 357, 358, **360**, 361, **361**, 364, 370, 372
standards 346–8, **347**

Stonehouse 55, 348, **349**, 361, 363–6, **363**, **364**, **365**, **366**
Tangier 343
transfer to army 352
Trincomalee 353, **353**
wards 347–8, **347**, 356, 357, 359, 361, 363–4, **363**, **367**, 368, 372, **372**
Wei Hai Wei 354
Woolwich 348, **348**
Yokohama 353–4, **355**
zymotic wards 351, **362**, 372, **372**
Naval Ordnance Store Department 315
Naval Works Act, 1895 44–7, 47, 50, 86, 186, 225, 235, 392
Naval Works Loan Act, 1895 384
navy, medieval 1
Navy Board
abolition 79, 81
and chapels 165–9
and Chatham 7
commissioners 54–5
the Great Rebuilding 59, 60–1, 62, 64–5
and Haulbowline 21
and the Industrial Revolution 67
lack of guidance 58
and local initiatives 53
and Malta 240
management system 53
and mechanisation 72
and naval hospitals 344–5
and overseas bases 212
oversight 58
and Pembroke 16, 17
Plymouth modernisation and enlargement proposals, 1761 6–7
relationship with Bentham 11
reorganisation, 1796 77
responsibility 4
and sail production 112
Seething Lane offices 53, **53**
and slip roofs 99, 101
Somerset House 53, 107, **108**, 109
staff 53
Nelson, HMS 382
Nelson, Horatio xvii, 239, 261–2, 370
Nelson, Richard 79–80
New Zealand xvii, 218, 293, 393
New Zealand Naval Forces 218
Newcastle 83
Newfoundland naval hospital 352
Niger River Expedition 31
Northfleet 11
numbers employed, home dockyards 5, *5*, *6*

O

oar makers 118
officers, accommodation 17, 19–20, **19**, 20, **56**. *see also* housing, senior officers
Ogle, Sir Chaloner 252–3, 358
Okanagan (Royal Canadian Navy submarine) **187**, 188, 192
Oneida, USS 263
Ordnance, Master of 315
Ordnance Department 315
ordnance yards xvii
Ascension Island 337
Bermuda 278–9, **278**, **282**, 336, 337, **338**, 339, **339**
blast walls 322, **322**
Chatham **318**, 322–7, **323**, **324**, **325**, **326**
Devonport 29, 79, 320, 331–6, **333**, **334**, **335**, **336**
Esquimalt 337
Gibraltar 341–2, **342**
Great Lakes 337
Great Yarmouth 319, **319**
Halifax 337
housing, senior officers 332–3, **333**
laboratories 318
Malta 337, 341–2, **341**
Marchwood depot 319
overseas bases 336–42, **338**, **339**, **340**, **341**, **342**
Port Antonio, Jamaica 337
Port Mahon 337
Port Royal, Jamaica 336–7, 337
Portsmouth 318, **320**, 327–31, **327**, **328**, **329**, **330**, **331**
powder magazines 316, 317–19, 333, **333**, 334, **335**, 336, **336**, 337
rifled gun era 320–2, **320**, **321**, **322**
role 317
shell-filling rooms 321–2, **322**, 330, 337
Simon's Town **321**, 337, **338**
smooth-bore era 315–19, **316**, **317**, **318**, **319**
storehouses 317, **318**, 322, **323**, 327–8, **328**, 332, **332**
Sydney 294, 298, 339, **340**, 341, **341**
Trincomalee 337
Oregon Boundary Treaty, 1846 219
Oregon Crisis, the 266, **266**, 272
Orlando, HMS **295**
outstationed commissioners 54–5
overseas bases **xii–xiii**. *see also* coaling depots; individual bases
19th century 217–25, **217**, **219**, **220**, **221**, **222**, **223**, **224**
advantages of 209–10
barracks 375
boathouses **220**, 221, **221**
building materials 214–15
careening wharves 210, **210**
chapels and churches 170
closures 225
command system 212
commissioners 212–13
construction 213–16
defences 210, 221, **221**
dry docks 210, 222–5, **222**, **223**, **224**
equipment 218, 221–2
establishment of 392
food supplies 215–16
housing, senior officers 154–5, **154**, 155–6, 214, **214**, 215
labour force *34*, 212, *212*, 213–14
local communities 374, 375
local standards 337
locations 217
naval hospitals 351–8, **352**, **353**, **354**, **355**, **356**, **357**, **358**, 364, 366–72, **367**, **368**, **371**, **372**
need for 209
ordnance yards 336–42, **338**, **339**, **340**, **341**, **342**
planning system 212–13
prefabricated timber buildings 215
resident engineers 218
sailing navy 209–16, **210**, **211**, **214**, **216**
site choice 213
strategic importance 220
structural ironwork 215
upgrading 220–5
victualling yards 302–4
water supplies 216
oversight 58

P

Pacific, the 219, 230
paddle wheels, vulnerability of 25
Palmer, Henry 188
Panama Canal 256
Panopticon design 12, **13**, 71, 72, 77
Paris, School of Naval Architecture 389
Parlby, Thomas 64, 68
Parry, W E 25
Pasley, Charles **36**, 79–80, 82, 84, **184**
Pater Town 17, 374
Pax Britannica, the 25, 217
pay offices 164–5, **164**
Peake, John 21
Pearce, Thomas 359
Pearse, James 210, 343
Pearson, Isaac 252, **252**
Pembroke Dockyard xvii, 3, *6*, 30, 68, 77, 95
accommodation 17
chapel 166, 169, 170, **170**
closure 52
Commissioner's House 19
costs 17, 18
dry dock 17, *176*
foundation 16
gateway 160–1
geological problems 17, 88
and growth in warship sizes 34
Hobbs Point 18
housing, senior officers 150, 151
labour force 17
lack of investment 187
local community 374
mast pond 19
No. 1 Storehouse 19
officers accommodation 19–20, **19**, **20**, 151
Officer's Offices 19
pay office 165
pitch house 144
role 17
ropewalk 113
sawmill 206
site 17
slips 17–18, **18**
slips expansion, 19th century 187
temporary facilities 17
warship-building yard 17–18, **18**
workshops 19

Pembroke, HMS 52
Penelope, HMS **233**
Peninsula and Orient shipping company (P&O) 225
Pepys Cockerell, Samuel 3, 21, 55, 70, **70**
Pering, Richard 99, **99**
permanent navy, establishment of 1
Persian Gulf, coaling stations 231, **231**
Peterhead harbour of refuge **42**, 43
Phaeton, HMS **274**
pile drivers 172, **173**
piles and piling 58, **59**
Pilkington, Henry 47, 86, 382
Pilkington, Robert 79, 316
Pilkington, William 349, **350**
Pioneer, HMS **289**
pitch 113
pitch houses 144, **144**
planning system 392
 1700–1760 53–89
 Admiralty Works Department 82–3
 the Great Rebuilding 59–65
 impact of the Industrial Revolution 65–70
 models 60–1, **61**
 overseas bases 212–13
 Victualling Board 303
Plumper, HMS 272
Plymouth Dockyard. *see also* Royal William Victualling Yard
 advantages 5
 apprentices 389
 boiler shops 27
 breakwater **xvi**, 41, 77, 103–6, **104**, **105**
 chapels 165–6, 166
 Commissioner's House 148, 155
 condition, 1761 58
 cordage production 133
 Devonport South Yard 30, 34, 101, 115–16, *176*, 195
 Dummer's buildings 56, **57**
 dry docks 56, **57**, 88, 89, 90
 foundation 3, **3**
 geology 89, 91
 the Great Rebuilding 5–6, **6**, 7, 8, 59, 60
 hoop house 144
 housing, senior officers 148, **148**, 149, 155
 introduction of steam power 121
 local community 374
 model, 1770s 60–1, 61, **61**
 mould loft 115, **115**
 naval hospital 343, 344, 345
 North Stone Dock 90
 numbers employed 6
 officers gardens 157
 officers' terrace 148, **148**, 149
 offices 162
 pay office 164
 Pocock's painting **10**
 Port Admiral's House 152, **152**, 153
 powder magazine 319
 pumping engines 95
 rise of 5
 ropery 56, 65, 78, 113, 131, 135–6
 ropery fire 132, 136
 sailmakers 142
 slips 8, 98, **99**, 103
 smithery 118, 194
 South Dock 99
 storehouses 61–2, **62**, 114
 tidal range 88
 victualling yard 301
 wet dock 90, 95
Plymouth Dock xvii, **3**, 4, 374
Plymouth Sound, breakwater **xvi**, 41, 77, 103–6, **104**, **105**
Popham, Home 111
Port Admirals 79, 152
 housing 152–4, **152**, **153**, **154**
Port Antonio, Jamaica xvii, 79, 210, 213, 215, 251, 374, 392
 climate 259
 closure 259
 construction 256, 258–9, **258**
 disadvantages 253, 259
 foundation 256–8
 housing, senior officers 258
 naval hospital 258–9
 ordnance yard 337
 site **256**, 257, **257**
Port Clarence 283
Port Mahon, Minorca 79, 210, 238–9, **238**, **239**, 393
 capture of 233, 238
 careening wharves 239, **239**
 construction 213
 foundation 209, 238
 housing, senior officers 239
 Isla del Ray 53, **54**
 naval hospital 343, 344, **345**, 347, **347**, 356–7, **356**, **357**
 ordnance yard 337
 return to Spain 239
 ropery 131
 ropewalk 239
 site choice 213
 strategic importance 238
 victualling storehouse 302
 wharves 88
Port Royal, Jamaica 79, 210
 capstan house **254**
 careening wharf 252, 253
 chapels 170
 closure 225, 256, 271
 coaling jetty 227, **227**, 255, **255**
 coaling station 231, 255, **255**, 256
 commodore's house 148, **149**, **255**
 construction 213, 215
 defences **220**, 221, 256
 equipment 218
 expansion, 19th century 253, **253**, 255–6, **255**
 fitting shop **255**
 foundation 251, 251–2
 housing, senior officers 253, **254**
 main storehouse 253, **254**
 naval hospital 15, 78, 203, 253, 352, 364, 366–70, **367**, **368**
 officers' gardens 158–9
 ordnance yard 336–7, 337
 Pearson's plan 252, **252**
 resident engineer 218
 ropery 131
 site choice 213
 smithery **255**
 strategic importance 251–2, 255, 256
 victualling store 255
 water supplies 304
 wharf walls 87
Port Stanley coaling station, Falkland Isles 230, **230**
portable housings 98
Portchester Castle 345
Portland 41, 43, 43–4, **43**, 44–5, 67, 82, 106
Portland naval hospital 351
Portsea xvii, 374
Portsmouth Dockyard **xiv**, xvii, **195**. *see also* Royal Clarence Victualling Yard
 1849 **29**
 advantages 5
 alluvial subsoil 88, 91
 anchor smiths' shop 119, **119**
 bakery 301, 305
 barracks 381, 382
 basin expansion, 19th century 174–5, 180, 182
 basins 39–40, 41, 46, 171
 Block Mills 123, **124–5**, 126
 boathouses 203–5, **204**, 394
 boiler shops 27
 brewery 301, 307, 309
 caissons 182
 Camber Wharf Rigging House **59**
 chain pumps 90, **90**
 chapels 165, 166, 167, **167**, 170
 coaling point 40, **40**, 46
 coffer-dams 91
 Commissioner's House 54–5, 55, 147, **147**, 155
 convict labour 40–1
 cooperage 301
 cordage production 133
 Cordite Cartridge Stores 331
 dry dock, 1492 1
 dry dock expansion, 19th century 179
 dry dock foundations 92–3
 dry docks 7, 8, 29, 39, 41, 45–6, 72, 88, **89**, 121, *176–7*, 179
 electrification 208
 estimates, 1857 84
 the Factory 46
 fire brigade **203**
 fire main water tank 203, **203**
 fortifications 39
 foundries 194
 Grand Storehouse 78, 327–8, **328**
 Great Basin caisson 88, 94–5, **94**
 the Great Extension, 1867 39–41, **40**
 Great Extension costs 40–1
 the Great Rebuilding 5–8, 7, **8**, 59, 60, 62–4
 Great Rebuilding accounts 62
 Gun Wharf **xiv**, 317, **320**, 327–8
 gun-mounting workshop 207, **207**
 housing, senior officers 147, **147**, 150, 155, 156–7
 importance, 16th century 4
 introduction of steam power 121–3, **122**

iron foundry 195, **195**
land reclamation 29
local community 374
locks 46, **46**
Marine Barracks 376
meat store 301
Middle Storehouse **63**, 64
mould loft 115
naval hospital 345
naval installations **xiv**
Naval Works Act extension 45–6, 46
the New Factory 208
New Gun Wharf 78
No. 1 Basin 11
No. 2 Ship Shop 29
numbers employed *6*
officers gardens 157
officers' terrace 150
offices 163, **163**
ordnance yard 318, **320**, 327–31, **327**, **328**, **329**, **330**, **331**
pay office 164, **164**
pitch house 144
plan, 1785 **327**
Port Admiral's House 152
Porter's Lodge 160
powder magazine 318, 319
power station 208, **208**
Priddy's Hard powder magazine **xiv**, **327**, 328, **329**, 330–1, **330**
pumping engines 95
pumping station 184, **184**
pumping systems 183
railway 195
reservoir 73
reservoir pump 121–2, **122**
rise of 5
ropery 7, **8**, 65–6, 113, 131, 133, 137
ropery fire 132, 137
St. Ann's church 166, 167, **167**
shell-filling rooms 330
slips 8, 96, **97**, 98, 99, 101
slips expansion, 19th century 185–6, **186**, 188–9, 192
smithery 119, 119–20, **119**, **124**, 194
South Dock 91
steam basin 28–9, **29**, 31
steam dredger 11
Steam Factory, 2 Ship Shop 193–5, **193**, **195**, 208
steam factory labour force *197*
storehouses 62–4, **62**, **63**, **66**, 67, 78, 394
structural ironwork 203–5, **203**, **204**
survival 393–4
tidal basin 39, 40, **40**, 41
tidal range 90
timber ground 39
torpedo workshop 207, **207**
Unicorn Gateway 41
victualling yard 301
wagon ways 84
wet dock 95
wharves 88
Wood Mills 76, 112, 118
workshops 118
Portsmouth Metal Mills 76
Portsmouth Naval Base Property Trust 394
Portsmouth Wood Mills 76, 112, 113
Post Office fleet 25, 42
Potemkin, Prince 12, 71
powder magazines 317–19, 337
costs 336
Devonport 333, **333**, 334, **335**, 336, **336**
Priddy's Hard **327**, 328, **329**, 330–1, **330**
Upnor Castle **xv**, 316, 318, 322, 324–5, **324**
power stations 208, **208**
Powerful, HMS 44–5, **222**, **231**
prefabrication 78, 258, 260, 344, 366
Preventive Squadron, the 216
Price & Co, J 46
Priddy's Hard powder magazine, Portsmouth **xiv**, **327**, 328, **329**, 330–1, **330**
Prince of Wales, HMS **185**, 190, 382
prismatic powder 320–1
Proby, Charles 356–7
protected harbours 41–2, **41**, **42**, 43, **43**
Provincial Marine, the 263
public-works prisons 34–5
Pulteney Malcolm, Sir Edward 371
pump houses
Chatham 128, **129**, 183, 183–4
Devonport 183, **183**
Sheerness 95
pumping stations 183–4, **183**, **184**, 235, 237

Q

Quadrangle, Devonport the 196–7, **196**, **197**
Quebec 211, *212*
Queen, HMS 30, **46**
Queen Elizabeth, HMS 186
Quick-Firing (QF) guns **320**, 321, 331

R

Raban, Edward 39, 86
railways 83, 83–4, **85**, 86, 105, **105**, 127, 174, 195, 219, 262, 290, 332
Railways Inspectorate 83–4
Raleigh, HMS **290**
Ramsden, Jesse 73
Ranger, William 79
Rattler, HMS 25
Regent (paddle tug) 25
Regent's Canal Ironworks 190
Rehe, Samuel 73
Rendel, James Meadows 82
Rennie, John, senior 11, 11–12, 13–15, 17, 68, **68**, 88, 95, 99, 101, 103, 105, 106, 120, 128, 183, 276–7, 392
Rennie, John, junior. 17, 95, 128, 164, 183, 305–9, 311, 392
Reynolds, William 74, 75
Rickman, Thomas 78
Rigby, Joseph and Charles 198
Rigging House, Camber Wharf, Portsmouth **59**
Rio de Janeiro 212, *212*
Ripley, Thomas 107
roads 113
Rochefort 88, 94
Rodger, N A M 302
Rodney, HMS 17
Roebuck, George 111
Roebuck, John **264**
Romulus (hulk) 78
rope manufacturing 113, 131–2, **131**
roperies 113, 130
Chatham **2**, 7, 35, 65, 74, 113, 130–1, **132**, 133, 394
conservation 394
cordage production **131**, 133
costs 133
dimensions 65, 131, 137, 138
fires 132, 136, 137
forming machines 134–5, **134**
hatchelling houses 131
hemp houses 131, 137, 141–2, **141**
introduction of steam power 132–6
labour force 132
laying floor 138–9, **139**, **140**
laying machines **132**
Malta 132, 240
Plymouth 56, 65, 78, 113, 130–1, 132, 135–6
Port Mahon 131
Port Royal 131
Portsmouth 7, **8**, 65–6, 113, 131, 132, 133
ropeyards 136–7
spinning floors 131, **131**, 135–6, **136**
spinning houses 138
Sunderland 133
ventilation 132, 139
winches 132, 135, **135**
winding drums 136, **136**
Woolwich 113, 130, 133
yarn houses 132, **132**, **136**, 138, 141
ropewalks 113, 131, 239, 240
Rosia Bay victualling yard, Gibraltar 237, **237**, 302–3, **303**
Ross, Charles 370–1
Rosyth Dockyard xvii
1918 **50**
basins **50**, 51, **52**
caissons 182
construction 50–2, **51**
costs 51
dry docks 51, *176–7*, 179, 236
establishment of 4, 171
foundations 174, **174**
local community 374–5
locks **52**
pumping station **51**
strategic importance 50
vulnerability 52
workshops 51–2
Rosyth Garden City 374–5
Rovehead, Alexander 363–4
Royal Albert Hall 80
Royal Australian Navy 218, 393
Royal Canadian Navy 225, 271, 275, 393
Royal Clarence Victualling Yard, Gosport **xiv**, 79, 84, 203, 309–12, **309**, **310**, **311**, 312, **327**, 394
Royal Commission on the Defence of the United Kingdom, 1859 35–6

royal dockyards. *see also* individual yards
corruption 69
Dummer's survey 56
establishment of 1–4
importance 391
numbers employed 5, *5*, *6*
value, 1698 56
Royal Edward Victualling Yard 295, 296, 304
Royal Engineers xvii, 20, 28, 53, 69, 79–81, 83, 84, 171, 235, 272, 298
Royal George, HMS 113
Royal Gun Factory, Woolwich 316
Royal Hospital for Seamen (Greenwich), [later, Royal Naval College, Greenwich] 55, 165, 366, 382, 394
Royal Hospital, Haslar **xiv**, 55, 58, 73, 165, **327**, 343, 345–6, **346**, 347, **347**, 358–62, **359**, **360**, **361**, **362**, 366
Royal Marines, barracks **xvi**, xvii, 77, 376
Royal Maritime Auxiliary Service 52
Royal Military Academy 80
Royal Military College, Kingston, Ontario 265, **265**, 266
Royal Naval College Osborne 385–6, **385**, **386**
Royal Naval Engineering College, Keyham 46, 383–4, **383**, 384–6, **384**
Royal Navy
architectural heritage xvii–xviii
Australia Station 293
decline 52
deployment, 18th century 211
deployment, overseas squadrons 220, *220*
dominance 25
East Indies squadron 287
expansion, 17th century 55–6
first iron vessel 31
first steam vessel 25
Fisher's reforms 225
foundation 1
Great Lakes freshwater fleet 262, 263, 265, 266
growth of the fleet, 18th century xvii, 4, 210, 391
Mediterranean Squadron 209, 218
modernisation 44
naval supremacy 217, 221, 393
North American squadron 270
North Pacific Squadron 219
Pacific Squadron 271, 272
post-1918 xvii
the Preventive Squadron 216
reforms, 19th century 220
role 217
steam vessel numbers 25
strength 59
Tudor 1–2, **2**
West Africa Squadron 283
West Indies presence 251
the Western Squadron 5
withdrawal from Esquimalt 274, 275
Royal New Zealand Navy 393
Royal Regiment of Artillery 79
Royal Sovereign, HMS 44, **44**
Royal Victoria Victualling Yard, Deptford 52, 109, 299–301, **300**, 302, 312, **312**, **313**, *313*, 314, **314**
Royal William, HMS 17, 91
Royal William Victualling Yard, Stonehouse **xvi**, 68, 164, 203, 305–9, **305**, **306**, **307**, **308**, *313*, 394
Rule, William 16
rum 309
Rush, Richard 265
Rush-Bagot Agreement 265, 266
Russia 71
Russian War of 1854–6 200

S

Sadler, James 73, **73**, 95, 121–2, **121**
sailmakers 112–13
sailmaking 112–13, 142–3, **142**, **143**
St. Ann's church, Portsmouth 166, 167, **167**
St. George, Bermuda 211
St. Helena 215, 230
St. Lawrence, HMS 211, 263, **264**
St. Lo, George 54, 94, 149–50
St. Lucia, Castries 229–30
St. Margaret's Hope 51
St. Mary's Island, Chatham 35, **36**, 39
St. Vincent, Earl 370, 389
Sandom, Captain William 266
Sandwich, Earl of 5, 7, 8, 59–60, 65–6, 98, 133, 309
Savage, Captain Henry John 20
saw frames 127
sawing, mechanical 123
sawmills 35, 123, 126–8, **126**, **127**, **128**, 206
sawpits 112, 116–17
sawyers 112, 117
Scamp, William 30, 35, 39, 81, 82, 84, 182, 199, 200, 233–4, **233**, 243–4, **243**, 245–6, 281, 348, **348**, 376
Scapa Flow 4, 52
Schank, John 21, 263
School of Military Engineering, Chatham 80
School of Naval Architecture, Paris 389
School of Naval Architecture, Portsmouth 389–90, **390**
Schurman, Donald 226
Scotland 3–4, 50–1
Scott, Henry 80
screw propeller, superiority of 25
scurvy 209
Second World War 52, 114, 250, 312, 393
Seething Lane, London 53, **53**
Selborne, Earl 51, 290
Selborne-Fisher Accord 384–6
semaphore telegraph system 110–11, **110**, **111**, 380, **380**
Seppings, Robert 25, 26, 72, 77, 100, 101, 188
Seven Years' War (1756–63) 5, 210, 262, 262–3, 267, 316
Severn Gorge, Iron Bridge 74, 78
sewerage systems 83
Sheerness Dockyard 2, 14, **14**, **15**, 77, 87
1774 **12**
access 11
barracks 375–6
basin expansion, 19th century 172–3, 182
basins 14, 171
Bentham plan 11–13, **13**
boatstore 82, 205, **205**
caissons 182
church 151, **151**, 168–9, **169**, 170
closure 52
coffer-dams 88
committee of 1812 12
convict labour 14
defences 13
dry dock expansion, 19th century 179
dry docks **92**, *177*, 181, **181**
establishment of 4
expansion and modernisation 11–15, **12**, **13**, **14**, **15**
foundations 14, **15**, 88, **92**, 93
gateway 160–1, **161**
the Great Basin 14
and growth in warship sizes 34
housing, senior officers 151, **151**, 155, **155**
hulks **12**
mast pond 14
modernisation costs 12, 13
Mud Dock 95
numbers employed *6*
officers' terrace 151, **151**
pay office 165
pitch house 144
plan 1813 13
Port Admiral's House 153, **153**, 155
Powder Monkey Bay 13
problems facing, 18th century 11
pump house 95
pumping engines 14
Quadrangle Storehouse 14, 15, **15**, 142
Rennie plan and redevelopment 11–12, 13–15, **14**, **15**
role 15
Rope Ground 131
sailmakers 142
sawmill 35
sawpits 117
size 13
slips 96, 98, 99, 101
slips expansion, 19th century 187
the Small Basin 14
steam factory 197
steam factory labour force *197*
storehouses 114
suppling boilers **145**
victualling yard 302
wagon ways 84
workers' accommodation 374
wrought ironwork 14–15
Sheffield 74
shell-filling rooms 321–2, **322**, 330, 337
shipbuilding reforms 59
ship-caissons 94, **94**
ships' blocks 123
ships surgeons 343
shipwrights 115, 117
shoaling 11

Shropshire Canal 75
Shrubsole, William 169
Sick and Hurt Board 167, 356, 357, 359, 363, 370
Simon's Town 10, 44, 82, 393
 additions, 19th century 89–90
 basin **289**
 boathouse **290**
 breakwater 106
 chapels 170, 288
 clocktower 288, **288**, **290**
 coal stores 289, **289**
 coaling shed 227
 defences 221
 dry docks *177*, 179, 289–90
 Dutch East India Company buildings 288, **288**
 East Yard 292
 establishment 288
 foundation 212, 287
 Furnace House 290
 the Main Factory 290, **292**
 mast house **288**, **290**
 modernisation 225
 naval hospital 353
 ordnance yard **321**, 337, **338**
 plan, 1900 **287**
 plan, 1909 **291**
 power station 208
 pumping station 184, **184**
 railway 290
 sail loft **288**, **290**
 slips 289, **290**
 space restrictions 289, **289**, **290**
 steam yard **287**
 storehouses 288, **288**
 strategic importance 287–8
 West Yard 292, **292**
Simoom, HMS 31
Sims, T 39, 274
Singapore xvii, 52, 231–2
Sirius, HMS 295
Skinner, William 328
Slade, Thomas 6, 59, 61–2, 65, 137
slaves 213, 216
sliding caissons 47, **48**
slips
 Chatham 8, 82, 98, 99, 101, **102**, 103, **103**, 185, **185**, 187–8, **187**, **188**, 189–90, **189**, **190**, **191**, 192–3, **192**
 construction 95–8, **96**, **97**
 covered 17, **18**, 35, **97**, 98, 98–103, **98**, **99**, **100**, **102**, **103**
 Deptford 96, 98, 100, **100**
 Devonport 30, **97**, 101, 186–7, **186**, 189
 dimensions 98, 185–7
 expansion, 19th century 185–93, **185**, **186**, **187**, **188**, **189**, **190**, **191**, **192**
 floors 187
 foundations 187–8
 glazing 101
 and growth in warship sizes 34
 Haslar Gunboat Yard 200
 Haulbowline 21
 Kingston, Ontario 263, **264**, 265
 land purchases 35
 location 96
 numbers 96, 98
 Pembroke 17–18, **18**, 187
 Plymouth 8, 98, **99**, 103
 Portsmouth 8, 96, 98, 99, 101, 185–6, **186**, 188–9, 192
 roof design 188–9
 roof spans 101, **102**
 roof supports 98, **98**, 101, 188, 189, 190
 roofs 81, 82, **186**, 188–90, **188**, **189**, **190**, **191**, 192–3, **192**, 203
 Sheerness 96, 98, 99, 101, 187
 Simon's Town 289, **289**
 slope 96
 Woolwich 98, 100–1, **100**, 189, 192–3, **192**
Smeaton, John 68
Smiles, Samuel 14, 106, 277
Smith, Edward 195
Smith, Percy 82
smitheries 112, 118–20, **119**, **120**, **124**, 193, 194, **194**, 198, 206, 245, **255**, 261, **261**
smiths 120
Snipe, Dr John 370, 372
Snodgrass, Gabriel 119
Society for the Improvement of Naval Architecture 69, 389
Society of Civil Engineers 67
Soho Foundry 27
Somerset, Duke of 247
Somerset House, London 53, 107, **108**, 109
South African Navy 393
South Queensferry naval hospital 351, **351**
South Western Railway Company 84
Southampton 1–2
Southampton Water, Marchwood depot 319
Spanish War (1739–48) 5
Spartan, HMS 119
specialist trades 118
Spectacle Island, Sydney 294, 295, 298, 339, **340**, 341, **341**
Spencer, Earl 72
Spenser, John 359
Spragge, Edward 209
Spry, Richard 267
steam battlefleet, the, impact of 31–5
steam engine, the xvii, 95
 Beddoes self-contained direct-acting 73
 costs 75
 first use afloat 11
 impact of 66
 limitations 25
 reliability 25–6, 31
 role 31
steam factories 193–9, **193**, **194**, **195**, **196**, **197**, *197*, **198**, **199**, 208, 285, **285**, 297
steam hammers **120**
steam power 193, 392
 early 121–3, **121**, **122**, **124**, **125**, 126–8, **126**, **127**, **128**, **129**, 130, **130**
 introduction of 121–3, **121**
 roperies 132–6
steam pumps 172, **172**, **173**, 174–5
steam sawing 117
steam technology
 development of 25–6
 role 31
steam yards **36**, 171
 Chatham 29, 35–9, **36**, **37–8**, **173**
 costs 29, 31
 Devonport 31
 Keyham 29–30, **30**, 31
 Portsmouth 28–9, **29**, 31
 Simon's Town **287**
 Woolwich 27–8, **27**, **28**
Stewart, Admiral Charles 256–8
Stonehouse barracks **xvi**, 376, **376**
Stonehouse naval hospital 55, 348, **349**, 361, 363–6, **363**, **364**, **365**, **366**
storehouses 113–14, **114**
 Bermuda 279, **280**, 281, **281**
 Chatham 65, **65**, 73, 114, **114**
 Deptford 301
 Devonport 332, **332**
 English Harbour, Antigua 260, **261**
 Esquimalt 275
 fireproofing **66**, 67
 Kingston, Ontario 263, **264**
 ordnance yards 317, **318**, 322, **323**, 327–8, **328**, 332, **332**
 Plymouth 61–2, **62**, 114
 Port Royal, Jamaica 253, **254**
 Portsmouth 62–4, **62**, **63**, **66**, 67, 78, 327–8, **328**, 394
 Royal Clarence Victualling Yard 311
 Royal William Victualling Yard 305, **306**, 307–8
 Sheerness 114
 Simon's Town 288, **288**
 Sydney 296, **296**
 victualling yards 301, 305, **306**, 307–8, 311
structural ironwork 78, 194, **197**, 202–3
 Bermuda 277
 Devonport 206
 Haulbowline 24, **24**
 overseas bases 215
 Port Royal naval hospital 366–7, **367**, **368**
 Portsmouth 203–5, **203**, **204**
 Royal Clarence Victualling Yard 311
 Sheerness boatstore 205, **205**
Strutt, William 74
Suez Canal 288
Sunderland, ropery 133
Suomenlinna 181
suppling boilers 145–6, **145**
supply chains 391
Surgeon-General 343
Surveyor of Buildings 77
Surveyor of Civil Architecture 70
Surveyor of the Navy 81
 appointment of building contractors 58
 Dummer's tenure 55–8
 and the Great Rebuilding 64
 responsibilities 55, 87–8
Sutherland, John 77
Sydney, New South Wales xvii, 223, **223**
 barracks 295, 298, **298**, 375
 Captain Cook Graving Dock 298
 Circular Quay 293–4, **293**
 clocktower 296
 Cockatoo Island 293, 298
 construction 295–6
 dry docks *177*, 295

electrification 297
engineer's shop **297**
foundation 293–4, 295
Garden Island 82, 294–5, **294**, **295**, 296, 298, **298**, 304, 339, 375, 393
Goat Island 294
offices 296, **297**
ordnance depot 294, 298
ordnance yard 339, **340**, 341, **341**
sail loft 296, 297
site 293, **293**
Spectacle Island 294, 295, 298, 339, **340**, 341, **341**
Steam Factory 297
storehouses 296, **296**
victualling yard 304
Symonds, William 26, 31

T

Table Bay 230
Tangier 209, 210, 343
tar 113
Taylor, G L 20, 77, 78, 79, 151, **151**, 153, 169, **169**, 170, **170**, 311, **350**, **351**
Teague, John 82, 275, 354, **355**
telegraph towers 111, **111**
Telford, Thomas 67, **67**
Templer, James 64, 68
tenders 81–2
Tenon, Jacques 364
Teredo navalis worm 11
Terrible, HMS 44–5
Thames, the 1–2, 10
Thompson, Thomas 77, 99
Thornbrough, Edward 21
Ticonderoga 263
timber seasoning sheds 117, **117**
timber supplies 112
timber trades, dockyard buildings 115–18, **115**, **116**, **117**, **118**
timber-bending kilns 144–6, **145**
timber-framed buildings 58
Tippetts, John 55
Tirpitz, Admiral 50
Titchfield, Jamaica 256, **256**, 257, **257**, 374
tobacco 301
Tonga 230
Topham, Jones and Railton 236
torpedo boats **220**, 221, **221**, 256, 271
torpedo workshops 207, **207**
torpedoes 320
training and training establishments 382, 389, 391
accommodation 384, 385, **385**
apprenticeships 382, 389
Britannia Royal Naval College 384, **385**
cadets 382–3, 384
Director of Naval Education 390
dockyard 389–90, **390**
engineering 383, 383–6, **384**, **385**, **386**
HMS *Excellent,* Whale Island, Portsmouth 387, **387**, **388**
meals 384, **385**
naval 382–7, **382**, **383**, **384**, **385**, **386**, **387**, **388**
Naval Academy, Portsmouth 381–2, **382**, **383**
reforms 384–6
Royal Naval College Osborne 385–6, **385**, **386**
Royal Naval Engineering College, Keyham 383–4, **383**, **384**
School of Naval Architecture, Portsmouth 389–90, **390**
staff 382
weapons 386–7
transport, land 113
Trent, HMS 23
Trincomalee 10, 156, 158, 158–9
Admiralty House 214, **214**
closure threatened 225
construction 213–14
dry docks *177*, 225
establishment of 212, 212–13, 218
naval hospital 353, **353**
ordnance yard 337
victualling yard 303
Trotter, Thomas 346
Troubridge, Thomas 370
Tudor navy 1–2, **2**
Twiss, William 79
typhus 344, 347

U

Upnor Castle
barracks **324**
powder magazine **xv**, 316, 318, 322, 324–5, **324**
Upnor Ordnance Depot **325**
Upper Canada Rebellion, 1837 266
Urgent, HMS **222**, **254**
US Navy 221, 256, 393

V

Valparaiso, Chile 219, 271
Vanbrugh, Sir John 107
Vancouver, George 68
Vau, François Le 88, 89
Vernon, Edward 213, 253, 347
Vernon, HMS 377
Vetch, James 84
Vickers 316
Victoria, HMS **26**, 34
Victory, HMS 34, 59, **60**, 93, 112, 116, 119, 123, 183, 324–5, 394
victualling agents 299, 302
Victualling Board 14, 20, 70, 79
contracts. 302
headquarters **108**, 109, 299–300
Napoleonic Wars 304
planning system 303
rented accommodation 302
responsibilities 299, 304
staff 299
Victualling Office, Dover 299, 302
victualling yards xvii, 302. *see also* Royal Clarence Victualling Yard; Royal Edward Victualling Yard; Royal Victoria Victualling Yard; Royal William Victualling Yard
Ascension Island 303
bakeries 301, 312
Bermuda 303–4
biscuit production 312, **312**
Chatham 301–2
cooperages 300–1, 309, **309**, 311, 314
English Harbour, Antigua 303
food production 300
foreign stations 302
Garden Island, Sydney 304
Gibraltar 237, **237**, 302–3, **303**, **304**
housing, senior officers 311, **311**
Malta 303, 312
meat processing 301, 306
mechanisation 312, **312**, **313**, 314, **314**
numbers employed *313*
numbers employed overseas 303, *303*
overseas bases 302–4
Plymouth 301
Port Mahon, Minorca 302
Portsmouth 301
rented accommodation 302
responsibility for 299
scale of operations 301
Sheerness 302
storehouses 301, 305, **306**, 307–8, 311
Trincomalee 303
water supplies 304
Yokohama 304
Vienna, Congress of 239
Vindictive, HMS **97**
Vittoriosa, Malta 370

W

wagon ways 84, **85**
Wales 3, 10
Walker, Baldwin 43
Waltham Abbey 317, 318, 320
War of 1812 263, 270
War of American Independence 211, 263, 352
War Office 41, 226, 315, 325
Warren, John Borlase 276, 284
Warren, Milbourn 356–7
Warren, Peter 260
Warrior, HMS 32, **32**, 34, *34*, 279, 394
warship building 96, 185
mechanisation 72
Pembroke 17–18, **18**
private yards 30
steam 28
warships
armament 315
coal bunkers 226–7
construction 101, 115–16
dimensions 31, 33, *34*, 44–5, 47, 81, 187, 189, 190, 236
first armoured 31–2
first iron-hulled 32, **32**
full sailing rig dispensed with 32
iron-hulled 31
modernisation 44
need for maintenance 391
provisions 299, *300*
responsibility for 55
Scamp's shore storage proposals 39

structural developments 26
technological developments 31–5, **32**, **33**, *34*
Warspite, HMS 34, 179, 186
Washington Treaty, 1922 52
water supplies 83, 216, 286, 304
watering points 304
Watt, James 12, 69, 95
Watts, Isaac 32, 389
weapons
supply system 315–16
technical development 315, 320–2
training and training establishments 386–7
Wei Hai Wei 218, 354
Wellesley Committee 382
Wellington, Duke of 25
West India Docks, London 114
wet docks. *see* basins
Whale Island, Portsmouth, *Excellent*, HMS 387, **387**, **388**
wharf walls 87, 88
Wharton, Admiral Sir William 51
wharves 88
Whidbey, Joseph 12, 68, 72, 77, 103, 105
White, William 44
Whitmore, George 370–1
Whitmore, William 75
Wilkinson, John 68, 75
Windsor Castle, HMS 24
Wood, Henry 81
wood mills 76, 112, 118
Woodgate, Thomas 275
woodworking machinery 206
Bentham's designs 71–2, 123
Woolwich 1, 71
18th century investment 11
1863 **27**
barracks **376**
basins 95
closure 34, 39
cordage production 133
dry docks 88, *177*
Fitting and Erecting Shop for Marine Engines 28
fitting out basin 28
foundries 28, **28**
hospital 348, **348**
influence 4
local community 374
numbers employed 6
pumping engines 95
railway 83–4
ropery 113, 130, 133
slips 98, 100–1, **100**
slips expansion, 19th century 189, 192–3, **192**
steam dredger 11
steam factory 27–8, **27**, **28**, 193
steam factory labour force *197*
Woolwich Arsenal 31, 317
Royal Gun Factory 316
workforce, numbers employed 5, *5*, *6*
workshops **118**, 201, 235, **235**
Wren, Christopher 55, 165
wrought iron 67, 78, 112, 368, **368**
Wyatt, James 72, 319
Wyatt, Jeffrey 277
Wyatt, Samuel 54–5, 122

Y

yarn houses 132, **132**, **136**
yellow fever 260
Yokohama 231, 304
coaling station **231**
naval hospital 353–4, **355**
York, Duke of 53